A Concise Introduction to Logic

Tenth Traditional Logic Edition

Patrick J. Hurley

CENGAGE
Learning™

Australia • Brazil • Japan • Korea • Mexico • Singapore • Spain • United Kingdom • United States

CENGAGE
Learning™

A Concise Introduction to Logic:
Tenth Traditional Logic Edition

Patrick J. Hurley

Executive Editors:
 Michele Baird
 Maureen Staudt
 Michael Stranz

Project Development Manager:
 Linda deStefano

Senior Marketing Coordinators:
 Sara Mecurio
 Lindsay Shapiro

Production/Manufacturing Manager:
 Donna M. Brown

PreMedia Services Supervisor:
 Rebecca A. Walker

Rights & Permissions Specialist:
 Kalina Hintz

Cover Image:
 Getty Images*

* Unless otherwise noted, all cover images used by Custom Solutions, a part of Cengage Learning, have been supplied courtesy of Getty Images with the exception of the Earthview cover image, which has been supplied by the National Aeronautics and Space Administration (NASA).

© 2008, 2006 Cengage Learning

For product information and
technology assistance, contact us at **Cengage Learning
Customer & Sales Support, 1-800-354-9706**

For permission to use material from this text or product,
submit all requests online at **cengage.com/permissions**
Further permissions questions can be emailed to
permissionrequest@cengage.com

ISBN-13: 978-0-495-49768-4

ISBN-10: 0-495-49768-1

Cengage Learning

5191 Natorp Boulevard
Mason, Ohio 45040
USA

Cengage Learning is a leading provider of customized learning solutions with office locations around the globe, including Singapore, the United Kingdom, Australia, Mexico, Brazil, and Japan. Locate your local office at: **international.cengage.com/region**

Cengage Learning products are represented in Canada by Nelson Education, Ltd.

For your lifelong learning solutions, visit **custom.cengage.com**

Visit our corporate website at **cengage.com**

Printed in the United States of America

*To the memory of my
brother Stephen*

*It is wrong always, everywhere, and for anyone,
to believe anything upon insufficient evidence.*

W. K. CLIFFORD

TABLE OF CONTENTS

Preface

The most immediate benefit derived from the study of logic is the skill needed to construct sound arguments of one's own and to evaluate the arguments of others. In accomplishing this goal, logic instills a sensitivity for the formal component in language, a thorough command of which is indispensable to clear, effective, and meaningful communication. On a broader scale, by focusing attention on the requirement for reasons or evidence to support our views, logic provides a fundamental defense against the prejudiced and uncivilized attitudes that threaten the foundations of our democratic society. Finally, through its attention to inconsistency as a fatal flaw in any theory or point of view, logic proves a useful device in disclosing ill-conceived policies in the political sphere and, ultimately, in distinguishing the rational from the irrational, the sane from the insane.

To realize the benefits offered by the study of logic, one must thoroughly understand the central concepts of the subject and be able to apply them in actual situations. To promote the achievement of these goals, this text presents the central concepts of logic clearly and simply. Examples are used extensively, key terms are introduced in boldface type and defined in the glossary/index, and major points are illustrated in graphic boxes. Furthermore, to ensure sufficient practice in applying the basic principles, the book includes over 2,000 exercises selected to illustrate the main points and guard against the most typical mistakes. In most cases, every third exercise is answered in the back of the book.

New to This Edition

- In this Tenth Edition, the coverage of **Inductive Logic** in Part III has been broken up into six separate chapters to allow for greater flexibility in using the text in class. This change also facilitates customization through our Custom program, which lets you select course materials to create an affordable text that matches your syllabus. For more information, visit www.thomsoncustom.com/makeityours/hurley10e.

- Also new in this edition, thirteen pages devoted to **"Eminent Logicians"** highlight the contributions of key logicians in history. The inclusion of these features should help to humanize logic and make it more interesting by connecting it with historical figures who devoted much of their lives to advancing the science of logic.

- A new method for testing sorites has been introduced into **Section 5.7.** This method, which resembles the rules method for syllogisms, is often simpler to apply because it does not require that intermediate conclusions be drawn.

- In **Section 8.6** the restriction on universal generalization for arguments involving relational predicates and overlapping quantifiers has been replaced by a slightly stricter version. To my considerable surprise, a very good logician came up with an invalid argument that got past the earlier formulation of this restriction.

- Also, in **Chapter 14** (formerly Section 9.6) more treatment is accorded Ockham's razor in connection with explanations.

- The **"Logic and Graduate-Level Admissions Tests"** appendix, which draws a connection between logic and earning a good score on tests such as the LSAT, GMAT, and MCAT, has been completely rewritten and expanded, paying greater attention to logical strategies.

- Beginning with this edition, the *Learning Logic* program is available online at **ThomsonNOW™** (www.thomsonedu.com/ThomsonNOW). As a result, the CD-ROM containing that program has been removed from the book, but it is available as a bundled item at no additional cost, and separately at minimal cost. *Learning Logic* is a multimedia program that vastly simplifies the teaching of logic, allowing classroom time to be spent on troubleshooting and special interests.

- Two new multimedia offerings are available with this edition. Audio files that help students comprehend and retain the central concepts of logic, and that can be used as a final preparation before taking an exam, are available as mp3 files. They can be purchased and downloaded at www.iChapters.com. Video clips will be available through **ThomsonNOW** (formerly **iLrn**), as well as on the multimedia manager. These clips cover topics that students often find difficult, such as the concept of validity, conversion, obversion, and contraposition, indirect truth tables, and natural deduction. Each video is devoted to a brief lecture on one of these topics, together with pointers on how to work the exercises at the end of the pertinent section.

- In addition, numerous smaller changes have been introduced throughout the book. A list of the more significant ones can be found in the instructor's manual.

Note to the Student

Imagine that you are interviewing for a job. The person across the desk asks about your strengths, and you reply that you are energetic, enthusiastic, and willing to work long hours. Also, you are creative and innovative, and you have good leadership skills. Then the interviewer asks about your weaknesses. You hadn't anticipated this question, but after a moment's thought you reply that your reasoning skills have never been very good.

> The interviewer quickly responds that this weakness could create big problems.
> "Why is that?" you ask.
> "Because reasoning skills are essential to good judgment. And without good judgment your creativity will lead to projects that make no sense. Your leadership skills will direct our other employees in circles. Your enthusiasm will undermine everything we have accomplished up until now. And your working long hours will make things even worse."

"But don't you think there is some position in your company that is right for me?" you ask.

The interviewer thinks for a moment and then replies, "We have a competitor on the other side of town. I hear they are hiring right now. Why don't you apply with them?"

The point of this little dialogue is that good reasoning skills are essential to doing anything right. The business person uses reasoning skills in writing a report or preparing a presentation; the scientist uses them in designing an experiment or clinical trial, the department manager uses them in maximizing worker efficiency, the lawyer uses them in composing an argument to a judge or jury. And that's where logic comes in. The chief purpose of logic is to develop good reasoning skills. In fact, logic is so important that when the liberal arts program of studies was formulated fifteen hundred years ago, logic was selected as one of the original seven liberal arts. Logic remains to this day a central component of a college or university education.

From a more pragmatic angle, logic is important to earning a good score on any of the several tests required for admission to graduate professional schools—the LSAT, GMAT, MCAT, and so on. Obviously, the designers of these tests recognize that the ability to reason logically is a prerequisite to success in these fields. The appendix in the back of the book, which has been expanded for this edition, contains sample questions and cues on answering them. Also, logic is a useful tool in relieving what has come to be called math anxiety. For whatever reason, countless students today are terrified of any form of reasoning that involves abstract symbols. If you happen to be one of these students, you should find it relatively easy to master the use of logical symbols, and your newly found comfort with these symbols will carry over into the other, more difficult fields.

To improve your performance in logic, I strongly urge you to take full advantage of a multimedia program called *Learning Logic*. This is an interactive tutorial that teaches the essentials of this textbook in a very user-friendly way. However, your computer must be equipped with loudspeakers or headphones, because the audio component is essential. With earlier editions of this textbook, *Learning Logic* was written on a CD that came bundled with the book, and if your instructor has ordered it (at no additional cost), it may still be bundled with the book. However, *Learning Logic* is now available online through ThomsonNOW, and new books contain an access card that gives instructions on how to open the program. If you have a used book, you can still access *Learning Logic* through ThomsonNOW for a small fee or, alternately, purchase the CD separately.

Also available online through www.thomsonedu.com/ThomsonNOW are brief video lectures on key topics. The videos include pointers on how to work the pertinent exercises in the textbook. They cover topics such as the concept of validity, conversion, obversion, and contraposition, indirect truth tables, and natural deduction. If, as you work through the content of this book, you encounter a subject that you have trouble understanding, one of these videos may solve the problem.

Additionally, a set of audio summaries for each chapter in the book is available online at www.thomsonedu.com/philosophy/hurley. These are designed so that you can download them onto your iPod, mp3 player, or computer and listen to them before taking a test.

Because proficiency in logic involves developing a skill, it helps to work through the practice problems in *Learning Logic* and the exercises in the textbook more than once. This will help you see that good reasoning (and bad reasoning, too) follows certain patterns whose identification is crucial to success in logic. As you progress, I think you will find that learning logic can be lots of fun, and working with the online resources should enhance your overall learning experience.

Note to the Instructor: Alternative Course Approaches to the Textbook

Depending on the instructor's preferences, this textbook can be approached in several ways. The following chart presents possible approaches for three different kinds of courses.

In general, the material in each chapter is arranged so that certain later sections can be skipped without affecting subsequent chapters. For example, those wishing a brief treatment of natural deduction in both propositional and predicate logic may want to skip the last three sections of Chapter 7 and the last four (or even five) sections of Chapter 8. Chapter 2 can be skipped altogether, although some may want to cover the first section of that chapter as an introduction to Chapter 3. Finally, Chapters 9 through 14 depend only slightly on earlier chapters, so these can be treated in any order one chooses. However, Chapter 14 does depend in part on Chapter 13.

Type of Course

	Traditional logic course	Informal logic course, critical reasoning course	Course emphasizing modern formal logic
Recommended material	Chapter 1 Chapter 3 Chapter 4 Chapter 5 Chapter 6 Sections 7.1–7.4	Chapter 1 Chapter 2 Chapter 3 Chapter 4 Sections 5.1–5.3 Sections 5.5–5.6 Sections 6.1–6.4 Section 6.6 Chapter 9 Chapter 12 Chapter 13 Chapter 14 Writing Supplement	Chapter 1 Sections 4.1–4.3 Section 4.7 Sections 6.1–6.5 Chapter 7 Chapter 8 Truth Tree Supplement
Optional material	Chapter 2 Sections 7.5–7.7 Chapters 9–14	Section 5.4 Section 5.7 Section 6.5 Chapter 10 Chapter 11	Chapter 3 Sections 4.4–4.6 Sections 5.1–5.2 Section 5.7 Section 6.6

Acknowledgements

For their reviews and suggestions leading to this tenth edition I want to thank the following:

Joseph Asike, Howard University
Jerome Balmuth, Colgate University
Ida Baltikauskas, Century College
Robert Barnard, University of Mississippi
Victoria Berdon, IUPU Columbus
Tom Browder, University of Nevada, Las Vegas
Kevin Browne, Indiana University Southeast
Michael Byron, Kent State University
Charles Carr, Arkansas State University
Jennifer Caseldine-Bracht, IUPU Fort Wayne
John Casey, Northern Illinois University
Robert Greg Cavin, Cypress College
Prakash Chenjeri, Southern Oregon University
Timothy Christion, University of North Texas
Michael Cole, College of William and Mary
William Cornwell, Salem State College
Victor Cosculluela, Polk Community College
Joseph DeMarco, Cleveland State University
Mary Domski, University of New Mexico
Paul Draper, Purdue University
Paul Eckstein, Bergen Community College
Anne M. Edwards, Austin Peay State University
Michael Epperson, California State University, Sacramento
Cassandra Evans, San Diego City College
Frank Fair, Sam Houston State University
Timothy C. Fout, University of Louisville
Craig Fox, California University of Pennsylvania
Shannon Grace, Edmunds Community College
James Granitto, Santiago Canyon College
Catherine Green, Rockhurst University
James Greene, Northern Michigan University
Harold Greenstein, SUNY Brockport
Shahrokh Haghighi, California State University
Alexander W. Hall, Clayton State University
Dean Hamden, Montclair State University
Larry Hauser, Alma College
Deborah Heikes, University of Alabama in Huntsville
Dale Lynn Holt, Mississippi State University
John B. Howell, III, Southwestern Baptist Theological Seminary
Peter Hutcheson, Texas State University
Sandra Johanson, Green River Community College
Glenn C. Joy, Texas State University, San Marcos
Grant Julin, St. Francis University
Phillip McReynolds, Pennsylvania State University

Richard Miller, East Carolina University
Len Olsen, Georgia Southern University
Brendan O'Sullivan, Rhodes College
Linda Peterson, University of San Diego
Cassandra Pinnick, Western Kentucky University
Bruce Reichenbach, Augsburg College
Michael Rooney, Pasadena City College
Michelle M. Rotert, Rock Valley College
Robert Rupert, University of Colorado, Boulder
Sam Russo, El Camino College
Eric Saidel, George Washington University
Kelly Salsbery, Stephen F. Austin State University
Phil Schneider, Coastal Carolina University
Stephanie Semler, Radford University
Pat Sewell, University of North Texas
Elizabeth Shadish, El Camino College
Dennis L. Slivinski, California State University, Channel Islands
Paula Smithka, University of Southern Mississippi
David Stern, University of Iowa
John Sullins, Sonoma State University
Ramon Tello, Shasta College
Phil Thompson, Eastern Illinois University
Ted Ulrich, Purdue University
Robert Urekew, University of Louisville
Andrew J. Waskey, Dalton State University
Chris Weigand, Our Lady of the Lake University
Robert Wengert, University of Illinois, Urbana/Champaign
Gerald Joseph Williams, Seton Hall University
Stephen Wykstra, Calvin College
Marie Zaccaria, Georgia Perimeter College
Jeffrey Zents, University of Texas

Of course any errors or omissions that may remain are the result of my own oversight.

Those who have contributed reviews and suggestions leading to the nine previous editions, and to whom I express my continued thanks, are the following:

James T. Anderson, University of San Diego; Carol Anthony, Villanova University; Harriet E. Baber, University of San Diego; Kent Baldner, Western Michigan University; James Baley, Mary Washington College; Jerome Balmuth, Colgate University; Victor Balowitz, State University of New York, College at Buffalo; Gary Baran, Los Angeles City College; Gregory Bassham, Kings College; Thora Bayer, Xavier University of Louisiana; David Behan, Agnes Scott College; John Bender, Ohio University, Athens; James O. Bennett, University of Tennessee, Knoxville; Robert Berman, Xavier University of Louisana; Joseph Bessie, Normandale Community College; John R. Bosworth, Oklahoma State University; Andrew Botterell, University of Toronto; Harold Brown, Northern Illinois University; Ken Buckman, University of Texas, Pan American; Robert Burch, Texas A&M University; Keith Burgess-Jackson, University of Texas, Arlington; James Campbell, University of Toledo; Joseph Keim Campbell, Washington State University; William Carroll, Coppin State University; Greg

Cavin, Cypress College; Ping-Tung Chang, University of Alaska; Drew Christie, University of New Hampshire; Ralph W. Clarke, West Virginia University; David Clowney, Rowan University; Michael J. Colson, Merced College; William F. Cooper, Baylor University; Mike Coste, Front Range Community College; Ronald R. Cox, San Antonio College; Houston A. Craighead, Winthrop University; Donald Cress, Northern Illinois University, DeKalb; Drew Christie, University of New Hampshire; Jack Crumley, University of San Diego; Linda Damico, Kennesaw State University; William J. DeAngelis, Northeastern University; Paul DeVries, Wheaton College; Jill Dieterle, Eastern Michigan University; Beverly R. Doss and Richard W. Doss, Orange Coast College; William A. Drumin, King's College, Pennsylvania; Clinton Dunagan, Saint Philips College; Lenore Erickson, Cuesta College; Evan Fales, University of Iowa; Lewis S. Ford, Old Dominion University; Gary Foulk, Indiana State University, Terre Haute; LeAnn Fowler, Slippery Rock University; Thomas H. Franks, Eastern Michigan University; Bernard D. Freydberg, Slippery Rock University; Dick Gaffney, Siena College; George Gale, University of Missouri, Kansas City; Pieranna Garavaso, University of Minnesota at Morris; Joseph Georges, El Camino College; Kevin Gibson, University of Colorado; Victor Grassian, Los Angeles Harbor College; J. Randall Groves, Ferris State University, Ken Hanly, Brandon University; Ronald Hill, University of San Diego; Lawrence Hinman, University of San Diego; Lynn Holt, Mississippi State University; R. I. G. Hughes, University of South Carolina, Columbia; Peter Hutcheson, Texas State University; Debby D. Hutchins, Boston College; William H. Hyde, Golden West College; Gary Jones, University of San Diego; Glenn C. Joy, Southwest Texas State University; Olin Joynton, North Harris County College; Glen Kessler, University of Virginia; Charles F. Kielkopf, Ohio State University; Moya Kinchla, Bakersfield College; Bernard W. Kobes, Arizona State University; Keith W. Krasemann, College of DuPage; Richard La Croix, State University College at Buffalo; Sandra LaFave, West Valley College, Saratoga, California; Richard Lee, University of Arkansas; Lory Lemke, University of Minnesota, Morris; Robert Levis, Pasadena City College; Chenyang Li, Monmouth College, Monmouth, Illinois; Ardon Lyon, City University of London; Scott MacDonald, University of Iowa; Krishna Mallick, Salem State College; Thomas Manig, University of Missouri, Columbia; James Manns, University of Kentucky; Dalman Mayer, Bellevue Community College; Larry D. Mayhew, Western Kentucky University; Leemon McHenry, California State University, Northridge; Robert McKay, Norwich University; Rick McKita, Colorado State University; Noel Merino, Humboldt State University; Kenneth R. Merrill, University of Oklahoma; Thomas Michaud, Wheeling Jesuit College; Dolores Miller, University of Missouri, Kansas City; George D. Miller, DePaul University; Frederick Mills, Bowie State University; Jeff Mitchell, Arkansas Tech University; John Mize, Long Beach City College; Dwayne Mulder, California State University, Fresno; John D. Mullen, Dowling College; Henry Nardone, Kings College; Theresa Norman, South Texas Community College; David O'Connor, Seton Hall University; Elane O'Rourke, Moorpark College; Rodney Peffer, University of San Diego; Linda Peterson, University of San Diego; Robert G. Pielke, El Camino College; Nelson Pole, Cleveland State University; Norman Prigge, Bakersfield State University; Gray Prince, West Los Angeles College; R. Puligandla, University of Toledo; T. R. Quigley, Oakland University; Nani Rankin, Indiana University at Kokomo; Robert Redmon, Virginia Commonwealth University; David Ring, Southern Methodist University; Tony Roark, Boise State University; Phyllis Rooney, Oakland University; Beth Rosdatter, University of Kentucky; Paul A. Roth, University of Missouri, Saint Louis; Daniel Rothbart, George Mason University; Paul Santelli, Siena College; Stephen Satris, Clemson University; Philip Schneider, George Mason University; James D. Schumaker, University of North Carolina at Charlotte; Joseph G. Shay, Boston

College; Arnold Smith, Youngstown State University; John-Christian Smith, Youngstown State University; Eric W. Snider, University of Toledo; Bob Snyder, Humboldt University; Joseph Snyder, Anne Arundel Community College; Lynne Spellman, University of Arkansas; Gordon Steinhoff, Utah State University; James Stuart, Bowling Green State University; John Sweigart, James Madison University; Clarendon Swift, Moorpark College; Wayne Swindall, California Baptist College; Bangs Tapscott, University of Utah; Ramon Tello, Shasta College; Jan Thomas, University of Arkansas at Little Rock; Richard Tieszen, San Jose State University; Larry Udell, West Chester University; William Uzgalis, Oregon State University; Thomas H. Warren, Solano College; Roy Weatherford, University of South Florida; David Weinburger, Stockton State College; Paul Weirich, University of Missouri, Columbia; Frank Wilson, Bucknell University; and W. Kent Wilson, University of Illinois, Chicago.

Finally, it has been a pleasure working with production supervisor Greg Hubit, copy editor Molly Roth, and development editor Shelley Murphy. Also, I am grateful to Worth Hawes, philosophy editor at Wadsworth Thomson; to marketing manager Christina Shea; to Julie Aguilar, technology project manager; to assistant editor Patrick Stockstill; and to editorial assistant Kamilah Lee for their help and support.

A Concise Introduction to Logic

TENTH EDITION

Basic Concepts

1.1 Arguments, Premises, and Conclusions

Logic may be defined as the organized body of knowledge, or science, that evaluates arguments. All of us encounter arguments in our day-to-day experience. We read them in books and newspapers, hear them on television, and formulate them when communicating with friends and associates. The aim of logic is to develop a system of methods and principles that we may use as criteria for evaluating the arguments of others and as guides in constructing arguments of our own. Among the benefits to be expected from the study of logic is an increase in confidence that we are making sense when we criticize the arguments of others and when we advance arguments of our own.

An **argument,** in its most basic form, is a group of statements, one or more of which (the premises) are claimed to provide support for, or reasons to believe, one of the others (the conclusion). All arguments may be placed in one of two basic groups: those in which the premises really do support the conclusion and those in which they do not, even though they are claimed to. The former are said to be good arguments (at least to that extent), the latter bad arguments. The purpose of logic, as the science that evaluates arguments, is thus to develop methods and techniques that allow us to distinguish good arguments from bad.

As is apparent from the given definition, the term *argument* has a very specific meaning in logic. It does not mean, for example, a mere verbal fight, as one might have with one's parent, spouse, or friend. Let us examine the features of this definition in greater detail. First of all, an argument is a group of statements. A **statement** is a sentence that is either true or false—in other words, typically a declarative sentence or a sentence component that could stand as a declarative sentence. The following sentences are statements:

> Chocolate truffles are loaded with calories.
> Melatonin helps relieve jet lag.
> Political candidates always tell the complete truth.
> No wives ever cheat on their husbands.
> Tiger Woods plays golf and Maria Sharapova plays tennis.

The first two statements are true, the second two false. The last one expresses two statements, both of which are true. Truth and falsity are called the two possible **truth values** of a statement. Thus, the truth value of the first two statements is true, the truth value of the second two is false, and the truth value of the last statement, as well as that of its components, is true.

Unlike statements, many sentences cannot be said to be either true or false. Questions, proposals, suggestions, commands, and exclamations usually cannot, and so are not usually classified as statements. The following sentences are not statements:

Where is Khartoum?	(question)
Let's go to a movie tonight.	(proposal)
I suggest you get contact lenses.	(suggestion)
Turn off the TV right now.	(command)
Fantastic!	(exclamation)

The statements that make up an argument are divided into one or more premises and one and only one conclusion. The **premises** are the statements that set forth the reasons or evidence, and the **conclusion** is the statement that the evidence is claimed to support or imply. In other words, the conclusion is the statement that is claimed to follow from the premises. Here is an example of an argument:

All film stars are celebrities.
Halle Berry is a film star.
Therefore, Halle Berry is a celebrity.

The first two statements are the premises; the third is the conclusion. (The claim that the premises support or imply the conclusion is indicated by the word "therefore.") In this argument the premises really do support the conclusion, and so the argument is a good one. But consider this argument:

Some film stars are men.
Cameron Diaz is a film star.
Therefore, Cameron Diaz is a man.

In this argument the premises do not support the conclusion, even though they are claimed to, and so the argument is not a good one.

One of the most important tasks in the analysis of arguments is being able to distinguish premises from conclusions. If what is thought to be a conclusion is really a premise, and vice versa, the subsequent analysis cannot possibly be correct. Many arguments contain indicator words that provide clues in identifying premises and conclusion. Some typical **conclusion indicators** are

therefore	accordingly	entails that
wherefore	we may conclude	hence
thus	it must be that	it follows that
consequently	for this reason	implies that
we may infer	so	as a result

Whenever a statement follows one of these indicators, it can usually be identified as the conclusion. By process of elimination the other statements in the argument are the premises. Example:

> Tortured prisoners will say anything just to relieve the pain. Consequently, torture is not a reliable method of interrogation.

The conclusion of this argument is "Torture is not a reliable method of interrogation," and the premise is "Tortured prisoners will say anything just to relieve the pain."

If an argument does not contain a conclusion indicator, it may contain a premise indicator. Some typical **premise indicators** are

since	in that	seeing that
as indicated by	may be inferred from	for the reason that
because	as	inasmuch as
for	given that	owing to

Any statement following one of these indicators can usually be identified as a premise. Example:

> Expectant mothers should never use recreational drugs, since the use of these drugs can jeopardize the development of the fetus.

The premise of this argument is "The use of these drugs can jeopardize the development of the fetus," and the conclusion is "Expectant mothers should never use recreational drugs."

In reviewing the list of indicators, note that "for this reason" is a conclusion indicator, whereas "for the reason that" is a premise indicator. "For this reason" (except when followed by a colon) means for the reason (premise) that was just given, so what follows is the conclusion. On the other hand, "for the reason that" announces that a premise is about to be stated.

Sometimes a single indicator can be used to identify more than one premise. Consider the following argument:

> It is vitally important that wilderness areas be preserved, for wilderness provides essential habitat for wildlife, including endangered species, and it is a natural retreat from the stress of daily life.

The premise indicator "for" goes with both "Wilderness provides essential habitat for wildlife, including endangered species," and "It is a natural retreat from the stress of daily life." These are the premises. By method of elimination, "It is vitally important that wilderness areas be preserved" is the conclusion.

Some arguments contain no indicators. With these, the reader/listener must ask such questions as: What single statement is claimed (implicitly) to follow from the others? What is the arguer trying to prove? What is the main point in the passage? The answers to these questions should point to the conclusion. Example:

> The space program deserves increased expenditures in the years ahead. Not only does the national defense depend on it, but the program will more than pay for itself in terms of technological spinoffs. Furthermore, at current funding levels the program cannot fulfill its anticipated potential.

The conclusion of this argument is the first statement, and all of the other statements are premises. The argument illustrates the pattern found in most arguments that lack indicator words: the intended conclusion is stated first, and the remaining statements are then offered in support of this first statement. When the argument is restructured according to logical principles, however, the conclusion is always listed *after* the premises:

> P_1: The national defense is dependent on the space program.
> P_2: The space program will more than pay for itself in terms of technological spinoffs.
> P_3: At current funding levels the space program cannot fulfill its anticipated potential.
> C: The space program deserves increased expenditures in the years ahead.

When restructuring arguments such as this, one should remain as close as possible to the original version, while at the same time attending to the requirement that premises and conclusion be complete sentences that are meaningful in the order in which they are listed.

Note that the first two premises are included within the scope of a single sentence in the original argument. For the purposes of this chapter, compound arrangements of statements in which the various components are all claimed to be true will be considered as separate statements.

Passages that contain arguments sometimes contain statements that are neither premises nor conclusions. Only statements that are actually intended to support the conclusion should be included in the list of premises. If, for example, a statement serves merely to introduce the general topic, or merely makes a passing comment, it should not be taken as part of the argument. Examples:

> The claim is often made that malpractice lawsuits drive up the cost of health care. But if such suits were outlawed or severely restricted, then patients would have no means of recovery for injuries caused by negligent doctors. Hence, the availability of malpractice litigation should be maintained intact.

> Currently 47 million Americans are without health insurance. When these people go to a hospital, they are routinely charged two to three times the normal cost for treatment. This practice, which covers the cost of treating indigent patients, is clearly unfair. For these reasons, a national health insurance program should be adopted. Politicians who oppose this change should be ashamed of themselves.

In the first argument, the opening statement serves merely to introduce the topic, so it is not part of the argument. The premise is the second statement, and the conclusion is the last statement. In the second argument, the final statement merely makes a passing comment, so it is not part of the argument. The premises are the first three statements, and the statement following "for these reasons" is the conclusion.

Closely related to the concepts of argument and statement are those of inference and proposition. An **inference,** in the narrow sense of the term, is the reasoning process expressed by an argument. In the broad sense of the term, "inference" is used interchangeably with "argument." Analogously, a **proposition,** in the narrow sense, is the meaning or information content of a statement. For the purposes of this book, however, "proposition" and "statement" are used interchangeably.

Note on the History of Logic

The person who is generally credited as the father of logic is the ancient Greek philosopher Aristotle (384–322 B.C.). Aristotle's predecessors had been interested in the art of constructing persuasive arguments and in techniques for refuting the arguments of others, but it was Aristotle who first devised systematic criteria for analyzing and evaluating arguments.

Aristotle's chief accomplishment is called **syllogistic logic,** a kind of logic in which the fundamental elements are *terms,* and arguments are evaluated as good or bad depending on how the terms are arranged in the argument. Chapters 4 and 5 of this textbook are devoted mainly to syllogistic logic. But Aristotle also deserves credit for originating **modal logic,** a kind of logic that involves such concepts as possibility, necessity, belief, and doubt. In addition, Aristotle catalogued several informal fallacies, a topic treated in Chapter 3 of this book.

After Aristotle's death, another Greek philosopher, Chrysippus (280–206 B.C.), one of the founders of the Stoic school, developed a logic in which the fundamental elements were *whole propositions.* Chrysippus treated every proposition as either true or false and developed rules for determining the truth or falsity of compound propositions from the truth or falsity of their components. In the course of doing so, he laid the foundation for the truth functional interpretation of the logical connectives presented in Chapter 6 of this book and introduced the notion of natural deduction, treated in Chapter 7.

For thirteen hundred years after the death of Chrysippus, relatively little creative work was done in logic. The physician Galen (A.D. 129–ca. 199) developed the theory of the compound categorical syllogism, but for the most part philosophers confined themselves to writing commentaries on the works of Aristotle and Chrysippus. Boethius (ca. 480–524) is a noteworthy example.

The first major logician of the Middle Ages was Peter Abelard (1079–1142). Abelard reconstructed and refined the logic of Aristotle and Chrysippus as communicated by Boethius, and he originated a theory of universals that traced the universal character of general terms to concepts in the mind rather than to "natures" existing outside the mind, as Aristotle had held. In addition, Abelard distinguished arguments that are valid because of their form from those that are valid because of their content, but he

Aristotle 384–322 B.C.

© Mansell/Time Life Pictures/Getty Images

Aristotle was born in Stagira, a small Greek town situated on the northern coast of the Aegean sea. His father was a physician in the court of King Amyntas II of Macedonia, and the young Aristotle was a friend of the King's son Philip, who was later to become king himself and the father of Alexander the Great. When he was about seventeen, Aristotle was sent to Athens to further his education in Plato's Academy, the finest institution of higher learning in the Greek world. After Plato's death Aristotle left for Assos, a small town on the coast of Asia Minor, where he married the niece of the local ruler.

Six years later Aristotle accepted an invitation to return to Macedonia to serve as tutor of the young Alexander. When Alexander ascended the throne following his father's assassination, Aristotle's tutorial job was finished, and he departed for Athens where he set up a school near the temple of Apollo Lyceus. The school came to be known as the Lyceum, and Alexander supported it with contributions of money and specimens of flora and fauna derived from his far-flung conquests. After Alexander's death, an anti-Macedonian rebellion forced Aristotle to leave Athens for Chalcis, about thirty miles to the north, where he died one year later at the age of sixty-two.

Aristotle is universally recognized as the originator of logic. He defined *logic* as the study of the process by which a statement follows by necessity from one or more other statements. The most fundamental kind of statement, he thought, is the categorical proposition, and he classified the four kinds of categorical propositions in terms of their being universal, particular, affirmative, and negative. He also developed the square of opposition, which shows how one such proposition implies the truth or falsity of another, and he identified the relations of conversion, obversion, and contraposition, which provide the basis for various immediate inferences.

His crowning achievement is the theory of the categorical syllogism, a kind of argument consisting of three categorical propositions. He showed how categorical syllogisms can be catalogued in terms of mood and figure, and he developed a set of rules for determining the validity of categorical syllogisms. Also, he showed how the modal concepts of possibility and necessity apply to categorical propositions. In addition to the theory of the syllogism, Aristotle advanced the theory of definition by genus and difference, and he showed how arguments could be defective in terms of thirteen forms of informal fallacy.

Aristotle made profound contributions to many areas of human learning including biology, physics, metaphysics, epistemology, psychology, aesthetics, ethics, and politics. However, his accomplishments in logic were so extensive and enduring that two thousand years after his death, the great philosopher Immanuel Kant said that Aristotle had discovered everything that could be known about logic. His logic was not superseded until the end of the nineteenth century when Frege, Whitehead, and Russell developed modern mathematical logic.

held that only formal validity is the "perfect" or conclusive variety. The present text follows Abelard on this point.

After Abelard, the study of logic during the Middle Ages flourished through the work of numerous philosophers. A logical treatise by William of Sherwood (ca. 1200–1271) contains the first expression of the "Barbara, Celarent . . ." poem quoted in Section 5.1 of this book, and the *Summulae Logicales* of Peter of Spain (ca. 1205–1277) became the standard textbook in logic for three hundred years. However, the most original contributions from this period were made by William of Ockham (ca. 1285–1347). Ockham extended the theory of modal logic, conducted an exhaustive study of the forms of valid and invalid syllogisms, and further developed the idea of a metalanguage, a higher-level language used to discuss linguistic entities such as words, terms, and propositions.

Toward the middle of the fifteenth century, a reaction set in against the logic of the Middle Ages. Rhetoric largely displaced logic as the primary focus of attention; the logic of Chrysippus, which had already begun to lose its unique identity in the Middle Ages, was ignored altogether, and the logic of Aristotle was studied only in highly simplistic presentations. A reawakening did not occur until two hundred years later through the work of Gottfried Wilhelm Leibniz (1646–1716).

Leibniz, a genius in numerous fields, attempted to develop a symbolic language or "calculus" that could be used to settle all forms of disputes, whether in theology, philosophy, or international relations. As a result of this work, Leibniz is sometimes credited with being the father of symbolic logic. Leibniz's efforts to symbolize logic were carried into the nineteenth century by Bernard Bolzano (1781–1848).

In the middle of the nineteenth century, logic commenced an extremely rapid period of development that has continued to this day. Work in symbolic logic was done by many philosophers and mathematicians, including Augustus De Morgan (1806–1871), George Boole (1815–1864), William Stanley Jevons (1835–1882), and John Venn (1834–1923). The rule bearing De Morgan's name is used in Chapter 7 of this book. Boole's interpretation of categorical propositions and Venn's method for diagramming them are covered in Chapters 4 and 5. At the same time a revival in inductive logic was initiated by the British philosopher John Stuart Mill (1806–1873), whose methods of induction are presented in Chapter 10.

Across the Atlantic, the American philosopher Charles Sanders Peirce (1839–1914) developed a logic of relations, invented symbolic quantifiers, and suggested the truth-table method for formulas in propositional logic. These topics are covered in Chapters 6 and 8 of this book. The truth-table method was completed independently by Emile Post (1897–1954) and Ludwig Wittgenstein (1889–1951).

Toward the end of the nineteenth century, the foundations of modern mathematical logic were laid by Gottlob Frege (1848–1925). His *Begriffsschrift* sets forth the theory of quantification presented in Chapter 8 of this text. Frege's work was continued into the twentieth century by Alfred North Whitehead (1861–1947) and Bertrand Russell (1872–1970), whose monumental *Principia Mathematica* attempted to reduce the whole of pure mathematics to logic. The *Principia* is the source of much of the symbolism that appears in Chapters 6, 7, and 8 of this text.

During the twentieth century, much of the work in logic has focused on the formalization of logical systems and on questions dealing with the completeness and consistency of such systems. A now-famous theorem proved by Kurt Gödel (1906–1978) states that in any formal system adequate for number theory there exists an undecidable formula—that is, a formula such that neither it nor its negation is derivable from the axioms of the system. Other developments include multivalued logics and the formalization of modal logic. Most recently, logic has made a major contribution to technology by providing the conceptual foundation for the electronic circuitry of digital computers.

EXERCISE 1.1

I. Each of the following passages contains a single argument. Using the letters "P" and "C," identify the premises and conclusion of each argument, writing premises first and conclusion last. List the premises in the order in which they make the most sense (usually the order in which they occur), and write both premises and conclusion in the form of separate declarative sentences. Indicator words may be eliminated once premises and conclusion have been appropriately labeled. The exercises marked with a star are answered in the back of the book.

★1. Titanium combines readily with oxygen, nitrogen, and hydrogen, all of which have an adverse effect on its mechanical properties. As a result, titanium must be processed in their absence.

(Illustrated World of Science Encyclopedia)

2. Since the good, according to Plato, is that which furthers a person's real interests, it follows that in any given case when the good is known, men will seek it.

(Avrum Stroll and Richard Popkin, *Philosophy and the Human Spirit*)

3. As the denial or perversion of justice by the sentences of courts, as well as in any other manner, is with reason classed among the just causes of war, it will follow that the federal judiciary ought to have cognizance of all causes in which the citizens of other countries are concerned.

(Alexander Hamilton, *Federalist Papers,* No. 80)

★4. When individuals voluntarily abandon property, they forfeit any expectation of privacy in it that they might have had. Therefore, a warrantless search or seizure of abandoned property is not unreasonable under the Fourth Amendment.

(Judge Stephanie Kulp Seymour, *United States v. Jones*)

5. Artists and poets look at the world and seek relationships and order. But they translate their ideas to canvas, or to marble, or into poetic images. Scientists try to find relationships between different objects and events. To express the order they find, they create hypotheses and theories. Thus the great scientific theories are easily compared to great art and great literature.

(Douglas C. Giancoli, *The Ideas of Physics,* 3rd ed.)

6. The fact that there was never a land bridge between Australia and mainland Asia is evidenced by the fact that the animal species in the two areas are very different. Asian placental mammals and Australian marsupial mammals have not been in contact in the last several million years.

(T. Douglas Price and Gary M. Feinman, *Images of the Past*)

★7. Cuba's record on disaster prevention is impressive. After October 1963, when Hurricane Flora devastated the island and killed more than a thousand people, the Cuban government overhauled its civil defense system. It was so successful that when six powerful hurricanes thumped Cuba between 1996 and 2002 only 16 people died. And when Hurricane Ivan struck Cuba in 2004 there was not a single casualty, but the same storm killed at least 70 people in other Caribbean countries.

(Newspaper clipping)

8. The classroom teacher is crucial to the development and academic success of the average student, and administrators simply are ancillary to this effort. For this reason, classroom teachers ought to be paid at least the equivalent of administrators at all levels, including the superintendent.

(Peter F. Falstrup, letter to the editor)

9. An agreement cannot bind unless both parties to the agreement know what they are doing and freely choose to do it. This implies that the seller who intends to enter a contract with a customer has a duty to disclose exactly what the customer is buying and what the terms of the sale are.

(Manuel G. Velasquez, "The Ethics of Consumer Production")

★10. Punishment, when speedy and specific, may suppress undesirable behavior, but it cannot teach or encourage desirable alternatives. Therefore, it is crucial to use positive techniques to model and reinforce appropriate behavior that the person can use in place of the unacceptable response that has to be suppressed.

(Walter Mischel and Harriet Mischel, *Essentials of Psychology*)

11. Profit serves a very crucial function in a free enterprise economy, such as our own. High profits are the signal that consumers want more of the output of the industry. High profits provide the incentive for firms to expand output and for more firms to enter the industry in the long run. For a firm of above-average efficiency, profits represent the reward for greater efficiency.

(Dominic Salvatore, *Managerial Economics*, 3rd ed.)

12. Cats can think circles around dogs! My cat regularly used to close and lock the door to my neighbor's doghouse, trapping their sleeping Doberman inside. Try telling a cat what to do, or putting a leash on him—he'll glare at you and say, "I don't think so. You should have gotten a dog."

(Kevin Purkiser, letter to the editor)

★13. Since private property helps people define themselves, since it frees people from mundane cares of daily subsistence, and since it is finite, no individual should accumulate so much property that others are prevented from accumulating the necessities of life.

(Leon P. Baradat, *Political Ideologies, Their Origins and Impact*)

14. To every existing thing God wills some good. Hence, since to love any thing is nothing else than to will good to that thing, it is manifest that God loves everything that exists.

(Thomas Aquinas, *Summa Theologica*)

15. [Women of the working class, especially wage workers, should not have more than two children at most.] The average working man can support no more and the average working woman can take care of no more in decent fashion.

(Margaret Sanger, *Family Limitations*)

★16. Radioactive fallout isn't the only concern in the aftermath of nuclear explosions. The nations of planet Earth have acquired nuclear weapons with an explosive power equal to more than a million Hiroshima bombs. Studies suggest that explosion of only half these weapons would produce enough soot, smoke, and dust to blanket the Earth, block out the sun, and bring on a nuclear winter that would threaten the survival of the human race.

(John W. Hill and Doris K. Kolb, *Chemistry for Changing Times*, 7th ed.)

17. An ant releases a chemical when it dies, and its fellows then carry it away to the compost heap. [Apparently the communication is highly effective;] a healthy ant painted with the death chemical will be dragged to the funeral heap again and again.

(Carol R. Ember and Melvin Ember, *Cultural Anthropology*, 7th ed.)

18. [Every art and every inquiry, and similarly every action and pursuit, is thought to aim at some good;] and for this reason the good has rightly been declared to be that at which all things aim.

(Aristotle, *Nicomachean Ethics*)

★19. Poverty offers numerous benefits to the nonpoor. Antipoverty programs provide jobs for middle-class professionals in social work, penology, and public health. Such workers' future advancement is tied to the continued growth of bureaucracies dependent on the existence of poverty.

(J. John Palen, *Social Problems*)

20. Corn is an annual crop. Butcher's meat, a crop which requires four or five years to grow. [As an acre of land, therefore, will produce a much smaller quantity of the one species of food than the other, the inferiority of the quantity must be compensated by the superiority of the price.]

(Adam Smith, *The Wealth of Nations*)

21. [Neither a borrower nor lender be]
    For loan oft loses both itself and friend,
    And borrowing dulls the edge of husbandry.

(William Shakespeare, *Hamlet* I, 3)

★22. The stakes in whistleblowing are high. Take the nurse who alleges that physicians enrich themselves in her hospital through unnecessary surgery; the engineer who discloses safety defects in the braking systems of a fleet of new rapid-transit vehicles; the Defense Department official who alerts Congress to military graft and overspending: all know that they pose a threat to those whom they denounce and that their own careers may be at risk.

(Sissela Bok, "Whistleblowing and Professional Responsibility")

23. If a piece of information is not "job relevant," then the employer is not entitled qua employer to know it. Consequently, since sexual practices, political beliefs, associational activities, etc., are not part of the description of most jobs, that is, since they do not directly affect one's job performance they are not legitimate information for an employer to know in the determination of the hiring of a job applicant.

(George G. Brenkert," Privacy, Polygraphs, and Work")

24. Many people believe that a dark tan is attractive and a sign of good health, but mounting evidence indicates that too much sun can lead to health problems. One of the most noticeable effects is premature aging of the skin. The sun also contributes to certain types of cataracts, and, what is most worrisome, it plays a role in skin cancer.

(Joseph M. Moran and Michael D. Morgan, *Meteorology*, 4th ed.)

★25. Contrary to the tales of some scuba divers, the toothy, gaping grin on the mouth of an approaching shark is not necessarily anticipatory. It is generally accepted that by constantly swimming with its mouth open, the shark is simply avoiding suffocation. This assures a continuous flow of oxygen-laden water into their mouths, over their gills, and out through the gill slits.

(Robert A. Wallace et al., *Biology: The Science of Life*)

26. Not only is the sky blue [as a result of scattering], but light coming from it is also partially polarized. You can readily observe this by placing a piece of Polaroid (for example, one lens of a pair of Polaroid sunglasses) in front of your eye and rotating it as you look at the sky on a clear day. You will notice a change in light intensity with the orientation of the Polaroid.

(Frank J. Blatt, *Principles of Physics,* 2nd ed.)

27. Since the secondary light [from the moon] does not inherently belong to the moon and is not received from any star or from the sun, and since in the whole universe there is no other body left but the earth, what must we conclude? What is to be proposed? Surely we must assert that the lunar body (or any other dark and sunless orb) is illuminated by the earth.

(Galileo Galilei, *The Starry Messenger*)

★28. Anyone familiar with our prison system knows that there are some inmates who behave little better than brute beasts. But the very fact that these prisoners exist is a telling argument against the efficacy of capital punishment as a deterrent. If the death penalty had been truly effective as a deterrent, such prisoners would long ago have vanished.

("The Injustice of the Death Penalty," *America*)

29. Though it is possible that REM sleep and dreaming are not necessary in the adult, REM deprivation studies seem to suggest otherwise. Why would REM pressure increase with deprivation if the system is unimportant in the adult?

(Herbert L. Petri, *Motivation: Theory and Research*, 2nd ed.)

30. |World government and the balance of power are in many ways opposites.| World government means one central authority, a permanent standing world police force, and clearly defined conditions under which this force will go into action. A balance of power system has many sovereign authorities, each controlling its own army, combining only when they feel like it to control aggression. To most people world government now seems unattainable.

(David W. Ziegler, *War, Peace, and International Politics,* 4th ed.)

II. The following arguments were taken from magazine and newspaper editorials and letters to the editor. In most instances the main conclusion must be rephrased to capture the full intent of the author. Write out what you interpret the main conclusion to be.

★1. University administrators know well the benefits that follow notable success in college sports: increased applications for admissions, increased income from licensed logo merchandise, more lucrative television deals, post-season game revenue and more successful alumni fund drives. The idea that there is something ideal and pure about the amateur athlete is self-serving bunk.

(Michael McDonnell, letter to the editor)

2. In a nation of immigrants, people of diverse ethnic backgrounds must have a common bond through which to exchange ideas. How can this bond be accomplished if there is no common language? It is those who shelter the immigrant from learning English by encouraging the development of a multilingual society who are creating a xenophobic atmosphere. They allow the immigrant to surround himself with a cocoon of language from which he cannot escape and which others cannot penetrate.

(Rita Toften, letter to the editor)

3. The health and fitness of our children has become a problem partly because of our attitude toward athletics. The purpose of sports, especially for children, should be to make healthy people healthier. The concept of team sports has failed to do this. Rather than learning to interact and cooperate with others, youngsters are taught to compete. Team sports have only reinforced the notion that the team on top is the winner, and all others are losers. This approach does not make sports appealing to many children, and some, especially among the less fit, burn out by the time they are twelve.

(Mark I. Pitman, "Young Jocks")

★4. College is the time in which a young mind is supposed to mature and acquire wisdom, and one can only do this by experiencing as much diverse intellectual stimuli as possible. A business student may be a whiz at accounting, but has he or she ever experienced the beauty of a Shakespearean sonnet or the boundless events composing Hebrew history? Most likely not. While many of these neoconservatives will probably go on to be financially successful, they are robbing themselves of the true purpose of collegiate academics, a sacrifice that outweighs the future salary checks.

(Robert S. Griffith, "Conservative College Press")

5. History has shown repeatedly that you cannot legislate morality, nor does anyone have a right to. The real problem is the people who have a vested interest in sustaining the multibillion-dollar drug industry created by the laws against drugs. The legalization of drugs would remove the thrill of breaking the law; it would end the suffering caused by unmetered doses, impurities, and substandard paraphernalia. A huge segment of the underground and extralegal economy would move into a legitimate economy, taking money away from criminals, eliminating crime and violence, and restoring many talented people to useful endeavor.

(Thomas L. Wayburn, letter to the editor)

6. Infectious disease is no longer the leading cause of death in this country, thanks to antibiotics, but there are new strains of bacteria that are resistant to—and others that grow only in the presence of—antibiotics. Yet Congress wants to cut the National Institutes of Health budget. Further cuts would leave us woefully unprepared to cope with the new microbes Mother Nature has cooking in her kitchen.

(Valina L. Dawson, letter to the editor)

★7. At a time when our religious impulses might help heal the pains and strains in our society, today's television pulpiteers preach intolerance, censure, and discrimination. They package a "believer life-style," and rail against everyone who doesn't fit it—homosexuals, communists, Jews and other non-Christians, sex educators, and so on. Such intolerance threatens to undermine the pluralism that marks our heritage. The packaging of that intolerance in slick Hollywood programming or under the guise of patriotic fervor is skillfully accomplished on many fronts. That, however, does not make it right.

(Peter G. Kreitler, "TV Preachers' Religious Intolerance")

8. Ideally, decisions about health care should be based on the doctor's clinical judgment, patient preference, and scientific evidence. Patients should always be presented with options in their care. Elective cesarean section, however, is not used to treat a problem but to avoid a natural process. An elective surgery like this puts the patient at unnecessary risk, increases the risk for complications in future deliveries, and increases health care costs.

(Anne Foster-Rosales, M.D., letter to the editor)

9. Parents who feel guilty for the little time they can (or choose to) spend with their children "pick up" after them—so the children don't learn to face the consequences of their own choices and actions. Parents who allow their children to fail are showing them greater love and respect.

(Susan J. Peters, letter to the editor)

★**10.** Most of the environmental problems facing us stem, at least in part, from the sheer number of Americans. The average American produces three quarters of a ton of garbage every year, consumes hundreds of gallons of gasoline, and uses large amounts of electricity (often from a nuclear power plant, coal burning, or a dam). The least painful way to protect the environment is to limit population growth.

(Craig M. Bradley, letter to the editor)

III. Define the following terms:

logic	conclusion	inference
argument	conclusion indicator	proposition
statement	premise indicator	truth value
premise		

IV. Answer "true" or "false" to the following statements:

1. The purpose of the premise or premises is to set forth the reasons or evidence given in support of the conclusion.
2. Some arguments have more than one conclusion.
3. All arguments must have more than one premise.
4. The words "therefore," "hence," "so," "since," and "thus" are all conclusion indicators.
5. The words "for," "because," "as," and "for the reason that" are all premise indicators.
6. In the strict sense of the terms, *inference* and *argument* have exactly the same meaning.
7. In most (but not all) arguments that lack indicator words, the conclusion is the first statement.
8. Any sentence that is either true or false is a statement.
9. Every statement has a truth value.
10. The person usually credited with being the father of logic is Aristotle.

1.2   **Recognizing Arguments**

Not all passages contain arguments. Because logic deals with arguments, it is important to be able to distinguish passages that contain arguments from those that do not. In general, a passage contains an argument if it purports to prove something; if it does not do so, it does not contain an argument. Two conditions must be fulfilled for a passage to purport to prove something:

1. At least one of the statements must claim to present evidence or reasons.
2. There must be a claim that the alleged evidence supports or implies something— that is, a claim that something follows from the alleged evidence or reasons.

As we have seen, the statements that claim to present the evidence or reasons are the premises, and the statement that the evidence is claimed to support or imply is the conclusion. It is not necessary that the premises present actual evidence or true reasons nor that the premises actually support the conclusion. But at least the premises must *claim* to present evidence or reasons, and there must be a *claim* that the evidence or reasons support or imply something.

The first condition expresses a **factual claim,** and deciding whether it is fulfilled often falls outside the domain of logic. Thus, most of our attention will be concentrated on whether the second condition is fulfilled. This second condition expresses what is called an **inferential claim.** The inferential claim is simply the claim that the passage expresses a certain kind of reasoning process—that something supports or implies something or that something follows from something. Also, you should recognize that this claim is not equatable with the intentions of the arguer. Intentions are subjective and, as such, are usually not accessible to the evaluator. Rather, the inferential claim is an objective feature of an argument grounded in its language or structure.

An inferential claim can be either explicit or implicit. An *explicit* inferential claim is usually asserted by premise or conclusion indicator words ("thus," "since," "because," "hence," "therefore," and so on). Example:

> Mad cow disease is spread by feeding parts of infected animals to cows, and this practice has yet to be completely eradicated. Thus, mad cow disease continues to pose a threat to people who eat beef.

The word "thus" expresses the claim that something is being inferred, so the passage is an argument.

An *implicit* inferential claim exists if there is an inferential relationship between the statements in a passage, but the passage contains no indicator words. Example:

> The genetic modification of food is risky business. Genetic engineering can introduce unintended changes into the DNA of the food-producing organism, and these changes can be toxic to the consumer.

The inferential relationship between the first statement and the other two constitutes an implicit claim that evidence supports something, so we are justified in calling the passage an argument. The first statement is the conclusion, and the other two are the premises.

In deciding whether there is a claim that evidence supports or implies something, keep an eye out for (1) indicator words and (2) the presence of an inferential relationship between the statements. In connection with these points, however, a word of caution is in order. First, the mere occurrence of an indicator word by no means guarantees the presence of an argument. For example, consider the following passages:

> Since Edison invented the phonograph, there have been many technological developments.

> Since Edison invented the phonograph, he deserves credit for a major technological development.

In the first passage the word "since" is used in a *temporal* sense. It means "from the time that." Thus, the first passage is not an argument. In the second passage "since" is used in a *logical* sense, and so the passage *is* an argument.

The second cautionary point is that it is not always easy to detect the occurrence of an inferential relationship between the statements in a passage, and one may have to review a passage several times before making a decision. In reaching such a decision, one may find it helpful to mentally insert the word "therefore" before the various statements to see whether it makes sense to interpret one of them as following from the others. Even with this mental aid, however, the decision whether a passage contains an inferential relationship (as well as the decision about indicator words) often involves a heavy dose of interpretation. As a result, not everyone will agree about every passage. Sometimes the only answer possible is a conditional one: "*If* this passage contains an argument, then these are the premises and that is the conclusion."

To assist in distinguishing passages that contain arguments from those that do not, let us now investigate some typical kinds of nonarguments. These include simple noninferential passages, expository passages, illustrations, explanations, and conditional statements.

Simple Noninferential Passages

Simple noninferential passages are unproblematic passages that lack a claim that anything is being proved. Such passages contain statements that could be premises or conclusions (or both), but what is missing is a claim that any potential premise supports a conclusion or that any potential conclusion is supported by premises. Passages of this sort include warnings, pieces of advice, statements of belief or opinion, loosely associated statements, and reports.

A **warning** is a form of expression that is intended to put someone on guard against a dangerous or detrimental situation. Examples:

> Watch out that you don't slip on the ice.
> Whatever you do, never confide personal secrets to Blabbermouth Bob.

If no evidence is given to prove that such statements are true, then there is no argument.

A **piece of advice** is a form of expression that makes a recommendation about some future decision or course of conduct. Examples:

> You should keep a few things in mind before buying a used car. Test drive the car at varying speeds and conditions, examine the oil in the crankcase, ask to see service records, and, if possible, have the engine and power train checked by a mechanic.

> Before accepting a job after class hours, I would suggest that you give careful consideration to your course load. Will you have sufficient time to prepare for classes and tests, and will the job produce an excessive drain on your energies?

As with warnings, if there is no evidence that is intended to prove anything, then there is no argument.

A **statement of belief** or **opinion** is an expression about what someone happens to believe or think about something. Examples:

> We believe that our company must develop and produce outstanding products that will perform a great service or fulfill a need for our customers. We believe that our

business must be run at an adequate profit and that the services and products we offer must be better than those offered by competitors.

(Robert D. Hay and Edmund R. Gray, "Introduction to Social Responsibility")

When I can read the latte menu through the hole in my server's earlobe, something is seriously out of whack. What happened to an earring, maybe two, in each lobe? Now any surface is game. Brow, lip, tongue, cheek, nose. I've adjusted to untied shoelaces and pants that make mooning irrelevant. But when it comes to piercings, I just can't budge.

(Debra Darvick, "Service with a Smile, and Plenty of Metal")

Because neither of these authors makes any claim that his or her belief or opinion is supported by evidence, or that it supports some conclusion, there is no argument.

Loosely associated statements may be about the same general subject, but they lack a claim that one of them is proved by the others. Example:

Not to honor men of worth will keep the people from contention; not to value goods that are hard to come by will keep them from theft; not to display what is desirable will keep them from being unsettled of mind.

(Lao-Tzu, *Thoughts from the Tao Te Ching*)

Because there is no claim that any of these statements provides evidence or reasons for believing another, there is no argument.

A **report** consists of a group of statements that convey information about some topic or event. Example:

Even though more of the world is immunized than ever before, many old diseases have proven quite resilient in the face of changing population and environmental conditions, especially in the developing world. New diseases, such as AIDS, have taken their toll in both the North and the South.

(Steven L. Spiegel, *World Politics in a New Era*)

These statements could serve as the premises of an argument, but because the author makes no claim that they support or imply anything, there is no argument. Another type of report is the news report:

Witnesses said they heard a loud crack before a balcony gave way at a popular nightspot, dropping dozens of screaming people fourteen feet. At least eighty people were injured at the Diamond Horseshoe casino when they fell onto broken glass and splintered wood. Investigators are waiting for an engineer's report on the deck's occupancy load.

(Newspaper clipping)

Again, because the reporter makes no claim that these statements imply anything, there is no argument.

One must be careful, though, with reports *about* arguments:

"The Air Force faces a serious shortage of experienced pilots in the years ahead, because repeated overseas tours and the allure of high paying jobs with commercial airlines are winning out over lucrative bonuses to stay in the service," says a prominent Air Force official.

(Newspaper clipping)

Properly speaking, this passage is not an argument, because the author of the passage does not claim that anything is supported by evidence. Rather, the author reports the claim by the Air Force official that something is supported by evidence. If such passages are interpreted as "containing" arguments, it must be made clear that the argument is not the author's but one made by someone about whom the author is reporting.

Expository Passages

An **expository passage** is a kind of discourse that begins with a topic sentence followed by one or more sentences that develop the topic sentence. If the objective is not to prove the topic sentence but only to expand it or elaborate it, then there is no argument. Examples:

There are three familiar states of matter: solid, liquid, and gas. Solid objects ordinarily maintain their shape and volume regardless of their location. A liquid occupies a definite volume, but assumes the shape of the occupied portion of its container. A gas maintains neither shape nor volume. It expands to fill completely whatever container it is in.

(John W. Hill and Doris K. Kolb, *Chemistry for Changing Times,* 7th ed.)

There is a stylized relation of artist to mass audience in the sports, especially in baseball. Each player develops a style of his own—the swagger as he steps to the plate, the unique windup a pitcher has, the clean-swinging and hard-driving hits, the precision quickness and grace of infield and outfield, the sense of surplus power behind whatever is done.

(Max Lerner, *America as a Civilization*)

In each passage the topic sentence is stated first, and the remaining sentences merely develop and flesh out this topic sentence. These passages are not arguments, because they lack an inferential claim. However, expository passages differ from simple noninferential passages (such as warnings and pieces of advice) in that many of them can also be taken as arguments. If the purpose of the subsequent sentences in the passage is not only to flesh out the topic sentence but also to prove it, then the passage is an argument. Example:

Skin and the mucous membrane lining the respiratory and digestive tracts serve as mechanical barriers to entry by microbes. Oil gland secretions contain chemicals that weaken or kill bacteria on skin. The respiratory tract is lined by cells that sweep mucus and trapped particles up into the throat, where they can be swallowed. The stomach has an acidic pH, which inhibits the growth of many types of bacteria.

(Sylvia S. Mader, *Human Biology,* 4th ed.)

In this passage the topic sentence is stated first, and the purpose of the remaining sentences is not only to *show how* the skin and mucous membranes serve as barriers to microbes but also to *prove* that they do this. Thus, the passage can be taken as both an expository passage and an argument.

In deciding whether an expository passage should be interpreted as an argument, try to determine whether the purpose of the subsequent sentences in the passage is merely to develop the topic sentence or also to prove that it is true. In borderline cases, ask yourself whether the topic sentence makes a claim that everyone accepts or agrees with. If it does, the passage is probably not an argument. In real-life situations authors rarely try to prove something is true when everyone already accepts it. However, if the topic sentence makes a claim that many people do not accept or have never thought about, then the purpose of the remaining sentences may be both to prove the topic sentence is true as well as to develop it. If this be so, the passage is an argument.

Finally, if even this procedure yields no definite answer, the only alternative may be to say that *if* the passage is taken as an argument, then the first statement is the conclusion and the others are the premises.

Illustrations

An **illustration** is an expression involving one or more examples that is intended to show what something means or how it is done. Illustrations are often confused with arguments because many illustrations contain indicator words such as "thus." Examples:

> Chemical elements, as well as compounds, can be represented by molecular formulas. Thus, oxygen is represented by "O_2," water by "H_2O," and sodium chloride by "NaCl."

> A deciduous tree is any tree that loses its leaves during the winter. For example, maples are deciduous. And so are elms, poplars, hawthorns, and alders.

These selections are not arguments, because they make no claim that anything is being proved. In the first selection, the word "thus" indicates how something is done— namely, how chemical elements and compounds can be represented by formulas. In the second, the examples cited are intended to illustrate the meaning of the word "deciduous." It pins down the meaning by providing concrete instances.

However, as with expository passages, many illustrations can be taken as arguments. Such arguments are often called **arguments from example.** Here is an instance of one:

> Although most forms of cancer, if untreated, can cause death, not all cancers are life-threatening. For example, basal cell carcinoma, the most common of all skin cancers, can produce disfigurement, but it almost never results in death.

In this passage the example given is intended to prove the truth of "Not all cancers are life-threatening." Thus, the passage is best interpreted as an argument.

In deciding whether an illustration should be interpreted as an argument, determine whether the passage merely shows how something is done or what something means, or whether it also purports to prove something. In borderline cases it helps to note whether the claim being illustrated is one that practically everyone accepts or agrees with. If it is, the passage is probably not an argument. As already noted, in real-life situations authors rarely attempt to prove what everyone already accepts. But if the claim being illustrated is one that many people do not accept or have never thought about, then the passage may be interpreted as an argument.

Thus, in reference to the first two examples we considered, most people are aware that elements and compounds can be expressed by formulas—practically everyone knows that water is H_2O—and most people have at least a vague idea of what a deciduous tree is. But they may not have ever considered whether some forms of cancer are not life-threatening. This is one of the reasons for evaluating the first two examples as mere illustrations and the last one as an argument.

Explanations

One of the most important kinds of nonargument is the explanation. An **explanation** is an expression that purports to shed light on some event or phenomenon. The event or phenomenon in question is usually accepted as a matter of fact. Examples:

> The sky appears blue from the earth's surface because light rays from the sun are scattered by particles in the atmosphere.

> The AIDS virus causes sickness and death because it infects certain white blood cells called T cells, and these cells are essential to the body's immune system.

> Naval oranges are called by that name because they have a growth that resembles a human naval on the end opposite the stem.

Every explanation is composed of two distinct components: the explanandum and explanans. The **explanandum** is the statement that describes the event or phenomenon to be explained, and the **explanans** is the statement or group of statements that purports to do the explaining. In the first example above, the explanandum is the statement "The sky appears blue from the earth's surface" and the explanans is "Light rays from the sun are scattered by particles in the atmosphere."

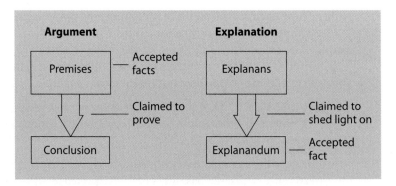

Explanations are sometimes mistaken for arguments because they often contain the indicator word "because." Yet explanations are not arguments, because in an explanation the purpose of the explanans is to shed light on, or to make sense of, the explanandum event—not to prove that it occurred. In other words, the purpose of the explanans is to show *why* something is the case, whereas in an argument, the purpose of the premises is to prove *that* something is the case.

In the first example given, the fact that the sky is blue is readily apparent to everyone. The statement that light rays from the sun are scattered by particles in the atmosphere is not intended to prove *that* the sky is blue, but rather to show *why* it is blue. In the second example, practically everyone knows that the AIDS virus causes sickness and death. The purpose of the passage is to explain *why* this happens—not to prove *that* it happens. Similarly, in the third example, it is obvious that naval oranges are called naval oranges. The purpose of the passage is to shed light on why they have this name.

Thus, to distinguish explanations from arguments, identify the statement that is either the explanandum or the conclusion (usually this is the statement that precedes the word "because"). If this statement describes an accepted matter of fact, and if the remaining statements purport to shed light on this statement, then the passage is an explanation.

This method usually works to distinguish arguments from explanations. However, some passages can be interpreted as both explanations and arguments. Example:

> Women become intoxicated by drinking a smaller amount of alcohol than men because men metabolize part of the alcohol before it reaches the bloodstream, whereas women do not.

The purpose of this passage could be to prove the first statement to those people who do not accept it as fact, and to shed light on that fact to those people who do accept it. Alternately, the passage could be intended to prove the first statement to a single person who accepts its truth on blind faith or incomplete experience, and simultaneously to shed light on this truth. Thus, the passage can be correctly interpreted as both an explanation and an argument.

Perhaps the greatest problem confronting the effort to distinguish explanations from arguments lies in determining whether something is an accepted matter of fact. Obviously, what is accepted by one person may not be accepted by another. Thus, the effort often involves determining which person or group of people the passage is directed to—the intended audience. Sometimes the source of the passage (textbook, newspaper, technical journal, etc.) will decide the issue. But when the passage is taken totally out of context, ascertaining the source may prove impossible. In those circumstances the only possible answer may be to say that *if* the passage is an argument, then such-and-such is the conclusion and such-and-such are the premises.

Conditional Statements

A **conditional statement** is an "if . . . then . . ." statement; for example:

> If professional football games incite violence in the home, then the widespread approval given to this sport should be reconsidered.

> If Lance Armstrong has won the Tour de France seven consecutive times, then he ranks as king of the hill in the world's most famous bicycle race.

Every conditional statement is made up of two component statements. The component statement immediately following the "if" is called the **antecedent,** and the one following the "then" is called the **consequent.** (Occasionally, the word "then" is left out, and occasionally the order of antecedent and consequent is reversed.) In the first example, the antecedent is "Professional football games incite violence in the home," and the consequent is "The widespread approval given to this sport should be reconsidered." In both of these examples, there is a meaningful relationship between antecedent and consequent. However, such a relationship need not exist for a statement to count as conditional. The statement "If Janet Jackson is a singer, then Denver is in Colorado" is just as much a conditional statement as those about professional football and Lance Armstrong.

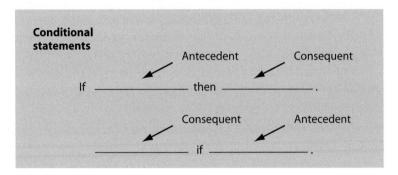

Conditional statements are not arguments, because they fail to meet the criteria given earlier. In an argument, at least one statement must claim to present evidence, and there must be a claim that this evidence implies something. In a conditional statement, there is no claim that either the antecedent or the consequent presents evidence. In other words, there is no assertion that either the antecedent or the consequent is true. Rather, there is only the assertion that *if* the antecedent is true, then so is the consequent. Of course, a conditional statement as a whole may present evidence because it asserts a relationship between statements. Yet when conditional statements are taken in this sense, there is still no argument, because there is then no separate claim that this evidence implies anything.

Some conditional statements are similar to arguments, however, in that they express the outcome of a reasoning process. As such, they may be said to have a certain inferential content. Consider the following:

> If Arnold Schwarzenegger was born a citizen of Austria, then he cannot be elected president of the United States.

> If Jennifer Lopez is Marc Anthony's wife, then Marc Anthony is Jennifer Lopez's husband.

The link between the antecedent and consequent of these conditional statements resembles the inferential link between the premises and conclusion of an argument. Yet there is a difference because the premises of an argument are claimed to be true, whereas no such claim is made for the antecedent of a conditional statement. Accordingly, these conditional statements are not arguments.* Yet their inferential content may be reexpressed to form arguments:

*In saying this we are temporarily ignoring the possibility of these statements being enthymemes. As we shall see in Chapter 5, an *enthymeme* is an argument in which a premise or conclusion (or both) is implied but not stated. If, to the second example, we add the premise "Jennifer Lopez is Marc Anthony's wife" and the conclusion "Therefore, Marc Anthony is Jennifer Lopez's husband," we have a complete argument. To decide whether a conditional statement is an enthymeme, we must be familiar with the context in which it occurs.

Arnold Schwarzenegger was born a citizen of Austria.
Therefore, he cannot be elected president of the United States.

Jennifer Lopez is Marc Anthony's wife.
Therefore, Marc Anthony is Jennifer Lopez's husband.

Finally, while no single conditional statement is an argument, a conditional statement may serve as either the premise or the conclusion (or both) of an argument, as the following examples illustrate:

If Iran is developing nuclear weapons, then Iran is a threat to world peace.
Iran is developing nuclear weapons.
Therefore, Iran is a threat to world peace.

If borders are secure, then terrorists cannot enter the country.
If terrorists cannot enter the country, then acts of terrorism will be reduced.
Therefore, if borders are secure, then acts of terrorism will be reduced.

The relation between conditional statements and arguments may now be summarized as follows:

1. A single conditional statement is not an argument.
2. A conditional statement may serve as either the premise or the conclusion (or both) of an argument.
3. The inferential content of a conditional statement may be reexpressed to form an argument.

The first two rules are especially pertinent to the recognition of arguments. According to the first rule, if a passage consists of a single conditional statement, it is not an argument. But if it consists of a conditional statement together with some other statement, then, by the second rule, it *may* be an argument, depending on such factors as the presence of indicator words and an inferential relationship between the statements.

Conditional statements are especially important in logic because they express the relationship between necessary and sufficient conditions. *A* is said to be a **sufficient condition** for *B* whenever the occurrence of *A* is all that is needed for the occurrence of *B*. For example, being a dog is a sufficient condition for being an animal. On the other hand, *B* is said to be a **necessary condition** for *A* whenever *A* cannot occur without the occurrence of *B*. Thus, being an animal is a necessary condition for being a dog. These relationships are expressed in the following conditional statements:

If *X* is a dog, then *X* is an animal.
If *X* is not an animal, then *X* is not a dog.

The first statement says that being a dog is a sufficient condition for being an animal, and the second that being an animal is a necessary condition for being a dog. However, a little reflection reveals that these two statements say exactly the same thing. Thus, each expresses in one way a necessary condition and in another way a sufficient condition. The terminology of sufficient and necessary conditions will be used in later chapters to express definitions and causal connections.

Summary

In deciding whether a passage contains an argument, you should look for three things: (1) indicator words such as "therefore," "since," "because," and so on; (2) an inferential relationship between the statements; and (3) typical kinds of nonarguments. But remember that the mere occurrence of an indicator word does not guarantee the presence of an argument. You must check to see that the statement identified as the conclusion is claimed to be supported by one or more of the other statements. Also keep in mind that in many arguments that lack indicator words, the conclusion is the first statement. Furthermore, it helps to mentally insert the word "therefore" before the various statements before deciding that a statement should be interpreted as a conclusion. The typical kinds of nonarguments that we have surveyed are as follows:

warnings	reports
pieces of advice	expository passages
statements of belief	illustrations
statements of opinion	explanations
loosely associated statements	conditional statements

Keep in mind that these kinds of nonargument are not mutually exclusive, and that, for example, one and the same passage can sometimes be interpreted as both a report and a statement of opinion, or as both an expository passage and an illustration. The precise kind of nonargument a passage might be is nowhere near as important as correctly deciding whether or not it is an argument.

After working the exercises in this section, you may, if you wish, proceed directly to Section 1.6 ("Extended Arguments").

EXERCISE 1.2

I. Determine which of the following passages are arguments. For those that are, identify the conclusion. For those that are not, determine the kind of nonargument.

★1. The turkey vulture is called by that name because its red featherless head resembles the head of a wild turkey.

2. If public education fails to improve the quality of instruction in both primary and secondary schools, then it is likely that it will lose additional students to the private sector in the years ahead.

3. Freedom of the press is the most important of our constitutionally guaranteed freedoms. Without it, our other freedoms would be immediately threatened. Furthermore, it provides the fulcrum for the advancement of new freedoms.

★4. A mammal is a vertebrate animal that nurses its offspring. Thus, cats and dogs are mammals, as are sheep, monkeys, rabbits, and bears.

5. It is strongly recommended that you have your house inspected for termite damage at the earliest possible opportunity.

6. Mosquito bites are not always the harmless little irritations most of us take them to be. For example, some mosquitoes carry West Nile virus, and people who are infected can become very sick or even die.

★7. If stem-cell research is restricted, then future cures will not materialize. If future cures do not materialize, then people will die prematurely. Therefore, if stem-cell research is restricted, then people will die prematurely.

8. Fictional characters behave according to the same psychological probabilities as real people. But the characters of fiction are found in exotic dilemmas that real people hardly encounter. Consequently, fiction provides us with the opportunity to ponder how people react in uncommon situations, and to deduce moral lessons, psychological principles, and philosophical insights from their behavior.

(J. R. McCuen and A. C. Winkler, *Readings for Writers*, 4th ed.)

9. I believe that it must be the policy of the United States to support free peoples who are resisting attempted subjugation by armed minorities or by outside pressures. I believe that we must assist free peoples to work out their own destinies in their own way. I believe that our help should be primarily through economic and financial aid, which is essential to economic stability and orderly political processes.

(President Truman, Address to Congress, 1947)

★10. Five college students who were accused of sneaking into the Cincinnati Zoo and trying to ride the camels pleaded no contest to criminal trespass yesterday. The students scaled a fence to get into the zoo and then climbed another fence to get into the camel pit before security officials caught them, zoo officials said.

(Newspaper clipping)

11. Mortality rates for women undergoing early abortions, where the procedure is legal, appear to be as low as or lower than the rates for normal childbirth. Consequently, any interest of the state in protecting the woman from an inherently hazardous procedure, except when it would be equally dangerous for her to forgo it, has largely disappeared.

(Justice Blackmun, *Roe v. Wade*)

12. The pace of reading, clearly, depends entirely upon the reader. He may read as slowly or as rapidly as he can or wishes to read. If he does not understand something, he may stop and reread it, or go in search of elucidation before continuing. The reader can accelerate his pace when the material is easy or less than interesting, and can slow down when it is difficult or enthralling. If what he reads is moving he can put down the book for a few moments and cope with his emotions without fear of losing anything.

(Marie Winn, *The Plug-In Drug*)

★13. I'm sick and tired of living in fear. I'm tired of plastic bags and duct tape. I'm tired of alerts telling me whether or not I can walk outside. America should be a bastion of hope. Jobs, affordable health care and respect from the world. These will bring hope, and hope is what prevents terrorism.

(Steve Mavros, letter to the editor)

14. Lions at Kruger National Park in South Africa are dying of tuberculosis. "All of the lions in the park may be dead within ten years because the disease is incurable, and the lions have no natural resistance," said the deputy director of the Department of Agriculture.

(Newspaper clipping)

15. Economics is of practical value in business. An understanding of the overall operation of the economic system puts the business executive in a better position to formulate policies. The executive who understands the causes and consequences of inflation is better equipped during inflationary periods to make more intelligent decisions than otherwise.

(Campbell R. McConnell, *Economics*, 8th ed.)

★16. Bear one thing in mind before you begin to write your paper: Famous literary works, especially works regarded as classics, have been thoroughly studied to the point where prevailing opinion on them has assumed the character of orthodoxy.

(J. R. McCuen and A. C. Winkler, *Readings for Writers*, 4th ed.)

17. Young people at universities study to achieve knowledge and not to learn a trade. We must all learn how to support ourselves, but we must also learn how to live. We need a lot of engineers in the modern world, but we do not want a world of modern engineers.

(Winston Churchill, *A Churchill Reader*, ed. Colin R. Coote)

18. No business concern wants to sell on credit to a customer who will prove unable or unwilling to pay his or her account. Consequently, most business organizations include a credit department which must reach a decision on the credit worthiness of each prospective customer.

(Walter B. Meigs and Robert F. Meigs, *Accounting*)

★19. For organisms at the sea surface, sinking into deep water usually means death. Plant cells cannot photosynthesize in the dark depths. Fishes and other animals that descend lose contact with the main surface food supply and themselves become food for strange deep-living predators.

(David H. Milne, *Marine Life and the Sea*)

20. Since the 1950s a malady called whirling disease has invaded U.S. fishing streams, frequently attacking rainbow trout. A parasite deforms young fish, which often chase their tails before dying, hence the name.

("Trout Disease—A Turn for the Worse," *National Geographic*)

21. Dachshunds are ideal dogs for small children, as they are already stretched and pulled to such a length that the child cannot do much harm one way or the other.

(Robert Benchley, quoted in *Cold Noses and Warm Hearts*)

★22. Atoms are the basic building blocks of all matter. They can combine to form molecules, whose properties are generally very different from those of the constituent atoms. Table salt, for example, a simple chemical compound formed from chlorine and sodium, resembles neither the poisonous gas nor the highly reactive metal.

(Frank J. Blatt, Principles of Physics, 2nd ed.)

23. The coarsest type of humor is the *practical joke:* pulling away the chair from the dignitary's lowered bottom. The victim is perceived first as a person of consequence, then suddenly as an inert body subject to the laws of physics: authority is debunked by gravity, mind by matter; man is degraded to a mechanism.

(Arthur Koestler, Janus: A Summing Up)

24. If a man holding a belief which he was taught in childhood or persuaded of afterwards keeps down and pushes away any doubts which arise about it in his mind, purposely avoids the reading of books and the company of men that call in question or discuss it, and regards as impious those questions which cannot easily be asked without disturbing it—the life of that man is one long sin against mankind.

(W. K. Clifford, "The Ethics of Belief")

★25. It is usually easy to decide whether or not something is alive. This is because living things share many common attributes, such as the capacity to extract energy from nutrients to drive their various functions, the power to actively respond to changes in their environment, and the ability to grow, to differentiate, and to reproduce.

(Donald Voet and Judith G. Voet, Biochemistry, 2nd ed.)

26. Words are slippery customers. The full meaning of a word does not appear until it is placed in its context. . . . And even then the meaning will depend upon the listener, upon the speaker, upon their entire experience of the language, upon their knowledge of one another, and upon the whole situation.

(C. Cherry, On Human Communication)

27. Haydn developed the string quartet from the eighteenth century *divertimento,* giving more substance to the light, popular form and scoring it for two violins, a viola, and a cello. His eighty-three quartets, written over the course of his creative lifetime, evolved slowly into a sophisticated form. Together they constitute one of the most important bodies of chamber music literature.

(Robert Hickok, Exploring Music)

★28. A person never becomes truly self-reliant. Even though he deals effectively with things, he is necessarily dependent upon those who have taught him to do so. They have selected the things he is dependent upon and determined the kinds and degrees of dependencies.

(B. F. Skinner, Beyond Freedom and Dignity)

29. There is no doubt that some businessmen conspire to shorten the useful life of their products in order to guarantee replacement sales. There is, similarly, no

doubt that many of the annual model changes with which American (and other) consumers are increasingly familiar are not technologically substantive.

(Alvin Toffler, *Future Shock*)

30. Water is a good solvent for many different substances, and it picks them up as it moves through the environment. For example, rain water flowing over and under the ground dissolves minerals such as limestone.

(Gilbert Castellan et al., *The World of Chemistry*)

★31. In areas where rats are a problem, it is very difficult to exterminate them with bait poison. That's because some rats eat enough poison to die but others eat only enough to become sick and then learn to avoid that particular poison taste in the future.

(Rod Plotnik, *Introduction to Psychology*, 4th ed.)

32. Men are less likely to develop osteoporosis until later in life than women and seldom suffer as severely because they have 30 percent more bone mass on the average and don't undergo the sudden drop in estrogen that occurs with menopause.

(Matt Clark, "The Calcium Craze," *Newsweek*)

33. Newspapers, radio, and television are essential for a democracy. They are the critical link between the people and their government. They provide information and analysis about policy issues, and they also sensitize policymakers to public opinion—which enables them to respond to the needs and desires of the population. Finally, the media play a critical role in reporting and evaluating the decisions of government.

(Stephen J. Wayne et al., *The Politics of American Government*)

★34. Nations are made in two ways, by the slow working of history or the galvanic force of ideas. Most nations are made the former way, emerging slowly from the mist of the past, gradually coalescing within concentric circles of shared sympathies, with an accretion of consensual institutions. But a few nations are formed and defined by the citizens' assent to a shared philosophy.

(George Will, "Lithuania and South Carolina")

35. Although the plane mirror is perhaps the oldest optical instrument known to man, it remains an important element in the modern arsenal of sophisticated optical devices. For example, the earth-moon laser-ranging experiments, initiated in 1969, rely on high-quality reflectors.

(Frank J. Blatt, *Principles of Physics,* 2nd ed.)

II. The following selections were originally submitted as letters to the editor of newspapers and magazines. Determine which of them can, with good reason, be considered arguments. In those that can, identify the conclusion.

★1. What this country needs is a return to the concept of swift and certain justice. If we need more courts, judges and prisons, then so be it. And as for capital punishment, I say let the punishment fit the crime. When criminals behave more like humans, then we can start to treat them more humanely. In the meantime, I would like to see the Night Stalkers of our society swiftly executed rather than coddled by our courts and prisons.

(John Pearson)

2. The big problem with computers in elementary schools isn't their minimal educational value but the fact that they often replace science in the budget and curriculum. Our local Parent Teachers Association is throwing away science equipment as fervently as it raises money for more computers. I use computers extensively in the college physics classes I teach, so I appreciate their value in communications and advanced computation. But in elementary schools, too much is being sacrificed so that children can have all those pricey beige boxes.

(Roger G. Tobin)

3. Is there any country in the world that worries more about its kids having fun in school, making lessons exciting and relevant, and then is more disappointed with the result than the United States? We think learning is like buying a car or smoking a cigarette. Just get into the thing or draw a breath and you will be effortlessly transported to lands of pleasure and excitement.

(Charles M. Breinin)

★4. After reading your cover story, I find that cable TV has simply flooded our airwaves with more sex, violence, and teen-age punk junk. Now our children can spend even less time studying and we can spend more time in blank-space stares at the idiot box. Cable would be fine with more educational channels—and fewer cheap thrills aimed at narrow-minded bubble brains.

(Jacqueline Murray)

5. In opposing obligatory prayer in the public schools, I am not deserting my god (and I would like to think of myself as a Christian). On the contrary, it is perfectly possible that I am thus serving my god, who I believe wants his children to pray to him of their own free will and not because some legislator, who may or may not be motivated by truly religious considerations, forces them to.

(Philip D. Walker)

6. My own son returned from his public elementary school with a book on dinosaurs loaned to him by his first-grade "science" teacher. It depicted the beasts as fire-breathing dragons and said the Bible informs us they were this way. God help us to achieve an educated and scientifically literate society, because these narrow-minded cretins won't.

(Bruce Strathdee)

★7. The poor quality of parenting and the lack in continuity of adult care provided to many U.S. children contribute to a passivity and a sense of helplessness that hobbles individuals for the remainder of their lives. Their subsequent unemployment, lack of education, and inability to make necessary life-style changes such as quitting an addiction can be attributed, in large part, to the helplessness they learned from childhood.

(William J. McCarthy)

8. Forty-one million Americans cannot afford health insurance in this time of global capitalism. At the same time, nine insurance executives earned more than $10 million last year, according to a recent study. If this is the celebrated triumph of capitalism over other forms of economic organization, what exactly did we win? Have we gained the world at the cost of our souls?

(Jason Reynolds)

9. The suggestion by sociobiologists that stepparent child abuse has evolutionary advantages is superficial. If there were evolutionary advantages to harming one's mate's offspring of a different parent, then by now there probably wouldn't be loving and generous stepparents around—and there are plenty. I know. I have a loving stepparent and am one.

(Ronald Cohen)

★10. The voting public is as full of bull as the politicians. As a result, we get the kind of officeholders we ask for. Show me a politician who will stand up and tell Americans the truth, and I'll show you a person who will never be elected.

(Huie Dixon)

III. The following statements represent conclusions for arguments. Each is expressed in the form of two alternatives. Select one of the alternatives for each conclusion, and then jot down several reasons that support it. Finally, incorporate your reasons into a written argument of at least 100 words that supports the conclusion. Include premise and conclusion indicators in some of your arguments, but not in all of them.

1. A constitutional amendment that outlaws flag burning should/should not be adopted.
2. Street drugs should/should not be legalized.
3. The death penalty should/should not be abolished.
4. Sanctions should/should not be imposed on students for using speech that is offensive to minorities.
5. Free health care should/should not be guaranteed to all citizens.
6. Same-sex marriages should/should not be recognized by the state.
7. The possession, ownership, and sale of handguns should/should not be outlawed.
8. Cigarettes should/should not be regulated as an addictive drug.
9. Affirmative action programs should/should not be abolished.
10. Doctors should/should not be allowed to assist terminally ill patients in committing suicide.

IV. Define the following terms:

argument from example   explanation
conditional statement   explanandum
antecedent   explanans
consequent   illustration
sufficient condition   expository passage
necessary condition

V. Answer "true" or "false" to the following statements:

1. Any passage that contains an argument must contain a claim that something is supported by evidence or reasons.

2. In an argument, the claim that something is supported by evidence or reasons is always explicit.

3. Passages that contain indicator words such as "thus," "since," and "because" are always arguments.

4. In deciding whether a passage contains an argument, we should always keep an eye out for indicator words and the presence of an inferential relationship between the statements.

5. Some expository passages can be correctly interpreted as arguments.

6. Some passages containing "for example" can be correctly interpreted as arguments.

7. In deciding whether an expository passage or an illustration should be interpreted as an argument, it helps to note whether the claim being developed or illustrated is one that is accepted by everyone.

8. Some conditional statements can be reexpressed to form arguments.

9. In an explanation, the explanandum usually describes an accepted matter of fact.

10. In an explanation, the explanans is the statement or group of statements that does the explaining.

VI. Fill in the blanks with "necessary" or "sufficient" to make the following statements true. After the blanks have been filled in, express the result in terms of conditional statements.

★1. Being a tiger is a _____ condition for being an animal.

2. Being an animal is a _____ condition for being a tiger.

3. Drinking water is a _____ condition for quenching one's thirst.

★4. Having a racket is a _____ condition for playing tennis.

5. Pulling the cork is a _____ condition for drinking an expensive bottle of wine.

6. Stepping on a cat's tail is a _____ condition for making the cat yowl.

★7. Burning leaves is a _____ condition for producing smoke.

8. Paying attention is a _____ condition for understanding a lecture.

9. Taking a swim in the North Sea is a _____ condition for cooling off.

★**10.** Opening a door is a _____ condition for crossing the threshold.

VII. Page through a book, magazine, or newspaper and find two arguments, one with indicator words, the other without. Copy the arguments as written, giving the appropriate reference. Then identify the premises and conclusion of each.

1.3   Deduction and Induction

In the previous section we saw that every argument involves an inferential claim—the claim that the conclusion is supposed to follow from the premises. The question we now address has to do with the strength of this claim. Just how strongly is the conclusion claimed to follow from the premises? If the conclusion is claimed to follow with strict certainty or necessity, the argument is said to be deductive; but if it is claimed to follow only probably, the argument is inductive.

Stated more precisely, a **deductive argument** is an argument incorporating the claim that it is *impossible* for the conclusion to be false given that the premises are true. Deductive arguments are those that involve necessary reasoning. On the other hand, an **inductive argument** is an argument incorporating the claim that it is *improbable* that the conclusion be false given that the premises are true. Inductive arguments involve probabilistic reasoning. Here are two examples:

> The meerkat is closely related to the suricat.
> The suricat thrives on beetle larvae.
> Therefore, probably the meerkat thrives on beetle larvae.

> The meerkat is a member of the mongoose family.
> All members of the mongoose family are carnivores.
> Therefore, it necessarily follows that the meerkat is a carnivore.

The first of these arguments is inductive, the second deductive.

In deciding whether an argument is inductive or deductive, we look to certain objective features of the argument. These features include (1) the occurrence of special indicator words, (2) the *actual* strength of the inferential link between premises and conclusion, and (3) the form or style of argumentation. However, we must acknowledge at the outset that many arguments in ordinary language are incomplete, and because of this, deciding whether the argument should best be interpreted as deductive or inductive may be impossible.

The occurrence of special indicator words is illustrated in the examples we just considered. The word "probably" in the conclusion of the first argument suggests that the argument should be taken as inductive, and the word "necessarily" in the conclusion of the second suggests that the second argument be taken as deductive. Additional inductive indicators are "improbable," "plausible," "implausible," "likely," "unlikely," and "reasonable to conclude." Additional deductive indicators are "certainly," "absolutely," and "definitely." (Note that the phrase "it must be the case that" is simply a conclusion indicator that can occur in either deductive or inductive argments.)

Inductive and deductive indicator words often suggest the correct interpretation. However, if they conflict with one of the other criteria (discussed shortly), we should probably ignore them. Arguers often use phrases such as "it certainly follows that" for rhetorical purposes to add impact to their conclusion and not to suggest that the argument be taken as deductive. Similarly, some arguers, not knowing the distinction between inductive and deductive, will claim to "deduce" a conclusion when their argument is more correctly interpreted as inductive.

The second factor that bears on our interpretation of an argument as inductive or deductive is the *actual* strength of the inferential link between premises and conclusion. If the conclusion actually does follow with strict necessity from the premises, the argument is clearly deductive. In such an argument it is impossible for the premises to be true and the conclusion false. On the other hand, if the conclusion does not follow with strict necessity but does follow probably, it is often best to consider the argument inductive. Examples:

> All entertainers are extroverts.
> David Letterman is an entertainer.
> Therefore, David Letterman is an extrovert.

> The vast majority of entertainers are extroverts.
> David Letterman is an entertainer.
> Therefore, David Letterman is an extrovert.

In the first example, the conclusion follows with strict necessity from the premises. If we assume that all entertainers are extroverts and that David Letterman is an entertainer, then it is impossible that David Letterman not be an extrovert. Thus, we should interpret this argument as deductive. In the second example, the conclusion does not follow from the premises with strict necessity, but it does follow with some degree of probability. If we assume that the premises are true, then based on that assumption it is probable that the conclusion is true. Thus, it is best to interpret the second argument as inductive.

Occasionally, an argument contains no special indicator words, and the conclusion does not follow either necessarily or probably from the premises; in other words, it does not follow at all. This situation points up the need for the third factor to be taken into account, which is the character or form of argumentation the arguer uses.

Deductive Argument Forms

Many arguments have a distinctive character or form that indicates that the premises are supposed to provide absolute support for the conclusion. Five examples of such forms or kinds of argumentation are arguments based on mathematics, arguments from definition, and categorical, hypothetical, and disjunctive syllogisms.

An **argument based on mathematics** is an argument in which the conclusion depends on some purely arithmetic or geometric computation or measurement. For example, a shopper might place two apples and three oranges into a paper bag and then conclude that the bag contains five pieces of fruit. Or a surveyor might measure a square piece of land and, after determining that it is 100 feet on each side, conclude that it contains 10,000 square feet. Since all arguments in pure mathematics are deductive, we can usually consider arguments that depend on mathematics to be deductive as well. A noteworthy exception, however, is arguments that depend on statistics. As we will see shortly, such arguments are usually best interpreted as inductive.

An **argument from definition** is an argument in which the conclusion is claimed to depend merely on the definition of some word or phrase used in the premise or conclusion. For example, someone might argue that because Claudia is mendacious, it follows that she tells lies, or that because a certain paragraph is prolix, it follows that it is excessively wordy. These arguments are deductive because their conclusions follow with necessity from the definitions of "mendacious" and "prolix."

A *syllogism*, in general, is an argument consisting of exactly two premises and one conclusion. Categorical syllogisms will be treated in greater depth in Chapter 5, but for now we will say that a **categorical syllogism** is a syllogism in which each statement begins with one of the words "all," "no," or "some." Example:

> All ancient forests are sources of wonder.
> Some ancient forests are targets of the timber industry.
> Therefore, some sources of wonder are targets of the timber industry.

Arguments such as these are nearly always best treated as deductive.

A **hypothetical syllogism** is a syllogism having a conditional statement for one or both of its premises. Examples:

> If estate taxes are abolished, then wealth will accumulate disproportionately.
> If wealth accumulates disproportionately, then democracy will be threatened.
> Therefore, if estate taxes are abolished, then democracy will be threatened.

> If Fox News is a propaganda machine, then it misleads its viewers.
> Fox News is a propaganda machine.
> Therefore, Fox News misleads its viewers.

Although certain forms of such arguments can sometimes be interpreted inductively, the deductive interpretation is usually the most appropriate.

A **disjunctive syllogism** is a syllogism having a disjunctive statement (i.e., an "either . . . or . . ." statement) for one of its premises. Example:

> Either global warming will be arrested, or hurricanes will become more intense.
> Global warming will not be arrested.
> Therefore, hurricanes will become more intense.

As with hypothetical syllogisms, such arguments are usually best taken as deductive. Hypothetical and disjunctive syllogisms will be treated in greater depth in Chapter 6.

Inductive Argument Forms

In general, inductive arguments are such that the content of the conclusion is in some way intended to "go beyond" the content of the premises. The premises of such an argument typically deal with some subject that is relatively familiar, and the conclusion then moves beyond this to a subject that is less familiar or that little is known about. Such an argument may take any of several forms: predictions about the future, arguments from analogy, inductive generalizations, arguments from authority, arguments based on signs, and causal inferences, to name just a few.

A **prediction** is an argument that proceeds from our knowledge of the past to a claim about the future. For example, someone might argue that because certain meteorological phenomena have been observed to develop over a certain region of central Missouri, a storm will occur there in six hours. Or again, one might argue that because certain fluctuations occurred in the prime interest rate on Friday, the value of the dollar will decrease against foreign currencies on Monday. Nearly everyone realizes that the future cannot be known with certainty; thus, whenever an argument makes a prediction about the future, one is usually justified in considering the argument inductive.

An **argument from analogy** is an argument that depends on the existence of an analogy, or similarity, between two things or states of affairs. Because of the existence of this analogy, a certain condition that affects the better-known thing or situation is concluded to affect the similar, lesser-known thing or situation. For example, someone might argue that because Christina's Porsche is a great handling car, it follows that Angela's Porsche must also be a great handling car. The argument depends on the existence of a similarity, or analogy, between the two cars. The certitude attending such an inference is probabilistic at best.

A **generalization** is an argument that proceeds from the knowledge of a selected sample to some claim about the whole group. Because the members of the sample have a certain characteristic, it is argued that all the members of the group have that same characteristic. For example, one might argue that because three oranges selected from a certain crate were especially tasty and juicy, all the oranges from that crate are especially tasty and juicy. Or again, one might argue that because six out of a total of nine members sampled from a certain labor union intend to vote for Johnson for union president, two-thirds of the entire membership intend to vote for Johnson. These examples illustrate the use of statistics in inductive argumentation.

An **argument from authority** is an argument that concludes something is true because a presumed expert or witness has said that it is. For example, a person might argue that earnings for Hewlett-Packard Corporation will be up in the coming quarter because of a statement to that effect by an investment counselor. Or a lawyer might argue that Mack the Knife committed the murder because an eyewitness testified to that effect under oath. Because the investment counselor and the eyewitness could be either mistaken or lying, such arguments are essentially probabilistic.

An **argument based on signs** is an argument that proceeds from the knowledge of a sign to a claim about the thing or situation that the sign symbolizes. The word "sign," as it is used here, means any kind of message (usually visual) produced by an intelligent being. For example, when driving on an unfamiliar highway one might see a sign indicating that the road makes several sharp turns one mile ahead. Based on this information, one might argue that the road does indeed make several sharp turns one mile ahead. Because the sign might be misplaced or in error about the turns, the conclusion is only probable.

A **causal inference** is an argument that proceeds from knowledge of a cause to a claim about an effect, or, conversely, from knowledge of an effect to a claim about a cause. For example, from the knowledge that a bottle of wine had been accidentally left in the freezer overnight, someone might conclude that it had frozen (cause to effect). Conversely, after tasting a piece of chicken and finding it dry and tough, one might conclude that it had been overcooked (effect to cause). Because specific instances of cause and effect can never be known with absolute certainty, one may usually interpret such arguments as inductive.

Further Considerations

It should be noted that the various subspecies of inductive arguments listed here are not intended to be mutually exclusive. Overlaps can and do occur. For example, many causal inferences that proceed from cause to effect also qualify as predictions. The purpose of this survey is not to demarcate in precise terms the various forms of induction but rather to provide guidelines for distinguishing induction from deduction.

Keeping this in mind, we should take care not to confuse arguments in geometry, which are always deductive, with arguments from analogy or inductive generalizations. For example, an argument concluding that a triangle has a certain attribute (such as a right angle) because another triangle, with which it is congruent, also has that attribute might be mistaken for an argument from analogy. Similarly, an argument that concludes that all triangles have a certain attribute (such as angles totaling two right angles) because any particular triangle has that attribute might be mistaken for an inductive generalization. Arguments such as these, however, are always deductive, because the conclusion follows necessarily and with complete certainty from the premises.

One broad classification of arguments not listed in this survey is scientific arguments. Arguments that occur in science can be either inductive or deductive, depending on the circumstances. In general, arguments aimed at the *discovery* of a law of nature are usually considered inductive. Suppose, for example, that we want to discover a law that governs the time required for a falling body to strike the earth. We drop bodies of various weights from various heights and measure the time it takes them to fall. Comparing our measurements, we notice that the time is approximately proportional to the square root of the distance. From this we conclude that the time required for any body to fall is proportional to the square root of the distance through which it falls. Such an argument is best interpreted as an inductive generalization.

Another type of argument that occurs in science has to do with the *application* of known laws to specific circumstances. Arguments of this sort are often considered to be deductive—but only with certain reservations. Suppose, for example, that we want to apply Boyle's law for ideal gases to a container of gas in our laboratory. Boyle's law states that the pressure exerted by a gas on the walls of its container is inversely proportional to the volume. Applying this law, we conclude that when we reduce the volume of our laboratory sample by half, the pressure will double. Considered purely as a mathematical computation, this argument is deductive. But if we acknowledge the fact that the conclusion pertains to the future and the possibility that Boyle's law may not work in the future, then the argument is best considered inductive.

A final point needs to be made about the distinction between inductive and deductive arguments. There is a tradition extending back to the time of Aristotle that holds that inductive arguments are those that proceed from the particular to the general, while deductive arguments are those that proceed from the general to the particular. (A **particular statement** is one that makes a claim about one or more particular members of a class, while a **general statement** makes a claim about *all* the members of a class.) It is true, of course, that many inductive and deductive arguments do work in this way; but this fact should not be used as a criterion for distinguishing induction from deduction. As a matter of fact, there are deductive arguments that proceed from the general to the general, from the particular to the particular, and from the particular to the general, as well as from the general to the particular; and there are inductive arguments that do the same. For example, here is a deductive argument that proceeds from the particular to the general:

> Three is a prime number.
> Five is a prime number.
> Seven is a prime number.
> Therefore, all odd numbers between two and eight are prime numbers.

And here is one that proceeds from the particular to the particular:

> Gabriel is a wolf.
> Gabriel has a tail.
> Therefore, Gabriel's tail is the tail of a wolf.

Here is an inductive argument that proceeds from the general to the particular:

> All emeralds previously found have been green.
> Therefore, the next emerald to be found will be green.

The other varieties are easy to construct. Thus, the progression from particular to general, and vice versa, cannot be used as a criterion for distinguishing induction and deduction.

Summary

To distinguish deductive arguments from inductive arguments, we attempt to evaluate the strength of the argument's inferential claim—how strongly the conclusion is claimed to follow from the premises. This claim is an objective feature of an argument, and it may or may not be related to the subjective intentions of the arguer.

To interpret an argument's inferential claim we look at three factors: special indicator words, the actual strength of the inferential link between premises and conclusion, and the character or form of argumentation. Given that we have more than one factor to look at, it is possible in a single argument for the occurrence of two of these factors to conflict with each other, leading to opposite interpretations. For example, in drawing a conclusion to a categorical syllogism (which is clearly deductive), an arguer might say "It probably follows that . . ." (which suggests induction). To help alleviate this conflict we can list the factors in order of importance:

1. Arguments in which the premises provide absolute support for the conclusion. Such arguments are always deductive.

2. Arguments having a specific deductive character or form (e.g., categorical syllogism). This factor is often of equal importance to the first, and, when present, it provides a clear-cut indication that the argument is deductive.

3. Arguments having a specific inductive character or form (e.g., a prediction). Arguments of this sort are nearly always best interpreted as inductive.

4. Arguments containing inductive indicator language (e.g., "It probably follows that . . ."). Since arguers rarely try to make their argument appear weaker than it really is, such language can usually be trusted. But if this language conflicts with one of the first two factors, it should be ignored.

5. Arguments containing deductive indicator language (e.g., "It necessarily follows that . . ."). Arguers occasionally use such language for rhetorical purposes, to make their argument appear stronger than it really is, so such language should be evaluated carefully.

6. Arguments in which the premises provide only probable support for the conclusion. This is the least important factor, and if it conflicts with any of the earlier ones, it should probably be ignored.

Unfortunately, many arguments in ordinary language are incomplete, so it often happens that none of these factors are clearly present. Determining the inductive or deductive character of such arguments may be impossible.

EXERCISE 1.3

I. Determine whether the following arguments are best interpreted as being inductive or deductive. Also state the criteria you use in reaching your decision (i.e., the presence of indicator words, the nature of the inferential link between premises and conclusion, or the character or form of argumentation).

★1. Because triangle A is congruent with triangle B, and triangle A is isosceles, it follows that triangle B is isosceles.

2. The plaque on the leaning tower of Pisa says that Galileo performed experiments there with falling objects. It must be the case that Galileo did indeed perform those experiments there.

3. The rainfall in Seattle has been more than 15 inches every year for the past thirty years. Therefore, the rainfall next year will probably be more than 15 inches.

★4. No e-mail messages are eloquent creations. Some love letters are eloquent creations. Therefore, some love letters are not e-mail messages.

5. Amoco, Exxon, and Texaco are all listed on the New York Stock Exchange. It must be the case that all major American oil companies are listed on the New York Stock Exchange.

6. The longer a pendulum is, the longer it takes to swing. Therefore, when the pendulum of a clock is lengthened, the clock slows down.

★7. Paying off terrorists in exchange for hostages is not a wise policy, since such action will only lead them to take more hostages in the future.

8. The Matterhorn is higher than Mount Whitney, and Mount Whitney is higher than Mount Rainier. The obvious conclusion is that the Matterhorn is higher than Mount Rainier.

9. Although both front and rear doors were found open after the burglary, there were pry marks around the lock on the rear door and deposits of mud near the threshold. It must be the case that the thief entered through the rear door and left through the front.

★10. The *Encylopaedia Britannica* has an article on symbiosis. The *Encyclopedia Americana,* like the *Britannica,* is an excellent reference work. Therefore, the *Americana* probably also has an article on symbiosis.

11. Cholesterol is endogenous with humans. Therefore, it is manufactured inside the human body.

12. Either classical culture originated in Greece, or it originated in Egypt. Classical culture did not originate in Egypt. Therefore, classical culture originated in Greece.

★13. World-renowned physicist Stephen Hawking says that the condition of the universe at the instant of the Big Bang was more highly ordered than it is today. In view of Hawking's stature in the scientific community, we should conclude that this description of the universe is correct.

14. If Alexander the Great died from typhoid fever, then he became infected in India. Alexander the Great did die from typhoid fever. Therefore, he became infected in India.

15. Crater Lake, the deepest lake in the United States, was caused by a huge volcanic eruption 7700 years ago. Since human beings have lived around the mountain for more than 10,000 years, it is likely that people witnessed that eruption.

(National Park Service, "Crater Lake—Its History")

★16. Each element, such as hydrogen and iron, has a set of gaps—wavelengths that it absorbs rather than radiates. So if those wavelengths are missing from the spectrum, you know that that element is present in the star you are observing.

(Rick Gore, "Eyes of Science")

17. Because the apparent daily movement which is common to both the planets and the fixed stars is seen to travel from the east to the west, but the far slower single movements of the single planets travel in the opposite direction from west to east, it is therefore certain that these movements cannot depend on the common movement of the world but should be assigned to the planets themselves.

(Johannes Kepler, *Epitomy of Copernican Astronomy*)

18. Reserves of coal in the United States have an energy equivalent 33 times that of oil and natural gas. On a worldwide basis the multiple is about 10. By shifting to a coal-based economy, we could satisfy our energy requirements for at least a century, probably longer.

(William L. Masterson and Emil J. Slowinski, *Principles of Chemistry*)

★19. When the Romans occupied England, coal was burned. Since coal produces quite a bit of soot and sulfur dioxide, there must have been days almost 2000 years ago when the air in the larger towns was badly polluted.

(Stanley Gedzelman, *The Science and Wonders of the Atmosphere*)

20. The graphical method for solving a system of equations is an approximation, since reading the point of intersection depends on the accuracy with which the lines are drawn and on the ability to interpret the coordinates of the point.

(Karl J. Smith and Patrick J. Boyle, *Intermediate Algebra for College Students*)

21. That [the moons of Jupiter] revolve in unequal circles is manifestly deduced from the fact that at the longest elongation from Jupiter it is never possible to see two of these moons in conjunction, whereas in the vicinity of Jupiter they are found united two, three, and sometimes all four together.

(Galileo Galilei, *The Starry Messenger*)

★22. Lenses function by refracting light at their surfaces. Consequently, their action depends not only on the shape of the lens surfaces, but also on the indices of refraction of the lens material and the surrounding medium.

(Frank J. Blatt, *Principles of Physics,* 2nd ed.)

23. Given present growth rates in underdeveloped countries, the limited practice of birth control, and the difficulty of slowing the current growth momentum, it can be said with virtual certainty that none of the people now reading this book will ever live in a world where the population is not growing.

(J. John Palen, *Social Problems*)

24. The interpretation of the laws is the proper and peculiar province of the courts. A constitution is, in fact, and must be regarded by the judges, as a fundamental law. It therefore belongs to them to ascertain its meaning, as well as the meaning of any particular act proceeding from the legislative body.

(Alexander Hamilton, *Federalist Papers,* No. 78)

★25. The Simpson incident had shown me that a dog was kept in the stables, and yet, though someone had been in and had fetched out a horse, he had not barked enough to arouse the two lads in the loft. Obviously the midnight visitor was someone whom the dog knew well.

(A. Conan Doyle, *Memoirs of Sherlock Holmes*)

26. Eternity is simultaneously whole. But time has a before and an after. Therefore time and eternity are not the same thing.

(Thomas Aquinas, *Summa Theologica*)

27. Ordinary things that we encounter every day are electrically neutral. Therefore, since negatively charged electrons are a part of everything, positively charged particles must also exist in all matter.

(James E. Brady and Gerard E. Humiston, *General Chemistry*)

★28. Animals that live on plant foods must eat large quantities of vegetation, and this consumes much of their time. Meat eaters, by contrast, have no need to eat so much or so often. Consequently, meat-eating hominines [early humans] may have had more leisure time available to explore and manipulate their environment; like lions and leopards, they would have time to spend lying around and playing.

(William A. Haviland, *Cultural Anthropology,* 8th ed.)

29. [Psychologists] Wirtshafter and Davis noted that the glycerol content of the blood is related to the size of the fat cells [in the body]. Since the size of the fat cells would indicate something about the amount of stored fats, increases in blood glycerol should indicate increases in body weight.

(Herbert L. Petri, *Motivation: Theory and Research,* 2nd ed.)

30. Because the moon moves relative to the earth so that it returns to the same position overhead after about 25 hours, there are two high and two low tides at any point every 25 hours.

(Douglas C. Giancoli, *The Ideas of Physics,* 3rd ed.)

II. Define the following terms:

deductive argument	argument from analogy
inductive argument	generalization
argument based on mathematics	prediction
	argument from authority
argument from definition	argument based on signs
categorical syllogism	causal inference
hypothetical syllogism	particular statement
disjunctive syllogism	general statement

III. Answer "true" or "false" to the following statements:

1. In an inductive argument, it is intended that the conclusion contain more information than the premises.

2. In a deductive argument, the conclusion is not supposed to contain more information than the premises.

3. The form of argumentation the arguer uses may allow one to determine whether an argument is inductive or deductive.

4. The actual strength of the link between premises and conclusion may allow one to determine whether an argument is inductive or deductive.

5. A geometrical proof is an example of an inductive argument.

6. Most arguments based on statistical reasoning are deductive.

7. If the conclusion of an argument follows merely from the definition of a word used in a premise, the argument is deductive.

8. An argument that draws a conclusion about a thing based on that thing's similarity to something else is a deductive argument.

9. An argument that draws a conclusion that something is true because someone has said that it is, is a deductive argument.

10. An argument that presents two alternatives and eliminates one, leaving the other as the conclusion, is an inductive argument.

11. An argument that proceeds from knowledge of a cause to knowledge of an effect is an inductive argument.

12. If an argument contains the phrase "it definitely follows that," then we know for certain that the argument is deductive.

13. An argument that predicts what will happen in the future, based on what has happened in the past, is an inductive argument.

14. Inductive arguments always proceed from the particular to the general.

15. Deductive arguments always proceed from the general to the particular.

IV. Page through a book, magazine, or newspaper and find two arguments, one inductive and the other deductive. Copy the arguments as written, giving the appropriate reference. Then identify the premises and conclusion of each.

1.4 Validity, Truth, Soundness, Strength, Cogency

This section introduces the central ideas and terminology required to evaluate arguments. We have seen that every argument makes two basic claims: a claim that evidence or reasons exist and a claim that the alleged evidence or reasons support something (or that something follows from the alleged evidence or reasons). The first is a factual claim, the second an inferential claim. The evaluation of every argument centers on the evaluation of these two claims. The more important of the two is the inferential claim, because if the premises fail to support the conclusion (that is, if the reasoning is bad), an argument is worthless. Thus we will always test the inferential claim first, and only if the premises do support the conclusion will we test the factual claim (that is, the claim that the premises present genuine evidence, or are true). The material that follows considers first deductive arguments and then inductive.

Deductive Arguments

The previous section defined a deductive argument as one incorporating the claim that it is impossible for the conclusion to be false given that the premises are true. If this claim is true, the argument is said to be valid. Thus, a **valid deductive argument** is an argument in which it is impossible for the conclusion to be false given that the premises are true. In these arguments the conclusion follows with strict necessity from the premises. Conversely, an **invalid deductive argument** is a deductive argument in which it *is* possible for the conclusion to be false given that the premises are true. In these arguments the conclusion does not follow with strict necessity from the premises, even though it is claimed to.

An immediate consequence of these definitions is that there is no middle ground between valid and invalid. There are no arguments that are "almost" valid and "almost" invalid. If the conclusion follows with strict necessity from the premises, the argument is valid; if not, it is invalid.

To test an argument for validity we begin by assuming that all the premises are true, and then we determine if it is possible, in light of that assumption, for the conclusion to be false. Here is an example:

> All television networks are media companies.
> NBC is a television network.
> Therefore, NBC is a media company.

In this argument both premises are actually true, so it is easy to *assume* that they are true. Next we determine, in light of this assumption, if it is possible for the conclusion to be false. Clearly this is not possible. If NBC is included in the group of television networks (second premise) and if the group of television networks is included in the group of media companies (first premise), it necessarily follows that NBC is included in the group of media companies (conclusion). In other words, assuming the premises to be true and the conclusion false entails a strict *contradiction*. Thus, the argument is valid.

Here is another example:

> All automakers are computer manufacturers.
> United Airlines is an automaker.
> Therefore, United Airlines is a computer manufacturer.

In this argument, both premises are actually false, but it is easy to assume that they are true. Every automaker could have a corporate division that manufactures computers. Also, in addition to flying airplanes, United Airlines could make cars. Next, in light of these assumptions, we determine if it is possible for the conclusion to be false. Again, we see that this is not possible, by the same reasoning as the previous example. Assuming the premises to be true and the conclusion false entails a contradiction. Thus, the argument is valid.

Another example:

> All banks are financial institutions.
> Wells Fargo is a financial institution.
> Therefore, Wells Fargo is a bank.

As in the first example, both premises of this argument are true, so it is easy to assume they are true. Next we determine, in light of this assumption, if it is possible for the conclusion to be false. In this case it *is* possible. If banks were included in one part of the group of financial institutions and Wells Fargo were included in another part, then Wells Fargo would *not* be a bank. In other words, assuming the premises to be true and the conclusion false does not involve any contradiction, and so the argument is invalid.

In addition to illustrating the basic idea of validity, these examples suggest an important point about validity and truth. In general, validity is not something that is uniformly determined by the actual truth or falsity of the premises and conclusion. Both the NBC example and the Wells Fargo example have actually true premises and an actually true conclusion, yet one is valid and the other invalid. The United Airlines example has actually false premises and an actually false conclusion, yet the argument is

Table 1.1 Deductive Arguments

	Valid	Invalid
True premises True conclusion	All wines are beverages. Chardonnay is a wine. Therefore, chardonnay is a beverage. [sound]	All wines are beverages. Chardonnay is a beverage. Therefore, chardonnay is a wine. [unsound]
True premises False conclusion	None exist.	All wines are beverages. Ginger ale is a beverage. Therefore, ginger ale is a wine. [unsound]
False premises True conclusion	All wines are soft drinks. Ginger ale is a wine. Therefore, ginger ale is a soft drink. [unsound]	All wines are whiskeys. Chardonnay is a whiskey. Therefore, chardonnay is a wine. [unsound]
False premises False conclusion	All wines are whiskeys. Ginger ale is a wine. Therefore, ginger ale is a whiskey. [unsound]	All wines are whiskeys. Ginger ale is a whiskey. Therefore, ginger ale is a wine. [unsound]

valid. Rather, validity is something that is determined by the *relationship* between premises and conclusion. The question is not whether the premises and conclusion are true or false, but whether the premises *support* the conclusion. In the examples of valid arguments the premises do support the conclusion, and in the invalid case they do not.

Nevertheless, there is *one* arrangement of truth and falsity in the premises and conclusion that does determine the issue of validity. Any deductive argument having actually true premises and an actually false conclusion is invalid. The reasoning behind this fact is fairly obvious. If the premises are actually true and the conclusion is actually false, then it certainly is *possible* for the premises to be true and the conclusion false. Thus, by the definition of invalidity, the argument is invalid.

The idea that any deductive argument having actually true premises and a false conclusion is invalid may be the most important point in all of deductive logic. The entire system of deductive logic would be quite useless if it accepted as valid any inferential process by which a person could start with truth in the premises and arrive at falsity in the conclusion.

Table 1.1 presents examples of deductive arguments that illustrate the various combinations of truth and falsity in the premises and conclusion. In the examples having false premises, both premises are false, but it is easy to construct other examples having only one false premise. When examining this table, note that the only combination of truth and falsity that does not allow for *both* valid and invalid arguments is true premises and false conclusion. As we have just seen, any argument having this combination is necessarily invalid.

The relationship between the validity of a deductive argument and the truth or falsity of its premises and conclusion, as illustrated in Table 1.1, is summarized as follows:

Premises	Conclusion	Validity
T	T	?
T	F	Invalid
F	T	?
F	F	?

A **sound argument** is a deductive argument that is *valid* and has *all true premises.* Both conditions must be met for an argument to be sound; if either is missing the argument is unsound. Thus, an **unsound argument** is a deductive argument that is invalid, has one or more false premises, or both. Because a valid argument is one such that it is impossible for the premises to be true and the conclusion false, and because a sound argument does in fact have true premises, it follows that every sound argument, by definition, will have a true conclusion as well. A sound argument, therefore, is what is meant by a "good" deductive argument in the fullest sense of the term.

In connection with this definition of soundness, a single proviso is required: For an argument to be unsound, the false premise or premises must actually be needed to support the conclusion. An argument with a conclusion that is validly supported by true premises but with a superfluous false premise would still be sound. By similar reasoning, no addition of a false premise to an originally sound argument can make the argument unsound. Such a premise would be superfluous and should not be considered part of the argument. Analogous remarks, incidentally, extend to induction.

Inductive Arguments

Section 1.3 defined an inductive argument as one incorporating the claim that it is improbable that the conclusion be false given that the premises are true. If this claim is true, the argument is said to be strong. Thus, a **strong inductive argument** is an inductive argument in which it is improbable that the conclusion be false given that the premises are true. In such arguments, the conclusion does in fact follow probably from the premises. Conversely, a **weak inductive argument** is an argument in which the conclusion does not follow probably from the premises, even though it is claimed to.

The procedure for testing the strength of inductive arguments runs parallel to the procedure for deduction. First we assume the premises are true, and then we determine whether, based on that assumption, the conclusion is probably true. Example:

> All dinosaur bones discovered to this day have been at least 50 million years old. Therefore, probably the next dinosaur bone to be found will be at least 50 million years old.

In this argument the premise is actually true, so it is easy to assume that it is true. Based on that assumption, the conclusion is probably true, so the argument is strong. Here is another example:

> All meteorites found to this day have contained sugar. Therefore, probably the next meteorite to be found will contain sugar.

The premise of this argument is obviously false. But if we assume the premise is true, then based on that assumption, the conclusion would probably be true. Thus, the argument is strong.

The next example is an argument from analogy:

> When a lighted match is slowly dunked into water, the flame is snuffed out. But gasoline is a liquid, just like water. Therefore, when a lighted match is slowly dunked into gasoline, the flame will be snuffed out.

In this argument the premises are actually true and the conclusion is probably false. Thus, if we assume the premises are true, then, based on that assumption, it is not probable that the conclusion is true. Thus, the argument is weak.

Another example:

> During the past fifty years, inflation has consistently reduced the value of the American dollar. Therefore, industrial productivity will probably increase in the years ahead.

In this argument, the premise is actually true and the conclusion is probably true in the actual world, but the probability of the conclusion is in no way based on the assumption that the premise is true. Because there is no direct connection between inflation and increased industrial productivity, the premise is irrelevant to the conclusion and it provides no probabilistic support for it. The conclusion is probably true independently of the premise. As a result, the argument is weak.

This last example illustrates an important distinction between strong inductive arguments and valid deductive arguments. As we will see in later chapters, if the conclusion of a deductive argument is necessarily true independently of the premises, the argument is still considered valid. But if the conclusion of an inductive argument is probably true independently of the premises, the argument is weak.

These four examples show that in general the strength or weakness of an inductive argument results not from the actual truth or falsity of the premises and conclusion, but from the probabilistic support the premises give to the conclusion. The dinosaur argument has a true premise and a probably true conclusion, and the meteorite argument has a false premise and a probably false conclusion; yet both are strong because the premise of each provides probabilistic support for the conclusion. The industrial productivity argument has a true premise and a probably true conclusion, but the argument is weak because the premise provides no probabilistic support for the conclusion. As in the evaluation of deductive arguments, the only arrangement of truth and

Table 1.2 Inductive Arguments

	Strong	Weak
True premise **Probably true conclusion**	All previous U.S. presidents were older than 40. Therefore, probably the next U.S. president will be older than 40. [cogent]	A few U.S. presidents were lawyers. Therefore, probably the next U.S. president will be older than 40. [uncogent]
True premise **Probably false conclusion**	None exist	A few U.S. presidents were unmarried. Therefore, probably the next U.S. president will be unmarried [uncogent]
False premise **Probably true conclusion**	All previous U.S. presidents were TV debaters. Therefore, probably the next U.S. president will be a TV debater. [uncogent]	A few U.S. presidents were dentists. Therefore, probably the next U.S. president will be a TV debater. [uncogent]
False premise **Probably false conclusion**	All previous U.S. presidents died in office. Therefore, probably the next U.S. president will die in office. [uncogent]	A few U.S. presidents were dentists. Therefore, probably the next U.S. president will be a dentist. [uncogent]

falsity that establishes anything is true premises and probably false conclusion (as in the lighted match argument). Any inductive argument having true premises and a probably false conclusion is weak.

Table 1.2 presents the various possibilities of truth and falsity in the premises and conclusion of inductive arguments. Note that the only arrangement of truth and falsity that is missing for strong arguments is true premises and probably false conclusion.

The relationship between the strength of an inductive argument and the truth or falsity of its premises and conclusion, as illustrated in Table 1.2, is summarized as follows:

Premises	Conclusion	Strength
T	prob. T	?
T	prob. F	Weak
F	prob. T	?
F	prob. F	?

Unlike the validity and invalidity of deductive arguments, the strength and weakness of inductive arguments admit of degrees. To be considered strong, an inductive argument must have a conclusion that is more probable than improbable. In other words, given that the premises are true, the likelihood that the conclusion is true must be more than 50 percent, and as the probability increases, the argument becomes stronger. For this purpose, consider the following pair of arguments:

> This barrel contains 100 apples.
> Three apples selected at random were found to be ripe.
> Therefore, probably all 100 apples are ripe.

> This barrel contains 100 apples.
> Eighty apples selected at random were found to be ripe.
> Therefore, probably all 100 apples are ripe.

The first argument is weak and the second is strong. However, the first is not absolutely weak nor the second absolutely strong. Both arguments would be strengthened or weakened by the random selection of a larger or smaller sample. For example, if the size of the sample in the second argument were reduced to seventy apples, the argument would be weakened. The incorporation of additional premises into an inductive argument will also generally tend to strengthen or weaken it. For example, if the premise "One unripe apple that had been found earlier was removed" were added to either argument, the argument would be weakened.

A **cogent argument** is an inductive argument that is *strong* and has *all true premises;* if either condition is missing, the argument is uncogent. Thus, an **uncogent argument** is an inductive argument that is weak, has one or more false premises, or both. A cogent argument is the inductive analogue of a sound deductive argument and is what is meant by a "good" inductive argument without qualification. Because the conclusion of a cogent argument is genuinely supported by true premises, it follows that the conclusion of every cogent argument is probably true.

There is a difference, however, between sound and cogent arguments in regard to the true premise requirement. In a sound argument it is necessary only that the premises be true and nothing more. Given such premises and good reasoning, a true conclusion is guaranteed. In a cogent argument, on the other hand, the premises must not only be true, but they must also not ignore some important piece of evidence that entails a quite different conclusion. This is called the *total evidence requirement.* As an illustration of the need for it, consider the following argument:

> Swimming in the Caribbean is usually lots of fun. Today the water is warm, the surf
> is gentle, and on this beach there are no dangerous currents. Therefore, it would
> be fun to go swimming here now.

If the premises reflect all the important factors, then the argument is cogent. But if they ignore the fact that several large dorsal fins are cutting through the water (suggesting sharks), then obviously the argument is not cogent. Thus, for cogency the premises must not only be true but also not overlook some important fact that requires a different conclusion.

Summary

For both deductive and inductive arguments, two separate questions need to be answered: (1) Do the premises support the conclusion? (2) Are all the premises true?

To answer the first question we begin by *assuming* the premises to be true. Then, for deductive arguments we determine whether, in light of this assumption, it *necessarily* follows that the conclusion is true. If it does, the argument is valid; if not, it is invalid. For inductive arguments we determine whether it *probably* follows that the conclusion is true. If it does, the argument is strong; if not, it is weak. For inductive arguments we keep in mind the requirements that the premises actually support the conclusion and that they not ignore important evidence. Finally, if the argument is either valid or strong, we turn to the second question and determine whether the premises are actually true. If all the premises are true, the argument is sound (in the case of deduction) or cogent (in the case of induction). All invalid deductive arguments are unsound, and all weak inductive arguments are uncogent.

The various alternatives open to statements and arguments may be diagrammed as follows. Note that in logic one never speaks of an argument as being "true" or "false," and one never speaks of a statement as being "valid," "invalid," "strong," or "weak."

Chrysippus 280–206 B.C.

© Araldo de Luca/CORBIS

Chrysippus was born in Soli, a city located in the south east coast of Asia Minor. Early in life he moved to Athens, where he studied under the Stoic philosopher Cleanthes, who in turn was a student of Zeno of Citium, the founder of Stoicism. Upon Cleanthes' death in 232 B.C., Chrysippus took over as leader of the school, and he produced over 700 treatises that systematized Stoic teaching. All of these works have been lost, but fragments survive in the writings of Cicero, Seneca, and others. Because of his extraordinary contribution, Chrysippus is considered to be the second founder of Stoicism.

Stoicism derives its name from the Greek word *stoa,* which means porch; stoic philosophers used to gather on a porch in the Agora (marketplace) in Athens to discuss their views. The stoics prized the virtue of self-sufficiency, and they emphasized the importance of not allowing oneself to be carried away by emotions or passions such as fear or love. Emotions are considered to be false judgments about the goodness or badness of something . The proper therapy for those victimized by emotions is to persuade them that these judgments are indeed false because they constitute obstacles to true happiness.

Chrysippus is often considered to be the originator of propositional logic. Unlike Aristotelian logic, where the fundamental components are terms, in propositional logic the fundamental components are whole propositions or statements. Aristotle had overlooked this kind of logic, but his close friend and successor Theophrastus worked out some of the logic of the pure hypothetical syllogism (If *A* then *B,* if *B* then *C;* therefore if *A* then *C*). Also, Philo of Megara introduced the truth functional interpretation of the material conditional (If *A,* then *B*). Beginning at this point, Chrysippus advanced propositional logic to a high level of development.

Chrysippus divided propositions into simple and compound, and he introduced a set of connectives that were used to produce compound propositions from one or more simple propositions. The compound propositions included negation, conjunction, exclusive disjunction, and implication, and Chrysippus showed how the truth value of a compound statement is a function of the truth values of its simple components. Chrysippus also introduced a set of rules of inference including what is today called *modus ponens, modus tollens,* disjunctive syllogism, and a rule similar to De Morgan's rule. Finally, he introduced the theory of natural deduction by which the conclusion of an argument can be derived from its premises through a series of discrete steps.

The broader philosophy of Chrysippus is characterized by monism and determinism. While most of us think that the universe is made up of millions of discrete entities, Chrysippus argued that in fact only one substance exists, and what appear to be individual substances are really parts of this one primary substance. Furthermore, everything that occurs is strictly governed by fate. Yet, in the face of this rigid causal determinism Chrysippus held that humans are responsible for their actions, and he tried in many ways to prove that the two viewpoints are in fact compatible with each other.

I. The following arguments are deductive. Determine whether each is valid or invalid, and note the relationship between your answer and the truth or falsity of the premises and conclusion. Finally, determine whether the argument is sound or unsound.

★1. Since *Moby Dick* was written by Shakespeare, and *Moby Dick* is a science fiction novel, it follows that Shakespeare wrote a science fiction novel.

2. Since London is north of Paris and south of Edinburgh, it follows that Paris is south of Edinburgh.

3. If George Washington was beheaded, then George Washington died. George Washington died. Therefore, George Washington was beheaded.

★4. The longest river in South America is the Amazon, and the Amazon flows through Brazil. Therefore, the longest river in South America flows through Brazil.

5. Since the Spanish-American War occurred before the U.S. Civil War, and the U.S. Civil War occurred after the Korean War, it follows that the Spanish-American War occurred before the Korean War.

6. The Empire State Building is taller than the Statue of Liberty, and the Statue of Liberty is taller than the Eiffel Tower. Therefore, the Empire State Building is taller than the Eiffel Tower.

★7. All leopards with lungs are carnivores. Therefore, all leopards are carnivores.

8. Chicago is a city in Michigan and Michigan is part of the United States. Therefore, Chicago is a city in the United States.

9. If Senator Hillary Clinton represents California, then she represents a western state. Hillary Clinton does not represent a western state. Therefore, she does not represent California.

★10. Every province in Canada has exactly one city as its capital. Therefore, since there are thirty provinces in Canada, there are thirty provincial capitals.

11. Since the Department of Defense Building outside Washington, D.C., has the shape of a hexagon, it follows that it has seven sides.

12. Since Winston Churchill was English, and Winston Churchill was a famous statesman, we may conclude that at least one Englishman was a famous statesman.

★13. Since some fruits are green, and some fruits are apples, it follows that some fruits are green apples.

14. All physicians are individuals who have earned degrees in political science, and some lawyers are physicians. Therefore, some lawyers are persons who have earned degrees in political science.

15. The United States Congress has more members than there are days in the year. Therefore, at least two members of Congress have the same birthday.

II. The following arguments are inductive. Determine whether each is strong or weak, and note the relationship between your answer and the truth or falsity of the premise(s) and conclusion. Then determine whether each argument is cogent or uncogent.

★1. The grave marker at Arlington National Cemetery says that John F. Kennedy is buried there. It must be the case that Kennedy really is buried in that cemetery.

2. The ebb and flow of the tides has been occurring every day for millions of years. But nothing lasts forever. Therefore, probably the motion of the tides will die out within a few years.

3. The vast majority of Rose Bowl games (in Pasadena, California) have been played in freezing cold weather. Therefore, probably the next Rose Bowl game will be played in freezing cold weather.

★4. Franklin Delano Roosevelt said that we have nothing to fear but fear itself. Therefore, women have no reason to fear serial rapists.

5. Most popular film stars are millionaires. Lindsay Lohan is a popular film star. Therefore, probably Lindsay Lohan is a millionaire.

6. Constructing the great pyramid at Giza required lifting massive stone blocks to great heights. Probably the ancient Egyptians had some antigravity device to accomplish this feat.

★7. People have been listening to rock and roll music for over a hundred years. Probably people will still be listening to it a year from now.

8. Paleontologists have unearthed the fossilized bones of huge reptiles, which we have named dinosaurs. Tests indicate that these bones are more than 50 million years old. Therefore, probably dinosaurs really did roam the earth 50 million years ago.

9. The Declaration of Independence says that all men are endowed by their creator with certain unalienable rights. Therefore it probably follows that a creator exists.

★10. Coca-Cola is an extremely popular soft drink. Therefore, probably someone, somewhere, is drinking a Coke right this minute.

11. Every map of the United States shows that Alabama is situated on the Pacific coast. Therefore, Alabama must be a western state.

12. When Neil Armstrong landed on the moon, he left behind a gold-plated Schwinn bicycle, which he used to ride around on the moon's surface. Probably that bicycle is still up there on the moon.

★13. The African American athlete LaDainian Tomlinson is able to withstand tremendous impacts on the football field. However, Serena Williams, like LaDainian Tomlinson, is a great African American athlete. Therefore, Serena Williams should be able to withstand tremendous impacts on the football field.

14. Unlike monkeys, today's humans have feet that are not suited for grasping objects. Therefore, a thousand years from now, probably humans will still have feet that are not suited for grasping objects.

15. A random sample of twenty-five famous country and western singers, including Garth Brooks and Dolly Parton, revealed that every single one of them

studied music in Tasmania. Therefore, probably the majority of famous country and western singers studied music in Tasmania.

III. Determine whether the following arguments are inductive or deductive. If an argument is inductive, determine whether it is strong or weak. If it is deductive, determine whether it is valid or invalid.

★1. Since Agatha is the mother of Raquel and the sister of Tom, it follows that Tom is the uncle of Raquel.

2. When a cook cannot recall the ingredients in a recipe, it is appropriate that she refresh her memory by consulting the recipe book. Similarly, when a student cannot recall the answers during a final exam, it is appropriate that she refresh her memory by consulting the textbook.

3. The sign on the highway leading into Denver, Colorado, says that the city's elevation is 5280 feet. It must be the case that Denver is 1 mile high.

★4. Since Christmas is always on a Thursday, it follows that the day after Christmas is always a Friday.

5. This figure is a Euclidean triangle. Therefore, the sum of its angles is equal to two right angles.

6. By accident Karen baked her brownies two hours longer than she should have. Therefore, they have probably been ruined.

★7. After taking LSD, Alice said she saw a flying saucer land in the shopping center parking lot. Since Alice has a reputation for always telling the truth, we must conclude that a flying saucer really did land there.

8. Since Phyllis is the cousin of Denise, and Denise is the cousin of Harriet, it follows necessarily that Harriet is the cousin of Phyllis.

9. The picnic scheduled in the park for tomorrow will most likely be cancelled. It's been snowing for six days straight.

★10. Circle A has exactly twice the diameter of circle B. From this we may conclude that circle A has exactly twice the area of circle B.

11. Robert has lost consistently at blackjack every day for the past several days. Therefore, it is very likely that he will win today.

12. Since John loves Nancy and Nancy loves Peter, it follows necessarily that John loves Peter.

★13. This cash register drawer contains over 100 coins. Three coins selected at random were found to have dates earlier than 1945. Therefore, probably all of the coins in the drawer have dates earlier than 1945.

14. The Japanese attack on Pearl Harbor happened in either 1941 or 1951. But it didn't happen in 1941. Therefore, it happened in 1951.

15. Harry will never be able to solve that difficult problem in advanced calculus in the limited time allowed. He has never studied anything beyond algebra, and in that he earned only a C−.

★16. Since $x + y = 10$, and $x = 7$, it follows that $y = 4$.

17. If acupuncture is hocus pocus, then acupuncture cannot relieve chronic pain. But acupuncture can relieve chronic pain. Therefore, acupuncture is not hocus pocus.

18. If inflation heats up, then interest rates will rise. If interest rates rise, then bond prices will decline. Therefore, if inflation heats up, then bond prices will decline.

★19. Statistics reveal that 86 percent of those who receive flu shots do not get the flu. Jack received a flu shot one month ago. Therefore, he should be immune, even though the flu is going around now.

20. Since Michael is a Pisces, it necessarily follows that he was born in March.

IV. Define the following terms:

valid argument	strong argument
invalid argument	weak argument
sound argument	cogent argument
unsound argument	uncogent argument

V. Answer "true" or "false" to the following statements:

1. Some arguments, while not completely valid, are almost valid.
2. Inductive arguments admit of varying degrees of strength and weakness.
3. Invalid deductive arguments are basically the same as inductive arguments.
4. If a deductive argument has true premises and a false conclusion, it is necessarily invalid.
5. A valid argument may have a false premise and a false conclusion.
6. A valid argument may have a false premise and a true conclusion.
7. A sound argument may be invalid.
8. A sound argument may have a false conclusion.
9. A strong argument may have false premises and a probably false conclusion.
10. A strong argument may have true premises and a probably false conclusion.
11. A cogent argument may have a probably false conclusion.
12. A cogent argument must be inductively strong.
13. If an argument has true premises and a true conclusion, we know that it is a perfectly good argument.
14. A statement may legitimately be spoken of as "valid" or "invalid."
15. An argument may legitimately be spoken of as "true" or "false."

1.5   Argument Forms: Proving Invalidity

This section explores the idea that the validity of a deductive argument is determined by the **argument form.** This idea was suggested in the arguments about wines and beverages presented in Table 1.1 in the previous section. All the arguments in the valid column have the same form, and all the arguments in the invalid column have the same form.

Yet, in the exercises at the end of that section we saw many cases of valid deductive arguments that did not have any recognizable form. How can we reconcile this fact with the claim that validity is determined by form? The answer is that these arguments are incomplete, so the form is not explicit. But once such arguments are completed and correctly phrased (which we address later in this book), the form becomes apparent. For example, consider the following valid argument:

Geese are migratory waterfowl, so they fly south for the winter.

This argument is missing a premise:

Migratory waterfowl fly south for the winter.

The argument can now be rephrased to make its form apparent:

All geese are migratory waterfowl.
All migratory waterfowl are birds that fly south for the winter.
Therefore, all geese are birds that fly south for the winter.

The form of the argument is

All *A* are *B*.
All *B* are *C*.
_____
All *A* are *C*.

This form is valid, and it captures the reasoning process of the argument. If we assume that the *A*s (whatever they might be) are included in the *B*s, and that the *B*s (whatever they might be) are included in the *C*s, then the *A*s must necessarily be included in the *C*s. This necessary relationship between the *A*s, *B*s, and *C*s is what makes the argument valid. This is what we mean when we say that the validity of a deductive argument is determined by its form.

Since validity is determined by form, it follows that any argument that has this valid form is a valid argument. Thus, we might substitute "daisies" for *A*, "flowers" for *B*, and "plants" for *C* and obtain the following valid argument:

All daisies are flowers.
All flowers are plants.
Therefore, all daisies are plants.

Any argument such as this that is produced by uniformly substituting terms or statements in place of the letters in an argument form is called a **substitution instance** of that form.

Let us now consider an invalid argument form:

All *A* are *B*.
All *C* are *B*.
_____
All *A* are *C*.

In this argument form, if we assume that the *A*s are in the *B*s and that the *C*s are in the *B*s, it does not *necessarily* follow that the *A*s are in the *C*s. It would not follow if the

*A*s were in one part of the *B*s and the *C*s were in another part, as the following diagram illustrates:

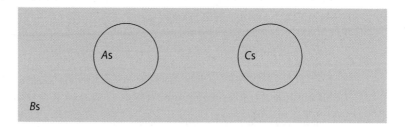

*B*s

This diagram suggests that we can prove the form invalid if we can find a substitution instance having actually true premises and an actually false conclusion. In such a substitution instance the *A*s and the *C*s would be separated from each other, but they would both be included in the *B*s. If we substitute "cats" for *A*, "animals" for *B*, and "dogs" for *C*, we have such a substitution instance:

All *A* are *B*.	All cats are animals.	True
All *C* are *B*.	All dogs are animals.	True
All *A* are *C*.	Therefore, all cats are dogs.	False

This substitution instance proves the form invalid, because it provides a concrete example of a case where the *A*s are in the *B*s, the *C*s are in the *B*s, but the *A*s are *not* in the *C*s.

Now, since the form is invalid, can we say that any argument that has this form is invalid? Unfortunately, the situation with invalid forms is not quite as simple as it is with valid forms. Every substitution instance of a valid form is a valid argument, but it is not the case that every substitution instance of an invalid form is an invalid argument. The reason is that some substitution instances of invalid forms are also substitution instances of valid forms.* However, we can say that any substitution instance of an invalid form is an invalid argument *provided* that it is not a substitution instance of any valid form. Thus we will say that an argument actually *has* an invalid form if it is a substitution instance of that form and it is not a substitution instance of any valid form.

The fact that some substitution instances of invalid forms are also substitution instances of valid forms means simply that we must exercise caution in identifying the

---

*For example, the following valid argument is a substitution instance of the invalid form we have been discussing:

All bachelors are persons.
All unmarried men are persons.
Therefore, all bachelors are unmarried men.

However, because "bachelors" is equivalent in meaning to "unmarried men," the argument is also a substitution instance of this valid form:

All *A* are *B*.
All *A* are *B*.
All *A* are *A*.

form of an argument. However, cases of ordinary language arguments that can be interpreted as substitution instances of both valid and invalid forms are so rare that this book chooses to ignore them. With this in mind, consider the following argument:

> All romantic novels are literary pieces.
> All works of fiction are literary pieces.
> Therefore, all romantic novels are works of fiction.

This argument clearly has the invalid form just discussed. This invalid form captures the reasoning process of the argument, which is obviously defective. Therefore, the argument is invalid, and it is invalid precisely because it has an invalid form.

Counterexample Method

A substitution instance having true premises and a false conclusion (like the cats-and-dogs example just constructed) is called a counterexample, and the method we have just used to prove the romantic-novels argument invalid is called the **counterexample method.** It consists of isolating the form of an argument and then constructing a substitution instance having true premises and a false conclusion. This proves the form invalid, which in turn proves the argument invalid. The counterexample method can be used to prove the invalidity of any invalid argument, but it cannot prove the validity of any valid argument. Thus, before the method is applied to an argument, the argument must be known or suspected to be invalid in the first place. Let us apply the counterexample method to the following invalid categorical syllogism:

> Since some employees are not social climbers and all vice presidents are employees, we may conclude that some vice presidents are not social climbers.

This argument is invalid because the employees who are not social climbers might not be vice presidents. Accordingly, we can *prove* the argument invalid by constructing a substitution instance having true premises and a false conclusion. We begin by isolating the form of the argument:

> Some *E* are not *S*.
> All *V* are *E*.
> ───────────────
> Some *V* are not *S*.

Next, we select three terms to substitute in place of the letters that will make the premises true and the conclusion false. The following selection will work:

> *E* = animals
> *S* = mammals
> *V* = dogs

The resulting substitution instance is this:

> Some animals are not mammals.
> All dogs are animals.
> Therefore, some dogs are not mammals.

The substitution instance has true premises and a false conclusion and is therefore, by definition, invalid. Because the substitution instance is invalid, the form is invalid, and therefore the original argument is invalid.

In applying the counterexample method to categorical syllogisms, it is useful to keep in mind the following set of terms: "cats," "dogs," "mammals," "fish," and "animals." Most invalid syllogisms can be proven invalid by strategically selecting three of these terms and using them to construct a counterexample. Because everyone agrees about these terms, everyone will agree about the truth or falsity of the premises and conclusion of the counterexample. Also, in constructing the counterexample, it often helps to begin with the conclusion. First, select two terms that yield a false conclusion, and then select a third term that yields true premises. Another point to keep in mind is that the word "some" in logic always means "at least one." For example, the statement "Some dogs are animals" means "At least one dog is an animal"—which is true. Also note that this statement does not imply that some dogs are not animals.

Not all deductive arguments, of course, are categorical syllogisms. Consider, for example, the following hypothetical syllogism:

> If the government imposes import restrictions, the price of automobiles will rise.
> Therefore, since the government will not impose import restrictions, it follows that the price of automobiles will not rise.

This argument is invalid because the price of automobiles might rise even though import restrictions are not imposed. It has the following form:

> If G, then P.
> Not G.
> Not P.

This form differs from the previous one in that its letters stand for complete statements. G, for example, stands for "The government imposes import restrictions." If we make the substitution

> G = Abraham Lincoln committed suicide.
> P = Abraham Lincoln is dead.

we obtain the following substitution instance:

> If Abraham Lincoln committed suicide, then Abraham Lincoln is dead.
> Abraham Lincoln did not commit suicide.
> Therefore, Abraham Lincoln is not dead.

Since the premises are true and the conclusion false, the substitution instance is clearly invalid. Therefore, the form is invalid, and this proves the original argument invalid.

When applying the counterexample method to an argument having a conditional statement as a premise (such as the one just discussed), it is recommended that the statement substituted in place of the conditional statement express some kind of necessary connection. In the Lincoln example, the first premise asserts the necessary connection between suicide and death. There can be no doubt about the truth of such a statement. Furthermore, if it should turn out that the conclusion is a conditional state-

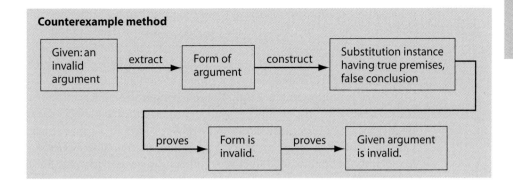

Counterexample method

Given: an invalid argument → *extract* → Form of argument → *construct* → Substitution instance having true premises, false conclusion

→ *proves* → Form is invalid. → *proves* → Given argument is invalid.

ment, note that one sure way of producing a false conditional statement is by joining a true antecedent with a false consequent. For example, the conditional statement "If Lassie is a dog, then Lassie is a cat" is clearly false.

Being able to identify the form of an argument with ease requires a familiarity with the basic deductive argument forms. The first task consists in distinguishing the premises from the conclusion. Always write the premises first and the conclusion last. The second task involves distinguishing what we may call "form words" from "content words." To reduce an argument to its form, leave the form words as they are, and replace the content words with letters. For categorical syllogisms, the words "all," "no," "some," "are," and "not" are form words, and for hypothetical syllogisms the words "if," "then," and "not" are form words. Additional form words for other types of arguments are "either," "or," "both," and "and." For various kinds of hybrid arguments, a more intuitive approach may be needed. Here is an example:

> All movie stars are actors who are famous, because all movie stars who are famous are actors.

If we replace "movie stars," "actors," and "famous" with the letters *M, A,* and *F,* this argument has the following form:

> All *M* who are *F* are *A*.
> _____
> All *M* are *A* who are *F*.

Here is one possible substitution instance for this form:

> All humans who are fathers are men.
> Therefore, all humans are men who are fathers.

Because the premise is true and the conclusion false, the form is invalid and so is the original argument.

Using the counterexample method to prove arguments invalid requires a little ingenuity because there is no rule that will automatically produce the required term or statement to be substituted into the form. Any term or statement will work, of course, provided that it yields a substitution instance that has premises that are indisputably true and a conclusion that is indisputably false. Ideally, the truth value of these statements should be known to the average individual; otherwise, the substitution instance cannot be depended on to prove anything. If, for example, *P* in the earlier hypothetical syllogism had been replaced by the statement "George Wilson is dead," the substitution instance would be useless, because nobody knows whether this statement is true or false.

The counterexample method is useful only for proving invalidity, because the only arrangement of truth and falsity that proves anything is true premises and false conclusion. If a substitution instance is produced having true premises and a true conclusion, it does *not* prove that the argument is valid. Furthermore, the method is useful only for deductive arguments because the strength and weakness of inductive arguments is only partially dependent on the form of the argument. Accordingly, no method that relates exclusively to the form of an inductive argument can be used to prove the argument weak.

EXERCISE 1.5

I. Use the counterexample method to prove the following categorical syllogisms invalid. In doing so, follow the suggestions given in the text.

★1. All galaxies are structures that contain black holes in the center, so all galaxies are quasars, since all quasars are structures that contain black holes in the center.

2. Some evolutionists are not people who believe in the Bible, for no creationists are evolutionists, and some people who believe in the Bible are not creationists.

3. No patents are measures that discourage research and development, and all patents are regulations that protect intellectual property. Thus, no measures that discourage research and development are regulations that protect intellectual property.

★4. Some farm workers are not people who are paid decent wages, because no illegal aliens are people who are paid decent wages, and some illegal aliens are not farm workers.

5. Some politicians are people who will stop at nothing to win an election, and no people who will stop at nothing to win an election are true statesmen. Hence, no politicians are true statesmen.

6. All meticulously constructed timepieces are true works of art, for all Swiss watches are true works of art and all Swiss watches are meticulously constructed timepieces.

★7. No patrons of fast-food restaurants are health-food addicts. Consequently, no patrons of fast-food restaurants are connoisseurs of fine desserts, since no connoisseurs of fine desserts are health-food addicts.

8. Some toxic dumps are sites that emit hazardous wastes, and some sites that emit hazardous wastes are undesirable places to live near. Thus, some toxic dumps are undesirable places to live near.

9. All persons who assist others in suicide are people guilty of murder. Accordingly, some individuals motivated by compassion are not persons guilty of murder, inasmuch as some people who assist others in suicide are individuals motivated by compassion.

★10. Some school boards are not groups that oppose values clarification, because some school boards are not organizations with vision, and some groups that oppose values clarification are not organizations with vision.

II. Use the counterexample method to prove each of the following arguments invalid.

★1. If animal species are fixed and immutable, then evolution is a myth. Therefore, evolution is not a myth, since animal species are not fixed and immutable.

2. If carbon dioxide is present in the atmosphere, then plants have a source of carbon. Hence, since plants have a source of carbon, carbon dioxide is present in the atmosphere.

3. If human rights are recognized, then civilization flourishes. If equality prevails, then civilization flourishes. Thus, if human rights are recognized, then equality prevails.

★4. If energy taxes are increased, then either the deficit will be reduced or conservation will be taken seriously. If the deficit is reduced, then inflation will be checked. Therefore, if energy taxes are increased, then inflation will be checked.

5. All homeless people who are panhandlers are destitute individuals. Therefore, all homeless people are destitute individuals.

6. Some wrestlers are colorful hulks, since some wrestlers are colorful and some wrestlers are hulks.

★7. All community colleges with low tuition are either schools with large enrollments or institutions supported by taxes. Therefore, all community colleges are institutions supported by taxes.

8. All merchandisers that are retailers are businesses that are inventory rotators. Therefore, all merchandisers are inventory rotators.

9. All diabetes victims are either insulin takers or glucose eliminators. Accordingly, some diabetes victims are glucose eliminators, since some diabetes victims are insulin takers.

★10. All FHA loans are living-standard enhancers for the following reasons. All reverse mortgages that are FHA loans are either living-standard enhancers or home equity depleters, and all reverse mortgages are home equity depleters.

1.6 Extended Arguments

The logical analysis of extended arguments, such as those found in editorials, essays, and lengthy letters to newspaper editors, involves numerous difficulties. Such arguments are often mixed together with fragments of reports, pieces of expository writing, illustrations, explanations, and statements of opinion. Proper analysis involves weeding out the extraneous material and isolating premises and conclusions. Another problem stems from the fact that lengthy arguments often involve complex arrangements of subarguments that feed into the main argument in various ways. Distinguishing one subargument from another is often a complicated task. And then there are some argumentative passages that involve completely separate strands of argumentation leading to separate conclusions. Again, distinguishing the strands and assigning premises to the right conclusion not only is problematic but often involves an element of creativity on the part of the analyst.

To facilitate the analysis of extended arguments, we will assign numerals to the various statements in the passage and use arrows to represent the inferential links. Example:

① The contamination of underground aquifers represents a pollution problem of catastrophic proportions. ② Half the nation's drinking water, which comes from these aquifers, is being poisoned by chemical wastes dumped into the soil for generations.

This argument is diagrammed as follows:

The diagram says that statement ②, the premise, supports statement ①, the conclusion.

In extended arguments we can identify two distinct patterns of argumentation, which we will name the vertical pattern and the horizontal pattern. The *vertical pattern* consists of a series of arguments in which a conclusion of a logically prior argument becomes a premise of a subsequent argument. Example:

① The selling of human organs, such as hearts, kidneys, and corneas, should be outlawed. ② Allowing human organs to be sold will inevitably lead to a situation in which only the rich will be able to afford transplants. This is so because ③ whenever something scarce is bought and sold as a commodity, the price always goes up. ④ The law of supply and demand requires it.

This argument is diagrammed as follows:

Vertical pattern

The diagram says that statement ①, which is the main conclusion, is supported by ②, which in turn is supported by ③, which in turn is supported by ④.

The *horizontal pattern* consists of a single argument in which two or more premises provide independent support for a single conclusion. If one of the premises were omitted, the other(s) would continue to support the conclusion in the same way. Example:

① The selling of human organs, such as hearts, kidneys, and corneas, should be outlawed. ② If this practice is allowed to get a foothold, people in desperate financial straits will start selling their own organs to pay their bills. Alternately, ③ those with a criminal bent will take to killing healthy young people and selling their organs on the black market. ④ In the final analysis, the buying and selling of human organs comes just too close to the buying and selling of life itself.

The diagram for this argument is as follows:

Horizontal pattern

This diagram says that statements ②, ③, and ④ support ① independently.

Two variations on the horizontal and vertical patterns occur when two or more premises support a conclusion *conjointly,* and when one or more premises support *multiple* conclusions. The first variation occurs when the premises depend on one another in such a way that if one were omitted, the support that the others provide would be diminished or destroyed. The following argument illustrates the occurrence of conjoint premises:

> ① Getting poor people off the welfare rolls requires that we modify their behavior patterns. ② The vast majority of people on welfare are high school dropouts, single parents, or people who abuse alcohol and drugs. ③ These behavior patterns frustrate any desire poor people may have to get a job and improve their condition in life.

Statement ① is the conclusion. Taken separately, statements ② and ③ provide little or no support for ①, but taken together they do provide support. That is, ② and ③ support ① *conjointly.* This relationship between the premises is illustrated by the use of the brace in the following diagram:

Conjoint premises

The next example illustrates the occurrence of a multiple conclusion:

> ① Dropping out of school and bearing children outside of marriage are two of the primary causes of poverty in this country. Therefore, ② to eliminate poverty we must offer incentives for people to get high school diplomas. Also, ③ we must find some way to encourage people to get married before they start having children.

In this passage statement ① supports both ② and ③. Since no single argument can have more than one conclusion, the passage is correctly evaluated as consisting of two arguments. For our purposes, however, we will treat it as if it were a single argument by joining the two conclusions with a brace:

Multiple conclusion

Our symbolism is now sufficiently developed to analyze most arguments found in editorials and letters to the editor of newspapers and magazines. Consider the following argument, taken from a newspaper editorial:

① Government mandates for zero-emission vehicles won't work because ② only electric cars qualify as zero-emission vehicles, and ③ electric cars won't sell. ④ They are too expensive, ⑤ their range of operation is too limited, and ⑥ recharging facilities are not generally available.

(William Campbell, "Technology Is Not Good Enough")

We immediately see that ① is the main conclusion, and ② and ③ support ① conjointly. Also, ④, ⑤, and ⑥ support ③ independently. The argument pattern is as follows:

The next argument is taken from a letter to the editor:

① Rhinos in Kenya are threatened with extinction because ② poachers are killing them for their horn. Since ③ the rhino has no natural predators, ④ it does not need its horn to survive. Thus ⑤ there should be an organized program to capture rhinos in the wild and remove their horn. ⑥ Such a program would eliminate the incentive of the poachers.

(Pamela C. Wagner, "Rhino Poaching")

First we search for the final conclusion. We select ⑤, because it is the ultimate point that the passage attempts to establish. Next we survey the premise and conclusion indicators. From this, we see that ② supports ① and ③ supports ④. Finally, we see that ①, ④, and ⑥ support ⑤. Yet these supporting statements depend on one another for their effect. Thus, they support the final conclusion conjointly. The argument pattern is as follows:

The next argument is taken from a magazine article:

① Skating is a wonderful form of exercise and relaxation, but ② today's rollerbladers are a growing menace and ③ something should be done to control them. ④ Roller-bladers are oblivious to traffic regulations as ⑤ they breeze through red lights and ⑥ skim down the wrong way on one-way streets. ⑦ They pose a threat to pedestrians because ⑧ a collision can cause serious injury. ⑨ Rollerbladers are even a hazard to shopkeepers as ⑩ they zoom through stores and ⑪ damage merchandise.

(Joan Schmidt, "Hell—On Wheels")

After reading the argument, we see that ① is merely an introductory sentence, and ② and ③ together compose the main conclusion. Also, ④, ⑦, and ⑨ support the main conclusion independently, while ⑤ and ⑥ support ④ independently, ⑧ supports ⑦, and ⑩ and ⑪ support ⑨ independently. The diagram is as follows:

The next argument is taken from the science column of a newspaper:

> ① We can expect small changes to occur in the length of our calendar year for an indefinite time to come. ② This is true for two reasons. ③ First, the rotation of the earth exhibits certain irregularities. ④ And why is this so? ⑤ The rotation of any body is affected by its distribution of mass, and ⑥ the earth's mass distribution is continually subject to change. For example, ⑦ earthquakes alter the location of the tectonic plates. Also, ⑧ the liquid core of the earth sloshes as the earth turns, and ⑨ rainfall redistributes water from the oceans. The second reason is that ⑩ the motion of the tides causes a continual slowing down of earth's rotation. ⑪ Tidal motion produces heat, and ⑫ the loss of this heat removes energy from the system.

(Isaac Asimov, "As the World Turns")

Preliminary analysis reveals that the final conclusion is ①. Also, ② tells us that the supporting statements are divided into two basic groups, but since ② does not add any support, we can leave it out of the diagram. In the first group, ⑤ and ⑥ support ③ conjointly, while ⑦, ⑧, and ⑨ support ⑥ independently. ④ will not appear in the diagram, because it serves merely as a premise indicator. In the second group, ⑪ and ⑫ support ⑩ conjointly. Thus, the argument pattern is as follows:

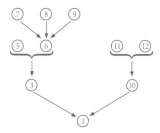

Our last example is taken from a letter to the editor of a newspaper:

> ① Community college districts save a great deal of money by hiring untenured part-time instructors, but ② the extensive use of these instructors is a disadvantage to

the students. ③ Most part-time instructors are paid only 60 percent of what a full-time teacher earns, and as a result, ④ they are forced to teach five or six courses just to survive. ⑤ This detracts from the opportunity to consult with students outside the classroom. To make matters worse, ⑥ many part-timers are not even given office space. Furthermore, ⑦ the lower pay demoralizes the part-timer, and ⑧ the lack of tenure makes for constant financial insecurity. ⑨ Obviously these conditions render the instructor less receptive to student needs. Lastly, because ⑩ these part-timers are burning the candle from both ends, ⑪ they have no spare energy to improve their courses, and ⑫ many lack the enthusiasm to motivate their students. As a result, ⑬ the educational process is impaired.

(Gordon Dossett et al., "Part-Time College Instructors")

Preliminary analysis reveals that the main conclusion is not ① but ②. Also, we see three main reasons why part-timers are a disadvantage to students: They have little opportunity to consult with students, they are less receptive to student needs, and the educational process is impaired by ⑪ and ⑫. In the first main branch, the indicator "as a result" shows that ③ supports ④, and ④ and ⑥ independently support ⑤. In the second branch, ⑦ and ⑧ independently support ⑨. In the third, ⑩ supports both ⑪ and ⑫, which in turn support ⑬ independently. Here is the argument pattern:

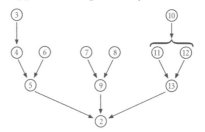

EXERCISE 1.6

I. The following arguments were abstracted from newspaper articles, editorials, and letters to the editor. Use the method presented in this section to construct argument patterns. If a statement is redundant or plays no role in the argument, do not include it in the pattern.

★1. ① The conditions under which many food animals are raised are unhealthy for humans. ② To keep these animals alive, large quantities of drugs must be administered. ③ These drugs remain in the animals' flesh and are passed on to the humans who eat it.

(Philip D. Oliver, "We Can Eat Ribs and Still Be Humane")

2. ① The development of carbon-embedded plastics, otherwise called "composits," is an important new technology because ② it holds the key for new aircraft and spacecraft designs. This is so because ③ these composits are not only stronger than steel but lighter than aluminum.

(Thomas H. Maugh II, "Composits—The Lightweight Champs of Aircraft Industry")

3. ① Homework stifles the thrill of learning in the mind of the student. ② It instills an oppressive learn-or-else discipline. ③ It quenches the desire for knowledge and the love of truth. For these reasons ④ homework should never be assigned.

(Colman McCarthy, "Homework's Tyranny Hobbles Promising Minds")

★4. ① When parents become old and destitute, the obligation of caring for them should be imposed on their children. ② Clearly, children owe a debt to their parents. ③ Their parents brought them into the world and cared for them when they were unable to care for themselves. ④ This debt could be appropriately discharged by having grown children care for their parents.

(Gary Jones, "The Responsibility of Parents")

5. ① Defending the war on drugs may not be fashionable, but the fact remains that ② hardcore drugs should remain illegal. ③ As long as hardcore drugs are illegal, they are harder to get, and ④ the social stigma of being arrested deters many users.

(Charles Van DeVenter, "I'm Proof: The War on Drugs Is Working")

6. ① The rain forest of Brazil produces oxygen for the whole world, yet ② it yields no monetary return to that country. Given that ③ the industrialized nations consume the most oxygen, ④ those nations ought to pay Brazil an annual fee for the use of its rain forest.

(Diane B. Robinson, letter to the editor)

★7. ① It appears that animals may be able to predict earthquakes. ② Prior to a major quake in China, hundreds of snakes suddenly appeared from hibernation and froze to death in the snow, ③ fish were seen leaping from rivers and lakes, and ④ cows and horses refused to enter barns. Also, ⑤ prior to a quake in Fremont, California, a flood of callers reported strange behavior from their pets and domestic animals.

(Michael Bowker, "Can Animals Really Predict Earthquakes?")

8. ① Contributions to relief organizations are often wasted. ② Food sent to war torn countries rarely reaches its destination, because ③ food distribution is controlled by the warring groups, and ④ these groups sell the food to buy weapons and ammunition.

(Michael Maren, "The Faces of Famine")

9. ① Research leading to the development of a scramjet engine is worthwhile. ② Commercial aircraft incorporating such an engine could cross the Pacific in as little as two hours. ③ This would relieve the fatigue of flights from New York to Tokyo. Also, ④ such an engine could power future orbiting spacecraft.

(T. A. Heppenheimer, "A Plane for Space")

★10. ① There is a lot of pressure on untenured college teachers to dumb down their courses. ② Administrators tend to rehire teachers who bring in more money, and ③ teachers who dumb down their classes do precisely this. Why? Because ④ easier classes attract more students, and ⑤ more students means more money for the school.

(Lynne Drury Lerych, "Meeting the Bottom Line in the College Biz")

II. The following arguments gradually increase in difficulty. Use the method presented in this section to construct argument patterns. If a statement is redundant or plays no role in the argument, do not include it in the pattern.

★1. ① Many people believe that the crime of bribery cannot extend to campaign contributions. ② From a legal standpoint, however, countless campaign contributions are in fact bribes. ③ A bribe is anything of value or advantage given with the intent to unlawfully influence the person to whom it is given in his official capacity. ④ A campaign contribution is certainly something of value or advantage. Furthermore, ⑤ every contribution from a lobbyist or special interest group is given with the intent to influence voting, and ⑥ thousands of such contributions are made in every important election.

(Daniel Hays Lowenstein, "Can Candidates Run for Political Office
Without Taking Bribes?")

2. ① America's farm policy desperately needs revamping. ② Seventy-three cents of every farm program dollar ends up in the pockets of the nation's super-farmers. As a result, ③ the mid-sized family farms are being squeezed out of existence. Also, ④ our farm policy courts environmental disaster. ⑤ Federal subsidies encourage farmers to use enormous amounts of fertilizer and pesticides. ⑥ These chemicals percolate down through the soil and pollute limited groundwater.

(Osha Gray Davidson, "Rise of America's Rural Ghetto")

3. ① Society values white lives more than black lives. This is clear from the fact that ② killers of whites are much more likely to be sentenced to death than killers of blacks. ③ Of the 1788 people currently on death row, 1713 were convicted of killing a white person. Yet ④ blacks are six times more likely to be murder victims than whites are. ⑤ In Florida, no one has ever been executed for murdering a black person, but ⑥ dozens have been executed for murdering white people.

(*Los Angeles Times* editorial, "Death and Race")

★4. ① Powerful new particle accelerators are important in high-energy physics, and ② they are worth their cost because ③ they will allow scientists to produce and capture significant quantities of Z particles. ④ Z particles result from the collision of positrons and electrons, and ⑤ particle accelerators are needed to achieve significant numbers of these collisions. ⑥ Z particles are thought to be the bearers of the weak nuclear force, and ⑦ learning the nature of this force may lead to the development of entirely new sources of energy.

(Lee Dye, "Linear Collider: Bold Gamble in Atomic Physics")

5. ① For years our country has been providing Japan unlimited access to our technology while getting little in return. ② Currently 7,000 Japanese graduate students study science and engineering in the U.S., ③ while only 1,000 Americans are engaged in similar studies in Japan. Also, ④ our government laboratories are open to the Japanese, but ⑤ Japanese laboratories are not open to Americans. ⑥ To remedy this imbalance, Japan should subsidize our universities, and also ⑦ it should help defray the costs of our laboratories.

(William C. Norris, "Technology Must Travel 2-Way Street")

6. ① All men crave material success because ② it serves as an insurance policy against sexual rejection. This is true because ③ women love men who are successful. ④ Both men and women want power, and ⑤ success is the form of power women feel most deprived of. Thus, ⑥ women try to achieve it vicariously through men. ⑦ As the 5-foot 6-inch Dustin Hoffman once put it, "When I was in high school, women wouldn't touch me with a 10-foot pole. Now I can't keep them away with a 10-foot pole."

(Warren Farrell, "Success Story: From Frog to Prince")

★7. ① Cigarette consumption could be easily reduced by simply outlawing tailor-made cigarettes. ② The manufacture of tailor-made cigarettes to American standards is a high-tech industry. ③ It cannot be done in small illicit labs like the processing of PCP, cocaine or heroin. ④ The availability of quality tobacco for hand-rolling would discourage the development of an illegal tailor-made market. ⑤ Most people would not pay the premium prices demanded by an illicit market for a product of unknown quality. ⑥ They could roll a high-quality product for themselves. ⑦ Truly addicted persons would continue to smoke no matter how inconvenient. But ⑧ most would give it up as too much bother before it became a deeply ingrained habit.

(Richard Sand, "An Easy Way to Reduce Cigarette Consumption")

8. ① Flesh food is not a necessity in the human diet, as ② nutritionally adequate alternatives are readily available. ③ Many people in the world thrive on a nonmeat diet. ④ Indeed, vegetarian Seventh-Day Adventists in this country live an average of six years longer than their meat-eating counterparts. ⑤ The National Academy of Science warns that our fat-laden diet is directly responsible for much of the heart disease and cancer that afflict so many. ⑥ At a time when people are starving in certain parts of the world, it should be noted that a steer must consume sixteen pounds of grain and soy to produce one pound of meat. ⑦ The grain and soybeans we feed our meat-producing animals would feed every hungry mouth in the world many times over. ⑧ Cattle are competing with humans for food. ⑨ Clearly, a reassessment of the whole concept of killing and eating animals is in order.

(Suzanne Sutton, "Killing Animals for Food—Time for a Second Look")

9. ① The argument has been made that to cut down on teenage drunk driving we should increase the federal excise tax on beer. ② Such a measure, however, would almost certainly fail to achieve its intended result. ③ Teenagers are notoriously insensitive to cost. ④ They gladly accept premium prices for the latest style in clothes or the most popular record albums. And then, ⑤ those who drink and drive already risk arrest and loss of driving privileges. ⑥ They would not think twice about paying a little more for a six-pack. Finally, ⑦ the situation is not as bleak as it has been made to appear. ⑧ The fatality rate for teenage drivers is lower today than it has been in years.

(James C. Sanders, "Increased U.S. Tax on Beer")

★10. ① It has been widely acknowledged that the quality of undergraduate education in this country is diminishing. ② An often unrecognized cause of this malady is the exploitative way that universities as employers treat their part-time and temporary faculty members. ③ In many universities there are no formal guidelines for evaluating the work of these instructors. As a result, ④ poor instructors who solicit the favor of the department chairman are often retained over better ones who do not. ⑤ Another factor is the low pay given to these instructors. ⑥ In order to survive, many of them must accept heavy teaching loads spread out over three or four institutions. ⑦ The quality of instruction can only suffer when faculty members stretch themselves so thin. Lastly, because ⑧ part-time and temporary faculty are rarely members of the faculty senate, ⑨ they have no voice in university governance. But ⑩ without a voice, the shoddy conditions under which they work are never brought to light.

(Michael Schwalbe, "Part-Time Faculty Members Deserve a Break")

11. ① Doctors who attend elderly people in nursing homes often prescribe tranquilizers to keep these people immobile. ② This practice is often unwarranted, and ③ it often impairs the health of the patients. ④ These tranquilizers often have damaging side effects in that ⑤ they accentuate the symptoms of senility, and ⑥ they increase the likelihood of a dangerous fall because ⑦ they produce unsteadiness in walking. Furthermore, since ⑧ these medications produce immobility, ⑨ they increase the risk of bedsores. ⑩ Doctors at the Center for Aging and Health say that physicians who care for the elderly are simply prescribing too much medication.

(Hal Willard, "At 90, the Zombie Shuffle")

12. ① All of us have encountered motorists who will go to any length to get a parking spot within 20 feet of the door they expect to enter. ② This obsession with good parking spots transcends all logic. ③ It might take 5 minutes to secure the ideal spot in a store parking lot, ④ while a more distant spot that is immediately available is only a 40-second walk from the door. ⑤ Waiting for that ideal spot also results in frenzied nerves and skyrocketing blood pressure. ⑥ Inevitably the occupant of the desired space will preen her hair before departing, and ⑦ all the while the cars backed up behind the waiting driver are blaring their horns. ⑧ Parking a little farther away is usually easier and safer

because ⑨ you can pull out more quickly, and ⑩ it avoids damage to car doors by adjacent parkers.

(Gwinn Owens, "A Ridiculous Addiction")

★13. ① The state has a right to intervene on behalf of unborn children, and ② this right should be implemented immediately. ③ While it may be true that a mere fetus has no rights, ④ surely a born child does have rights, and ⑤ these rights project backward to the time it was in the womb. This is true because ⑥ what happens to the child in the womb can have an impact throughout the child's life. ⑦ It is well known that alcohol and drug abuse by expectant mothers cause birth defects, and ⑧ these defects are not correctable after birth. ⑨ Granted, an expectant mother has the right to treat her own body as she chooses, but ⑩ this right does not extend to her unborn child. ⑪ Once a pregnant woman decides to give birth, she effectively transfers part of her rights over to her unborn child. ⑫ Unfortunately, however, the unborn child is incapable of securing these rights for itself. Thus, ⑬ the intervention of a higher power is justified.

(Alan Dershowitz, "Drawing the Line on Prenatal Rights")

14. ① A manned trip to Mars is a justified scientific goal because ② it affords a unique opportunity to explore the origins of the solar system and the emergence of life. However, ③ from a scientific standpoint, an initial landing on the tiny Martian moons, Phobos and Deimos, would be more rewarding than a landing on the planet itself. Because ④ the Martian terrain is rugged, ⑤ humans would not be able to venture far, ⑥ nor could they operate a robot vehicle without the use of a satellite, since ⑦ Mars's mountains would block their view. ⑧ Explorers on Phobos and Deimos could easily send robot vehicles to the planet's surface. ⑨ Using Mars's moons as a base would also be better than unmanned exploration directed from the Houston space center. Because ⑩ the distance is so great, ⑪ radio signals to and from Mars can take as long as an hour. Thus, ⑫ driving an unmanned rover from Earth, step by step, would be a time-consuming operation. ⑬ Sample returns to Earth would take months instead of hours, and ⑭ follow-on missions would be years apart instead of days, further slowing the process of exploration.

(S. Fred Singer, "The Case for Going to Mars")

15. ① There are lots of problems with the U.S. airline system, but ② deregulation isn't one of them. ③ Airline deregulation has delivered most of what it promised when enacted in 1978. ④ It has held down fares, ⑤ increased competition, ⑥ and raised the industry's efficiency. ⑦ Despite claims to the contrary, airline safety has not suffered. And, ⑧ with some exceptions, service to some cities and towns has improved. ⑨ On average, fares are lower today than in 1980. ⑩ Morrison and Winston estimate that fares are 20% to 30% below what they would be under regulation. ⑪ Competition has increased because ⑫ prior to deregulation airlines had protected routes. ⑬ After deregulation this changed. ⑭ Efficiency has also improved. ⑮ After deregulation the percentage of occupied seats jumped by 10% and miles traveled by 32%. ⑯ Despite fears that

airlines would cut unprofitable service to small communities, most smaller cities and towns experienced a 20% to 30% increase in flight frequency. Lastly, ⑰ travel on U.S. airlines remains among the safest forms of transportation. ⑱ Between 1975 and 1985, deaths resulting from crashes totaled fewer than 3000.

(Robert J. Samuelson, "Let's Not Regulate the Deregulated Airlines")

III. Turn to the editorial pages of a newspaper and select an editorial that contains an argument. Keep in mind that some editorials are really reports and contain no arguments at all. Also, few editorials are as neat and straightforward as the selections presented in Parts I and II of this exercise. Guest editorials on the opinion-editorial page (usually opposite the editorial page) are often better written than those on the editorial page. Analyze the argument (or arguments) according to the method presented in this section. Begin by placing a numeral at the beginning of each statement. Compound statements having components that are claimed to be true may be broken up into parts and the parts enumerated accordingly. Numerals should usually be placed after genuine premise and conclusion indicators even when they occur in the middle of a statement. Do *not*, however, break up conditional statements into antecedent and consequent. Proceed to identify the main conclusion (or conclusions) and determine how the other statements provide support. Any statement that does not play a direct role in the argument should be left out of the final argument pattern.

Summary

Logic is the study of the evaluation of arguments, which are lists of statements consisting of one or more premises and one conclusion. Premises can be distinguished from conclusion by the occurrence of indicator words ("hence," "therefore," "since," and so on) or an inferential relation among the statements. Because not all groups of statements are arguments, it is important to be able to distinguish arguments from nonarguments. This is done by attending to indicator words, the presence of an inferential relation among the statements, and typical kinds of nonarguments. Typical nonarguments include warnings, loosely associated statements, reports, expository passages, illustrations, conditional statements, and explanations.

Arguments are customarily described as deductive or inductive. Deductive arguments are those in which the conclusion is claimed to follow necessarily from the premises, while inductive arguments are those in which the conclusion is claimed to follow only probably from the premises. The two can be distinguished by attending to special indicator words ("it necessarily follows that," "it probably follows that," and so on), the actual strength of the inferential relation, and typical forms or styles of deductive and inductive argumentation. Typical deductive arguments include arguments based on mathematics, arguments from definition, and categorical, hypothetical, and disjunctive syllogisms. Typical inductive arguments include predictions, arguments from analogy, generalizations, arguments from authority, arguments based on signs, and causal inferences.

The evaluation of arguments involves two steps: evaluating the link between premises and conclusion, and evaluating the truth of the premises. Deductive arguments in which the conclusion actually follows from the premises are said to be valid, and those that also have true premises are said to be sound. Inductive arguments in which the conclusion actually follows from the premises are said to be strong, and those that also have true premises are said to be cogent. The terms "true" and "false" apply not to arguments, but to statements. The truth and falsity of premises and conclusion is only indirectly related to validity, but any deductive argument having true premises and a false conclusion is invalid.

The validity of a deductive argument is determined by the form of the argument. An argument form that allows for a substitution instance having true premises and a false conclusion is an invalid form, and any argument having that form is an invalid argument. This fact leads to the counterexample method for proving invalidity. This method consists in identifying the form of a given invalid argument and then constructing a counterexample having premises that are indisputably true and a conclusion that is indisputably false.

The structure of longer arguments may be disclosed by the application of a method consisting of arrows and braces that show how the various premises support intermediate conclusions, and how the latter in turn support the main conclusion. Four basic argument patterns are the vertical pattern, horizontal pattern, conjoint premises, and multiple conclusion.

3

Informal Fallacies

3.1 Fallacies in General

A **fallacy** is a defect in an argument that consists in something other than false premises alone. The fallacies introduced in this chapter involve defective patterns of arguing that occur so often they have been given specific names. Such defects comprise either mistakes in reasoning or the creation of an illusion that makes a bad argument appear good. The term *non sequitur* ("it does not follow") is another name for fallacy. Both deductive and inductive arguments may contain fallacies; if they do, they are either unsound or uncogent, depending on the kind of argument. Conversely, if an argument is unsound or uncogent, it has one or more false premises or it contains a fallacy (or both).

Fallacies are usually divided into two groups: formal and informal. A **formal fallacy** is one that may be identified by merely examining the form or structure of an argument. Fallacies of this kind are found only in deductive arguments that have identifiable forms. Chapter 1 presented some of these forms: categorical syllogisms, disjunctive syllogisms, and hypothetical syllogisms. The following categorical syllogism contains a formal fallacy:

> All bullfights are grotesque rituals.
> All executions are grotesque rituals.
> Therefore, all bullfights are executions.

This argument has the following form:

> All *A* are *B*.
> All *C* are *B*.
> All *A* are *C*.

By merely examining this form, one can see that it is invalid. The fact that *A*, *B*, and *C* stand respectively for "bullfights," "grotesque rituals," and "executions" is irrelevant in detecting the fallacy. The problem may be traced to the second premise. If the letters *C* and *B* are interchanged, the form becomes valid, and the original argument, with the same change introduced, also becomes valid (but unsound).

Here is an example of a formal fallacy that occurs in a hypothetical syllogism:

If apes are intelligent, then apes can solve puzzles.
Apes can solve puzzles.
Therefore, apes are intelligent.

This argument has the following form:

If A then B.
B.
_____
A.

In this case, if A and B are interchanged in the first premise, the form becomes valid, and the original argument, with the same change, also becomes valid. This fallacy and the one that precedes it will be discussed in later chapters.

In distinguishing formal from informal fallacies, remember that formal fallacies occur only in deductive arguments. Thus, if a given argument is inductive, it cannot contain a formal fallacy. Also, keep an eye out for standard deductive argument forms such as categorical syllogisms and hypothetical syllogisms. If such an argument is invalid because of an improper arrangement of terms or statements, it commits a formal fallacy. Section 1.5 investigated some of these forms and gave instruction on distinguishing the form from the content of an argument. All of the exercises at the end of that section commit formal fallacies.

Informal fallacies are those that can be detected only by examining the content of the argument. Consider the following example:

The Brooklyn Bridge is made of atoms.
Atoms are invisible.
Therefore, the Brooklyn Bridge is invisible.

To detect this fallacy one must know something about bridges—namely, that they are large visible objects, and even though their atomic components are invisible, this does not mean that the bridges themselves are invisible.

Or consider this example:

A chess player is a person.
Therefore, a bad chess player is a bad person.

To detect this fallacy one must know that the meaning of the word "bad" depends on what it modifies, and that being a bad chess player is quite different from being a bad person.

The various informal fallacies accomplish their purpose in so many different ways that no single umbrella theory covers them all. Some fallacies work by getting the reader or listener to feel various emotions, such as fear, pity, or camaraderie, and then attaching a certain conclusion to those emotions. Others attempt to discredit an opposing argument by associating it with certain pejorative features of its author. And then there are those that appeal to various dispositions on the part of the reader or listener, such as superstition or mental laziness, to get him or her to accept a conclusion. By studying the typical ways in which arguers apply these techniques, one is less likely to be fooled by the fallacious arguments posed by others or to stumble blindly into fallacies when constructing arguments for one's own use.

Since the time of Aristotle, logicians have attempted to classify the various informal fallacies. Aristotle himself identified thirteen and separated them into two groups. The work of subsequent logicians has produced dozens more, rendering the task of classifying them even more difficult. The presentation that follows divides twenty-two informal fallacies into five groups: fallacies of relevance, fallacies of weak induction, fallacies of presumption, fallacies of ambiguity, and fallacies of grammatical analogy. The final section of the chapter considers the related topics of detecting and avoiding fallacies in the context of ordinary language.

EXERCISE 3.1

Determine whether the fallacies committed by the following arguments are formal fallacies or informal fallacies.

★1. If Rasputin was really mad, then he deceived Czar Nicholas II. Rasputin was not really mad. Therefore, he did not deceive Czar Nicholas II.

2. Everything that runs has feet. The Columbia River runs very swiftly. Therefore, the Columbia River has feet.

3. All people who believe we create our own reality are people who lack social responsibility. All people governed by selfish motives are people who lack social responsibility. Therefore, all people who believe we create our own reality are people governed by selfish motives.

★4. The ship of state is like a ship at sea. No sailor is ever allowed to protest orders from the captain. For the same reason, no citizen should ever be allowed to protest presidential policies.

5. Renowned violinist Pinchas Zukerman has said, "When it comes to vodka, Smirnoff plays second fiddle to none." We must therefore conclude that Smirnoff is the best vodka available.

6. If the Chinese government systematically kills its unwanted orphans, then the Chinese government is immoral. The Chinese government is indeed immoral. Therefore, the Chinese government systematically kills its unwanted orphans.

★7. Sarah Jessica Parker, Ben Affleck, and Julia Roberts are Democrats. Therefore, it must be the case that all Hollywood stars are Democrats.

8. Venezuelan President Hugo Chavez argues that the United States has no right to decide what's good or bad for the whole world. But who is this Chavez? He's nothing but an autocratic demagogue who assaults democracy at every opportunity. Clearly his arguments are nonsense.

9. If plastic guns are sold to the public, then terrorists will carry them aboard airliners undetected. If plastic guns are sold to the public, then airline hijackings will increase. Therefore, if terrorists carry plastic guns aboard airliners undetected, then airline hijackings will increase.

★10. Some corporate mergers are arrangements that produce layoffs. Some arrangements that produce layoffs are occasions of economic unrest. Therefore, some corporate mergers are occasions of economic unrest.

Fallacies of Relevance

The **fallacies of relevance** share the common characteristic that the arguments in which they occur have premises that are *logically* irrelevant to the conclusion. Yet the premises may appear to be *psychologically* relevant, so the conclusion may *seem* to follow from the premises, even though it does not follow logically. In a good argument the premises provide genuine evidence in support of the conclusion. In an argument that commits a fallacy of relevance, on the other hand, the connection between premises and conclusion is emotional. To identify a fallacy of relevance, therefore, one must be able to distinguish genuine evidence from various forms of emotional appeal.

1. Appeal to Force
(*Argumentum ad Baculum*: Appeal to the "Stick")

The fallacy of **appeal to force** occurs whenever an arguer poses a conclusion to another person and tells that person either implicitly or explicitly that some harm will come to him or her if he or she does not accept the conclusion. The fallacy always involves a threat by the arguer to the physical or psychological well-being of the listener or reader, who may be either an individual or a group of people. Obviously, such a threat is logically irrelevant to the subject matter of the conclusion, so any argument based on such a procedure is fallacious. The *ad baculum* fallacy often occurs when children argue with one another:

> *Child to playmate: Sesame Street* is the best show on TV; and if you don't believe it, I'm going to call my big brother over here and he's going to beat you up.

But it occurs among adults as well:

> *Secretary to boss:* I deserve a raise in salary for the coming year. After all, you know how friendly I am with your wife, and I'm sure you wouldn't want her to find out what's been going on between you and that sexpot client of yours.

The first example involves a physical threat, the second a psychological one. While neither threat provides any genuine evidence that the conclusion is true, both provide evidence that someone might be injured. If the two types of evidence are confused with each other, both arguer and listener may be deluded into thinking that the conclusion is supported by evidence, when in fact it is not.

The appeal to force fallacy usually accomplishes its purpose by psychologically impeding the reader or listener from acknowledging a missing premise that, if acknowl-

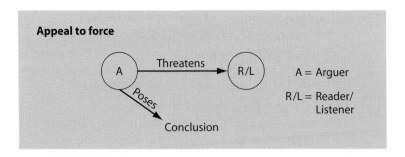

Appeal to force

A → Threatens → R/L

A Poses → Conclusion

A = Arguer

R/L = Reader/ Listener

edged, would be seen to be false or at least questionable. The two examples just given can be interpreted as concealing the following premises, both of which are most likely false:

> If my brother forces you to admit that *Sesame Street* is the best show on TV, then *Sesame Street* is in fact the best show.

> If I succeed in threatening you, then I deserve a raise in salary.

The conclusion of the first argument is that *Sesame Street* is the best show on TV. But just because someone is forced into saying that it is does not mean that such is the case. Similarly, the conclusion of the second argument is that the secretary deserves a raise in salary. But if the boss is threatened into raising the secretary's salary, this does not mean that the secretary deserves a raise. Many of the other informal fallacies can be interpreted as accomplishing their purpose in this way.

2. Appeal to Pity
(*Argumentum ad Misericordiam*)

The **appeal to pity** fallacy occurs when an arguer attempts to support a conclusion by merely evoking pity from the reader or listener. This pity may be directed toward the arguer or toward some third party. Example:

> *Taxpayer to judge:* Your Honor, I admit that I declared thirteen children as dependents on my tax return, even though I have only two. But if you find me guilty of tax evasion, my reputation will be ruined. I'll probably lose my job, my poor wife will not be able to have the operation that she desperately needs, and my kids will starve. Surely I am not guilty.

The conclusion of this argument is "Surely I am not guilty." Obviously, the conclusion is not *logically* relevant to the arguer's set of pathetic circumstances, although it is *psychologically* relevant. If the arguer succeeds in evoking pity from the listener or reader, the latter is likely to exercise his or her desire to help the arguer by accepting the argument. In this way the reader or listener may be fooled into accepting a conclusion that is not supported by any evidence. The appeal to pity is quite common and is often used by students on their instructors at exam time and by lawyers on behalf of their clients before judges and juries.

Of course, some arguments that attempt to evoke sympathetic feelings from the reader or listener are not fallacious. We might call them *arguments from compassion*. Such arguments differ from the fallacious appeal to pity in that, in addition to evoking

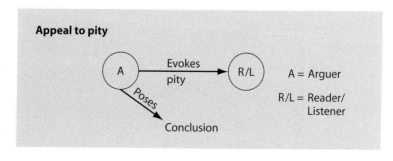

compassion on behalf of some person, they supply information about why that person is genuinely deserving of help or special consideration. Whenever possible these nonfallacious arguments should show that the person in question is a victim of circumstances and not responsible for the dire straits he finds himself in, that the recommended help or special consideration is not illegal or inappropriate, and that it will genuinely help the person in question. In contrast to such arguments, the appeal to pity proceeds by ignoring all of these considerations and attempts to support a conclusion by merely evoking pity from the reader or listener.

3. Appeal to the People (*Argumentum ad Populum*)

Nearly everyone wants to be loved, esteemed, admired, valued, recognized, and accepted by others. The **appeal to the people** uses these desires to get the reader or listener to accept a conclusion. Two approaches are involved: one of them direct, the other indirect.

The *direct approach* occurs when an arguer, addressing a large group of people, excites the emotions and enthusiasm of the crowd to win acceptance for his or her conclusion. The objective is to arouse a kind of mob mentality. This is the strategy used by nearly every propagandist and demagogue. Adolf Hitler was a master of the technique, but speech makers at Democratic and Republican national conventions also use it with some measure of success. Waving flags and blaring music add to the overall effect. Because the individuals in the audience want to share in the camaraderie, the euphoria, and the excitement, they find themselves accepting a variety of conclusions with ever-increasing fervor.

An appeal to negative emotions, such as suspicion and fear, can also generate a mob mentality. These emotions have produced many lynchings, and they led to the internment of Japanese Americans during World War II. Also, the direct approach is not limited to oral discourse. The same effect can be accomplished in writing. By using such emotionally charged phrasing as "fighter of communism," "champion of the free enterprise system," and "defender of the working man," polemicists can awaken the same kind of mob mentality as they would if they were speaking.

In the *indirect approach* the arguer aims his or her appeal not at the crowd as a whole but at one or more individuals separately, focusing on some aspect of their relationship to the crowd. The indirect approach includes such specific forms as the bandwagon argument, the appeal to vanity, and the appeal to snobbery. All are standard techniques of the advertising industry.

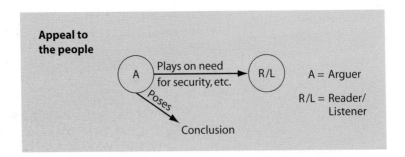

Here is an example of the **bandwagon argument:**

> Of course you want to buy Zing toothpaste. Why, 90 percent of America brushes with Zing.

The idea is that you will be left behind or left out of the group if you do not use the product.

The **appeal to vanity** often associates the product with someone who is admired, pursued, or imitated, the idea being that you, too, will be admired and pursued if you use it. The recent television and billboard ads for the U.S. Marine Corps provide an example. The ads show a strong, handsome man in uniform holding a gleaming sword, and the caption reads:

> The Few, the Proud, the Marines.

The message is that if you join the Marines, then you, too, will be admired and respected, just like the handsome man in the uniform.

The **appeal to snobbery** depends on a similar kind of association.

> A Rolls-Royce is not for everyone. If you qualify as one of the select few, this distinguished classic may be seen and driven at British Motor Cars, Ltd.
> (By appointment only, please.)

Needless to say, the indirect approach is used not only by advertisers:

> *Mother to child:* You want to grow up and be just like Wonder Woman, don't you? Then eat your liver and carrots.

These examples illustrate how the indirect version of the appeal to the people can overlap the false cause fallacy, which is presented in Section 3.3. Thus, the previous example might be interpreted to suggest that eating liver and carrots will *cause* one to become just like Wonder Woman. If so, the fallacy could be identified as false cause.

Both the direct and indirect approaches of the *ad populum* fallacy have the same basic structure:

> You want to be accepted/included in the group/loved/esteemed.... Therefore, you should accept XYZ as true.

In the direct approach the arousal of a mob mentality produces an immediate feeling of belonging. Each person feels united with the crowd, and this feeling evokes a sense of strength and security. When the crowd roars its approval of the conclusions that are then offered, anyone who does not accept them automatically cuts himself or herself off from the crowd and risks the loss of his or her security, strength, and acceptance. The same thing happens in the indirect approach, but the context and technique are somewhat subtler.

4. Argument Against the Person (*Argumentum ad Hominem*)

This fallacy always involves two arguers. One of them advances (either directly or implicitly) a certain argument, and the other then responds by directing his or her attention not to the first person's argument but to the first person *himself.* When this occurs, the second person is said to commit an **argument against the person.**

The argument against the person occurs in three forms: the *ad hominem* abusive, the *ad hominem* circumstantial, and the *tu quoque.* In the ***ad hominem* abusive,** the second person responds to the first person's argument by verbally abusing the first person. Example:

> Before he died, poet Allen Ginsberg argued in favor of legalizing pornography. But Ginsberg's arguments are nothing but trash. Ginsberg was a marijuana-smoking homosexual and a thoroughgoing advocate of the drug culture.

Because Ginsberg's being a marijuana-smoking homosexual and advocate of the drug culture is irrelevant to whether the premises of this argument support the conclusion, the argument is fallacious.

Not all cases of the *ad hominem* abusive are so blunt, but they are just as fallacious. Example:

> William Buckley has argued in favor of legalizing drugs such as cocaine and heroin. But Buckley is just another one of those upper-crust intellectuals who is out of touch with real America. No sensible person should listen to his pseudosolutions.

Again, whether Buckley is an upper-crust intellectual has nothing to do with whether his premises support his conclusion.

The ***ad hominem* circumstantial** begins the same way as the *ad hominem* abusive, but instead of heaping verbal abuse on his or her opponent, the respondent attempts to discredit the opponent's argument by alluding to certain circumstances that affect the opponent. By doing so the respondent hopes to show that the opponent is predisposed to argue the way he or she does and should therefore not be taken seriously. Here is an example:

> The Dalai Lama argues that China has no business in Tibet and that the West should do something about it. But the Dalai Lama just wants the Chinese to leave so he can return as leader. Naturally he argues this way. Therefore, we should reject his arguments.

The author of this argument ignores the substance of the Dalai Lama's argument and attempts to discredit it by calling attention to certain circumstances that affect the Dalai Lama—namely, that he wants to return to Tibet as its leader. But the fact that the Dalai Lama happens to be affected by these circumstances is irrelevant to whether

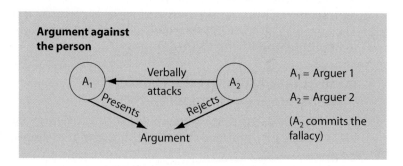

Argument against the person

A_1 — Verbally attacks — A_2
A_1 Presents — Argument — Rejects A_2

A_1 = Arguer 1

A_2 = Arguer 2

(A_2 commits the fallacy)

his premises support a conclusion. The *ad hominem* circumstantial is easy to recognize because it always takes this form: "Of course Mr. X argues this way; just look at the circumstances that affect him."

The ***tu quoque*** ("you too") fallacy begins the same way as the other two varieties of the *ad hominem* argument, except that the second arguer attempts to make the first appear to be hypocritical or arguing in bad faith. The second arguer usually accomplishes this by citing features in the life or behavior of the first arguer that conflict with the latter's conclusion. In effect, the second arguer says, "How dare you argue that I should stop doing *X*; why, you do (or have done) *X* yourself." Example:

> *Child to parent:* Your argument that I should stop stealing candy from the corner store is no good. You told me yourself just a week ago that you, too, stole candy when you were a kid.

Obviously, whether the parent stole candy is irrelevant to whether the parent's premises support the conclusion that the child should not steal candy.

Keep in mind that the purpose of an *ad hominem* argument is to discredit another person's argument by placing its author in a bad light. Thus, for the fallacy to be committed, there must always be two arguers (at least implicitly). If it should turn out that the person being attacked is not an arguer, then the personal comments made by the attacker may well be relevant to the conclusion that is drawn. In general, personal observations are relevant to conclusions about what kind of person someone is (good, bad, stingy, trustworthy, and so forth) and whether a person has done something. Example:

> International terrorist Osama bin Laden planned the destruction of the World Trade Center, killing thousands of innocent people, and he supports terrorist causes all over the world. Bin Laden is therefore a wicked and irresponsible person.

The conclusion is not that Bin Laden's argument is bad but that Bin Laden himself is bad. Because the premises give relevant support to this conclusion, the argument commits no fallacy. Another example:

> Shakespeare cannot possibly have written the thirty-six plays attributed to him, because the real Shakespeare was a two-bit country businessman who barely finished the fourth grade in school and who never left the confines of his native England.

The conclusion is not that some argument of Shakespeare's is bad but that Shakespeare did not write certain plays. Again, since the premises are relevant to this conclusion, the argument commits no *ad hominem* fallacy.

Determining what kind of person someone is includes determining whether that person is trustworthy. Thus, personal comments are often relevant in evaluating whether a person's proclamations or statements, unsupported by evidence, warrant our belief. Examples of such statements include promises to do something, testimony given by a witness, and testimonials in support of a product or service. Here is an example of an argument that discredits a witness:

> Mickey has testified that he saw Freddy set fire to the building. But Mickey was recently convicted on ten counts of perjury, and he hates Freddy with a passion and would love to see him sent to jail. Therefore, you should not believe Mickey's testimony.

This argument commits no fallacy. The conclusion is not that you should reject Mickey's argument but rather that you should reject his testimony. Testimony is not argument, and the fact that the witness is a known liar and has a motive to lie now is relevant to whether we should believe him. Furthermore, note that the conclusion is not that Mickey's statement is literally false but rather that we should not *believe* the statement. It is quite possible that Mickey really did see Freddy set fire to the building and that Mickey's statement to that effect is true. But if our only reason for believing this statement is the mere fact that Mickey has made it, then given the circumstances, we are not justified in that belief. Personal factors are never relevant to truth and falsity as such, but they are relevant to believability.

Yet there is often a close connection between truth and believability, and this provides one of the reasons why *ad hominem* arguments are often effective. In evaluating any argument there are always two issues to be considered: the quality of the reasoning and the truth of the premises. As noted, both are irrelevant to the personal characteristics of the arguer. But whether we *accept* the premises as true may depend on the credibility of the arguer. Knowing that the arguer is biased or has a motive to lie may provide good grounds for distrusting the premises. Another reason why *ad hominem* arguments are effective is that they engage the emotions of readers and listeners and thereby motivate them to transfer their negative feelings about the arguer onto the argument.

5. Accident

The fallacy of **accident** is committed when a general rule is applied to a specific case it was not intended to cover. Typically, the general rule is cited (either directly or implicitly) in the premises and then wrongly applied to the specific case mentioned in the conclusion. Two examples:

> Freedom of speech is a constitutionally guaranteed right. Therefore, John Q. Radical should not be arrested for his speech that incited the riot last week.

> Property should be returned to its rightful owner. That drunken sailor who is starting a fight with his opponents at the pool table lent you his .45-caliber pistol, and now he wants it back. Therefore, you should return it to him now.

In the first example, the general rule is that freedom of speech is normally guaranteed, and the specific case is the speech made by John Q. Radical. Because the speech incited

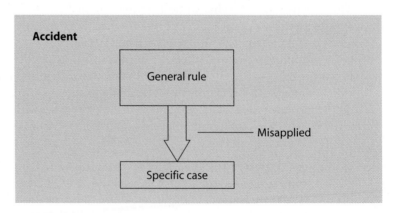

Accident

General rule

Misapplied

Specific case

a riot, the rule does not apply. In the second example, the general rule is that property should be returned to its rightful owner, and the specific case is the sailor who wants his gun returned. The rule does not apply, because the return of the property might result in serious injury or death.

The fallacy of accident gets its name from the fact that one or more accidental features of the specific case make it an exception to the rule. In the first example the accidental feature is that the speech incited a riot; in the second example the accidental features are that the sailor is drunk, that he is starting a fight, and that the property in question is dangerous.

6. Straw Man

The **straw man** fallacy is committed when an arguer distorts an opponent's argument for the purpose of more easily attacking it, demolishes the distorted argument, and then concludes that the opponent's real argument has been demolished. By so doing, the arguer is said to have set up a straw man and knocked it down, only to conclude that the real man (opposing argument) has been knocked down as well. Example:

> Mr. Goldberg has argued against prayer in the public schools. Obviously Mr. Goldberg advocates atheism. But atheism is what they used to have in Russia. Atheism leads to the suppression of all religions and the replacement of God by an omnipotent state. Is that what we want for this country? I hardly think so. Clearly Mr. Goldberg's argument is nonsense.

Like the argument against the person fallacy, the straw man fallacy involves two arguers. Mr. Goldberg, who is the first arguer, has presented an argument against prayer in the public schools. The second arguer then attacks Goldberg's argument by equating it with an argument for atheism. He then attacks atheism and concludes that Goldberg's argument is nonsense. Since Goldberg's argument had nothing to do with atheism, the second argument commits the straw man fallacy.

As this example illustrates, the kind of distortion the second arguer resorts to is often an attempt to exaggerate the first person's argument or make it look more extreme than it really is. Here are two more examples:

> The garment workers have signed a petition arguing for better ventilation on the work premises. Unfortunately, air-conditioning is expensive. Air ducts would have to be run throughout the factory, and a massive heat exchange unit installed on the roof. Also, the cost of operating such a system during the summer would be astronomical. In view of these considerations the petition must be rejected.

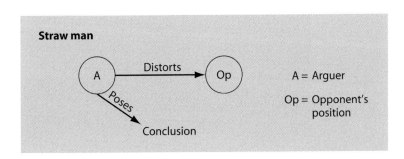

Straw man

A — Distorts → Op

Poses ↓

Conclusion

A = Arguer

Op = Opponent's position

> The student status committee has presented us with an argument favoring alcohol privileges on campus. What do the students want? Is it their intention to stay boozed up from the day they enter as freshmen until the day they graduate? Do they expect us to open a bar for them? Or maybe a chain of bars all over campus? Such a proposal is ridiculous!

In the first argument, the petition is merely for better ventilation in the factory—maybe a fan in the window during the summer. The arguer exaggerates this request to mean an elaborate air-conditioning system installed throughout the building. He then points out that this is too expensive and concludes by rejecting the petition. A similar strategy is used in the second argument. The arguer distorts the request for alcohol privileges to mean a chain of bars all over campus. Such an idea is so patently outlandish that no further argument is necessary.

7. Missing the Point (*Ignoratio Elenchi*)

All the fallacies we have discussed thus far have been instances of cases where the premises of an argument are irrelevant to the conclusion. **Missing the point** illustrates a special form of irrelevance. This fallacy occurs when the premises of an argument support one particular conclusion, but then a different conclusion, often vaguely related to the correct conclusion, is drawn. Whenever one suspects that such a fallacy is being committed, he or she should be able to identify the *correct* conclusion, the conclusion that the premises *logically* imply. This conclusion must be significantly different from the conclusion that is actually drawn. Examples:

> Crimes of theft and robbery have been increasing at an alarming rate lately. The conclusion is obvious: We must reinstate the death penalty immediately.

> Abuse of the welfare system is rampant nowadays. Our only alternative is to abolish the system altogether.

At least two correct conclusions are implied by the premise of the first argument: either "We should provide increased police protection in vulnerable neighborhoods" or "We should initiate programs to eliminate the causes of the crimes." Reinstating the death

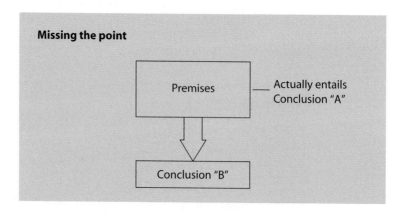

Missing the point

Premises —— Actually entails Conclusion "A"

Conclusion "B"

penalty is not a logical conclusion at all. Among other things, theft and robbery are not capital crimes. In the second argument the premises logically suggest some systematic effort to eliminate the cheaters rather than eliminating the system altogether.

Ignoratio elenchi means "ignorance of the proof." The arguer is ignorant of the logical implications of his or her own premises and, as a result, draws a conclusion that misses the point entirely. The fallacy has a distinct structure all its own, but in some ways it serves as a catchall for arguments that are not clear instances of one or more of the other fallacies. An argument should not be identified as a case of missing the point, however, if one of the other fallacies fits.

8. Red Herring

This fallacy is closely associated with missing the point (*ignoratio elenchi*). The **red herring** fallacy is committed when the arguer diverts the attention of the reader or listener by changing the subject to a different but sometimes subtly related one. He or she then finishes by either drawing a conclusion about this different issue or by merely presuming that some conclusion has been established. By so doing, the arguer purports to have won the argument. The fallacy gets its name from a procedure used to train hunting dogs to follow a scent. A red herring (or bag of them) is dragged across the trail with the aim of leading the dogs astray. Since red herrings have an especially potent scent (caused in part by the smoking process used to preserve them), only the best dogs will follow the original scent.

To use the red herring fallacy effectively, the arguer must change the original subject of the argument without the reader or listener noticing it. One way of doing this is to change the subject to one that is subtly related to the original subject. Here are two examples of this technique:

> Environmentalists are continually harping about the dangers of nuclear power. Unfortunately, electricity is dangerous no matter where it comes from. Every year hundreds of people are electrocuted by accident. Since most of these accidents are caused by carelessness, they could be avoided if people would just exercise greater caution.

> There is a good deal of talk these days about the need to eliminate pesticides from our fruits and vegetables. But many of these foods are essential to our health. Carrots are an excellent source of vitamin A, broccoli is rich in iron, and oranges and grapefruit have lots of vitamin C.

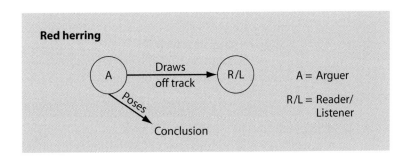

Both arguments commit the red herring fallacy. In the first, the original issue is whether nuclear power is dangerous. The arguer changes this subject to the danger of electrocution and proceeds to draw a conclusion about that. The new subject is clearly different from the possibility of nuclear explosion or meltdown, but the fact that both are related to electricity facilitates the arguer's goal of leading someone off the track. In the second argument, the original issue is pesticides, and the arguer changes it to the value of fruits and vegetables in one's diet. Again, the fact that the second topic is related to the first assists the arguer in committing the fallacy. In neither case does the arguer draw a conclusion about the original topic, but by merely diverting the attention of the reader or listener, the arguer creates the presumption of having won the argument.

A second way of using the red herring effectively is to change the subject to some flashy, eye-catching topic that is virtually guaranteed to distract the listener's attention. Topics of this sort include sex, crime, scandal, immorality, death, and any other topic that might serve as the subject of gossip. Here is an example of this technique:

> Professor Conway complains of inadequate parking on our campus. But did you know that last year Conway carried on a torrid love affair with a member of the English Department? The two used to meet every day for clandestine sex in the copier room. Apparently they didn't realize how much you can see through that fogged glass window. Even the students got an eyeful. Enough said about Conway.

The red herring fallacy can be confused with the straw man fallacy because both have the effect of drawing the reader/listener off the track. This confusion can usually be avoided by remembering the unique ways in which they accomplish this purpose. In the straw man, the arguer begins by distorting an opponent's argument and concludes by knocking down the distorted argument. In the red herring, the arguer ignores the opponent's argument (if there is one) and subtly changes the subject. Thus, to distinguish the two fallacies, one should attempt to determine whether the arguer has knocked down a distorted argument or simply changed the subject. Also keep in mind that straw man always involves two arguers, at least implicitly, whereas a red herring often does not.

Both the red herring and straw man fallacies are susceptible of being confused with missing the point, because all three involve a similar kind of irrelevancy. To avoid this confusion, one should note that both red herring and straw man proceed by generating a new set of premises, whereas missing the point does not. Straw man draws a conclusion from new premises that are obtained by distorting an earlier argument, and red herring, if it draws any conclusion at all, draws one from new premises obtained by changing the subject. Missing the point, however, draws a conclusion from the original premises. Also, in the red herring and straw man, the conclusion, if there is one, is *relevant* to the premises from which it is drawn; but in missing the point, the conclusion is *irrelevant* to the premises from which it is drawn. Finally, remember that missing the point serves in part as a kind of catchall fallacy, and a fallacious argument should not be identified as a case of missing the point if one of the other fallacies clearly fits.

EXERCISE 3.2

I. Identify the fallacies of relevance committed by the following arguments, giving a brief explanation for your answer. If no fallacy is committed, write "no fallacy."

★1. The position open in the accounting department should be given to Frank Thompson. Frank has six hungry children to feed, and his wife desperately needs an operation to save her eyesight.

2. Erica Evans, who takes orders at the local Taco Bell, argues persuasively in favor of increasing the minimum wage. But this is exactly what you would expect. Erica is paid the minimum wage, and if the minimum wage is increased, then her own salary will go up. Obviously Erica's arguments are worthless.

3. The school board argues that our schools are in desperate need of repair. But the real reason our students are falling behind is that they spend too much time with their computers. Becoming educated means a lot more than learning how to point and click. The school board should send a letter to the parents urging them to monitor their kids' computer time.

★4. Whoever thrusts a knife into another person should be arrested. But surgeons do precisely this when operating. Therefore, surgeons should be arrested.

5. You should read Irving Stone's latest novel right away. It's sold over a million copies, and practically everyone in the Manhattan cocktail circuit is talking about it.

6. Friedrich Nietzsche's philosophy is not worth the paper it's printed on. Nietzsche was an immoral reprobate who went completely insane from syphilis before he died.

★7. Surely you welcome the opportunity to join our protective organization. Think of all the money you will lose from broken windows, overturned trucks, and damaged merchandise in the event of your not joining.

8. Senator Barrow advocates increased Social Security benefits for the poor. It is regrettable that the senator finds it necessary to advocate socialism. Socialism defeats initiative, takes away promised rewards, and leads directly to inefficiency and big government. It was tried for years in Eastern Europe, and it failed miserably. Clearly, socialism is no good.

9. Something is seriously wrong with high school education these days. After ten years of decline, SAT scores are still extremely low, and high school graduates are practically incapable of reading and writing. The obvious conclusion is that we should close the schools.

★10. The editors of the *Daily Register* have accused our company of being one of the city's worst water polluters. But the *Daily Register* is responsible for much more pollution than we are. After all, they own the Western Paper Company, and that company discharges tons of chemical residue into the city's river every day.

11. If 20 percent of adult Americans are functionally illiterate, then it's no wonder that morons get elected to public office. In fact, 20 percent of adult Americans *are* functionally illiterate. Therefore, it's no wonder that morons get elected to public office.

12. Ladies and gentlemen, today the lines of battle have been drawn. When the din of clashing armor has finally died away, the Republican party will emerge

victorious! We are the true party of the American people! We embody the values that all real Americans hold sacred! We cherish and protect our founding fathers' vision that gave birth to the Constitution! We stand for decency and righteousness; for self-determination and the liberty to conduct our affairs as each of us freely chooses! In the coming election, victory will be ours, so help us God!

★13. We've all heard the argument that too much television is the reason our students can't read and write. Yet many of today's TV shows are excellent. *Grey's Anatomy* unveils the personal lives of interns at an urban hospital, *Law and Order* explores ethical issues in our criminal justice system, and *American Idol* uncovers hidden musical talent. Today's TV is just great!

14. Surely architect Norris is not responsible for the collapse of the Central Bank Tower. Norris has had nothing but trouble lately. His daughter eloped with a child molester, his son committed suicide, and his alcoholic wife recently left for Las Vegas with his retirement savings.

15. The First Amendment to the Constitution prevents the government from interfering with the free exercise of religion. The liturgical practice of the Religion of Internal Enlightenment involves human sacrifice. Therefore, it would be wrong for the government to interfere with this religious practice.

★16. Former antiterrorism czar Richard Clark argues in his book that the Iraq war was a terrible mistake and that it undermines the war on terrorism. But it's clear that Clark makes these outlandish claims merely to drum up sales for his book. Thus, we really shouldn't take his arguments seriously.

17. Professor Pearson's arguments in favor of the theory of evolution should be discounted. Pearson is a cocaine-snorting sex pervert and, according to some reports, a member of the Communist party.

18. Rudolf Höss, commandant of the Auschwitz concentration camp, confessed to having exterminated one million people, most of whom were Jews, in the Auschwitz gas chamber. We can only conclude that Höss was either insane or an extremely evil person.

★19. TV commentator Larry Kudlow argues that government should get off the back of the American businessman. Obviously, Kudlow wants to abolish government altogether. Yet without government there would be no defense, no judicial system, no Social Security, and no health and safety regulations. None of us wants to forgo these benefits. Thus, we can see that Kudlow's argument is absurd.

20. I know that some of you oppose the appointment of David Cole as the new sales manager. On further consideration, however, I am confident you will find him well qualified for the job. If Cole is not appointed, it may become necessary to make severe personnel cutbacks in your department.

21. Animal rights activists say that animals are abused in biomedical research labs. But consider this: Pets are abused by their owners every day. Probably 25 percent of pet owners should never get near animals. Some cases of abuse are enough to make you sick.

★22. Of course you want to buy a pair of Slinky fashion jeans. Slinky jeans really show off your figure, and all the Hollywood starlets down on the Strip can be seen wearing them these days.

23. Actress Andie MacDowell says that it's healthy to drink milk. But the dairy industry pays MacDowell thousands of dollars to make these ads. Therefore, we should not take her testimonials too seriously.

24. Dr. Morrison has argued that smoking is responsible for the majority of health problems in this country and that every smoker who has even the slightest concern for his or her health should quit. Unfortunately, however, we must consign Dr. Morrison's argument to the trash bin. Only yesterday I saw none other than Dr. Morrison himself smoking a cigar.

★25. Mr. Rhodes is suffering from amnesia and has no recollection whatever of the events of the past two weeks. We can only conclude that he did not commit the crime of murdering his wife a week ago, as he has been accused of doing.

II. Answer "true" or "false" to the following statements:

1. In the appeal to force, the arguer physically attacks the listener.

2. In the direct variety of the appeal to the people, the arguer attempts to create a kind of mob mentality.

3. If an arguer attempts to discredit court room testimony or a promise by pointing out that the witness or the person making the promise is a liar, then the arguer commits an *argumentum ad hominem* (argument against the person) fallacy.

4. The *argumentum ad hominem* always involves two arguers.

5. In the *argumentum ad hominem* circumstantial, the circumstances cited by the second arguer are intended precisely to malign the character of the first arguer.

6. In the *tu quoque* fallacy, the arguer threatens the reader or listener.

7. In the fallacy of accident, a general rule is applied to a specific case where it does not fit.

8. In the straw man fallacy, an arguer often distorts another person's argument by making it look more extreme than it really is.

9. Whenever one suspects that a missing the point fallacy is being committed, one should be able to state the conclusion that is logically implied by the premises.

10. In the red herring fallacy, the arguer attempts to lead the reader or listener off the track.

III. Identify the arguments in the following dialogue, then discuss each of them in terms of the fallacies presented in this section. You should be able to find at least one case of each fallacy.

"Thanks for saving us a seat," Jodie says to her friend Frank, as she and Liz sit down with coffee cups in hand in the crowded cafeteria.

"No problem," Frank says.

"We were late getting out of Professor Conklin's social problems class," Jodie says disgustedly. "He's such a jerk! He always keeps us late, and he's the most arrogant snob I've ever met."

"I've heard that," Frank says. "What's he covering in class now?"

"Sexual harassment in the workplace," Jodie replies. "But that *is* a real problem these days."

"How so?"

"Well, my friend Amelia is a dispatcher for a trucking company, and she's told me about dozens of times she's been a victim of sexual harassment. The truckers have *Playboy* centerfolds tacked up all over the place, they constantly leer at her, they're always asking her for dates. One of them even pats her rear when she leans over at the drinking fountain."

Frank laughs. "Well, there is such a thing as the First Amendment, which supposedly guarantees freedom of expression. You wouldn't want to deny these guys their freedom of expression, would you?"

"Freedom of expression, my eye!" explodes Jodie, looking incredulously at Frank. "Patting someone's rear isn't freedom of expression, it's abusive physical contact. So it's not protected by the First Amendment. Men! The trouble with you, Frank, is you're a typical man. If you were a woman, you'd see these things for what they are," she says, looking at Liz for support.

Liz nods her head in strong agreement.

"Well," says Frank, "I think your friend is lucky to have a job, what with all the people out of work these days. I've got a friend who's spent half his retirement savings just putting food on the table for his family, after losing his job. He was in the construction business, which is dead right now. And in other parts of the country it's even worse. You should tell Amelia to quit complaining."

"Stop giving me the runaround," demands Jodie, offended. "The trouble with you men is, you always look at women as sex objects. That makes sexual harassment inevitable."

"What do you mean?" protests Frank. "It's you women who treat us men like sex objects. What about all your makeup and perfume? And the tight pants and all the see-through stuff you wear? You think men are just a pack of animals—nothing but instinct—and you think that will make us fall for you. Isn't that how you see us?"

"I won't dignify that with a reply," fumes Jodie. "Anyone who isn't blind can see that Amelia's being victimized by those truckers. If you can't see it, maybe pouring this hot coffee over your thick head will wake you up!" she threatens.

"Calm down," says Frank with a startled look. "Everyone is beginning to stare at us. Okay, suppose I agree that Amelia is a victim. The question is, what do we do about it?"

"To begin with," says Jodie firmly, "the trucking company should transfer Amelia out of dispatch and give her a better job, like executive secretary in the regional office. Her husband ran out on her recently, leaving her with all five kids—and little Tommy needs braces. She could really use the extra money."

"You're joking!" Frank laughs sarcastically. "Didn't you tell me once that Amelia never finished high school and is functionally illiterate? She could never handle a job like that."

Thinking for a moment, Jodie then replies, "Well, maybe you're right. But at least the company should adopt a policy forbidding all forms of sexual harassment. Maybe that would make the truckers see how abusive they are, and then they might stop acting that way. Practically every company in the country has such a policy, but Amelia's bosses are dragging their feet."

"Okay. But then how do you define sexual harassment?" Frank asks. "'Cause if you can't define it, any policy is useless."

"Well, I don't exactly know," Jodie hesitates. "I'll have to think about that."

"Aha! I knew it!" exclaims Frank, triumphantly. "You can't define it, which means you don't even know if it exists! If you weren't such a radical feminist, you would see that all these claims of sexual harassment are hooey."

"Me, radical?" Jodie explodes. "The truth is you're a radical sexist. What you're saying is, women are only chattel, like they were 200 years ago, and men can use or abuse them any way they please. Liz, that's what he's saying, isn't it?"

"Absolutely," Liz affirms.

"What a crazy argument," says Frank scornfully. "What you're saying is, we should abolish all distinctions between men and women and create a unisex society in which everyone acts like a bunch of robots. Isn't that right, Liz?"

"No, not at all," insists Liz. "She's trying to—"

"You're completely insane, Frank," Jodie interrupts, rising determinedly from her chair, "and your arguments are wacko!" She then throws the remains of her coffee at Frank. The other students who have been listening to the heated argument rise up shouting, "Right on, Jodie!" Some begin chanting, "End sex harassment! End sex harassment!" As more students join the demonstration, they surround Frank, gesturing crudely.

Angry and humiliated, he breaks away and dashes out the door.

3.3 Fallacies of Weak Induction

The **fallacies of weak induction** occur not because the premises are logically irrelevant to the conclusion, as is the case with the eight fallacies of relevance, but because the connection between premises and conclusion is not strong enough to support the conclusion. In each of the following fallacies, the premises provide at least a shred of evidence in support of the conclusion, but the evidence is not nearly good enough to cause a reasonable person to believe the conclusion. Like the fallacies of relevance, however, the fallacies of weak induction often involve emotional grounds for believing the conclusion.

9. Appeal to Unqualified Authority
(*Argumentum ad Verecundiam*)

We saw in Chapter 1 that an argument from authority is an inductive argument in which an arguer cites the authority or testimony of another person in support of some conclusion. The **appeal to unqualified authority** fallacy is a variety of the argument from authority and occurs when the cited authority or witness lacks credibility. There are several reasons why an authority or witness might lack credibility. The person might lack the requisite expertise, might be biased or prejudiced, might have a motive

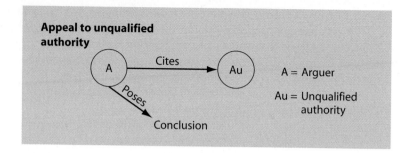

Appeal to unqualified authority

Cites

A → Au

A = Arguer

Au = Unqualified authority

Poses

Conclusion

to lie or disseminate "misinformation," or might lack the requisite ability to perceive or recall. The following examples illustrate these reasons:

> Dr. Bradshaw, our family physician, has stated that the creation of muonic atoms of deuterium and tritium hold the key to producing a sustained nuclear fusion re-action at room temperature. In view of Dr. Bradshaw's expertise as a physician, we must conclude that this is indeed true.

This conclusion deals with nuclear physics, and the authority is a family physician. Because it is unlikely that a physician would be an expert in nuclear physics, the argument commits an appeal to unqualified authority.

> David Duke, former Grand Wizard of the Ku Klux Klan, has stated, "Jews are not good Americans. They have no understanding of what America is." On the basis of Duke's authority, we must therefore conclude that the Jews in this country are un-American.

As an authority, David Duke is clearly biased, so his statements cannot be trusted.

> James W. Johnston, Chairman of R. J. Reynolds Tobacco Company, testified before Congress that tobacco is not an addictive substance and that smoking cigarettes does not produce any addiction. Therefore, we should believe him and conclude that smoking does not in fact lead to any addiction.

If Mr. Johnston had admitted that tobacco is addictive, it would have opened the door to government regulation, which could put his company out of business. Thus, because Johnston had a clear motive to lie, we should not believe his statements.

> Old Mrs. Furguson (who is practically blind) has testified that she saw the defendant stab the victim with a bayonet while she was standing in the twilight shadows 100 yards from the incident. Therefore, members of the jury, you must find the defendant guilty.

Here the witness lacks the ability to perceive what she has testified to, so her testimony is untrustworthy.

Of course if an authority is credible, the resulting argument will contain no fallacy. Example:

> The county tax collector issued a press release stating that property tax revenues are higher this year than last. Therefore, we conclude that these revenues are indeed higher this year.

Normally a county tax collector would be considered a qualified expert in the area of tax revenues, so assuming the tax collector has no reason to lie, this argument is inductively strong.

In deciding whether a person is a qualified authority, one should keep two important points in mind. First, the person might be an authority in more than one field. For example, a chemist might also be an authority in biology, or an economist might also be an authority in law. The second point is that there are some areas in which practically no one can be considered an authority. Such areas include politics, morals, and religion. For example, if someone were to argue that abortion is immoral because a certain philosopher or religious leader has said so, the argument would be weak regardless of the authority's qualifications. Many questions in these areas are so hotly contested that there is no conventional wisdom an authority can depend on.

10. Appeal to Ignorance
(*Argumentum ad Ignorantiam*)

When the premises of an argument state that nothing has been proved one way or the other about something, and the conclusion then makes a definite assertion about that thing, the argument commits an **appeal to ignorance.** The issue usually involves something that is incapable of being proved or something that has not yet been proved. Example:

> People have been trying for centuries to provide conclusive evidence for the claims of astrology, and no one has ever succeeded. Therefore, we must conclude that astrology is a lot of nonsense.

Conversely, the following argument commits the same fallacy.

> People have been trying for centuries to disprove the claims of astrology, and no one has ever succeeded. Therefore, we must conclude that the claims of astrology are true.

The premises of an argument are supposed to provide positive evidence for the conclusion. The premises of these arguments, however, tell us nothing about astrology; rather, they tell us about what certain unnamed and unidentified people have tried unsuccessfully to do. This evidence may provide some slight reason for believing the conclusion, but certainly not sufficient reason.

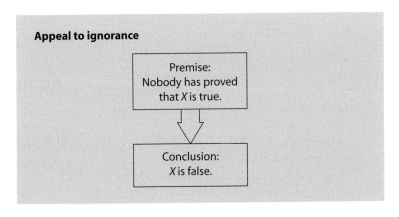

Appeal to ignorance

Premise:
Nobody has proved
that *X* is true.

Conclusion:
X is false.

These examples do, however, lead us to the first of two important exceptions to the appeal to ignorance. The first stems from the fact that if qualified researchers investigate a certain phenomenon within their range of expertise and fail to turn up any evidence that the phenomenon exists, this fruitless search by itself constitutes positive evidence about the question. Consider, for example, the following argument:

> Teams of scientists attempted over several decades to detect the existence of the luminiferous aether, and all failed to do so. Therefore, the luminiferous aether does not exist.

The premises of this argument are true. Given the circumstances, it is likely that the scientists in question would have detected the aether if in fact it did exist. Since they did not detect it, it probably does not exist. Thus, we can say that the given argument is inductively strong (but not deductively valid).

As for the two arguments about astrology, if the attempts to prove or disprove the astrological claims had been done in a systematic way by qualified experts, the arguments would more likely be good. Exactly what is required to qualify someone to investigate astrological claims is, of course, difficult to say. But as these arguments stand, the premises state nothing about the qualifications of the investigators, and so the arguments remain fallacious.

It is not always necessary, however, that the investigators have *special* qualifications. The kinds of qualifications needed depend on the situation. Sometimes the mere ability to see and report what one sees is sufficient. Example:

> No one has ever seen Mr. Andrews drink a glass of wine, beer, or any other alcoholic beverage. Probably Mr. Andrews is a nondrinker.

Because it is highly probable that if Mr. Andrews were a drinker, somebody would have seen him drinking, this argument is inductively strong. No special qualifications are needed to be able to see someone take a drink.

The second exception to the appeal to ignorance relates to courtroom procedure. In the United States and a few other countries, a person is presumed innocent until proven guilty. If the prosecutor in a criminal trial fails to prove the guilt of the defendant beyond reasonable doubt, counsel for the defense may justifiably argue that his or her client is not guilty. Example:

> Members of the jury, you have heard the prosecution present its case against the defendant. Nothing, however, has been proved beyond a reasonable doubt. Therefore, under the law, the defendant is not guilty.

This argument commits no fallacy because "not guilty" means, in the legal sense, that guilt beyond a reasonable doubt has not been proved. The defendant may indeed have committed the crime of which he or she is accused, but if the prosecutor fails to prove guilt beyond a reasonable doubt, the defendant is considered "not guilty."

11. Hasty Generalization (Converse Accident)

Hasty generalization is a fallacy that affects inductive generalizations. In Chapter 1 we saw that an inductive generalization is an argument that draws a conclusion about all members of a group from evidence that pertains to a selected sample. The fallacy oc-

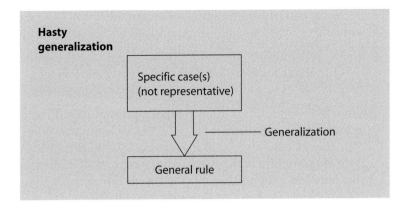

Hasty generalization

Specific case(s) (not representative)

Generalization

General rule

3

curs when there is a reasonable likelihood that the sample is not representative of the group. Such a likelihood may arise if the sample is either too small or not randomly selected. Here are two examples:

> After only one year the alternator went out in Mr. O'Grady's new Chevrolet. Mrs. Dodson's Oldsmobile developed a transmission problem after six months. The obvious conclusion is that cars made by General Motors are just a pile of junk these days.

> Ten Arab fundamentalists hijacked planes and crashed them into the World Trade Center in New York City. The message is clear: Arabs are nothing but a pack of religious fanatics prone to violence.

In these arguments a conclusion about a whole group is drawn from premises that mention only a few instances. Because such small, atypical samples are not sufficient to support a general conclusion, each argument commits a hasty generalization. The second example indicates how hasty generalization plays a role in racial and religious prejudice.

The mere fact that a sample is small, however, does not necessarily mean that it is atypical. On the other hand, the mere fact that a sample is large does not guarantee that it is typical. In the case of small samples, various factors may intervene that render such sample typical of the larger group. Examples:

> Ten milligrams of substance Z was fed to four mice, and within two minutes all four went into shock and died. Probably substance Z, in this amount, is fatal to mice in general.

> On three separate occasions I drank a bottle of Figowitz beer and found it flat and bitter. Probably I would find every bottle of Figowitz beer flat and bitter.

Neither of these arguments commits the fallacy of hasty generalization, because in neither case is there any likelihood that the sample is atypical of the group. In the first argument the fact that the mice died in only two minutes suggests the existence of a causal connection between eating substance Z and death. If there is such a connection, it would hold for other mice as well. In the second example the fact that the taste of beer typically remains constant from bottle to bottle causes the argument to be strong, even though only three bottles were sampled.

In the case of large samples, if the sample is not random, it may not be typical of the larger group. Example:

> One hundred thousand voters from Orange County, California, were surveyed on their choice for governor, and 68 percent said they intend to vote for the Republican candidate. Clearly the Republican candidate will be elected.

Even though the sample cited in this argument is large, the argument commits a hasty generalization. The problem is that Orange County is overwhelmingly Republican, so the mere fact that 68 percent intend to vote for the Republican candidate is no indication of how others in the state intend to vote. In other words, the survey was not conducted randomly, and for this reason the argument is fatally flawed. The need for randomness in samples is discussed further in Chapter 12 of this book.

Hasty generalization is otherwise called "converse accident" because it proceeds in a direction opposite to that of accident. Whereas accident proceeds from the general to the particular, converse accident moves from the particular to the general. The premises cite some characteristic affecting one or more atypical instances of a certain class, and the conclusion then applies that characteristic to all members of the class.

12. False Cause

The fallacy of **false cause** occurs whenever the link between premises and conclusion depends on some imagined causal connection that probably does not exist. Whenever an argument is suspected of committing the false cause fallacy, the reader or listener should be able to say that the conclusion depends on the supposition that X causes Y, whereas X probably does not cause Y at all. Examples:

> During the past two months, every time that the cheerleaders have worn blue ribbons in their hair, the basketball team has been defeated. Therefore, to prevent defeats in the future, the cheerleaders should get rid of those blue ribbons.

> Successful business executives are paid salaries in excess of $100,000. Therefore, the best way to ensure that Ferguson will become a successful executive is to raise his salary to at least $100,000.

> There are more laws on the books today than ever before, and more crimes are being committed than ever before. Therefore, to reduce crime we must eliminate the laws.

The first argument depends on the supposition that the blue ribbons caused the defeats, the second on the supposition that a high salary causes success, and the third on the supposition that laws cause crime. In no case is it likely that any causal connection exists.

The first argument illustrates a variety of the false cause fallacy called *post hoc ergo propter hoc* ("after this, therefore on account of this"). This variety of the fallacy presupposes that just because one event precedes another event, the first event causes the second. Obviously, mere temporal succession is not sufficient to establish a causal connection. Nevertheless, this kind of reasoning is quite common and lies behind most forms of superstition. (Example: "A black cat crossed my path and later I tripped and sprained my ankle. It must be that black cats really are bad luck.")

The second and third arguments illustrate a variety of the false cause fallacy called *non causa pro causa* ("not the cause for the cause"). This variety is committed when

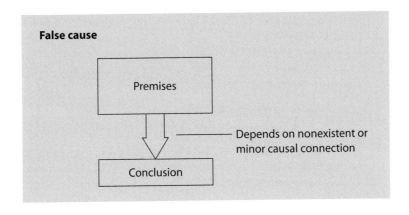

False cause

Premises

Depends on nonexistent or minor causal connection

Conclusion

what is taken to be the cause of something is not really the cause at all and the mistake is based on something other than mere temporal succession. In reference to the second argument, success as an executive causes increases in salary—not the other way around—so the argument mistakes the cause for the effect. In reference to the third argument, the increase in crime is, for the most part, only coincidental with the increase in the number of laws. Obviously, the mere fact that one event is coincidental with another is not sufficient reason to think that one caused the other.

A third variety of the false cause fallacy, and one that is probably committed more often than either of the others in their pure form, is *oversimplified cause*. This variety occurs when a multitude of causes is responsible for a certain effect but the arguer selects just one of these causes and represents it as if it were the sole cause. Here are some examples:

> The quality of education in our grade schools and high schools has been declining for years. Clearly, our teachers just aren't doing their job these days.

> Today, all of us can look forward to a longer life span than our parents and grandparents. Obviously we owe our thanks to the millions of dedicated doctors who expend every effort to ensure our health.

In reference to the first argument, the decline in the quality of education is caused by many factors, including lack of discipline in the home, lack of parental involvement, too much television, and drug use by students. Poor teacher performance is only one of these factors and probably a minor one at that. In the second argument, the efforts of doctors are only one among many factors responsible for our longer life span. Other, more important factors include a better diet, more exercise, reduced smoking, safer highways, and more stringent occupational safety standards.

The oversimplified cause fallacy is usually motivated by self-serving interests. Sometimes the arguer wants to take undeserved credit for himself or herself or give undeserved credit to some movement with which he or she is affiliated. At other times, the arguer wants to heap blame on an opponent or shift blame from himself or herself onto some convenient occurrence. Instances of the fallacy can resemble either the *post hoc* or the *non causa pro causa* varieties in that the alleged cause can occur either prior to or concurrently with the effect. It differs from the other varieties of false cause fallacy in that the single factor selected for credit or blame is often partly responsible for the effect, but responsible to only a minor degree.

The last variety of false cause we will consider is called the *gambler's fallacy*. This fallacy is committed whenever the conclusion of an argument depends on the supposition that independent events in a game of chance are causally related. Here is an example:

> A fair coin was flipped five times in a row, and each time it came up heads. Therefore, it is extremely likely that it will come up tails on the next flip.

In fact, it is no more likely that the coin will come up tails on the next flip than it was on the first flip. Each flip is an independent event, so earlier flips have no causal influence on later ones. Thus, the fact that the earlier flips came up heads does not increase the likelihood that the next flip will come up tails.

For the gambler's fallacy to be committed, the events must be independent or nearly independent. Such events include rolls of a pair of fair (unloaded) dice, spins of a fair roulette wheel, and selections of lottery winning numbers. Events are not completely independent whenever the skill of the gambler affects the outcome. Thus, poker, blackjack, and horse-race betting provide less-than-perfect candidates for the gambler's fallacy.

The false cause fallacy is often convincing because it is often difficult to determine whether two phenomena are causally related. A lengthy time lapse between the operation of the cause and the occurrence of the effect can exacerbate the problem. For example, the thirty-year interval between exposure to asbestos and the onset of asbestosis impeded the recognition of a causal connection. Also, when two events are causally related, determining the degree of relatedness may be hard. Thus, there may be some connection between the electromagnetic field produced by high voltage transmission lines and leukemia, but the connection may be extremely slight. Finally, when a causal connection is recognized, it may be difficult to determine which is the cause and which is the effect. For example, an allergic reaction may be connected with an episode of anxiety, but it may be hard to tell if the reaction causes the anxiety or if the anxiety causes the reaction.

The realm of human action constitutes another area in which causal connections are notoriously difficult to establish. For example, the attorneys for accused murderer Dan White argued that Twinkies, Coke, and potato chips caused him to kill San Francisco mayor George Moscone. Other attorneys have blamed their clients' crimes on PMS, rap music, childhood abuse, mental retardation, and hallucinations. The complex nature of human motivation renders all such causal claims difficult to evaluate. The situation may become even worse when a whole nation of people are involved. Thus, the recent drop in crime rates has been attributed to "three strikes" laws, but it is difficult to say whether this or some other factor is really responsible.

One point that should be kept in mind when establishing causal connections is that statistical correlations by themselves often reveal little about what is actually going on. For example, if all that we knew about smoking and lung cancer was that the two frequently occur together, we might conclude any number of things. We might conclude that both have a common cause, such as a genetic predisposition, or we might conclude that lung cancer is a disease contracted early in life and that it manifests itself in its early stages by a strong desire for tobacco. Fortunately, in this case we have more evidence than a mere statistical correlation. This additional evidence inclines us to believe that the smoking is a cause of the cancer.

13. Slippery Slope

The fallacy of **slippery slope** is a variety of the false cause fallacy. It occurs when the conclusion of an argument rests on an alleged chain reaction and there is not sufficient reason to think that the chain reaction will actually take place. Here is an example:

> Immediate steps should be taken to outlaw pornography once and for all. The continued manufacture and sale of pornographic material will almost certainly lead to an increase in sex-related crimes such as rape and incest. This in turn will gradually erode the moral fabric of society and result in an increase in crimes of all sorts. Eventually a complete disintegration of law and order will occur, leading in the end to the total collapse of civilization.

Because there is no good reason to think that the mere failure to outlaw pornography will result in all these dire consequences, this argument is fallacious. An equally fallacious counterargument is as follows:

> Attempts to outlaw pornography threaten basic civil rights and should be summarily abandoned. If pornography is outlawed, censorship of newspapers and news magazines is only a short step away. After that there will be censorship of textbooks, political speeches, and the content of lectures delivered by university professors. Complete mind control by the central government will be the inevitable result.

Both arguments attempt to persuade the reader or listener that the welfare of society rests on a "slippery slope" and that a single step in the wrong direction will result in an inevitable slide all the way to the bottom.

The slippery slope fallacy can involve various kinds of causality. For example, someone might argue that removing a single brick from a building would set off a chain reaction leading to the destruction of the building, or that chopping down a tall tree would set off a cascade of falling trees leading to the destruction of the forest. These arguments depend on pure physical causality. On the other hand, someone might argue that starting a rumor about the health of the economy would set off a chain reaction leading to the collapse of the stock market. Such an argument would depend on the kind of causality found in interpersonal communications. Or someone might argue that planting a seed of doubt in a person's mind about the faithfulness of his or her spouse would gnaw away at that person, leading to the breakup of the marriage. Such an argument would depend on the kind of causality that links mental states.

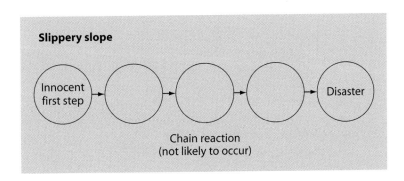

Slippery slope

Innocent first step → → → → Disaster

Chain reaction
(not likely to occur)

Deciding whether a slippery slope fallacy has been committed can be difficult when one is uncertain whether the alleged chain reaction will or will not occur. This question is discussed in Section 3.5. But many slippery slopes rest on a mere emotional conviction on the part of the arguer that a certain action or policy is bad, and the arguer attempts to trump up support for his or her position by citing all sorts of dire consequences that will result if the action is taken or the policy followed. In such cases there is usually little problem in identifying the argument as a slippery slope.

14. Weak Analogy

This fallacy affects inductive arguments from analogy. As we saw in Chapter 1, an argument from analogy is an argument in which the conclusion depends on the existence of an analogy, or similarity, between two things or situations. The fallacy of **weak analogy** is committed when the analogy is not strong enough to support the conclusion that is drawn. Example:

> Harper's new car is bright blue, has leather upholstery, and gets excellent gas mileage. Crowley's new car is also bright blue and has leather upholstery. Therefore, it probably gets excellent gas mileage, too.

Because the color of a car and the choice of upholstery have nothing to do with gasoline consumption, this argument is fallacious.

The basic structure of an argument from analogy is as follows:

> Entity A has attributes a, b, c, and z.
> Entity B has attributes a, b, c.
> Therefore, entity B probably has attribute z also.

Evaluating an argument having this form requires a two-step procedure: (1) Identify the attributes a, b, c, ... that the two entities A and B share, and (2) determine how the attribute z, mentioned in the conclusion, relates to the attributes a, b, c, ... If some causal or systematic relation exists between z and a, b, or c, the argument is strong; otherwise, it is weak. In the example argument, the two entities share the attributes of being cars; the attributes entailed by being a car, such as having four wheels; and the attributes of color and upholstery material. Because none of these attributes is systematically or causally related to good gas mileage, the argument is fallacious.

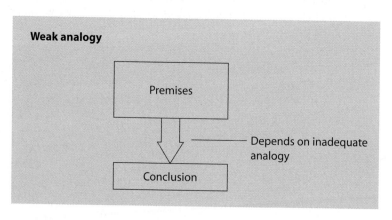

Weak analogy

Premises

Conclusion

Depends on inadequate analogy

William of Ockham ca. 1285–1347

The English philosopher and theologian, William of Ockham, was born in or near the village of Ockham not far from London. Little is known about his childhood, and his biographers are not even certain about the year of his birth, with estimates running from 1280 to 1290. However, they are certain that while Ockham was still a small boy, his parents delivered him to the nearest Franciscan monastery to be brought up in the monastic way of life. His parents' intentions were realized when he entered the Franciscan Order and was ordained in 1306.

© The Granger Collection, New York

Ockham studied theology at Oxford, possibly under Duns Scotus, and he lectured there. He also studied and taught at the University of Paris, where he wrote extensively on theology and philosophy. Ockham's theological views generated controversy among theologians of the day, some of whom vehemently opposed him. In 1324, he was called to Avignon, then the location of the papal court, to answer charges of heresy.

A panel of scholars had been appointed to review the charges made against Ockham, and he was obliged to remain at a Franciscan house in Avignon throughout the investigation, which lasted four years. During this time, the Franciscan minister general, Michael of Cesena, was called to Avignon, because he had become embroiled in a controversy with Pope John XXII over the issue of the poverty of Jesus and the apostles. Michael held that Jesus and the apostles did not own property but instead survived through goodwill offerings of people in the community. The Franciscans regarded themselves as emulating the model set by Jesus and the apostles, but the pope, who lived in luxury, obviously disagreed.

Though Ockham had more than enough problems of his own, the minister general asked him to research the issue to see which position was right—the pope's or the minister general's. Ockham ultimately came out on the side of the minister general, claiming that the pope was a heretic and had no business even being pope. This got the Avignon Franciscans into a great deal of trouble, and to extricate themselves they purloined several horses and rode out of town in the middle of the night. Ludwig of Bavaria, the Holy Roman Emperor, gave them protection, and Ockham lived out the rest of his life in Munich. While there he turned his attention to politics and political philosophy. He was a staunch advocate of the separation of church and state, claiming that the pope had no right to intervene in state affairs. The pope retaliated by excommunicating him.

Ockham is best known for endorsing a principle of parsimony that has come to be called "Ockham's razor." This principle states that, among alternative explanations, the simplest one is the best. Ockham emphasized the importance of keeping the number of entities hypothesized in an explanation to an absolute minimum. In the area of logic, he is known for his theory of truth conditions for categorical propositions, for work in the foundations of inductive reasoning, for preliminary work on a three-valued logic, and for developing a close approximation to what would later come to be known as De Morgan's rule.

As an illustration of when the requisite systematic or causal relation does and does not exist, consider the following arguments:

> The flow of electricity through a wire is similar to the flow of water through a pipe. Obviously a large-diameter pipe will carry a greater flow of water than a pipe of small diameter. Therefore, a large-diameter wire should carry a greater flow of electricity than a small-diameter wire.

> The flow of electricity through a wire is similar to the flow of water through a pipe. When water runs downhill through a pipe, the pressure at the bottom of the hill is greater than it is at the top. Thus, when electricity flows downhill through a wire, the voltage should be greater at the bottom of the hill than at the top.

The first argument is good and the second is fallacious. Both arguments depend on the similarity between water molecules flowing through a pipe and electrons flowing through a wire. In both cases there is a systematic relation between the diameter of the pipe/wire and the amount of flow. In the first argument this systematic relation provides a strong link between premises and conclusion, and so the argument is a good one. But in the second argument a causal connection exists between difference in elevation and increase in pressure that holds for water but not for electricity. Water molecules flowing through a pipe are significantly affected by gravity, but electrons flowing through a wire are not. Thus, the second argument is fallacious.

The theory and evaluation of arguments from analogy is one of the most complex and elusive subjects in all of logic. Additional material on arguments from analogy appears in Section 3.5 and Chapter 9 of this text.

EXERCISE 3.3

I. Identify the fallacies of weak induction committed by the following arguments, giving a brief explanation for your answer. If no fallacy is committed, write "no fallacy."

★1. The *Daily News* carried an article this morning about three local teenagers who were arrested on charges of drug possession. Teenagers these days are nothing but a bunch of junkies.

2. If a car breaks down on the freeway, a passing mechanic is not obligated to render emergency road service. For similar reasons, if a person suffers a heart attack on the street, a passing physician is not obligated to render emergency medical assistance.

3. There must be something to psychical research. Three famous physicists—Oliver Lodge, James Jeans, and Arthur Stanley Eddington—took it seriously.

★4. The secretaries have asked us to provide lounge areas where they can spend their coffee breaks. This request will have to be refused. If we give them lounge areas, next they'll be asking for spas and swimming pools. Then it will be racquetball courts, tennis courts, and fitness centers. Expenditures for these facilities will drive us into bankruptcy.

5. The accumulation of pressure in a society is similar to the buildup of pressure in a boiler. If the pressure in a boiler increases beyond a critical point, the

boiler will explode. Accordingly, if a government represses its people beyond a certain point, the people will rise up in revolt.

6. A few minutes after Governor Harrison finished his speech on television, a devastating earthquake struck southern Alaska. For the safety of the people up there, it is imperative that Governor Harrison make no more speeches.

★7. No one has ever been able to prove the existence of extrasensory perception. We must therefore conclude that extrasensory perception is a myth.

8. Lester Brown, universally respected author of the yearly *State of the World* report, has said that the destruction of tropical rain forests is one of the ten most serious worldwide problems. Thus, it must be the case that this is indeed a very serious problem.

9. America's business leaders are all a bunch of crooks. Just look at the facts. Dennis Kowslowski ripped off millions of dollars from Tyco Corporation, Jeffrey Skilling and Andy Fastow did the same with Enron, Bernie Ebbers defrauded the investors of WorldCom, and the Rigas family stole millions from Adelphia.

★10. Iranian President Mahmoud Ahmadinejad says that the holocaust is a fairy tale promoted for the purpose of garnering sympathy for Israel. In view of Ahmadinejad's apparent expertise in this area, we must conclude that the holocaust is indeed a fairy tale, just as he says.

11. Probably no life exists on Venus. Teams of scientists have conducted exhaustive studies of the planet's surface and atmosphere, and no living organisms have been found.

12. We don't dare let the animal rights activists get their foot in the door. If they sell us on the idea that dogs, cats, and dolphins have rights, next it will be chickens and cows. That means no more chicken Kiev or prime rib. Next it will be worms and insects. This will lead to the decimation of our agricultural industry. The starvation of the human race will follow close behind.

★13. No one would buy a pair of shoes without trying them on. Why should anyone be expected to get married without premarital sex?

14. No one has proved conclusively that America's nuclear power plants constitute a danger to people living in their immediate vicinity. Therefore, it is perfectly safe to continue to build nuclear power plants near large metropolitan centers.

15. There are more churches in New York City than in any other city in the nation, and more crimes are committed in New York City than anywhere else. So, if we are to eliminate crime, we must abolish the churches.

II. Answer "true" or "false" to the following statements:

1. If an arguer cites a statement by a recognized expert in support of a conclusion and the statement falls within the expert's range of expertise, then the arguer commits an appeal to unqualified authority.

2. If an arguer cites a statement in support of a conclusion and the statement reflects the strong bias of its author, then the arguer commits an appeal to unqualified authority.

3. In the appeal to ignorance, the arguer accuses the reader or listener of being ignorant.

4. If an attorney for the defense in an American or Canadian criminal trial argues that the prosecution has proved nothing beyond a reasonable doubt about the guilt of the defendant, then the attorney commits an appeal to ignorance.

5. Hasty generalization always proceeds from the particular to the general.

6. The *post hoc ergo propter hoc* variety of the false cause fallacy presumes that X causes Y merely because X happens before Y.

7. If an argument concludes that X causes Y simply because X and Y occur over the same time interval, then the argument commits the *non causa pro causa* variety of the false cause fallacy.

8. If the conclusion of an argument depends on the occurrence of a chain reaction of events, and there is good reason to believe that the chain reaction will actually occur, the argument commits a slippery slope fallacy.

9. The fallacy of weak analogy always depends on an alleged similarity between two things or situations.

10. If an argument from analogy depends on a causal or systematic relationship between certain attributes, and there is good reason to believe that this relationship exists, then the argument commits no fallacy.

III. Identify the fallacies of relevance and weak induction committed by the following arguments. If no fallacy is committed, write "no fallacy."

★1. On our first date, George had his hands all over me, and I found it nearly impossible to keep him in his place. A week ago Tom gave me that stupid line about how, in order to prove my love, I had to spend the night with him. Men are all alike. All any of them want is sex.

2. Tagging by graffiti artists has become a terrible problem in recent years. Obviously our schools are stifling the creative spirit of these young people.

3. North Korean dictator Kim Jong Il has promised not to let any of his nuclear weapons fall into the hands of terrorists. But Kim is erratic, dishonest, corrupt, and possibly even insane. Therefore, we should not trust his promises for a minute.

★4. House speaker Nancy Pelosi has argued strongly against oil and gas exploration in the Arctic National Wildlife Refuge. But what would you expect? She represents the city of San Francisco, which is loaded with environmentalists. If she didn't take this position, she would be run out of office. Thus, her arguments on this issue really have no merit.

5. What the farmer sows in the spring he reaps in the fall. In the spring he sows $8-per-bushel soybeans. Therefore, in the fall he will reap $8-per-bushel soybeans.

6. World-renowned physicist Stephen Hawking claims that black holes do not gobble up everything that falls into them without leaving a trace, but that something is always left behind. Given Hawking's stature as a scientist and the

many years he has worked on this problem, we should conclude that this is indeed the case.

★7. Emily has bought over 100 tickets on the weekly state lottery, and she has never won anything. Therefore, the likelihood increases every week that she will win something if she continues to buy tickets.

8. Johnny, of course I deserve the use of your bicycle for the afternoon. After all, I'm sure you wouldn't want your mother to find out that you played hooky today.

9. Practically everyone downloads music free of charge from the Internet these days. Therefore, you should have no qualms about doing this yourself.

★10. Ellen Quinn has argued that logic is not the most important thing in life. Apparently Ellen advocates irrationality. It has taken two million years for the human race to achieve the position that it has, and Ellen would throw the whole thing into the garbage. What utter nonsense!

11. When water is poured on the top of a pile of rocks, it always trickles down to the rocks on the bottom. Similarly, when rich people make lots of money, we can expect this money to trickle down to the poor.

12. Extensive laboratory tests have failed to prove any deleterious side effects of the new painkiller lexaprine. We conclude that lexaprine is safe for human consumption.

★13. Environmentalists accuse us of blocking the plan to convert Antarctica into a world park. In fact, nothing could be further from the truth. Antarctica is a huge continent teeming with life. It is the home of millions of penguins, seals, sea birds, and sea lions. Also, great schools of finfish and whales inhabit its coastal waters.

14. Media host Howard Stern claims that leaders of the religious right are nothing but a pack of racketeers bent on destroying every vestige of free speech, and he gives numerous reasons to support this claim. But Stern is just a vulgar, smut-mouthed freak who will say anything for shock value. Nobody should listen to this nonsense.

15. The operation of a camera is similar in many ways to the operation of an eye. If you are to see anything in a darkened room, the pupils of your eyes must first dilate. Accordingly, if you are to take a photograph (without flash) in a darkened room, the aperture of the camera lens must first be increased.

★16. Certainly Miss Malone will be a capable and efficient manager. She has a great figure, a gorgeous face, and tremendous poise and she dresses very fashionably.

17. James Dobson, director of Focus on the Family, says that men have the divine obligation to lead their families, and women have the divine obligation to submit to their husband's authority. Given Dobson's apparent ability to receive messages from God, we must conclude that this statement is absolutely true.

18. Dear Internal Revenue Service: I received a notice that my taxes are being audited for last year. But you have no right to do this. The deadline for filing a return was April 15, and I filed my tax return on April 12—a full three days before the deadline.

★19. To prevent dangerous weapons from being carried aboard airliners, those seeking to board must pass through a magnetometer and submit to a possible pat-down search. Therefore, to prevent alcohol and drugs from being carried into rock concerts, those entering should submit to similar search procedures.

20. Mr. Flemming's arguments against the rent control initiative on the September ballot should be taken with a grain of salt. As a landlord he would naturally be expected to oppose the initiative.

21. India is suffering a serious drought, thousands of children are dying of starvation in their mothers' arms, and homeless beggars line the streets of the major cities. Surely we must give these poor downtrodden people the chance of bettering their condition in America, the land of wealth and opportunity.

★22. Members of the jury, you have heard Shirley Gaines testify that the defendant did not offer to perform acts of prostitution for the undercover police officer. But Gaines is a known prostitute herself and a close friend of the defendant. Also, only a year ago she was convicted of twelve counts of perjury. Therefore, you should certainly discount Gaines's testimony.

23. It is ridiculous to hear that man from Peru complaining about America's poverty. Peru has twice as much poverty as America has ever had.

24. Angela complains that the problems on the algebra test were too hard. But have you ever seen the way Angela flirts with that good-looking quarterback on the football team? She's constantly batting those long, black eyelashes at him, and her tight-fitting sweaters leave nothing to the imagination. Angela should pay more attention to her studies.

★25. Nobody has ever proved that immoral behavior by elected officials erodes public morality. Therefore, we must conclude that such behavior does not erode public morality.

26. Freedom of speech is guaranteed by the First Amendment. Therefore, your friend was acting within his rights when he shouted "Fire! Fire!" in that crowded theater, even though it was only a joke.

27. No one, on encountering a watch lying on a forest trail, would expect that it had simply appeared there without having been made by someone. For the same reason, no one should expect that the universe simply appeared without having been made by some being.

★28. On Monday I drank ten rum and Cokes, and the next morning I woke up with a headache. On Wednesday I drank eight gin and Cokes, and the next morning I woke up with a headache. On Friday I drank nine bourbon and Cokes, and the next morning I woke up with a headache. Obviously, to prevent further headaches I must give up Coke.

29. Radio entertainer Rush Limbaugh claims there is not a shred of evidence to prove that nicotine is addictive or that cigarettes cause emphysema, lung cancer, or any other disease. Given Limbaugh's apparent expertise in medical science, we can only conclude that what he says about nicotine and cigarettes is true.

30. Some of the parents in our school district have asked that we provide bilingual education in Spanish. This request will have to be denied. If we provide this service, then someone will ask for bilingual education in Greek. Then it will be German, French, and Hungarian. Polish, Russian, Chinese, Japanese, and Korean will follow close behind. We certainly can't accommodate all of them.

IV. Identify the arguments in the following dialogue, then discuss each of them in terms of the fallacies presented in this section and the previous section. You should be able to find at least one case of each fallacy.

"Hi! Glad you could make it," Ralph says to his friend Claudia at a Friday night party. "Hey, you just missed a great discussion that Tom, Ruben, and I were having about abduction by extraterrestrials. Ruben just left, but he said he's been reading this book by Whitley Strieber—I think it's called *Transformation*—in which Strieber describes being kidnapped by creatures from outer space."

"Good grief! You don't actually believe that nonsense, do you?" Claudia asks incredulously.

"Well, I don't think Strieber would lie. Also, Ruben told us an amazing personal story. He was out camping a year ago, and after he'd killed off a couple of six-packs of Moosehead, he says he saw a UFO. So, I think we have to conclude there really are UFOs."

"What a joke!" Claudia laughs scornfully. "Ruben was probably hallucinating. By the way, didn't he fail most of his classes last semester? His parents are spending a fortune for his education, and all he does is party, sleep, and ignore his studies. I think that's immoral. As for Strieber, does he give any evidence?"

"As a matter of fact, he does," Ralph replies smugly. "Apparently, a few years ago, he was driving with his wife on some country road, when both of them experienced an unusual blackout. When they woke up, they were thirty-five miles further down the road, and they had no recollection of how they got there. Later, both began having dreams about extraterrestrials performing experiments on them while they were on board their spacecraft. Extraterrestrials must have abducted them, then hypnotized them so they wouldn't remember what had happened."

"Oh yeah, now I remember who Strieber is," answers Claudia, caustically. "He's that weirdo who dreams up all kinds of fantastic stories just so he can write books about them and make lots of money. If you give that sickie one minute of your time, then you're crazier than he is."

"I think you're prejudiced," Ralph says. "Why, recent surveys show that 64 percent of the American public believe in UFOs, and the number is growing every day. That alone should convince you they're real."

"You've got to be kidding," Claudia mutters, shaking her head in disbelief.

"Well then, consider this," insists Ralph. "There are hundreds of people out there who've had similar dreams and the same unaccounted-for time lapses. They can't all be fantasizing."

"I know that Strieber is a kook," Claudia persists, "so all the others must be, too."

"Now, now, aren't we jumping to conclusions?" her friend asks condescendingly.

"Not at all. First it was UFOs and little green men. Now those little creatures are abducting people and experimenting on them. Before long they'll be manipulating our genes and trying to infiltrate the human race. In the end, everyone will suspect everyone else of being an alien, mass terror will prevail, and civilization will collapse!" Claudia exclaims in mock horror.

"Don't be a fool!" Ralph barks, irritated. "The problem with you is, you're an agnostic. Obviously, you're saying we should refuse to believe in anything we can't clearly see or touch. So, logically, God doesn't exist, and there is no immortal soul. Tom, that's what she's saying, isn't it?"

"More or less," Tom agrees halfheartedly.

"Again, not at all," Claudia responds. "What I'm saying is, people have to be just a little bit critical about what they believe. Apparently you believe any cockamamie story that comes your way. You're just so gullible. If you keep it up, everyone and their dog will take you for a ride."

"Oh yeah? If I were you, I'd take a close look at my own beliefs," Ralph gibes. "Didn't I see you reading the astrology column just the other day? Nobody in their right mind believes in astrology. Maybe I should start screaming 'Claudia believes in astrology! Claudia believes in astrology!' Then everyone will gawk at you, and that sexy physics major you're dying to get a date with will think you're a nut."

"Oh, shut up!" says Claudia, blushing. "I may read the astrology column, but I certainly don't believe it. I just read it for fun. But, the fact is, during the past twenty-five years there have been thousands of alleged sightings of UFOs, and not a single one has led to any solid evidence of their existence. What do you make of that?"

"I think we should look at this situation the other way around," Ralph says. "Up until now, nobody has shown that UFOs *don't* exist, so I think we should give those people who claim they have seen them the benefit of the doubt. We should believe in UFOs and extraterrestrials until the sightings are proved false."

"Well, okay. Let's suppose, just for the sake of argument, that I admit the existence of UFOs and their little green drivers. How are we supposed to respond to them? What are we supposed to do?" Claudia asks.

"For starters, we should extend an open invitation to them," answers Ralph. "They may come from a dying planet where millions of their compatriots desperately struggle for survival. Their sun may be burning out, their water supply exhausted, and their soil poisoned with toxic chemicals. Surely they deserve a second chance on a new planet."

"Maybe so," Claudia says in a patronizing tone. "And now that you mention it, we probably have a legal obligation to let them in. Our current immigration laws say that we have to admit at least ten thousand applicants annually, from every major nation. If those aliens would just sign the right papers, we'd have to give them permanent residency. However, what worries me is, they may have the wrong intentions. After all, didn't they conduct experiments on those people they abducted?"

"Yes, but don't we experiment on animals? If the animals don't complain, why should we? Also, medical experimentation often leads to wonderful new cures. I'm certain we have nothing to worry about," says Ralph, proud of his logic.

"Humph! I hope you're right. Well, I've got to go now—and don't let any green men kidnap you," Claudia says with a barb.

"And you, either," Ralph answers.

Fallacies of Presumption, Ambiguity, and Grammatical Analogy

The **fallacies of presumption** include begging the question, complex question, false dichotomy, and suppressed evidence. These fallacies arise not because the premises are irrelevant to the conclusion or provide insufficient reason for believing the conclusion but because the premises presume what they purport to prove. *Begging the question* presumes that the premises provide adequate support for the conclusion when in fact they do not, and *complex question* presumes that a question can be answered by a simple "yes," "no," or other brief answer when a more sophisticated answer is needed. *False dichotomy* presumes that an "either . . . or . . ." statement presents jointly exhaustive alternatives when in fact it does not, and *suppressed evidence* presumes that no important evidence has been overlooked by the premises when in fact it has.

The **fallacies of ambiguity** include *equivocation* and *amphiboly*. These fallacies arise from the occurrence of some form of ambiguity in either the premises or the conclusion (or both). As we saw in Section 2.1, an expression is ambiguous if it is susceptible to different interpretations in a given context. The words "light" and "bank" are ambiguous, as is the statement "Tuna are biting off the Washington coast." When the conclusion of an argument depends on a shift in meaning of an ambiguous word or phrase or on the wrong interpretation of an ambiguous statement, the argument commits a fallacy of ambiguity.

The **fallacies of grammatical analogy** include *composition* and *division*. Arguments that commit these fallacies are grammatically analogous to other arguments that are good in every respect. Because of this similarity in linguistic structure, such fallacious arguments may appear good yet be bad.

15. Begging the Question (*Petitio Principii*)

The fallacy of **begging the question** is committed whenever the arguer creates the illusion that inadequate premises provide adequate support for the conclusion by leaving out a possibly false (shaky) key premise, by restating a possibly false premise as the conclusion, or by reasoning in a circle. The Latin name for this fallacy, *petitio principii*, means "request for the source." The actual source of support for the conclusion is not apparent, and so the argument is said to beg the question. After reading or hearing the argument, the observer is inclined to ask, "But how do you know *X*?" where *X* is the needed support.

The first, and most common, way of committing this fallacy is by leaving a possibly false key premise out of the argument while creating the illusion that nothing more is needed to establish the conclusion. Examples:

> Murder is morally wrong. This being the case, it follows that abortion is morally wrong.

> Of course humans and apes evolved from common ancestors. Just look how similar they are.

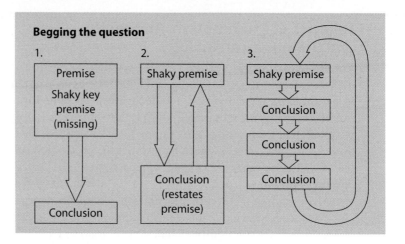

Begging the question

1.

Premise
Shaky key premise (missing)

↓

| Conclusion |

2.

| Shaky premise |

↓↓

| Conclusion (restates premise) |

3.

| Shaky premise |

↓↓

| Conclusion |

↓

| Conclusion |

↓

| Conclusion |

It's obvious that the poor in this country should be given handouts from the government. After all, these people earn less than the average citizen.

Clearly, terminally ill patients have a right to doctor-assisted suicide. After all, many of these people are unable to commit suicide by themselves.

The first of these arguments begs the question "How do you know that abortion is a form of murder?" The second begs the question "Does the mere fact that humans and apes look similar imply that they evolved from common ancestors?" And the third and fourth beg the questions "Just because the poor earn less than the average citizen, does this imply that the government should give them handouts?" and "Just because terminally ill patients cannot commit suicide by themselves, does it follow that they have a right to a doctor's assistance?"

These questions indicate that something has been left out of the original arguments. Thus, the first argument is missing the premise "Abortion is a form of murder"; the second is missing the premise "If humans and apes look similar, then they have common ancestors"; and so on. These premises are crucial for the soundness of the arguments. If the arguer is unable to establish the truth of these premises, then the arguments prove nothing. However, in most cases of begging the question, this is precisely the reason why such premises are left unstated. The arguer is *not* able to establish their truth, and by employing rhetorical phraseology such as "of course," "clearly," "this being the case," and "after all," the arguer hopes to create the illusion that the stated premise, by itself, provides adequate support for the conclusion when in fact it does not.

The same form of begging the question often appears in arguments concerning religious topics to justify conclusions about the existence of God, the immortality of the soul, and so on. Example:

The world in which we live displays an amazing degree of organization. Obviously this world was created by an intelligent God.

This argument begs the question "How do you know that the organization in the world could only have come from an intelligent creator?" Of course the claim that it did come from an intelligent creator may well be true, but the burden is on the arguer to prove it. Without supporting reasons or evidence, the argument proves nothing. Yet most people who are predisposed to believe the conclusion are likely to accept the argument as a good one. The same can be said of most arguments that beg the question, and this fact suggests another reason why arguers resort to this fallacy: Such arguments tend to reinforce preexisting inclinations and beliefs.

The second form of *petitio principii* occurs when the conclusion of an argument merely restates a possibly false premise in slightly different language. In such an argument, the premise supports the conclusion, and the conclusion tends to reinforce the premise. Examples:

> Capital punishment is justified for the crimes of murder and kidnapping because it is quite legitimate and appropriate that someone be put to death for having committed such hateful and inhuman acts.

> Anyone who preaches revolution has a vision of the future for the simple reason that if a person has no vision of the future he could not possibly preach revolution.

In the first argument, saying that capital punishment is "justified" means the same thing as saying that it is "legitimate and appropriate," and in the second argument the premise and the conclusion say exactly the same thing. However, by repeating the same thing in slightly different language, the arguer creates the illusion that independent evidence is being presented in support of the conclusion, when in fact it is not. Both arguments contain rhetorical phraseology ("hateful and inhuman," "*simple* reason," and "could not possibly") that help effect the illusion. The first argument begs the question "How do you know that capital punishment really is legitimate and appropriate?" and the second begs the question "How do you know that people who preach revolution really do have a vision of the future?"

The third form of *petitio principii* involves circular reasoning in a chain of inferences having a first premise that is possibly false. Example:

> Ford Motor Company clearly produces the finest cars in the United States. We know they produce the finest cars because they have the best design engineers. This is true because they can afford to pay them more than other manufacturers. Obviously they can afford to pay them more because they produce the finest cars in the United States.

On encountering this argument, the attentive reader is inclined to ask, "Where does this reasoning begin? What is its source?" Since the argument goes in a circle, it has no beginning or source, and as a result it proves nothing. Of course, in this example the circularity is rather apparent, so the argument is not likely to convince anyone. Cases in which circular reasoning may convince involve long and complex arguments having premises that depend on one another in subtle ways and a possibly false key premise that depends on the conclusion.

In all cases of begging the question, the arguer uses some linguistic device to create the illusion that inadequate premises provide adequate support for a conclusion. Without such an illusion, the fallacy is not committed. Thus, the following arguments commit no fallacy:

No dogs are cats.
Therefore, no cats are dogs.

London is in England and Paris is in France.
Therefore, Paris is in France and London is in England.

In both of these examples, the premise amounts to little more than a restatement of the conclusion. Yet both arguments are sound because they are valid and have true premises. No fallacy is committed, because no illusion is created to make inadequate premises appear as adequate. We will study arguments of this sort in Chapters 4 and 7.

Here is another example:

Rome is in Germany or Rome is in Germany.
Therefore, Rome is in Germany.

This argument is valid, but it is unsound because it has a false premise. However, it commits no fallacy because, again, no illusion is created to cover anything up. Arguments having this form also appear in Chapter 7.

As with these examples, arguments that beg the question are normally valid. This is easy to see. Any argument that includes the conclusion as one of the premises is clearly valid, and those forms of the fallacy that leave a key premise out of the argument become valid when that key premise is introduced. The problem with arguments that beg the question is that they are usually unsound, or at least not clearly sound, because the premise needed to provide adequate support for the conclusion is, at best, of uncertain truth value. Because such arguments presume the truth of this premise, begging the question is called a fallacy of presumption.

16. Complex Question

The fallacy of **complex question** is committed when two (or more) questions are asked in the guise of a single question and a single answer is then given to both of them. Every complex question presumes the existence of a certain condition. When the respondent's answer is added to the complex question, an argument emerges that establishes the presumed condition. Thus, although not an argument as such, a complex question involves an implicit argument. This argument is usually intended to trap the respondent into acknowledging something that he or she might otherwise not want to acknowledge. Examples:

Have you stopped cheating on exams?

Where did you hide the marijuana you were smoking?

Let us suppose the respondent answers "yes" to the first question and "under the bed" to the second. The following arguments emerge:

You were asked whether you have stopped cheating on exams. You answered, "Yes." Therefore, it follows that you have cheated in the past.

You were asked where you hid the marijuana you were smoking. You replied, "Under the bed." It follows that you were in fact smoking marijuana.

On the other hand, let us suppose that the respondent answers "no" to the first question and "nowhere" to the second. We then have the following arguments:

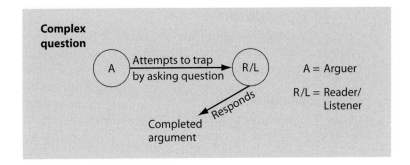

Complex question

A — Attempts to trap by asking question → R/L — Responds → Completed argument

A = Arguer
R/L = Reader/Listener

You were asked whether you have stopped cheating on exams. You answered, "No." Therefore, you continue to cheat.

You were asked where you hid the marijuana you were smoking. You answered, "Nowhere." It follows that you must have smoked all of it.

Obviously, each of the questions is really two questions:

Did you cheat on exams in the past? If you did cheat in the past, have you stopped now?

Were you smoking marijuana? If you were smoking it, where did you hide it?

If respondents are not sophisticated enough to identify a complex question when one is put to them, they may answer quite innocently and be trapped by a conclusion that is supported by no evidence at all; or, they may be tricked into providing the evidence themselves. The correct response lies in resolving the complex question into its component questions and answering each separately.

The fallacy of complex question should be distinguished from another kind of question known in law as a leading question. A *leading question* is one in which the answer is in some way suggested in the question. Whether or not a question is a leading one is important in the direct examination of a witness by counsel. Example:

Tell us, on April 9, did you see the defendant shoot the deceased?	(leading question)
Tell us, what did you see on April 9?	(straight question)

Leading questions differ from complex questions in that they involve no logical fallacies—that is, they do not attempt to trick the respondent into admitting something he or she does not want to admit. To distinguish the two, however, one sometimes needs to know whether prior questions have been asked. Here are some additional examples of complex questions:

Are you going to be a good little boy and eat your hamburger?
Is George Hendrix still telling lies?
How long must I put up with your snotty behavior?
When are you going to stop talking nonsense?

17. False Dichotomy

The fallacy of **false dichotomy** is committed when a disjunctive ("either . . . or . . .") premise presents two unlikely alternatives as if they were the only ones available, and the arguer then eliminates the undesirable alternative, leaving the desirable one as the conclusion. Such an argument is clearly valid, but since the disjunctive premise is false, or at least probably false, the argument is typically unsound. The fallacy is often committed by children when arguing with their parents, by advertisers, and by adults generally. Here are three examples:

> Either you let me attend the Dixie Chicks concert or I'll be miserable for the rest of my life. I know you don't want me to be miserable for the rest of my life, so it follows that you'll let me attend the concert.

> Either you use Ultra Guard deodorant or you risk the chance of perspiration odor. Surely you don't want to risk the chance of perspiration odor. Therefore, you will want to use Ultra Guard deodorant.

> Either you buy only American-made products or you don't deserve to be called a loyal American. Yesterday you bought a new Toyota. It's therefore clear that you don't deserve to be called a loyal American.

In none of these arguments does the disjunctive premise present the only alternatives available, but in each case the arguer tries to convey that impression. For example, in the first argument, the arguer tries to convey the impression that he or she either goes to the concert or faces a lifetime of misery, and that no other alternatives are possible. Clearly, however, this is not the case.

The fallacious nature of false dichotomy lies in the illusion created by the arguer that the disjunctive premise presents jointly exhaustive alternatives. If it did, the premise would be true of necessity. For example, the statement "Either Reno is in Nevada, or it is not in Nevada" presents jointly exhaustive alternatives and is true of necessity. But in the fallacy of false dichotomy, not only do the two alternatives fail to be jointly exhaustive, but they are not even likely. As a result, the disjunctive premise is false, or at least probably false. Thus, the fallacy amounts to making a false or probably false premise appear true.

If one of the alternatives in the disjunctive premise is true, then the fallacy is not committed. For example, the following argument is valid and sound:

> Either Seattle is in Washington, or it is in Oregon.
> Seattle is not in Oregon.
> Therefore, Seattle is in Washington

False dichotomy is otherwise called "false bifurcation" and the "either-or fallacy." Also, in most cases the arguer expresses only the disjunctive premise and leaves it to the reader or listener to supply the missing statements:

> Either you buy me a new mink coat, or I'll freeze to death when winter comes.
> Either I continue smoking, or I'll get fat and you'll hate to be seen with me.

The missing premise and conclusion are easily introduced.

18. Suppressed Evidence

Chapter 1 explained that a cogent argument is an inductive argument with good reasoning and true premises. The requirement of true premises includes the proviso that the premises not ignore some important piece of evidence that outweighs the presented evidence and entails a very different conclusion. If an inductive argument does indeed ignore such evidence, then the argument commits the fallacy of **suppressed evidence.** Consider, for example, the following argument:

> Most dogs are friendly and pose no threat to people who pet them. Therefore, it would be safe to pet the little dog that is approaching us now.

If the arguer ignores the fact that the little dog is excited and foaming at the mouth (which suggests rabies), then the argument commits a suppressed evidence fallacy. This fallacy is classified as a fallacy of presumption because it works by creating the presumption that the premises are both true and complete when in fact they are not.

Perhaps the most common occurrence of the suppressed evidence fallacy appears in inferences based on advertisements. Nearly every ad neglects to mention certain negative features of the product advertised. As a result, an observer who sees or hears an advertisement and then draws a conclusion from it may commit the fallacy of suppressed evidence. Example:

> The ad for Kentucky Fried Chicken says, "Buy a bucket of chicken and have a barrel of fun!" Therefore, if we buy a bucket of that chicken, we will be guaranteed to have lots of fun.

The ad fails to state that the fun does not come packaged with the chicken but must be supplied by the buyer. Also, of course, the ad fails to state that the chicken is loaded with fat and that the buyer's resultant weight gain may not amount to a barrel of fun. By ignoring these facts, the argument based on the ad is fallacious.

Another way that an arguer can commit the suppressed evidence fallacy is by ignoring important events that have occurred with the passage of time that render an inductive conclusion improbable. Here is an example:

> During the past sixty years, Poland has enjoyed a rather low standard of living. Therefore, Poland will probably have a low standard of living for the next sixty years.

Suppressed evidence

Premises ⎯ Ignores stronger evidence that supports a different conclusion

Conclusion

This argument ignores the fact that Poland was part of the Soviet bloc during most of the past sixty years, and this fact accounts for its rather low standard of living. However, following the collapse of the Soviet Union, Poland became an independent nation, and its economy is expected to improve steadily during the next sixty years.

Yet another form of suppressed evidence is committed by arguers who quote passages out of context from sources such as the Bible, the Constitution, and the Bill of Rights to support a conclusion that the passage was not intended to support. Consider, for example, the following argument against gun control:

> The Second Amendment to the Constitution states that the right of the people to keep and bear arms shall not be infringed. But a law controlling handguns would infringe the right to keep and bear arms. Therefore, a law controlling handguns would be unconstitutional.

In fact, the Second Amendment reads, "A well regulated militia being necessary to the security of a free state, the right of the people to keep and bear arms shall not be infringed." In other words, the amendment states that the right to bear arms shall not be infringed when the arms are necessary for the preservation of a well-regulated militia. Because a law controlling handguns (pistols) would have little effect on the preservation of a well-regulated militia, it is unlikely that such a law would be unconstitutional.

The suppressed evidence fallacy is similar to the form of begging the question in which the arguer leaves a key premise out of the argument. The difference is that suppressed evidence leaves out a premise that requires a *different* conclusion, while that form of begging the question leaves out a premise that is needed to support the *stated* conclusion. However, because both fallacies proceed by leaving a premise out of the argument, there are cases where the two fallacies overlap.

19. Equivocation

The fallacy of **equivocation** occurs when the conclusion of an argument depends on the fact that a word or phrase is used, either explicitly or implicitly, in two different senses in the argument. Such arguments are either invalid or have a false premise, and in either case they are unsound. Examples:

> Some triangles are obtuse. Whatever is obtuse is ignorant. Therefore, some triangles are ignorant.
>
> Any law can be repealed by the legislative authority. But the law of gravity is a law. Therefore, the law of gravity can be repealed by the legislative authority.
>
> We have a duty to do what is right. We have a right to speak out in defense of the innocent. Therefore, we have a duty to speak out in defense of the innocent.
>
> A mouse is an animal. Therefore, a large mouse is a large animal.

In the first argument "obtuse" is used in two different senses. In the first premise it describes a certain kind of angle, while in the second it means dull or stupid. The second argument equivocates on the word "law." In the first premise it means statutory law, and in the second it means law of nature. The third argument uses "right" in two senses. In the first premise "right" means morally correct, but in the second it means a

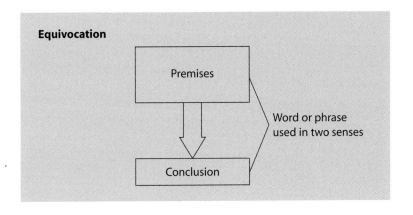

Equivocation

Premises

Word or phrase
used in two senses

Conclusion

just claim or power. The fourth argument illustrates the ambiguous use of a relative word. The word "large" means different things depending on the context. Other relative words that are susceptible to this same kind of ambiguity include "small," "good," "bad," "light," "heavy," "difficult," "easy," "tall," and "short."

To be convincing, an argument that commits an equivocation must use the equivocal word in ways that are subtly related. Of the examples just given, only the third might fulfill this requirement. Since both uses of the word "right" are related to ethics, the unalert observer may not notice the shift in meaning. Another technique is to spread the shift in meaning out over the course of a lengthy argument. Political speech makers often use phrases such as "equal opportunity," "gun control," "national security," and "environmental protection" in one way at the beginning of a speech and in quite another way at the end. A third technique consists in using such phrases one way in a speech to one group and in a different way in a speech to an opposing group. If the same people are not present at both speeches, the equivocation is not detected.

20. Amphiboly

The fallacy of **amphiboly** occurs when the arguer misinterprets an ambiguous statement and then draws a conclusion based on this faulty interpretation. The original statement is usually asserted by someone other than the arguer, and the ambiguity usually arises from a mistake in grammar or punctuation—a missing comma, a dangling modifier, an ambiguous antecedent of a pronoun, or some other careless arrangement of words. Because of this ambiguity, the statement may be understood in two clearly distinguishable ways. The arguer typically selects the unintended interpretation and proceeds to draw a conclusion based on it. Here are some examples:

> The tour guide said that standing in Greenwich Village, the Empire State Building could easily be seen. It follows that the Empire State Building is in Greenwich Village.

> John told Henry that he had made a mistake. It follows that John has at least the courage to admit his own mistakes.

> Professor Johnson said that he will give a lecture about heart failure in the biology lecture hall. It must be the case that a number of heart failures have occurred there recently.

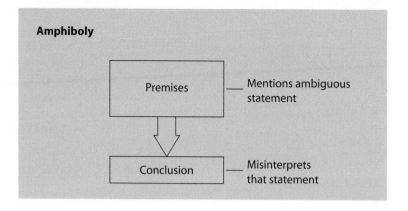

Amphiboly

Premises —— Mentions ambiguous statement

Conclusion —— Misinterprets that statement

The premise of the first argument contains a dangling modifier. Is it the observer or the Empire State Building that is supposed to be standing in Greenwich Village? The factually correct interpretation is the former. In the second argument the pronoun "he" has an ambiguous antecedent; it can refer either to John or to Henry. Perhaps John told Henry that *Henry* had made a mistake. In the third argument the ambiguity concerns what takes place in the biology lecture hall; is it the lecture or the heart failures? The correct interpretation is probably the former. The ambiguity can be eliminated by inserting commas ("Professor Johnson said that he will give a lecture, about heart failure, in the biology lecture hall") or by moving the ambiguous modifier ("Professor Johnson said that he will give a lecture in the biology lecture hall about heart failure"). Ambiguities of this sort are called *syntactical ambiguities.*

Two areas where cases of amphiboly cause serious problems involve contracts and wills. The drafters of these documents often express their intentions in terms of ambiguous statements, and alternate interpretations of these statements then lead to different conclusions. Examples:

> Mrs. Hart stated in her will, "I leave my 500-carat diamond necklace and my pet chinchilla to Alice and Theresa." Therefore, we conclude that Alice gets the necklace and Theresa gets the chinchilla.

> Mr. James signed a contract that reads, "In exchange for painting my house, I promise to pay David $5,000 and give him my new Cadillac only if he finishes the job by May 1." Therefore, since David did not finish until May 10, it follows that he gets neither the $5,000 nor the Cadillac.

In the first example the conclusion obviously favors Alice. Theresa is almost certain to argue that the gift of the necklace and chinchilla should be shared equally by her and Alice. Mrs. Hart could have avoided the dispute by adding either "respectively" or "collectively" to the end of the sentence. In the second example, the conclusion favors Mr. James. David will argue that the condition that he finish by May 1 affected only the Cadillac and that he therefore is entitled to the $5,000. The dispute could have been avoided by properly inserting a comma in the language of the promise.

Amphiboly differs from equivocation in two important ways. First, equivocation is always traced to an ambiguity in the meaning of a *word* or *phrase*, whereas amphiboly involves a syntactical ambiguity in a *statement*. The second difference is that amphiboly usually involves a mistake made by the arguer in interpreting an ambiguous statement made by someone else, whereas the ambiguity in equivocation is typically the arguer's own creation. If these distinctions are kept in mind, it is usually easy to distinguish amphiboly from equivocation. Occasionally, however, the two fallacies occur together, as the following example illustrates:

> The *Great Western Cookbook* recommends that we serve the oysters when thoroughly stewed. Apparently the delicate flavor is enhanced by the intoxicated condition of the diners.

First, it is unclear whether "stewed" refers to the oysters or to the diners, and so the argument commits an amphiboly. But if "stewed" refers to the oysters it means "cooked," and if it refers to the diners it means "intoxicated." Thus, the argument also involves an equivocation.

21. Composition

The fallacy of **composition** is committed when the conclusion of an argument depends on the erroneous transference of an attribute from the parts of something onto the whole. In other words, the fallacy occurs when it is argued that because the parts have a certain attribute, it follows that the whole has that attribute, too, and the situation is such that the attribute in question cannot be legitimately transferred from parts to whole. Examples:

> Maria likes anchovies. She also likes chocolate ice cream. Therefore, it is certain that she would like a chocolate sundae topped with anchovies.

> Each player on this basketball team is an excellent athlete. Therefore, the team as a whole is excellent.

> Each atom in this teacup is invisible. Therefore, this teacup is invisible.

> Sodium and chlorine, the atomic components of salt, are both deadly poisons. Therefore, salt is a deadly poison.

In these arguments the attributes that are transferred from the parts onto the whole are designated by the words "Maria likes," "excellent," "invisible," and "deadly poison," respectively. In each case the transference is illegitimate, and so the argument is fallacious.

Not every such transference is illegitimate, however. Consider the following arguments:

> Every atom in this teacup has mass. Therefore, this teacup has mass.

> Every component in this picket fence is white. Therefore, the whole fence is white.

In each case an attribute (having mass, being white) is transferred from the parts onto the whole, but these transferences are quite legitimate. Indeed, the fact that the atoms have mass is the very reason *why* the teacup has mass. The same reasoning extends to the fence. Thus, the acceptability of these arguments is attributable, at least in part, to the *legitimate* transference of an attribute from parts onto the whole.

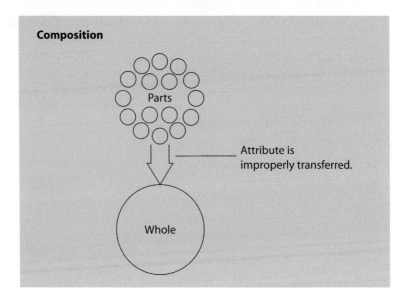

Composition

Parts

Attribute is improperly transferred.

Whole

These examples illustrate the fact that the fallacy of composition is indeed an informal fallacy. It cannot be discovered by a mere inspection of the form of an argument—that is, by the mere observation that an attribute is being transferred from parts onto the whole. In addition, detecting this fallacy requires a general knowledge of the situation and of the nature of the attribute being transferred. The critic must be certain that, given the situation, the transference of this particular attribute is not allowed.

Further caution is required by the fact that composition is sometimes confused with hasty generalization. The only time this confusion is possible is when the "whole" is a class (such as the class of people in a city or the class of trees in a forest), and the "parts" are the members of the class. In such a case composition proceeds from the members of the class to the class itself. Hasty generalization, on the other hand, proceeds from the specific to the general. Because it is sometimes easy to mistake a statement about a class for a general statement, composition can be mistaken for hasty generalization. Such a mistake can be avoided if one is careful to keep in mind the distinction between these two kinds of statements. This distinction falls back on the difference between the **collective** and the **distributive** predication of an attribute. Consider the following statements:

Fleas are small.
Fleas are numerous.

The first statement is a general statement. The attribute of being small is predicated distributively; that is, it is assigned (or distributed) to each and every flea in the class. Each and every flea in the class is said to be small. The second statement, on the other hand, is a statement about a class as a whole, or what we will call a "class statement." The attribute of being numerous is predicated collectively; in other words, it is assigned not to the individual fleas but to the *class* of fleas. The meaning of the statement is not that each and every flea is numerous but that the class of fleas is large.

To distinguish composition from hasty generalization, therefore, the following procedure should be followed. Examine the conclusion of the argument. If the conclusion is a general statement—that is, a statement in which an attribute is predicated distributively to each and every member of a class—the fallacy committed is hasty generalization. But if the conclusion is a class statement—that is, a statement in which an attribute is predicated collectively to a class as a whole—the fallacy is composition. Example:

> Less gasoline is consumed by a car than by a truck. Therefore, less gasoline is consumed in the United States by cars than by trucks.

At first sight this argument might appear to proceed from the specific to the general and, consequently, to commit a hasty generalization. But in fact the conclusion is not a general statement at all but a class statement. The conclusion states that the whole class of cars uses less gas than does the whole class of trucks (which is false, because there are many more cars than trucks). Since the attribute of using less gasoline is predicated collectively, the fallacy committed is composition.

22. Division

The fallacy of **division** is the exact reverse of composition. As composition goes from parts to whole, division goes from whole to parts. The fallacy is committed when the conclusion of an argument depends on the erroneous transference of an attribute from a whole (or a class) onto its parts (or members). Examples:

> Salt is a nonpoisonous compound. Therefore, its component elements, sodium and chlorine, are nonpoisonous.

> This jigsaw puzzle, when assembled, is circular in shape. Therefore, each piece is circular in shape.

> The Royal Society is over 300 years old. Professor Thompson is a member of the Royal Society. Therefore, Professor Thompson is over 300 years old.

In each case the attribute, designated respectively by the terms "nonpoisonous," "circular in shape," and "over 300 years old," is illegitimately transferred from the whole or class onto the parts or members. As with the fallacy of composition, however, this kind of transference is not always illegitimate. The following arguments contain no fallacy:

> This teacup has mass. Therefore, the atoms that compose this teacup have mass.

> This field of poppies is uniformly orange. Therefore, the individual poppies are orange.

Obviously, one must be acquainted with the situation and the nature of the attribute being transferred to decide whether the fallacy of division is actually committed.

Just as composition can sometimes be confused with hasty generalization (converse accident), division can sometimes be confused with accident. As with composition, this confusion can occur only when the "whole" is a class. In such a case, division proceeds from the class to the members, whereas accident proceeds from the general to the specific. Thus, if a class statement is mistaken for a general statement, division may be mistaken for accident. To avoid such a mistake, one should analyze the premises of

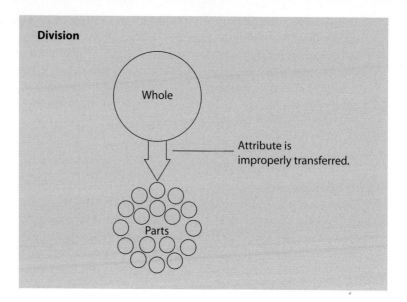

Division

Whole

Attribute is
improperly transferred.

Parts

the argument. If the premises contain a general statement, the fallacy committed is accident; but if they contain a class statement, the fallacy is division. Example:

Stanley Steamers have almost disappeared.
This car is a Stanley Steamer.
Therefore, this car has almost disappeared.

The first premise is not a general statement but a class statement. The attribute of having almost disappeared is predicated collectively. Accordingly, the fallacy committed is division, not accident.

This example also illustrates how cases of division that involve class statements can include a subtle form of equivocation. In the conclusion, the word "disappeared" means fading from vision, as when the lights are turned down; but in the first premise it means rarely seen. The equivocation is a kind of secondary fallacy that results from the primary fallacy, which is division.

The next example shows how division turns up in arguments dealing with averages.

The average American family has 2.5 children.
The Jones family is an average American family.
Therefore, the Jones family has 2.5 children.

The statement "The average American family has 2.5 children" is not a general statement, but rather a class statement. The sense of the statement is not that each and every family has 2.5 children, but that the class of families is reducible to about 55 percent children and 45 percent adults. Thus, once again, the fallacy is division, and not accident.

In our account of composition and division, we have presented examples of arguments that commit these fallacies in conjunction with other, structurally similar arguments that do not. Because of the structural similarity between arguments that do and do not commit these fallacies, composition and division are classified as fallacies of grammatical analogy.

SUMMARY OF INFORMAL FALLACIES

Fallacies of Relevance

Appeal to force: Arguer threatens reader/listener.

Appeal to pity: Arguer elicits pity from reader/listener.

Appeal to the people (direct): Arguer arouses mob mentality.

Appeal to the people (indirect): Arguer appeals to reader/listener's desire for security, love, respect, etc.

Argument against the person (abusive): Arguer verbally abuses other arguer.

Argument against the person (circumstantial): Arguer presents other arguer as predisposed to argue this way.

Argument against the person (*tu quoque*): Arguer presents other arguer as hypocrite.

Accident: General rule is applied to a specific case it was not intended to cover.

Straw man: Arguer distorts opponent's argument and then attacks the distorted argument.

Missing the point: Arguer draws conclusion different from that supported by premises.

Red herring: Arguer leads reader/listener off track.

Fallacies of Weak Induction

Appeal to unqualified authority: Arguer cites untrustworthy authority.

Appeal to ignorance: Premises report that nothing is known or proved, and then a conclusion is drawn.

Hasty generalization: Conclusion is drawn from an atypical sample.

False cause: Conclusion depends on nonexistent or minor causal connection.

Slippery slope: Conclusion depends on unlikely chain reaction.

Weak analogy: Conclusion depends on defective analogy.

Fallacies of Presumption

Begging the question: Arguer creates the illusion that inadequate premises are adequate by leaving out a key premise, by restating the conclusion as a premise, or by reasoning in a circle.

Complex question: Multiple questions are concealed in a single question.

False dichotomy: "Either ... or ..." statement hides additional alternatives.

Suppressed evidence: Arguer ignores important evidence that requires a different conclusion.

Fallacies of Ambiguity
Equivocation: Conclusion depends on a shift in meaning of a word or phrase.

Amphiboly: Conclusion depends on the wrong interpretation of a syntactically ambiguous statement.

Fallacies of Grammatical Analogy
Composition: Attribute is wrongly transferred from parts to whole.

Division: Attribute is wrongly transferred from whole to parts.

EXERCISE 3.4

I. Identify the fallacies of presumption, ambiguity, and grammatical analogy committed by the following arguments, giving a brief explanation for your answer. If no fallacy is committed, write "no fallacy."

★1. Either we require forced sterilization of Third World peoples or the world population will explode and all of us will die. We certainly don't want to die, so we must require forced sterilization.

2. Every sentence in this paragraph is well written. Therefore, the paragraph is well written.

3. An athlete is a human being. Therefore, a good athlete is a good human being.

★4. James said that he saw a picture of a beautiful girl stashed in Stephen's locker. We can only conclude that Stephen has broken the rules, because girls are not allowed in the locker room.

5. Why is it so difficult for you to reach a decision?

6. Water will quench one's thirst. Water is composed of hydrogen and oxygen. Therefore, hydrogen and oxygen will quench one's thirst.

★7. People who lack humility have no sense of beauty, because everyone who has a sense of beauty also has humility.

8. Butane is combustible. Therefore, it burns.

9. Twenty years ago, Kung Fong, the great sumo wrestler, could have yanked up one of the fir trees in the new municipal arboretum with a single pull. Therefore, since Mr. Fong is as strong today as he was then, he could just as easily pull up one of those trees today.

★10. If Thomas gives Marie a ring, then Thomas and Marie will be engaged. Thomas did give Marie a ring. In fact, he phoned her just the other night. Therefore, Thomas and Marie are engaged.

11. Alex, I heard your testimony in court earlier today. Tell me, why did you lie on the witness stand?

12. Johnson is employed by the General Services Administration, and everyone knows that the GSA is the most inefficient branch of the government. Therefore, Johnson must be an inefficient worker.

★13. All men are mortal. Therefore, some day man will disappear from the earth.

14. Each and every cell in this carrot is 90 percent water. Therefore, the entire carrot is 90 percent water.

15. George said that he was interviewing for a job drilling oil wells in the supervisor's office. We can only conclude that the supervisor must have an awfully dirty office.

★16. During the fifty years that Mr. Jones worked, he contributed $90,000 to Social Security. Now that he is retired, he stands to collect $200,000 from the system. Obviously he will collect a much greater monetary value than he contributed.

17. Either you marry me right now or I'll be forced to leave you and never speak to you again. I'm sure you wouldn't want me to do that. Therefore, you'll marry me right now.

18. Either Meg Ryan or Britney Spears is a popular singer. Meg Ryan is not a popular singer. Therefore, Britney Spears is a popular singer.

★19. Switzerland is 48 percent Protestant. Heidi Gilsing is a Swiss. Therefore, Heidi Gilsing is 48 percent Protestant.

20. Picasso is the greatest artist of the twentieth century. We know that this is so because art critics have described him in these terms. These art critics are correct in their assessment because they have a more keenly developed sense of appreciation than the average person. This is true because it takes a more keenly developed sense of appreciation to realize that Picasso is the greatest artist of the twentieth century.

21. An atomic bomb causes more damage than a conventional bomb. Therefore, during World War II more damage was caused by atomic bombs than by conventional bombs.

★22. Sylvia, I saw you shopping for wine the other day. Incidentally, are you still drinking excessively?

23. The author warns about numerous computational errors in his accounting text. Therefore, he must have written it very carelessly.

24. Emeralds are seldom found in this country, so you should be careful not to misplace your emerald ring.

★25. Of course abortion is permissible. After all, a woman has a right to do as she pleases with her own body.

II. Answer "true" or "false" to the following statements:

1. Arguments that commit the fallacy of begging the question are normally valid.
2. The effect of begging the question is to hide the fact that a premise may not be true.
3. The correct way of responding to a complex question is to divide the question into its component questions and answer each separately.
4. False dichotomy always involves an "either . . . or . . ." statement, at least implicitly.
5. The fallacy of equivocation arises from a syntactical defect in a statement.
6. The fallacy of amphiboly usually involves the ambiguous use of a single word.
7. Amphiboly usually arises from the arguer's misinterpreting a statement made by someone else.
8. The fallacy of composition always proceeds from whole to parts.
9. The fallacy of division always proceeds from parts to whole.
10. A general statement makes an assertion about each and every member of a class.
11. A class statement makes an assertion about a class as a whole.
12. In the statement "Divorces are increasing," an attribute is predicated distributively.
13. In the statement "Waistlines are increasing," an attribute is predicated distributively.
14. Composition and division involve the distributive predication of an attribute.
15. Equivocation and amphiboly are classified as fallacies of ambiguity.

III. Identify the fallacies of relevance, weak induction, presumption, ambiguity, and grammatical analogy committed by the following arguments, giving a brief explanation for your answer. If no fallacy is committed, write "no fallacy."

★1. In his *History of the American Civil War*, Jeffry Noland argues that the war had little to do with slavery. However, as a historian from Alabama, Noland could not possibly present an accurate account. Therefore, his arguments should be discounted.

2. Mr. Wilson said that on July 4 he went out on the veranda and watched the fireworks go up in his pajamas. We conclude that Mr. Wilson must have had an exciting evening.

3. Televangelist Jerry Falwell said that God's anger with feminism led to the destruction of the World Trade Center. Given Falwell's closeness to God, we have no alternative than to blame the feminists for this atrocity.

★4. A crust of bread is better than nothing. Nothing is better than true love. Therefore, a crust of bread is better than true love.

5. Every member of the Delta Club is over 70 years old. Therefore, the Delta Club must be over 70 years old.

6. Of course you should eat Wheaties. Wheaties is the breakfast of champions, you know.

★7. It's obvious that animals have rights. Just look at how powerless they are in comparison with modern humans.

8. The idea that black people in this country live in poverty is ridiculous. Look at Bill Cosby. He's a millionaire. And so are Denzel Washington and Oprah Winfrey.

9. No one has ever proved that the human fetus is not a person with rights. Therefore, abortion is morally wrong.

★10. California condors are rapidly disappearing. This bird is a California condor. Therefore, this bird should disappear any minute now.

11. When a car breaks down so often that repairs become pointless, the car is thrown on the junk heap. Similarly, when a person becomes old and diseased, he or she should be mercifully put to death.

12. The twenty-story Carson Building is constructed of concrete blocks. Each and every concrete block in the structure can withstand an earthquake of 9.5 on the Richter scale. Therefore, the building can withstand an earthquake of 9.5 on the Richter scale.

★13. Terrorists from the Middle East have crossed our borders and traveled through the country at will. Obviously the Immigration Service has not been doing its job.

14. This administration is not anti-German, as it has been alleged. Germany is a great country. It has contributed immensely to the world's artistic treasury. Goethe and Schiller made magnificent contributions to literature, and Bach, Beethoven, Wagner, and Brahms did the same in music.

15. Paul, it was great to see you at the party the other night. Everyone there was doing crack. Incidentally, how long have you been dealing that stuff?

★16. Duane Richards, CEO of the Western Fuels Association, an organization that supplies coal to electric utilities, says that there is no evidence that burning fossil fuels causes global warming. In view of Mr. Richards's wealth of expertise in the area of fossil fuels, we must conclude that what he says about global warming is true.

17. Senator Kennedy's arguments in favor of health care for the poor and aged should be ignored. Kennedy is a do-gooder who supports this kind of legislation only to get his name in the newspapers.

18. Professor Andrews, surely I deserve a B in logic. I know that I have gotten Fs on all the tests, but if you give me an F for my final grade, I will lose my scholarship. That will force me to drop out of school, and my poor, aged parents, who yearn to see me graduate, will be grief stricken for the rest of their lives.

★19. Molecules are in constant random motion. The Statue of Liberty is composed of molecules. Therefore, the Statue of Liberty is in constant random motion.

20. Either we have prayer in our public schools or the moral fabric of society will disintegrate. The choice should be obvious.

21. White sheep eat more than black sheep (because there are more of them). Therefore, this white sheep eats more than that black sheep.

★22. If someone rents a piece of land and plants crops on it, the landlord is never permitted to come and take those crops for himself when harvest time arrives. Similarly, if couples enlist the services of a surrogate mother to provide them with a baby, the mother should never be allowed to welch on the deal and keep the baby for herself once it is born.

23. Motives and desires exert forces on people, causing them to choose one thing over another. But force is a physical quantity, governed by the laws of physics. Therefore, human choices are governed by the laws of physics.

24. Each and every brick in the completely brick-faced Wainright Building has a reddish brown color. Therefore, the Wainright Building has a reddish brown color.

★25. Humanitarian groups have argued in favor of housing for the poor. Apparently what they want is another high-density project. Unfortunately, these projects have been tried in the past and have failed. In no time they turn into ghettos with astronomical rates of crime and delinquency. Chicago's Cabrini-Green is a prime example. Clearly, these humanitarian arguments are not what they seem.

26. Pauline said that after she had removed her new mink coat from the shipping carton she threw it into the trash. We conclude that Pauline has no appreciation for fine furs.

27. We know that induction will provide dependable results in the future because it has always worked in the past. Whatever has consistently worked in the past will continue to work in the future, and we know that this is true because it has been established by induction.

★28. What goes up must come down. The price of housing has been going up for years. Therefore, it will surely come down soon.

29. Mr. Prime Minister, I am certain you will want to release the members of our National Liberation Group whom you currently hold in prison. After all, I'm sure you will want to avoid having car bombs go off in the centers of your most heavily populated cities.

30. San Diego has the same latitude as Yuma, Arizona, and San Diego enjoys moderate temperatures through the summer months. Therefore, probably Yuma enjoys moderate temperatures through the summer months.

★31. We're all familiar with the complaint that over 40 million Americans are without health insurance. But America's doctors, nurses, and hospitals are among the best in the world. Thousands of people come from abroad every year to be treated here. Clearly there is nothing wrong with our health care system.

32. Real estate mogul Donald Trump argues that good management is essential to any business. But who is he to talk? Trump's own mismanagement drove Trump Hotels and Casino Resorts into bankruptcy twice in twelve years.

33. The farmers of our state have asked that we introduce legislation to provide subsidies for soybeans. Unfortunately, we will have to turn down their request. If we give subsidies to the soybean farmers, then the corn and wheat growers

will ask for the same thing. Then it will be the cotton growers, citrus growers, truck farmers, and cattle raisers. In the end, the cost will be astronomical.

★34. The travel brochure states that walking up O'Connell Street, the statue of Parnell comes into view. Apparently that statue has no trouble getting around.

35. Criminals are basically stupid, because anyone who isn't basically stupid wouldn't be a criminal.

36. Professor Glazebrooks's theory about the origin of the Martian craters is undoubtedly true. Rudolph Orkin, the great concert pianist, announced his support of the theory in this morning's newspaper.

★37. Mr. Franklin has lost at the craps table for the last ten throws of the dice. Therefore, it is extremely likely that he will win on the next throw.

38. Raising a child is like growing a tree. Sometimes violent things, such as cutting off branches, have to be done to force the tree to grow straight. Similarly, corporal punishment must sometimes be inflicted on children to force them to develop properly.

39. Good steaks are rare these days, so don't order yours well done.

★40. The Book of Mormon is true because it was written by Joseph Smith. Joseph Smith wrote the truth because he was divinely inspired. We know that Joseph Smith was divinely inspired because the Book of Mormon says that he was, and the Book of Mormon is true.

41. The students attending Bradford College come from every one of the fifty states. Michelle attends Bradford College. Therefore, Michelle comes from every one of the fifty states.

42. Rhubarb pie is a dessert. Therefore, whoever eats rhubarb pie eats a dessert.

★43. The vast majority of car accidents occur within twenty miles of one's home. Apparently it is much more dangerous to drive close to home than far away from home.

44. Either you're with us or you're with the terrorists. The choice should be easy.

45. Nobody has ever proved that weapons of mass destruction do not exist in Iraq. Therefore, those weapons must be in that country somewhere.

★46. On Friday I took Virginia out to dinner. She told me that if I wasn't interested in a serious relationship, I should forget about dating her. On Saturday I took Margie to a film. When we discussed it afterward over a drink, she couldn't understand why I wasn't interested in babies. Women are all alike. All they want is a secure marriage.

47. Dozens of species of plants and animals are being wiped out every year, even though we have laws to prevent it. Clearly, we should repeal the Endangered Species Act.

48. People are driving their cars like maniacs tonight. There must be a full moon.

★49. A line is composed of points. Points have no length. Therefore, a line has no length.

50. Are you in favor of the ruinous economic policy of the Democratic Platform Committee?

IV. Identify the arguments in the following dialogue, then discuss each of them in terms of the fallacies presented in this section and the previous section. You should be able to find at least one case of each fallacy.

"Thanks for giving me a lift home," Paul says to his friend Steve, as they head toward the freeway.

"No problem; it's on my way," says Steve.

"Uh oh," warns Paul suddenly, "watch out ahead. Looks like the police have pulled somebody over."

"Thanks," Steve says. "Hope they don't beat the guy up."

"Not a chance," says Paul. "Why would you say that?"

"You're an optimist," answers Steve. "Most cops are animals; they beat up on anybody they want to. You remember Rodney King, don't you? Those cops in L.A. put King in the hospital for no reason at all. That should prove I'm right."

"I think you're overreacting," Paul says. "Daryl Gates, the L.A. police chief at the time, said the King incident was an aberration. Since he was chief, I think we should take him at his word."

"But Gates was a lunatic who refused to acknowledge even our most basic rights," Steve persists. "Also, if you recall, he was forced to resign after the King incident. I know we don't live in L.A., but our police department is just as bad as theirs. So you can bet that our friend back there is just as abusive as any of them."

"Wait a minute," Paul argues. "As far as I know, nobody has ever proved that our police force is the slightest bit violent. You've no right to draw such a conclusion."

"Well, listen to this," Steve counters, as he changes lanes and turns onto the freeway. "About a week ago, I was with my friend Casey. When I left him, he was perfectly okay, but he was picked up for going through a stop sign on the way home. I saw him a couple of days later, and he had a big bruise under his right eye. The cop who stopped Casey must have hit him with his baton."

"Hold on. Did you ask Casey what happened?"

"No. I didn't have to," says Steve, a bit righteously. "I asked Casey's wife what happened between Casey and the cop, and she said he hit him. Those were her exact words, so that was good enough for me. I bet the cop's a maniac."

"Good grief," answers his friend. "How long will it take you to get over your warped view of things?"

"My way of looking at things isn't warped," Steve insists. "The problem is, you and I are both white. If you were black, you'd see things differently. Police brutality toward African Americans is way out of hand."

"Well," counters Paul, "a study done recently by an independent agency might interest you. According to that study, for every African American whom the police use force against, there's a white person they also use force against. That proves the police treat African Americans no worse than they do whites."

"I've never heard of that study, but it seems to me there must be something wrong with it," insists Steve.

"Well, the results of that study are borne out in my experience," says Paul. "I've been pulled over three or four times in the past couple of years, and the officers have always been extremely courteous. I can only conclude that the vast majority of these allegations of police brutality are the product of fertile imaginations."

"Again, your naïveté amazes me," Steve answers, dumbfounded. "First of all, you forget that you're white and you drive a new Mercedes. Don't you think that makes a difference? In fact, that's the trouble with all these arguments that downplay police brutality. They're all concocted by white people."

"Well, the fact remains that we have a major crime problem in this country," Paul argues. "Combating crime requires a few concessions, and you do want to combat crime, don't you?"

"Sure," Steve replies grudgingly, "but at what expense? Do innocent people have to get their heads bashed in?"

"Well, I think what it comes down to is this," says Paul. "Either you allow the police to use whatever force they find necessary, or the criminals will take over this country. Now you certainly don't want that to happen, do you?"

"No, but that's the crucial question," Steve says, exiting from the freeway. "When and how much force is necessary?"

"Well, you remember when the police apprehended that serial killer a few weeks ago? When the police made the arrest, the killer attacked them. So, the police can use force when attacked."

"I agree," responds Steve thoughtfully. "But what about the way the police treated those peaceful right-to-lifers who were demonstrating in front of the abortion clinic the other day? Many of them were elderly and posed no physical threat. But the cops used those contraptions—what do you call them, nimchucks, nomchucks, I don't know—to squeeze the old folks' wrists, causing great pain and injury, and they hit the old people on the head with their batons. Do you think that was necessary?"

"Of course it was," answers Paul, agitatedly. "Those people attacked the police—they hurled epithets at them."

"Honestly, I don't know how we've managed to stay friends all these years," Steve says with some frustration. "By the way, do you know what it says on the back of all police cars? It says 'To Protect and Serve.' Now if you hired a servant to take care of you, you'd get rid of him if he disobeyed you. Right?"

"Probably."

"Well, isn't it true," Steve asks, "that whenever a police officer disobeys one of us taxpayers, that officer should be fired?"

"That may be stretching it a bit," Paul laughs.

"But seriously," continues Steve, "I think what we need is some screening device to keep violent types from ever becoming cops."

"Well, you'll be happy to know that exactly such a device has been used for the past twenty-one years," Paul states. "Before entering the police academy, every applicant goes through a battery of psychological tests that positively eliminates all the macho types and the ones prone to violence. This ensures the individual officers are nonviolent, so we know the entire police force is nonviolent."

"Hmm. Maybe your so-called solution is really the problem," Steve suggests, as he pulls up in front of Paul's house. "We've had psychological testing for twenty-one years, and all that time, police violence has been on the rise. Perhaps we should get rid of the testing program."

"Well, I don't know about the logic of that," Paul muses, stepping out of the car. "But like you said, we've been friends for a long time, so I guess we can disagree. Thanks for the ride and the discussion. See you tomorrow!"

"Sure," Steve murmurs. "Tomorrow."

3.5   Fallacies in Ordinary Language

This section addresses two topics. The first concerns the challenge of detecting the fallacies of others in ordinary language, and the second relates to the goal of avoiding fallacies in one's own arguments.

Detecting Fallacies

Most of the informal fallacies that we have seen thus far have been clear-cut, easily recognizable instances of a specific mistake. When fallacies occur in ordinary usage, however, they are often neither clear-cut nor easily recognizable. The reason is that there are innumerable ways of making mistakes in arguing, and variations inevitably occur that may not be exact instances of any specifically named fallacy. In addition, one fallacious mode of arguing may be mixed with one or more others, and the strands of reasoning may have to be disentangled before the fallacies can be named. Yet another problem arises from the fact that arguments in ordinary language are rarely presented in complete form. A premise or conclusion often is left unexpressed, which may obscure the nature of the evidence that is presented or the strength of the link between premises and conclusion.

Consider, for example, the following letter that appeared in a newspaper:

> God, I am sick of "women's rights"! Every time one turns on the news we hear about some form of discrimination against some poor female who wants to be a fireman—or some "remark" that suggests or implies women are inferior to men.
>
> I, for one, do not want to be rescued by a "woman fireman," especially if I am a 6-foot-2 male and she is a 5-foot-6 female.
>
> Why is it that women find their "role" so degrading? What is wrong with being a wife and mother, staying home while the male goes out and "hunts for food" and brings it home to his family?
>
> I don't think women have proven themselves to be as inventive, as capable (on the average) of world leadership, as physically capable, or as "courageous" as men. They have yet to fight a war (the average American woman) and let's face it ladies, who wants to?
>
> Whether a person is female, black, white, handicapped—whatever—*ability* is what counts in the final analysis. Women cannot demand "equality"—no one can—unless it is earned.
>
> When push comes to shove and a damsel is in distress, she is hard-pressed to protect herself and usually has to be rescued by a man. Until I can move a piano, beat off a potential robber or rapist, or fight a war, I am quite content to be a woman, thank you.
>
> (Patricia Kelley)

This letter presents numerous fallacies. The phrase "poor female who wants to be a fireman" suggests a mild *ad hominem* abusive, and equating women's rights in general with the right to be a firefighter suggests a straw man. The second paragraph commits another straw man fallacy by supposing that the job of firefighter inevitably entails such activities as climbing up ladders and rescuing people. Surely there are many male firefighters who cannot do this. The same paragraph also can be interpreted as begging the question: Do women who want to be firefighters want the specific job of rescuing tall men?

The third paragraph throws out a red herring. The issue is whether women have the right to be considered for a job of their choice and whether they must be paid as much as a man in the same situation. Whether there is something wrong with being a wife and mother is quite a different issue. Also, the reference to men hunting for food suggests a possible begging of the question: Are we still locked into a "hunter-gatherer" social structure?

The paragraph about whether women have proved themselves to be as inventive, capable, and courageous as men begs yet another question: Assuming, for the sake of argument, that this is true, have women been allowed to occupy roles in society where such inventiveness, capability, and courageousness can be demonstrated? Furthermore, this paragraph commits a red herring fallacy and/or misses the point: Even if women have not proved this, what does that have to do with the issue? Most jobs do not require any high degree of inventiveness or courage or a capacity for world leadership.

The paragraph about ability begs yet another question: Is it in fact the case that women have less ability? I am not aware that anything of the sort has ever been proved. Finally, the last paragraph throws out another red herring. What does moving pianos and beating off rapists have to do with most jobs or the question of equal pay for equal work?

Probably the single most important requirement for detecting fallacies in ordinary language is alertness. The reader or listener must pay close attention to what the arguer is saying. What is the conclusion? What are the reasons given in support of the conclusion? Are the reasons relevant to the conclusion? Do the reasons support the conclusion? If the reader or listener is half asleep or lounging in that passive, drugged-out state that attends much television viewing, then none of these questions will receive answers. Under those circumstances the reader or listener will never be able to detect informal fallacies, and he or she will accept even the worst reasoning without the slightest hesitation.

Avoiding Fallacies

Why do people commit informal fallacies? Unfortunately, this question admits of no simple, straightforward answer. The reasons underlying the commission of fallacies are complex and interconnected. However, we can identify three factors that lead to most of the informal mistakes in reasoning. The first is intent. Many fallacies are committed intentionally. The arguer may know full well that his or her reasoning is defective but goes ahead with it anyway because of some benefit for himself or herself or some other person. All of the informal fallacies we have studied can be used for that purpose, but some of them are particularly well suited to it. These include the appeal to force, appeal to pity, appeal to the people, straw man, *ad hominem*, complex question, false dichotomy, and suppressed evidence. Here is such a case of appeal to force:

> I deserve a chocolate sundae for dessert, and if you don't buy me one right now, I'll start screaming and embarrass you in front of all of the people in this restaurant.

And here is a case of false dichotomy that conveys the appearance of being intentionally committed:

> Either you take me on a Caribbean cruise, or I'll have a nervous breakdown. It's up to you.

The key to avoiding fallacies that are intentionally committed probably lies in some form of moral education. The arguer must come to realize that using intellectually dishonest means to acquire something he or she does not deserve is just another form of cheating.

The situation becomes more complicated, however, when the sought-after goal is morally justified. Arguers sometimes use fallacious reasoning intentionally to trick a person into doing something that is really for that person's own good. Here is a false dichotomy of that sort:

> Either you control your eating and get regular exercise, or you'll have a heart attack and die. The choice is yours.

Given the beneficial consequences of controlled eating and regular exercise, some moral philosophers will find nothing wrong with this argument. Others will contend that manipulating someone into doing something violates human dignity. In either case, such arguments are logically unacceptable.

The second factor that leads to the commission of informal fallacies is a careless mental posture combined with an emotional disposition favoring or opposing some person or thing. The careless mental posture opens the door, so to speak, to fallacious reasoning, and the emotional disposition pushes the arguer through it. Even people who are thoroughly versed in the informal fallacies occasionally succumb to the deadly combination of mental carelessness and emotional impetus. For example, arguments such as the following *ad hominem* abusive can sometimes be heard in the halls of university philosophy departments:

> Professor Ballard's argument in favor of restructuring our course offering isn't worth a hoot. But what would you expect from someone who publishes in such mediocre journals? And did you hear Ballard's recent lecture on Aristotle? It was total nonsense.

When people who should know better are confronted with the fact that their argument commits a common fallacy, they often admit with embarrassment that they have not been thinking and then revise their argument according to logical principles. In contrast, people who are not familiar with the distinction between good and fallacious reasoning will likely deny that there is anything wrong with their argument. Thus, the key to avoiding fallacies that arise from mental carelessness lies in developing a thorough familiarity with the informal fallacies, combined with a habitual realization of how emotions affect people's reasoning. Everyone should realize that unchecked emotions are an open invitation to illogical reasoning, and they can lead a person to commit quite blindly every one of the fallacies we have studied thus far.

The third factor that leads to the commission of informal fallacies is far more difficult to contend with than the first two. It consists in the influence of what we might call the "worldview" of the arguer. By worldview we mean a cognitive network of beliefs, attitudes, habits, memories, values, and other elements that conditions and renders meaningful the world in which we live. Beginning in infancy, our worldview emerges quietly and unconsciously from enveloping influences—culture, language, gender, religion, politics, and social and economic status. As we grow older, it continues to develop through the shaping forces of education and experience. Once it has taken root, our worldview determines how each of us sizes up the world in which we live. Given a set of circumstances, it indicates what is reasonable to believe and what is unreasonable.

In connection with the construction and evaluation of arguments, an arguer's worldview determines the answer to questions about importance, relevance, causal connections, the qualifications of authorities, whether a sample is typical or atypical of a group, what can and cannot be taken for granted, and other factors. However, because these determinations inevitably involve unexamined presuppositions, the arguer's worldview can lead to the commission of informal fallacies. All of the fallacies we have studied so far are likely candidates, but the ones especially susceptible are appeal to pity, straw man, missing the point, appeal to unqualified authority, hasty generalization, false cause, slippery slope, weak analogy, begging the question, false dichotomy, and suppressed evidence.

Thus, a person with a victim mentality may think that his pathetic circumstances really justify some favorable treatment; an uncritical conservative may cite with complete confidence the authority of Rush Limbaugh; a person with a racist worldview may conclude that the errant behavior of a handful of Asians, African Americans, or Hispanics really is typical of the larger class; a person with a liberal worldview may quite innocently distort an opponent's argument by equating it with fascism; a pro-life arguer may consider it obvious that the fetus is a person with rights, while a pro-choice arguer may take it for granted that the fetus is not a person with rights, and so on. Consider, for example, the following argument from analogy:

> A court trial is like a professional football game. In a professional football game, the most important thing is winning. Similarly, in a trial, the most important thing is winning.

This argument is consistent with the worldview of many, if not most, lawyers. Lawyers are trained as advocates, and when they enter a courtroom they see themselves going into battle for their clients. In any battle, winning is the most important objective. But this viewpoint presupposes that truth and justice are either unattainable in the courtroom or of secondary importance. Thus, while many lawyers would evaluate this argument as nonfallacious, many nonlawyers would reject it as a weak analogy.

For another example, consider the following causal inference:

> After enslaving most of Eastern Europe for nearly fifty years, the evil Soviet empire finally collapsed. Obviously God listened to our prayers.

This argument reflects the worldview of many theists. It presupposes that there is a God, that God listens to prayers, that God is affected by prayers, that God has the power to influence the course of history, and that God does influence the course of history. While the theist is likely to consider this argument a good one, the atheist will reject it as a blatant case of false cause.

To avoid fallacies that arise from the influence of worldviews, the arguer must acknowledge and critique his or her presuppositions. Doing so inclines the arguer to couch his or her arguments in language that takes those presuppositions into account. The result is nearly always an argument that is more intelligently crafted, and, it is hoped, more persuasive. However, the task of recognizing and critiquing one's presuppositions is not easy. Presuppositions are intrinsically linked to one's worldview, and many people are not even aware that they have a worldview. The reason is that worldviews are formed through a process that is largely unconscious. Thus, the arguer must first recognize that he or she has a worldview and must then exercise constant vigilance over the presuppositions it comprises.

Even after one's presuppositions have been exposed and thoroughly critiqued, however, there is no guarantee that one's arguments will agree with the arguments of others who have critiqued their worldviews. This is because a person's worldview reflects the unique perspective that person has on the world. No two people share exactly the same perspective. Nevertheless, disclosing and critiquing the presuppositions in one's worldview lays a foundation for meaningful communication with other reasonable arguers, and it provides a context of reasonableness for working out disagreements.

In summary, the three factors that are probably responsible for most informal fallacies are intent, mental carelessness combined with emotional dispositions, and unexamined presuppositions in the arguer's worldview. However, these factors rarely occur in isolation. In the vast majority of cases, two or all three conspire to produce fallacious reasoning. This fact exacerbates the difficulty in avoiding informal fallacies in one's own arguments and in detecting fallacies in the arguments of others.

Now let us consider some cases of real-life arguments in light of the factors we have just discussed. All are taken from letters to the editors of newspapers and magazines. The first relates to affirmative action programs:

> I'm a nonracist, nonsexist, white male born in 1969, who has never owned a slave, treated anyone as inferior because of his or her race, or sexually harassed a female co-worker. In other words, I don't owe women or minorities a thing. Since when are people required to pay for the sins of their predecessors simply because they belong to the same race or gender?
>
> (Ben Gibbons)

The author of this argument presupposes that racist and sexist patterns in society have not benefited him in any way. Among other things, he presupposes that his white ancestors in no way benefited from their being white and that none of these benefits passed down to him. On the other hand, given that he has received such benefits, he may presuppose that he is not obligated to pay any of them back. Of course, none of these things may have occurred, but the author should at least address these issues. Because he does not address them, the argument begs the question.

The next argument relates to second-hand smoke from cigarettes:

> Now, besides lung cancer and other nasty business, second-hand smoke causes deafness and impotence. Was second-hand smoke a problem when people heated their homes solely by fireplaces? How about those romantic teepees with the smoke hole at the top? And what about fireplaces in new homes? Let's have some research

about the problems caused by these as well as barbecues. A little cancer with your
hot dog, anyone?

(Pat Sharp)

This argument seems to commit the fallacy of equivocation. The arguer begins by
using "second-hand smoke" to refer to the smoke from burning tobacco, and then
uses the term to refer to the smoke from fireplaces, teepee fires, and barbecues. Smoke
from burning tobacco is clearly not the same thing as smoke from burning wood or
charcoal. Alternately, the argument might be seen to beg the question: "But do people
burn tobacco in their fireplaces and barbecues?" These fallacies probably arise either
from the intentions of the author or from carelessness in failing to distinguish the two
kinds of second-hand smoke. In either event, the author is probably hostile to government efforts to control second-hand tobacco smoke in confined areas.

The next argument deals with gun control:

> Detroit, the seventh largest city and one with strict gun laws, had 596 homicides last
> year. In the same year Phoenix, the ninth largest city and one that at the time did
> not require gun owners to be licensed, had 136 homicides. Criminals don't fear the
> toothless criminal-justice system, but they do fear armed citizens.
>
> (Paul M. Berardi)

This argument commits a false cause fallacy. The author presupposes that the availability of guns caused Phoenix to have a lower homicide rate than Detroit. The arguer
also presupposes that Detroit and Phoenix are comparable as to homicide rate merely
because they are roughly the same size. As a result, the argument involves a weak analogy and also begs the question. The additional factors of emotion and intent may also
be present. The arguer probably hates the prospect of gun control, and he may be fully
aware of the fact that Phoenix and Detroit are not comparable for his purpose, but he
went ahead with the comparison anyway.

The next argument deals with religious fundamentalism:

> If we compromise God's word, we compromise the truth. To say that the fundamen-
> talist is a loud shrill voice drowning out religious moderation implies that diluted
> truth is better than absolute truth.
>
> (Gerald Gleason)

This argument begs the question. The arguer presupposes that there is a God, that
God has spoken, that God has revealed his intentions to fundamentalist preachers,
and that those preachers accurately report the word of God. The argument also seems
to reflect an emotional disposition in favor of religious fundamentalism.

The last argument we will consider relates to English as the official U.S. language:

> This great country has been held together for more than 200 years because of one
> simple thing: the English language.
> There are two things we must do: Make English the official language of the
> United States and do away with bilingual education.
>
> (David Moisan)

This argument misses the point. The arguer presupposes that making English the official
language would guarantee that all citizens speak it and that doing away with bilingual

education would accelerate the learning process of immigrant children. The argument may also reflect the fear that many feel in connection with the changes U.S. society is experiencing as a result of recent immigration.

EXERCISE 3.5

I. Most of the following selections were taken from letters to the editors of newspapers and magazines. Identify any fallacies that may be committed, giving a brief explanation for your answer. Then, if a fallacy is identified, discuss the possible factors that led the arguer to commit the fallacy.

★1. Exporting cigarettes [to Asia] is good business for America; there is no reason we should be prohibited from doing so. Asians have been smoking for decades; we are only offering variety in their habit. If the Asians made tobacco smoking illegal, that would be a different situation. But as long as it is legal, the decision is up to the smokers. The Asians are just afraid of American supremacy in the tobacco industries.

(Pat Monohan)

2. When will these upper-crust intellectuals realize that the masses of working people are not in cozy, cushy, interesting, challenging, well-paying jobs, professions and businesses? My husband is now 51; for most of the last 33 years he has worked in the same factory job, and only the thought of retiring at 62 has sustained him. When he reaches that age in 11 years, who will tell him that his aging and physically wracked body must keep going another two years? My heart cries out for all the poor souls who man the assembly lines, ride the trucks or work in the fields or mines, or in the poorly ventilated, hot-in-summer, cold-in-winter factories and garages. Many cannot afford to retire at 62, 65, or even later. Never, never let them extend the retirement age. It's a matter of survival to so many.

(Isabel Fierman)

3. Women in military combat is insane. No society in its right mind would have such a policy. The military needs only young people and that means the only women who go are those in their child-bearing years. Kill them off and society will not be able to perpetuate itself.

(Jack Carman)

★4. Dear Ann: I've read that one aspirin taken every other day will reduce the risk of heart attack. Why not take two and double the protection?

(Boston)

5. The American Civil Liberties Union did a study that found that in the last 80 years it believes twenty-five innocent people have been executed in the United States. This is unfortunate. But, there are innocent people who die each year in highway accidents. Out of 40,000 deaths, how many deaths are related to driving while intoxicated? How many more thousands are injured and incur financial ruin or are invalids and handicapped for the remainder of their lives?

(Mahlon R. Braden)

6. Mexico's president expresses legitimate concern when he questions supplying oil to Americans who are unwilling to apply "discipline" in oil consumption. In view of the fact that his country's population is expected to double in only twenty-two years, isn't it legitimate for us to ask when Mexicans will apply the discipline necessary to control population growth and quit dumping their excess millions over our borders?

(Wayne R. Bartz)

★7. A parent would never give a ten-year-old the car keys, fix him or her a martini, or let him or her wander at night through a dangerous part of town. The same holds true of the Internet. Watch what children access, but leave the Net alone. Regulation is no substitute for responsibility.

(Bobby Dunning)

8. How would you feel to see your children starving and have all doors slammed in your face? Isn't it time that all of us who believe in freedom and human rights stop thinking in terms of color and national boundaries? We should open our arms and hearts to those less fortunate and remember that a time could come when we might be in a similar situation.

(Lorna Doyle)

9. A capital gains tax [reduction] benefits everyone, not just the "rich," because everyone will have more money to invest or spend in the private economy, resulting in more jobs and increasing prosperity for all. This is certainly better than paying high taxes to a corrupt, self-serving and incompetent government that squanders our earnings on wasteful and useless programs.

(David Miller)

★10. After reading "Homosexuals in the Churches," I'd like to point out that I don't know any serious, capable exegetes who stumble over Saint Paul's denunciation of homosexuality. Only a fool (and there seem to be more and more these days) can fail to understand the plain words of Romans, Chapter one. God did not make anyone "gay." Paul tells us in Romans 1 that homosexuals become that way because of their own lusts.

(LeRoy J. Hopper)

11. When will they ever learn—that the Republican Party is not for the people who voted for it?

(Alton L. Stafford)

12. Before I came to the United States in July, 1922, I was in Berlin where I visited the famous zoo. In one of the large cages were a lion and a tiger. Both respected each other's strength. It occurred to me that it was a good illustration of "balance of power." Each beast followed the other and watched each other's moves. When one moved, the other did. When one stopped, the other stopped.

In today's world, big powers or groups of powers are trying to maintain the status quo, trying to be as strong as or stronger than the other. They realize a conflict may result in mutual destruction. As long as the countries believe there is a balance of power we may hope for peace.

(Emilie Lackow)

★13. Doctors say the birth of a baby is a high point of being a doctor. Yet a medical survey shows one out of every nine obstetricians in America has stopped delivering babies.

Expectant mothers have had to find new doctors. In some rural areas, women have had to travel elsewhere to give birth.

How did this happen? It's part of the price of the lawsuit crisis.

The number of lawsuits Americans file each year is on the rise. Obstetricians are among the hardest hit—almost three out of four have faced a malpractice claim. Many have decided it isn't worth the risk.

(Magazine ad by the Insurance Information Institute)

14. The conservative diatribe found in campus journalism comes from the mouths of a handful of affluent brats who were spoon-fed through the '80s. Put them on an ethnically more diverse campus, rather than a Princeton or a Dartmouth, and then let us see how long their newspapers survive.

(David Simons)

15. I see that our courts are being asked to rule on the propriety of outlawing video games as a "waste of time and money."

It seems that we may be onto something here. A favorable ruling would open the door to new laws eliminating show business, spectator sports, cocktail lounges, the state of Nevada, public education and, of course, the entire federal bureaucracy.

(A. G. Dobrin)

★16. The death penalty is the punishment for murder. Just as we have long jail terms for armed robbery, assault and battery, fraud, contempt of court, fines for speeding, reckless driving and other numerous traffic violations, so must we have a punishment for murder. Yes, the death penalty will not deter murders any more than a speeding ticket will deter violating speed laws again, but it is the punishment for such violation!

(Lawrence J. Barstow)

17. Would you rather invest in our nation's children or Pentagon waste? The choice is yours.

(Political ad)

18. My gun has protected me, and my son's gun taught him safety and responsibility long before he got hold of a far more lethal weapon—the family car. Cigarettes kill many times more people yearly than guns and, unlike guns, have absolutely no redeeming qualities. If John Lennon had died a long, painful and expensive death from lung cancer, would you have devoted a page to a harangue against the product of some of your biggest advertisers—the cigarette companies?

(Silvia A. DeFreitas)

★19. If the advocates of prayers in public schools win on this issue, just where will it end? Perhaps next they will ask for prayers on public transportation? Prayers by government workers before they start their job each day? Or maybe, mandatory prayers in public restaurants before starting each meal might be a good idea.

(Leonard Mendelson)

20. So you want to ban smoking in all eating establishments? Well, you go right ahead and do that little thing. And when the 40 percent of smokers stop eating out, the restaurants can do one of two things: close, or raise the price of a $20 dinner 40 percent to $28.

(Karen Sawyer)

21. Pigeons are forced to leave our city to battle for life. Their struggle is an endless search for food. What manner of person would watch these hungry creatures suffer from want of food and deny them their survival? These helpless birds are too often ignored by the people of our city, with not the least bit of compassion shown to them. Pigeons are God's creatures just as the so-called human race is. They need help.

(Leslie Ann Price)

★22. You take half of the American population every night and set them down in front of a box watching people getting stabbed, shot and blown away. And then you expect them to go out into the streets hugging each other?

(Mark Hustad)

23. So you think that putting the worst type of criminal out of his misery is wrong. How about the Americans who were sent to Korea, to Vietnam, to Beirut, to Central America? Thousands of good men were sacrificed supposedly for the good of our country. At the same time we were saving and protecting Charles Manson, Sirhan Sirhan [Robert Kennedy's murderer], and a whole raft of others too numerous to mention.

(George M. Purvis)

24. The fact is that the hype over "acid rain" and "global warming" is just that: hype. Take, for example, Stephen Schneider, author of *Global Warming*. In his current "study" he discusses a "greenhouse effect of catastrophic proportions," yet twenty years ago Schneider was a vocal proponent of the theory of a "new ice age."

(Urs Furrer)

★25. Just as our parents did for us, my husband and I rely solely on Christian Science for all the health needs of our four sons and find it invaluable for the quick cure of whatever ailments and contagions they are subject to. One particular healing that comes to mind happened several years ago when our youngest was a toddler. He had a flu-type illness that suddenly became quite serious. We called a Christian Science practitioner for treatment and he was completely well the next morning.

(Ellen Austin)

26. As somebody who has experienced the tragedy of miscarriage—or spontaneous abortion—at eight weeks, I greatly resent the position that a fetus is not

a baby. I went through the grief of losing a baby, and no one should tell me otherwise.

(Ann Fons)

27. How can we pledge allegiance to the flag of the United States of America and not establish laws to punish people who burn the flag to make a statement? We are a people who punish an individual who libels another person but will not seek redress from an individual who insults every citizen of this great country by desecrating the flag.

(William D. Lankford)

★28. The notion of "buying American" is as misguided as the notion of buying Wisconsin, or Oshkosh, Wisconsin, or South Oshkosh, Wisconsin. For the same reasons that Wisconsin increases its standard of living by trading with the rest of the nation, America increases its standard of living by trading with the rest of the world.

(Phillip Smith)

29. We've often heard the saying, "Far better to let 100 guilty men go free than to condemn one innocent man." What happens then if we apply the logic of this argument to the question, "Is a fetus an unborn human being?" Then is it not better to let 100 fetuses be born rather than to mistakenly kill one unborn human being? This line of reasoning is a strictly humanist argument against abortion.

(James Sebastian)

30. In our society it is generally considered improper for a man to sleep, shower, and dress amid a group of women to whom he normally would be sexually attracted. It seems to me, then, to be equally unacceptable that a gay man sleep, shower, and dress in a company of men to whom, we assume, he would be no less sexually attracted.

(Mark O. Temple)

★31. I say "bravo" and "right on!" Now we have some real-life humane heroes to look up to! These brave people [a group of animal liberators] went up against the insensitive bureaucratic technology, and won, saving former pet animals from senseless torture.

  If researchers want to experiment, let them use computers, or themselves—but not former pet animals! I know it's bad enough they use monkeys and rats, but if those animals are bred knowing nothing else but these Frankensteins abusing them it's different (but not better) than dogs or cats that have been loved and petted all their lives to suddenly be tortured and mutilated in the name of science. End all animal research! Free all research animals!

  Right on, animal liberators!

(Linda Magee)

32. Dear Ann: Recently I was shopping downtown in 20-below-zero weather. A stranger walked up to me and said, "I wonder how many beautiful rabbits died so you could have that coat?" I noticed she was wearing a down coat, so I asked

if the geese they got the down from to make her coat were still alive. She looked surprised. Obviously she had never given it a thought.

If people are so upset about cruelty to animals, why don't they go after the folks who refuse to spend the money to have their pets neutered and spayed? Thousands of dogs are put to death every year because the animal pounds can't feed and house them. Talk about cruelty to animals—that's the best example there is.

("Baby It's Cold Outside")

33. I prayed for the U.S. Senate to defeat the prayer amendment—and it did. There is a God.

(Richard Carr)

★34. People of the Philippines, I have returned! The hour of your redemption is here! Rally to me! Let the indomitable spirit of Bataan and Corregidor lead on! As the lines of battle roll forward to bring you within the zone of operations, rise and strike! For future generations of your sons and daughters, strike! Let no heart be faint! Let every arm be steeled! The guidance of divine God points the way! Follow in his name to the Holy Grail of righteous victory!

(General Douglas MacArthur)

35. As the oldest of eleven children (all married), I'd like to point out our combined family numbers more than 100 who vote only for pro-life candidates. Pro-lifers have children, pro-choicers do not.

(Mrs. Kitty Reickenback)

36. I am 12 years old. My class had a discussion on whether police used unnecessary force when arresting the people from Operation Rescue.

My teacher is an ex-cop, and he demonstrated police holds to us. They don't hurt at all unless the person is struggling or trying to pull away. If anybody was hurt when they were arrested, then they must have been struggling with the officers trying to arrest them.

(Ben Torre-Bueno)

★37. As corporate farms continue to gobble up smaller family farms, they control a larger percentage of the grain and produce raised in the United States. Some have already reached a point in size where, if they should decide to withhold their grain and produce from the marketplace, spot shortages could occur and higher prices would result. The choice is to pay us family farmers now or pay the corporations later.

(Delwin Yost)

38. If you buy our airline ticket now you can save 60 percent, and that means 60 percent more vacation for you.

(Radio ad)

39. Why all the flap about atomic bombs? The potential for death is always with us. Of course, if you just want something to worry about, go ahead. Franklin D. Roosevelt said it: "The only thing we have to fear is fear itself."

(Lee Flemming Reese)

★40. September 17 marked the anniversary of the signing of the U.S. Constitution. How well have we, the people, protected our rights? Consider what has happened to our private-property rights.

"Property has divine rights, and the moment the idea is admitted into society that property is not as sacred as the laws of God, anarchy and tyranny begin." John Quincy Adams, 1767–1848, Sixth President of the United States.

Taxes and regulations are the two-edged sword which gravely threatens the fabric of our capitalistic republic. The tyranny of which Adams speaks is with us today in the form of government regulators and regulations which have all but destroyed the right to own property. Can anarchy be far behind?

(Timothy R. Binder)

41. Evolution would have been dealt serious setbacks if environmentalists had been around over the eons trying to save endangered species.

Species are endangered because they just do not fit the bigger picture any more as the world changes. That's not bad. It's just life.

In most cases we have seen the "endangered species" argument is just a ruse; much deeper motives usually exist, and they are almost always selfish and personal.

(Tom Gable)

42. The problem that I have with the pro-choice supporters' argument is that they make "choice" the ultimate issue. Let's face facts. No one has absolute freedom of choice sanctioned by the law. One can choose to rob a bank, but it's not lawful. Others can choose to kill their one-year-old child, but it is not legal. Why then should a woman have the legal right to take the life of her unborn child?

(Loretta S. Horn)

★43. If a car or truck kills a person, do politicians call for car control or truck control? And call in all cars/trucks?

If a child burns down a house do we have match control or child control and call in all of each?

Gun control and confiscation is equally as pathetic a thought process in an age of supposed intelligence.

(Pete Hawes)

44. I was incensed to read in your article about the return of anti-Semitism that New York City Moral Majority Leader Rev. Dan C. Fore actually said that "Jews have a God-given ability to make money, almost a supernatural ability . . ." I find it incredibly ironic that he and other Moral Majority types conveniently overlook the fact that they, too, pack away a pretty tidy sum themselves through their fund-raising efforts. It is sad that anti-Semitism exists, but to have this prejudice voiced by leaders of religious organizations is deplorable. These people are in for quite a surprise come Judgment Day.

(John R. Murks)

45. Are Americans so stupid they don't realize that every time they pay thousands of dollars for one of those new "economical" Japanese cars, they are simulta-

neously making the U.S. bankrupt and giving the Japanese enough money to buy all of America?

(Sylvia Petersen Young)

★46. Why are people so shocked that Susan Smith apparently chose to kill her children because they had become an inconvenience? Doesn't this occur every day in abortion clinics across the country? We suspect Smith heard very clearly the message many feminists have been trying to deliver about the expendable nature of our children.

(Kevin and Diana Cogan)

47. What's wrong with kids today? Answer: nothing, for the majority of them. They are great.

Witness the action of two San Diego teenage boys recently, when the Normal Heights fire was at its worst. They took a garden hose to the roof of a threatened house—a house belonging to four elderly sisters, people they didn't even know. They saved the house, while neighboring houses burned to the ground.

In the Baldwin Hills fire, two teenage girls rescued a blind, retired Navy man from sure death when they braved the flames to find him, confused, outside his burning house. He would probably have perished if they hadn't run a distance to rescue him.

(Theodore H. Wickham)

48. Now that Big Brother has decided that I must wear a seatbelt when I ride in a car, how long will it take before I have to wear an inner tube when I swim in my pool, a safety harness when I climb a ladder, and shoes with steel-reinforced toecaps when I carry out the garbage?

(G. R. Turgeon)

★49. Dear Ann: I was disappointed in your response to the girl whose mother used the strap on her. The gym teacher noticed the bruises on her legs and backside and called it "child abuse." Why are you against strapping a child when the Bible tells us in plain language that this is what parents should do?

The Book of Proverbs mentions many times that the rod must be used. Proverbs 23:13 says: "Withhold not correction from the child for if thou beatest him with the rod he shall not die." Proverbs 23:14 says: "Thou shalt beat him with the rod and shalt deliver his soul from death."

There is no substitute for a good whipping. I have seen the results of trying to reason with kids. They are arrogant, disrespectful and mouthy. Parents may wish for a more "humane" way, but there is none. Beating children is God's way of getting parents to gain control over their children.

(Davisville, W.Va.)

50. The Fourth Amendment guarantees our right to freedom from unreasonable search and seizure. It does not prohibit *reasonable* search and seizure. The matter of sobriety roadblocks to stop drunk drivers boils down to this: Are such roadblocks reasonable or unreasonable? The majority of people answer:

"Reasonable." Therefore, sobriety roadblocks should not be considered to be unconstitutional.

(Haskell Collier)

51. The Supreme Court recently ruled that a police department in Florida did not violate any rights of privacy when a police helicopter flew over the back yard of a suspected drug dealer and noticed marijuana growing on his property. Many people, including groups like the Anti-Common Logic Union, felt that the suspect's right to privacy outweighed the police department's need to protect the public at large.

The simple idea of sacrificing a right to serve a greater good should be allowed in certain cases. In this particular case the danger to the public wasn't extremely large; marijuana is probably less dangerous than regular beer. But anything could have been in that back yard—a load of cocaine, an illegal stockpile of weapons, or other major threats to society.

(Matt Cookson)

★52. I am 79 and have been smoking for 60 years. My husband is 90 and has inhaled my smoke for some 50 years with no bad effects.

I see no reason to take further steps to isolate smokers in our restaurants and public places, other than we now observe.

Smokers have taken punishment enough from neurotic sniffers, some of whom belong in bubbles. There are plenty of injudicious fumes on our streets and freeways.

(Helen Gans)

53. The mainstream press finds itself left behind by talk radio, so they try to minimize its importance. Americans are finding the true spirit of democracy in community and national debate. Why should we be told what to believe by a news weekly or the nightly news when we can follow public debate as it unfolds on talk radio?

(Adam Abbott)

54. The issue is not whether we should subsidize the arts, but whether anyone should be able to force someone else to subsidize the arts. You and I are free to *give* any amount of our money to any artistic endeavor we wish to support. When the government gets involved, however, a group of bureaucrats is given the power to *take* our money and give it to the arts they wish to support. We are not consulted. That is not a way to promote a responsible culture. That is tyranny.

(Jerry Harben)

★55. Who are these Supreme Court justices who have the guts to OK the burning of our flag?

If the wife or daughter of these so-called justices were raped, could the rapist be exonerated because he took the First Amendment? That he was just expressing himself? How about murder in the same situation?

(Robert A. Lewis)

56. I have one question for those bleeding hearts who say we should not have used the atomic bomb: If the nation responsible for the Rape of Nanking, the Manchurian atrocities, Pearl Harbor and the Bataan Death March had invented the bomb first, don't you think they would have used it? So do I.

(Bill Blair)

57. Since when did military service become a right, for gays or anyone else? The military has always been allowed to discriminate against people who don't meet its requirements, including those who are overweight or too tall or too short. There is an adequate supply of personnel with the characteristics they need. And there is no national need for gays in the military.

(William R. Cnossen)

★58. There is something very wrong about the custom of tipping. When we go to a store, we don't decide what a product is worth and pay what we please; we pay the price or we leave. Prices in coffee bars and restaurants should be raised, waiters should be paid a decent wage, and the words "no tipping" should be clearly visible on menus and at counters.

(George Jochnowitz)

59. Most Americans do not favor gun control. They know that their well-being depends on their own ability to protect themselves. So-called "assault rifles" are used in few crimes. They are not the weapon of choice of criminals, but they are for people trying to protect themselves from government troops.

(Larry Herron)

60. Holding a gun, a thief robs John Q. Public of thousands of dollars. Holding a baby, an unmarried mother robs taxpayers of thousands of dollars. If one behavior is considered a crime, then so should the other.

(Louis R. Ward)

II. Turn to the editorial pages of a newspaper or the letters column of a magazine and find an instance of a fallacious argument in the editorials or letters to the editor. Identify the premises and conclusion of the argument and write an analysis at least one paragraph in length identifying the fallacy or fallacies committed and the factors that may have led the arguer to commit them.

Summary

A fallacy is a mistake in an argument that arises from something other than merely false premises. Usually fallacies involve defects in reasoning or the creation of an illusion that makes a bad argument appear good. Fallacies can be either formal or informal. A formal fallacy is one that can be detected by analyzing the form of an argument; such fallacies affect only deductive arguments. An informal fallacy is one that can be identified only by analyzing the content of an argument; such fallacies can affect both deductive and inductive arguments.

The fallacies of relevance occur when the premises of an argument are not relevant to the conclusion. Cases of such irrelevance occur in premises that threaten the observer, elicit pity from the observer, create a mob mentality in a group of observers, appeal to the observer's desire for security, verbally abuse an opposing arguer, present an opposing arguer as predisposed to argue as he does, present an opposing arguer as a hypocrite, misapply a general rule, distort an opponent's argument, or lead the observer off the track. A kind of catchall fallacy, missing the point, occurs when an arguer draws a conclusion different from the one implied by the premises.

The fallacies of weak induction occur when the premises, although possibly relevant to the conclusion, provide insufficient support for the conclusion. Cases of such inadequate support occur when the arguer cites an authority who is not qualified, draws a conclusion from premises that give no positive evidence, draws a conclusion from an atypical sample, depends on a nonexistent or minor causal connection, depends on a chain reaction that is unlikely to occur, or draws a conclusion from an analogy that is not close enough to support it.

The fallacies of presumption occur when the premises presume what they purport to prove. Such presumptions occur when the arguer creates the illusion that inadequate premises are adequate, asks a question that comprises two or more questions, uses a disjunctive statement that falsely claims to exhaust the available alternatives, or ignores important evidence that requires a different conclusion.

The fallacies of ambiguity occur when the conclusion depends on some form of linguistic ambiguity. Either a word or phrase is used in more than one sense or the wrong interpretation is given to an ambiguous statement.

The fallacies of grammatical analogy occur when a defective argument appears good owing to a grammatical similarity to some argument that is not fallacious. Such grammatical similarities occur in arguments that wrongly transfer an attribute from parts to a whole or from a whole to its parts.

Fallacies that occur in real-life argumentation are harder to detect than those in manufactured examples because they may not exactly fit the structure of the named fallacies and because several fallacies can be woven together in a single passage. Three factors that underlie the commission of fallacies in real-life argumentation are the intent of the arguer, mental carelessness combined with unchecked emotions, and unexamined presuppositions in the arguer's worldview.

4 Categorical Propositions

4.1 The Components of Categorical Propositions

In Chapter 1 we saw that a proposition (or statement—here we are ignoring the distinction) is a sentence that is either true or false. A proposition that relates two classes, or categories, is called a **categorical proposition.** The classes in question are denoted respectively by the **subject term** and the **predicate term,** and the proposition asserts that either all or part of the class denoted by the subject term is included in or excluded from the class denoted by the predicate term. Here are some examples of categorical propositions:

> *American Idol* contestants hope for recognition.
> Snowmobiles do not belong in Yellowstone National Park.
> Many of today's cell phones contain cameras.
> Not all romances have a happy ending.
> Oprah Winfrey publishes magazines.

The first statement asserts that the entire class of *American Idol* contestants is included in the class of people who hope for recognition, the second that the entire class of snowmobiles is excluded from the class of things that belong in Yellowstone National Park, and the third that part of the class of today's cell phones is included in the class of things that contain cameras. The fourth statement asserts that part of the class of romances is excluded from the class of things that have a happy ending, and the last statement asserts that the class that has Oprah Winfrey as its single member is included in the class of people who publish magazines.

Since any categorical proposition asserts that either all or part of the class denoted by the subject term is included in or excluded from the class denoted by the predicate term, it follows that there are exactly four types of categorical propositions: (1) those that assert that the whole subject class is included in the predicate class, (2) those that assert that part of the subject class is included in the predicate class, (3) those that assert that the whole subject class is excluded from the predicate class, and (4) those that assert that part of the subject class is excluded from the predicate class. A categorical proposition that expresses these relations with complete clarity is called a **standard-form**

categorical proposition. A categorical proposition is in standard form if and only if it is a substitution instance of one of the following four forms:

All *S* are *P*.
No *S* are *P*.
Some *S* are *P*.
Some *S* are not *P*.

Many categorical propositions, of course, are not in standard form because, among other things, they do not begin with the words "all," "no," or "some." In the final section of this chapter we will develop techniques for translating categorical propositions into standard form, but for now we may restrict our attention to those that are already in standard form.

The words "all," "no," and "some" are called **quantifiers** because they specify how much of the subject class is included in or excluded from the predicate class. The first form asserts that the whole subject class is included in the predicate class, the second that the whole subject class is excluded from the predicate class, and so on. (Incidentally, in formal deductive logic the word "some" always means at least one.) The letters *S* and *P* stand respectively for the subject and predicate terms, and the words "are" and "are not" are called the **copula** because they link (or "couple") the subject term with the predicate term.

Consider the following example:

All members of the American Medical Association are people holding degrees from recognized academic institutions.

This standard-form categorical proposition is analyzed as follows:

quantifier:	all
subject term:	members of the American Medical Association
copula:	are
predicate term:	people holding degrees from recognized academic institutions

In resolving standard-form categorical propositions into their four components, one must keep these components separate. They do not overlap. In this regard, note that "subject term" and "predicate term" do not mean the same thing in logic that "subject" and "predicate" mean in grammar. The *subject* of the example statement includes the quantifier "all," but the *subject term* does not. Similarly, the *predicate* includes the copula "are," but the *predicate term* does not.

Two additional points should be noted about standard-form categorical propositions. The first is that the form "All *S* are not *P*" is *not* a standard form. This form is ambiguous and can be rendered as either "No *S* are *P*" or "Some *S* are not *P*," depending on the content. The second point is that there are exactly three forms of quantifiers and two forms of copulas. Other texts allow the various forms of the verb "to be" (such as "is," "is not," "will," and "will not") to serve as the copula. For the sake of uniformity, this book restricts the copula to "are" and "are not." The last section of this chapter describes techniques for translating these alternate forms into the two accepted ones.

Originated by Aristotle, the theory of categorical propositions has constituted one of the core topics in logic for over 2,000 years. It remains important even today because many of the statements we make in ordinary discourse are either categorical propositions as they stand or are readily translatable into them. Standard-form categorical propositions represent an ideal of clarity in language, and a familiarity with the relationships that prevail among them provides a backdrop of precision for all kinds of linguistic usage. In Chapter 5 we will see how categorical propositions may be combined to produce *categorical syllogisms*, a kind of argumentation that is closely related to the most basic forms of human reasoning.

EXERCISE 4.1

In the following categorical propositions identify the quantifier, subject term, copula, and predicate term.

★1. Some airport screeners are officials who harass frail grandmothers.

2. No stressful jobs are occupations conducive to a healthy lifestyle.

3. All oil-based paints are products that contribute to photochemical smog.

★4. Some preachers who are intolerant of others' beliefs are not television evangelists.

5. All trials in which a coerced confession is read to the jury are trials in which a guilty verdict can be reversed.

6. Some artificial hearts are mechanisms that are prone to failure.

★7. No sex education courses that are taught competently are programs that are currently eroding public morals.

8. Some universities that emphasize research are not institutions that neglect undergraduate education.

4.2   Quality, Quantity, and Distribution

Quality and quantity are attributes of categorical propositions. In order to see how these attributes pertain, it is useful to rephrase the meaning of categorical propositions in class terminology:

Proposition	Meaning in class notation
All S are P.	Every member of the S class is a member of the P class; that is, the S class is included in the P class.
No S are P.	No member of the S class is a member of the P class; that is, the S class is excluded from the P class.
Some S are P.	At least one member of the S class is a member of the P class.
Some S are not P.	At least one member of the S class is not a member of the P class.

The **quality** of a categorical proposition is either affirmative or negative depending on whether it affirms or denies class membership. Accordingly, "All S are P" and "Some S are P" have **affirmative** quality, and "No S are P" and "Some S are not P" have **negative** quality. These are called **affirmative statements** and **negative statements,** respectively.

The **quantity** of a categorical proposition is either universal or particular, depending on whether the statement makes a claim about *every* member or just *some* member of the class denoted by the subject term. "All S are P" and "No S are P" each assert something about every member of the S class and thus are **universal statements.** "Some S are P" and "Some S are not P" assert something about one or more members of the S class and hence are **particular statements.**

Note that the quantity of a categorical proposition may be determined through mere inspection of the quantifier. "All" and "no" immediately imply universal quantity, while "some" implies particular. But categorical propositions have no "qualifier." In universal propositions the quality is determined by the quantifier, and in particular propositions it is determined by the copula.

Particular propositions mean no more and no less than the meaning assigned to them in class notation. The statement "Some S are P" does *not* imply that some S are not P, and the statement "Some S are not P" does *not* imply that some S are P. It often *happens*, of course, that substitution instances of these statement forms are both true. For example, "Some apples are red" is true, as is "Some apples are not red." But the fact that one is true does not *necessitate* that the other be true. "Some zebras are animals" is true (because at least one zebra is an animal), but "Some zebras are not animals" is false. Similarly, "Some turkeys are not fish" is true, but "Some turkeys are fish" is false. Thus, the fact that one of these statement forms is true does not *logically imply* that the other is true, as these substitution instances clearly prove.

Since the early Middle Ages the four kinds of categorical propositions have commonly been designated by letter names corresponding to the first four vowels of the Roman alphabet: **A, E, I, O.** The universal affirmative is called an **A proposition,** the universal negative an **E proposition,** the particular affirmative an **I proposition,** and the particular negative an **O proposition.** Tradition has it that these letters were derived from the first two vowels in the Latin words *affirmo* ("I affirm") and *nego* ("I deny"), thus:

		n
Universal	A	E
	f	
	f	g
Particular	I	O
	r	
	m	
	o	

The material presented thus far in this section may be summarized as follows:

Proposition	Letter name	Quantity	Quality
All S are P.	**A**	universal	affirmative
No S are P.	**E**	universal	negative
Some S are P.	**I**	particular	affirmative
Some S are not P.	**O**	particular	negative

Unlike quality and quantity, which are attributes of *propositions*, **distribution** is an attribute of the *terms* (subject and predicate) of propositions. A term is said to be distributed if the proposition makes an assertion about every member of the class denoted by the term; otherwise, it is undistributed. Stated another way, a term is distributed if and only if the statement assigns (or distributes) an attribute to every member of the class denoted by the term. Thus, if a statement asserts something about every member of the S class, then S is distributed; if it asserts something about every member of the P class, then P is distributed; otherwise S and P are undistributed.

Let us imagine that the members of the classes denoted by the subject and predicate terms of a categorical proposition are contained respectively in circles marked with the letters "S" and "P." The meaning of the statement form "All S are P" may then be represented by the following diagram:

The S circle is contained in the P circle, which represents the fact that every member of S is a member of P. (Of course, should S and P represent terms denoting identical classes, the two circles would overlap exactly.) As the diagram shows, "All S are P" makes a claim about every member of the S class, since the statement says that every member of S is in the P class. But the statement does not make a claim about every member of the P class, since there may be some members of P that are outside of S. Thus, by the definition of "distributed term" given above, S is distributed and P is not. In other words, for any universal affirmative (**A**) proposition, the subject term, whatever it may be, is distributed, and the predicate term is undistributed.

Let us now consider the universal negative (**E**) proposition. "No S are P" states that the S and P classes are separate, which may be represented as follows:

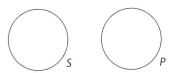

This statement makes a claim about every member of S and every member of P. It asserts that every member of S is separate from every member of P, and also that every member of P is separate from every member of S. Accordingly, by our definition, both the subject and predicate terms of universal negative (**E**) propositions are distributed.

The particular affirmative (**I**) proposition states that at least one member of S is a member of P. If we represent this one member of S that we are certain about by an asterisk, the resulting diagram looks like this:

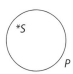

Since the asterisk is inside the P class, it represents something that is simultaneously an S and a P; in other words, it represents a member of the S class that is also a member of the P class. Thus, the statement "Some S are P" makes a claim about one member (at least) of S and also one member (at least) of P, but not about all members of either class. Hence, by the definition of distribution, neither S nor P is distributed.

The particular negative (**O**) proposition asserts that at least one member of S is not a member of P. If we once again represent this one member of S by an asterisk, the resulting diagram is as follows:

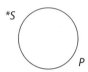

Since the other members of S may or may not be outside of P, it is clear that the statement "Some S are not P" does not make a claim about every member of S, so S is not distributed. But, as may be seen from the diagram, the statement does assert that every member of P is separate and distinct from this one member of S that is outside the P circle. Thus, in the particular negative (**O**) proposition, P is distributed and S is undistributed.

At this point the notion of distribution may be somewhat vague and elusive. Unfortunately, there is no simple and easy way to make the idea graphically clear. The best that can be done is to repeat some of the things that have already been said. First of all, distribution is an attribute or quality that the subject and predicate terms of a categorical proposition may or may not possess, depending on the kind of proposition. If the proposition in question is an **A** type, then the subject term, whatever it may be, is distributed. If it is an **E** type, then both terms are distributed; if an **I** type, then neither; and if an **O** type, then the predicate. If a certain term is *distributed* in a proposition, this simply means that the proposition says something about every member of the class that the term denotes. If a term is *undistributed*, the proposition does not say something about every member of the class.

An easy way to remember the rule for distribution is to keep in mind that universal (**A** and **E**) statements distribute their subject terms and negative (**E** and **O**) statements distribute their predicate terms. As an aid to remembering this arrangement, the following mnemonic may be useful: "Unprepared Students Never Pass." Attending to the first letter in these words may help one recall that Universals distribute Subjects, and Negatives distribute Predicates. Another mnemonic that accomplishes the same purpose is "Any Student Earning B's Is Not On Probation." In this mnemonic the first letters may help one recall that **A** statements distribute the Subject, **E** statements distribute Both terms, **I** statements distribute Neither term, and **O** statements distribute the Predicate.

	Two mnemonic devices for distribution	
"Unprepared Students Never Pass"	"Any Student Earning B's Is Not On Probation"
Universals distribute Subjects. Negatives distribute Predicates.	A distributes Subject. E distributes Both. I distributes Neither. O distributes Predicate.

Finally, note that the attribute of distribution, while not particularly important to subsequent developments in this chapter, is essential to the evaluation of syllogisms in the next chapter.

The material of this section may now be summarized as follows:

Proposition	Letter name	Quantity	Quality	Terms distributed
All S are P.	A	universal	affirmative	S
No S are P.	E	universal	negative	S and P
Some S are P.	I	particular	affirmative	none
Some S are not P.	O	particular	negative	P

EXERCISE 4.2

I. For each of the following categorical propositions identify the letter name, quantity, and quality. Then state whether the subject and predicate terms are distributed or undistributed.

★1. No butterfly ballots are trustworthy election tools.

2. All governments that bargain with terrorists are governments that encourage terrorism.

3. Some symphony orchestras are organizations on the brink of bankruptcy.

★4. Some Chinese leaders are not thoroughgoing opponents of capitalist economics.

5. All human contacts with benzene are potential causes of cancer.

6. No labor strikes are events welcomed by management.

★7. Some hospitals are organizations that overcharge the Medicare program.

8. Some affirmative action plans are not programs that result in reverse discrimination.

II. Change the quality but not the quantity of the following statements.

★1. All drunk drivers are threats to others on the highway.

2. No wildlife refuges are locations suitable for condominium developments.

3. Some slumlords are people who eventually wind up in jail.

★4. Some CIA operatives are not champions of human rights.

III. Change the quantity but not the quality of the following statements.

★1. All owners of pit bull terriers are people who can expect expensive lawsuits.

2. No tax proposals that favor the rich are fair proposals.

3. Some grade school administrators are people who choke the educational process.

★4. Some residents of Manhattan are not people who can afford to live there.

IV. Change both the quality and the quantity of the following statements.

★1. All oil spills are events catastrophic to the environment.

2. No alcoholics are people with a healthy diet.

3. Some Mexican vacations are episodes that end with gastrointestinal distress.

★4. Some corporate lawyers are not people with a social conscience.

4.3   Venn Diagrams and the Modern Square of Opposition

Aristotle and Boole

Before we can address the two main topics of this section, we must look further at the meaning of universal (**A** and **E**) propositions. Consider these two **A** propositions:

All Tom Cruise's movies are hits.

All unicorns are one-horned animals.

The first proposition implies that Tom Cruise has indeed made some movies. In other words, the statement has existential import. It implies that one or more things denoted by the subject term actually exist. On the other hand, no such implication is made by the statement about unicorns. The statement is true, because unicorns, by definition, have a single horn. But the statement does not imply that unicorns actually exist.

Thus, the question arises: Should universal propositions be interpreted as implying that the things talked about actually exist? Or should they be interpreted as implying no such thing? In response to this question, logicians have taken two different approaches. Aristotle held that universal propositions about existing things have existential import. In other words, such statements imply the existence of the things talked about:

Aristotelian standpoint

All pheasants are birds.	Implies the existence of pheasants.
No pine trees are maples.	Implies the existence of pine trees.
All satyrs are vile creatures.	Does not imply the existence of satyrs.

The first two statements have existential import because their subject terms denote actually existing things. The third statement has no existential import, because satyrs do not exist.

On the other hand, the nineteenth-century logician George Boole held that no universal propositions have existential import. Such statements never imply the existence of the things talked about:

George Boole 1815–1864

© Bettmann/CORBIS

The English mathematician and philosopher George Boole is known primarily for the development of Boolean algebra—a type of logic based on the three fundamental operations of *and, or,* and *not.* The American logician Charles Sanders Peirce was captivated by Boole's ideas, and he saw a possible application in the area of electrical circuitry. One of Peirce's students, Claude Shannon, actually succeeded in putting theory to practice when he showed how Boole's system could be used in designing telephone routing switches. This innovation subsequently led to the development of electronic digital computers.

Boole's early years were marked by struggle. His father, John, was a cobbler, and his mother, Mary Ann, a lady's maid. They could afford only the most basic education for their son, which John supplemented by teaching mathematics and science to young George and by hiring a Latin tutor for him. Boole taught himself Greek, French, and German. His father, a leading member of the Mechanics Institute, was intrigued by the application of mathematics in making instruments, and he passed this interest to his son. Though poverty limited the resources available to him, Boole used borrowed mathematics journals from the institute to further his mathematics education on his own.

When George was only sixteen, his father's shoemaking business folded, and it fell to him to support the family by working as an assistant teacher. When he was twenty-two, he took over the operation of a boarding school after its former director had died, and his whole family assisted him in running it. Throughout this period, Boole continued his study of mathematics, and at age twenty-nine he published a paper on the use of algebraic methods in solving differential equations. In recognition of this work he received the Royal Society Medal, which brought him considerable fame in the mathematical world.

Three years later Boole published *The Mathematical Analysis of Logic,* which brought to fruition some of Leibniz's earlier speculations on the relationship between mathematics and logic. It also showed how the symbolism of mathematics could be imported into logic. This work won him a professorship at Queens College, in Cork, Ireland, where he remained for the rest of his life. Seven years later he published a much larger and more mature work on the same subject, *An Investigation of the Laws of Thought, on Which Are Founded the Mathematical Theories of Logic and Probabilities.* This later work presented a complete system of symbolic reasoning.

Boole married Mary Everest (the niece of Sir George Everest, after whom Mt. Everest is named). He met her when she came to visit her famous uncle in Cork, and the relationship developed through his giving her lessons on differential equations. The couple had five daughters, but when Boole was only forty-nine his life was cut short from what was probably pneumonia. Boole had walked two miles in the pouring rain to lecture at Queens, and he delivered the lecture in wet clothing. After he developed a high fever and became desperately ill, his wife, thinking that a good cure always mirrors the cause, poured cold water on him as he lay in bed. He died shortly thereafter.

Boolean standpoint

All trucks are vehicles.	Does not imply the existence of trucks.
No roses are daisies.	Does not imply the existence of roses.
All werewolves are monsters.	Does not imply the existence of werewolves.

We might summarize these results by saying that the Aristotelian standpoint is "open" to existence. When things exist, the Aristotelian standpoint recognizes their existence, and universal statements about those things have existential import. In other words, existence counts for something. On the other hand, the Boolean standpoint is "closed" to existence. When things exist, the Boolean standpoint does not recognize their existence, and universal statements about those things have no existential import.

The Aristotelian standpoint differs from the Boolean standpoint only with regard to universal (**A** and **E**) propositions. The two standpoints are identical with regard to particular (**I** and **O**) propositions. Both the Aristotelian and the Boolean standpoints recognize that particular propositions make a positive assertion about existence. For example, from both standpoints, the statement "Some cats are animals" asserts that at least one cat exists, and that cat is an animal. Also, from both standpoints, "Some fish are not mammals" asserts that at least one fish exists, and that fish is not a mammal. Thus, from both standpoints, the word "some" implies existence.*

Adopting either the Aristotelian or the Boolean standpoint amounts to accepting a set of ground rules for interpreting the meaning of universal propositions. Either standpoint can be adopted for any categorical proposition or any argument composed of categorical propositions. Taking the Aristotelian standpoint amounts to recognizing that universal statements about existing things convey evidence about existence. Conversely, for a statement to convey such evidence, the Aristotelian standpoint must be taken and the subject of the statement must denote actually existing things. Taking the Boolean standpoint, on the other hand, amounts to ignoring any evidence about existence that universal statements might convey.

Because the Boolean standpoint is neutral about existence, it is simpler than the Aristotelian standpoint, which recognizes existential implications. For this reason, we will direct our attention first to arguments considered from the Boolean standpoint. Later, in Section 4.5, we will extend our treatment to the Aristotelian standpoint.

Venn Diagrams

From the Boolean standpoint, the four kinds of categorical propositions have the following meaning. Notice that the first two (universal) propositions imply nothing about the existence of the things denoted by *S:*

---

*In ordinary language, the word "some" occasionally implies something less than actual existence. For example, the statement "Some unicorns are tenderhearted" does not seem to suggest that unicorns actually exist, but merely that among the group of imaginary things called "unicorns," there is a subclass of tenderhearted ones. In the vast majority of cases, however, "some" in ordinary language implies existence. The logical "some" conforms to these latter uses.

All *S* are *P*. = No members of *S* are outside *P*.
No *S* are *P*. = No members of *S* are inside *P*.
Some *S* are *P*. = At least one *S* exists, and that *S* is a *P*.
Some *S* are not *P*. = At least one *S* exists, and that *S* is not a *P*.

Adopting this interpretation of categorical propositions, the nineteenth-century logician John Venn developed a system of diagrams to represent the information they express. These diagrams have come to be known as **Venn diagrams.**

A Venn diagram is an arrangement of overlapping circles in which each circle represents the class denoted by a term in a categorical proposition. Because every categorical proposition has exactly two terms, the Venn diagram for a single categorical proposition consists of two overlapping circles. Each circle is labeled so that it represents one of the terms in the proposition. Unless otherwise required, we adopt the convention that the left-hand circle represents the subject term, and the right-hand circle the predicate term. Such a diagram looks like this:

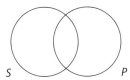

The members of the class denoted by each term should be thought of as situated inside the corresponding circle. Thus, the members of the *S* class (if any such members exist) are situated inside the *S* circle, and the members of the *P* class (if any such members exist) are situated inside the *P* circle. If any members are situated inside the area where the two circles overlap, then such members belong to both the *S* class and the *P* class. Finally, if any members are situated outside both circles, they are members of neither *S* nor *P*.

Suppose, for example, that the *S* class is the class of Americans and the *P* class is the class of farmers. Then, if we use numerals to identify the four possible areas, the diagram looks like this:

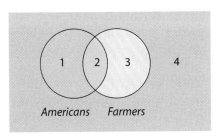

Anything in the area marked "1" is an American but not a farmer, anything in the area marked "2" is both an American and a farmer, and anything in the area marked "3" is a farmer but not an American. The area marked "4" is the area outside both circles; thus, anything in this area is neither a farmer nor an American.

We can now use Venn diagrams to represent the information expressed by the four kinds of categorical proposition. To do this we make a certain kind of mark in a diagram.

Two kinds of marks are used: shading an area and placing an X in an area. Shading an area means that the shaded area is empty,* and placing an X in an area means that at least one thing exists in that area. The X may be thought of as representing that one thing. If no mark appears in an area, this means that nothing is known about that area; it may contain members or it may be empty. Shading is always used to represent the content of universal (**A** and **E**) propositions, and placing an X in an area is always used to represent the content of particular (**I** and **O**) propositions. The content of the four kinds of categorical propositions is represented as follows:

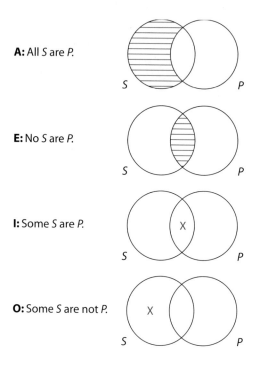

A: All *S* are *P.*

E: No *S* are *P.*

I: Some *S* are *P.*

O: Some *S* are not *P.*

Recall that the **A** proposition asserts that no members of *S* are outside *P*. This is represented by shading the part of the *S* circle that lies outside the *P* circle. The **E** proposition asserts that no members of *S* are inside *P*. This is represented by shading the part of the *S* circle that lies inside the *P* circle. The **I** proposition asserts that at least one *S* exists and that *S* is also a *P*. This is represented by placing an X in the area where the *S* and *P* circles overlap. This X represents an existing thing that is both an *S* and a *P*. Finally, the **O** proposition asserts that at least one *S* exists, and that *S* is not a *P*. This is represented by placing an X in the part of the *S* circle that lies outside the *P* circle. This X represents an existing thing that is an *S* but not a *P*.

Because there is no X in the diagrams that represent the universal propositions, these diagrams say nothing about existence. For example, the diagram for the **A** proposition merely asserts that nothing exists in the part of the *S* circle that lies outside the *P*

---

*In many mathematics texts, shading an area of a Venn diagram indicates that the area is *not* empty. The significance of shading in logic is exactly the opposite.

circle. The area where the two circles overlap and the part of the *P* circle that lies outside the *S* circle contain no marks at all. This means that something might exist in these areas, or they might be completely empty. Similarly, in the diagram for the **E** proposition, no marks appear in the left-hand part of the *S* circle and the right-hand part of the *P* circle. This means that these two areas might contain something or, on the other hand, they might not.

The Modern Square of Opposition

Let us compare the diagram for the **A** proposition with the diagram for the **O** proposition. The diagram for the **A** proposition asserts that the left-hand part of the *S* circle is empty, whereas the diagram for the **O** proposition asserts that this same area is not empty. These two diagrams make assertions that are the exact opposite of each other. As a result, their corresponding statements are said to contradict each other. Analogously, the diagram for the **E** proposition asserts that the area where the two circles overlap is empty, whereas the diagram for the **I** proposition asserts that the area where the two circles overlap is not empty. Accordingly, their corresponding propositions are also said to contradict each other. This relationship of mutually contradictory pairs of propositions is represented in a diagram called the **modern square of opposition.** This diagram, which arises from the modern (or Boolean) interpretation of categorical propositions, is represented as follows:

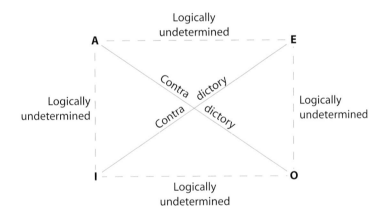

If two propositions are related by the **contradictory relation,** they necessarily have opposite truth value. Thus, if a certain **A** proposition is given as true, the corresponding **O** proposition must be false. Similarly, if a certain **I** proposition is given as false, the corresponding **E** proposition must be true. But no other inferences are possible. In particular, given the truth value of an **A** or **O** proposition, nothing can be determined about the truth value of the corresponding **E** or **I** propositions. These propositions are said to have **logically undetermined truth value.** Like all propositions, they do have a truth value, but logic alone cannot determine what it is. Similarly, given the truth value of an **E** or **I** proposition, nothing can be determined about the truth value of the corresponding **A** or **O** propositions. They, too, are said to have logically undetermined truth value.

Testing Immediate Inferences

Since the modern square of opposition provides logically necessary results, we can use it to test certain arguments for validity. We begin by assuming the premise is true, and we enter the pertinent truth value in the square. We then use the square to compute the truth value of the conclusion. If the square indicates that the conclusion is true, the argument is valid; if not, the argument is invalid. Here is an example:

> Some trade spies are not masters at bribery.
> Therefore, it is false that all trade spies are masters at bribery.

Arguments of this sort are called **immediate inferences** because they have only one premise. Instead of reasoning from one premise to the next, and then to the conclusion, we proceed immediately to the conclusion. To test this argument for validity, we begin by assuming that the premise, which is an **O** proposition, is true, and we enter this truth value in the square of opposition. We then use the square to compute the truth value of the corresponding **A** proposition. By the contradictory relation, the **A** proposition is false. Since the conclusion claims that the **A** proposition is false, the conclusion is true, and therefore the argument is valid. Arguments that are valid from the Boolean standpoint are said to be **unconditionally valid** because they are valid regardless of whether their terms refer to existing things.

Note that the conclusion of this argument has the form "It is false that all *S* are *P*." Technically, statements of this type are not standard-form propositions because, among other things, they do not begin with a quantifier. To remedy this difficulty we adopt the convention that statements having this form are equivalent to " 'All *S* are *P*' is false." Analogous remarks apply to the negations of the **E, I**, and **O** statements.

Here is another example:

> It is false that all meteor showers are common spectacles.
> Therefore, no meteor showers are common spectacles.

We begin by assuming that the premise is true. Since the premise claims that an **A** proposition is false, we enter "false" into the square of opposition. We then use the square to compute the truth value of the corresponding **E** proposition. Since there is no relation that links the **A** and **E** propositions, the **E** proposition has undetermined truth value. Thus, the conclusion of the argument has undetermined truth value, and the argument is invalid.

We can also use Venn diagrams to test immediate inferences for validity. To do so we begin by using letters to represent the terms, and we then draw Venn diagrams for the premise and conclusion. If the information expressed by the conclusion diagram is contained in the premise diagram, the argument is valid; if not, it is invalid. Here is the symbolized form of the trade spies argument that we tested earlier.

> Some *T* are not *M*.
> Therefore, it is false that all *T* are *M*.

The next step is to draw two Venn diagrams, one for the premise and the other for the conclusion. The premise diagram is easy; all we need do is place an X in the left-hand part of the *T* circle. But drawing the conclusion is a bit more complicated. First we consider how we would diagram "All *T* are *M*." We would shade the left-hand part of the *T* circle. But since the conclusion asserts that "All *T* are *M*" is *false*, we do just the opposite: we place an X in the left-hand part of the *T* circle. Here are the completed diagrams:

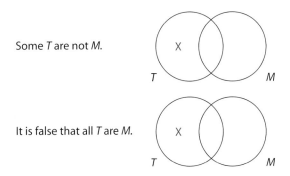

Some *T* are not *M*.

It is false that all *T* are *M*.

To evaluate the argument, we look to see whether the information expressed by the conclusion diagram is also expressed by the premise diagram. The conclusion diagram asserts that something exists in the left-hand part of the *T* circle. Since this information is also expressed by the premise diagram, the argument is valid. In this case, the diagram for the conclusion is identical to the diagram for the premise, so it is clear that premise and conclusion assert exactly the same thing. However, as we will see in Sections 4.5 an 4.6, for an argument to be valid, it is not necessary that premise and conclusion assert exactly the same thing. It is only necessary that the premise assert *at least as much* as the conclusion.

Here is the symbolized version of the second argument evaluated earlier:

It is false that all *M* are *C*.
Therefore, no *M* are *C*.

In diagramming the premise, we do just the opposite of what we would do to diagram "All *M* are *C*." Instead of shading the left-hand part of the *M* circle, we place an X in that area. For the conclusion we shade the area where the two circles overlap:

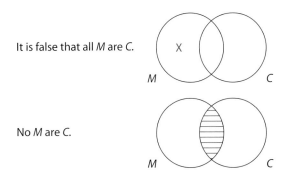

It is false that all *M* are *C*.

No *M* are *C*.

Here, the conclusion diagram asserts that the overlap area is empty. Since this information is not contained in the premise diagram, the argument is invalid.

We conclude with a special example:

> All cell phones are wireless devices.
> Therefore, some cell phones are wireless devices.

The completed Venn diagrams are as follows:

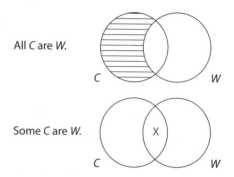

All C are W.

Some C are W.

The information of the conclusion diagram is not contained in the premise diagram, so the argument is invalid. However, if the premise were interpreted as having existential import, then the C circle in the premise diagram would not be empty. Specifically, there would be members in the overlap area. This would make the argument valid.

Arguments of this sort are said to commit the existential fallacy. From the Boolean standpoint, the **existential fallacy** is a formal fallacy that is committed whenever an argument is invalid merely because the premise is interpreted as lacking existential import. In Section 4.5, additional forms of this fallacy will be explored. For now, we can identify two forms of the fallacy that arise from the Boolean standpoint:

Existential fallacy

All A are B.
Therefore, some A are B.

No A are B.
Therefore, some A are not B.

EXERCISE 4.3

I. Draw Venn diagrams for the following propositions.

★1. No life decisions are happenings based solely on logic.

2. All electric motors are machines that depend on magnetism.

3. Some political campaigns are mere attempts to discredit opponents.

★4. Some rock music lovers are not fans of Madonna.

5. All redistricting plans are sources of controversy.

6. No tax audits are pleasant experiences for cheaters.

★7. Some housing developments are complexes that exclude children.

8. Some cruise ships are not steam-driven vessels.

II. Use the modern square of opposition to determine whether the following immediate inferences are valid or invalid from the Boolean standpoint.

★1. No sculptures by Rodin are boring creations.
Therefore, all sculptures by Rodin are boring creations.

2. It is false that some lunar craters are volcanic formations.
Therefore, no lunar craters are volcanic formations.

3. All trial lawyers are people with stressful jobs.
Therefore, some trial lawyers are people with stressful jobs.

★4. All dry martinis are dangerous concoctions.
Therefore, it is false that some dry martinis are not dangerous concoctions.

5. It is false that no jazz musicians are natives of New Orleans.
Therefore, some jazz musicians are not natives of New Orleans.

6. Some country doctors are altruistic healers.
Therefore, some country doctors are not altruistic healers.

★7. No fertility drugs are solutions to every problem.
Therefore, it is false that all fertility drugs are solutions to every problem.

8. It is false that no credit cards are things that contain holograms.
Therefore, some credit cards are things that contain holograms.

9. It is false that some stunt pilots are not colorful daredevils.
Therefore, it is false that some stunt pilots are colorful daredevils.

★10. No vampires are avid connoisseurs of garlic bread.
Therefore, it is false that some vampires are avid connoisseurs of garlic bread.

11. No talk radio shows are accurate sources of information.
Therefore, some talk radio shows are not accurate sources of information.

12. Some stellar constellations are spiral-shaped objects.
Therefore, no stellar constellations are spiral-shaped objects.

★13. It is false that some soap bubbles are not occasions of glee.
Therefore, some soap bubbles are occasions of glee.

14. It is false that all weddings are light-hearted celebrations.
Therefore, some weddings are not light-hearted celebrations.

15. It is false that some chocolate soufflés are desserts containing olives.
Therefore, it is false that all chocolate soufflés are desserts containing olives.

III. Use Venn diagrams to evaluate the immediate inferences in Part II of this exercise. Identify any that commit the existential fallacy.

4.4 Conversion, Obversion, and Contraposition

For a preliminary glimpse into the content of this section, consider the statement "No dogs are cats." This statement claims that the class of dogs is separated from the class of cats. But the statement "No cats are dogs" claims the same thing. Thus, the two statements have the same meaning and the same truth value. For another example, consider the statement "Some dogs are not retrievers." This statement claims there is at least one dog outside the class of retrievers. But the statement "Some dogs are non-retrievers" claims the same thing, so again, the two statements have the same meaning and the same truth value.

Conversion, obversion, and contraposition are operations that can be performed on a categorical proposition, resulting in a new statement that may or may not have the same meaning and truth value as the original statement. Venn diagrams are used to determine how the two statements relate to each other.

Conversion

The simplest of the three operations is **conversion,** and it consists in switching the subject term with the predicate term. For example, if the statement "No foxes are hedgehogs" is converted, the resulting statement is "No hedgehogs are foxes." This new statement is called the *converse* of the given statement. To see how the four types of categorical propositions relate to their converse, compare the following sets of Venn diagrams:

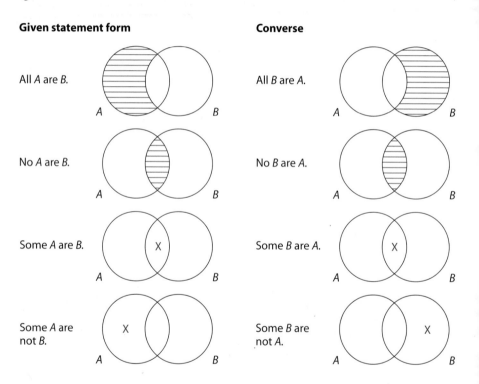

Given statement form

All *A* are *B*.

No *A* are *B*.

Some *A* are *B*.

Some *A* are not *B*.

Converse

All *B* are *A*.

No *B* are *A*.

Some *B* are *A*.

Some *B* are not *A*.

If we examine the diagram for the **E** statement, we see that it is identical to that of its converse. Also, the diagram for the **I** statement is identical to that of its converse. This means that the **E** statement and its converse are logically equivalent, and the **I** statement and its converse are logically equivalent. Two statements are said to be **logically equivalent statements** when they necessarily have the same truth value (as we will see again in Chapter 6). Thus, converting an **E** or **I** statement gives a new statement that always has the same truth value (and the same meaning) as the given statement. These equivalences are strictly proved by the Venn diagrams for the **E** and **I** statements.

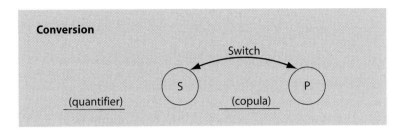

On the other hand, the diagram for the **A** statement is clearly not identical to the diagram for its converse, and the diagram for the **O** statement is not identical to the diagram for its converse. Also, these pairs of diagrams are not the exact opposite of each other, as is the case with contradictory statements. This means that an **A** statement and its converse are logically unrelated as to truth value, and an **O** statement and its converse are logically unrelated as to truth value. In other words, converting an **A** or **O** statement gives a new statement whose truth value is logically undetermined in relation to the given statement. The converse of an **A** or **O** statement does have a truth value, of course, but logic alone cannot tell us what it is.

Because conversion yields necessarily determined results for **E** and **I** statements, it can be used as the basis for immediate inferences having these types of statements as premises. The following argument forms are valid:

No *A* are *B*.
Therefore, no *B* are *A*.

Some *A* are *B*.
Therefore, some *B* are *A*.

Since the conclusion of each argument form necessarily has the same truth value as the premise, if the premise is assumed true, it follows necessarily that the conclusion is true. On the other hand, the next two argument forms are invalid. Each commits the fallacy of **illicit conversion:**

All *A* are *B*.
Therefore, all *B* are *A*.

Some *A* are not *B*.
Therefore, some *B* are not *A*.

Here are two examples of arguments that commit the fallacy of illicit conversion:

All cats are animals.   (True)
Therefore, all animals are cats.   (False)

Some animals are not dogs.   (True)
Therefore, some dogs are not animals.   (False)

Obversion

More complicated than conversion, **obversion** requires two steps: (1) changing the quality (without changing the quantity), and (2) replacing the predicate with its term complement. The first part of this operation was treated in Exercise 4.2. It consists in changing "No *S* are *P*" to "All *S* are *P*" and vice versa, and changing "Some *S* are *P*" to "Some *S* are not *P*" and vice versa.

The second step requires understanding the concept of *class complement.* The complement of a class is the group consisting of everything outside the class. For example, the complement of the class of dogs is the group that includes everything that is not a dog (cats, fish, trees, and so on). The **term complement** is the word or group of words that denotes the class complement. For terms consisting of a single word, the term complement is usually formed by simply attaching the prefix "non" to the term. Thus, the complement of the term "dog" is "non-dog," the complement of the term "book" is "non-book," and so on.

The relationship between a term and its complement can be illustrated by a Venn diagram. For example, if a single circle is allowed to represent the class of dogs, then everything outside the circle represents the class of non-dogs:

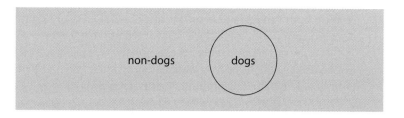

We now have everything we need to form the *obverse* of categorical propositions. First we change the quality (without changing the quantity), and then we replace the predicate term with its term complement. For example, if we are given the statement "All horses are animals," then the obverse is "No horses are non-animals"; and if we are given the statement "Some trees are maples," then the obverse is "Some trees are not non-maples." To see how the four types of categorical propositions relate to their obverse, compare the following sets of Venn diagrams:

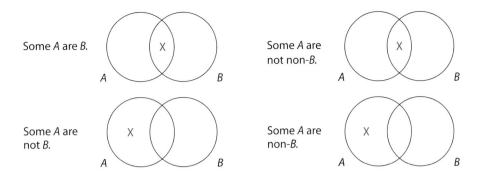

Some A are B.

A   X   B

Some A are not non-B.

A   X   B

Some A are not B.

A   X   B

Some A are non-B.

A   X   B

To see how the obverse diagrams are drawn, keep in mind that "non-*B*" designates the area outside the *B* circle. Thus, "No *A* are non-*B*" asserts that the area where *A* overlaps non-*B* is empty. This is represented by shading the left-hand part of the *A* circle. "All *A* are non-*B*" asserts that all members of *A* are outside *B*. This means that no members of *A* are inside *B*, so the area where *A* overlaps *B* is shaded. "Some *A* are not non-*B*" asserts that at least one member of *A* is not outside *B*. This means that at least one member of *A* is inside *B*, so an X is placed in the area where *A* and *B* overlap. Finally, "Some *A* are non-*B*" asserts that at least one member of *A* is outside *B*, so an X is placed in the left-hand part of the *A* circle.

If we examine these pairs of diagrams, we see that the diagram for each given statement form is identical to the diagram for its obverse. This means that each of the four types of categorical proposition is logically equivalent to (and has the same meaning as) its obverse. Thus, if we obvert an **A** statement that happens to be true, the resulting statement will be true; if we obvert an **O** statement that happens to be false, the resulting statement will be false, and so on.

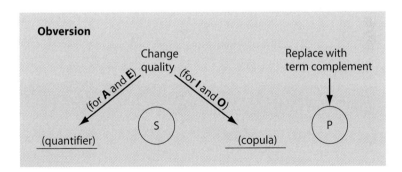

Obversion

Change quality

Replace with term complement

(for **A** and **E**)   (for **I** and **O**)

(quantifier)   S   (copula)   P

It is easy to see that if a statement is obverted and then obverted again, the resulting statement will be identical to the original statement. For example, the obverse of "All horses are animals" is "No horses are non-animals." To obvert the latter statement we again change the quality ("no" switches to "all") and replace "non-animals" with its term complement. The term complement is produced by simply deleting the prefix "non." Thus, the obverse of the obverse is "All horses are animals."

When a term consists of more than a single word, more ingenuity is required to form its term complement. For example, if we are given the term "animals that are not native to America," it would not be appropriate to form the term complement by writing "non-animals that are not native to America." Clearly it would be better to write "animals native to America." Even though this is technically not the complement of the given term, the procedure is justified if we allow a reduction in the scope of discourse. This can be seen as follows. Technically the term complement of "animals that are not native to America" denotes all kinds of things such as ripe tomatoes, battleships, gold rings, and so on. But if we suppose that we are talking *only* about animals (that is, we reduce the scope of discourse to animals), then the complement of this term is "animals native to America."

As is the case with conversion, obversion can be used to supply the link between the premise and the conclusion of immediate inferences. The following argument forms are valid:

All *A* are *B*.   Some *A* are *B*.
Therefore, no *A* are non-*B*.   Therefore, some *A* are not non-*B*.

No *A* are *B*.   Some *A* are not *B*.
Therefore, all *A* are non-*B*.   Therefore, some *A* are non-*B*.

Because the conclusion of each argument form necessarily has the same truth value as its premise, if the premise is assumed true, it follows necessarily that the conclusion is true.

Contraposition

Like obversion, **contraposition** requires two steps: (1) switching the subject and predicate terms and (2) replacing the subject and predicate terms with their term complements. For example, if the statement "All goats are animals" is contraposed, the resulting

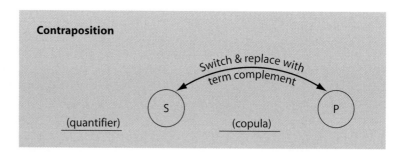

statement is "All non-animals are non-goats." This new statement is called the contrapositive of the given statement. To see how all four types of categorical propositions relate to their contrapositive, compare the following sets of diagrams:

Given statement form **Contrapositive**

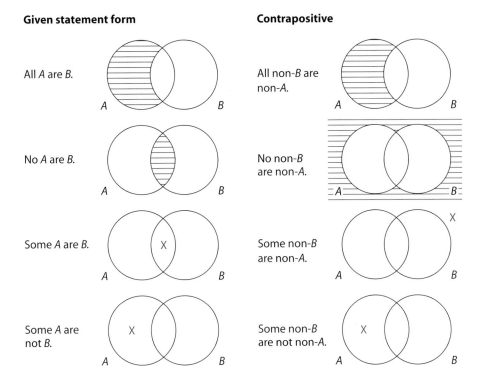

Given statement form		Contrapositive	
All *A* are *B*.		All non-*B* are non-*A*.	
No *A* are *B*.		No non-*B* are non-*A*.	
Some *A* are *B*.		Some non-*B* are non-*A*.	
Some *A* are not *B*.		Some non-*B* are not non-*A*.	

To see how the first diagram on the right is drawn, remember that "non-*A*" designates the area outside *A*. Thus, "All non-*B* are non-*A*" asserts that all members of non-*B* are outside *A*. This means that no members of non-*B* are inside *A*. Thus, we shade the area where non-*B* overlaps *A*. "No non-*B* are non-*A*" asserts that the area where non-*B* overlaps non-*A* is empty. Since non-*B* is the area outside the *B* circle and non-*A* is the area outside the *A* circle, the place where these two areas overlap is the area outside both circles. Thus, we shade this area. "Some non-*B* are non-*A*" asserts that something exists in the area where non-*B* overlaps non-*A*. Again, this is the area outside both circles, so we place an X in this area. Finally, "Some non-*B* are not non-*A*" asserts that at least one member of non-*B* is outside non-*A*. This means that at least one member of non-*B* is inside *A*, so we place an X in the area where non-*B* overlaps *A*.

Now, inspection of the diagrams for the **A** and **O** statements reveals that they are identical to the diagrams of their contrapositive. Thus, the **A** statement and its contrapositive are logically equivalent (and have the same meaning), and the **O** statement and its contrapositive are logically equivalent (and have the same meaning). On the other hand, the diagrams of the **E** and **I** statements are neither identical to nor the exact opposite of the diagrams of their contrapositives. This means that contraposing an **E** or **I** statement gives a new statement whose truth value is logically undetermined in relation to the given statement.

To help remember when conversion and contraposition yield logically equivalent results, note the second and third vowels in the words:

CONVER**SI**ON

CONTRA**PO**SITION

As with conversion and obversion, contraposition may provide the link between the premise and the conclusion of an argument. The following argument forms are valid:

All *A* are *B*.
Therefore, all non-*B* are non-*A*.

Some *A* are not *B*.
Therefore, some non-*B* are not non-*A*.

On the other hand, the following argument forms are invalid. Each commits the fallacy of **illicit contraposition:**

Some *A* are *B*.
Therefore, some non-*B* are non-*A*.

No *A* are *B*.
Therefore, no non-*B* are non-*A*.

Here are two examples of arguments that commit the fallacy of illicit contraposition:

No dogs are cats.	(True)
Therefore, no non-cats are non-dogs.	(False)
Some animals are non-cats.	(True)
Therefore, some cats are non-animals.	(False)

In regard to the first argument, an example of something that is both a non-cat and a non-dog is a pig. Thus, the conclusion implies that no pigs are pigs, which is false. In regard to the second argument, if both premise and conclusion are obverted, the premise becomes "Some animals are not cats," which is true, and the conclusion becomes "Some cats are not animals," which is false.

Both illicit conversion and illicit contraposition are formal fallacies: They can be detected through mere examination of the form of an argument.

Finally, note that the Boolean interpretation of categorical propositions has prevailed throughout this section. This means that the results obtained are unconditional, and they hold true regardless of whether the terms in the propositions denote actually existing things. Thus, they hold for propositions about unicorns and leprechauns just as they do for propositions about dogs and animals. These results are summarized in the following table.

Conversion: Switch subject and predicate terms.

Given statement	Converse	Truth value
E: No A are B.	No B are A.	Same truth value as given statement
I: Some A are B.	Some B are A.	
A: All A are B.	All B are A.	Undetermined truth value
O: Some A are not B.	Some B are not A.	

Obversion: Change quality, and replace predicate term with term complement.

Given statement	Obverse	Truth value
A: All A are B.	No A are non-B.	Same truth value as given statement
E: No A are B.	All A are non-B.	
I: Some A are B.	Some A are not non-B.	
O: Some A are not B.	Some A are non-B.	

Contraposition: Switch subject and predicate terms, and replace each with its term complement.

Given statement	Contrapositive	Truth value
A: All A are B.	All non-B are non-A.	Same truth value as given statement
O: Some A are not B.	Some non-B are not non-A.	
E: No A are B.	No non-B are non-A.	Undetermined truth value
I: Some A are B.	Some non-B are non-A.	

EXERCISE 4.4

I. Exercises 1 through 6 provide a statement, its truth value in parentheses, and an operation to be performed on that statement. Supply the new statement and the truth value of the new statement. Exercises 7 through 12 provide a statement, its truth value in parentheses, and a new statement. Determine how the new statement was derived from the given statement and supply the truth value of the new statement.

Given statement	Operation	New statement	Truth value
★1. No A are non-B. (T)	conv.	_____	_____
2. Some A are B. (T)	contrap.	_____	_____
3. All A are non-B. (F)	obv.	_____	_____
★4. All non-A are B. (F)	contrap.	_____	_____
5. Some non-A are not B. (T)	conv.	_____	_____
6. Some non-A are non-B. (T)	obv.	_____	_____
★7. No non-A are non-B. (F)	_____	No B are A.	_____
8. Some A are not non-B. (T)	_____	Some A are B.	_____
9. All A are non-B. (F)	_____	All non-B are A.	_____
★10. No non-A are B. (F)	_____	All non-A are non-B.	_____
11. Some non-A are not B. (T)	_____	Some non-B are not A.	_____
12. Some A are non-B. (F)	_____	Some non-B are A.	_____

II. Perform the operations of conversion, obversion, and contraposition as indicated.

1. Convert the following propositions and state whether the converse is logically equivalent or not logically equivalent to the given proposition.

★a. All hurricanes are storms intensified by global warming.

b. No sex-change operations are completely successful procedures.

c. Some murals by Diego Rivera are works that celebrate the revolutionary spirit.

d. Some forms of carbon are not substances with a crystalline structure.

2. Obvert the following propositions and state whether the obverse is logically equivalent or not logically equivalent to the given proposition.

★a. All radically egalitarian societies are societies that do not preserve individual liberties.

b. No cult leaders are people who fail to brainwash their followers.

c. Some college football coaches are people who do not slip money to their players.

d. Some budgetary cutbacks are not actions fair to the poor.

3. Contrapose the following propositions and state whether the contrapositive is logically equivalent or not logically equivalent to the given proposition.

★a. All physicians whose licenses have been revoked are physicians ineligible to practice.

b. No unpersecuted migrants are migrants granted asylum.

c. Some politicians who do not defend Social Security are politicans who do not want to increase taxes.

d. Some opponents of gay marriage are not opponents of civil unions.

III. Use conversion, obversion, and contraposition to determine whether the following arguments are valid or invalid. For those that are invalid, name the fallacy committed.

★1. All commodity traders are gamblers who risk sudden disaster.
Therefore, all gamblers who risk sudden disaster are commodity traders.

2. No child abusers are people who belong in day-care centers.
Therefore, all child abusers are people who do not belong in day-care centers.

3. Some states having limited powers are not slave states.
Therefore, some free states are not states having unlimited powers.

★4. Some insane people are illogical people.
Therefore, some logical people are sane people.

5. Some organ transplants are not sensible operations.
Therefore, some organ transplants are senseless operations.

6. No individuals who laugh all the time are people with a true sense of humor.
Therefore, no people with a true sense of humor are individuals who laugh all the time.

★7. All periods when interest rates are high are times when businesses tend not to expand.
Therefore, all times when businesses tend to expand are periods when interest rates are low.

8. Some swimsuits are not garments intended for the water.
Therefore, some garments intended for the water are not swimsuits.

9. No promises made under duress are enforceable contracts.
Therefore, no unenforceable contracts are promises made in the absence of duress.

★10. All ladies of the night are individuals with low self-esteem.
Therefore, no ladies of the night are individuals with high self-esteem.

11. Some graffiti writers are artists relieving pent-up frustrations.
Therefore, some artists relieving pent-up frustrations are graffiti writers.

12. Some peaceful revolutions are episodes that erupt in violence.
Therefore, some episodes that do not erupt in violence are non-peaceful revolutions.

★13. Some insurance companies are not humanitarian organizations.
Therefore, some humanitarian organizations are not insurance companies.

14. Some fossil fuels are unrenewable energy sources.
Therefore, some fossil fuels are not renewable energy sources.

15. All hired killers are criminals who deserve the death penalty.
Therefore, all criminals who deserve the death penalty are hired killers.

★16. No nonprescription drugs are medicines without adverse effects.
Therefore, no medicines with adverse effects are prescription drugs.

17. All fire-breathing dragons are lizards that languish in soggy climates.
Therefore, no fire-breathing dragons are lizards that flourish in soggy climates.

18. Some distant galaxies are not spiral-shaped arrangements.
Therefore, some spiral-shaped arrangements are not distant galaxies.

★19. All unpleasant experiences are things we do not like to remember.
Therefore, all things we like to remember are pleasant experiences.

20. Some pro-lifers are not people concerned with child welfare.
Therefore, some pro-lifers are people unconcerned with child welfare.

4.5   The Traditional Square of Opposition

In Section 4.3 we adopted the Boolean standpoint, and we saw how the modern square of opposition applies regardless of whether the propositions refer to actually existing things. In this section, we adopt the Aristotelian standpoint, which recognizes that universal propositions about existing things have existential import. For such propositions the traditional square of opposition becomes applicable. Like the modern square, the **traditional square of opposition** is an arrangement of lines that illustrates logically necessary relations among the four kinds of categorical propositions. However, because the Aristotelian standpoint recognizes the additional factor of existential import, the traditional square supports more inferences than does the modern square. It is represented as follows:

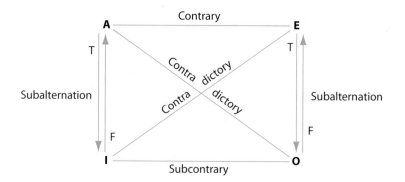

The four relations in the traditional square of opposition may be characterized as follows:

Contradictory = opposite truth value
Contrary = at least one is false (not both true)
Subcontrary = at least one is true (not both false)
Subalternation = truth flows downward, falsity flows upward

The **contradictory relation** is the same as that found in the modern square. Thus, if a certain **A** proposition is given as true, the corresponding **O** proposition is false, and vice versa, and if a certain **A** proposition is given as false, the corresponding **O** proposition is true, and vice versa. The same relation holds between the **E** and **I** propositions. The contradictory relation thus expresses complete opposition between propositions.

The **contrary relation** differs from the contradictory in that it expresses only partial opposition. Thus, if a certain **A** proposition is given as true, the corresponding **E** proposition is false (because at least one must be false), and if an **E** proposition is given as true, the corresponding **A** proposition is false. But if an **A** proposition is given as false, the corresponding **E** proposition could be *either* true or false without violating the "at least one is false" rule. In this case, the **E** proposition has logically undetermined truth value. Similarly, if an **E** proposition is given as false, the corresponding **A** proposition has logically undetermined truth value.

These results are borne out in ordinary language. Thus, if we are given the actually true **A** proposition "All cats are animals," the corresponding **E** proposition "No cats are animals" is false, and if we are given the actually true **E** proposition "No cats are dogs," the corresponding **A** proposition "All cats are dogs" is false. Thus, the **A** and **E** propositions cannot both be true. However, they can both be false. "All animals are cats" and "No animals are cats" are both false.

The **subcontrary relation** also expresses a kind of partial opposition. If a certain **I** proposition is given as false, the corresponding **O** proposition is true (because at least one must be true), and if an **O** proposition is given as false, the corresponding **I** proposition is true. But if either an **I** or an **O** proposition is given as true, then the corresponding proposition could be either true or false without violating the "at least one is true" rule. Thus, in this case the corresponding proposition would have logically undetermined truth value.

Again, these results are borne out in ordinary language. If we are given the actually false **I** proposition "Some cats are dogs," the corresponding **O** proposition "Some cats are not dogs" is true, and if we are given the actually false **O** proposition "Some cats are not animals," the corresponding **I** proposition "Some cats are animals" is true. Thus, the **I** and **O** propositions cannot both be false, but they can both be true. "Some animals are cats" and "Some animals are not cats" are both true.

The **subalternation relation** is represented by two arrows: a downward arrow marked with the letter T (true), and an upward arrow marked with an F (false). These arrows can be thought of as pipelines through which truth values "flow." The downward arrow "transmits" only truth, and the upward arrow only falsity. Thus, if an **A** proposition is given as true, the corresponding **I** proposition is true also, and if an **I** proposition is given as false, the corresponding **A** proposition is false. But if an **A** proposition is given as false, this truth value cannot be transmitted downward, so the corresponding **I** proposition will have logically undetermined truth value. Conversely, if an **I** proposition is given as true, this truth value cannot be transmitted upward, so the corresponding **A** proposition will have logically undetermined truth value. Analogous reasoning prevails for the subalternation relation between the **E** and **O** propositions. To remember the direction of the arrows for subalternation, imagine that truth descends from "above," and falsity rises up from "below."

Now that we have examined these four relations individually, let us see how they can be used together to determine the truth values of corresponding propositions. The first rule of thumb that we should keep in mind when using the square to compute more than one truth value is always to use contradiction first. Now, let us suppose that we are told that the nonsensical proposition "All adlers are bobkins" is true. Suppose further that adlers actually exist, so we are justified in using the traditional square of opposition. By the contradictory relation, "Some adlers are not bobkins" is false. Then, by either the contrary or the subalternation relation, "No adlers are bobkins" is false. Finally, by either contradictory, subalternation, or subcontrary, "Some adlers are bobkins" is true.

Next, let us see what happens if we assume that "All adlers are bobkins" is false. By the contradictory relation, "Some adlers are not bobkins" is true, but nothing more can be determined. In other words, given a false **A** proposition, both contrary and subalternation yield undetermined results, and given a true **O** proposition (the one whose truth value we just determined), subcontrary and subalternation yield undetermined results. Thus, the corresponding **E** and **I** propositions have logically undetermined truth value. This result illustrates two more rules of thumb. Assuming that we always use the contradictory relation first, if one of the remaining relations yields a logically undetermined truth value, the others will as well. The other rule is that whenever one statement turns out to have logically undetermined truth value, its contradictory will also. Thus, statements having logically undetermined truth value will always occur in pairs, at opposite ends of diagonals on the square.

Testing Immediate Inferences

Next, let us see how we can use the traditional square of opposition to test immediate inferences for validity. Here is an example:

> All Swiss watches are true works of art.
> Therefore, it is false that no Swiss watches are true works of art.

To evaluate this argument, we begin, as usual, by assuming the premise is true. Since the premise is an **A** proposition, by the contrary relation the corresponding **E** proposition is false. But this is exactly what the conclusion says, so the argument is valid.

Here is another example:

> Some viruses are structures that attack T cells.
> Therefore, some viruses are not structures that attack T cells.

Here the premise and conclusion are linked by the subcontrary relation. According to that relation, if the premise is assumed true, the conclusion has logically undetermined truth value, and so the argument is invalid. It commits the formal fallacy of **illicit subcontrary.** Analogously, arguments that depend on an incorrect application of the contrary relation commit the formal fallacy of **illicit contrary,** and arguments that depend on an illicit application of subalternation commit the formal fallacy of **illicit subalternation.** Some forms of these fallacies are as follows:

Illicit contrary

It is false that all *A* are *B*.
Therefore, no *A* are *B*.

It is false that no *A* are *B*.
Therefore, all *A* are *B*.

Illicit subcontrary

Some *A* are *B*.
Therefore, it is false that some *A* are not *B*.

Some *A* are not *B*.
Therefore, some *A* are *B*.

Illicit subalternation

Some *A* are not *B*.
Therefore, no *A* are *B*.

It is false that all *A* are *B*.
Therefore, it is false that some *A* are *B*.

Cases of the incorrect application of the contradictory relation are so infrequent that an "illicit contradictory" fallacy is not usually recognized.

As we saw at the beginning of this section, for the traditional square of opposition to apply, the Aristotelian standpoint must be adopted, and the propositions to which it is applied must assert something about actually existing things. The question may now be asked, What happens when the Aristotelian standpoint is adopted but the propositions are about things that do not exist? The answer is that another fallacy, the **existential fallacy,** is committed. From the Aristotelian standpoint the existential fallacy is committed whenever contrary, subcontrary, and subalternation are used (in an otherwise correct way) with propositions about things that do not exist. The existential fallacy occurs only in connection with these three relations. It does not occur in connection with the contradictory relation, which holds in the same way with nonexisting things as it does with existing things. Also, for the same reason, it does not occur in connection with conversion, obversion, and contraposition. The following inferences commit the existential fallacy:

> All witches who fly on broomsticks are fearless women.
> Therefore, some witches who fly on broomsticks are fearless women.

> No wizards with magical powers are malevolent beings.
> Therefore, it is false that all wizards with magical powers are malevolent beings.

The first depends on an otherwise correct use of the subalternation relation, and the second on an otherwise correct use of the contrary relation. If flying witches and magical wizards actually existed, both arguments would be valid. But since they do not exist, both arguments are invalid and commit the existential fallacy.

In summary, the existential fallacy can be committed in either of two ways. As we saw in Section 4.3, from the Boolean standpoint, the existential fallacy is committed whenever an argument is invalid merely because the premise is interpreted as lacking existential import. Thus, the argument "All cats are animals; therefore, some cats are animals" commits the existential fallacy from the Boolean standpoint. On the other hand, from the Aristotelian standpoint, the existential fallacy is committed whenever the validity of an argument depends on existential import and the requisite things do not exist. Thus, the argument "All unicorns are animals; therefore, some unicorns are animals" commits the existential fallacy from the Aristotelian standpoint. Any argument that commits the existential fallacy from the Aristotelian standpoint also commits it from the Boolean standpoint, but the converse obviously is not true.

> **Existential fallacy examples—Two standpoints**
>
> All cats are animals.   } Boolean: Invalid, existential fallacy
> Some cats are animals.   Aristotelian: Valid
>
> All unicorns are animals.   } Boolean: Invalid, existential fallacy
> Some unicorns are animals.   Aristotelian: Invalid, existential fallacy

The phrase **conditionally valid** applies to an argument after the Aristotelian standpoint has been adopted and we are not certain if the subject term of the premise denotes actually existing things. For example, the following argument is conditionally valid:

> All students who failed the exam are students on probation.
> Therefore, some students who failed the exam are students on probation.

The validity of this argument rests on whether there were in fact any students who failed the exam. The argument is either valid or invalid, but we lack sufficient information about the meaning of the premise to tell which is the case. Once it becomes known that there are indeed some students who failed the exam, we can assert that the argument is valid from the Aristotelian standpoint. But if there are no students who failed the exam, the argument is invalid because it commits the existential fallacy.

Similarly, all argument *forms* that depend on valid applications of contrary, subcontrary, and subalternation are conditionally valid because we do not know if the letters in the propositions denote actually existing things. For example, the following argument form, which depends on the contrary relation, is conditionally valid:

> All *A* are *B*.
> Therefore, it is false that no *A* are *B*.

If "dogs" and "animals" are substituted in place of *A* and *B*, respectively, the resulting argument is valid. But if "unicorns" and "animals" are substituted, the resulting argument is invalid because it commits the existential fallacy. In Section 4.3, we noted that all arguments (and argument forms) that are valid from the Boolean standpoint are *unconditionally valid*. They are valid regardless of whether their terms denote actually existing things.

Now that we have seen how the traditional square of opposition, by itself, is used to test arguments for validity, let us see how it can be used together with the operations of conversion, obversion, and contraposition to prove the validity of arguments that are given as valid. Suppose we are given the following valid argument:

> All inappropriate remarks are faux pas.
> Therefore, some faux pas are not appropriate remarks.

To prove this argument valid, we select letters to represent the terms, and then we use some combination of conversion, obversion, and contraposition together with the traditional square to find the intermediate links between premise and conclusion:

> All non-*A* are *F*.   (assumed true)
> Some non-*A* are *F*.   (true by subalternation)
> Some *F* are non-*A*.   (true by conversion)
> Therefore, some *F* are not *A*.   (true by obversion)

The premise is the first line in this proof, and each succeeding step is validly derived from the one preceding it by the relation written in parentheses at the right. Since the conclusion (which is the last step) follows by a series of three necessary inferences, the argument is valid.

Various strategies can be used to construct proofs such as this, but one useful procedure is first to concentrate on obtaining the individual terms as they appear in the conclusion, then to attend to the order of the terms, and finally to use the square of opposition to adjust quality and quantity. As the example proof illustrates, however, variations on this procedure are sometimes necessary. The fact that the predicate of the conclusion is "*A*," while "non-*A*" appears in the premise, leads us to think of obversion. But using obversion to change "non-*A*" into "*A*" requires that the "non-*A*" in the premise be moved into the predicate position via conversion. The latter operation, however, is valid only on **E** and **I** statements, and the premise is an **A** statement. The fact that the conclusion is a particular statement suggests subalternation as an intermediate step, thus yielding an **I** statement that can be converted.

I. Use the traditional square of opposition to find the answers to these problems. When a statement is given as false, simply enter an "F" into the square of opposition and compute (if possible) the other truth values.

★1. If "All fashion fads are products of commercial brainwashing" is true, what is the truth value of the following statements?

   a. No fashion fads are products of commercial brainwashing.
   b. Some fashion fads are products of commercial brainwashing.
   c. Some fashion fads are not products of commercial brainwashing.

2. If "All fashion fads are products of commercial brainwashing" is false, what is the truth value of the following statements?

   a. No fashion fads are products of commercial brainwashing.
   b. Some fashion fads are products of commercial brainwashing.
   c. Some fashion fads are not products of commercial brainwashing.

3. If "No sting operations are cases of entrapment" is true, what is the truth value of the following statements?

   a. All sting operations are cases of entrapment.
   b. Some sting operations are cases of entrapment.
   c. Some sting operations are not cases of entrapment.

★4. If "No sting operations are cases of entrapment" is false, what is the truth value of the following statements?

   a. All sting operations are cases of entrapment.
   b. Some sting operations are cases of entrapment.
   c. Some sting operations are not cases of entrapment.

5. If "Some assassinations are morally justifiable actions" is true, what is the truth value of the following statements?

   a. All assassinations are morally justifiable actions.
   b. No assassinations are morally justifiable actions.
   c. Some assassinations are not morally justifiable actions.

6. If "Some assassinations are morally justifiable actions" is false, what is the truth value of the following statements?

   a. All assassinations are morally justifiable actions.
   b. No assassinations are morally justifiable actions.
   c. Some assassinations are not morally justifiable actions.

★7. If "Some obsessive-compulsive behaviors are not curable diseases" is true, what is the truth value of the following statements?

   a. All obsessive-compulsive behaviors are curable diseases.
   b. No obsessive-compulsive behaviors are curable diseases.
   c. Some obsessive-compulsive behaviors are curable diseases.

8. If "Some obsessive-compulsive behaviors are not curable diseases" is false, what is the truth value of the following statements?

   a. All obsessive-compulsive behaviors are curable diseases.

   b. No obsessive-compulsive behaviors are curable diseases.

   c. Some obsessive-compulsive behaviors are curable diseases.

II. Use the traditional square of opposition to determine whether the following arguments are valid or invalid. Name any fallacies that are committed.

★1. All advocates of school prayer are individuals who insist on imposing their views on others.
    Therefore, some advocates of school prayer are individuals who insist on imposing their views on others.

2. It is false that no jailhouse informants are people who can be trusted.
   Therefore, some jailhouse informants are not people who can be trusted.

3. All homemakers are people with real jobs.
   Therefore, it is false that no homemakers are people with real jobs.

★4. It is false that some trolls are not creatures who live under bridges.
    Therefore, it is false that no trolls are creatures who live under bridges.

5. Some campus romances are episodes plagued by violence.
   Therefore, some campus romances are not episodes plagued by violence.

6. Some pornographic publications are materials protected by the First Amendment.
   Therefore, it is false that no pornographic publications are materials protected by the First Amendment.

★7. It is false that all mainstream conservatives are people who support free legal services for the poor.
    Therefore, no mainstream conservatives are people who support free legal services for the poor.

8. It is false that some forms of human creativity are activities amenable to mathematical analysis.
   Therefore, it is false that all forms of human creativity are activities amenable to mathematical analysis.

9. It is false that some tooth fairies are daytime visitors.
   Therefore, some tooth fairies are not daytime visitors.

★10. It is false that some orthodox psychoanalysts are not individuals driven by a religious fervor.
    Therefore, it is false that some orthodox psychoanalysts are individuals driven by a religious fervor.

11. Some starship captains are not members of the Federation.
    Therefore, it is false that all starship captains are members of the Federation.

12. It is false that some network news programs are exercises in mediocrity.
    Therefore, it is false that no network news programs are exercises in mediocrity.

★13. No flying reindeer are animals who get lost in the fog.
Therefore, it is false that all flying reindeer are animals who get lost in the fog.

14. It is false that no leveraged buyouts are deals unfair to workers.
Therefore, all leveraged buyouts are deals unfair to workers.

15. It is false that some wood ticks are not carriers of Lyme disease.
Therefore, some wood ticks are carriers of Lyme disease.

III. Exercises 1 through 10 provide a statement, its truth value in parentheses, and an operation to be performed on that statement. Supply the new statement and the truth value of the new statement. Exercises 11 through 20 provide a statement, its truth value in parentheses, and a new statement. Determine how the new statement was derived from the given statement and supply the truth value of the new statement. Take the Aristotelian standpoint in working these exercises and assume that the terms refer to actually existing things.

Given statement	Operation/relation	New statement	Truth value
★1. All non-A are B. (T)	contrap.	_____	_____
2. Some A are non-B. (F)	subalt.	_____	_____
3. No A are non-B. (T)	obv.	_____	_____
★4. Some non-A are not B. (T)	subcon.	_____	_____
5. No A are non-B. (F)	contradic.	_____	_____
6. No A are B. (T)	contrap.	_____	_____
★7. All non-A are B. (T)	contrary	_____	_____
8. Some A are not non-B. (F)	obv.	_____	_____
9. No A are non-B. (F)	conv.	_____	_____
★10. Some non-A are non-B. (F)	subcon.	_____	_____
11. Some non-A are not B. (T)	_____	All non-A are B.	_____
12. Some A are non-B. (T)	_____	Some non-B are A.	_____
★13. All non-A are B. (F)	_____	No non-A are non-B.	_____
14. Some non-A are not B. (T)	_____	No non-A are B.	_____
15. All A are non-B. (F)	_____	All non-B are A.	_____
★16. Some non-A are non-B. (F)	_____	No non-A are non-B.	_____
17. Some A are not non-B. (T)	_____	Some B are not non-A.	_____
18. No non-A are B. (T)	_____	Some non-A are not B.	_____
★19. No A are non-B. (F)	_____	All A are non-B.	_____
20. Some non-A are B. (F)	_____	Some non-A are not B.	_____

IV. Use either the traditional square of opposition or conversion, obversion, or contraposition to determine whether the following arguments are valid or invalid. For those that are invalid, name the fallacy committed.

★1. It is false that some jogging events are not aerobic activities.
Therefore, it is false that no jogging events are aerobic activities.

2. No meat-eating vegetarians are individuals with a high-protein diet.
Therefore, no individuals with a high-protein diet are meat-eating vegetarians.

3. Some jobs in health care are not glamorous occupations.
Therefore, some jobs in health care are glamorous occupations.

★4. Some terminally ill patients are patients who do not want to live.
Therefore, some patients who want to live are recovering patients.

5. All Barbie dolls are toys that engender a false sense of values.
Therefore, no Barbie dolls are toys that engender a true sense of values.

6. All flying elephants are jolly pachyderms.
Therefore, some flying elephants are jolly pachyderms.

★7. It is false that some international terrorists are political moderates.
Therefore, some international terrorists are not political moderates.

8. No pet hamsters are animals that need much attention.
Therefore, it is false that all pet hamsters are animals that need much attention.

9. Some hedge-fund managers are not responsible investors.
Therefore, some responsible investors are not hedge-fund managers.

★10. It is false that all substances that control cell growth are hormones.
Therefore, no substances that control cell growth are hormones.

11. Some cases of whistle-blowing are actions disloyal to employers.
Therefore, some cases of whistle-blowing are not actions loyal to employers.

12. No stolen computer chips are easy items to trace.
Therefore, no difficult items to trace are computer chips that are not stolen.

★13. Some economists are followers of Ayn Rand.
Therefore, some economists are not followers of Ayn Rand.

14. All porcelain figurines are fragile artifacts.
Therefore, it is false that some porcelain figurines are not fragile artifacts.

15. Some pleasant recollections are not missed opportunities.
Therefore, some availed opportunities are not unpleasant recollections.

V. Use the traditional square of opposition together with conversion, obversion, and contraposition to prove that the following arguments are valid. Show each intermediate step in the deduction.

★1. All insurance policies are cryptically written documents.
Therefore, some cryptically written documents are insurance policies.

2. No gemstones that do not contain chromium are emeralds.
Therefore, some stones that are not emeralds are not gemstones that contain chromium.

3. It is false that some *Ficus benjaminas* are untemperamental house plants.
Therefore, all *Ficus benjaminas* are temperamental house plants.

★4. All exogenous morphines are addictive substances.
Therefore, it is false that all addictive substances are endogenous morphines.

5. No people who do not advocate free-enterprise economics are fundamental-ist Christians.
   Therefore, it is false that some fundamentalist Christians are not people who advocate free-enterprise economics.

6. It is false that some Gothic cathedrals are buildings that do not feature pointed arches.
   Therefore, some buildings that feature pointed arches are Gothic cathedrals.

★7. Some people who recognize paranormal events are not non-scientists.
   Therefore, it is false that no scientists are people who recognize paranormal events.

8. It is false that no unhealthy things to ingest are food additives.
   Therefore, some food additives are not healthy things to ingest.

9. It is false that some illegal searches are not sobriety checkpoints.
   Therefore, some sobriety checkpoints are not legal searches.

★10. It is false that some feminists are not advocates of equal pay for equal work.
   Therefore, it is false that all advocates of equal pay for equal work are non-feminists.

4.6   Venn Diagrams and the Traditional Standpoint

Earlier in this chapter we saw how Venn diagrams can be used to represent the content of categorical propositions from the Boolean standpoint. With a slight modification they can also be used to represent the content of categorical propositions from the tra-ditional, or Aristotelian, standpoint. These modified Venn diagrams can then be used to prove the relationships of the traditional square of opposition, and also to test the validity of immediate inferences from the traditional standpoint.

The difference between the Boolean standpoint and the Aristotelian standpoint concerns only universal (**A** and **E**) propositions. From the Boolean standpoint, univer-sal propositions have no existential import, but from the Aristotelian standpoint they do have existential import when their subject terms refer to actually existing things. For example, from the Boolean standpoint the statement "All raccoons are pests" does not imply the existence of anything, but from the Aristotelian standpoint it implies the existence of raccoons. Thus, if we are to construct a Venn diagram to represent such a statement from the Aristotelian standpoint, we need to use some symbol that represents this implication of existence.

The symbol that we will use for this purpose is an X surrounded by a circle. Like the X's that we have used up until now, this circled X signifies that something exists in the area in which it is placed. However, the two symbols differ in that the uncircled X represents the positive claim of existence made by particular (**I** and **O**) propositions, whereas the circled X represents the implication of existence made by universal propo-sitions about actually existing things. Such statements may be diagrammed from the Aristotelian standpoint as follows:

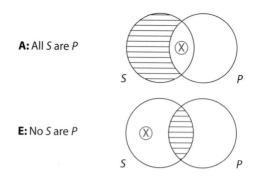

A: All *S* are *P*

E: No *S* are *P*

In the diagram for the **A** statement, the left-hand part of the *S* circle is shaded, so if there are any members of *S*, they must be in the area where the two circles overlap. Thus, a circled X is placed in the overlap area. In the diagram for the **E** statement, the overlap area is shaded, so if there are any members of *S* they must be in the left-hand part of the *S* circle. Thus, a circled X is placed in this area.

The diagrams for the **I** and **O** statements are the same from the Aristotelian standpoint as they are from the Boolean:

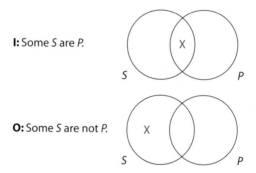

I: Some *S* are *P.*

O: Some *S* are not *P.*

Proving the Traditional Square of Opposition

We can now use this modified Venn diagram technique to prove the relations of the traditional square of opposition. Having such a proof is important because up until now these relations have only been illustrated with various examples; they have not been proved. The accompanying figure reproduces the traditional square of opposition together with Venn diagrams that represent the Aristotelian interpretation of the four standard-form propositions.

Let us begin with the contradictory relation. If the **A** statement is given as true, then the left-hand part of the *S* circle is empty. This makes the **O** statement false, because it claims that the left-hand part of the *S* circle is not empty. And if the **O** state-

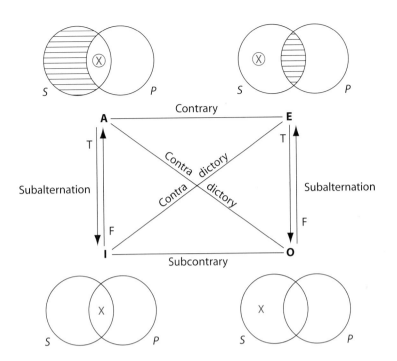

ment is given as true, then the left-hand part of the *S* circle is not empty, which makes the **A** statement false. On the other hand, if the **O** statement is given as false, then the left-hand part of the *S* circle is empty. However, given that some members of *S* exist, they must be in the overlap area. This double outcome makes the **A** statement true. Also, if the **A** statement is given as false, then either the left-hand part of the *S* circle is not empty, or the overlap area is empty (or both). If the left-hand part of the *S* circle is not empty, then the **O** statement is true. Alternately, if the overlap area is empty, then, given that some members of *S* exist, they must be in the left-hand part of the *S* circle, and, once again, the **O** statement is true. Analogous reasoning applies for the relation between the **E** and **I** statements.

Next, we turn to the contrary relation. If the **A** statement is given as true, then the overlap area is not empty, which makes the **E** statement false. By analogous reasoning, if the **E** statement is given as true, the overlap area is empty, which makes the **A** statement false. However, if the **A** statement is given as false (making the **O** statement true), then the **E** statement could be either true or false depending on whether or not the overlap area is empty. Thus, in this case the **E** statement would have logically undetermined truth value. By analogous reasoning, if the **E** statement is given as false (making the **I** statement true), the **A** statement could be either true or false depending on whether or not the left-hand part of the *S* circle is empty. Thus, the **A** statement would have logically undetermined truth value.

Turning next to the subcontrary relation, if the **I** statement is given as false, then the area where the *S* and *P* circles overlap is empty. Given that at least one *S* exists, there must be something in the left-hand part of the *S* circle, which makes the **O** statement true. By analogous reasoning, if the **O** statement is given as false, there must be something in the overlap area, making the **I** statement true. But if the **I** statement is given as true, then the **O** statement could be either true or false depending on whether something exists in the left-hand part of the *S* circle. Thus, the **O** statement would have undetermined truth value. Similarly, if the **O** statement is given as true, then the **I** statement could be either true or false depending on whether something exists in the overlap area. Thus, the **I** statement would have undetermined truth value.

Finally, we consider subalternation. If the **A** statement is given as true, then something exists in the area where the *S* and *P* circles overlap, which makes the **I** statement true as well. And if the **I** statement is given as false, then the overlap area is empty, making the **A** statement false. But if the **A** statement is given as false (making the **O** statement true), then the **I** statement could be either true or false depending on whether something exists in the overlap area. Thus, the **I** statement would have logically undetermined truth value. And if the **I** statement is given as true, then the **A** statement could be either true or false depending on whether or not the left-hand part of the *S* circle is empty. Thus, the **A** statement would have logically undetermined truth value. Analogous reasoning applies for the subalternation relation between the **E** and **O** statements.

Testing Immediate Inferences

From the Aristotelian standpoint, the modified Venn diagram technique involving circled X's can be used to test immediate inferences. The only requirement is that the subject and predicate terms of the conclusion be the same as those of the premise. Such inferences depend on the square of opposition and do not involve the operations of conversion, obversion, and contraposition. Venn diagrams can also be used to test inferences involving these latter operations, but a further modification must be introduced.

Since any argument that is valid from the Boolean standpoint is also valid from the Aristotelian standpoint, testing the argument from the Boolean standpoint is often simpler. If the argument is valid, then it is valid from both standpoints. But if the argument is invalid from the Boolean standpoint and has a particular conclusion, then it may be useful to test it from the Aristotelian standpoint. Let us begin by testing an inference *form* for validity:

> All *A* are *B*.
> Therefore, some *A* are *B*.

First, we draw Venn diagrams from the Boolean standpoint for the premise and conclusion:

All *A* are *B*.

Some *A* are *B*.

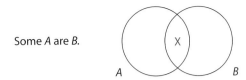

The information of the conclusion diagram is not represented in the premise diagram, so the inference form is not valid from the Boolean standpoint. Thus, noting that the conclusion is particular, we adopt the Aristotelian standpoint and assume for the moment that the subject of the premise (*A*) denotes at least one existing thing. This thing is represented by placing a circled X in the open area of that circle:

All *A* are *B*.

Some *A* are *B*.

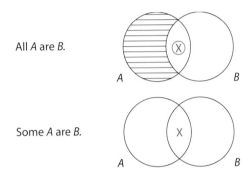

Now the information of the conclusion diagram *is* represented in the premise diagram. Thus, the inference form is conditionally valid from the Aristotelian standpoint. It is valid on condition that the circled X represents at least one existing thing.

To test a complete inference we begin by testing its form. Here is an example:

No penguins are birds that can fly.
Therefore, it is false that all penguins are birds that can fly.

First, we reduce the immediate inference to its form and test it from the Boolean standpoint:

No *P* are *B*.

It is false that
all *P* are *B*.

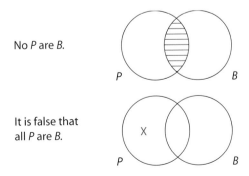

Since the inference form is not valid from the Boolean standpoint, we adopt the Aristotelian standpoint and assume for the sake of this test that the subject of the premise (*P*) denotes at least one existing thing:

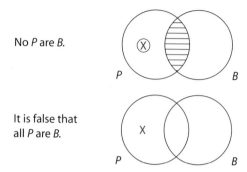

No *P* are *B*.

It is false that all *P* are *B*.

The Venn diagrams show that the inference form is conditionally valid from the Aristotelian standpoint. It is valid on condition that the circled X represents at least one existing thing. Since the circled X is in the *P* circle, the final step is to see if the term in the inference corresponding to *P* denotes something that exists. The term in question is "penguins," and at least one penguin actually exists. Thus, the condition is fulfilled, and the inference is valid from the Aristotelian standpoint.

Another example:

    All sugarplum fairies are delicate creatures.
    Therefore, some sugarplum fairies are delicate creatures.

This immediate inference has the same form as the first one we tested. The form is not valid from the Boolean standpoint, but it is conditionally valid from the Aristotelian standpoint:

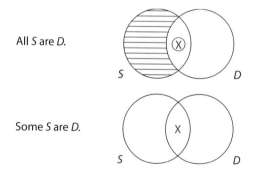

All *S* are *D*.

Some *S* are *D*.

The final step is to see if the circled X represents at least one existing thing. The circled X is in the *S* circle and *S* stands for "sugarplum fairies," which do not exist. Thus, the requisite condition is not fulfilled, and the inference is not valid from the Aristotelian standpoint. The inference commits the existential fallacy.

    The steps involved in testing an immediate inference from the Aristotelian standpoint may now be summarized:

1. Reduce the inference to its form and test it from the Boolean standpoint. If the form is valid, proceed no further. The inference is valid from both standpoints.

2. If the inference form is invalid from the Boolean standpoint and has a particular conclusion, then adopt the Aristotelian standpoint and look to see if the left-hand premise circle is partly shaded. If it is, enter a circled X in the unshaded part and retest the form.

3. If the inference form is conditionally valid, determine if the circled X represents something that exists. If it does, the condition is fulfilled, and the inference is valid from the Aristotelian standpoint. If it does not, the inference is invalid, and it commits the existential fallacy from the Aristotelian standpoint.

EXERCISE 4.6

I. Use the modified Venn diagram technique to determine if the following immediate inference forms are valid from the Boolean standpoint, conditionally valid from the Aristotelian standpoint, or invalid.

★1. Some *A* are not *B*.
   Therefore, no *A* are *B*.

2. It is false that some *A* are *B*.
   Therefore, it is false that all *A* are *B*.

3. It is false that no *A* are *B*.
   Therefore, some *A* are *B*.

★4. All *A* are *B*.
   Therefore, it is false that no *A* are *B*.

5. Some *A* are *B*.
   Therefore, it is false that some *A* are not *B*.

6. Some *A* are not *B*.
   Therefore, it is false that all *A* are *B*.

★7. It is false that some *A* are *B*.
   Therefore, no *A* are *B*.

8. It is false that some *A* are not *B*.
   Therefore, some *A* are *B*.

9. It is false that all *A* are *B*.
   Therefore, no *A* are *B*.

★10. No *A* are *B*.
   Therefore, some *A* are not *B*.

II. Use the modified Venn diagram technique to determine if the following immediate inferences are valid from the Boolean standpoint, valid from the Aristotelian standpoint, or invalid. Identify any inferences that commit the existential fallacy from either standpoint.

★1. No summer romances are banal pastimes.
   Therefore, it is false that some summer romances are banal pastimes.

2. It is false that some people who hunger for wealth are not victims of their obsession.
   Therefore, some people who hunger for wealth are victims of their obsession.

3. No lamps containing genies are ordinary sources of light.
   Therefore, some lamps containing genies are not ordinary sources of light.

★4. It is false that some duck hunters are animal rights activists.
   Therefore, some duck hunters are not animal rights activists.

5. All repressive political regimes are insults to human dignity.
   Therefore, no repressive political regimes are insults to human dignity.

6. It is false that all skating rinks are playgrounds for amateurs.
   Therefore, some skating rinks are not playgrounds for amateurs.

★7. All pixies who slide down moonbeams are fun-loving daredevils.
   Therefore, it is false that no pixies who slide down moonbeams are fun-loving daredevils.

8. It is false that some graduate teaching assistants are not underpaid laborers.
   Therefore, it is false that no graduate teaching assistants are underpaid laborers.

9. Some housing projects are developments riddled with crime.
   Therefore, it is false that no housing projects are developments riddled with crime.

★10. It is false that some thunderstorms are quiescent phenomena.
   Therefore, all thunderstorms are quiescent phenomena.

11. No flower gardens are creations that feature skunk weed.
   Therefore, it is false that all flower gardens are creations that feature skunk weed.

12. It is false that no incendiary devices are contraptions that misfire.
   Therefore, some incendiary devices are not contraptions that misfire.

★13. It is false that some pet lovers are people who think that animals are mere machines.
   Therefore, it is false that all pet lovers are people who think that animals are mere machines.

14. No werewolves are creatures who lurk about in the daytime.
   Therefore, it is false that all werewolves are creatures who lurk about in the daytime.

15. Some soccer games are not thrilling events to watch.
   Therefore, no soccer games are thrilling events to watch.

4.7 Translating Ordinary Language Statements into Categorical Form

Although few statements that occur in ordinary written and oral expression are categorical propositions in standard form, many of them can be translated into standard-form propositions. Such translation has two chief benefits. The first is that the operations and inferences pertinent to standard-form categorical propositions (contrary, subcontrary, etc.) become applicable to these statements. The second is that such statements, once translated, are completely clear and unambiguous as to their meaning. Many statements in ordinary language are susceptible to multiple interpretations, and each interpretation represents one possible mode of translation. The effort to translate such statements discloses the various interpretations and thus helps prevent misunderstanding and confusion.

Translating statements into categorical form is like any other kind of translation in that no set of specific rules will cover every possible form of phraseology. Yet, one general rule always applies: Understand the *meaning* of the given statement, and then reexpress it in a new statement that has a quantifier, subject term, copula, and predicate term. Some of the forms of phraseology that are typically encountered are terms without nouns, nonstandard verbs, singular propositions, adverbs and pronouns, unexpressed and nonstandard quantifiers, conditional statements, exclusive propositions, "the only," and exceptive propositions.

1. Terms Without Nouns

The subject and predicate terms of a categorical proposition must contain either a plural noun or a pronoun that serves to denote the class indicated by the term. Nouns and pronouns denote classes, while adjectives (and participles) connote attributes. If a term consists of only an adjective, a plural noun or pronoun should be introduced to make the term genuinely denotative. Examples:

Some roses are red.	Some roses are red *flowers*.
All tigers are carnivorous.	All tigers are carnivorous *animals*.

2. Nonstandard Verbs

According to the position adopted earlier in this chapter, the only copulas that are allowed in standard-form categorical propositions are "are" and "are not." Statements in ordinary usage, however, often incorporate other forms of the verb "to be." Such statements may be translated as the following examples illustrate:

Some college students will become educated.	Some college students *are people who* will become educated.
Some dogs would rather bark than bite.	Some dogs *are animals that* would rather bark than bite.

In other statements no form of the verb "to be" occurs at all. These may be translated as the following examples indicate:

Some birds fly south during the winter.	Some birds *are animals that* fly south during the winter.
All ducks swim.	All ducks *are swimmers*.
	or
	All ducks *are animals that* swim.

3. Singular Propositions

A **singular proposition (statement)** is a proposition that makes an assertion about a specific person, place, thing, or time. Singular propositions are typically translated into universals by means of a parameter. A **parameter** is a phrase that, when introduced into a statement, affects the form but not the meaning. Some parameters that may be used to translate singular propositions are these:

> people identical to
> places identical to
> things identical to
> cases identical to
> times identical to

For example, the statement "Socrates is mortal" may be translated as "All people identical to Socrates are people who are mortal." Because only one person is identical to Socrates, namely Socrates himself, the term "people identical to Socrates" denotes the class that has Socrates as its only member. In other words, it simply denotes Socrates. Such a translation admittedly leaves some of the original information behind, because singular statements usually have existential import, whereas universal statements do not—at least from the Boolean standpoint. But if such translations are interpreted from the Aristotelian standpoint, the existential import is preserved. Here are some examples:

George went home.	All *people identical to* George are *people who* went home.
Sandra did not go shopping.	No *people identical to* Sandra are *people who* went shopping.
There is a radio in the bedroom.	All *places identical to* the bedroom are *places* there is a radio. or *Some* radios are *things* in the bedroom.
The moon is full tonight.	All *things identical to* the moon are *things that* are full tonight. or All *times identical to* tonight are *times* the moon is full.
I hate gin.	All *people identical to* me are *people who* hate gin. or All *things identical to* gin are *things that* I hate.

In translating singular statements, note that the parameter "people identical to" is *not* the same as "people similar to" or "people like." There may be many people *like* Socrates, but there is only one person *identical to* Socrates. Also note that parameters should *not* be used when the term in question already has a plural noun (or pronoun) that denotes the intended class. Such use is not wrong, technically, but it is redundant. Example:

Diamonds are carbon allotropes.

Correct: All diamonds are carbon allotropes.

Redundant: All things identical to diamonds are things identical to carbon allotropes.

4. Adverbs and Pronouns

When a statement contains a spatial adverb such as "where," "wherever," "anywhere," "everywhere," or "nowhere," or a temporal adverb such as "when," "whenever," "anytime," "always," or "never," it may be translated in terms of "places" or "times," respectively. Statements containing pronouns such as "who," "whoever," "anyone," "what," "whatever," or "anything" may be translated in terms of "people" or "things," respectively. Examples:

He always wears a suit to work.

All *times* he goes to work are *times* he wears a suit.

He is always clean shaven.

All *times* are *times* he is clean shaven.

She never brings her lunch to school.

No *times* she goes to school are *times* she brings her lunch.

Nowhere on earth are there any unicorns.

No *places* on earth are *places* there are unicorns.

Whoever works hard will succeed.

All *people* who work hard are *people* who will succeed.

Whenever he wins he celebrates.

All *times* he wins are *times* he celebrates.

She goes where she chooses.

All *places* she chooses to go are *places* she goes.

She does what she wants.

All *things* she wants to do are *things* she does.

Notice the order of the subject and predicate terms in the last four examples. When translating statements such as these it is often easy to confuse the subject term with the predicate term. However, since these statements are all translated as **A** type categorical propositions, such a mix-up amounts to committing the fallacy of illicit conversion. To prevent it from happening, keep this rule in mind: For "W" words ("who," "what," "when," "where," "whoever," "whatever," "whenever," "wherever"), the language following the "W" word goes into the subject term of the categorical proposition.

5. Unexpressed Quantifiers

Many statements in ordinary usage have quantifiers that are implied but not expressed. In introducing the quantifiers one must be guided by the most probable meaning of the statement. Examples:

Emeralds are green gems.	*All* emeralds are green gems.
There are lions in the zoo.	*Some* lions are animals in the zoo.
A tiger is a mammal.	*All* tigers are mammals.
A fish is not a mammal.	*No* fish are mammals.
A tiger roared.	*Some* tigers are animals that roared.
Children are human beings.	*All* children are human beings.
Children live next door.	*Some* children are people who live next door.

6. Nonstandard Quantifiers

In some ordinary language statements, the quantity is indicated by words other than the three standard-form quantifiers. Such words include "few," "a few," "not every," "anyone," and various other forms. Another problem occurs when the quantifier "all" is combined with the copula "are not." As we have already seen, statements of the form "All *S* are not *P*" are *not* standard-form propositions. Depending on their meaning, they should be translated as either "No *S* are *P*" or "Some *S* are not *P*." When the intended meaning is "Some *S* are not *P*," the meaning may be indicated by placing oral emphasis on the word "all." For example, "*All* athletes are not superstars" means "Some athletes are not superstars." Here are some additional examples:

A few soldiers are heroes.	*Some* soldiers are heroes.
Anyone who votes is a citizen.	*All* voters are citizens.
Not everyone who votes is a Democrat.	*Some* voters are not Democrats.
Not a single dog is a cat.	*No* dogs are cats.
All newborns are not able to talk.	*No* newborns are people able to talk.
All prisoners are not violent.	*Some* prisoners are not violent people.
Many entertainers are comedians	*Some* entertainers are comedians.
Several demonstrators were arrested.	*Some* demonstrators are people who were arrested.
Few sailors entered the regatta.	*Some* sailors are people who entered the regatta *and some* sailors are not people who entered the regatta.

Notice that this last statement beginning with "few" cannot be translated as a single categorical proposition. Such statements (and some beginning with "a few") must be translated as a compound arrangement of an **I** proposition and an **O** proposition. Statements beginning with "almost all" and "not quite all" must be handled in the same way. When these statements occur in arguments, the arguments must be treated in the same way as those containing exceptive propositions, which will be discussed shortly.

7. Conditional Statements

When the antecedent and consequent of a conditional statement refer to the same class of things, the statement can usually be translated into categorical form. Such statements are always translated as universals. Language following the word "if" goes in the subject term of the categorical proposition, and language following "only if" goes in the predicate term. Examples:

If it's a mouse, then it's a mammal.	All mice are mammals.
If a bear is hungry, then it is dangerous.	All hungry bears are dangerous animals.
Jewelry is expensive if it is made of gold.	All pieces of jewelry made of gold are expensive things.
A car is a Camry only if it's a Toyota.	All Camrys are Toyotas.

Conditional statements having a negated consequent are usually best translated as **E** propositions. Examples:

If it's a turkey, then it's not a mammal.	No turkeys are mammals.
If an animal has four legs, then it is not a bird.	No four-legged animals are birds.
A knife will cut only if it isn't dull.	No knives that cut are dull knives.

The word "unless" means "if not." Since language following the word "if" goes in the subject, statements containing "unless" are translated as categorical propositions having negated subject terms. Examples:

Tomatoes are edible unless they are spoiled.	All unspoiled tomatoes are edible tomatoes.
Unless a boy misbehaves he will be treated decently.	All boys who do not misbehave are boys who will be treated decently.

8. Exclusive Propositions

Many propositions that involve the words "only," "none but," "none except," and "no . . . except" are exclusive propositions. Efforts to translate them into categorical propositions often lead to confusing the subject term with the predicate term. To avoid such confusion keep in mind that language following "only," "none but," "none except," and "no . . . except" goes in the predicate term of the categorical proposition. For example, the statement "Only executives can use the silver elevator" is translated "All people who can use the silver elevator are executives." If it were translated "All executives are people who can use the silver elevator," the translation would be incorrect. Examples:

Only elected officials will attend the convention.	All people who will attend the convention are elected officials.
None but the brave deserve the fair.	All people who deserve the fair are brave people.

No birds except peacocks are proud of their tails.	All birds proud of their tails are peacocks.
He owns only blue-chip stocks.	All stocks he owns are blue-chip stocks.
She invited only wealthy socialites.	All people she invited are wealthy socialites.

For a statement involving "only," "none but," "none except," and "no . . . except" to be a genuinely exclusive proposition, the word that follows these words must be a *plural* noun or pronoun. If the word that follows "only," "none but," or the like designates an *individual*, the statement really asserts two things. For example, the statement "Only Megan painted a picture" asserts that Megan painted a picture *and* that no other person painted a picture. Thus it would be translated as two statements: "All people identical to Megan are people who painted a picture, *and* all people who painted a picture are people identical to Megan." This section of the book will ignore cases where the word following "only," "none but," or the like designates an individual.

Also note that many English statements containing "only" are ambiguous because "only" can be interpreted as modifying alternate words in the statement. Consider, for example, the statement "He only jogs after sunset." Does this mean "He is the only person who jogs after sunset" or "He jogs and does not walk after sunset" or "The only time he jogs is after sunset"? If the statement's context does not provide an answer, the translator is free to pick any of these senses for translation. This same ambiguity, incidentally, affects the last two examples in the earlier list. Accordingly, they might also be translated "All things he owns are blue-chip stocks" and "All socialites she invited are wealthy people."

9. "The Only"

Statements beginning with the words "the only" are translated differently from those beginning with "only." For example, the statement "The only cars that are available are Chevrolets" means "If a car is available, then it is a Chevrolet." This in turn is translated as "All cars that are available are Chevrolets." In other words, language following "the only" goes in the subject term of the categorical proposition. Examples:

| The only animals that live in this canyon are skunks. | All animals that live in this canyon are skunks. |
| Accountants are the only ones who will be hired. | All those who will be hired are accountants. |

Statements involving "the only" are similar to those involving "only" in this one respect: When the statement is about an *individual*, two statements are needed to translate it. For example, "The only person who painted a picture is Megan" means that Megan painted a picture, *and* no other person painted a picture. The statement is equivalent in meaning to "Only Megan painted a picture." Thus, it is translated "All people identical to Megan are people who painted a picture, *and* all people who painted a picture are people identical to Megan." Statements involving "the only" that refer to individuals are ignored throughout the remainder of this chapter.

10. Exceptive Propositions

Propositions of the form "All except S are P" and "All but S are P" are exceptive propositions. They must be translated not as single categorical propositions but as pairs of conjoined categorical propositions. Statements that include the phrase "none except," on the other hand, are exclusive (not exceptive) propositions. "None except" is synonymous with "none but." Here are some examples of exceptive propositions:

All except students are invited.	No students are invited people, and all nonstudents are invited people.
All but managers must report to the president.	No managers are people who must report to the president, and all nonmanagers are people who must report to the president.

Because exceptive propositions cannot be translated into single categorical propositions, many of the simple inferences and operations pertinent to categorical propositions cannot be applied to them. Arguments that contain exceptive propositions as premises or conclusion can be evaluated only through the application of extended techniques. This topic is taken up in the next chapter.

Key word (to be eliminated)	Translation hint
whoever, wherever, always, anyone, never, etc.	use "all" together with people, places, times
a few, several, many	use "some"
if . . . then	use "all" or "no"
unless	use "if not"
only, none but, none except, no . . . except	use "all"
the only	use "all"
all but, all except, few	two statements required
not every, not all	use "some . . . are not"
there is, there are	use "some"

Rule for A propositions

Language following these words goes in the subject term: "if," "the only," and "W" words ("who," "what," "when," "where," "whoever," "whatever," "whenever," "wherever").

Language following these words goes in the predicate term: "only if," "only," "none but," "none except," and "no . . . except."

I. Translate the following into standard-form categorical propositions.

★1. Any bank that makes too many risky loans will fail.

2. Women military officers are not eligible for combat duty.

3. Terrorist attacks succeed whenever security measures are lax.

★4. Bromine is extractable from seawater.

5. Not all guilt feelings are psychological aberrations.

6. Every jazz fan admires Duke Ellington.

★7. If it's a halogen, then it isn't chemically inert.

8. A television show that depicts violence incites violence.

9. Manipulators do not make good marriage partners.

★10. None but pirate ships fly the Jolly Roger.

11. She gains weight whenever she's depressed.

12. She's depressed whenever she gains weight.

★13. A man is a bachelor only if he is unmarried.

14. Warmth always relieves pain.

15. Joseph J. Thomson discovered the electron.

★16. A few organic silicones are used as lubricants.

17. Only nuclear-powered vehicles are suitable for deep-space exploration.

18. Comets are the only heavenly bodies with tails.

★19. There is a giant star in the Tarantula Nebula.

20. If a pregnant woman drinks alcohol, she risks giving birth to a deformed child.

21. No shellfish except oysters make pearls.

★22. Only diabetics require insulin treatments.

23. The electroscope is a device for detecting static electricity.

24. Occasionally there are concerts in Central Park.

★25. Berlin was the setting for the 1936 Olympic Games.

26. The Kentucky Derby is never run in January.

27. The only way to get rid of a temptation is to yield to it.

★28. Where there's smoke, there's fire.

29. Lunar eclipses do not occur unless the moon is full.

30. Radio transmissions are disrupted whenever sunspot activity increases.

★31. If an ore isn't radioactive, then it isn't pitchblende.

32. All but the rats left the sinking ship.

33. A pesticide is dangerous if it contains DDT.

★34. John Grisham writes only novels about lawyers.

35. He who hesitates is lost.

36. Modern corporations are all run in the interest of their managers.

★37. Unless the sun is shining, a rainbow cannot occur.

38. Whoever suffers allergic reactions has a weakened immune system.

39. All fruits except pineapples ripen after they are picked.

★40. Few corporate raiders are known for their integrity.

41. Monkeys are found in the jungles of Guatemala.

42. Monkeys are mammals.

★43. I like strawberries.

44. All passengers are not allowed to smoke on board the aircraft.

45. All flowers are not fragrant.

★46. Cynthia travels where she wants.

47. Bats are the only true flying mammals.

48. Not every river runs to the sea.

★49. Physicists do not understand the operation of superconductors.

50. Many apartment dwellers are victimized by noise.

51. There are forced labor camps in China.

★52. Whatever increases efficiency improves profitability.

53. Dolphins are swimming between the breakers.

54. Feathers are not heavy.

★55. Few picnics are entirely free of ants.

56. A civil right is unalienable if it is a human right.

57. She says what she pleases.

★58. Several contestants won prizes.

59. An animal is a feline only if it is a cat.

60. Renee does whatever she is told to do.

II. The following exercises contain typical mistakes that students make in attempting to translate statements into standard form. Correct the errors and redundancies in these attempted translations.

★1. Some of the third-generation computers are things that are machines that take dictation.

2. All cars identical to BMWs are the only cars that young lawyers drive.

3. All vertebrates except cartilaginous fishes are animals with a bony skeleton.

★4. No downhill skiers are effective competitors if they suffer from altitude sickness.

5. All substances like cobalt are things that are substances identical to ferromagnetic metals.

6. No people identical to nuclear pacifists are people who believe a just war is possible.

★7. All people identical to matadors are not performers who succumb easily to fear.

8. All companies identical to Google are looking forward to a bright future.

9. No toxic dumps are ecological catastrophes unless they leak.

★10. All crocodiles are things identical to dangerous animals when they are hungry.

Summary

A categorical proposition is a proposition that relates two classes (or categories). Standard-form categorical propositions occur in four forms and are composed of a quantifier ("all," "no," "some"), a subject term, a copula ("are," "are not"), and a predicate term. A standard-form categorical proposition has either affirmative or negative *quality*, depending on whether it joins or separates the subject and predicate classes, and universal or particular *quantity*, depending on whether it relates all or only a part of the subject class to the predicate class. The subject and predicate terms are said to be *distributed* or *undistributed* depending on whether the proposition makes an assertion about all or only a part of the class denoted by the term in question. Each standard-form proposition is given a letter name (**A, E, I, O**) that reflects its quantity and quality.

Categorical propositions having universal quantity allow for two different interpretations. According to the Aristotelian interpretation, **A** and **E** propositions about actually existing things imply the existence of those things, but according to the Boolean interpretation, **A** and **E** propositions never imply the existence of anything. The content of a standard-form proposition may be represented in a Venn diagram, which consists of two overlapping circles. Placing an X in an area indicates that the area is not empty, and shading an area indicates that the area is empty. The modern square of opposition is a diagram that applies to the Boolean interpretation; it indicates that the **A** and **O** propositions contradict each other and that the **E** and **I** propositions contradict each other.

Conversion, obversion, and contraposition are operations that can be performed on standard-form propositions; they result in a new proposition that is either logically equivalent or not logically equivalent to the original proposition. Two propositions that are logically equivalent necessarily have the same truth value. Conversion gives logically equivalent results for **E** and **I** propositions, obversion does so for all four, and contraposition does so for **A** and **O**. The formal fallacies of illicit conversion and illicit contraposition result from the application of conversion and contraposition to propositions that do not yield logically equivalent results.

The traditional square of opposition applies to the Aristotelian interpretation of categorical propositions when the subject term refers to actually existing things; it shows how each kind of proposition relates to the other three. The contrary relation, holding between the **A** and **E** propositions, asserts that at least one is false. The subcontrary relation, holding between **I** and **O**, asserts that at least one is true. Subalternation, holding between **A** and **I** and between **E** and **O**, indicates that truth "flows" downward and falsity upward. Contradiction holds as in the modern square. The formal fallacies of illicit contrary, illicit subcontrary, and illicit subalternation result from incorrect applications of these relations. The existential fallacy results from applying the traditional square to propositions whose subject terms denote nonexistent things.

The Venn diagram technique, which typically applies to the Boolean interpretation of categorical propositions, can be modified to apply to the Aristotelian interpretation. The modification consists in introducing a circled X, which represents the temporary assumption of existence, into the unshaded part of the subject circle for **A** and **E** propositions. Once modified, the Venn diagram technique can be used to prove the relationships of the traditional square of opposition and to test immediate inferences from the Aristotelian standpoint.

Categorical propositions that are not in standard form can be translated into standard-form propositions. The chief requirements are that the new proposition have a proper quantifier, subject term, copula, and predicate term and that it have the same meaning as the original proposition.

4

5

Categorical Syllogisms

5.1   Standard Form, Mood, and Figure

In the general sense of the term, a **syllogism** is a deductive argument consisting of two premises and one conclusion. Provisionally I will define a *categorical syllogism* as a syllogism consisting of three categorical propositions and containing a total of three different terms, each of which appears twice in distinct propositions. (I will give a more precise definition shortly.) The following argument is a categorical syllogism:

> All soldiers are patriots.
> No traitors are patriots.
> Therefore, no traitors are soldiers.

Each of the three terms in a categorical syllogism has its own name depending on its position in the argument. The **major term,** by definition, is the predicate of the conclusion, and the **minor term** is the subject of the conclusion. The **middle term,** which provides the middle ground between the two premises, is the one that occurs once in each premise and does not occur in the conclusion. Thus, for the argument just given, the major term is "soldiers," the minor term is "traitors," and the middle term is "patriots."

The premises of a categorical syllogism also have their own names. The **major premise,** by definition, is the one that contains the major term, and the **minor premise** is the one that contains the minor term. Thus, in the syllogism just given the major premise is "All soldiers are patriots," and the minor premise is "No traitors are patriots." Now that we are supplied with these definitions, we may proceed to the idea of standard form. A **standard-form categorical syllogism** is one that meets the following four conditions:

1. All three statements are standard-form categorical propositions.
2. The two occurrences of each term are identical.
3. Each term is used in the same sense throughout the argument.
4. The major premise is listed first, the minor premise second, and the conclusion last.

The first condition requires that each statement have a proper quantifier, subject term, copula, and predicate term. The second condition is clear. The third rules out the possibility of equivocation. For example, if a syllogism containing the word "men" used that term in the sense of human beings in one statement and in the sense of male human beings in another statement, the syllogism would really contain more than three terms and would therefore not be in standard form. Finally, the fourth condition merely requires that the three statements be listed in the right order.

The syllogism about soldiers is in standard form because all four conditions are fulfilled. However, the following syllogism is not in standard form, because the fourth condition is violated:

> All watercolors are paintings.
> Some watercolors are masterpieces.
> Therefore, some paintings are masterpieces.

To put this syllogism into standard form the order of the premises must be reversed. The major premise (the one containing "masterpieces," which is the predicate term in the conclusion) must be listed first, and the minor premise (the one containing "paintings," which is the subject term in the conclusion) must be listed second.

Now that we have a definition of standard-form categorical syllogism, we can give a more precise definition of categorical syllogism. A **categorical syllogism** is a deductive argument consisting of three categorical propositions that is capable of being translated into standard form. For an argument to qualify as a categorical syllogism, all three statements need not be standard-form categorical propositions; but if they are, the analysis is greatly simplified. For this reason, all of the syllogisms presented in the first four sections of this chapter will consist of statements that are in standard form. In later sections, techniques will be developed for translating non-standard-form syllogisms into equivalent arguments that are in standard form.

After a categorical syllogism has been put into standard form, its validity or invalidity may be determined through mere inspection of the form. The individual form of a syllogism consists of two factors: mood and figure. The **mood** of a categorical syllogism consists of the letter names of the propositions that make it up. For example, if the major premise is an **A** proposition, the minor premise an **O** proposition, and the conclusion an **E** proposition, the mood is **AOE**. To determine the mood of a categorical syllogism, one must first put the syllogism into standard form; the letter name of the statements may then be noted to the side of each. The mood of the syllogism is then designated by the order of these letters, reading the letter for the major premise first, the letter for the minor premise second, and the letter for the conclusion last.

The **figure** of a categorical syllogism is determined by the location of the two occurrences of the middle term in the premises. Four different arrangements are possible. If we let S represent the subject of the conclusion (minor term), P the predicate of the conclusion (major term), and M the middle term, and leave out the quantifiers and copulas, the four possible arrangements may be illustrated as follows:

Figure 1		**Figure 2**		**Figure 3**		**Figure 4**	
Ⓜ	P	P	Ⓜ	Ⓜ	P	P	Ⓜ
S	Ⓜ	S	Ⓜ	Ⓜ	S	Ⓜ	S
S	P	S	P	S	P	S	P

In the first figure the middle term is top left, bottom right; in the second, top right, bottom right, and so on. Example:

> No painters are sculptors.
> Some sculptors are artists.
> Therefore, some artists are not painters.

This syllogism is in standard form. The mood is **EIO** and the figure is four. The form of the syllogism is therefore designated as **EIO**-4.

To remember how the four figures are defined, imagine the four possible arrangements of the middle term as depicting the outline of a shirt collar:

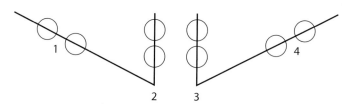

The only problem with this device is that it may lead you to confuse the second figure with the third. To avoid this confusion, keep in mind that for these two figures the S and P terms go on the same "collar flap" as the middle term. Thus, for the second figure, S and P are to the left of the middle term, and for the third figure they are to the right.

Since there are four kinds of categorical propositions and there are three categorical propositions in a categorical syllogism, there are 64 possible moods ($4 \times 4 \times 4 = 64$). And since there are four different figures, there are 256 different forms of categorical syllogisms ($4 \times 64 = 256$).

Once the mood and figure of a syllogism is known, the validity of the syllogism can be determined by checking the mood and figure against a list of valid syllogistic forms. To do this, first adopt the Boolean standpoint and see if the syllogism's form appears in the following table of unconditionally valid forms. If it does, the syllogism is valid from the Boolean standpoint. In other words, it is valid regardless of whether its terms denote actually existing things.

Figure 1	Figure 2	Figure 3	Figure 4
AAA	EAE	IAI	AEE
EAE	AEE	AII	IAI
AII	EIO	OAO	EIO
EIO	AOO	EIO	

If the syllogism does not appear on the list of unconditionally valid forms, then adopt the Aristotelian standpoint and see if the syllogism's form appears in the following table of conditionally valid forms. If it does, the syllogism is valid from the Aristotelian standpoint on condition that a certain term (the "critical" term) denotes actually existing things. The required condition is stated in the last column.

Conditionally valid forms

Figure 1	Figure 2	Figure 3	Figure 4	Required condition
AAI	AEO		AEO	*S* exists
EAO	EAO			
		AAI	EAO	*M* exists
		EAO		
			AAI	*P* exists

For example, the **AAI**-1 is valid from the Aristotelian standpoint if the subject of the conclusion (the minor term) denotes actually existing things. The **EAO**-3 is valid if the middle term denotes actually existing things. Thus, if we are given an **AAI**-1 syllogism and the minor term is "cats," then the syllogism is valid from the Aristotelian standpoint. But if the minor term is "unicorns," then the syllogism is invalid. On the other hand, if the minor term is "students who failed the exam" and we are not certain if there are any such students, then the syllogism is conditionally valid.

The relationship between the Aristotelian standpoint and the Boolean standpoint is illustrated in the following bar graph:

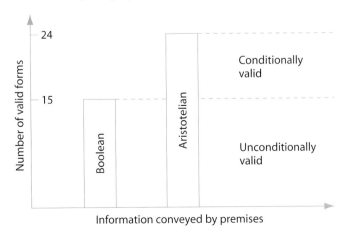

The graph shows that when the premises of a syllogistic form are recognized as conveying information about existence, an additional nine forms become valid.

Interestingly, during the Middle Ages logic students used to memorize a little poem that served as a rule of thumb for distinguishing valid from invalid syllogisms. The vowels in the words identified the mood, and the words "prioris," "secundae," and so on the figure.

Barbara, Celarent, Darii, Ferioque prioris;
Cesare, Camestres, Festino, Baroco secundae;
Tertia, Darapti, Disamis, Datisi, Felapton,
Bocardo, Ferison habet: quarta insuper addit
Bramantip, Camenes, Dimaris, Fesapo, Fresison.

For example, the "Barbara" syllogism (this designation is still encountered today) is **AAA**-1, "Celarent" is **EAE**-1, and so on. This poem conforms substantially to the two tables given earlier, except that five forms have been left out. The reason these forms were left out is that the logicians of that time considered them weak: They draw a particular conclusion from premises that would support a (stronger) universal conclusion. For example, the weaker **AAI**-1 is left out in favor of the stronger **AAA**-1. Needless to say, few students today depend on this poem to distinguish valid from invalid syllogisms.

We have seen how, given the syllogism, we can obtain the mood and figure. But sometimes we need to go in the reverse direction: from the mood and figure to the syllogistic form. Suppose we are given the form **EIO**-4. To reconstruct the syllogistic form is easy. First use the mood to determine the skeleton of the form:

E	No _____ are _____.
I	Some _____ are _____.
O	Some _____ are not _____.

Then use the figure to determine the arrangement of the middle terms:

E	No _____ are *M*.
I	Some *M* are _____.
O	Some _____ are not _____.

Finally, supply the major and minor terms, using the letters *S* and *P* to designate the subject and predicate of the conclusion. The predicate of the conclusion is always repeated in the first premise, and the subject of the conclusion is repeated in the second premise:

E	No *P* are *M*.
I	Some *M* are *S*.
O	Some *S* are not *P*.

EXERCISE 5.1

iLrn I. The following syllogisms are in standard form. Identify the major, minor, and middle terms, as well as the mood and figure of each. Then use the two lists of valid syllogistic forms to determine whether each is valid from the Boolean standpoint, valid from the Aristotelian standpoint, or invalid.

★1. All neutron stars are things that produce intense gravity.
   All neutron stars are extremely dense objects.
   Therefore, all extremely dense objects are things that produce intense gravity.

2. No insects that eat mosquitoes are insects that should be killed.
   All dragonflies are insects that eat mosquitoes.
   Therefore, no dragonflies are insects that should be killed.

3. No environmentally produced diseases are inherited afflictions.
   Some psychological disorders are not inherited afflictions.
   Therefore, some psychological disorders are environmentally produced diseases.

★4. No people who mix fact with fantasy are good witnesses.
   Some hypnotized people are people who mix fact with fantasy.
   Therefore, some hypnotized people are not good witnesses.

5. All ozone molecules are good absorbers of ultraviolet rays.
   All ozone molecules are things destroyed by chlorine.
   Therefore, some things destroyed by chlorine are good absorbers of ultraviolet rays.

II. Put the following syllogisms into standard form, using letters to represent the terms, and name the mood and figure. Then use the two lists of valid syllogistic forms to determine whether each is valid from the Boolean standpoint, valid from the Aristotelian standpoint, or invalid.

★1. No Republicans are Democrats, so no Republicans are big spenders, since all big spenders are Democrats.

2. Some latchkey children are not kids who can stay out of trouble, for some youngsters prone to boredom are latchkey children, and no kids who can stay out of trouble are youngsters prone to boredom.

3. No rent-control proposals are regulations welcomed by landlords, and all regulations welcomed by landlords are measures that allow a free hand in raising rents. Therefore, some rent-control proposals are measures that allow a free hand in raising rents.

★4. Some insects that feed on milkweed are not foods suitable for birds, inasmuch as no monarch butterflies are foods suitable for birds and all monarch butterflies are insects that feed on milkweed.

5. No illegal aliens are people who have a right to welfare payments, and some migrant workers are illegal aliens. Thus, some people who have a right to welfare payments are migrant workers.

6. Some African nations are not countries deserving military aid, because some African nations are not upholders of human rights, and all countries deserving military aid are upholders of human rights.

★7. All pranksters are exasperating individuals, consequently some leprechauns are exasperating individuals, since all leprechauns are pranksters.

8. Some racists are not people suited to be immigration officials, given that some humanitarians are not people suited to be immigration officials, and no humanitarians are racists.

9. No people who respect human life are terrorists, and all airline hijackers are terrorists. Hence, no airline hijackers are people who respect human life.

★10. Some silicates are crystalline substances, because all silicates are oxygen compounds, and some oxygen compounds are not crystalline substances.

III. Reconstruct the syllogistic forms from the following combinations of mood and figure.

★1. **OAE**-3

2. **EIA**-4

3. **AII**-3

★4. **IAE**-1

5. **AOO**-2

6. **EAO**-4

★7. **AAA**-1

8. **EAO**-2

9. **OEI**-3

★10. **OEA**-4

IV. Construct the following syllogisms.

★1. An **EIO**-2 syllogism with these terms: *major:* dogmatists; *minor:* theologians; *middle:* scholars who encourage free thinking.

2. An unconditionally valid syllogism in the first figure with a particular affirmative conclusion and these terms: *major:* people incapable of objectivity; *minor:* Supreme Court justices; *middle:* lockstep ideologues.

3. An unconditionally valid syllogism in the fourth figure having two universal premises and these terms: *major:* teenage suicides; *minor:* heroic episodes; *middle:* tragic occurrences.

★4. A valid syllogism having mood **OAO** and these terms: *major:* things capable of replicating by themselves; *minor:* structures that invade cells; *middle:* viruses.

5. A valid syllogism in the first figure having a universal negative conclusion and these terms: *major:* guarantees of marital happiness; *minor:* prenuptial agreements; *middle:* legally enforceable documents.

V. Answer "true" or "false" to the following statements.

1. Every syllogism is a categorical syllogism.

2. Some categorical syllogisms cannot be put into standard form.

3. The statements in a categorical syllogism need not be expressed in standard form.

4. The statements in a standard-form categorical syllogism need not be expressed in standard form.

5. In a standard-form categorical syllogism the two occurrences of each term must be identical.

6. The major premise of a standard-form categorical syllogism contains the subject of the conclusion.

7. To determine its mood and figure, a categorical syllogism must first be put into standard form.

8. In a standard-form syllogism having Figure 2, the two occurrences of the middle term are on the right.

9. The unconditionally valid syllogistic forms are valid from both the Boolean and the Aristotelian standpoints.

10. The conditionally valid syllogistic forms are invalid if the requisite condition is not fulfilled.

5.2   Venn Diagrams

Venn diagrams provide the most intuitively evident and, in the long run, easiest to remember technique for testing the validity of categorical syllogisms. The technique is basically an extension of the one developed in Chapter 4 to represent the informational content of categorical propositions. Because syllogisms contain three terms, whereas propositions contain only two, the application of Venn diagrams to syllogisms requires three overlapping circles.

These circles should be drawn so that seven areas are clearly distinguishable within the diagram. The second step is to label the circles, one for each term. The precise order of the labeling is not critical, but we will adopt the convention of always assigning the lower-left circle to the subject of the conclusion, the lower-right circle to the predicate of the conclusion, and the top circle to the middle term. This convention is easy to remember because it conforms to the arrangement of the terms in a standard-form syllogism: The subject of the conclusion is on the lower left, the predicate of the conclusion is on the lower right, and the middle term is in the premises, above the conclusion.

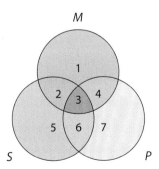

Anything in the area marked "1" is an *M* but neither an *S* nor a *P*, anything in the area marked "2" is both an *S* and an *M* but not a *P*, anything in the area marked "3" is a member of all three classes, and so on.

Reproduced by permission of the Master and Fellows of Gonville and Caius College, Cambridge

John Venn 1834–1923

John Venn is known mainly for his circle diagrams, which have contributed to work in many areas of mathematics and logic, including computer science, set theory, and statistics. His book *The Logic of Chance* (1866) advanced probability theory by introducing the relative frequency interpretation of probability; it significantly influenced later developments in statistical theory as well. In *Symbolic Logic* (1881) he defended George Boole against various critics and rendered the new logic intelligible to nonmathematical thinkers. Finally, in *The Principles of Empirical and Inductive Logic* (1889) he criticized Mill's methods of induction as being of limited application as an engine of discovery in science.

John Venn was born in Hull, England, the son of Henry Venn, the Drypool parish rector, and Martha Sykes Venn, who died when Venn was a child. The Venns were prominent members of the evangelical movement within the Church of England. John Venn's grandfather had been an evangelical leader, as was his father, whom his contemporaries regarded as the head of the evangelical movement. His father served for many years in an administrative capacity for the Church Missionary Society, and John was expected to follow in the family tradition. In 1858, after graduating from Gonville and Caius (pronounced "keys") College, Cambridge, he was ordained and served for a time as a curate in parishes near London.

Perhaps owing to his contact with Henry Sidgwick and other Cambridge agnostics, Venn's confidence in the Thirty-nine Articles of the Church of England began to erode. Also, as a result of his reading the works of De Morgan, Boole, and Mill, his interest shifted almost totally from theological matters to issues related to logic. At age twenty-eight, Venn returned to Cambridge to become a lecturer in logic and probability theory. Five years later, he married Susanna Carnegie Edmonstone, the daughter of an Anglican cleric, and they had one child, John Archibald Venn. In 1883, at age forty-nine, Venn became a fellow of the Royal Society and received the degree of Doctor of Science.

The greater part of Venn's life centered completely on his association with Cambridge. In 1857 he became a fellow of Caius, and he remained a member of the college foundation for sixty-six years, until his death. During the last twenty years of his life he served as college president, during which time he wrote a history of the college. Also, in collaboration with his son, he completed Part I of the massive *Alumni Cantabrigienses,* which contains short biographies of 76,000 graduates and office holders ranging from the university's earliest days through 1751.

John Venn's son said of his father that he was a "fine walker and mountain climber." Also, in keeping with his view that abstract subjects such as logic and mathematics ought to serve practical utility, Venn loved to use this knowledge to build machines. He invented a cricket bowling machine that was used against the best batsman of an Australian team. The machine "clean bowled" this batsman four times. Today Venn is memorialized by a stained glass window in the dining hall of Caius College, which contains a representation of a Venn diagram.

The test procedure consists of transferring the information content of the premises to the diagram and then inspecting the diagram to see whether it necessarily implies the truth of the conclusion. If the information in the diagram does do this, the argument is valid; otherwise it is invalid.

The use of Venn diagrams to evaluate syllogisms usually requires a little practice at first. Perhaps the best way of learning the technique is through illustrative examples, but a few pointers are needed first:

1. Marks (shading or placing an X) are entered only for the premises. No marks are made for the conclusion.

2. If the argument contains one universal premise, this premise should be entered first in the diagram. If there are two universal premises, either one can be done first.

3. When entering the information contained in a premise, one should concentrate on the circles corresponding to the two terms in the statement. While the third circle cannot be ignored altogether, it should be given only minimal attention.

4. When inspecting a completed diagram to see whether it supports a particular conclusion, one should remember that particular statements assert two things. "Some S are P" means "At least one S exists *and* that S is a P"; "Some S are not P" means "At least one S exists *and* that S is not a P."

5. When shading an area, one must be careful to shade *all* of the area in question. Examples:

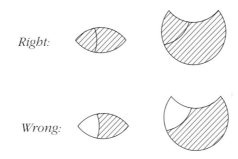

6. The area where an X goes is always initially divided into two parts. If one of these parts has already been shaded, the X goes in the unshaded part. Examples:

If one of the two parts is not shaded, the X goes on the line separating the two parts. Examples:

Right:

This means that the X may be in either (or both) of the two areas—but it is not known which one.

7. An X should never be placed in such a way that it dangles outside of the diagram, and it should never be placed on the intersection of two lines.

Wrong: *Wrong:*

Boolean Standpoint

Because the Boolean standpoint does not recognize universal premises as having existential import, its approach to testing syllogisms is simpler and more general than that of the Aristotelian standpoint. Hence, we will begin by testing syllogisms from that standpoint and later proceed to the Aristotelian standpoint. Here is an example:

1. No *P* are *M*.   **EAE**-2
   All *S* are *M*.
   No *S* are *P*.

Since both premises are universal, it makes no difference which premise we enter first in the diagram. To enter the major premise, we concentrate our attention on the *M* and *P* circles, which are highlighted with color:

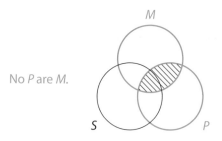

We now complete the diagram by entering the minor premise. In doing so, we concentrate our attention on the *S* and *M* circles, which are highlighted with color:

All S are M.

The conclusion states that the area where the *S* and *P* circles overlap is shaded. Inspection of the diagram reveals that this area is indeed shaded, so the syllogistic form is valid. Because the form is valid from the Boolean standpoint, it is *unconditionally valid.* In other words, it is valid regardless of whether its premises are recognized as having existential import.

Here is another example:

2. All *M* are *P.*   **AEE**-1
    No *S* are *M.*
    No *S* are *P.*

Again, both premises are universal, so it makes no difference which premise we enter first in the diagram. To enter the major premise, we concentrate our attention on the *M* and *P* circles:

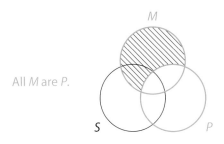

All *M* are *P.*

To enter the minor premise, we concentrate our attention on the *M* and *S* circles:

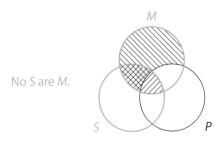

No *S* are *M.*

Again, the conclusion states that the area where the S and P circles overlap is shaded. Inspection of the diagram reveals that only part of this area is shaded, so the syllogistic form is invalid.

Another example:

3. Some *P* are *M*. **IAI**-4
   All *M* are *S*.
   Some *S* are *P*.

We enter the universal premise first. To do so, we concentrate our attention on the *M* and *S* circles:

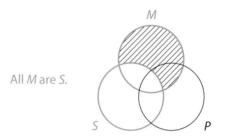

To enter the particular premise, we concentrate our attention on the *M* and *P* circles. This premise tells us to place an X in the area where the *M* and *P* circles overlap. Because part of this area is shaded, we place the X in the remaining area:

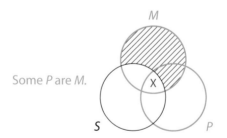

The conclusion states that there is an X in the area where the *S* and *P* circles overlap. Inspection of the diagram reveals that there is indeed an X in this area, so the syllogistic form is valid.

The examples that follow are done in a single step.

4. All *P* are *M*.   **AOO**-2
   Some *S* are not *M*.
   Some *S* are not *P*.

The universal premise is entered first. The particular premise tells us to place an X in the part of the *S* circle that lies outside the *M* circle. Because part of this area is shaded, we place the X in the remaining area. The conclusion states that there is an X that is inside the *S* circle but outside the *P* circle. Inspection of the diagram reveals that there is indeed an X in this area, so the syllogistic form is valid.

5. Some *M* are *P*.
   All *S* are *M*.
   Some *S* are *P*.

IAI-1

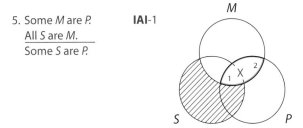

As usual, we enter the universal premise first. In entering the particular premise, we concentrate on the area where the *M* and *P* circles overlap. (For emphasis, this area is colored in the diagram.) Because this overlap area is divided into two parts (the areas marked "1" and "2"), we place the X on the line (arc of the *S* circle) that separates the two parts. The conclusion states that there is an X in the area where the *S* and *P* circles overlap. Inspection of the diagram reveals that the single X is dangling outside of this overlap area. We do not know if it is in or out. Thus, the syllogistic form is invalid.

6. All *M* are *P*.
   Some *S* are not *M*.
   Some *S* are not *P*.

AOO-1

In entering the particular premise, we concentrate our attention on the part of the *S* circle that lies outside the *M* circle (colored area). Because this area is divided into two parts (the areas marked "1" and "2"), we place the X on the line (arc of the *P* circle) separating the two areas. The conclusion states that there is an X that is inside the *S* circle but outside the *P* circle. There *is* an X in the *S* circle, but we do not know whether it is inside or outside the *P* circle. Hence, the argument is invalid.

7. All *M* are *P*.
   All *S* are *M*.
   All *S* are *P*.

AAA-1

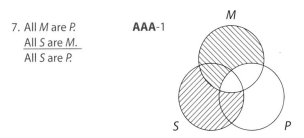

This is the "Barbara" syllogism. The conclusion states that the part of the S circle that is outside the P circle is empty. Inspection of the diagram reveals that this area is indeed empty. Thus, the syllogistic form is valid.

8. Some *M* are not *P.*   **OIO**-1
   Some *S* are M.
   Some *S* are not *P.*

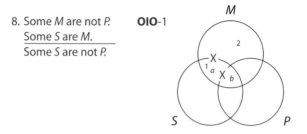

In this diagram no areas have been shaded, so there are two possible areas for each of the two X's. The X from the first premise goes on the line (arc of the S circle) separating areas 1 and 2, and the X from the second premise goes on the line (arc of the P circle) separating areas *a* and *b*. The conclusion states that there is an X that is inside the S circle but outside the P circle. We have no certainty that the X from the first premise is inside the S circle, and while the X from the second premise is inside the S circle, we have no certainty that it is outside the P circle. Hence, the syllogistic form is invalid.

We have yet to explain the rationale for placing the X on the boundary separating two areas when neither of the areas is shaded. Consider this argument:

No *P* are *M.*
Some *S* are not *M.*
Some *S* are *P.*

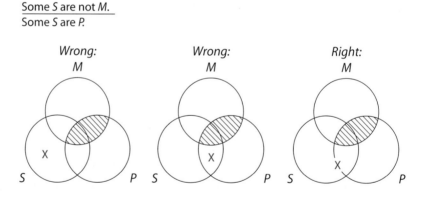

In each of the three diagrams the content of the first premise is represented correctly. The problem concerns placing the X from the second premise. In the first diagram the X is placed inside the S circle but outside both the M circle and the P circle. This diagram asserts: "At least one S is not an M and it is also not a P." Clearly the diagram says more than the premise does, and so it is incorrect. In the second diagram the X is placed inside the S circle, outside the M circle, and inside the P circle. This diagram asserts: "At least one S is not an M, but it is a P." Again, the diagram says more than the premise says, and so it is incorrect. In the third diagram, which is done correctly, the X is placed on the boundary between the two areas. This diagram asserts: "At least one *S* is not an *M*, and it may or may not be a *P*." In other words, nothing at all is said about *P*, and so the diagram represents exactly the content of the second premise.

Aristotelian Standpoint

The syllogistic forms we have tested thus far are valid or invalid from the Boolean standpoint, which does not recognize universal premises as having existential import. We now shift to the Aristotelian standpoint, where existential import can make a difference to validity. To test a syllogism from the Aristotelian standpoint, we follow basically the same procedure we followed in Section 4.6 to test immediate inferences:

1. Reduce the syllogism to its form and test it from the Boolean standpoint. If the form is valid, proceed no further. The syllogism is valid from both standpoints.
2. If the syllogistic form is invalid from the Boolean standpoint and has a particular conclusion, then adopt the Aristotelian standpoint and look to see if there is a Venn circle that is completely shaded except for one area. If there is, enter a circled X in that area and retest the form.
3. If the syllogistic form is conditionally valid, determine if the circled X represents something that exists. If it does, the condition is fulfilled, and the syllogism is valid from the Aristotelian standpoint.

In regard to step 2, if the diagram contains no Venn circle completely shaded except for one area, then the syllogism is invalid from the Aristotelian standpoint. However, if it does contain such a Venn circle and the syllogism has a particular conclusion, then we place a circled X in the one unshaded area. This circled X represents the temporary assumption that the Venn circle in question is not empty.

In regard to step 3, if the circled X does not represent something that exists, then the syllogism is invalid. As we will see in Section 5.3, such syllogisms commit the existential fallacy from the Aristotelian standpoint.

The table of conditionally valid syllogistic forms presented in Section 5.1 names nine forms that are valid from the Aristotelian standpoint if a certain condition is fulfilled. The following syllogism has one of those forms:

9. No fighter pilots are tank commanders.
    All fighter pilots are courageous individuals.
    Therefore, some courageous individuals are not tank commanders.

First we replace the terms with letters and test the syllogism from the Boolean standpoint:

The conclusion asserts that there is an X that is inside the *C* circle but outside the *T* circle. Inspection of the diagram reveals no X's at all, so the syllogism is invalid from the Boolean standpoint. Proceeding to step 2, we adopt the Aristotelian standpoint and, noting that the conclusion is particular and that the *F* circle is all shaded except for one area, we enter a circled X in that area:

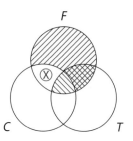

The diagram now indicates that the syllogism is conditionally valid, so we proceed to step 3 and determine whether the circled X represents something that actually exists. Since the circled X represents an *F*, and since *F* stands for fighter pilots, the circled X does represent something that exists. Thus, the condition is fulfilled, and the syllogism is valid from the Aristotelian standpoint.

Here is another example:

10. All reptiles are scaly animals.
    All currently living tyrannosaurs are reptiles.
    Therefore, some currently living tyrannosaurs are scaly animals.

First we test the syllogism from the Boolean standpoint:

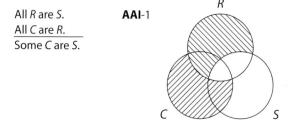

All *R* are *S*. **AAI-1**
All *C* are *R*.
Some *C* are *S*.

The conclusion asserts that there is an X in the area where the *C* and *S* circles overlap. Since the diagram contains no X's at all, the syllogism is invalid from the Boolean standpoint. Proceeding to step 2, we adopt the Aristotelian standpoint. Then, after noticing that the conclusion is particular and that the *C* circle is all shaded except for one area, we enter a circled X in that area:

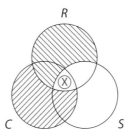

The diagram now indicates that the syllogism is conditionally valid, so we proceed to the third step and determine whether the circled X represents something that actually exists. Since the circled X represents a *C,* and *C* stands for currently living tyrannosaurs, the circled X does not represent something that actually exists. Thus, the condition is not fulfilled, and the syllogism is invalid. As we will see in the next section of this chapter, the syllogism commits the existential fallacy from the Aristotelian standpoint.

In determining whether the circled X stands for something that exists, we always look to the Venn circle that is all shaded except for one area. If the term corresponding to that circle denotes existing things, then the circled X represents one of those things. In some diagrams, however, there may be two Venn circles that are all shaded except for one area, and each may contain a circled X in the unshaded area. In these cases we direct our attention only to the circled X needed to draw the conclusion. If that circled X stands for something that exists, the argument is valid; if not, it is invalid.

EXERCISE 5.2

I. Use Venn diagrams to determine whether the following standard-form categorical syllogisms are valid from the Boolean standpoint, valid from the Aristotelian standpoint, or invalid. Then, identify the mood and figure, and cross-check your answers with the tables of valid syllogisms found in Section 5.1.

★1. All corporations that overcharge their customers are unethical businesses.
Some unethical businesses are investor-owned utilities.
Therefore, some investor-owned utilities are corporations that overcharge their customers.

2. No AIDS victims are people who pose an immediate threat to the lives of others.
Some kindergarten children are AIDS victims.
Therefore, some kindergarten children are not people who pose an immediate threat to the lives of others.

3. No individuals truly concerned with the plight of suffering humanity are people motivated primarily by self-interest.
All television evangelists are people motivated primarily by self-interest.
Therefore, some television evangelists are not individuals truly concerned with the plight of suffering humanity.

★4. All high-fat diets are diets high in cholesterol.
Some diets high in cholesterol are not healthy food programs.
Therefore, some healthy food programs are not high-fat diets.

5. No concertos are symphonies.
   No symphonies are string quartets.
   Therefore, no string quartets are concertos.

6. All compounds that destroy the ozone layer are environmental hazards.
   All chlorofluorocarbons are compounds that destroy the ozone layer.
   Therefore, all chlorofluorocarbons are environmental hazards.

★7. No pediatricians are individuals who jeopardize the health of children.
   All faith healers are individuals who jeopardize the health of children.
   Therefore, no faith healers are pediatricians.

8. Some individuals prone to violence are not men who treat others humanely.
   Some police officers are individuals prone to violence.
   Therefore, some police officers are not men who treat others humanely.

9. Some automated teller machines are places criminals lurk.
   All places criminals lurk are places to be avoided at night.
   Therefore, some places to be avoided at night are automated teller machines.

★10. No corporations that defraud the government are organizations the government should deal with.
   Some defense contractors are not organizations the government should deal with.
   Therefore, some defense contractors are not corporations that defraud the government.

11. All circular triangles are plane figures.
   All circular triangles are three-sided figures.
   Therefore, some three-sided figures are plane figures.

12. All supernovas are objects that emit massive amounts of energy.
   All quasars are objects that emit massive amounts of energy.
   Therefore, all quasars are supernovas.

★13. No people who profit from the illegality of their activities are people who want their activities legalized.
   All drug dealers are people who profit from the illegality of their activities.
   Therefore, no drug dealers are people who want their activities legalized.

14. Some individuals who risk heart disease are people who will die young.
   Some smokers are individuals who risk heart disease.
   Therefore, some smokers are people who will die young.

15. Some communications satellites are rocket-launched failures.
   All communications satellites are devices with antennas.
   Therefore, some devices with antennas are rocket-launched failures.

★16. All currently living dinosaurs are giant reptiles.
   All giant reptiles are ectothermic animals.
   Therefore, some ectothermic animals are currently living dinosaurs.

17. All survivalists are people who enjoy simulated war games.
   No people who enjoy simulated war games are soldiers who have tasted the agony of real war.
   Therefore, all soldiers who have tasted the agony of real war are survivalists.

18. No people majoring in greed are individuals concerned about the welfare of society.
Some college students are people majoring in greed.
Therefore, some college students are not individuals concerned about the welfare of society.

★19. No aspirin-based pain relievers are ibuprofens.
All aspirin-based pain relievers are analgesics.
Therefore, some analgesics are not ibuprofens.

20. Some snowflakes are not uniform solids.
All snowflakes are six-pointed crystals.
Therefore, some six-pointed crystals are not uniform solids.

II. Use Venn diagrams to obtain the conclusion that is validly implied by each of the following sets of premises. If no conclusion can be validly drawn, write "no conclusion."

★1. No *P* are *M*.
All *S* are *M*.

6. No *M* are *P*.
Some *S* are not *M*.

2. Some *P* are not *M*.
Some *M* are *S*.

★7. All *M* are *P*.
All *S* are *M*.

3. Some *M* are *P*.
All *S* are *M*.

8. All *P* are *M*.
All *S* are *M*.

★4. Some *M* are not *P*.
All *M* are *S*.

9. No *P* are *M*.
Some *M* are *S*.

5. Some *P* are *M*.
All *M* are *S*.

★10. No *P* are *M*.
No *M* are *S*.

III. Answer "true" or "false" to the following statements.

1. In the use of Venn diagrams to test the validity of syllogisms, marks are sometimes entered in the diagram for the conclusion.

2. When an X is placed on the arc of a circle, it means that the X could be in either (or both) of the two areas that the arc separates.

3. If an X lies on the arc of a circle, the argument cannot be valid.

4. When representing a universal statement in a Venn diagram, one always shades two of the seven areas in the diagram (unless one of these areas is already shaded).

5. If a completed diagram contains two X's, the argument cannot be valid.

6. If the conclusion asserts that a certain area is shaded, and inspection of the diagram reveals that only half that area is shaded, the argument is valid.

7. If the conclusion asserts that a certain area contains an X and inspection of the diagram reveals that only half an X appears in that area, the argument is valid.

8. If the conclusion is in the form "All *S* are *P*," and inspection of the diagram reveals that the part of the *S* circle that is outside the *P* circle is shaded, then the argument is valid.

9. If, in a completed diagram, three areas of a single circle are shaded, and placing a circled X in the one remaining area would make the conclusion true, then the argument is valid from the Aristotelian standpoint but not from the Boolean standpoint.

10. If, in a completed diagram, three areas of a single circle are shaded, but the argument is not valid from the Boolean standpoint, then it must be valid from the Aristotelian standpoint.

5.3   Rules and Fallacies

The idea that valid syllogisms conform to certain rules was first expressed by Aristotle. Many such rules are discussed in Aristotle's own account, but logicians of today generally settle on five or six.* If any one of these rules is violated, a specific formal fallacy is committed and, accordingly, the syllogism is invalid. Conversely, if none of the rules is broken, the syllogism is valid. These rules may be used as a convenient cross-check against the method of Venn diagrams. We will first consider the rules as they apply from the Boolean standpoint, and then shift to the Aristotelian standpoint.

Boolean Standpoint

Of the five rules presented in this section, the first two depend on the concept of distribution, the second two on the concept of quality, and the last on the concept of quantity. In applying the first two rules, you may want to recall either of the two mnemonic devices presented in Chapter 4: "Unprepared Students Never Pass" and "Any Student Earning B's Is Not On Probation." These mnemonics help one remember that the four categorical propositions distribute their terms as follows:

Statement type	Terms distributed
A	subject
E	subject, predicate
I	none
O	predicate

Here is the first rule.

---

*Some texts include a rule stating that the three terms of a categorical syllogism must be used in the same sense throughout the argument. In this text this requirement is included as part of the definition of *standard-form categorical syllogism* and is subsequently incorporated into the definition of *categorical syllogism*. See Section 5.1.

Rule 1: The middle term must be distributed at least once.

Fallacy: **Undistributed middle.**

Example: All sharks are fish.
All salmon are fish.
_____
All salmon are sharks.

In this standard-form categorical syllogism the middle term is "fish." In both premises "fish" occurs as the predicate of an **A** proposition and therefore it is not distributed in either premise. Thus, the syllogism commits the fallacy of undistributed middle and is invalid. If the major premise were rewritten to read "All fish are sharks," then "fish" would be distributed in that premise and the syllogism would be valid. But, of course, it would still be unsound because the rewritten premise would be false.

The logic behind Rule 1 may be explained by recounting how the middle term accomplishes its intended purpose, which is to provide a common ground between the subject and predicate terms of the conclusion. Let us designate the minor, major, and middle terms by the letters S, P, and M, respectively, and let us suppose that M is distributed in the major premise. By definition, P is related to the *whole* of the M class. Then, when the M class is related either in whole or in part to S, S and P necessarily become related. Analogous reasoning prevails if we suppose that M is distributed in the minor premise. But if M is undistributed in both premises, S and P may be related to *different parts* of the M class, in which case there is no common ground for relating S and P. This is exactly what happens in our fish example. The terms "salmon" and "sharks" are related to different parts of the fish class, so no common ground exists for relating them.

Rule 2: If a term is distributed in the conclusion, then it must be distributed in a premise.

Fallacies: **Illicit major; illicit minor.**

Examples: All horses are animals.
Some dogs are not horses.
_____
Some dogs are not animals.

All tigers are mammals.
All mammals are animals.
_____
All animals are tigers.

In the first example the major term, "animals," is distributed in the conclusion but not in the major premise, so the syllogism commits the fallacy of illicit major, or, more precisely, "illicit process of the major term." In the second example the minor term, "animals," is distributed in the conclusion but not in the minor premise. The second example therefore commits the fallacy of illicit minor, or "illicit process of the minor term."

In applying this rule, one must always examine the conclusion first. If no terms are distributed in the conclusion, Rule 2 cannot be violated. If one or both terms in the conclusion are distributed, then the appropriate premise must be examined. If the term distributed in the conclusion is also distributed in the premise, then the rule is not violated. But, if the term is not distributed in the premise, the rule is violated and the syllogism is invalid. In applying Rule 2 (and also Rule 1), you may find it helpful to begin by marking all the distributed terms in the syllogism—either by circling them or by labeling them with a small letter "d."

The logic behind Rule 2 is easy to understand. Let us once again designate the minor, major, and middle terms by the letters *S*, *P*, and *M*, respectively, and let us suppose that a certain syllogism commits the fallacy of illicit major. The conclusion of that syllogism then makes an assertion about every member of the *P* class, but the major premise makes an assertion about only some members of the *P* class. Because the minor premise, by itself, says nothing at all about the *P* class, the conclusion clearly contains information not contained in the premises, and the syllogism is therefore invalid. Analogous reasoning applies to the fallacy of illicit minor.

Rule 2 becomes intuitively plausible when it is recognized that distribution is a positive attribute. Granting this, an argument that has a term distributed in the conclusion but not in the premises has *more* in the conclusion than it does in the premises and is therefore invalid. Of course, it is always permissible to have more in a premise than appears in the conclusion, so it is perfectly all right for a term to be distributed in a premise but not in the conclusion.

Rule 3: Two negative premises are not allowed.

Fallacy: **Exclusive premises.**

Example: No fish are mammals.
           Some dogs are not fish.
           _____
           Some dogs are not mammals.

This syllogism may be seen as invalid because it has true premises and a false conclusion. The defect stems from the fact that it has two negative premises.

On reflection, Rule 3 should be fairly obvious. Let *S*, *P*, and *M* once again designate the minor, major, and middle terms. Now, if the *P* class and the *M* class are separate either wholly or partially, and the *S* class and the *M* class are separate either wholly or partially, nothing is said about the relation between the *S* class and the *P* class. These two classes may be either distinct or identical in whole or in part. Venn diagrams may be used effectively to illustrate the fact that no conclusion can be validly drawn from two negative premises.

Rule 4: A negative premise requires a negative conclusion, and a negative conclusion requires a negative premise.

Fallacy: **Drawing an affirmative conclusion from a negative premise.**
                                    or
           Drawing a negative conclusion from affirmative premises.

Examples: All crows are birds.
            Some wolves are not crows.
            _____
            Some wolves are birds.

            All triangles are three-angled polygons.
            All three-angled polygons are three-sided polygons.
            _____
            Some three-sided polygons are not triangles.

These arguments may be seen as invalid because each has true premises and a false conclusion. The first draws an affirmative conclusion from a negative premise, and the second draws a negative conclusion from affirmative premises.

The logic behind Rule 4 may be seen as follows. If S, P, and M once again designate the minor, major, and middle terms, an affirmative conclusion always states that the S class is contained either wholly or partially in the P class. The only way that such a conclusion can follow is if the S class is contained either wholly or partially in the M class, and the M class wholly in the P class. In other words, it follows only when both premises are affirmative. But if, for example, the S class is contained either wholly or partially in the M class, and the M class is separate either wholly or partially from the P class, such a conclusion will never follow. Thus, an affirmative conclusion cannot be drawn from negative premises.

Conversely, a negative conclusion asserts that the S class is separate either wholly or partially from the P class. But if both premises are affirmative, they assert class inclusion rather than separation. Thus, a negative conclusion cannot be drawn from affirmative premises.

As a result of the interaction of these first four rules, it turns out that no valid syllogism can have two particular premises. This result is convenient to keep in mind, because it allows us to identify as invalid any standard-form syllogism in which both premises start with "some." Because it is logically derivable from the first four rules, a separate rule to this effect is not given here.

Rule 5: If both premises are universal, the conclusion cannot be particular.

Fallacy: **Existential fallacy.**

Example: All mammals are animals.
All tigers are mammals.
Some tigers are animals.

The example has two universal premises and a particular conclusion, so it violates Rule 5. It commits the existential fallacy from the Boolean standpoint. The reason the syllogism is invalid from the Boolean standpoint is that the conclusion asserts that tigers exist, whereas the premises are interpreted as making no such assertion. From the Boolean standpoint, universal premises are not recognized as having existential import.

Aristotelian Standpoint

Any categorical syllogism that breaks one of the first four rules is invalid from the Aristotelian standpoint. However, if a syllogism breaks only Rule 5, it is valid from the Aristotelian standpoint on condition that the critical term denotes at least one existing thing. (The critical term is the term listed in the farthest right-hand column of the table of conditionally valid syllogistic forms.) In the example given in connection with Rule 5, the critical term is "tigers," and the syllogism breaks no other rules, so it is valid from the Aristotelian standpoint. The conclusion asserts that tigers exist, and the Aristotelian standpoint recognizes that the premises convey evidence of their existence. On the other hand, consider the following example:

All mammals are animals.
All unicorns are mammals.
―――――――――――――――
Some unicorns are animals.

In this example, the critical term is "unicorns." Since unicorns do not exist, the Aristotelian standpoint does not recognize that the premises convey evidence of their existence. Thus, the syllogism is invalid from the Aristotelian standpoint, and it commits the existential fallacy from that standpoint. Of course, it also commits the existential fallacy from the Boolean standpoint.

In addition to consulting the list, one way of identifying the critical term is to draw a Venn diagram. The critical term is the one that corresponds to the circle that is all shaded except for one area. In the case of two such circles, it is the one that corresponds to the Venn circle containing the circled X on which the conclusion depends. Another way of identifying the critical term is through examination of the distributed terms in the syllogism. The critical term is the one that is *superfluously distributed*. In other words, it is the term that, in the premises, is distributed in more occurrences than is necessary for the syllogism to obey all the rules. Here are three examples:

All M^d are P.	No M^d are P^d.	All P^d are M.
All S^d are M.	All M^d are S.	All M^d are S.
―――――――	―――――――	―――――――
Some S are P.	Some S are not P^d.	Some S are P.

The distributed terms are tagged with a small "d." In the first syllogism, M must be distributed to satisfy Rule 1, but S, in the second premise, need not be distributed to satisfy any rule. Thus, by the *superfluous distribution rule,* S is the term that must denote actually existing things for the syllogism to be valid from the Aristotelian standpoint. In the second syllogism, P must be distributed in the first premise to satisfy Rule 2, and M must be distributed once to satisfy Rule 1; but M is distributed twice. Thus, M is the term that must denote existing things for the syllogism to be valid from the Aristotelian standpoint. In the third syllogism, M must be distributed to satisfy Rule 1, but P need not be distributed to satisfy any rule. Thus, in this syllogism, P is the critical term.

You may recall that the existential fallacy from the Boolean standpoint first appeared in Section 4.3, where it arose in connection with the modern square of opposition. Also, the existential fallacy from the Aristotelian standpoint first appeared in Section 4.5, where it arose in connection with the traditional square of opposition. The two versions of the existential fallacy that appear in connection with Rule 5 stem from the same mistake as it relates to categorical syllogisms.

Proving the Rules

The foregoing discussion has shown that if a syllogism breaks any one of the five rules, it cannot be valid from the Boolean standpoint. Thus, we have shown that each of the rules is a *necessary* condition for validity. The question remains, however, whether a syllogism's breaking none of the rules is a *sufficient* condition for validity. In other words, does the fact that a syllogism breaks none of the rules guarantee its validity? The answer to this question is "yes," but unfortunately there appears to be no quick method for proving this fact. Therefore, if you are willing to take your instructor's word for it, you may stop reading this section now and proceed to the exercises. The proof that follows is somewhat tedious, and it proceeds by considering four classes of syllogisms having **A, E, I,** and **O** propositions for their conclusions.

Let us first suppose we are given a valid syllogism having an **A** proposition for its conclusion. Once again, suppose that *P*, *S*, and *M* designate the major, minor, and middle terms, respectively. Then, by Rules 1 and 2, both *M* and *S* are distributed in the premises. Further, by Rule 4, both premises are affirmative. Now, since **I** propositions distribute neither term, and **A** propositions distribute only one term, both premises must be **A** propositions, and *S* must be distributed in one and *M* in the other. Accordingly, the premises are "All *S* are *M*" and "All *M* are *P*." If we now combine these premises with the conclusion, "All *S* are *P*," we can determine by simple reasoning or a Venn diagram that the syllogism is valid. Note that only Rules 1, 2, and 4 were used in producing this first step in our proof, but the resulting syllogism obeys the unused rules as well. A similar process applies to the steps that follow.

Next, we consider a syllogism having an **E** proposition for its conclusion. By Rules 1 and 2, all three terms are distributed in the premises, and by Rules 3 and 4, one premise is negative and the other affirmative. Because three terms are distributed in the premises and there are only two premises, one of the premises must distribute two terms. Accordingly, this premise must be an **E** proposition. Furthermore, the other premise, which is affirmative and which distributes the third term, must be an **A** proposition. From this we conclude that there are four possible sets of premises: "All *S* are *M*" and "No *M* are *P*" (or its converse), and "All *P* are *M*" and "No *M* are *S*" (or its converse). Since converting an **E** proposition has no effect on validity, we may ignore the converse of these propositions. If we now combine the two given sets of premises with the conclusion, "No *S* are *P*," simple reasoning or a pair of Venn diagrams will establish the validity of the two resulting syllogisms.

Next, consider a syllogism having an **I** proposition for its conclusion. By Rule 1, *M* is distributed in at least one premise, and by Rule 4, both premises are affirmative. Further, by Rule 5, both premises cannot be universal. Thus, at least one premise is an **I** proposition. However, since the other premise distributes a term, that premise must be an **A** proposition. Accordingly, the four possible sets of premises are "All *M* are *S*" and "Some *M* are *P*" (or its converse), and "All *M* are *P*" and "Some *M* are *S*" (or its converse). Again, since converting an **I** proposition has no effect on validity, we may ignore the converse of these propositions. Then if we combine the two given pairs of premises with the conclusion, "Some *S* are *P*," simple reasoning or a pair of Venn diagrams will establish the validity of the two resulting syllogisms.

Last, we consider a syllogism having an **O** proposition for its conclusion. By Rules 1 and 2, both *M* and *P* are distributed in the premises. Also, by Rules 3 and 4, one premise is negative and the other affirmative, and by Rule 5, both premises cannot be universal. However, both premises cannot be particular (**I** and **O**), because then only one term would be distributed. Therefore, the premises are either **A** and **O** or **E** and **I**. In regard to the first of these alternatives, either *M* is the subject of the **A** statement and *P* is the predicate of the **O**, or *P* is the subject of the **A** statement and *M* is the predicate of the **O**.

This gives the premises as "All *M* are *S*" and "Some *M* are not *P*," and "All *P* are *M*" and "Some *S* are not *M*." When these pairs of premises are combined with the conclusion, "Some *S* are not *P*," simple reasoning or a pair of Venn diagrams will establish the validity of the two resulting syllogisms. Finally, considering the other alternative (**E** and **I**), the resulting four sets of premises are "No *M* are *P*" (or its converse) and "Some *M* are *S*" (or its converse). Again ignoring the converted propositions, simple reasoning or a Venn diagram will establish the validity of the single resulting syllogism.

This procedure proves that the five rules collectively provide a sufficient condition for the validity of any syllogism from the Boolean standpoint. Since eight distinct inferences or Venn diagrams were needed to accomplish it, this shows that there are really only eight significantly distinct syllogisms that are valid from the Boolean standpoint. The other seven are variations of these that result from converting one of the premises. For syllogisms having particular conclusions and universal premises about existing things, an analogous procedure can be used to prove that the first four rules collectively provide a sufficient condition for the validity of any syllogism from the Aristotelian standpoint.

EXERCISE 5.3

I. Reconstruct the following syllogistic forms and use the five rules for syllogisms to determine if they are valid from the Boolean standpoint, conditionally valid from the Aristotelian standpoint, or invalid. For those that are conditionally valid, identify the condition that must be fulfilled. For those that are invalid from either the Boolean or Aristotelian standpoint, name the fallacy or fallacies committed. Check your answers by constructing a Venn diagram for each.

★1. **AAA**-3	11. **AII**-2
2. **IAI**-2	12. **AIO**-3
3. **EIO**-1	★13. **AEE**-4
★4. **AAI**-2	14. **EAE**-4
5. **IEO**-1	15. **EAO**-3
6. **EOO**-4	★16. **EEE**-1
★7. **EAA**-1	17. **EAE**-1
8. **AII**-3	18. **OAI**-3
9. **AAI**-4	★19. **AOO**-2
★10. **IAO**-3	20. **EAO**-1

II. Use the five rules to determine whether the following standard-form syllogisms are valid from the Boolean standpoint, conditionally valid from the Aristotelian standpoint, or invalid. For those that are invalid from either the Boolean or Aristotelian standpoint, name the fallacy or fallacies committed. Check your answer by constructing a Venn diagram for each.

★1. Some nebulas are clouds of gas.
Some clouds of gas are objects invisible to the naked eye.
Therefore, some objects invisible to the naked eye are nebulas.

2. No individuals sensitive to the difference between right and wrong are people who measure talent and success in terms of wealth.
All corporate takeover experts are people who measure talent and success in terms of wealth.
Therefore, no corporate takeover experts are individuals sensitive to the difference between right and wrong.

3. No endangered species are creatures loved by the timber industry.
All spotted owls are endangered species.
Therefore, some spotted owls are not creatures loved by the timber industry.

★4. Some cases of affirmative action are not measures justified by past discrimination.
No cases of affirmative action are illegal practices.
Therefore, some illegal practices are not measures justified by past discrimination.

5. All transparent metals are good conductors of heat.
All transparent metals are good conductors of electricity.
Therefore, some good conductors of electricity are good conductors of heat.

6. All members of the National Rifle Association are people opposed to gun control.
All members of the National Rifle Association are law-abiding citizens.
Therefore, all law-abiding citizens are people opposed to gun control.

★7. No searches based on probable cause are violations of Fourth Amendment rights.
Some warrantless searches are violations of Fourth Amendment rights.
Therefore, some warrantless searches are not searches based on probable cause.

8. All war zones are places where abuse of discretion is rampant.
Some places where abuse of discretion is rampant are international borders.
Therefore, some international borders are war zones.

9. All inside traders are people subject to prosecution.
Some executives with privileged information are not people subject to prosecution.
Therefore, some executives with privileged information are inside traders.

★10. All successful flirts are masters at eye contact.
All masters at eye contact are people genuinely interested in others.
Therefore, some people genuinely interested in others are successful flirts.

III. Answer "true" or "false" to the following statements.

1. If a categorical syllogism violates one of the first four rules, it may still be valid.

2. If a valid syllogism has an **E** statement as its conclusion, then both the major and minor terms must be distributed in the premises.

3. If a syllogism has two **I** statements as premises, then it is invalid.

4. If a syllogism has an **E** and an **O** statement as premises, then no conclusion follows validly.

5. If a syllogism has an **I** statement as its conclusion, then Rule 2 cannot be violated.

6. If a valid syllogism has an **O** statement as its conclusion, then its premises can be an **A** and an **I** statement.

7. If a valid syllogism has an **E** statement as a premise, then its conclusion can be an **A** statement.

8. If a syllogism breaks only Rule 5 and its three terms are "dogs," "cats," and "animals," then the syllogism is valid from the Boolean standpoint.

9. If a syllogism breaks only Rule 5 and its three terms are "dogs," "cats," and "animals," then the syllogism is valid from the Aristotelian standpoint.

10. If a syllogism breaks only Rule 5 and its three terms are "elves," "trolls," and "gnomes," then the syllogism is valid from the Aristotelian standpoint.

5.4   Reducing the Number of Terms

Categorical syllogisms, as they occur in ordinary spoken and written expression, are seldom phrased according to the precise norms of the standard-form syllogism. Sometimes quantifiers, premises, or conclusions are left unexpressed, chains of syllogisms are strung together into single arguments, and terms are mixed together with their negations in a single argument. The final four sections of this chapter are concerned with developing techniques for reworking such arguments in order to render them testable by Venn diagrams or by the rules for syllogisms.

In this section we consider arguments that contain more than three terms but that can be modified to reduce the number of terms to three. Consider the following:

> All photographers are non-writers.
> Some editors are writers.
> Therefore, some non-photographers are not non-editors.

This syllogism is clearly not in standard form because it has six terms: "photographers," "editors," "writers," "non-photographers," "non-editors," and "non-writers." But because three of the terms are complements of the other three, the number of terms can be reduced to a total of three, each used twice in distinct propositions. To accomplish the reduction, we can use the three operations of conversion, obversion, and contraposition discussed in Chapter 4. But, of course, since the reworked syllogism must be equivalent in meaning to the original one, we must use these operations only on the kinds of statements for which they yield logically equivalent results. That is, we must use conversion only on **E** and **I** statements and contraposition only on **A** and **O** statements. Obversion yields logically equivalent results for all four kinds of categorical statements.

Let us rewrite our six-term argument using letters to represent the terms, and then obvert the first premise and contrapose the conclusion in order to eliminate the negated letters:

Symbolized argument	**Reduced argument**
All *P* are non-*W*.	No *P* are *W*.
Some *E* are *W*.	Some *E* are *W*.
Some non-*P* are not non-*E*.	Some *E* are not *P*.

Because the first premise of the original argument is an **A** statement and the conclusion an **O** statement, and because the operations performed on these statements yield logically equivalent results, the reduced argument is equivalent in meaning to the original argument. The reduced argument is in standard syllogistic form and may be evaluated either with a Venn diagram or by the five rules for syllogisms. The application of these methods indicates that the reduced argument is valid. We conclude, therefore, that the original argument is also valid.

It is not necessary to eliminate the negated terms in order to reduce the number of terms. It is equally effective to convert certain nonnegated terms into negated ones. Thus, instead of obverting the first premise of the example argument and contraposing the conclusion, we could have contraposed the first premise and converted and then obverted the second premise. The operation is performed as follows:

Symbolized argument	**Reduced argument**
All *P* are non-*W*.	All *W* are non-*P*.
Some *E* are *W*.	Some *W* are not non-*E*.
Some non-*P* are not non-*E*.	Some non-*P* are not non-*E*.

The reduced argument is once again equivalent to the original one, but now we must reverse the order of the premises to put the syllogism into standard form:

Some *W* are not non-*E*.
All *W* are non-*P*.
Some non-*P* are not non-*E*.

When tested with a Venn diagram or by means of the five rules, this argument will, of course, also be found valid, and so the original argument is valid. When using a Venn diagram, no unusual method is needed; the diagram is simply lettered with the three terms "*W*," "non-*E*," and "non-*P*."

The most important point to remember in reducing the number of terms is that conversion and contraposition must never be used on statements for which they yield undetermined results. That is, conversion must never be used on **A** and **O** statements, and contraposition must never be used on **E** and **I** statements. The operations that are allowed are summarized as follows:

Conversion:	No *A* are *B*.	No *B* are *A*.
	Some *A* are *B*.	Some *B* are *A*.
Obversion:	All *A* are *B*.	No *A* are non-*B*.
	No *A* are *B*.	All *A* are non-*B*.
	Some *A* are *B*.	Some *A* are not non-*B*.
	Some *A* are not *B*.	Some *A* are non-*B*.
Contraposition:	All *A* are *B*.	All non-*B* are non-*A*.
	Some *A* are not *B*.	Some non-*B* are not non-*A*.

EXERCISE 5.4

Rewrite the following arguments using letters to represent the terms, reduce the number of terms, and put the arguments into standard form. Then test the new forms with Venn diagrams or by means of the five rules for syllogisms to determine the validity or invalidity of the original arguments.

★1. Some intelligible statements are true statements, because all unintelligible statements are meaningless statements and some false statements are meaningful statements.

2. Some people who do not regret their crimes are convicted murderers, so some convicted murderers are people insusceptible of being reformed, since all people susceptible of being reformed are people who regret their crimes.

3. All Peace Corps volunteers are people who have witnessed poverty and desolation, and all people insensitive to human need are people who have failed to witness poverty and desolation. Thus, all Peace Corps volunteers are people sensitive to human need.

★4. Some unintentional killings are not punishable offenses, inasmuch as all cases of self-defense are unpunishable offenses, and some intentional killings are cases of self-defense.

5. All aircraft that disintegrate in flight are unsafe planes. Therefore, no poorly maintained aircraft are safe planes, because all well-maintained aircraft are aircraft that remain intact in flight.

6. No objects that sink in water are chunks of ice, and no objects that float in water are things at least as dense as water. Accordingly, all chunks of ice are things less dense than water.

★7. Some proposed flights to Mars are inexpensive ventures, because all unmanned space missions are inexpensive ventures, and some proposed flights to Mars are not manned space missions.

8. All schools driven by careerism are institutions that do not emphasize liberal arts. It follows that some universities are not institutions that emphasize liberal arts, for some schools that are not driven by careerism are universities.

9. No cases of AIDS are infections easily curable by drugs, since all diseases that infect the brain are infections not easily curable by drugs, and all diseases that do not infect the brain are cases other than AIDS.

★10. Some foreign emissaries are people without diplomatic immunity, so some people invulnerable to arrest and prosecution are foreign emissaries, because no people with diplomatic immunity are people vulnerable to arrest and prosecution.

5.5 Ordinary Language Arguments

Many arguments that are not standard-form categorical syllogisms as written can be translated into standard-form syllogisms. In doing so we often use techniques developed in the last section of Chapter 4—namely, inserting quantifiers, modifying subject and predicate terms, and introducing copulas. The goal, of course, is to produce an argument consisting of three standard-form categorical propositions that contain a total of three different terms, each of which occurs twice in distinct propositions. Once translated, the argument can be tested by means of a Venn diagram or the rules for syllogisms.

Since the task of translating arguments into standard-form syllogisms involves not only converting the component statements into standard form but adjusting these statements one to another so that their terms occur in matched pairs, a certain amount of practice may be required before it can be done with facility. In reducing the terms to three matched pairs it is often helpful to identify some factor common to two or all three propositions and to express this common factor through the strategic use of parameters. For example, if all three statements are about people, the term "people" or "people identical to" might be used; or if they are about times or places, the term "times" or "times identical to" or the term "places" or "places identical to" might be used. Here is an example:

> Whenever people put off marriage until they are older, the divorce rate decreases. Today, people are putting off marriage until they are older. Therefore, the divorce rate is decreasing today.

The temporal adverbs "whenever" and "today" suggest that "times" should be used as the common factor. Following this suggestion, we have this:

> All times people put off marriage until they are older are times the divorce rate decreases. All present times are times people put off marriage until they are older. Therefore, all present times are times the divorce rate decreases.

This is a standard-form categorical syllogism. Notice that each of the three terms is matched with an exact duplicate in a different proposition. To obtain such a match, it is sometimes necessary to alter the wording of the original statement just slightly. Now if we adopt the convention

> M = times people put off marriage until they are older
> D = times the divorce rate decreases
> P = present times

the syllogism may be symbolized as follows:

> All M are D.
> All P are M.
> All P are D.

This is the so-called "Barbara" syllogism and is, of course, valid. Here is another example:

> Boeing must be a manufacturer because it hires riveters, and any company that hires riveters is a manufacturer.

For this argument the parameter "companies" suggests itself:

> All companies identical to Boeing are manufacturers, because all companies identical to Boeing are companies that hire riveters, and all companies that hire riveters are manufacturers.

The first statement, of course, is the conclusion. When the syllogism is written in standard form, it will be seen that it has, like the previous syllogism, the form **AAA**-1.
Here is another example:

> If a piece of evidence is trustworthy, then it should be admissible in court. Polygraph tests are not trustworthy. Therefore, they should not be admissible in court.

To translate this argument, using a single common factor is not necessary:

> All trustworthy pieces of evidence are pieces of evidence that should be admissible in court. No polygraph tests are trustworthy pieces of evidence. Therefore, no polygraph tests are pieces of evidence that should be admissible in court.

This syllogism commits the fallacy of illicit major and is therefore invalid.

As was mentioned in Section 4.7, arguments containing an exceptive proposition must be handled in a special way. Let us consider one that contains an exceptive proposition as a premise:

> All of the jeans except the Levi's are on sale. Therefore, since the Calvin Klein jeans are not Levi's, they must be on sale.

The first premise is translated as two conjoined categorical propositions: "No Levi's are jeans on sale," and "All jeans that are not Levi's are jeans on sale." These give rise to two syllogisms:

> No Levi's are jeans on sale.
> No Calvin Klein jeans are Levi's.
> Therefore, all Calvin Klein jeans are jeans on sale.

> All jeans that are not Levi's are jeans on sale.
> No Calvin Klein jeans are Levi's.
> Therefore, all Calvin Klein jeans are jeans on sale.

The first syllogism, which is in standard form, is invalid because it has two negative premises. The second one, on the other hand, is not in standard form, because it has four terms. If the second premise is obverted, so that it reads "All Calvin Klein jeans are jeans that are not Levi's," the syllogism becomes an **AAA**-1 standard-form syllogism, which is valid.

Each of these two syllogisms may be viewed as a pathway in which the conclusion of the original argument might follow necessarily from the premises. Since it does follow via the second syllogism, the original argument is valid. If both of the resulting syllogisms turned out to be invalid, the original argument would be invalid.

EXERCISE 5.5

Translate the following arguments into standard-form categorical syllogisms, then use Venn diagrams or the rules for syllogisms to determine whether each is valid or invalid. See Section 4.7 for help with the translation.

★1. Physicists are the only scientists who theorize about the nature of time, and Stephen Hawking certainly does that. Therefore, Stephen Hawking must be a physicist.

2. Whenever suicide rates decline, we can infer that people's lives are better adjusted. Accordingly, since suicide rates have been declining in recent years, we can infer that people's lives have been better adjusted in recent years.

3. Environmentalists purchase only fuel-efficient cars. Hence, Hummers must not be fuel efficient, since environmentalists do not purchase them.

★4. Whoever wrote the Declaration of Independence had a big impact on civilization, and Thomas Jefferson certainly had that. Therefore, Thomas Jefferson wrote the Declaration of Independence.

5. There are public schools that teach secular humanism. Therefore, since secular humanism is a religion, there are public schools that teach religion.

6. Anyone who led America into the space age will live in history. Therefore, John Glenn will live in history, because he led America into the space age.

★7. Shania Twain sings what she wants. Hence, since Shania sings country songs, it follows that she must want to sing country songs.

8. Not all interest expenses are tax deductible. Home mortgage payments are interest expenses. Thus, they are not tax deductible.

9. If a marriage is based on a meshing of neuroses, it allows little room for growth. If a marriage allows little room for growth, it is bound to fail. Therefore, if a marriage is based on a meshing of neuroses, it is bound to fail.

★10. TV viewers cannot receive scrambled signals unless they have a decoder. Whoever receives digital satellite signals receives scrambled signals. Therefore, whoever receives digital satellite signals has a decoder.

11. Wherever icebergs are present, threats to shipping exist. Icebergs are not present in the South Pacific. Hence, there are no threats to shipping in the South Pacific.

12. According to surveys, there are college students who think that Africa is in North America. But anyone who thinks that has no knowledge of geography. It follows that there are college students who have no knowledge of geography.

★13. Diseases carried by recessive genes can be inherited by offspring of two carriers. Thus, since cystic fibrosis is a disease carried by recessive genes, it can be inherited by offspring of two carriers.

14. All of the movies except the chick flicks were exciting. Hence, the action films were exciting, because none of them is a chick flick.

15. Autistic children are occasionally helped by aversive therapy. But aversive therapy is sometimes inhumane. Thus, autistic children are sometimes helped by inhumane therapy.

5.6   Enthymemes

An **enthymeme** is an argument that is expressible as a categorical syllogism but that is missing a premise or a conclusion. Examples:

> The corporate income tax should be abolished; it encourages waste and high prices.

> Animals that are loved by someone should not be sold to a medical laboratory, and lost pets are certainly loved by someone.

The first enthymeme is missing the premise "Whatever encourages waste and high prices should be abolished," and the second is missing the conclusion "Lost pets should not be sold to a medical laboratory."

Enthymemes occur frequently in ordinary spoken and written English for several reasons. Sometimes it is simply boring to express every statement in an argument. The listener or reader's intelligence is called into play when he or she is required to supply a missing statement, thereby sustaining his or her interest. On other occasions the arguer may want to slip an invalid or unsound argument past an unwary listener or reader, and this aim may be facilitated by leaving a premise or conclusion out of the picture.

Many enthymemes are easy to convert into syllogisms. The reader or listener must first determine what is missing, whether premise or conclusion, and then introduce the missing statement with the aim of converting the enthymeme into a good argument. Attention to indicator words will often provide the clue as to the nature of the missing statement, but a little practice can render this task virtually automatic. The missing statement need not be expressed in categorical form; expressing it in the general context of the other statements is sufficient and is often the easier alternative. Once this is done, the entire argument may be translated into categorical form and then tested with a Venn diagram or by the rules for syllogisms. Example:

Venus completes its orbit in less time than the Earth, because Venus is closer to the sun.

Missing premise: Any planet closer to the sun completes its orbit in less time than the Earth.

Translating this argument into categorical form, we have

All planets closer to the sun are planets that complete their orbit in less time than the Earth.
All planets identical to Venus are planets closer to the sun.
All planets identical to Venus are planets that complete their orbit in less time than the Earth.

This syllogism is valid (and sound).

Any enthymeme (such as the one about Venus) that contains an indicator word is missing a premise. This may be seen as follows. If an enthymeme contains a conclusion indicator, then the conclusion follows it, which means that the missing statement is a premise. On the other hand, if the enthymeme contains a premise indicator, then the conclusion precedes it, which means, again, that the missing statement is a premise.

If, however, an enthymeme contains no indicator words at all (such as the two enthymemes at the beginning of this section), then the missing statement could be either a premise or a conclusion. If the two given statements are joined by a word such as "and," "but," "moreover," or some similar conjunction, the missing statement is usually a conclusion. If not, the first statement is usually the conclusion, and the missing statement is a premise. To test this latter alternative, it may help to mentally insert the word "because" between the two statements. If this insertion makes sense, the missing statement is a premise.

After the nature of the missing statement has been determined, the next task is to write it out. To do so, one must first identify its terms. This can be done by taking account of the terms that are given. Two of the terms in the given statements will match up with each other. Once this pair of terms is found, attention should be focused on the other two terms. These are the ones that will be used to form the missing statement. In constructing the missing statement, attention to the rules for syllogisms may be helpful (if the resulting syllogism is to be valid). For example, if the missing statement is a conclusion and one of the given premises is negative, the missing conclusion must be negative. Or if the missing statement is a premise and the stated conclusion is universal, the missing premise must be universal.

The enthymemes that we have considered thus far have been fairly straightforward. The kinds of enthymemes that occur in letters to the editor of magazines and newspapers often require a bit more creativity to convert into syllogisms. Consider the following:

> The motorcycle has served as basic transportation for the poor for decades. It deserves to be celebrated.
>
> (William B. Fankboner)

The conclusion is the last statement, and the missing premise is that any vehicle that has served as basic transportation for the poor for decades deserves to be celebrated. The enthymeme may be written as a standard-form syllogism as follows:

> All vehicles that have served as basic transportation for the poor for decades are vehicles that deserve to be celebrated.
> All vehicles identical to the motorcycle are vehicles that have served as basic transportation for the poor for decades.
> Therefore, all vehicles identical to the motorcycle are vehicles that deserve to be celebrated.

The syllogism is valid and arguably sound. Here is another example:

> I know several doctors who smoke. In a step toward my own health, I will no longer be their patient. It has occurred to me that if they care so little about their own health, how can they possibly care about mine?
>
> (Joan Boyer)

In this argument the author draws three connections: the connection between doctors' smoking and doctors' caring about their own health, between doctors' caring about their own health and doctors' caring about the author's health, and between doctors' caring about the author's health and doctors who will have the author as a patient. Two arguments are needed to express these connections:

> All doctors who smoke are doctors who do not care about their own health.
> All doctors who do not care about their own health are doctors who do not care about my health.
> Therefore, all doctors who smoke are doctors who do not care about my health.

And,

> All doctors who smoke are doctors who do not care about my health.
> All doctors who do not care about my health are doctors who will not have me as a patient.
> Therefore, all doctors who smoke are doctors who will not have me as a patient.

Notice that the conclusion of the first argument becomes a premise in the second argument. To put these arguments into final standard form the order of the premises must be reversed. Both arguments are valid, but probably not sound.

I. In the following enthymemes determine whether the missing statement is a premise or a conclusion. Then supply the missing statement, attempting whenever possible to convert the enthymeme into a valid argument. The missing statement need not be expressed as a standard-form categorical proposition.

★1. Some police chiefs undermine the evenhanded enforcement of the law, because anyone who fixes parking tickets does that.

2. Any form of cheating deserves to be punished, and plagiarism is a form of cheating.

3. Carrie Underwood is a talented singer. After all, she's won several Grammy awards.

★4. A few fraternities have dangerous initiation rites, and those that do have no legitimate role in campus life.

5. Only nonprofit organizations are exempt from paying taxes, so churches must be exempt.

6. All of the operas except Mozart's were well performed, and *Carmen* was not written by Mozart.

★7. Not all phone calls are welcome, but those from friends are.

8. Higher life forms could not have evolved through merely random processes, because no organized beings could have evolved that way.

9. None but great novels are timeless, and *The Brothers Karamazov* is a great novel.

★10. The humpback whale population has been decreasing in recent years because the humpback is being overhunted.

11. Wherever water exists, human life can be sustained, and water exists on the moon.

12. If a symphony orchestra has effective fund-raisers, it will survive; and the Cleveland symphony has survived for years.

★13. Mechanistic materialists do not believe in free will, because they think that everything is governed by deterministic laws.

14. A contract to buy land is not enforceable unless it's in writing, but our client's contract to buy land *is* in writing.

15. The only telescopes that are unaffected by the atmosphere are orbiting telescopes, and the Hubble telescope is in orbit.

II. Translate the enthymemes in Part I of this exercise into standard-form categorical syllogisms and test them for validity.

III. The following enthymemes were originally submitted as letters to the editor of magazines and newspapers. Convert them into valid standard-form syllogisms. In some cases two syllogisms may be required.

★1. If the Defense Department is so intent on fighting alcohol abuse, why does it make alcohol so readily available and acceptable? Alcohol is tax free at post liquor stores, and enlisted men's and officers' clubs make drinking almost a mandatory facet of military life.

(Diane Lynch)

2. All aid to Israel should be stopped at once. Why should the American taxpayer be asked to send billions of dollars to Israel when every city in the United States is practically broke and millions of people are out of work?

(Bertha Grace)

3. Suicide is not immoral. If a person decides that life is impossible, it is his or her right to end it.

(Donald S. Farrar)

★4. The best way to get people to read a book is to ban it. The fundamentalist families in Church Hill, Tennessee, have just guaranteed sales of *Macbeth, The Diary of Anne Frank, The Wizard of Oz* and other stories.

(Paula Fleischer)

5. The budget deficit will not be brought under control because to do so would require our elected leaders in Washington to do the unthinkable—act courageously and responsibly.

(Bruce Crutcher)

6. The Constitution bans any law that is so vague that "men of common intelligence must necessarily guess at its meaning." Sexual harassment laws, however, are so vague that no one knows what they mean.

(Hans Bader)

★7. College students of today are the higher-income taxpayers of tomorrow. Congress should consider financial aid as an investment in the financial future of our country.

(Carol A. Steimel)

8. Our genes and our environment control our destinies. The idea of conscious choice is ridiculous. Yes, prisons should be designed to protect society, but they should not punish the poor slobs who were headed for jail from birth.

(Paul R. Andrews)

9. Encouraging toy-gun play gives children a clear message that the best way to deal with frustration and conflict is with a gun. Is this the message that we want to be sending our kids?

(Patricia Owen)

★10. The U.S. surgeon general's latest report on cigarettes and cancer is an interesting example of natural selection in the late twentieth century. The intelligent members of our species will quit smoking, and survive. The dummies will continue to puff away.

(Kelly Kinnon)

IV. Page through a magazine or newspaper and identify five topics of current interest. Construct an enthymeme involving each topic.

5.7   Sorites

A **sorites** is a chain of categorical syllogisms in which the intermediate conclusions have been left out. The name is derived from the Greek word *soros*, meaning "heap," and is pronounced "sō rī tēz," with the accent on the second syllable. The plural form is also "sorites." Here is an example:

> All bloodhounds are dogs.
> All dogs are mammals.
> No fish are mammals.
> Therefore, no fish are bloodhounds.

The first two premises validly imply the intermediate conclusion "All bloodhounds are mammals." If this intermediate conclusion is then treated as a premise and put together with the third premise, the final conclusion follows validly. The sorites is thus composed of two valid categorical syllogisms and is therefore valid. The rule in evaluating a sorites is based on the idea that a chain is only as strong as its weakest link. If any of the component syllogisms in a sorites is invalid, the entire sorites is invalid.

A **standard-form sorites** is one in which each of the component propositions is in standard form, each term occurs twice, the predicate of the conclusion is in the first premise, and each successive premise has a term in common with the preceding one.* The sorites in the example is in standard form. Each of the propositions is in standard form, each term occurs twice; the predicate of the conclusion, "bloodhounds," is in the first premise; the other term is in the first premise; "dogs," is in the second premise, and so on.

I will now introduce two techniques for testing a sorites for validity. The first technique involves three steps: (1) put the sorites into standard form, (2) introduce the intermediate conclusions, and (3) test each component syllogism for validity. If each component is valid, the sorites is valid. Consider the following sorites form:

> No *B* are *C*.
> Some *E* are *A*.
> All *A* are *B*.
> All *D* are *C*.
> _____
> Some *E* are not *D*.

To put the sorites form into standard form, the premises must be rearranged:

> All *D* are *C*.
> No *B* are *C*.
> All *A* are *B*.
> Some *E* are *A*.
> _____
> Some *E* are not *D*.

Next, the intermediate conclusions are drawn. Venn diagrams are useful in performing this step, and they serve simultaneously to check the validity of each component syllogism:

---

*Actually, there are two definitions of standard-form sorites: the Goclenian and the Aristotelian. The one given here is the Goclenian. In the Aristotelian version, the premises are arranged so that the *subject* of the conclusion occurs in the first premise.

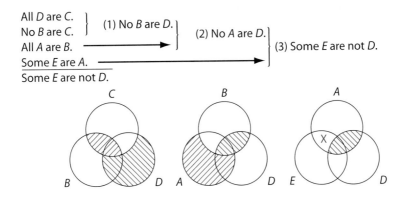

All *D* are *C*.
No *B* are *C*. } (1) No *B* are *D*.
All *A* are *B*. ⟶ } (2) No *A* are *D*.
Some *E* are *A*. ⟶ } (3) Some *E* are not *D*.
Some *E* are not *D*.

The first intermediate conclusion, "No *B* are *D*," is drawn from the first two premises. The second, "No *A* are *D*," is drawn from the first intermediate conclusion and the third premise. And the third conclusion, which is identical to the final conclusion, is drawn from the second intermediate conclusion and the fourth premise. Since all conclusions are drawn validly, the sorites is valid. On the other hand, if at some step in the procedure no conclusion can be drawn, the sorites is invalid.

The second technique for testing the validity of a sorites is faster and simpler than the first one because it does not require that the intermediate conclusions be derived. This second technique consists in applying five rules that closely resemble the rules for syllogisms. The rules are as follows:

Rule 1: Each of the middle terms must be distributed at least once.

Rule 2: If a term is distributed in the conclusion, then it must be distributed in a premise.

Rule 3: Two negative premises are not allowed.

Rule 4: A negative premise requires a negative conclusion, and a negative conclusion requires a negative premise.

Rule 5: If all the premises are universal, the conclusion cannot be particular.

Rule 1 refers to the "middle terms" in the sorites. These are the terms that occur in matched pairs in the premises. The conclusion referred to in Rules 2, 4, and 5 is the final conclusion of the sorites. Also, as with categorical syllogisms, if a sorites breaks only Rule 5, it is valid from the Aristotelian standpoint on condition that its terms refer to existing things.

Before applying the rules, it helps to put the sorites into standard form; in either event the sorites must be written so that the terms occur in matched pairs. The following sorites is in standard form, and the distributed terms are marked with a small "d." As is apparent, there are three middle terms: *M, K,* and *R.*

All S^d are *M*.
All K^d are *M*.
No K^d are R^d.
Some *F* are *R*.
Some *F* are not S^d.

This sorites breaks Rule 1 because neither occurrence of *M* in the first two premises is distributed. Thus, the sorites is invalid. Note that no other rule is broken. Both of the *K*'s in lines 2 and 3 are distributed, one of the *R*'s in lines 3 and 4 is distributed, *S* is distributed in the conclusion and also in the first premise, there is a negative conclusion and only one negative premise, and while the conclusion is particular so is one of the premises.

The logic behind the five rules is as follows. For Rule 1, each of the middle terms in the sorites is also a middle term in one of the component syllogisms. Thus, if Rule 1 is broken, one of the component syllogisms has an undistributed middle, making the entire sorites invalid.

For Rule 2, when the sorites is in standard form, the predicate of the conclusion must appear in each of the intermediate conclusions. Thus, if the predicate of the conclusion is distributed, it must also be distributed in each of the intermediate conclusions, and also in the first premise. Otherwise, one of the component syllogisms would have either an illicit major or an illicit minor, making the entire sorites invalid. Analogously, if the subject of the conclusion is distributed, it must also be distributed in the last premise. Otherwise, the last component syllogism would have an illicit minor, making the entire sorites invalid.

For Rule 3, when a negative premise appears in the list of premises, the conclusion derived from that premise must be negative, as must all subsequent conclusions. Otherwise, one of the component syllogisms would break Rule 4 for syllogisms. If a second negative premise should appear, the syllogism consisting of that premise and the prior intermediate conclusion would commit the fallacy of exclusive premises, making the entire sorites invalid.

Similarly, for Rule 4, when a negative premise appears in the list of premises, all subsequent conclusions must be negative. Otherwise, one of the component syllogisms would break Rule 4 for syllogisms. Conversely, if the conclusion of the sorites is negative, either the last premise or the last intermediate conclusion must be negative. Otherwise, the last component syllogism would break Rule 4 for syllogisms. If the last intermediate conclusion is negative, then either the prior premise or the prior intermediate conclusion must be negative. If we continue this reasoning, we see that some prior premise must be negative.

For Rule 5, a particular conclusion has existential import, while universal premises (from the Boolean standpoint) do not. Thus, if all the premises are universal and the conclusion is particular, the sorites as a whole commits the existential fallacy.

One of the advantages of the rules method for testing a sorites is that invalidity can often be detected through immediate inspection. Once a sorites has been put into standard form, any sorites having more than one negative premise is invalid, and any sorites having a negative premise and an affirmative conclusion (or vice versa) is invalid. Also, as with syllogisms, any sorites having more than one particular premise is invalid. This last requirement is implied by the other rules.

EXERCISE 5.7

I. Rewrite the following sorites in standard form, reducing the number of terms when necessary. Then supply the intermediate conclusions and test with Venn diagrams.

★1. No *B* are *C*.
Some *D* are *C*.
All *A* are *B*.
_____
Some *D* are not *A*.

2. No *C* are *D*.
All *A* are *B*.
Some *C* are not *B*.
_____
Some *D* are not *A*.

3. No *S* are *M*.
All *F* are *S*.
Some *M* are *H*.
All *E* are *F*.
_____
Some *H* are not *E*.

★4. Some *T* are *K*.
No *K* are *N*.
Some *C* are *Q*.
All *T* are *C*.
_____
Some *Q* are not *N*.

5. No *A* are non-*B*.
No *C* are *B*.
All non-*A* are non-*D*.
_____
No *D* are *C*.

6. All *M* are non-*P*.
Some *M* are *S*.
All *K* are *P*.
_____
Some non-*K* are not non-*S*.

★7. All non-*U* are non-*V*.
No *U* are non-*W*.
All *V* are *Y*.
No *X* are *W*.
_____
All *Y* are non-*X*.

8. All *D* are non-*C*.
All non-*B* are non-*A*.
Some *E* are *D*.
All *B* are *C*.
_____
Some non-*A* are not non-*E*.

9. All non-*L* are non-*K*.
Some *K* are *M*.
All *P* are non-*L*.
No non-*N* are *M*.
No *Q* are non-*P*.
_____
Some *N* are not *Q*.

★10. All *R* are *S*.
No non-*V* are *T*.
No *Q* are non-*R*.
No non-*Q* are *P*.
All *T* are non-*S*.
_____
All *V* are non-*P*.

II. For the sorites in Part I, rewrite each in standard form, reducing the number of terms when necessary. Then use the five rules for sorites to test each for validity.

III. The following sorites are valid. Rewrite each sorites in standard form, using letters to represent the terms and reducing the number of terms whenever necessary. Then use Venn diagrams or the rules method to prove each one valid.

★1. Whatever produces oxygen supports human life.
Rain forests produce oxygen.
Nothing that supports human life should be destroyed.
_____
Rain forests should not be destroyed.

2. No restrictive trade policies fail to invite retaliation.
Trade wars threaten our standard of living.
Some Japanese trade policies are restrictive.
Policies that invite retaliation lead to a trade war.
_____
Some Japanese trade policies threaten our standard of living.

3. Anything that poisons drinking water causes disease and death.
Chemicals percolating through the soil contaminate aquifers.
Dumped chemicals percolate through the soil.
Whatever contaminates aquifers poisons drinking water.
Dumped chemicals cause disease and death.

★4. Nothing that is brittle is ductile.
Superconductors are all ceramics.
Only ductile things can be pulled into wires.
Ceramics are brittle.
Superconductors cannot be pulled into wires.

5. Some college students purchase their term papers.
Any cheat is expelled from college.
No one will achieve his career goals who is expelled.
No one who purchases term papers is other than a cheat.
Some college students will not achieve their career goals.

6. Creation science does not favor the teaching of evolution.
Nothing should be taught that frustrates the understanding of life.
Whatever opposes the teaching of evolution impedes the learning of biology.
Anything that enhances the understanding of life fosters the learning of biology.
Creation science should not be taught.

★7. Whoever gives birth to crack babies increases future crime rates.
Some pregnant women use crack.
None but criminals increase future crime rates.
Pregnant crack users never give birth to anything but crack babies.
Some pregnant women are criminals.

8. Whatever retards population growth increases food availability.
Anything that prevents starvation enhances life.
Birth control measures never accelerate population growth.
Anything that enhances life should be encouraged.
Whatever increases food availability prevents starvation.
Birth control measures should not be discouraged.

9. A few countries allow ivory trading.
Whatever country resists elephant killing discourages poachers.
Any country that allows ivory trading encourages poachers.
No country that promotes the extinction of elephants should escape the condemnation of the civilized world.
Any country that supports elephant killing promotes the extinction of elephants.
A few countries should be condemned by the civilized world.

★10. Anything that promotes skin cancer causes death.
Whatever preserves the ozone layer prevents the release of CFCs.
Nothing that resists skin cancer increases UV radiation.
Anything that destroys the ozone layer increases UV radiation.
There are packaging materials that release CFCs.
Nothing that causes death should be legal.
Some packaging materials should be illegal.

IV. The following sorites are taken from Lewis Carroll's *Symbolic Logic*. All are valid. Rewrite each sorites in standard form, using letters to represent the terms and reducing the number of terms whenever necessary. Then use Venn diagrams or the rules method to prove each one valid.

★1. No ducks waltz.
No officers ever decline to waltz.
All my poultry are ducks.
My poultry are not officers.

2. No experienced person is incompetent.
Jenkins is always blundering.
No competent person is always blundering.
Jenkins is inexperienced.

3. No terriers wander among the signs of the zodiac.
Nothing that does not wander among the signs
of the zodiac is a comet.
Nothing but a terrier has a curly tail.
No comet has a curly tail.

★4. All hummingbirds are richly colored.
No large birds live on honey.
Birds that do not live on honey are dull in color.
All hummingbirds are small.

5. All unripe fruit is unwholesome.
All these apples are wholesome.
No fruit grown in the shade is ripe.
These apples were grown in the sun.

6. All my sons are slim.
No child of mine is healthy who takes no exercise.
All gluttons who are children of mine are fat.
No daughter of mine takes any exercise.
All gluttons who are children of mine are unhealthy.

★7. The only books in this library that I do not recommend for reading
are unhealthy in tone.
The bound books are all well-written.
All the romances are healthy in tone.
I do not recommend you to read any of the unbound books.
All the romances in this library are well-written.

8. No interesting poems are unpopular among people of real taste.
No modern poetry is free from affectation.
All your poems are on the subject of soap bubbles.
No affected poetry is popular among people of real taste.
No ancient poem is on the subject of soap bubbles.
All your poems are uninteresting.

9. All writers who understand human nature are clever.
   No one is a true poet unless he can stir the hearts of men.
   Shakespeare wrote *Hamlet*.
   No writer who does not understand human nature can stir the hearts of men.
   None but a true poet could have written *Hamlet*.

   Shakespeare was clever.

★10. I trust every animal that belongs to me.
   Dogs gnaw bones.
   I admit no animals into my study unless they beg when told to do so.
   All the animals in the yard are mine.
   I admit every animal that I trust into my study.
   The only animals that are really willing to beg when told to do so are dogs.

   All the animals in the yard gnaw bones.

Summary

A categorical syllogism is a deductive argument consisting of three categorical propositions and containing a total of three different terms, each of which appears twice in distinct propositions. In a standard-form categorical syllogism, the propositions are all in standard form, the two occurrences of each term are identical, each term is used in the same sense throughout the argument, and the major premise is listed first, the minor premise second, and the conclusion last. The major premise is the one that contains the major term (which by definition is the predicate of the conclusion), and the minor premise is the one that contains the minor term (which by definition is the subject of the conclusion). The middle term is the one that appears twice in the premises.

The validity of a standard-form syllogism is determined by its form, and the form is identified in terms of mood and figure. The mood consists of the letter names of the propositions that compose the syllogism, and the figure is determined by the location of the two occurrences of the middle term in the premises. From the Boolean standpoint, a syllogism is either valid or invalid regardless of whether its terms denote actually existing things. From the Aristotelian standpoint, a syllogism is either valid, conditionally valid, or invalid. A conditionally valid syllogism is called valid once it is known that the critical term denotes actually existing things.

Venn diagrams for syllogisms consist of three overlapping circles, with each circle representing a term. To test a syllogism for validity, the content of the premises is represented in the diagram, and the diagram is then inspected to see if it supports the conclusion. In representing the content of the premises, X's and shading are entered into the diagram in basically the same way as they are for two-circle diagrams. The Venn diagram technique applies immediately to syllogisms interpreted from the Boolean standpoint, but it can be modified to test syllogisms from the Aristotelian standpoint.

The validity of categorical syllogisms can also be tested by the application of five rules. A syllogism is valid if and only if (1) its middle term is distributed in at least one premise, (2) a term distributed in the conclusion is also distributed in the premise, (3) at least one premise is affirmative, (4) a negative conclusion occurs with a negative premise and vice versa, and (5) a particular conclusion (should there be one) occurs with a particular premise. If only the last rule is violated, the syllogism is valid from the Aristotelian standpoint on condition that the critical term denotes actually existing things, but it is not valid from the Boolean standpoint.

An argument containing more than three terms, wherein one is a complement of another, may be reduced to a standard-form syllogism by applying the operations of conversion, obversion, and contraposition. These operations must be used only when they yield logically equivalent results, and the goal is to produce an argument containing three terms wherein each is matched with an identical term in a different proposition.

Syllogisms expressed in ordinary language can be translated into standard form by applying the techniques developed in Section 4.7. Enthymemes are quasi-syllogisms that are missing a premise or conclusion. They can be converted into syllogisms by supplying the missing statement. A sorites is a chain of syllogisms in which the intermediate conclusions have been deleted. Testing a sorites consists in putting it into standard form, supplying the intermediate conclusions, and testing each syllogism in the chain.

5

6 Propositional Logic

6.1 Symbols and Translation

Earlier chapters showed that the validity of a deductive argument is purely a function of its form. By knowing the form of an argument, we can often tell immediately whether it is valid or invalid. Unfortunately, however, ordinary linguistic usage often obscures the form of an argument. To dispel this obscurity, logic introduces various simplifying procedures. In Chapter 5, letters were used to represent the terms in a syllogism, and techniques were developed to reduce syllogisms to what is called standard form. In this chapter, form recognition is facilitated through the introduction of special symbols called **operators,** or **connectives.** When arguments are expressed in terms of these symbols, determining validity often becomes a matter of mere visual inspection.

In the two previous chapters, the fundamental elements were terms. In **propositional logic,** however, the fundamental elements are whole statements (or propositions). Statements are represented by letters, and these letters are then combined by means of the operators to form more-complex symbolic representations.

To understand the symbolic representation used in propositional logic, we must distinguish simple statements from compound statements. A **simple statement** is one that does not contain any other statement as a component. Here are some examples:

> Fast foods tend to be unhealthy.
>
> James Joyce wrote *Ulysses.*
>
> Parakeets are colorful birds.
>
> The monk seal is threatened with extinction.

Any convenient uppercase letter may be selected to represent each statement. Thus F might be selected to represent the first, J the second, P the third, and M the fourth. As will be explained shortly, lowercase letters are reserved for use as statement variables.

A **compound statement** is one that contains at least one simple statement as a component. Here are some examples:

It is not the case that Al Qaeda is a humanitarian organization.

Dianne Reeves sings jazz, and Christina Aguilera sings pop.

Either people get serious about conservation or energy prices will skyrocket.

If the world's nations spurn international law, then future wars are guaranteed.

The Broncos will win if and only if they run the ball.

Using letters to stand for the simple statements, these compound statements may be represented as follows:

It is not the case that *A*.
D and *C*.
Either *P* or *E*.
If *W* then *F*.
B if and only if *R*.

In the first example, note that the statement is compound even though it contains only a single component (*A*). In general, negative statements are interpreted as compound units consisting of an affirmative statement and the phrase "it is not the case that."

The expressions "it is not the case that," "and," "or," "if . . . then . . . ," and "if and only if" are translated by logical operators. The five logical operators are as follows:

Operator	Name	Logical function	Used to translate
~	tilde	negation	not, it is not the case that
•	dot	conjunction	and, also, moreover
v	wedge	disjunction	or, unless
⊃	horseshoe	implication	if . . . then . . . , only if
≡	triple bar	equivalence	if and only if

Saying that logical operators are used to "translate" these English expressions does not mean that the expressions and the operators are identical. As in any translation (from English to French, for example), a certain distortion of meaning occurs. The meaning of such English expressions as "and," "or," and "if and only if" is often vague and may vary with context, whereas the meaning of the logical operators is clear, precise, and invariable. Thus, when we say that the logical operators may be used to translate expressions in ordinary language, we mean that the operators capture a certain aspect of their correlative English expressions. The precise character of this aspect is spelled out in the next section of this chapter. The purpose of this section is to develop a familiarity with the logical operators through practice in translation.

When we use the operators to translate the previous examples of compound statements, the results are as follows:

It is not the case that *A*.	~*A*
D and *C*.	*D* • *C*
Either *P* or *E*.	*P* v *E*
If *W* then *F*.	*W* ⊃ *F*
B if and only if *R*.	*B* ≡ *R*

The statement ~A is called a **negation.** The statement $D \cdot C$ is called a **conjunctive statement** (or a **conjunction**), and the statement $P \vee E$ is called a **disjunctive statement** (or a **disjunction**); in the conjunctive statement, the components D and C are called **conjuncts,** and in the disjunctive statement the components P and E are called **disjuncts.** The statement $W \supset F$ is called a **conditional statement** (or a **conditional**), and it expresses the relation of **material implication.** Its components are called **antecedent** (W) and **consequent** (F). Lastly, $B \equiv R$ is called a **biconditional statement** (or a **biconditional**), and it expresses the relation of **material equivalence.**

Let us now use the logical operators to translate additional English statements. The tilde symbol is used to translate any negated simple proposition:

Rolex does not make computers.	~R
It is not the case that Rolex makes computers.	~R
It is false that Rolex makes computers.	~R

As these examples show, the tilde is always placed *in front* of the proposition it negates. All of the other operators are placed *between* two propositions. Also, unlike the other operators, the tilde cannot be used to connect two propositions. Thus, $G \sim H$ is not a proper expression. But the tilde is the only operator that can immediately follow another operator. Thus, it would be proper to write $G \cdot \sim H$. In the Rolex examples, the tilde is used to negate a simple proposition, but it can also be used to negate a compound proposition—for example ~$(G \cdot F)$. In this case the tilde negates the entire expression inside the parentheses.

This last example allows us the opportunity to define what is called the main operator in a statement. The **main operator** is that operator in a compound statement that governs the largest component(s) in the statement. In the example just given, the main operator is the tilde, because it governs everything that follows it—namely, $(G \cdot F)$. The dot, on the other hand, is not the main operator because it governs only the two simple statements inside the parentheses. On the other hand, in the statement $H \cdot \sim(K \vee M)$, the dot is the main operator because it governs both H and $\sim(K \vee M)$, whereas the tilde governs only the expression in parentheses.

These statements are all **negations.** The main operator is a tilde.

~B
~$(G \supset H)$
~$[(A \equiv F) \cdot (C \equiv G)]$

The dot symbol is used to translate such conjunctions as "and," "also," "but," "however," "yet," "still," "moreover," "although," and "nevertheless":

Tiffany sells jewelry, and Gucci sells cologne.	$T \cdot G$
Tiffany sells jewelry, but Gucci sells cologne.	$T \cdot G$
Tiffany sells jewelry; however, Gucci sells cologne.	$T \cdot G$
Tiffany and Ben Bridge sell jewelry.	$T \cdot B$

Note that the last example is equivalent in meaning to "Tiffany sells jewelry, and Ben Bridge sells jewelry." To translate such a statement as a conjunction of two simple statements, the original statement must be equivalent to a compound statement in English. For example, the statement "Mary and Louise are friends" is *not* equivalent in meaning to "Mary is a friend, and Louise is a friend," so this statement cannot be translated as $M \cdot L$.

These statements are all **conjunctions.** The main operator is a dot.

$K \cdot \sim L$

$(E \vee F) \cdot (G \vee H)$

$[(R \supset T) \vee (S \supset U)] \cdot [(W \equiv X) \vee (Y \equiv Z)]$

The wedge symbol is used to translate "or" and "unless." A previous chapter explained that "unless" is equivalent in meaning to "if not." This equivalence holds in propositional logic as well, but in propositional logic it is usually simpler to equate "unless" with "or." For example, the statement "You won't graduate unless you pass freshman English" is equivalent to "Either you pass freshman English or you won't graduate" and also to "If you don't pass freshman English, then you won't graduate." As the next section demonstrates, the wedge symbol has the meaning of "and/or"— that is, "or" in the inclusive sense. Although "or" and "unless" are sometimes used in an exclusive sense, the wedge is usually used to translate them as well.

The word "either," which is often used to introduce disjunctive statements, has primarily a punctuational meaning. The placement of this word often tells us where parentheses and brackets must be introduced in the symbolic expression. If parentheses or brackets are not needed, "either" does not affect the translation. A similar point applies to the word "both," which is often used to introduce conjunctive statements. Here are some disjunctive statements:

Aspen allows snowboards or Telluride does.	$A \vee T$
Either Aspen allows snowboards or Telluride does.	$A \vee T$
Aspen allows snowboards unless Telluride does.	$A \vee T$
Unless Aspen allows snowboards, Telluride does.	$A \vee T$

From the English sense of these statements, it should be clear that $A \vee T$ is logically equivalent to $T \vee A$. Also $T \cdot G$ is logically equivalent to $G \cdot T$. Logically equivalent propositions necessarily have the same truth value.

These statements are all **disjunctions.** The main operator is a wedge.

$\sim C \vee \sim D$

$(F \cdot H) \vee (\sim K \cdot \sim L)$

$[S \cdot (T \supset U)] \vee [X \cdot (Y \equiv Z)]$

The horseshoe symbol is used to translate "if ... then ...," "only if," and similar expressions that indicate a conditional statement. The expressions "in case," "provided that," "given that," and "on condition that" are usually translated in the same way as "if." By customary usage, the horseshoe symbol is also used to translate "implies." Although "implies" is used most properly to describe the relationship between the premises and conclusion of an argument, we may accept this translation as an alternate meaning for "implies."

The function of "only if" is, in a sense, just the reverse of "if." For example, the statement "You will catch a fish only if your hook is baited" does not mean "If your hook is baited, then you will catch a fish." If it meant this, then everyone with a baited hook would catch a fish. Rather, the statement means "If your hook is not baited, then you will not catch a fish," which is logically equivalent to "If you catch a fish, then your hook was baited." To avoid mistakes in translating "if" and "only if" remember this rule: The statement that follows "if" is always the antecedent, and the statement that follows "only if" is always the consequent. Thus "C only if H" is translated $C \supset H$, whereas "C if H" is translated $H \supset C$. Additional examples:

If Purdue raises tuition, then so does Notre Dame.	$P \supset N$
Notre Dame raises tuition if Purdue does.	$P \supset N$
Purdue raises tuition only if Notre Dame does.	$P \supset N$
Cornell cuts enrollment provided that Brown does.	$B \supset C$
Cornell cuts enrollment on condition that Brown does.	$B \supset C$
Brown's cutting enrollment implies that Cornell does.	$B \supset C$

In translating conditional statements, it is essential not to confuse antecedent with consequent. The statement $A \supset B$ is not logically equivalent to $B \supset A$.

These statements are all **conditionals** (material implications). The main operator is a horseshoe.

$H \supset \sim J$
$(A \lor C) \supset (D \cdot E)$
$[K \lor (S \cdot \sim T)] \supset [\sim F \lor (M \cdot O)]$

The horseshoe symbol is also used to translate statements phrased in terms of sufficient conditions and necessary conditions. Event A is said to be a **sufficient condition** for event B whenever the occurrence of A is all that is required for the occurrence of B. On the other hand, event A is said to be a **necessary condition** for event B whenever B cannot occur without the occurrence of A. For example, having the flu is a sufficient condition for feeling miserable, whereas having air to breathe is a necessary condition for survival. Other things besides having the flu might cause a person to feel miserable, but that by itself is sufficient; other things besides having air to breathe are required for survival, but without air survival is impossible. In other words, air is necessary.

6

To translate statements involving sufficient and necessary conditions into symbolic form, place the statement that names the sufficient condition in the antecedent of the conditional and the statement that names the necessary condition in the consequent. The mnemonic device "SUN" may be conveniently used to keep this rule in mind. Turning the U sideways creates $S \supset N$, wherein S and N designate sufficient and necessary conditions, respectively. Whatever is given as a sufficient condition goes in the place of the S, and whatever is given as a necessary condition goes in the place of the N:

> Hilton's opening a new hotel is a sufficient condition
>   for Marriott's doing so. $H \supset M$

> Hilton's opening a new hotel is a necessary condition
>   for Marriott's doing so. $M \supset H$

The triple bar symbol is used to translate the expressions "if and only if" and "is a sufficient and necessary condition for":

> JFK tightens security if and only if O'Hare does. $J \equiv O$

> JFK's tightening security is a sufficient and
>   necessary condition for O'Hare's doing so. $J \equiv O$

Analysis of the first statement reveals that $J \equiv O$ is logically equivalent to $(J \supset O) \cdot (O \supset J)$. The statement "JFK tightens security only if O'Hare does" is translated $J \supset O$, and "JFK tightens security if O'Hare does" is translated $O \supset J$. Combining the two English statements, we have $(J \supset O) \cdot (O \supset J)$, which is just a longer way of writing $J \equiv O$. A similar analysis applies to the second statement. Because the order of the two conjuncts can be reversed, $J \equiv O$ is logically equivalent to $O \equiv J$. However, when translating such statements, we adopt the convention that the letter representing the first English statement is written to the left of the triple bar, and the letter representing the second English statement is written to the right of the triple bar. Thus, the examples above are translated $J \equiv O$, and not $O \equiv J$.

> These statements are all **biconditionals** (material equivalences).
> The main operator is a triple bar.
>
> $M \equiv \sim T$
> $(B \lor D) \equiv (A \cdot C)$
> $[K \lor (F \supset I)] \equiv [\sim L \cdot (G \lor H)]$

Whenever more than two letters appear in a translated statement, we must use parentheses, brackets, or braces to indicate the proper range of the operators. The statement $A \cdot B \lor C$, for example, is ambiguous. When parentheses are introduced, this statement becomes either $(A \cdot B) \lor C$ or $A \cdot (B \lor C)$. These two statements are not logically equivalent. Thus, with statements such as these, some clue must be found in the English statement that indicates the correct placement of the parentheses in the symbolic statement. Such clues are usually given by commas and semicolons, by such words as "either" and "both," and by the use of a single predicate in conjunction with two or more subjects. The following examples illustrate the correct placement of parentheses and brackets:

Prozac relieves depression and Allegra combats allergies, or Zocor lowers cholesterol.	$(P \cdot A) \vee Z$
Prozac relieves depression, and Allegra combats allergies or Zocor lowers cholesterol.	$P \cdot (A \vee Z)$
Either Prozac relieves depression and Allegra combats allergies or Zocor lowers cholesterol.	$(P \cdot A) \vee Z$
Prozac relieves depression and either Allegra combats allergies or Zocor lowers cholesterol.	$P \cdot (A \vee Z)$
Prozac relieves depression or both Allegra combats allergies and Zocor lowers cholesterol.	$P \vee (A \cdot Z)$
Prozac relieves depression and Allegra or Zocor lowers cholesterol.	$P \cdot (A \vee Z)$
If Merck changes its logo, then if Pfizer increases sales, then Lilly will reorganize.	$M \supset (P \supset L)$
If Merck's changing its logo implies that Pfizer increases sales, then Lilly will reorganize.	$(M \supset P) \supset L$
If Schering and Pfizer lower prices or Novartis downsizes, then Warner will expand production.	$[(S \cdot P) \vee N] \supset W$

Do not confuse these three statement forms:

A if B	$B \supset A$
A only if B	$A \supset B$
A if and only if B	$A \equiv B$

When a tilde appears in a symbolic expression, by convention it is considered to affect only the unit that immediately follows it. For example, in the expression $\sim K \vee M$ the tilde affects only the K; in the expression $\sim(K \vee M)$ it affects the entire expression inside the parentheses. In English, the expression "It is not the case that K or M" is ambiguous, because the range of the negating words is indefinite. To eliminate this ambiguity, we now adopt the convention that the negating words are considered to affect only the unit that follows them. Thus, "It is not the case that K or M" is translated $\sim K \vee M$.

The statement "Not both S and T" is translated $\sim(S \cdot T)$. By an important rule called *De Morgan's rule*, this statement is logically equivalent to $\sim S \vee \sim T$. For example, the statement "Not both Steven and Thomas were fired" is equivalent in meaning to "Either Stephen was not fired or Thomas was not fired." Because the former statement is *not* equivalent in meaning to "Stephen was not fired and Thomas was not fired," $\sim(S \cdot T)$ is *not* logically equivalent to $\sim S \cdot \sim T$. Analogously, the statement "Not either S or T"

is translated $\sim(S \lor T)$, which by De Morgan's rule is logically equivalent to $\sim S \cdot \sim T$. For example, "Not either Steven or Thomas was fired" is equivalent in meaning to "Steven was not fired and Thomas was not fired." Thus $\sim(S \lor T)$ is *not* logically equivalent to $\sim S \lor \sim T$. The following examples illustrate these points:

Megan is not a winner, but Kathy is.	$\sim M \cdot K$
Not both Megan and Kathy are winners.	$\sim(M \cdot K)$
Both Megan and Kathy are not winners.	$\sim M \cdot \sim K$
Not either Megan or Kathy is a winner.	$\sim(M \lor K)$
Neither Megan nor Kathy is a winner.	$\sim(M \lor K)$
Either Megan or Kathy is not a winner.	$\sim M \lor \sim K$

Notice the function of "either" and "both":

Not either A or B.	$\sim(A \lor B)$
Either not A or not B.	$\sim A \lor \sim B$
Not both A and B.	$\sim(A \cdot B)$
Both not A and not B.	$\sim A \cdot \sim B$

The symbolic expressions that we have used throughout this section to translate meaningful, unambiguous English statements are called **well-formed formulas (WFFs).** "WFFs" is usually pronounced "woofs." A well-formed formula is a *syntactically* correct arrangement of symbols. In English, for example, the expression "there is a cat on the porch" is syntactically correct, but "Porch on the is cat a there" is not syntactically correct. Some examples of symbolic arrangements that are *not* well-formed formulas are "$A \supset \lor B$," "$A \cdot B (\lor C)$," and "$\sim\lor B \equiv \supset C$."

Summary	Operator
not, it is not the case that, it is false that	$\sim$
and, yet, but, however, moreover, nevertheless, still, also, although, both, additionally, furthermore	$\cdot$
or, unless	$\lor$
if . . . then, only if, implies, given that, in case, provided that, on condition that, sufficient condition for, necessary condition for (Note: Do not confuse antecedent with consequent!)	$\supset$
if and only if, is equivalent to, sufficient and necessary condition for	$\equiv$

Gottfried Wilhelm Leibniz 1646–1716

© Bildarchiv Preussischer Kulturbestiz/Art Resource, NY

Gottfried Wilhelm Leibniz was a polymath who knew virtually everything that could be known at the time about nearly every area of intellectual endeavor. He also made important contributions to many of them, including physics, engineering, philosophy, theology, history, law, politics, and philology. In mathematics Leibniz invented differential and integral calculus (independently of Newton) and the theory of differential equations. He also discovered the binary number system (used by all of today's digital computers), and he created the first calculating machine that could add, subtract, multiply, and divide. In metaphysics he created the famous theory of monads which, among other things, explained the relation between the soul and the body.

Leibniz was born in Leipzig to prominent parents. His father (who died when Leibniz was six) was a professor of moral philosophy at the city's university, and his mother was the daughter of a famous lawyer. As a child Leibniz proved himself a prodigy. By age twelve he was fluent in Latin and had a passing knowledge of Greek, both of which he had learned by himself. By thirteen he was deep into the works of Aristotle and scholastic philosophy, and at fourteen he entered the University of Leipzig, where he studied philosophy, mathematics, and law. After completing that program he began a doctoral program in law; however, when he applied for the degree at age twenty, he was refused because of his youth. Not to be outdone, Leibniz presented his thesis to the University of Altdorf, and the professors there were so impressed that they immediately awarded him the degree of Doctor of Laws and offered him a professorship.

As he grew older Leibniz developed a taste for the finer things in life, including expensive clothing, flowing wigs, fancy carriages, and luxurious accommodations. However, following the death of his mother when he was eighteen, an uncle received what should have been Leibniz's inheritance. When this happened Leibniz figured that the best way of satisfying his expensive tastes was to attach himself to the wealthy and the powerful, which he did with great success. He entered the employment of the elector of Mainz, and by the age of twenty-four he held the rank of privy counselor of justice, one of the highest ranks in the government. His work as a diplomat allowed him the opportunity to travel widely and meet most of the prominent figures in Europe. Later he worked for the Duke of Hanover, which also allowed much time for travel and independent study.

Leibniz is sometimes called the father of symbolic logic for his work in developing the *universal characteristic,* a symbolic language in which any item of information can be represented in a natural and systematic way, together with the *calculus ratiocinator,* a deductive system for manipulating the symbols and deriving consequences. Given the dispassionate nature of this enterprise, Leibniz thought that it would serve to resolve differences of opinion in religion, theology, and philosophy. However, at age seventy he died in Hanover before completing the project.

I. Translate the following statements into symbolic form using capital letters to represent affirmative English statements.

★1. Cartier does not make cheap watches.

2. Arizona has a national park but Nebraska does not.

3. Either Stanford or Tulane has an architecture school.

★4. Both Harvard and Baylor have medical schools.

5. If Chanel has a rosewood fragrance, then so does Lanvin.

6. Chanel has a rosewood fragrance if Lanvin does.

★7. Lindsay Lohan will check into rehab if and only if Britney Spears does.

8. Reese Witherspoon wins best actress only if Martin Scorsese wins best director.

9. Armani will launch a leather collection given that Gucci rejects skinny models.

★10. The Colts' winning most of their games implies that Peyton Manning is a great quarterback.

11. Bill Gates does not support malaria research unless Warren Buffet does.

12. Mercedes will introduce a hybrid model only if Lexus and BMW do.

★13. Mariah Carey sings pop and either Elton John sings rock or Diana Krall sings jazz.

14. Either Mariah Carey sings pop and Elton John sings rock or Diana Krall sings jazz.

15. Not both Jaguar and Porsche make motorcycles.

★16. Both Jaguar and Porsche do not make motorcycles.

17. Either Nokia or Seiko makes cell phones.

18. Not either Ferrari or Maserati makes economy cars.

★19. Neither Ferrari nor Maserati makes economy cars.

20. Either Ferrari or Maserati does not make economy cars.

21. If Bill O'Reilly spins the news, then if Katie Couric charms her viewers, then Paula Zahn has sex appeal.

★22. If Bill O'Reilly's spinning the news implies that Katie Couric charms her viewers, then Paula Zahn has sex appeal.

23. Tommy Hilfiger celebrates casual if and only if neither Ralph Lauren nor Calvin Klein offers street chic.

24. If Saks promotes gift cards, then either Macy's or Bloomingdale's puts on a fashion show.

★25. Either Rado does not make a sapphire watch or if Movado makes one then so does Pulsar.

26. If either Renée Zellweger or Michelle Pfeiffer accepts a dramatic role, then neither Charlie Sheen nor Ethan Hawke will make an action film.

27. If Kate Winslet and Jessica Biel do a comedy, then either Forest Whitaker will make a documentary or Paris Hilton will do a skin flick.

★28. Mercury is a planet given that both Pluto and Ceres are not.

29. Saturn has rings, and Neptune is windy or Jupiter is massive.

30. Saturn has rings and Neptune is windy, or Jupiter is massive.

★31. Tiffany and Ben Bridge will release an emerald collection unless Zales and Kay do not.

32. Brad Pitt will travel abroad provided that Angelina Jolie does, but Shiloh and Maddox will stay home.

33. Either Jennifer Lopez or Ben Affleck will attend the premier, but it is not the case that both will.

★34. Hillary Clinton will not admit she was wrong; however, if Iraq totally disintegrates, then either Brian Williams or Charles Gibson will report it.

35. It is not the case that both Iran gives up its nuclear program and Syria or Pakistan combats terrorism.

36. It is not the case that either Hezbollah will renounce violence or Al Qaeda and the Taliban will be defeated.

★37. If Spike Lee writes a screen play, then if Denzel Washington stars in the movie, then Paramount and MGM will compete to produce it.

38. If Tom Cruise is gay, then if Diane Sawyer interviews him, then Scientology's being nonsense implies that Katie Holmes is in for a surprise.

39. It is not the case that either Tiger Woods and Maria Sharapova play professional football or Bonnie Blair and Lance Armstrong play professional baseball.

★40. It is not the case that both Kobe Bryant or Shaquille O'Neal plays professional tennis and LaDainian Tomlinson or Brett Favre plays professional basketball.

41. Israel's abandoning its settlements is a sufficient condition for the Palestinians' declaring an end to hostilities.

42. Israel's abandoning its settlements is a necessary condition for the Palestinian's declaring an end to hostilities.

★43. Israel's abandoning its settlements is a sufficient and necessary condition for the Palestinians' declaring an end to hostilities.

44. The UN's sending a peacekeeping force is a sufficient condition for ending Darfur's genocide only if the Janjaweed's being disarmed is a necessary condition for Sudan's taking control of the region.

45. Lou Dobbs and Anderson Cooper focus on illegal immigration if and only if Jim Lehrer and Tim Russert report political events.

★46. It is not the case that both Atari's releasing a stalker game implies that Nintendo does and Sega's releasing a molester game implies that Commodore does.

47. Natalie Maines is a true patriot if Emily Robinson speaks the truth, provided that Martie Maguire campaigns for peace.

48. The Dixie Chicks' opening the show implies that the Chili Peppers close it, given that the Black Eyed Peas' showing up implies that neither Gnarls Barkley nor Rascal Flatts will perform.

★49. If Christina Aguilera's singing soul and Justin Timberlake's singing pop are sufficient and necessary conditions for Kelly Clarkson's singing rock, then neither Beyoncé nor Shakira will sing rap.

50. Nassau's advertising sizzling night clubs is a necessary condition for Puerto Vallarta's offering luxury hotels; moreover, Cancun's having turquoise waters and Acapulco's promising powder-white beaches is a sufficient condition for Jamaica's offering reggae music.

II. Translate the following statements into symbolic form using capital letters to represent affirmative English statements.

★1. Unless we reduce the incidence of child abuse, future crime rates will increase.

2. If pharmaceutical makers conceal test results, they are subject to substantial fines.

3. High-definition television is a technological marvel, but it is expensive.

★4. Cigarette manufacturers are neither honest nor socially responsible.

5. Psychologists and psychiatrists do not both prescribe antidepressant drugs.

6. If health maintenance organizations cut costs, then either preventive medicine is emphasized or the quality of care deteriorates.

★7. A necessary condition for a successful business venture is good planning.

8. If cocaine is legalized, then its use may increase but criminal activity will decline.

9. Ozone depletion in the atmosphere is a sufficient condition for increased cancer rates.

★10. If affirmative action programs are dropped, then if new programs are not created, then minority applicants will suffer.

11. If Internet use continues to grow, then more people will become cyberaddicts and normal human relations will deteriorate.

12. Human life will not perish unless either we poison ourselves with pollution or a large asteroid collides with the earth.

★13. Cooling a group of atoms to absolute zero and keeping them bunched together is a necessary and sufficient condition for producing a Bose-Einstein condensate.

14. If motion pictures contain subliminal sex messages or if they challenge the traditional family, then conservative politicians call for censorship.

15. Either clear-cutting in national forests is halted and old-growth trees are allowed to stand, or salmon runs will be destroyed and bird habitats obliterated.

★16. Three-strikes laws will be enforced and longer sentences imposed only if hundreds of new prisons are built, and that will happen only if taxes are increased.

17. The Ebola virus is deadly, but it will become a major threat to humanity if and only if it becomes airborne and a vaccine is not developed.

18. If evolutionary biology is correct, then higher life-forms arose by chance, and if that is so, then it is not the case that there is any design in nature and divine providence is a myth.

★19. If banks charge fees for teller-assisted transactions, then more people will use ATMs; and if that happens and ATM fees increase, then banks will close branches and profits will skyrocket.

20. If corporate welfare continues, then taxpayer interests will be ignored and billions of tax dollars will go to giant corporations; and if the latter occurs, then there will not be anything left for the poor and the budget will not be balanced.

III. Determine which of the following are *not* well-formed formulas.

1. $(S \cdot {\sim} T) \vee ({\sim} U \cdot W)$
2. ${\sim}(K \vee L) \cdot (\supset G \vee H)$
3. $(E {\sim} F) \vee (W \equiv X)$
4. $(B \supset {\sim} T) \equiv {\sim}({\sim} C \supset U)$
5. $(F \equiv {\sim} Q) \cdot (A \supset E \vee T)$
6. ${\sim} D \vee {\sim}[(P \supset Q) \cdot (T \supset R)]$
7. $[(D \cdot \vee Q) \supset (P \vee E)] \vee [A \supset (\cdot H)]$
8. $M(N \supset Q) \vee ({\sim} C \cdot D)$
9. ${\sim}(F \vee {\sim} G) \supset [(A \equiv E) \cdot {\sim} H]$
10. $(R \equiv S \cdot T) \supset {\sim}({\sim} W \cdot {\sim} X)$

6.2   Truth Functions

The truth value of a compound proposition expressed in terms of one or more logical operators is said to be a function of the truth values of its components. This means that the truth value of the compound proposition is completely determined by the truth values of its components. If the truth values of the components are known, then the truth value of the compound proposition can be calculated from the definitions of the logical operators. Accordingly, a **truth function** is any compound proposition whose truth value is completely determined by the truth values of its components.

Many compound propositions in ordinary language are not truth functions. For example, the statement "Mary believes that Paul is dishonest" is compound because it contains the statement "Paul is dishonest" as a component. Yet the truth value of the compound statement is not determined by the truth value of the component, because Mary's beliefs about Paul are not compelled by any attribute that Paul may or may not possess.

The first part of this section presents the definitions of the five logical operators, the second part shows how they are used to compute the truth values of more complicated propositions, and the third examines further the degree to which symbolized expressions match the meaning of expressions in ordinary language.

Definitions of the Logical Operators

The definitions of the logical operators are presented in terms of **statement variables,** which are lowercase letters (p, q, r, s) that can stand for any statement. For example, the statement variable p could stand for the statements A, $A \supset B$, $B \vee C$, and so on.

Statement variables are used to construct statement forms. A **statement form** is an arrangement of statement variables and operators such that the uniform substitution of statements in place of the variables results in a statement. For example, ~p and $p \supset q$ are statement forms because substituting the statements A and B in place of p and q, respectively, results in the statements ~A and $A \supset B$. A compound statement is said to have a certain form if it can be produced by substituting statements in place of the letters in that form. Thus ~A, ~$(A \lor B)$, and ~$[A \cdot (B \lor C)]$ are negations because they can be produced by substituting statements in place of p in the form ~p.

Now let us consider the definition of the tilde operator (negation). This definition is given by a **truth table,** an arrangement of truth values that shows in every possible case how the truth value of a compound proposition is determined by the truth values of its simple components. The truth table for negation shows how any statement having the form of a negation (~p) is determined by the truth value of the statement that is negated (p):

Negation

p	~p
T	F
F	T

The truth table shows that ~p is false when p is true and that ~p is true when p is false. This is exactly what we would expect, because it perfectly matches ordinary English usage. Examples:

It is not the case that McDonald's makes hamburgers.   ~M

It is not the case that Starbucks makes hamburgers.   ~S

The first statement is false because M is true, and the second is true because S is false.

Let us now consider the definition of the dot operator (conjunction). The truth table that follows shows how any statement having the form of a conjunction ($p \cdot q$) is determined by the truth values of its conjuncts (p, q):

Conjunction

p	q	$p \cdot q$
T	T	T
T	F	F
F	T	F
F	F	F

This truth table shows that a conjunction is true when its two conjuncts are true and is false in all other cases. This definition reflects ordinary language usage almost as perfectly as negation. Consider the following conjunctive statements:

Ferrari and Maserati make sports cars. $F \cdot M$

Ferrari and GMC make sports cars. $F \cdot G$

GMC and Jeep make sports cars. $G \cdot J$

The first statement is true, because both conjuncts are true; but the second and third statements are false, because at least one of their conjuncts is false.

Turning now to the definition of the wedge operator (disjunction), the truth table is as follows:

Disjunction

p	q	p ∨ q
T	T	T
T	F	T
F	T	T
F	F	F

The truth table indicates that the disjunction is true when at least one of the disjuncts is true and that otherwise it is false. The truth-functional interpretation of "or" is that of *inclusive* disjunction: Cases in which the disjunction is true include the case when both disjuncts are true. This inclusive sense of "or" corresponds to many instances of ordinary usage, as the following examples illustrate:

Either Steven King or Cate Blanchett is a novelist.	*S* ∨ *C*
Either Steven King or Danielle Steel is a novelist.	*S* ∨ *D*
Either Kobe Bryant or Tiger Woods is a novelist.	*K* ∨ *T*

The first two statements are true, because in each case at least one of the disjuncts is true. The third is false, because both disjuncts are false.

The match between the truth-functional definition of disjunction and ordinary usage is not perfect, however. Sometimes the sense of a statement in ordinary language is that of *exclusive* disjunction. Examples:

The Orient Express is on either track A or track B.

You can have either soup or salad with this meal.

Tammy is either ten or eleven years old.

The sense of these statements excludes the possibility of both alternatives being true. Thus, if these statements were translated using the wedge, a portion of their ordinary meaning would be lost. If the exclusive aspect of these "either . . . or . . ." statements is essential, the symbolic equivalent of "but not both" can be attached to their translations. Thus the first statement could be translated (*A* ∨ *B*) • ~(*A* • *B*).

Let us now consider the horseshoe operator (material implication, or conditional). Its truth table is as follows:

Conditional
(material implication)

p	q	p ⊃ q
T	T	T
T	F	F
F	T	T
F	F	T

The truth table shows that a conditional statement is false when the antecedent is true and the consequent false and is true in all other cases. This truth-functional interpretation of conditional statements conforms in part with the ordinary meaning of "if . . . then . . ." and in part it diverges. Consider the following examples:

If Nicole Kidman is an actor, then so is Meryl Streep.	*N* ⊃ *M*
If Nicole Kidman is an actor, then so is Wolf Blitzer.	*N* ⊃ *W*

If Wolf Blitzer is an actor, then so is Helen Hunt.	$W \supset H$
If Wolf Blitzer is an actor, then so is Larry King.	$W \supset L$

In these statements N, M, and H are true and W and L are false. Thus, according to the truth-functional interpretation, the first statement is true and the second false. This result conforms in large measure to our expectations. But the truth-functional interpretation of the last two statements is true. Although this result may not conflict with our expectations, it is not at all clear why these statements should be considered true.

For an intuitive approach to this problem, imagine that your logic instructor made the following statement: "If you get an A on the final exam, then you will get an A for the course." Under what conditions would you say that your instructor had lied to you? Clearly, if you got an A on the final exam but did not get an A for the course, you would say that she had lied. This outcome corresponds to a true antecedent and a false consequent. On the other hand, if you got an A on the final exam and also got an A for the course, you would say that she had told the truth (true antecedent, true consequent). But what if you failed to get an A on the final exam? Two alternatives are then possible: Either you got an A for the course anyway (false antecedent, true consequent) or you did not get an A for the course (false antecedent, false consequent). In neither case, though, would you say that your instructor had lied to you. Giving her the benefit of the doubt, you would say that she had told the truth.

Lastly, let us consider the definition of the triple bar operator (material equivalence, or biconditional). Its truth table is as follows:

Biconditional
(material equivalence)

p	q	$p \equiv q$
T	T	T
T	F	F
F	T	F
F	F	T

The truth table shows that the biconditional is true when its two components have the same truth value and that otherwise it is false. These results conform reasonably well with our expectations. However, given that $p \equiv q$ is simply a shorter way of writing $(p \supset q) \cdot (q \supset p)$, the truth-table results are required by the definition of material implication. If p and q are either both true or both false, then $p \supset q$ and $q \supset p$ are both true, making their conjunction true. But if p is true and q is false, then $p \supset q$ is false, making the conjunction false. Similarly, if p is false and q is true, then $q \supset p$ is false, again making the conjunction false. Thus $p \equiv q$ is true when p and q have the same truth value and false when they have opposite truth values.

The truth table definition of the triple bar symbol conforms quite closely with ordinary usage, as the following examples illustrate:

Bill Maher is a show host if and only if Jay Leno is.	$B \equiv J$
Bill Maher is a show host if and only if Meg Ryan is.	$B \equiv M$
Meg Ryan is a show host if and only if Al Pacino is.	$M \equiv A$

In these statements, *B* and *J* are true and *M* and *A* false. Thus, from the truth-functional standpoint, the first is true and the second false. This is what we would ordinarily expect. The third statement, however, turns out to be true because both of its components are false. While this result may not be what we would expect, it does not violate our expectations either. Other biconditional statements having false components are more obviously true. Example:

> Ralph Nader was elected president if and only if he received a majority vote from the electoral college.

This statement asserts what is required for any candidate to be elected or not elected, and so it is clearly true.

In summary, the definitions of the five logical operators conform reasonably well with ordinary linguistic usage. However, as the last part of this section shows, the match is less than perfect. Before considering this question, though, let us use the operator definitions to compute the truth values of more-complicated statements.

Computing the Truth Value of Longer Propositions

To compute the truth value of a more complicated expression, use this procedure: Enter the truth values of the simple components directly beneath the letters. Then use these truth values to compute the truth values of the compound components. The truth value of a compound statement is written beneath the operator representing it. Let us suppose, for example, that we are told in advance that the simple propositions *A, B,* and *C* are true and *D, E,* and *F* are false. We may then compute the truth value of the following compound proposition:

$$(A \lor D) \supset E$$

First we write the truth values of the simple propositions immediately below the respective letters and bring the operators and parentheses down:

$$(A \lor D) \supset E$$
$$(T \lor F) \supset F$$

Next we compute the truth value of the proposition in parentheses and write it beneath the operator to which it pertains:

$$(A \lor D) \supset E$$
$$(T \lor F) \supset F$$
$$\quad T \quad \supset F$$

Finally, we use the last-completed line to obtain the truth value of the conditional, which is the "main operator" in the proposition:

$$(A \lor D) \supset E$$
$$(T \lor F) \supset F$$
$$\quad T \quad \supset F$$
$$\qquad \textcircled{F}$$

The final answer is circled. This is the truth value of the compound proposition given that A is true and D and E are false.

The general strategy is to build the truth values of the larger components from the truth values of the smaller ones. In general, the order to be followed in entering truth values is this:

1. Individual letters representing simple propositions
2. Tildes immediately preceding individual letters
3. Operators joining letters or negated letters
4. Tildes immediately preceding parentheses
5. And so on

Here are some additional examples. As before, let A, B, and C be true, D, E, and F false. Note that the computed truth values are written beneath the operators to which they pertain. The final answers, which are written beneath the main operators, are circled.

$(B \cdot C) \supset (E \supset A)$

$(T \cdot T) \supset (F \supset T)$

   T $\supset$ T

       Ⓣ

$\sim (C \vee \sim A) \supset \sim B$

$\sim (T \vee \sim T) \supset \sim T$

$\sim (T \vee F) \quad \supset F$

$\sim \quad T \quad\;\; \supset F$

F $\supset$ F

        Ⓣ

$[\sim (D \vee F) \cdot (B \vee \sim A)] \supset \sim (F \supset \sim C)$

$[\sim (F \vee F) \cdot (T \vee \sim T)] \supset \sim (F \supset \sim T)$

$[\sim (F \vee F) \cdot (T \vee F\;)] \supset \sim (F \supset F\;)$

$[\sim \quad F \quad \cdot \quad T \quad] \supset \sim \quad T$

$[T \qquad \cdot \quad T \quad] \supset F$

        T $\supset$ F

        Ⓕ

If preferred, the truth values of the compound components may be entered directly beneath the operators, without using the line-by-line approach illustrated in these examples. The following examples illustrate this second approach, which is used in the next section:

$$[(D \equiv \sim A) \cdot \sim (C \cdot \sim B)] \equiv \sim [(A \supset \sim D) \vee (C \equiv E)]$$

F T F T T T T F F T (F) F T T T F T T F F

$$\sim \{[(C \cdot \sim E) \supset \sim (A \cdot \sim B)] \supset [\sim (B \vee D) \equiv (\sim C \vee E)]\}$$

(F) T T T F T T T F F T T F T T F T F T F F

Further Comparison with Ordinary Language

The first part of this section showed that the definitions of the five logical operators conform reasonably well with ordinary linguistic usage. This part further examines the extent of this match in meaning.

In regard to the dot operator, which is used to translate "and" and "but," the match is often good; but it fails, at least in part, when the meaning of a conjunctive statement depends on the order of the conjuncts. Consider the following statements:

She got married and had a baby.	$M \cdot B$
She had a baby and got married.	$B \cdot M$

The first statement implies that the marriage occurred first, and the baby came later, while the second statement implies that the baby came first. This implied meaning is lost in the truth-functional interpretation, because $M \cdot B$ is logically equivalent to $B \cdot M$.

For another example, consider the following:

This car is ugly, but it's economical to drive.	$U \cdot E$
This car is economical to drive, but it's ugly.	$E \cdot U$

If these statements are taken as single premises of separate arguments, they might suggest different conclusions. The first suggests "Therefore, we should buy this car," whereas the second suggests "Therefore, we shouldn't buy this car." Yet given that the word "but" is translated in the same way as "and," the two statements are logically equivalent when interpreted truth-functionally. When subtleties of expression are important in the interpretation of a statement, using logical operators to translate the statement may not be appropriate.

Another instance where the truth-functional interpretation of "and" differs from the ordinary linguistic meaning is offered by slang statements like this one:

You go for that gun, and you'll regret it.

The sense of this statement is not that you will in fact go for the gun but rather that, *if* you go for that gun, then . . . Accordingly, if this statement were interpreted as a truth-functional conjunction, its meaning would be distorted.

In regard to the wedge operator, which is used to translate "or" and "unless," we saw that the wedge is defined as inclusive disjunction, but we observed that the English word "or" sometimes has the sense of exclusive disjunction. This same observation applies to "unless." In the following statements, "unless" has an inclusive sense:

You won't win the lottery unless you buy a ticket.

It will not rain unless there are clouds in the sky.

The meaning of the first statement includes the case of buying a ticket and not winning, and the meaning of the second includes the case of there being clouds and no rain. In statements like these, where "unless" has an inclusive sense, using the wedge symbol to translate "unless" results in no loss of meaning.

On the other hand, in the following statements "unless" is used in the exclusive sense:

> Pork is not properly cooked unless the meat is white.

> These logs will make a nice campfire unless they are wet.

The first statement suggests that the meat cannot be white and at the same time not be properly cooked, and the second suggests that the logs cannot be wet and at the same time be used to make a nice campfire. Thus, if these statements are translated using the wedge operator, part of the meaning will be left out. If this additional part is essential, it can be included by adding the symbolic equivalent of "but not both" to the translation.

In connection with the horseshoe operator, we saw that a question arose when the antecedent of a conditional statement turned out to be false. Why, under this circumstance, should the conditional statement be said to be true? For an example of some conditional statements that conform to the truth-functional interpretation, consider the following:

> If the temperature rises above 32°F, then the snow will begin to melt.

> If Figure A is a triangle, then Figure A has three sides.

> If all *A* are *B* and all *B* are *C*, then all *A* are *C*.

In all three examples the statement remains true even though the antecedent might be false. In the first, even though the temperature does not rise above 32°F at any particular moment, the law that governs the melting point of snow holds true. In other words, the statement (which expresses this law) is true regardless of the truth value of the antecedent. In the second, the mere fact that Figure A might not be a triangle does not affect the fact that a triangle, by definition, has three sides. Thus, the statement (which expresses this fact) is true regardless of the truth value of the antecedent. The third statement expresses a logical relationship between statements. This logical relationship remains unchanged regardless of what the terms *A*, *B*, and *C* are taken to represent. Thus, if *A*, *B*, and *C* represent "dogs," "cats," and "birds," respectively, both antecedent and consequent turn out to be false, but the conditional statement remains true.

As these examples illustrate, the definition of the horseshoe operator matches the meaning of some conditional statements in ordinary language very well. However, in general, the match is far from perfect. The source of the mismatch stems from the fact that the horseshoe operator designates the *material* conditional, or *truth-functional* conditional. The material conditional is a kind of conditional statement whose truth value depends purely on the truth or falsity of the antecedent and consequent and not on any inferential connection *between* antecedent and consequent. Since many conditional statements in ordinary language express such an inferential connection, when the horseshoe operator is used to translate them, part of their meaning is left out. For example, compare the following two statements:

> If Shakespeare wrote *Hamlet,* then the sun rises in the east.

> If ice is lighter than water, then ice floats in water.

The first statement expresses no inferential connection between antecedent and consequent, so using the horseshoe operator to translate it results in no loss of meaning. However, the second statement does express such a connection. The fact that ice is lighter than water is the reason why it floats. Accordingly, when the horseshoe operator is used to translate the second statement, this special meaning is lost.

The fact that the material conditional ignores inferential connections between antecedent and consequent allows for conflicts between the truth-functional interpretation of a conditional statement and the ordinary interpretation. Consider, for example, the following:

> If Barbara Boxer advocates the use of cocaine, then she is a good senator.

> If Chicago is in Michigan, then Chicago is very close to Miami.

According to their ordinary language interpretation, both of these statements are false. Good senators do not advocate the use of cocaine, and Michigan is far from Miami. Yet, when these statements are interpreted as material conditionals, both turn out to be true, because their antecedents are false. In cases like these, when the truth-functional interpretation of a conditional statement conflicts with the ordinary language interpretation, using the horseshoe operator to translate it may not be appropriate.

While inferential relations between antecedent and consequent often play some role in conditionals expressed in the indicative mood (such as those we just considered), they play a dominant role in conditional statements expressed in the subjunctive mood. Consider, for example, the following:

> If I were Bill Gates, then I would be rich.

> If dolphins were fish, then they would be cold-blooded.

> If the Washington Monument were made of lead, then it would be lighter than air.

> If President Kennedy had committed suicide, then he would be alive today.

Subjunctive conditionals are often called counterfactual conditionals because their antecedents are typically false. As a result, the *only* way of determining their truth value in ordinary language is through some kind of inference. Thus, from our knowledge that Bill Gates is rich, we reason that if I were he, then I would be rich. Similarly, from our knowledge that all fish are cold-blooded, we conclude that if dolphins were fish, then they would be cold-blooded. On the other hand, we reason that the second two are false from our knowledge that lead is heavier than air and our knowledge that suicide results in death. Because the truth value of subjunctive conditionals is so closely tied to inferences like these and is so unrelated to the truth or falsity of the components, subjunctive conditionals are generally not considered to be truth functional at all, and the horseshoe operator is not used to translate them. But if they were interpreted truth-functionally, note that all four of these statements would turn out true, because they have false antecedents.

These observations about conditional statements apply equally to biconditionals. Just as the horseshoe operator expresses *material* implication, the triple bar operator expresses *material* equivalence. As such, it ignores any inferential connection between its component statements, and, as a result, conflicts can arise between the ordinary meaning of a biconditional and its truth-functional meaning. Here are two examples of biconditionals expressed in the indicative mood that illustrate such a conflict:

Adolf Hitler was justified in killing millions of Jews if and only if he always confessed his sins to a priest.

The Department of Defense building is a hexagon if and only if it has eight sides.

According to the ordinary interpretation, these statements are false. Confessing one's sins to a priest does not justify anything, and hexagons, by definition, have six sides, not eight. Yet, when these statements are interpreted as expressing material biconditionals, both are true, because in each case the component statements are false. In cases like these, when the ordinary meaning of a biconditional conflicts with the truth-functional meaning, using the triple bar operator to translate it may not be appropriate. Furthermore, as with subjunctive conditionals, subjunctive biconditionals are generally not considered to be truth-functional at all, so the triple bar operator is not used to translate them.

EXERCISE 6.2

I. Identify the main operator in the following propositions:

★1. $\sim(A \lor M) \cdot \sim(C \supset E)$

2. $(G \cdot \sim P) \supset \sim(H \lor \sim W)$

3. $\sim[P \cdot (S \equiv K)]$

★4. $\sim(K \cdot \sim O) \equiv \sim(R \lor \sim B)$

5. $(M \cdot B) \lor \sim[E \equiv \sim(C \lor I)]$

6. $\sim[(P \cdot \sim R) \supset (\sim E \lor F)]$

★7. $\sim[(S \lor L) \cdot M] \supset (C \lor N)$

8. $[\sim F \lor (N \cdot U)] \equiv \sim H$

9. $E \cdot [(F \supset A) \equiv (\sim G \lor H)]$

★10. $\sim[(X \lor T) \cdot (N \lor F)] \lor (K \supset L)$

II. Write the following compound statements in symbolic form, then use your knowledge of the historical events referred to by the simple statements to determine the truth value of the compound statements.

★1. It is not the case that Hitler ran the Third Reich.

2. Nixon resigned the presidency and Lincoln wrote the Gettysburg Address.

3. France bombed Pearl Harbor, or Lindbergh crossed the Atlantic.

★4. Hitler ran the Third Reich and Nixon did not resign the presidency.

5. Edison invented the telephone, or Custer was killed by the Indians.

6. Alexander the Great civilized America if Napoleon ruled France.

★7. Washington was assassinated only if Edison invented the telephone.

8. Lincoln wrote the Gettysburg Address if and only if France bombed Pearl Harbor.

9. It is not the case that either Alexander the Great civilized America or Washington was assassinated.

★10. If Hitler ran the Third Reich, then either Custer was killed by the Indians or Einstein discovered aspirin.

11. Either Lindbergh crossed the Atlantic and Edison invented the telephone or both Nixon resigned the presidency and it is false that Edison invented the telephone.

12. Lincoln's having written the Gettysburg Address is a sufficient condition for Alexander the Great's having civilized America if and only if Washington's being assassinated is a necessary condition for Custer's having been killed by the Indians.

★13. Both Hitler ran the Third Reich and Lindbergh crossed the Atlantic if neither Einstein discovered aspirin nor France bombed Pearl Harbor.

14. It is not the case that Custer was killed by the Indians unless both Nixon resigned the presidency and Edison invented the telephone.

15. Custer was killed by the Indians, and Lincoln wrote the Gettysburg Address only if either Washington was assassinated or Alexander the Great civilized America.

III. Determine the truth values of the following symbolized statements. Let A, B, and C be true and X, Y, and Z be false. Circle your answer.

★1. $A \cdot X$

2. $B \cdot \sim Y$

3. $X \vee \sim Y$

★4. $\sim C \vee Z$

5. $B \supset \sim Z$

6. $Y \supset \sim A$

★7. $\sim X \supset Z$

8. $B \equiv Y$

9. $\sim C \equiv Z$

★10. $\sim(A \cdot \sim Z)$

11. $\sim B \vee (Y \supset A)$

12. $A \supset \sim(Z \vee \sim Y)$

★13. $(A \cdot Y) \vee (\sim Z \cdot C)$

14. $\sim(X \vee \sim B) \cdot (\sim Y \vee A)$

15. $(Y \supset C) \cdot \sim(B \supset \sim X)$

★16. $(C \equiv \sim A) \vee (Y \equiv Z)$

17. $\sim(A \cdot \sim C) \supset (\sim X \supset B)$

18. $\sim[(B \vee \sim C) \cdot \sim(X \vee \sim Z)]$

★19. $\sim[\sim(X \supset C) \equiv \sim(B \supset Z)]$

20. $(X \supset Z) \supset [(B \equiv \sim X) \cdot \sim(C \vee \sim A)]$

21. $[(\sim X \vee Z) \supset (\sim C \vee B)] \cdot [(\sim X \cdot A) \supset (\sim Y \cdot Z)]$

★22. $\sim[(A \equiv X) \vee (Z \equiv Y)] \vee [(\sim Y \supset B) \cdot (Z \supset C)]$

23. $[(B \cdot \sim C) \vee (X \cdot \sim Y)] \supset \sim[(Y \cdot \sim X) \vee (A \cdot \sim Z)]$

24. $\sim\{\sim[(C \vee \sim B) \cdot (Z \vee \sim A)] \cdot \sim[\sim(B \vee Y) \cdot (\sim X \vee Z)]\}$

★25. $(Z \supset C) \supset \{[(\sim X \supset B) \supset (C \supset Y)] \equiv [(Z \supset X) \supset (\sim Y \supset Z)]\}$

IV. When possible, determine the truth values of the following symbolized statements. Let A and B be true, Y and Z false. P and Q have unknown truth value. If the truth value of the statement cannot be determined, write "undetermined."

★1. $A \lor P$

2. $Q \lor Z$

3. $Q \cdot Y$

★4. $Q \cdot A$

5. $P \supset B$

6. $Z \supset Q$

★7. $A \supset P$

8. $P \equiv {\sim}P$

9. $(P \supset A) \supset Z$

★10. $(P \supset A) \equiv (Q \supset B)$

11. $(Q \supset B) \supset (A \supset Y)$

12. ${\sim}(P \supset Y) \lor (Z \supset Q)$

★13. ${\sim}(Q \cdot Y) \equiv {\sim}(Q \lor A)$

14. $[(Z \supset P) \supset P] \supset P$

15. $[Q \supset (A \lor P)] \equiv [(Q \supset B) \supset Y]$

6.3   Truth Tables for Propositions

The previous section showed how the truth value of a compound proposition could be determined, given a *designated* truth value for each simple component. A truth table gives the truth value of a compound proposition for *every possible* truth value of its simple components. Each line in the truth table represents one such possible arrangement of truth values.

In constructing a truth table the first step is to determine the number of lines (or rows). Because each line represents one possible arrangement of truth values, the total number of lines is equal to the number of possible combinations of truth values for the simple propositions. Where L designates the number of lines and n the number of *different* simple propositions, the number of lines may be computed by the following formula:

$L = 2^n$

By means of this formula we obtain the following table:

Number of different simple propositions	Number of lines in truth table
1	2
2	4
3	8
4	16
5	32
6	64

Let us now construct a truth table for a compound proposition. We may begin with a fairly simple one:

$(A \lor \sim B) \supset B$

The number of different simple propositions is two. Thus the number of lines in the truth table is four. We draw these lines beneath the proposition as follows:

$(A \lor \sim B) \supset B$

_____

_____

_____

_____

The next step is to divide the number of lines in half. The result is 2. Then we go to the first letter on the left (*A*) and enter T on the first two lines and F on the remaining two lines.

$(A \lor \sim B) \supset B$

T _____

T _____

F _____

F _____

Next we divide that number (two) in half and, since the result is one, write one T, one F, one T, and one F beneath the next letter (*B*):

$(A \lor \sim B) \supset B$

T   T _____

T   F _____

F   T _____

F   F _____

Inspection of the truth table at this stage reveals that every possible combination of truth and falsity has now been assigned to *A* and *B*. In other words, the truth table exhausts the entire range of possibilities. The next step is to duplicate the *B* column under the second *B*.

$(A \lor \sim B) \supset B$

T   T   T

T   F   F

F   T   T

F   F   F

This much has been automatic.

Now, using the principles developed in the previous section, we compute the remaining columns. First, the column under the tilde is computed from the column under *B*:

$(A \lor \sim B) \supset B$

T   F T   T

T   T F   F

F   F T   T

F   T F   F

Next, the column under the wedge is computed from the column under *A* and the column under the tilde:

```
(A  v  ~  B)  ⊃  B
 T  T  F  T      T
 T  T  T  F      F
 F  F  F  T      T
 F  T  T  F      F
```

Last, the column under the horseshoe is computed from the column under the wedge and the column under *B*:

```
(A  v  ~  B)  ⊃  B
 T  T  F  T  |T|  T
 T  T  T  F  |F|  F
 F  F  F  T  |T|  T
 F  T  T  F  |F|  F
```

The column under the main operator is outlined to indicate that it represents the entire compound proposition. Inspecting the completed truth table, we see that the truth value of the compound proposition is true when *B* is true and false when *B* is false, regardless of the truth value of *A*.

Let us consider another example: $(C \cdot \sim D) \supset E$. The number of different letters is three, so the number of lines is eight. Under *C* we make half this number true, half false (that is, four true, four false). Then, under *D* we make half *this* number true, half false, and so on (two true, two false, two true, two false). Finally, under *E* the truth value alternates on every line. The truth table thus exhausts every possible arrangement of truth values:

```
(C  •  ~  D)  ⊃  E
 T        T      T
 T        T      F
 T        F      T
 T        F      F
 F        T      T
 F        T      F
 F        F      T
 F        F      F
```

Now we compute the truth values for the remaining columns—first for the tilde, then for the dot, and finally for the horseshoe:

```
(C  •  ~  D)  ⊃  E
 T  F  F  T  |T|  T
 T  F  F  T  |T|  F
 T  T  T  F  |T|  T
 T  T  T  F  |F|  F
 F  F  F  T  |T|  T
 F  F  F  T  |T|  F
 F  F  T  F  |T|  T
 F  F  T  F  |T|  F
```

Inspecting the completed truth table, we see that the compound proposition is false only when C is true and D and E are false.

An alternate method for constructing truth tables, which turns out to be faster for certain compound propositions, replicates the type of truth table used to define the meaning of the five logical operators in Section 6.2. Suppose, for example, that we are given this proposition: $[(A \lor B) \cdot (B \supset A)] \supset B$. We would begin by constructing columns for the simple propositions A and B, writing them to the left of the given proposition:

A	B	$[(A \lor B) \cdot (B \supset A)] \supset B$
T	T	
T	F	
F	T	
F	F	

We would then use the columns on the left to derive the truth values of the compound propositions. We would compute first the truth values of the expressions in parentheses, then the dot, and finally the right-hand horseshoe:

A	B	$[(A \lor B)$	$\cdot$	$(B \supset A)]$	$\supset$	B
T	T	T	T	T	T	
T	F	T	T	T	F	
F	T	T	F	F	T	
F	F	F	F	T	T	

Classifying Statements

Truth tables may be used to determine whether the truth value of a compound statement depends solely on its form or whether it also depends on the specific truth values of its components. A compound statement is said to be a **logically true** or **tautologous statement** if it is true regardless of the truth values of its components. It is said to be a **logically false** or **self-contradictory statement** if it is false regardless of the truth values of its components. And it is said to be a **contingent statement** if its truth value varies depending on the truth values of its components. By inspecting the column of truth values under the main operator, we can determine how the compound proposition should be classified:

Column under main operator	Statement classification
all true	tautologous (logically true)
all false	self-contradictory (logically false)
at least one true, at least one false	contingent

As the truth table we developed earlier indicates, $(C \cdot {\sim}D) \supset E$ is a contingent proposition. The column under the main operator contains at least one T and at least one F. In other words, the truth value of the compound proposition is "contingent" on the truth values of its components. Sometimes it is true, sometimes false, depending on the truth values of the components.

On the other hand, consider the following truth tables:

$$[(G \supset H) \cdot G] \supset H \qquad\qquad (G \lor H) \equiv (\sim G \cdot \sim H)$$

T T T	T T	**T**	T				
T F F	F T	**T**	F				
F T T	F F	**T**	T				
F T F	F F	**T**	F				

T T T	**F**	F T F F T					
T T F	**F**	F T F T F					
F T T	**F**	T F F F T					
F F F	**F**	T F T T F					

The proposition on the left is tautologous (logically true or a **tautology**) because the column under the main operator is all true. The one on the right is self-contradictory (logically false) because the main operator column is all false. In neither case is the truth value of the compound proposition contingent on the truth values of the components. The one on the left is true regardless of the truth values of its components—in other words, *necessarily* true. The one on the right is *necessarily* false.

If a proposition is either logically true or logically false, its truth value depends merely on its form and has nothing to do with its content. As a result, such statements do not make any genuine assertions about things in the world. For example, the tautologous statement "It is either raining or it is not raining" provides no information about the weather. Similarly, the self-contradictory statement "It is raining and it is not raining" provides no information about the weather. On the other hand, the contingent statement "It is raining in the mountains" does provide information about the weather.

Comparing Statements

Truth tables may also be used to determine how two propositions are related to each other. Two propositions are said to be **logically equivalent statements** if they have the same truth value on each line under their main operators, and they are **contradictory statements** if they have opposite truth values on each line under their main operators. If neither of these relations hold, the propositions are either consistent or inconsistent. Two (or more) propositions are **consistent statements** if there is at least one line on which both (or all) of them turn out to be true, and they are **inconsistent statements** if there is no line on which both (or all) of them turn out to be true. By comparing the main operator columns, one can determine which is the case. However, because the first two relations are stronger than (and may overlap) the second two, the first two relations should be considered first.

Columns under main operators	Relation
same truth value on each line	logically equivalent
opposite truth value on each line	contradictory
there is at least one line on which the truth values are both true	consistent
there is no line on which the truth values are both true	inconsistent

For example, the following two propositions are logically equivalent. The main operator columns of their respective truth tables are identical. Note that for proper comparison the columns under K must be identical and the columns under L must be identical.

```
   K ⊃ L                  ~ L ⊃ ~ K
  T [T] T               F T [T] F T
  T [F] F               T F [F] F T        Logically equivalent
  F [T] T               F T [T] T F
  F [T] F               T F [T] T F
```

For any two propositions that are logically equivalent, the biconditional statement formed by joining them with a triple bar is tautologous. Thus, $(K \supset L) \equiv (\sim L \supset \sim K)$ is tautologous. This is easy to see because the columns under the main operators of $K \supset L$ and $\sim L \supset \sim K$ are identical.

The next two propositions are contradictory:

```
   K ⊃ L                  K • ~ L
  T [T] T               T [F] F T
  T [F] F               T [T] T F          Contradictory
  F [T] T               F [F] F T
  F [T] F               F [F] T F
```

The next two propositions are consistent. On the first line of each truth table the column under the main operator turns out true. This means that it is possible for both propositions to be true, which is the meaning of consistency:

```
   K v L                  K • L
  T [T] T               T [T] T
  T [T] F               T [F] F            Consistent
  F [T] T               F [F] T
  F [F] F               F [F] F
```

Finally, the next two propositions are inconsistent. There is no line in the columns under the main operators where the truth values are both true:

```
   K ≡ L                  K • ~ L
  T [T] T               T [F] F T
  T [F] F               T [T] T F          Inconsistent
  F [F] T               F [F] F T
  F [T] F               F [F] T F
```

Any pair of propositions is either consistent or inconsistent. Furthermore, some consistent propositions are also logically equivalent, and some inconsistent propositions are either contradictory or logically equivalent. Because of this partial overlap, pairs of propositions are usually first classified in terms of the stronger of these relations, which are logical equivalence and contradiction. If neither of these stronger relations applies, then the pair of propositions is classified in terms of the weaker relations, consistency and inconsistency.

Unlike logical equivalence and contradiction, which usually relate exactly two propositions, consistency and inconsistency often apply to larger groups of propositions. For consistency, the only requirement is that there be at least one line in the group of truth tables where all of the propositions are true, and for inconsistency the only requirement is that there be no such line. As a result of these requirements, the statement consisting of the conjunction of a group of inconsistent propositions will always be self-contradictory, whereas the statement consisting of the conjunction of a group of consistent propositions will never be self-contradictory.

Consistency and inconsistency are important because, among other things, they can be used to evaluate the overall rationality of a person's stated position on something. If the statements expressing such a position are consistent, then there is at least a possibility that the position makes sense. This is so because there will be at least one line in the group of truth tables where all of the person's statements are true. On the other hand, if the statements are inconsistent, then there is no possibility that the position makes sense. In this case there is no line in the truth tables where all of the statements are true. The group of statements, conjoined together, amounts to a self-contradiction.

The truth tables for consistency and logical equivalence also illustrate the important difference between two propositions being factually true and their being logically equivalent. For example, the statements "Water boils at 100°C" and "The current population of the United States is over 200 million" are both true in the present actual world. This real-world situation conforms to the one truth-table line on which both statements are true. As a result of this line, the two statements are consistent. However, they are not logically equivalent, because their truth values are not *necessarily* the same. The truth value of the second proposition might change in the future, while that of the first would remain the same. An analogous distinction, incidentally, holds between two statements having actually opposite truth values and their being contradictory.

EXERCISE 6.3

I. Use truth tables to determine whether the following symbolized statements are tautologous, self-contradictory, or contingent.

★1. $N \supset (N \supset N)$

2. $(G \supset G) \supset G$

3. $(S \supset R) \cdot (S \cdot \sim R)$

★4. $[(E \supset F) \supset F] \supset E$

5. $(\sim K \supset H) \equiv \sim(H \lor K)$

6. $(M \supset P) \lor (P \supset M)$

★7. $[(Z \supset X) \cdot (X \lor Z)] \supset X$

8. $[(C \supset D) \cdot \sim C] \supset \sim D$

9. $[X \supset (R \supset F)] \equiv [(X \supset R) \supset F]$

★10. $[G \supset (N \supset \sim G)] \cdot [(N \equiv G) \cdot (N \lor G)]$

11. $[(Q \supset P) \cdot (\sim Q \supset R)] \cdot \sim(P \lor R)$

12. $[(H \supset N) \cdot (T \supset N)] \supset [(H \lor T) \supset N]$

★13. $[U \cdot (T \lor S)] \equiv [(\sim T \lor \sim U) \cdot (\sim S \lor \sim U)]$

14. $\{[(G \cdot N) \supset H] \cdot [(G \supset H) \supset P]\} \supset (N \supset P)$

15. $[(F \lor E) \cdot (G \lor H)] \equiv [(G \cdot E) \lor (F \cdot H)]$

II. Use truth tables to determine whether the following pairs of symbolized statements are logically equivalent, contradictory, consistent, or inconsistent. First determine whether the pairs of propositions are logically equivalent or contradictory; then, if these relations do not apply, determine if they are consistent or inconsistent.

★1. $\sim D \vee B$	$\sim(D \cdot \sim B)$
2. $F \cdot M$	$\sim(F \vee M)$
3. $\sim K \supset L$	$K \supset \sim L$
★4. $R \vee \sim S$	$S \cdot \sim R$
5. $\sim A \equiv X$	$(X \cdot \sim A) \vee (A \cdot \sim X)$
6. $H \equiv \sim G$	$(G \cdot H) \vee (\sim G \cdot \sim H)$
★7. $(E \supset C) \supset L$	$E \supset (C \supset L)$
8. $N \cdot (A \vee \sim E)$	$\sim A \cdot (E \vee \sim N)$
9. $M \supset (K \supset P)$	$(K \cdot M) \supset P$
★10. $W \equiv (B \cdot T)$	$W \cdot (T \supset \sim B)$
11. $G \cdot (E \vee P)$	$\sim(G \cdot E) \cdot \sim(G \cdot P)$
12. $R \cdot (Q \vee S)$	$(S \vee R) \cdot (Q \vee R)$
★13. $H \cdot (K \vee J)$	$(J \cdot H) \vee (H \cdot K)$
14. $Z \cdot (C \equiv P)$	$C \equiv (Z \cdot \sim P)$
15. $Q \supset \sim(K \vee F)$	$(K \cdot Q) \vee (F \cdot Q)$

III. Use truth tables to obtain the answers to the following exercises.

★1. Renowned economist Harold Carlson makes the following prediction: "The balance of payments will decrease if and only if interest rates remain steady; however, it is not the case that either interest rates will not remain steady or the balance of payments will decrease." What can we say about Carlson's prediction?

2. A high school principal made this statement to the school board: "Either music is not dropped from the curriculum or the students will become cultural philistines; furthermore, the students will not become cultural philistines if and only if music is dropped from the curriculum." Assuming the principal is correct, what has she told us about music and the students? (Hint: Construct a truth table for the principal's statement and examine the line on which the statement turns out true.)

3. Christina and Thomas are having a discussion about their plans for the evening. Christina: "If you don't love me, then I'm certainly not going to have sex with you." Thomas: "Well, that means that if I do love you, then you will have sex with me, right?" Is Thomas correct? (Hint: Construct a truth table for each statement and compare them.)

★4. Two astronomers are discussing supernovas. Dr. Frank says, "Research has established that if a supernova occurs within ten light years of the earth, then life on earth will be destroyed." Dr. Harris says, "Research has also established that either a supernova will not occur within ten light years of the earth or life on earth will not be destroyed." Is it possible that both astronomers are correct? If so, what can we determine about the occurrence of a supernova?

5. Antonia Martinez, who is running for the state senate, makes this statement: "Either a tax reduction is feasible only if both educational costs do not increase and the welfare program is abolished, or a tax reduction is feasible and either

the welfare program will not be abolished or educational costs will increase." What has Martinez told us about taxes, educational costs, and welfare?

6. Automotive expert Frank Goodbody has this to say about Japanese imports: "If Mitsubishi is the sportiest, then both Toyota is the most trouble-free and Isuzu is not the lowest priced. If Isuzu is the lowest priced, then both Toyota is not the most trouble-free and Mitsubishi is the sportiest." Is it possible that Goodbody is correct in his assessment? If so, what may we conclude about Mitsubishi, Toyota, and Isuzu?

★7. Two stockbrokers are having a discussion. One claims that Netmark will introduce a new product if and only if both Datapro cuts its work force and Compucel expands production. The other claims that Datapro will cut its work force, and Compucel will expand production if and only if Netmark introduces a new product. Is it possible that both stockbrokers are right? If so, what have they told us about these companies?

8. Eric Carson sums up his beliefs about God as follows: "God exists if and only if either life is meaningful or the soul is not immortal. God exists and the soul is immortal. If God exists, then life is not meaningful." Is it possible that Eric's beliefs make sense?

9. Cindy, Jane, and Amanda witnessed a bank robbery. At trial, Cindy testified that Lefty did not enter the bank, and if Howard pulled a gun, then Conrad collected the money. Jane testified that if Howard did not pull a gun, then Lefty entered the bank. Amanda testified that if Conrad collected the money, then Howard pulled a gun. Is it possible that all three witnesses told the truth? If so, what can we conclude about Lefty, Howard, and Conrad?

★10. Nicole Evans expresses her philosophy as follows: "If the mind is identical to the brain, then personal freedom does not exist and humans are not responsible for their actions. If personal freedom does not exist, then the mind is identical to the brain. Either humans are responsible for their actions or the mind is not identical to the brain. If personal freedom exists, then humans are responsible for their actions." Is it possible that Nicole's philosophy makes sense? If so, what does it say about the mind, personal freedom, and responsibility?

6

6.4 Truth Tables for Arguments

Truth tables provide the standard technique for testing the validity of arguments in propositional logic. To construct a truth table for an argument, follow these steps:

1. Symbolize the arguments using letters to represent the simple propositions.
2. Write out the symbolized argument, placing a single slash between the premises and a double slash between the last premise and the conclusion.
3. Draw a truth table for the symbolized argument as if it were a proposition broken into parts, outlining the columns representing the premises and conclusion.
4. Look for a line in which all of the premises are true and the conclusion is false. If such a line exists, the argument is invalid; if not, it is valid.

For example, let us test the following argument for validity:

> If juvenile killers are as responsible for their crimes as adults, then execution is a justifiable punishment.
> Juvenile killers are not as responsible for their crimes as adults.
> Therefore, execution is not a justifiable punishment.

The first step is to symbolize the argument:

$$J \supset E$$
$$\underline{\sim J}$$
$$\sim E$$

Now a truth table may be constructed. Since the symbolized argument contains two different letters, the truth table has four lines. Make sure that identical letters have identical columns beneath them. Here are the columns for the individual letters:

```
J ⊃ E / ~ J // ~ E
T   T    T      T
T   F    T      F
F   T    F      T
F   F    F      F
```

The truth table is now completed, and the columns representing the premises and conclusion are outlined:

```
J  ⊃  E /  ~  J // ~  E
T [T] T   [F] T    [F] T
T [F] F   [F] T    [T] F
F (T) T   (T) F    (F) T
F [T] F   [T] F    [T] F
```

Inspection of the third line reveals that both of the premises are true and the conclusion is false. The argument is therefore invalid.

Another example:

> If insider trading occurs, then investors will not trust the securities markets. If investors do not trust the securities markets, then business in general will suffer. Therefore, if insider trading occurs, then business in general will suffer.

The completed truth table is this:

```
O ⊃ ~ T /  ~ T ⊃ B // O ⊃ B
T [F] F T   F T [T] T    T [T] T
T [F] F T   F T [T] F    T [F] F
T [T] T F   T F [T] T    T [T] T
T [T] T F   T F [F] F    T [F] F
F [T] F T   F T [T] T    F [T] T
F [T] F T   F T [T] F    F [T] F
F [T] T F   T F [T] T    F [T] T
F [T] T F   T F [F] F    F [T] F
```

Inspection of the truth table reveals that there is no line on which both premises are true and the conclusion is false. The argument is therefore valid.

The logic behind the method of truth tables is easy to understand. By definition, a valid argument is one in which it is not possible for the premises to be true and the conclusion false. A truth table presents every possible combination of truth values that the components of an argument may have. Therefore, if no line exists on which the premises are true and the conclusion false, then it is not possible for the premises to be true and the conclusion false, in which case the argument is valid. Conversely, if there *is* a line on which the premises are true and the conclusion false, then it *is* possible for the premises to be true and the conclusion false, and the argument is invalid. Accordingly, to test the validity of an argument, use this procedure:

> **Look for a line that has all true premises and a false conclusion. If you find such a line, the argument is invalid. If not, the argument is valid.**

Truth tables provide a convenient illustration of the fact that any argument having inconsistent premises is valid regardless of what its conclusion may be, and any argument having a tautologous conclusion is valid regardless of what its premises may be. Example:

The sky is blue.
The sky is not blue.
Therefore, Paris is the capital of France.

$S \ / \sim S \ // \ P$

T	F T	T
T	F T	F
F	T F	T
F	T F	F

Since the premises of this argument are inconsistent, there is no line on which the premises are both true. Accordingly, there is no line on which the premises are both true and the conclusion false, so the argument is valid. Of course, the argument is unsound, because it has a false premise. Another example:

Bern is the capital of Switzerland. Therefore, it is either raining or it is not raining.

$B \ // \ R \ v \sim R$

T	T T F T
T	F T T F
F	T T F T
F	F T T F

The conclusion of this argument is a tautology. Accordingly, there is no line on which the premise is true and the conclusion false, and so the argument is valid. Incidentally, it is also sound, because the premise is true.

The conditional statement having the conjunction of an argument's premises as its antecedent and the conclusion as its consequent is called the argument's **corresponding conditional.** For example, the corresponding conditional of the second argument tested in this section is $[(O \supset \sim T) \cdot (\sim T \supset B)] \supset (O \supset B)$. For any valid argument (such as this one), the corresponding conditional is a tautology. This is easy to see. In any valid argument, there is no line on which the premises are all true and the conclusion false. Thus, in the corresponding conditional, there is no line on which the antecedent is true and the consequent false, so the corresponding conditional is true on every line.

EXERCISE 6.4

I. Translate the following arguments into symbolic form. Then determine whether each is valid or invalid by constructing a truth table for each.

★1. If national elections deteriorate into TV popularity contests, then smooth-talking morons will get elected. Therefore, if national elections do not deteriorate into TV popularity contests, then smooth-talking morons will not get elected.

2. Brazil has a huge foreign debt. Therefore, either Brazil or Argentina has a huge foreign debt.

3. If fossil fuel combustion continues at its present rate, then a greenhouse effect will occur. If a greenhouse effect occurs, then world temperatures will rise. Therefore, if fossil fuel combustion continues at its present rate, then world temperatures will rise.

★4. If there are dried-up riverbeds on Mars, then water once flowed on the Martian surface. There are dried-up riverbeds on Mars. Therefore, water once flowed on the Martian surface.

5. If high school graduates are deficient in reading, they will not be able to compete in the modern world. If high school graduates are deficient in writing, they will not be able to compete in the modern world. Therefore, if high school graduates are deficient in reading, then they are deficient in writing.

6. The disparity between rich and poor is increasing. Therefore, political control over economic equality will be achieved only if restructuring the economic system along socialist lines implies that political control over economic equality will be achieved.

★7. Einstein won the Nobel Prize either for explaining the photoelectric effect or for the special theory of relativity. But he did win the Nobel Prize for explaining the photoelectric effect. Therefore, Einstein did not win the Nobel Prize for the special theory of relativity.

8. If microchips are made from diamond wafers, then computers will generate less heat. Computers will not generate less heat and microchips will be made from diamond wafers. Therefore, synthetic diamonds will be used for jewelry.

9. Either the USS *Arizona* or the USS *Missouri* was not sunk in the attack on Pearl Harbor. Therefore, it is not the case that either the USS *Arizona* or the USS *Missouri* was sunk in the attack on Pearl Harbor.

★10. If racial quotas are adopted for promoting employees, then qualified employees will be passed over; but if racial quotas are not adopted, then prior discrimination will go unaddressed. Either racial quotas will or will not be adopted for promoting employees. Therefore, either qualified employees will be passed over or prior discrimination will go unaddressed.

II. Determine whether the following symbolized arguments are valid or invalid by constructing a truth table for each.

★1. $K \supset \sim K$
$\sim K$

2. $R \supset R$
R

3. $P \equiv \sim N$
$N \vee P$

★4. $\sim(G \cdot M)$
$M \vee \sim G$
$\sim G$

5. $K \equiv \sim L$
$\sim(L \cdot \sim K)$
$K \supset L$

6. Z
$E \supset (Z \supset E)$

★7. $\sim(W \cdot \sim X)$
$\sim(X \cdot \sim W)$
$X \vee W$

8. $C \equiv D$
$E \vee \sim D$
$E \supset C$

9. $A \equiv (B \vee C)$
$\sim C \vee B$
$A \supset B$

★10. $J \supset (K \supset L)$
$K \supset (J \supset L)$
$(J \vee K) \supset L$

11. $\sim(K \equiv S)$
$S \supset \sim(R \vee K)$
$R \vee \sim S$

12. $E \supset (F \cdot G)$
$F \supset (G \supset H)$
$E \supset H$

★13. $A \supset (N \vee Q)$
$\sim(N \vee \sim A)$
$A \supset Q$

14. $G \supset H$
$R \equiv G$
$\sim H \vee G$
$R \equiv H$

15. $L \supset M$
$M \supset N$
$N \supset L$
$L \vee N$

★16. $S \supset T$
$S \supset \sim T$
$\sim T \supset S$
$S \vee \sim T$

17. $W \supset X$
$X \supset W$
$X \supset Y$
$Y \supset X$
$W \equiv Y$

18. $K \equiv (L \vee M)$
$L \supset M$
$M \supset K$
$K \vee L$
$K \supset L$

★19. $A \supset B$
$(A \cdot B) \supset C$
$A \supset (C \supset D)$
$A \supset D$

20. $\sim A \vee R$
$\sim(N \cdot \sim C)$
$R \supset C$
$C \supset \sim N$
$A \vee C$

6.5   Indirect Truth Tables

Indirect truth tables provide a shorter and faster method for testing the validity of arguments than do ordinary truth tables. This method is especially applicable to arguments that contain a large number of different simple propositions. For example, an argument containing five different simple propositions would require an ordinary truth table having thirty-two lines. The indirect truth table for such an argument, on the other hand, would usually require only a single line and could be constructed in a fraction of the time required for the ordinary truth table.

Indirect truth tables can also be used to test a series of statements for consistency. In Section 6.3 we showed how ordinary truth tables are used to test pairs of statements for consistency and we noted that consistency was a relation that applied to any group of propositions. In this section we use indirect truth tables to test groups of three, four, five, and six propositions for consistency. Given the abbreviated nature of indirect truth tables, this evaluation can usually be done much more quickly than it can with ordinary truth tables.

Testing Arguments for Validity

To construct an indirect truth table for an argument, we begin by assuming that the argument is invalid. That is, we assume that it is possible for the premises to be true and the conclusion false. Truth values corresponding to true premises and false conclusion are entered beneath the main operators for the premises and conclusion. Then, working backward, the truth values of the separate components are derived. If no contradiction is obtained in the process, this means that it is indeed possible for the premises to be true and the conclusion false, as originally assumed, so the argument is therefore invalid. If, however, the attempt to make the premises true and the conclusion false necessarily leads to a contradiction, it is not possible for the premises to be true and the conclusion false, in which case the argument is valid. Consider the following symbolized argument:

$$\sim A \supset (B \vee C)$$
$$\underline{\sim B}$$
$$C \supset A$$

We begin as before by writing the symbolized argument on a single line, placing a single slash between the premises and a double slash between the last premise and the conclusion. Then we assign T to the premises and F to the conclusion:

```
~ A ⊃ (B ∨ C) / ~ B // C ⊃ A
    T              T        F
```

We can now derive the truth values of B, C, and A, as follows:

```
~ A ⊃ (B ∨ C) / ~ B // C ⊃ A
    T             T F    T F F
```

These truth values are now transferred to the first premise:

```
~ A ⊃ (B ∨ C) /  ~ B // C ⊃ A
T F T  F T T      T F    T F F
```

We thus have a perfectly consistent assignment of truth values, which makes the premises true and the conclusion false. The argument is therefore invalid. If an ordinary truth table were constructed for this argument, it would be seen that the argument fails on the line on which *A* is false, *B* is false, and *C* is true. This is the exact arrangement presented in the indirect truth table just presented.

Here is another example. As always, we begin by assigning T to the premises and F to the conclusion:

$$A \supset (B \lor C) \:/\: B \supset D \:/\: A \:/\!/ \sim C \supset D$$
$$\text{T} \qquad\qquad \text{T} \quad\; \text{T} \qquad \text{F}$$

From the conclusion we can now derive the truth values of *C* and *D*, which are then transferred to the first two premises:

$$A \supset (B \lor C) \:/\: B \supset D \:/\: A \:/\!/ \sim C \supset D$$
$$\text{T} \qquad\; \text{F} \qquad \text{T F} \quad \text{T} \qquad \text{T F F F}$$

The truth value of *B* is now derived from the second premise and transferred, together with the truth value of *A*, to the first premise:

$$A \supset (B \lor C) \:/\: B \supset D \:/\: A \:/\!/ \sim C \supset D$$
$$\boxed{\text{T T F F}}\,\text{F} \qquad \text{F T F} \quad \text{T} \qquad \text{T F F F}$$

A contradiction now appears in the truth values assigned to the first premise, since T ⊃ F is F. The inconsistent truth values are circled. Because every step was strictly necessitated by some prior step, we have shown that it is impossible for the premises to be true and the conclusion false. The argument is therefore valid.

Sometimes a single row of truth values is not sufficient to prove an argument valid. Example:

$$\sim A \supset B \:/\: B \supset A \:/\: A \supset \sim B \:/\!/ A \cdot \sim B$$
$$\text{T} \qquad\; \text{T} \qquad\; \text{T} \qquad\qquad \text{F}$$

Since a conditional statement can be true in any one of three ways, and a conjunctive statement can be false in any one of three ways, merely assigning truth to the premises and falsity to the conclusion of this argument is not sufficient to obtain the truth values of any of the component statements. When faced with a situation such as this, we must list all of the possible ways that one of the premises can be true or the conclusion false, and proceed from there. If we list all of the possible ways the conclusion may be false, we obtain the following:

$$\sim A \supset B \:/\: B \supset A \:/\: A \supset \sim B \:/\!/ A \cdot \sim B$$
$$\text{T} \qquad\quad \text{T} \qquad\quad \text{T} \qquad\qquad \text{T F F T}$$
$$\text{T} \qquad\quad \text{T} \qquad\quad \text{T} \qquad\qquad \text{F F T F}$$
$$\text{T} \qquad\quad \text{T} \qquad\quad \text{T} \qquad\qquad \text{F F F T}$$

Extending the truth values of *A* and *B* to the premises, we obtain the following result:

$$\sim A \supset B \:/\: B \supset A \:/\: A \supset \sim B \:/\!/ A \cdot \sim B$$
$$\text{T} \qquad\quad \text{T} \quad \boxed{\text{T T F}}\,\text{T} \qquad \text{T F F T}$$
$$\boxed{\text{T F T F}} \quad \text{T} \qquad \text{T} \qquad\qquad \text{F F T F}$$
$$\text{T} \qquad \boxed{\text{T T F}} \quad \text{T} \qquad\qquad \text{F F F T}$$

Since each line necessarily leads to a contradiction, the argument is valid. If a contradiction had been avoided on some line, the argument would, of course, be invalid, because it would be possible for the premises to be true and the conclusion false. Note that in this argument it is not necessary to fill out all the truth values on any one line to be forced into a contradiction. On each line the contradiction is necessarily derived within the context of a single premise.

If an indirect truth table requires more than one line, the method to be followed is this. Either select one of the premises and compute all of the ways it can be made true, or select the conclusion and compute all of the ways it can be made false. This selection should be dictated by the requirement of simplicity. For example, if the conclusion can be made false in only two ways, while each of the premises can be made true in three ways, then select the conclusion. On the other hand, if one of the premises can be made true in only two ways while the conclusion can be made false in three ways, then select that premise. If neither of these situations prevails, then select the conclusion.

Having made your selection, proceed to compute the truth values of each line, beginning with the first. If no contradiction is derived on this line, stop! The argument has been proved invalid. If a contradiction *is* derived on the first line, proceed to the second line. If no contradiction is derived on this line, then, again, the argument has been proved invalid. If a contradiction *is* derived, proceed to the third line, and so on. Remember, the objective is to produce a line having no contradiction. Once such a line is produced, the argument has been proved invalid, and no further work need be done. If, on the other hand, each line necessarily leads to a contradiction, the argument is valid.

Three final points need to be made about indirect truth tables for arguments. First, if a contradiction is obtained in the assignment of truth values, every step leading to it must be logically implied by some prior step. In other words, the contradiction must be unavoidable. If a contradiction is obtained after truth values are assigned haphazardly or by guessing, then nothing has been proved. The objective is not to produce a contradiction but to *avoid* one (if possible).

For example, in the following indirect truth table a contradiction is apparent in the first premise:

$$A \supset B \ / \ C \supset B \ / / \ A \supset C$$
$$\boxed{\text{T T F}} \quad \text{F T F} \quad \text{T F F}$$

Yet the argument is invalid. The contradiction that appears is not *required* by the assignment of truth to the premises and falsity to the conclusion. The following indirect truth table, which is done correctly, proves the argument invalid:

$$A \supset B \ / \ C \supset B \ / / \ A \supset C$$
$$\text{T T T} \quad \text{F T T} \quad \text{T F F}$$

The second point is that for valid arguments the order in which the truth values are assigned may affect where the contradiction is obtained. That is, depending on the order of assignment, the contradiction may appear in the first premise, second premise, third premise, and so on. But, of course, the order of assignment does not affect the final determination of validity.

The last point is that it is essential that identical letters be assigned identical truth values. For example, if the letter *A* appears three times in a certain symbolized argument and the truth value T is assigned to it in one occurrence, then the same truth value must be assigned to it in the other occurrences as well. After the truth table has

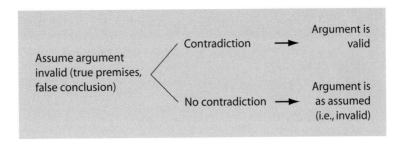

Assume argument invalid (true premises, false conclusion)
— Contradiction → Argument is valid
— No contradiction → Argument is as assumed (i.e., invalid)

been completed, each letter should be rechecked to ensure that one and the same truth value has been assigned to its various occurrences.

Testing Statements for Consistency

The method for testing a series of statements for consistency is similar to the method for testing arguments. We begin by writing the statements on a line, separating each with a single slash mark. (Since we have no conclusion, we use no double slash marks.) Then we assume that the statements are consistent. We assign a T to the main operator of each, and we then compute the truth values of the components. If this computation leads necessarily to a contradiction, the statements are not as we assumed them to be. That is, they are inconsistent. But if no contradiction is reached, the statements are consistent. Here is an example:

A v B
B ⊃ (C v A)
C ⊃ ~B
~A

First we write the statements on a single line separated by a single slash mark; we then assign T to each of the main operators:

A v B / B ⊃ (C v A) / C ⊃ ~ B / ~ A
  T   T   T   T

Next, we compute the truth values of the components. First we compute the truth value of A. Next, we enter this truth value in the first statement and compute the truth value of B. Next, we enter the truth value of B in the second statement and compute the truth value of C. Finally, the truth values of C and B are carried to the third statement:

A v B / B ⊃ (C v A) / C ⊃ ~ B / ~ A
F T T T T T T F (T T F) T T F

Since this computation leads necessarily to a contradiction (third statement), the group of statements is inconsistent.

Here is another example. The statements are written on a single line, and a T is assigned to each of the main operators:

A ⊃ (B • C) / C ⊃ ~ A / B v A / B ⊃ C
  T   T   T   T

© Hulton Archive/Getty Images

Augustus De Morgan 1806–1871

The English logician and mathematician Augustus De Morgan is famous for the development of predicate quantification and the invention of relational algebra—an algebra fundamental to the work of Russell and Whitehead in their *Principia Mathematica*. He is known to all students of symbolic logic owing to his formulation of what came to be known as De Morgan's rule of inference.

De Morgan was born in Madura, India, where his father was employed by the East India Company. He became blind in one eye not long after birth, and after his family returned to England his fellow students often taunted him and played cruel tricks on him because of his disability. When he was ten, his father died coming home from another trip to India. This left the boy under the influence of his mother, a devout Anglican who wanted her son to become an Anglican priest.

De Morgan obtained a B.A. from Trinity College, Cambridge, and might have received a Masters degree but for the fact that Cambridge then required all candidates to take a theological test. Because of his commitment to the ideal of religious neutrality, De Morgan refused to take this test. Perhaps in rebellion against his mother's influence, he developed a lifelong habit of avoiding churches, claiming that he could not bear hearing sermons. Following his refusal to take the exam, he continued his studies at University College London, a new institution founded on the principle of religious neutrality. At age twenty-two, he became the first professor of mathematics there.

Three years into his professorship, De Morgan became involved in a disagreement with the administration regarding its treatment of a colleague. De Morgan led a faculty protest, and in the end he resigned his position on the faculty. Five years later, he returned to his former position after his replacement accidentally drowned. He remained there for thirty years, until at age sixty he became involved in another administrative dispute—this time over a decision that De Morgan considered to be in violation of the university's stated policy of religious neutrality. He again resigned in protest, bringing his academic career to an end. Though active in academic politics, he curiously abstained from all involvement in national politics. An acquaintance once remarked that "he never voted in an election, and never visited the House of Commons."

De Morgan was proud of his son, George, who became a distinguished mathematician in his own right, and he was disconsolate at his son's untimely death, which occurred when De Morgan was sixty-two. The death of a daughter, during that same period, compounded his grief, and De Morgan died three years later, possibly owing to grief and stress.

De Morgan was known for his sense of humor and his interest in odd facts. He produced an almanac of full moons spanning a four-thousand-year period. A lunar crater is named after him. He liked to point out that he was x years old in the year x^2 (43 in 1849). He also enjoyed composing bits of verse in imitation of famous poets—for example, "Great fleas have little fleas upon their backs to bite 'em, and little fleas have lesser fleas, and so *ad infinitum*" (after Jonathan Swift).

6

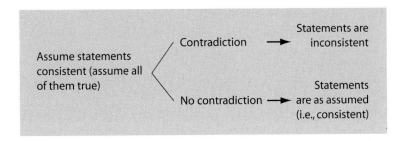

Since all of the statements can be true in three ways, we select one of them (the fourth) and figure all of the ways it can be true:

A ⊃ (B • C) / C ⊃ ~ A / B v A / B ⊃ C
T   T   T   T T T
                                    F T T
                                    F T F

Filling out the first line leads to no contradiction, so the statements are consistent:

A ⊃ (B • C) / C ⊃ ~ A / B v A / B ⊃ C
F T   T T T   T T T F   T T F   T T T
                                    F T T
                                    F T F

As with testing arguments, the objective is to *avoid* a contradiction. As soon as no contradiction is reached, we stop. The statements are consistent. Only if all three lines had led to a contradiction would these statements be inconsistent.

Rule for all multiline indirect truth tables

Contradiction is derived ⟶ Go to next line (if there is one).

No contradiction is derived ⟶ Stop. Argument is invalid/
                                             Statements are consistent.

6

EXERCISE 6.5

I. Use indirect truth tables to determine whether the following arguments are valid or invalid.

★1. B ⊃ C
    ~C
    ―――
    ~B

2. ~E v F
    ~E
    ――――
    ~F

3. P ⊃ (Q • R)
    R ⊃ S
    ―――――
    P ⊃ S

★4. ~(I ≡ J)
    ――――――
    ~(I ⊃ J)

5. W ⊃ (X ⊃ Y)
    X ⊃ (Y ⊃ Z)
    ――――――――
    W ⊃ (X ⊃ Z)

6. A ⊃ (B v C)
    C ⊃ (D • E)
    ~B
    ――――――
    A ⊃ ~E

★7. $G \supset H$
$H \supset I$
$\sim J \supset G$
$\underline{\sim I}$
J

8. $J \supset (\sim L \supset \sim K)$
$K \supset (\sim L \supset M)$
$\underline{(L \lor M) \supset N}$
$J \supset N$

9. $P \cdot (Q \lor R)$
$(P \cdot R) \supset \sim (S \lor T)$
$\underline{(\sim S \lor \sim T) \supset \sim (P \cdot Q)}$
$S \equiv T$

★10. $(M \lor N) \supset O$
$O \supset (N \lor P)$
$M \supset (\sim Q \supset N)$
$\underline{(Q \supset M) \supset \sim P}$
$N \equiv O$

11. $(A \lor B) \supset (C \cdot D)$
$\underline{(\sim A \lor \sim B) \supset E}$
$(\sim C \lor \sim D) \supset E$

12. $F \supset G$
$\sim H \lor I$
$(G \lor I) \supset J$
$\underline{\sim J}$
$\sim (F \lor H)$

★13. $(A \lor B) \supset (C \cdot D)$
$(X \lor \sim Y) \supset (\sim C \cdot \sim W)$
$\underline{(X \lor Z) \supset (A \cdot E)}$
$\sim X$

14. $\sim G \supset (\sim H \cdot \sim I)$
$J \supset H$
$K \supset (L \cdot M)$
$\underline{K \lor J}$
$L \cdot G$

15. $N \lor \sim O$
$P \lor O$
$P \supset Q$
$(N \lor Q) \supset (R \cdot S)$
$S \supset (R \supset T)$
$\underline{O \supset (T \supset U)}$
U

II. Use indirect truth tables to determine whether the following groups of statements are consistent or inconsistent.

★1. $K \equiv (R \lor M)$
$K \cdot \sim R$
$M \supset \sim K$

2. $F \equiv (A \cdot \sim P)$
$A \supset (P \cdot S)$
$S \supset \sim F$
$A \cdot \sim F$

3. $(G \lor \sim Q) \supset (F \lor B)$
$\sim (F \lor Q)$
$B \supset N$
$(F \lor N) \supset Q$

★4. $(N \lor C) \equiv E$
$N \supset \sim (C \lor H)$
$H \supset E$
$C \supset H$

5. $P \lor \sim S$
$S \lor \sim T$
$T \lor \sim X$
$X \lor \sim J$
$J \lor \sim P$

6. $(Q \lor K) \supset C$
$(C \cdot F) \supset (N \lor L)$
$C \supset (F \cdot \sim L)$
$Q \cdot \sim N$

★7. $S \supset (R \equiv A)$
$A \supset (W \cdot \sim R)$
$R \equiv (W \lor T)$
$S \cdot U$
$U \supset T$

8. $(E \lor H) \supset (K \cdot D)$
$D \supset (M \cdot B)$
$B \supset \sim E$
$\sim (H \lor K)$
$D \supset B$

9. $G \supset P$
$P \supset (A \cdot \sim G)$
$(R \lor T) \supset G$
$Y \supset R$
$B \supset T$
$Y \lor B$

★10. $A \lor Z$
$\quad A \supset (T \cdot F)$
$\quad Z \supset (M \cdot Q)$
$\quad Q \supset \sim F$
$\quad T \supset \sim M$
$\quad M \supset A$

6.6   Argument Forms and Fallacies

Many of the arguments that occur in propositional logic have forms that bear specific names and can be immediately recognized as either valid or invalid. The first part of this section presents some of the more common ones and explains how they are recognized. The second part discusses ways of refuting two of these forms, constructive and destructive dilemmas. The third part presents a word of caution relating to invalid forms. Finally, the fourth part applies to real-life arguments some of the principles developed in the first part.

Common Argument Forms

An **argument form** is an arrangement of statement variables and operators such that the uniform replacement of the variables by statements results in an argument. A *valid* argument form is any argument form that satisfies the truth-table test.

The first valid argument form to consider is **disjunctive syllogism,** which is defined as follows:

Disjunctive syllogism (DS):
$$p \lor q$$
$$\underline{\sim p}$$
$$q$$

The validity of this form can be easily checked by a truth table. Now, given that validity is purely a function of the form of an argument, any argument produced by uniformly substituting statements in place of the variables in this argument form is a valid argument. Such an argument is said to *have* the form of a disjunctive syllogism. The following argument was produced in this way and is therefore valid:

Either Harvard or Princeton is in New Jersey. $H \lor P$
Harvard is not in New Jersey. $\underline{\sim H}$
Therefore, Princeton is in New Jersey. P

The validity of a disjunctive syllogism arises from the fact that one of the premises presents two alternatives and the other premise eliminates one of those alternatives, leaving the other as the conclusion. This so-called "method of elimination" is essential to the validity of a disjunctive syllogism. If one premise should present two alternatives and the other premise should *affirm* one of those alternatives, the argument is invalid (unless the conclusion is a tautology). Example:

Either Harvard or Amherst is in Massachusetts. $H \lor A$
Harvard is in Massachusetts. H
Therefore, Amherst is not in Massachusetts. $\overline{\sim A}$

Since both Harvard and Amherst are in Massachusetts, the premises are true and the conclusion is false. Thus, the argument is invalid. Because the wedge symbol designates inclusive disjunction, the disjunctive premise includes the possibility of both disjuncts being true. Thus, for the argument to be valid, the other premise must eliminate one of the disjuncts.

The next valid argument form we consider is **pure hypothetical syllogism.** It consists of two premises and one conclusion, all of which are hypothetical (conditional) statements, and is defined as follows:

Pure hypothetical syllogism (HS):

$$p \supset q$$
$$q \supset r$$
$$\overline{p \supset r}$$

Any argument that has the form of a pure hypothetical syllogism (that is, any argument that can be produced by uniformly substituting statements in place of the variables in the form) is a valid argument. Example:

If world population continues to grow, then cities will become hopelessly overcrowded.	$W \supset C$
If cities become hopelessly overcrowded, then pollution will become intolerable.	$C \supset P$
Therefore, if world population continues to grow, then pollution will become intolerable.	$\overline{W \supset P}$

The validity of a pure hypothetical syllogism is grounded in the fact that the premises link together like a chain. In the population argument, the consequent of the first premise is identical to the antecedent of the second. If the premises fail to link together in this way, the argument may be invalid. Example:

If Bill Gates is a man, then Bill Gates is a human being.	$M \supset H$
If Bill Gates is a woman, then Bill Gates is a human being.	$W \supset H$
Therefore, if Bill Gates is a man, then Bill Gates is a woman.	$\overline{M \supset W}$

The premises of this argument are true, and the conclusion is false. Thus, the argument is invalid.

Another important valid argument form is called *modus ponens* ("asserting mode"). It consists of a conditional premise, a second premise that asserts the antecedent of the conditional premise, and a conclusion that asserts the consequent:

Modus ponens **(MP):**

$$p \supset q$$
$$\underline{p }$$
$$q$$

Any argument having the form of *modus ponens* is a valid argument. Example:

If twelve million children die yearly from starvation, then something is wrong with food distribution.	$T \supset S$
Twelve million children die yearly from starvation.	T
Therefore, something is wrong with food distribution.	$\overline{S}$

Closely associated with *modus ponens* is **modus tollens** ("denying mode"). *Modus tollens* is a valid argument form consisting of one conditional premise, a second premise that denies the consequent of the conditional premise, and a conclusion that denies the antecedent. It is defined as follows:

Modus tollens (MT):

$$p \supset q$$
$$\frac{\sim q}{\sim p}$$

Although a little harder to understand than *modus ponens, modus tollens* can be understood by the following reasoning process: The conclusion states that we do not have p, because if we did have p, then (by the first premise) we would have q, and we do not have q (by the second premise). Any argument that has the form of *modus tollens* is a valid argument. Example:

If Japan cares about endangered species, then it has
    stopped killing whales.
Japan has not stopped killing whales.

Therefore, Japan does not care about endangered
    species.

$$C \supset S$$
$$\frac{\sim S}{\sim C}$$

Two invalid forms are closely associated with *modus ponens* and *modus tollens*. These are **affirming the consequent** and **denying the antecedent.** Affirming the consequent consists of one conditional premise, a second premise that asserts the consequent of the conditional, and a conclusion that asserts the antecedent:

Affirming the consequent (AC):

$$p \supset q$$
$$\frac{q}{p}$$

Any argument that has the form of affirming the consequent is an invalid argument.[*] The following argument has this form and is therefore invalid:

If Napoleon was killed in a plane crash, then Napoleon is dead.
Napoleon is dead.

Therefore, Napoleon was killed in a plane crash.

$$K \supset D$$
$$\frac{D}{K}$$

Given that this argument has true premises and a false conclusion, it is clearly invalid.

Denying the antecedent consists of a conditional premise, a second premise that denies the antecedent of the conditional, and a conclusion that denies the consequent:

Denying the antecedent (DA):

$$p \supset q$$
$$\frac{\sim p}{\sim q}$$

Any argument that has the form of denying the antecedent is an invalid argument. Example:

If Napoleon was killed in a plane crash, then Napoleon is dead.
Napoleon was not killed in a plane crash.

Therefore, Napoleon is not dead.

$$K \supset D$$
$$\frac{\sim K}{\sim D}$$

Again, this argument has true premises and a false conclusion, so it is clearly invalid.

---

[*]See "Note on Invalid Forms" later in this section.

A **constructive dilemma** is a valid argument form that consists of a conjunctive premise made up of two conditional statements, a disjunctive premise that asserts the antecedents in the conjunctive premise (like *modus ponens*), and a disjunctive conclusion that asserts the consequents of the conjunctive premise. It is defined as follows:

Constructive dilemma (CD):

$$(p \supset q) \cdot (r \supset s)$$
$$\underline{p \lor r}$$
$$q \lor s$$

Any argument that has the form of a constructive dilemma is a valid argument. Example:

If we choose nuclear power, then we increase the risk
    of a nuclear accident; but if we choose conventional
    power, then we add to the greenhouse effect. $(N \supset I) \cdot (C \supset A)$
We must choose either nuclear power or conventional
    power. $N \lor C$
Therefore, we either increase the risk of nuclear accident
    or add to the greenhouse effect. $I \lor A$

The **destructive dilemma** is also a valid argument form. It is similar to the constructive dilemma in that it includes a conjunctive premise made up of two conditional statements and a disjunctive premise. However, the disjunctive premise denies the consequents of the conditionals (like *modus tollens*), and the conclusion denies the antecedents:

Destructive dilemma (DD):

$$(p \supset q) \cdot (r \supset s)$$
$$\underline{\sim q \lor \sim s}$$
$$\sim p \lor \sim r$$

Any argument that has the form of a destructive dilemma is a valid argument. Example:

If we are to reverse the greenhouse effect, then we
    must choose nuclear power; but if we are to lower
    the risk of a nuclear accident, then we must
    choose conventional power. $(R \supset N) \cdot (L \supset C)$
We will either not choose nuclear power or not
    choose conventional power. $\sim N \lor \sim C$
Therefore, we will either not reverse the greenhouse
    effect or not lower the risk of a nuclear accident. $\sim R \lor \sim L$

Refuting Constructive and Destructive Dilemmas

Now that we are familiar with several argument forms in propositional logic, we may return for a closer look at two of them, constructive and destructive dilemmas. Arguments having these forms occur frequently in public debate, where an arguer may use them to trap an opponent. Since both forms are valid, the only direct mode of defense available to the opponent is to prove the dilemma unsound. This can be done by proving at least one of the premises false. If the conjunctive premise (otherwise called the "horns of the dilemma") is proven false, the opponent is said to have "grasped the dilemma by the horns." This, of course, may be done by proving either one of the conditional statements false. If, on the other hand, the disjunctive premise is proven false, the opponent is said to have "escaped between the horns of the dilemma." The latter strategy often involves finding a third alternative that excludes the two that are given in the disjunctive premise. If such a third alternative can be found, both of the given disjuncts will be proved false. Consider the following constructive dilemma:

> If taxes increase, the economy will suffer, and if taxes decrease, needed government services will be curtailed. Since taxes must either increase or decrease, it follows that the economy will suffer or that needed government services will be curtailed.

It is easy to escape between the horns of this dilemma by arguing that taxes could be kept as they are, in which case they would neither increase nor decrease.

Some dilemmas, however, do not allow for the possibility of escaping between the horns. Consider the following constructive dilemma:

> If we encourage competition, we will have no peace, and if we do not encourage competition, we will make no progress. Since we must either encourage competition or not encourage it, we will either have no peace or make no progress.

Since the disjunctive premise of this dilemma is a tautology, it cannot be proven false. This leaves the strategy of grasping the dilemma by the horns, which may be done by proving either of the conditional statements in the conjunctive premise false. One debater might want to attack the first conditional and argue that competition and peace can coexist, while another might want to attack the second and argue that progress can be achieved through some means other than encouraging competition.

The strategy to be followed in refuting a dilemma is therefore this: Examine the disjunctive premise. If this premise is a tautology, attempt to grasp the dilemma by the horns by attacking one or the other of the conditional statements in the conjunctive premise. If the disjunctive premise is not a tautology, then either escape between the horns by, perhaps, finding a third alternative, or grasp the dilemma by the horns—whichever is easier.

A third, indirect strategy for refuting a dilemma involves constructing a counterdilemma. This is typically done by changing either the antecedents or the consequents of the conjunctive premise while leaving the disjunctive premise as it is, so as to obtain a different conclusion. If the dilemma in question is a constructive dilemma, the consequents of the conjunctive premise are changed. Here are possible counterdilemmas for the two dilemmas just presented:

If taxes increase, needed government services will be extended, and if taxes decrease, the economy will improve. Since taxes must either increase or decrease, it follows that needed government services will be extended or the economy will improve.

If we encourage competition, we will make progress, and if we do not encourage competition, we will have peace. Since we must either encourage competition or not encourage it, we will either make progress or have peace.

Constructing a counterdilemma falls short of a refutation of a given dilemma because it merely shows that a different approach can be taken to a certain problem. It does not cast any doubt on the soundness of the original dilemma. Yet the strategy is often effective because it testifies to the cleverness of the debater who can accomplish it successfully. In the heat of debate the attending audience is often persuaded that the original argument has been thoroughly demolished.

Note on Invalid Forms

Throughout this book we have seen that any substitution instance of a valid argument form is a valid argument. For example, consider *modus ponens:*

$$p \supset q$$
$$\underline{p}$$
$$q$$

Literally any two statements uniformly substituted in the place of p and q will result in a valid argument. Thus, the following symbolized arguments both have the form of *modus ponens*, and are accordingly valid:

$$S \supset T \qquad\qquad (K \lor B) \supset (N \cdot R)$$
$$\underline{S} \qquad\qquad\qquad\quad \underline{K \lor B}$$
$$T \qquad\qquad\qquad\quad N \cdot R$$

In the first argument S and T are uniformly substituted in the place of p and q, and in the second argument $K \lor B$ and $N \cdot R$ are uniformly substituted in the place of p and q.

However, this result does not extend to invalid argument forms. Consider, for example, affirming the consequent:

$$p \supset q$$
$$\underline{q}$$
$$p$$

Sometimes the uniform substitution of statements in the place of p and q results in an invalid argument, and sometimes it does not. Both of the following symbolized arguments are substitution instances of affirming the consequent, but the one on the left is invalid while the one on the right is valid:

$$G \supset N \qquad\qquad (F \lor D) \supset (F \cdot D)$$
$$\underline{N} \qquad\qquad\qquad\quad \underline{F \cdot D}$$
$$G \qquad\qquad\qquad\quad F \lor D$$

To deal with this problem we adopt a convention about when an argument will be said to *have* an invalid form. We will say that an argument has an invalid form if it is a substitution instance of that form *and* it is not a substitution instance of any valid form. According to this convention only the argument on the left has the form of affirming the consequent. The argument on the right does not have this form because it is a substitution instance of the following valid form:

$$(p \lor q) \supset (p \cdot q)$$
$$\underline{p \cdot q}$$
$$p \lor q$$

The validity of this form results from the fact that the conclusion follows from the second premise alone, without any involvement of the first premise. This fact may be easily checked with a truth table.

Here is another invalid form:

$$p \supset q$$
$$\underline{r \supset q}$$
$$p \supset r$$

Both of the following symbolized arguments are substitution instances of this form, but only the one on the left is invalid:

$K \supset L$	$\sim C \supset A$
$\underline{R \supset L}$	$\underline{(C \supset E) \supset A}$
$K \supset R$	$\sim C \supset (C \supset E)$

The argument on the right is valid because its conclusion is a tautology. Accordingly, only the argument on the left will be said to have the invalid form in question.

The point of this discussion is that when we attempt to determine the validity of arguments through mere inspection, we have to exert caution with invalid forms. The mere fact that an argument is a substitution instance of an invalid form does not guarantee that it is invalid. Before judging it invalid we must make sure that it is not valid for some other reason, such as its conclusion being a tautology. However, as concerns the exercises at the end of this section, all of the arguments that are substitution instances of invalid forms are invalid. In other words, none of them is like either of the right-hand examples considered in these paragraphs.

Summary and Application

Any argument having one of the following forms is valid:

$p \lor q$	disjunctive	$p \supset q$	pure hypothetical
$\underline{\sim p}$	syllogism	$\underline{q \supset r}$	syllogism (HS)
q	(DS)	$p \supset r$	
$p \supset q$	*modus ponens*	$p \supset q$	*modus tollens*
$\underline{p}$	(MP)	$\underline{\sim q}$	(MT)
q		$\sim p$	

$(p \supset q) \cdot (r \supset s)$	constructive	$(p \supset q) \cdot (r \supset s)$	destructive
$\dfrac{p \lor r}{q \lor s}$	dilemma (CD)	$\dfrac{\sim q \lor \sim s}{\sim p \lor \sim r}$	dilemma (DD)

Any argument having either of the following forms is invalid:

$p \supset q$	affirming the	$p \supset q$	denying the
$\dfrac{q}{p}$	consequent (AC)	$\dfrac{\sim p}{\sim q}$	antecedent (DA)

In identifying arguments as having these argument forms, use the following procedure. First symbolize the argument, using uppercase letters for the simple propositions. Then see whether the symbolized argument fits the pattern of one of these forms. For example, the following symbolized argument has the form of *modus ponens*, and is therefore valid:

$$K \supset R$$
$$\dfrac{K}{R}$$

If K and R are substituted respectively in place of p and q in the *modus ponens* form, we obtain the symbolized argument in question.

However, not every attempt at argument recognition is as simple as this. For more complicated cases it helps to keep two points in mind:

The order of the premises never affects the argument's form.
Negated letters can be substituted in place of the p, q, r, and s of an argument form just as can non-negated letters.

In regard to the first point, consider these symbolized arguments:

N	$\sim S$
$\dfrac{N \supset B}{B}$	$\dfrac{S \lor F}{F}$

The argument on the left is *modus ponens*, and the one on the right is a disjunctive syllogism. To see this more clearly, simply switch the order of the premises.

In regard to the second point (involving negated letters), consider these examples:

$\sim G \supset \sim H$	$\sim K \supset \sim M$
$\dfrac{\sim G}{\sim H}$	$\dfrac{\sim\sim M}{\sim\sim K}$

The argument on the left is *modus ponens*, and the one on the right is *modus tollens*. To produce the argument on the left, substitute $\sim G$ in the place of p in the *modus ponens* form, and $\sim H$ in the place of q. For the argument on the right, substitute $\sim K$ in the place of p in the *modus tollens* form, and $\sim M$ in the place of q.

Another problem that complicates the task of argument recognition arises from the fact that many arguments can be translated in alternate ways. Consider, for example, this argument:

Either the witness lied or Bob is guilty.
The witness told the truth.
Therefore, Bob is guilty.

If we select *L* to represent "The witness lied," then the argument can be translated into symbols as follows:

L ∨ B
~L
———
B

This symbolized argument is clearly an instance of disjunctive syllogism.

On the other hand, if we select *T* to represent "The witness told the truth," then we have this translation:

~T ∨ B
T
———
B

Technically this is not an instance of disjunctive syllogism, because the second premise, *T*, is not preceded by a tilde. To avoid this kind of difficulty in connection with alternative translations, we introduce two rules. They should be obvious, but if there is any doubt about them they can be proved using truth tables. The rules are as follows:

p is logically equivalent to ~~*p*.   (Double Negation)
p ∨ *q* is logically equivalent to *q* ∨ *p*.   (Commutativity)

According to the first rule, double tildes may be either inserted or deleted prior to any statement, and according to the second rule the order of the components in a disjunctive statement may be reversed. Applying the double negation rule to the second premise of the symbolized argument above, we have

~T ∨ B
~~T
———
B

After this change, the argument is now an instance of disjunctive syllogism.

For examples of how the commutativity rule is applied, consider these symbolized arguments:

M ∨ E	(R ⊃ L) • (T ⊃ K)
~E	T ∨ R
———	———
M	L ∨ K

Technically the argument on the left is not an instance of disjunctive syllogism because the letters in the first premise are in the wrong order, and the argument on the right is not an instance of constructive dilemma because the letters in the second premise are in the wrong order. We can reverse the order of these letters by applying the commutativity rule:

E ∨ M	(R ⊃ L) • (T ⊃ K)
~E	R ∨ T
———	———
M	L ∨ K

After these changes, the argument on the left is now clearly an instance of disjunctive syllogism, and the one on the right is an instance of constructive dilemma.

Here are some additional examples. In some cases the symbolized argument must be rewritten using double negation or commutativity before it fits the pattern of the argument form indicated.

$\sim\!A \supset \sim\!B$			$A \supset \sim\!B$		
$\sim\!B \supset C$	HS—valid		$B \supset \sim\!C$	invalid	
$\overline{\sim\!A \supset C}$			$\overline{A \supset \sim\!C}$		
$\sim\!A \supset \sim\!B$			$\sim\!A \supset B$		
B	MT—valid		A	DA—invalid	
$\overline{A}$			$\overline{\sim\!B}$		
$\sim\!A \lor \sim\!B$			$\sim\!A \lor B$		
A	DS—valid		$\sim\!A$	invalid	
$\overline{\sim\!B}$			$\overline{B}$		
$(A \supset \sim\!B) \cdot (\sim\!C \supset D)$			$(\sim\!A \supset B) \cdot (C \supset \sim\!D)$		
$A \lor \sim\!C$	CD—valid		$B \lor \sim\!D$	invalid	
$\overline{\sim\!B \lor D}$			$\overline{A \lor \sim\!C}$		
$A \lor \sim\!B$			$A \supset \sim\!B$		
B	DS—valid		$\sim\!B$	AC—invalid	
$\overline{A}$			$\overline{A}$		
A			$A \lor C$		
$A \supset B$	MP—valid		$(A \supset B) \cdot (C \supset D)$	CD—valid	
$\overline{B}$			$\overline{B \lor D}$		

Let us now see how the argument forms presented in this section can be used to interpret the structure of some real-life arguments. Consider the following letter to the editor of a newspaper:

> If U.S. servicemen are indeed being held in Southeast Asia, what is the motivation of their captors? No government there has asked for anything in return, as might be expected if they were deliberately holding Americans.
>
> (Norm Oshrin)

This argument is enthymematic; in other words, it is missing certain parts. The author intends to prove that U.S. servicemen are not being held in Southeast Asia—because if they were, their captors would be demanding something for their return. The argument can thus be structured as a *modus tollens*:

> If U.S. servicemen are being held in Southeast Asia, then their captors have demanded something for their return.
> Their captors have not demanded something for their return.
> Therefore, U.S. servicemen are not being held in Southeast Asia.

Here is another example:

> In a time when an entire nation believes in Murphy's law (that if anything can go wrong, it surely will) and has witnessed serious accidents in the highly regulated,

supposedly fail-safe nuclear industry, it's fascinating that people can persist in the fantasy that an error will not occur in the area of nuclear weaponry.

(Burk Gossom, Newsweek)

Although this argument allows for more than one analysis, clearly the arguer presents two main reasons why we can expect an accident in the area of nuclear weaponry: "Murphy's law" (which everyone believes to be true) dictates it, and accidents have occurred in the area of nuclear power (which is presumed fail-safe). Thus, at the very least, we can extract two *modus ponens* arguments from this selection:

> If everyone believes Murphy's law, then we can expect accidents in nuclear weaponry.
> Everyone believes Murphy's law.
> Therefore, we can expect accidents in nuclear weaponry.

> If accidents have occurred in nuclear power, then we can expect accidents in nuclear weaponry.
> Accidents have occurred in nuclear power.
> Therefore, we can expect accidents in nuclear weaponry.

Many arguments that we encounter in ordinary life can be interpreted as instances of valid argument forms. After being so interpreted, however, not all will turn out sound. The invalid forms (denying the antecedent and affirming the consequent) should be reserved for the relatively few arguments that are clearly invalid as originally expressed.

EXERCISE 6.6

I. Interpret the following symbolized arguments in light of the eight argument forms presented in this section. In some cases a symbolized argument must be rewritten using commutativity or double negation before it becomes an instance of one of these forms. Those not having a named form are invalid.

★1. $N \supset C$
$\dfrac{\sim C}{\sim N}$

2. $S \supset F$
$\dfrac{F \supset \sim L}{S \supset \sim L}$

3. $A \vee \sim Z$
$\dfrac{\sim Z}{A}$

★4. $(S \supset \sim P) \cdot (\sim S \supset D)$
$\dfrac{S \vee \sim S}{\sim P \vee D}$

5. $\sim N$
$\dfrac{\sim N \supset T}{T}$

6. $M \vee \sim B$
$\dfrac{\sim M}{\sim B}$

★7. $(E \supset N) \cdot (\sim L \supset \sim K)$
$\dfrac{\sim N \vee K}{\sim E \vee L}$

8. $W \supset \sim M$
$\dfrac{\sim M}{W}$

9. $\sim B \supset \sim L$
$\dfrac{G \supset \sim B}{G \supset \sim L}$

★10. $F \supset O$
$\dfrac{\sim F}{\sim O}$

11. $(K \vee B) \cdot (N \vee Q)$
$\dfrac{K \vee N}{B \vee Q}$

12. X
$\dfrac{X \supset \sim E}{\sim E}$

★13. $P \vee \sim S$
$\underline{S}$
P

14. $B \cdot T$
$\underline{T}$
$\sim B$

15. $\sim R \vee \sim Q$
$\underline{(G \supset Q) \cdot (H \supset R)}$
$\sim G \vee \sim H$

★16. $\sim G \supset H$
$\underline{H}$
$\sim G$

17. $K \supset \sim C$
$\underline{C}$
$\sim K$

18. $(I \supset M) \cdot (\sim O \supset A)$
$\underline{\sim O \vee I}$
$M \vee A$

★19. $X \supset \sim F$
$\underline{W \supset \sim F}$
$W \supset X$

20. $\sim L \supset U$
$\underline{L}$
$\sim U$

II. Translate the following arguments into symbolic notation and then interpret them in light of the eight argument forms presented in this section. In some cases a symbolized argument must be rewritten using commutativity or double negation before it becomes an instance of one of these forms. Those not having a named form are invalid.

★1. Future presidents will be allowed to serve a third term only if the Twenty-second Amendment is repealed. The Twenty-second Amendment will not be repealed. Therefore, future presidents will not be allowed to serve a third term.

2. If Michelangelo painted the ceiling of the Sistine Chapel, then he was familiar with stories from the Old Testament. Michelangelo was familiar with stories from the Old Testament. Therefore, Michelangelo painted the ceiling of the Sistine Chapel.

3. If you enter the teaching profession, you will have no money for vacations; and if you do not enter the teaching profession, you will have no time for vacations. Since you must either enter or not enter the teaching profession, it follows that either you will have no money or no time for vacations.

★4. Either the wealthiest people are the happiest, or it is not the case that money can buy everything. The wealthiest people are not the happiest. Therefore, money cannot buy everything.

5. Either tortured political prisoners in Turkey can openly complain of their mistreatment or Turkey is not a democracy. Tortured political prisoners in Turkey can openly complain of their mistreatment. Therefore, Turkey is a democracy.

6. If the sun is a variable star, then its energy will drop drastically at some point in the future. If the sun's energy drops drastically at some point in the future, then the earth will become a giant ice-ball. Therefore, if the sun is a variable star, then the earth will become a giant ice-ball.

★7. Twenty percent of America's children have never seen a dentist. But if that is so, health care in America is not properly distributed. Therefore, health care in America is not properly distributed.

8. If TV viewing provides genuine relaxation, then TV enhances the quality of life. But TV viewing does not provide genuine relaxation. Therefore, TV does not enhance the quality of life.

9. If high school clinics are to stem the tide of teenage pregnancy, then they must dispense birth control devices; but if they want to discourage illicit sex, then they must not dispense these devices. Since high school clinics must either dispense or not dispense birth control devices, either they will not stem the tide of teenage pregnancy, or they will not discourage illicit sex.

★10. If limits are imposed on medical malpractice suits, then patients will not be adequately compensated for their injuries; but if the cost of malpractice insurance continues to rise, then physicians will be forced out of business. Limits will not be imposed, and the cost of malpractice insurance will not continue to rise. Therefore, patients will be adequately compensated and physicians will not be forced out of business.

11. If Prohibition succeeded in the 1920s, then the war on drugs will succeed today. But Prohibition did not succeed in the 1920s. Therefore, the war on drugs will not succeed today.

12. If life is always better than death, then people do not commit suicide. People do commit suicide. Therefore, life is not always better than death.

★13. If we want to arrest criminals, then police must engage in high-speed chases; but if we want to protect motorists, then police must not engage in high-speed chases. Since police must either engage or not engage in high-speed chases, either we will not arrest criminals or not protect motorists.

14. Either industrial pollutants will be more stringently controlled, or acid rain will continue to fall. Industrial pollutants will be more stringently controlled. Therefore, acid rain will not continue to fall.

15. Insurance companies contribute millions of dollars to political campaigns. But if that is so, then meaningful insurance reform is impossible. Therefore, meaningful insurance reform is impossible.

★16. If Mexico does not get its population growth under control, then its unemployment problem will never be solved. Mexico's unemployment problem will never be solved. Therefore, Mexico will not get its population growth under control.

17. Either the dinosaurs were not cold-blooded or they were not the ancestors of modern birds. The dinosaurs were the ancestors of modern birds. Therefore, the dinosaurs were not cold-blooded.

18. If coal burning continues, then heavy metals will be released into the atmosphere. If heavy metals are not released into the atmosphere, then nervous system damage will decrease. Therefore, if coal burning does not continue, then nervous system damage will decrease.

★19. If sea levels rise twenty feet worldwide, then coastal cities from New York to Sydney will be inundated. If the ice sheets on Antarctica slip into the sea, then sea levels will rise twenty feet worldwide. Therefore, if the ice sheets on Antarctica slip into the sea, then coastal cities from New York to Sydney will be inundated.

20. If tax credits are given for private education, then the government will be supporting religion; but if tax credits are not given for private education, then some parents will end up paying double tuition. Either tax credits will or will not be given for private education. Therefore, either the government will be supporting religion, or some parents will end up paying double tuition.

III. Identify the following dilemmas as either constructive or destructive. Then suggest a refutation for each by escaping between the horns, grasping by the horns, or constructing a counterdilemma.

★1. If Melinda spends the night studying, she will miss the party; but if she does not spend the night studying, she will fail the test tomorrow. Melinda must either spend the night studying or not studying. Therefore, she will either miss the party or fail the test.

2. If we build our home in the valley, it will be struck by floods; and if we build it on the hilltop, it will be hit by lightning. Since we must either build it in the valley or on the hilltop, our home will either be struck by floods or hit by lightning.

3. If psychotherapists respect their clients' right to confidentiality, then they will not report child abusers to the authorities; but if they have any concern for the welfare of children, then they will report them. Psychotherapists must either report or not report child abusers to the authorities. Therefore, psychotherapists either have no respect for their clients' right to confidentiality or no concern for the welfare of children.

★4. If corporations are to remain competitive, then they must not spend money to neutralize their toxic waste; but if the environment is to be preserved, then corporations must spend money to neutralize their toxic waste. Corporations either will or will not spend money to neutralize their toxic waste. Therefore, either they will not remain competitive, or the environment will be destroyed.

5. If physicians pull the plug on terminally ill patients, then they risk being charged with murder; but if they do not pull the plug, they prolong their patients' pain and suffering. Since physicians with terminally ill patients must do one or the other, either they risk being charged with murder or they prolong their patients' pain and suffering.

6. If the Mitchells get a divorce, they will live separately in poverty; but if they stay married, they will live together in misery. Since they must either get a divorce or stay married, they will either live separately in poverty or together in misery.

★7. If college students want courses that are interesting and rewarding, then they must major in liberal arts; but if they want a job when they graduate, then they must major in business. College students will either not major in liberal arts, or they will not major in business. Therefore, either they will not take courses that are interesting and rewarding, or they will not have a job when they graduate.

8. If merchants arrest suspected shoplifters, then they risk false imprisonment; but if they do not arrest them, they risk loss of merchandise. Merchants must either arrest or not arrest suspected shoplifters. Therefore, they will either risk false imprisonment or loss of merchandise.

9. If women threatened with rape want to avoid being maimed or killed, then they must not resist their assaulter; but if they want to ensure successful prosecution of the assailant, they must resist him. Since women threatened with rape must do one or the other, either they will risk being maimed or killed or they will jeopardize successful prosecution of the assailant.

★10. If we prosecute suspected terrorists, then we risk retaliation by other terrorists; but if we release them, then we encourage terrorism. Since we must either prosecute or release suspected terrorists, we either risk retaliation by other terrorists or we encourage terrorism.

IV. The following selections were taken from letters to the editor of newspapers. Each contains one or more arguments, but the exact form of the argument may be hidden or ambiguous. Use the argument forms presented in this section to structure the selections as specifically named arguments.

★1. Anyone who is wondering how well Oral Roberts receives messages from God will be interested in our experience. Two weeks after my mother died, a letter came from Oral Roberts saying God had told him to write to her that day and ask for money! It makes one wonder.

(Hazel Woodsmall)

2. OK, I've tried it for a week again this year, but I still don't like daylight-saving time. My grass is brown enough already—it doesn't need another hour of daylight each day. Let's turn the clocks back to the way God intended—standard time.

(Jim Orr)

3. The religious right, in its impassioned fervor to correct our alleged moral wrongs and protect the rights of our unborn "children," may one day realize its ultimate goal of a constitutional amendment banning abortion. And what will the punishment be for those caught performing or receiving an abortion? The death penalty, of course.

(David Fisher)

★4. Most educators believe math instructors ought to emphasize group problem solving. If *group* problem solving is so important (and I think it is), why do we place such emphasis on individual testing? The national math test is a mistake.

(Frederick C. Thayer)

5. If voluntary school prayer for our children is going to make them more moral, then just think what mandatory church attendance on Sunday could do for the rest of us.

(Roderick M. Boyes)

6

6. A country that replaces the diseased hearts of old white men but refuses to feed schoolchildren, pay women adequately, educate adolescents, or care for the elderly—that country is doomed. We are acting as if there is no tomorrow. Where is our shame?

(Robert Birch)

★7. We cannot afford to close the library at Central Juvenile Hall. These young people in particular need to have access to ideas, dreams, and alternative ways of living. It can make the difference for many students who might become interested in reading for the first time in their lives while in Juvenile Hall.

(Natalie S. Field)

8. If the death penalty deters one person from becoming a murderer, it is effective. There are also some other important reasons for having the death penalty. First, the families and friends of innocent victims have the right to see effective retribution. Second, terminating the life of a killer is more economical than keeping him in jail at the taxpayer's expense. Third, everyone will have greater respect for the judicial system when justice is carried out.

(Doug Kroker)

9. Regarding the bill to require parental consent for a minor's abortion, I would like to point out that the pious platitudes about parental authority quickly fall by the wayside when the minor wants to keep the baby and the parents say, "Don't be silly! You have an abortion and finish your education." If the parents can veto a minor's abortion, shouldn't they also be able to require one? Better the choice, either pro or con, be left to the girl/woman herself.

(Jane Roberts)

★10. More than a million adult videocassettes are rented each week. Nor, as the propagandists would have you believe, does viewing such material lead to violent sex crimes. If it did, there would be over one million such crimes per week.

(Lybrand P. Smith)

Summary

Propositional logic is characterized by the fact that the fundamental units are whole statements. Simple statements, represented by capital letters, are combined through the use of logical operators to form compound statements. The five operators are the tilde, which is used to form negations; the dot, which forms conjunctions; the wedge, which forms disjunctions; the horseshoe, which forms conditional statements; and the triple bar, which forms biconditional statements. These operators roughly translate the English words "not," "and," "or," "if . . . then . . . ," and "if and only if," respectively.

The truth-functional meaning of the logical operators is defined in terms of truth tables. A truth table is an arrangement of truth values that shows in every possible case how the truth value of a compound statement is determined by the truth value of its simple components. The truth value of longer statements is computed by assigning truth values to the simple components and then working outward to the larger ones. The meaning of statements symbolized in terms of the logical operators conforms fairly closely to that of English statements, but it occasionally breaks down, especially with conditional and biconditional statements.

Truth tables can be used to classify individual compound statements and to compare one compound statement with another. A compound statement is tautologous if the truth values under the main operator are all true, it is self-contradictory if they are all false, and it is contingent if at least one is true and at least one is false. Two statements are logically equivalent if the truth values under the main operators are the same on each line, and they are contradictory if they are the opposite on each line. Two or more statements are consistent if there is at least one line under the main operators where all of the truth values are true, and they are inconsistent if there is no such line.

One may test arguments for validity by using either ordinary truth tables or indirect truth tables. For the ordinary method, if there is a line on which the premises turn out true and the conclusion false, the argument is invalid; if not, the argument is valid. The indirect method begins by assuming the premises true and the conclusion false. If this assumption leads necessarily to a contradiction, the argument is valid; if not, it is invalid. To use the indirect method to test a series of statements for consistency, the statements are assumed to be true. If this assumption leads necessarily to a contradiction, the statements are inconsistent; if not, they are consistent.

Once an argument is symbolized, mere inspection will often determine whether it is valid or invalid. This determination is facilitated by a familiarity with a few common argument forms. Six such forms that are valid are disjunctive syllogism, pure hypothetical syllogism, *modus ponens, modus tollens,* constructive dilemma, and destructive dilemma. Two common invalid forms are affirming the consequent and denying the antecedent. A dilemma expressed in ordinary language may be refuted by proving it unsound. Two methods are grasping the dilemma by the horns and escaping between the horns. A third method, which falls short of strict refutation, is constructing a counterdilemma.

6

7 Natural Deduction in Propositional Logic

7.1   Rules of Implication I

Natural deduction is a method for establishing the validity of propositional type arguments that is both simpler and more enlightening than the method of truth tables. By means of this method, the conclusion of an argument is actually derived from the premises through a series of discrete steps. In this respect natural deduction resembles the method used in geometry to derive theorems relating to lines and figures; but whereas each step in a geometrical proof depends on some mathematical principle, each step in a logical proof depends on a **rule of inference.** This chapter will present eighteen rules of inference.

The first eight rules of inference are called **rules of implication** because they consist of basic argument forms whose premises *imply* their conclusions. The following four rules of implication should be familiar from the previous chapter:

1. *Modus ponens* (MP):
$$p \supset q$$
$$\underline{p}$$
$$q$$

3. Pure hypothetical syllogism (HS):
$$p \supset q$$
$$\underline{q \supset r}$$
$$p \supset r$$

2. *Modus tollens* (MT):
$$p \supset q$$
$$\underline{\sim q}$$
$$\sim p$$

4. Disjunctive syllogism (DS):
$$p \lor q$$
$$\underline{\sim p}$$
$$q$$

In constructing proofs, *modus ponens* allows us to assert the consequent of a conditional statement on a line by itself, and *modus tollens* allows us to assert the negation of the antecedent. Pure hypothetical syllogism ("hypothetical syllogism" for short) is used to derive a conditional statement from two other conditionals, and disjunctive syllogism allows us to assert the right-hand disjunct of a disjunctive statement on a line by itself.

These four rules will be sufficient to derive the conclusion of many simple arguments in propositional logic. Further, once we are supplied with all eighteen rules together with conditional proof, the resulting system will be sufficient to derive the conclusion of any valid argument in propositional logic. Conversely, since each rule is

See information on our website: **www.thomsonexercises.com**

a valid argument form unto itself, any conclusion derived from their correct use results in a valid argument. The method of natural deduction is thus equal in power to the truth-table method as far as proving validity is concerned. However, since natural deduction cannot be used with any facility to prove invalidity, we still need the truth-table method for that purpose.

A proof in natural deduction consists of a sequence of propositions, each of which is either a premise or is derived from preceding propositions by application of a rule of inference and the last of which is the conclusion of the original argument. For an example of how the rules of inference are used in constructing such a proof, consider the following argument:

> If the Astros win the playoff, then the Braves will lose the pennant. If the Astros do not win the playoff, then either Connolly or Davis will be fired. The Braves will not lose the pennant. Furthermore, Connolly will not be fired. Therefore, Davis will be fired.

The first step is to symbolize the argument, numbering the premises and writing the conclusion to the right of the last premise, separated by a slash mark:

1. $A \supset B$
2. $\sim A \supset (C \lor D)$
3. $\sim B$
4. $\sim C$ / D

The conclusion is now derived from the premises via steps 5 through 7. The justification for each line is written to the immediate right:

5. $\sim A$ 1, 3, MT
6. $C \lor D$ 2, 5, MP
7. D 4, 6, DS

Line 5 is obtained from lines 1 and 3 via *modus tollens*. In other words, when A and B in these lines are substituted respectively for the p and q of the *modus tollens* rule, line 5 follows as the conclusion. Then, when $\sim A$ and $C \lor D$ in lines 2 and 5 are substituted respectively for the p and q of the *modus ponens* rule, line 6 follows as the conclusion. Finally, when C and D in lines 4 and 6 are substituted respectively for the p and q of the disjunctive syllogism rule, line 7 follows as the final conclusion. These lines constitute a valid derivation of the conclusion from the premises because each line is a substitution instance of a valid argument form.

These arguments are all instances of ***modus ponens*** (MP)		
$\sim F \supset (G \equiv H)$	$(A \lor B) \supset \sim (C \cdot D)$	$K \cdot L$
$\sim F$	$A \lor B$	$(K \cdot L) \supset [(R \supset S) \cdot (T \supset U)]$
$G \equiv H$	$\sim (C \cdot D)$	$(R \supset S) \cdot (T \supset U)$

Here is an example of another completed proof. The conclusion to be obtained is written to the right of the last premise (line 4). Lines 5 through 7 are used to derive the conclusion:

1. $F \supset G$
2. $F \lor H$
3. $\sim G$
4. $H \supset (G \supset I)$ / $F \supset I$
5. $\sim F$ 1, 3, MT
6. H 2, 5, DS
7. $G \supset I$ 4, 6, MP
8. $F \supset I$ 1, 7, HS

When the letters in lines 1 and 3 are substituted into the *modus tollens* rule, line 5 is obtained. Then, when the letters in lines 2 and 5 are substituted into the disjunctive syllogism rule, line 6 is obtained. Line 7 is obtained by substituting H and $G \supset I$ from lines 4 and 6 into the *modus ponens* rule. Finally, line 8 is obtained by substituting the letters in lines 1 and 7 into the hypothetical syllogism rule. Notice that the conclusion, stated to the right of line 4, is not (and never is) part of the proof. It merely indicates what the proof is supposed to yield in the end.

These arguments are all instances of **modus tollens** (MT)

$$\frac{\begin{array}{c}(D \lor F) \supset K \\ \sim K\end{array}}{\sim (D \lor F)} \qquad \frac{\begin{array}{c}\sim G \supset \sim(M \lor N) \\ \sim\sim(M \lor N)\end{array}}{\sim\sim G} \qquad \frac{\begin{array}{c}\sim T \\ [(H \lor K) \bullet (L \lor N)] \supset T\end{array}}{\sim[(H \lor K) \bullet (L \lor N)]}$$

The successful use of natural deduction to derive a conclusion from one or more premises depends on the ability of the reasoner to visualize more or less complex arrangements of simple propositions as instances of the basic rules of inference. Here is a slightly more complex example:

1. $\sim(A \bullet B) \lor [\sim(E \bullet F) \supset (C \supset D)]$
2. $\sim\sim(A \bullet B)$
3. $\sim(E \bullet F)$
4. $D \supset G$ / $C \supset G$
5. $\sim(E \bullet F) \supset (C \supset D)$ 1, 2, DS
6. $C \supset D$ 3, 5, MP
7. $C \supset G$ 4, 6, HS

Line 4 is the last premise. To obtain line 5, $\sim(A \bullet B)$ and $[\sim(E \bullet F) \supset (C \supset D)]$ are substituted respectively for the p and q of the disjunctive syllogism rule, yielding $[\sim(E \bullet F) \supset (C \supset D)]$ as the conclusion. Next, $\sim(E \bullet F)$ and $C \supset D$ are substituted respectively for the p and q of *modus ponens*, yielding $C \supset D$ on line 6. Finally, lines 6 and 4 are combined to yield line 7 via the hypothetical syllogism rule.

These arguments are all instances of **pure hypothetical syllogism** (HS)

$A \supset (D \bullet F)$	$\sim M \supset (R \supset S)$	$(L \supset N) \supset [(S \lor T) \bullet K]$
$(D \bullet F) \supset \sim H$	$(C \lor K) \supset \sim M$	$(C \equiv F) \supset (L \supset N)$
$A \supset \sim H$	$(C \lor K) \supset (R \supset S)$	$(C \equiv F) \supset [(S \lor T) \bullet K]$

The proofs that we have investigated thus far have been presented in ready-made form. We turn now to the question of how the various lines are obtained, leading in the end to the conclusion. What strategy is used in deriving these lines? While the answer is somewhat complex, we have a few basic rules of thumb to follow. Always begin by looking at the conclusion and by then attempting to locate the conclusion in the premises. Let us suppose that the conclusion is a single letter L. We begin by looking for L in the premises. Let us suppose we find it in a premise that reads

$K \supset L$

Immediately we see that we can obtain L via *modus ponens* if we first obtain K. We now begin searching for K. Let us suppose that we find K in another premise that reads

$J \lor K$

From this we see that we could obtain K via disjunctive syllogism if we first obtain $\sim J$. The process continues until we isolate the required statement on a line by itself. Let us suppose that we find $\sim J$ on a line by itself. The thought process is then complete, and the various steps may be written out in the reverse order in which they were obtained mentally. The proof would look like this:

1. $\sim J$
2. $J \lor K$
3. $K \supset L$ / L
4. K 1, 2, DS
5. L 3, 4, MP

These arguments are all instances of **disjunctive syllogism** (DS)

$U \lor \sim (W \bullet X)$	$\sim (E \lor F)$	$\sim B \lor [(H \supset M) \bullet (S \supset T)]$
$\sim U$	$(E \lor F) \lor (N \supset K)$	$\sim \sim B$
$\sim (W \bullet X)$	$N \supset K$	$(H \supset M) \bullet (S \supset T)$

Turning now to a different example, let us suppose that the conclusion is the conditional statement $R \supset U$. We begin by attempting to locate $R \supset U$ in the premises. If we cannot find it, we look for its separate components, R and U. Let us suppose we find R in the antecedent of the conditional statement:

$R \supset S$

Furthermore, let us suppose we find *U* in the consequent of the conditional statement:

$T \supset U$

We then see that we can obtain $R \supset U$ via a series of hypothetical syllogism steps if we first obtain $S \supset T$. Let us suppose that we find $S \supset T$ on a line by itself. The proof has now been completely thought through and may be written out as follows:

1. $S \supset T$
2. $T \supset U$
3. $R \supset S$ / $R \supset U$
4. $R \supset T$ 1, 3, HS
5. $R \supset U$ 2, 4, HS

At this point a word of caution is in order about the meaning of a proposition being "obtained." Let us suppose that we are searching for *E* and we find it in a premise that reads $E \supset F$. The mere fact that we have located the letter *E* in this line does not mean that we have obtained *E*. $E \supset F$ means that *if* we have *E*, then we have *F*; it does *not* mean that we *have* either *E* or *F*. From such a line we could obtain *F* (via *modus ponens*) if we first obtain *E*, or we could obtain ~*E* (via *modus tollens*) if we first obtain ~*F*. The proposition $E \supset F$ by itself gives us nothing, and even if we combine it with other lines, there is no way that we could ever obtain *E* from such a line.

Here is a sample argument:

1. $A \lor B$
2. $\sim C \supset \sim A$
3. $C \supset D$
4. $\sim D$ / B

We begin by searching for *B* in the premises. Finding it in line 1, we see that it can be obtained via disjunctive syllogism if we first obtain ~*A*. This in turn can be gotten from line 2 via *modus ponens* if we first obtain ~*C*, and this can be gotten from line 3 via *modus tollens* once ~*D* is obtained. Happily, the latter is stated by itself on line 4. The proof has now been completely thought through and can be written out as follows:

1. $A \lor B$
2. $\sim C \supset \sim A$
3. $C \supset D$
4. $\sim D$ / B
5. $\sim C$ 3, 4, MT
6. $\sim A$ 2, 5, MP
7. B 1, 6, DS

Another example:

1. $E \supset (K \supset L)$
2. $F \supset (L \supset M)$
3. $G \lor E$
4. $\sim G$
5. F / $K \supset M$

We begin by searching for $K \supset M$ in the premises. Not finding it, we search for the separate components, *K* and *M*, and locate them in lines 1 and 2. The fact that *K* appears in the antecedent of a conditional statement, and *M* in the consequent of another, immediately suggests hypothetical syllogism. But first we must obtain these conditional statements on lines by themselves. We can obtain $K \supset L$ via *modus ponens* if we first obtain *E*. This, in turn, we can obtain from line 3 via disjunctive syllogism if we first obtain ~*G*. Since ~*G* appears by itself on line 4, the first part of the thought process is now complete. The second part requires that we obtain $L \supset M$. This we can get from line 2 via *modus ponens* if we can get *F*, and we do have *F* by itself on line 5. All of the steps leading to the conclusion have now been thought through, and the proof can be written out:

1. $E \supset (K \supset L)$
2. $F \supset (L \supset M)$
3. $G \lor E$
4. ~G
5. F / $K \supset M$
6. E 3, 4, DS
7. $K \supset L$ 1, 6, MP
8. $L \supset M$ 2, 5, MP
9. $K \supset M$ 7, 8, HS

The thought process behind these proofs illustrates an important point about the construction of proofs by natural deduction. Ideally, we should never write down a line in a proof unless we know why we are doing it and where it leads. Typically, good proofs are not produced haphazardly or by luck; rather, they are produced by organized logical thinking. Occasionally, of course, we may be baffled by an especially difficult proof, and random deductive steps noted on the side may be useful. But we should not commence the actual writing out of the proof until we have used logical thinking to discover the path leading to the conclusion.

This section ends with some strategies for applying the first four rules of inference.

Strategy 1: Always begin by attempting to "find" the conclusion in the premises.

Strategy 2: If the conclusion contains a letter that appears in the consequent of a conditional statement in the premises, consider obtaining that letter via *modus ponens*:

1. $A \supset B$
2. $C \lor A$
3. A / B
4. B 1, 3, MP

Strategy 3: If the conclusion contains a negated letter that appears in the antecedent of a conditional statement in the premises, consider obtaining the negated letter via *modus tollens*:

1. $C \supset B$
2. $A \supset B$
3. ~B / ~A
4. ~A 2, 3, MT

Strategy 4: If the conclusion is a conditional statement, consider obtaining it via pure hypothetical syllogism:

1. $B \supset C$
2. $C \supset A$
3. $A \supset B$ / $A \supset C$
4. $A \supset C$ 1, 3, HS

Strategy 5: If the conclusion contains a letter that appears in a disjunctive statement in the premises, consider obtaining that letter via disjunctive syllogism:

1. $A \supset B$
2. $A \lor C$
3. $\sim A$ / C
4. C 2, 3, DS

Of course, these strategies apply to obtaining any line prior to the conclusion, just as they apply to obtaining the conclusion.

EXERCISE 7.1

I. For each of the following lists of premises, derive the conclusion and supply the justification for it. There is only one possible answer for each problem.

★(1) 1. $G \supset F$
     2. $\sim F$
     3. _____ ____

(2) 1. S
     2. $S \supset M$
     3. _____ ____

(3) 1. $R \supset D$
     2. $E \supset R$
     3. _____ ____

★(4) 1. $B \lor C$
     2. $\sim B$
     3. _____ ____

(5) 1. N
     2. $N \lor F$
     3. $N \supset K$
     4. _____ ____

(6) 1. $\sim J \lor P$
     2. $\sim J$
     3. $S \supset J$
     4. _____ ____

★(7) 1. $H \supset D$
     2. $F \supset T$
     3. $F \supset H$
     4. _____ ____

(8) 1. $S \supset W$
     2. $\sim S$
     3. $S \lor N$
     4. _____ ____

(9) 1. $F \supset \sim A$
     2. $N \supset A$
     3. $\sim F$
     4. $\sim A$
     5. _____ ____

★(10) 1. $H \supset A$
     2. A
     3. $A \lor M$
     4. $G \supset H$
     5. _____ ____

(11) 1. $W \lor B$
     2. W
     3. $B \supset T$
     4. $W \supset A$
     5. _____ ____

(12) 1. $K \supset \sim R$
     2. $\sim R$
     3. $R \lor S$
     4. $R \supset T$
     5. _____ ____

★(13) 1. ~C ⊃ ~F
    2. L ⊃ F
    3. ~~F
    4. F ∨ ~L
    5. _____ ____

(14) 1. N ⊃ ~E
    2. ~~S
    3. ~E ∨ ~S
    4. ~S ∨ N
    5. _____ ____

(15) 1. ~R ⊃ ~T
    2. ~T ∨ B
    3. C ⊃ ~R
    4. ~C
    5. _____ ____

★(16) 1. ~K
    2. ~K ⊃ ~P
    3. ~K ∨ G
    4. G ⊃ Q
    5. _____ ____

(17) 1. F ∨ (A ⊃ C)
    2. A ∨ (C ⊃ F)
    3. A
    4. ~F
    5. _____ ____

(18) 1. (R ⊃ M) ⊃ D
    2. M ⊃ C
    3. D ⊃ (M ∨ E)
    4. ~M
    5. _____ ____

★(19) 1. (S ∨ C) ⊃ L
    2. ~S
    3. ~L
    4. S ⊃ (K ⊃ L)
    5. _____ ____

(20) 1. (A ∨ W) ⊃ (N ⊃ Q)
    2. Q ⊃ G
    3. ~A
    4. (Q ⊃ G) ⊃ (A ∨ N)
    5. _____ ____

II. The following symbolized arguments are missing a premise. Write the premise needed to derive the conclusion (last line), and supply the justification for the conclusion. Try to construct the simplest premise needed to derive the conclusion.

★(1) 1. B ∨ K
    2. _____
    3. K   ____

(2) 1. N ⊃ S
    2. _____
    3. S   ____

(3) 1. K ⊃ T
    2. _____
    3. ~K   ____

★(4) 1. C ⊃ H
    2. _____
    3. R ⊃ H   ____

(5) 1. F ⊃ N
    2. N ⊃ T
    3. _____
    4. ~F   ____

(6) 1. W ∨ T
    2. A ⊃ W
    3. _____
    4. A ⊃ T   ____

★(7) 1. M ⊃ B
    2. Q ⊃ M
    3. _____
    4. M   ____

(8) 1. C ∨ L
    2. L ⊃ T
    3. _____
    4. L   ____

(9) 1. E ⊃ N
    2. T ∨ ~E
    3. S ⊃ E
    4. _____
    5. E   ____

★(10) 1. $H \supset A$
      2. $S \supset H$
      3. $\sim M \lor H$
      4. _____
      5. $\sim H$ ____

(11) 1. $T \supset N$
      2. $G \supset T$
      3. $H \lor T$
      4. _____
      5. $F \supset T$ ____

(12) 1. $G \supset C$
      2. $M \lor G$
      3. $T \lor \sim G$
      4. _____
      5. G ____

★(13) 1. $\sim S \supset \sim B$
      2. $R \lor \sim B$
      3. $\sim B \supset \sim S$
      4. _____
      5. $\sim\sim B$ ____

(14) 1. $\sim R \supset D$
      2. $\sim J \supset \sim R$
      3. $N \lor \sim R$
      4. _____
      5. $\sim F \supset \sim R$ ____

(15) 1. $\sim S \lor \sim P$
      2. $\sim K \supset P$
      3. $\sim P \supset F$
      4. _____
      5. $\sim P$ ____

★(16) 1. $J \supset E$
      2. $B \lor \sim J$
      3. $\sim Z \supset J$
      4. _____
      5. J ____

(17) 1. $(H \supset C) \supset A$
      2. $N \supset (F \supset K)$
      3. $(E \cdot R) \supset K$
      4. _____
      5. $H \supset K$ ____

(18) 1. $(S \supset M) \supset G$
      2. $S \supset (M \cdot G)$
      3. $G \supset (R \supset \sim S)$
      4. _____
      5. $\sim S$ ____

★(19) 1. $(W \lor \sim F) \supset H$
      2. $(H \lor G) \supset \sim F$
      3. $T \supset (F \supset G)$
      4. _____
      5. $\sim F$ ____

(20) 1. $(H \cdot A) \lor T$
      2. $\sim S \supset (P \supset T)$
      3. $(N \lor T) \supset P$
      4. _____
      5. T ____

III. Use the first four rules of inference to derive the conclusions of the following symbolized arguments.

★(1) 1. $\sim C \supset (A \supset C)$
     2. $\sim C$ / $\sim A$

(2) 1. $F \lor (D \supset T)$
    2. $\sim F$
    3. D / T

(3) 1. $(K \cdot B) \lor (L \supset E)$
    2. $\sim(K \cdot B)$
    3. $\sim E$ / $\sim L$

★(4) 1. $P \supset (G \supset T)$
    2. $Q \supset (T \supset E)$
    3. P
    4. Q / $G \supset E$

(5) 1. $\sim W \supset [\sim W \supset (X \supset W)]$
    2. $\sim W$ / $\sim X$

(6) 1. $J \supset (K \supset L)$
    2. $L \lor J$
    3. $\sim L$ / $\sim K$

★(7) 1. $\sim S \supset D$
    2. $\sim S \lor (\sim D \supset K)$
    3. $\sim D$ / K

(8) 1. $A \supset (E \supset \sim F)$
    2. $H \lor (\sim F \supset M)$
    3. A
    4. $\sim H$ / $E \supset M$

(9) 1. $\sim G \supset (G \vee \sim A)$
   2. $\sim A \supset (C \supset A)$
   3. $\sim G$ / $\sim C$

★(10) 1. $N \supset (J \supset P)$
   2. $(J \supset P) \supset (N \supset J)$
   3. N / P

(11) 1. $G \supset [\sim O \supset (G \supset D)]$
   2. $O \vee G$
   3. $\sim O$ / D

(12) 1. $\sim M \vee (B \vee \sim T)$
   2. $B \supset W$
   3. $\sim\sim M$
   4. $\sim W$ / $\sim T$

★(13) 1. $R \supset (G \vee \sim A)$
   2. $(G \vee \sim A) \supset \sim S$
   3. $G \supset S$
   4. R / $\sim A$

(14) 1. $(L \equiv N) \supset C$
   2. $(L \equiv N) \vee (P \supset \sim E)$
   3. $\sim E \supset C$
   4. $\sim C$ / $\sim P$

(15) 1. $\sim J \supset [\sim A \supset (D \supset A)]$
   2. $J \vee \sim A$
   3. $\sim J$ / $\sim D$

★(16) 1. $(B \supset \sim M) \supset (T \supset \sim S)$
   2. $B \supset K$
   3. $K \supset \sim M$
   4. $\sim S \supset N$ / $T \supset N$

(17) 1. $H \vee (Q \vee F)$
   2. $R \vee (Q \supset R)$
   3. $R \vee \sim H$
   4. $\sim R$ / F

(18) 1. $\sim A \supset (B \supset \sim C)$
   2. $\sim D \supset (\sim C \supset A)$
   3. $D \vee \sim A$
   4. $\sim D$ / $\sim B$

★(19) 1. $\sim G \supset [G \vee (S \supset G)]$
   2. $(S \vee L) \supset \sim G$
   3. $S \vee L$ / L

(20) 1. $H \supset [\sim E \supset (C \supset \sim D)]$
   2. $\sim D \supset E$
   3. $E \vee H$
   4. $\sim E$ / $\sim C$

(21) 1. $\sim B \supset [(A \supset K) \supset (B \vee \sim K)]$
   2. $\sim J \supset K$
   3. $A \supset \sim J$
   4. $\sim B$ / $\sim A$

★(22) 1. $(C \supset M) \supset (N \supset P)$
   2. $(C \supset N) \supset (N \supset M)$
   3. $(C \supset P) \supset \sim M$
   4. $C \supset N$ / $\sim C$

(23) 1. $(R \supset F) \supset [(R \supset \sim G) \supset (S \supset Q)]$
   2. $(Q \supset F) \supset (R \supset Q)$
   3. $\sim G \supset F$
   4. $Q \supset \sim G$ / $S \supset F$

(24) 1. $\sim A \supset [A \vee (T \supset R)]$
   2. $\sim R \supset [R \vee (A \supset R)]$
   3. $(T \vee D) \supset \sim R$
   4. $T \vee D$ / D

★(25) 1. $\sim N \supset [(B \supset D) \supset (N \vee \sim E)]$
   2. $(B \supset E) \supset \sim N$
   3. $B \supset D$
   4. $D \supset E$ / $\sim D$

IV. Translate the following arguments into symbolic form and use the first four rules of inference to derive the conclusion of each. The letters to be used for the simple statements are given in parentheses after each exercise. Use these letters in the order in which they are listed.

★1. If the average child watches more than five hours of television per day, then either his power of imagination is improved or he becomes conditioned to expect constant excitement. The average child's power of imagination is not improved by watching television. Also, the average child does watch more than five hours of television per day. Therefore, the average child is conditioned to expect constant excitement. (*W, P, C*)

2. If a ninth planet exists, then its orbit is perpendicular to that of the other planets. Either a ninth planet is responsible for the death of the dinosaurs, or its

orbit is not perpendicular to that of the other planets. A ninth planet is not responsible for the death of the dinosaurs. Therefore, a ninth planet does not exist. (*E, O, R*)

3. If quotas are imposed on textile imports only if jobs are not lost, then the domestic textile industry will modernize only if the domestic textile industry is not destroyed. If quotas are imposed on textile imports, the domestic textile industry will modernize. The domestic textile industry will modernize only if jobs are not lost. Therefore, if quotas are imposed on textile imports, the domestic textile industry will not be destroyed. (*Q, J, M, D*)

★4. If teachers are allowed to conduct random drug searches on students only if teachers are acting in loco parentis, then if teachers are acting in loco parentis, then students have no Fourth Amendment protections. Either students have no Fourth Amendment protections or if teachers are allowed to conduct random drug searches on students, then teachers are acting in loco parentis. It is not the case that students have no Fourth Amendment protections. Therefore, teachers are not allowed to conduct random drug searches on students. (*R, L, F*)

5. Either funding for nuclear fusion will be cut or if sufficiently high temperatures are achieved in the laboratory, nuclear fusion will become a reality. Either the supply of hydrogen fuel is limited, or if nuclear fusion becomes a reality, the world's energy problems will be solved. Funding for nuclear fusion will not be cut. Furthermore, the supply of hydrogen fuel is not limited. Therefore, if sufficiently high temperatures are achieved in the laboratory, the world's energy problems will be solved. (*C, H, R, S, E*)

6. Either the continents are not subject to drift or if Antarctica was always located in the polar region, then it contains no fossils of plants from a temperate climate. If the continents are not subject to drift, then Antarctica contains no fossils of plants from a temperate climate. But it is not the case that Antarctica contains no fossils of plants from a temperate climate. Therefore, Antarctica was not always located in the polar region. (*D, L, F*)

★7. If terrorists take more hostages, then terrorist demands will be met if and only if the media give full coverage to terrorist acts. Either the media will voluntarily limit the flow of information or if the media will recognize they are being exploited by terrorists, they will voluntarily limit the flow of information. Either the media will recognize they are being exploited by terrorists or terrorists will take more hostages. The media will not voluntarily limit the flow of information. Therefore, terrorist demands will be met if and only if the media give full coverage to terrorist acts. (*H, D, A, V, R*)

8. Either we take recycling seriously or we will be buried in garbage. If we incinerate our garbage only if our health is jeopardized, then we do not take recycling seriously. If our landfills are becoming exhausted, then if we incinerate our garbage, then toxic ash will be produced. If toxic ash is produced, then our health is jeopardized. Our landfills are becoming exhausted. Therefore, we will be buried in garbage. (*R, B, I, H, L, T*)

9. If the drug interdiction program is strengthened only if cocaine becomes more readily available, then either the number of addicts is decreasing or the war on

drugs is failing. If the drug interdiction program is strengthened, then smugglers will shift to more easily concealable drugs. If smugglers shift to more easily concealable drugs, then cocaine will become more readily available. Furthermore, the number of addicts is not decreasing. Therefore, the war on drugs is failing. (D, C, N, W, S)

★10. If the death penalty is not cruel and unusual punishment, then either it is cruel and unusual punishment or if society is justified in using it, then it will deter other criminals. If the death penalty is cruel and unusual punishment, then it is both cruel and unusual and its use degrades society as a whole. It is not the case that both the death penalty is cruel and unusual and its use degrades society as a whole. Furthermore, the death penalty will not deter other criminals. Therefore, society is not justified in using the death penalty. (C, J, D, U)

7.2 Rules of Implication II

Four additional rules of implication are listed here. Constructive dilemma should be familiar from Chapter 6. The other three are new.*

5. Constructive dilemma (CD):

$$(p \supset q) \cdot (r \supset s)$$
$$\underline{p \lor r}$$
$$q \lor s$$

6. Simplification (Simp):

$$\underline{p \cdot q}$$
$$p$$

7. Conjunction (Conj):

$$p$$
$$\underline{q}$$
$$p \cdot q$$

8. Addition (Add):

$$\underline{p}$$
$$p \lor q$$

Like the previous four rules, these are fairly easy to understand, but if there is any doubt about them their validity may be proven by means of a truth table.

Constructive dilemma can be understood as involving two *modus ponens* steps. The first premise states that if we have *p* then we have *q*, and if we have *r* then we have *s*. But since, by the second premise, we do have either *p* or *r*, it follows by *modus ponens* that we have either *q* or *s*. Constructive dilemma is the only form of dilemma that will be included as a rule of inference. By the rule of transposition, which will be presented in Section 7.4, any argument that is a substitution instance of the destructive dilemma form can be easily converted into a substitution instance of constructive dilemma. Destructive dilemma, therefore, is not needed as a rule of inference.

7

These arguments are both instances of **constructive dilemma** (CD)	
$\sim M \lor N$	$[(K \supset T) \supset (A \cdot B)] \cdot [(H \supset P) \supset (A \cdot C)]$
$(\sim M \supset S) \cdot (N \supset \sim T)$	$(K \supset T) \lor (H \supset P)$
$S \lor \sim T$	$(A \cdot B) \lor (A \cdot C)$

*Some texts include a rule called *absorption* by which the statement form $p \supset (q \cdot p)$ is deduced from $p \supset q$. This rule is necessary only if conditional proof is not presented. This text opts in favor of conditional proof, to be presented shortly.

Simplification states that if two propositions are given as true on a single line, then each of them is true separately. According to the strict interpretation of the simplification rule, only the left-hand conjunct may be stated in the conclusion. Once the commutativity rule for conjunction has been presented, however (see Section 7.3), we will be justified in replacing a statement such as $H \cdot K$ with $K \cdot H$. Once we do this, the K will appear on the left, and the appropriate conclusion is K.

These arguments are all instances of **simplification** (Simp)

$$\frac{\sim F \cdot (U \equiv E)}{\sim F} \qquad \frac{(M \vee T) \cdot (S \supset R)}{(M \vee T)} \qquad \frac{[(X \supset Z) \cdot M] \cdot (G \supset H)}{[(X \supset Z) \cdot M]}$$

Conjunction states that two propositions—for example, H and K—asserted separately on different lines may be conjoined on a single line. The two propositions may be conjoined in whatever order we choose (either $H \cdot K$ or $K \cdot H$) without appeal to the commutativity rule for conjunction.

These arguments are all instances of **conjunction** (Conj)

$$\frac{\sim E}{\sim E \cdot \sim G} \qquad \frac{C \supset M}{(C \supset M) \cdot (D \supset N)} \qquad \frac{R \supset (H \cdot T)}{[R \supset (H \cdot T)] \cdot [K \supset (H \cdot O)]}$$

Addition states that whenever a proposition is asserted on a line by itself it may be joined disjunctively with any proposition we choose. In other words, if G is asserted to be true by itself, it follows that $G \vee H$ is true. This may appear somewhat puzzling at first, but once one realizes that $G \vee H$ is a much weaker statement than G by itself, the puzzlement should disappear. The new proposition must, of course, always be joined disjunctively (not conjunctively) to the given proposition. If G is stated on a line by itself, we are *not* justified in writing $G \cdot H$ as a consequence of addition.

These arguments are all instances of **addition** (Add)

$$\frac{S}{S \vee \sim T} \qquad \frac{C \cdot D}{(C \cdot D) \vee (K \cdot \sim P)} \qquad \frac{W \equiv Z}{(W \equiv Z) \vee [A \supset (M \supset O)]}$$

The use of these four rules may now be illustrated. Consider the following argument form:

1. $A \supset B$
2. $(B \vee C) \supset (D \cdot E)$
3. A / D

As usual, we begin by looking for the conclusion in the premises. D appears in the consequent of the second premise, which we can obtain via simplification if we first obtain *B* ∨ *C*. This expression as such does not appear in the premises, but from lines 1 and 3 we see that we can obtain *B* by itself via *modus ponens*. Having obtained *B*, we can get *B* ∨ *C* via addition. The proof has now been thought through and can be written out as follows:

1. $A \supset B$
2. $(B \lor C) \supset (D \cdot E)$
3. A / D
4. B 1, 3, MP
5. $B \lor C$ 4, Add
6. $D \cdot E$ 2, 5, MP
7. D 6, Simp

Another example:

1. $K \supset L$
2. $(M \supset N) \cdot S$
3. $N \supset T$
4. $K \lor M$ / $L \lor T$

Seeing that *L* ∨ *T* does not appear as such in the premises, we look for the separate components. Finding *L* and *T* as the consequents of two distinct conditional statements causes us to think that the conclusion can be obtained via constructive dilemma. If a constructive dilemma can be set up, it will need a disjunctive statement as its second premise, and such a statement appears on line 4. Furthermore, each of the components of this statement, *K* and *M*, appears as the antecedent of a conditional statement, exactly as they both should for a dilemma. The only statement that is missing now is *M* ⊃ *T*. Inspecting line 2 we see that we can obtain *M* ⊃ *N* via simplification, and putting this together with line 3 gives us *M* ⊃ *T* via hypothetical syllogism. The completed proof may now be written out:

1. $K \supset L$
2. $(M \supset N) \cdot S$
3. $N \supset T$
4. $K \lor M$ / $L \lor T$
5. $M \supset N$ 2, Simp
6. $M \supset T$ 3, 5, HS
7. $(K \supset L) \cdot (M \supset T)$ 1, 6, Conj
8. $L \lor T$ 4, 7, CD

Another example:

1. $\sim M \cdot N$
2. $P \supset M$
3. $Q \cdot R$
4. $(\sim P \cdot Q) \supset S$ / $S \lor T$

When we look for *S* ∨ *T* in the premises we find *S* in the consequent of line 4 but no *T* at all. This signals an important principle: Whenever the conclusion of an argument contains a letter not found in the premises, addition must be used to introduce the missing letter. Addition is the *only* rule of inference that can introduce new letters. To introduce *T* by addition, however, we must first obtain *S* on a line by itself. *S* can be obtained from line 4 via *modus ponens* if we first obtain ~*P* • *Q*. This, in turn, can be gotten via conjunction, but first ~*P* and *Q* must be obtained individually on separate lines. *Q* can be obtained from line 3 via simplification and ~*P* from line 2 via *modus tollens*, but the latter step requires that we first obtain ~*M* on a line by itself. Since this can be gotten from line 1 via simplification, the proof is now complete. It may be written out as follows:

1. ~*M* • *N*		
2. *P* ⊃ *M*		
3. *Q* • *R*		
4. (~*P* • *Q*) ⊃ *S*	/ *S* v *T*	
5. ~*M*	1, Simp	
6. ~*P*	2, 5, MT	
7. *Q*	3, Simp	
8. ~*P* • *Q*	6, 7, Conj	
9. *S*	4, 8, MP	
10. *S* v *T*	9, Add	

Addition is used together with disjunctive syllogism to derive the conclusion of arguments having inconsistent premises. As we saw in Chapter 6, such arguments are always valid. The procedure is illustrated as follows:

1. *S*		
2. ~*S*	/ *T*	
3. *S* v *T*	1, Add	
4. *T*	2, 3, DS	

With arguments of this sort the conclusion is always introduced via addition and then separated via disjunctive syllogism. Since addition can be used to introduce any letter or arrangement of letters we choose, it should be clear from this example that inconsistent premises validly entail any conclusion whatever.

To complete this presentation of the eight rules of implication, let us consider some of the typical ways in which they are *misapplied*. Examples are as follows:

1. *A* ⊃ (*B* ⊃ *C*)	
2. *B*	
3. *C*	1, 2, MP (invalid—*B* ⊃ *C* must first be obtained on a line by itself)

1. *P* v (*S* • *T*)	
2. *S*	1, Simp (invalid—*S* • *T* must first be obtained on a line by itself)

1. *K*	
2. *K* • *L*	1, Add (invalid—the correct form of addition is "*K* v *L*")

1. *M* v *N*	
2. *M*	1, Simp (invalid—simplification is possible only with a conjunctive premise; line 1 is a disjunction)

1. *G* ⊃ *H*	
2. *G* ⊃ (*H* v *J*)	1, Add (improper—*J* must be added to the whole line, not just to the consequent: (*G* ⊃ *H*) v *J*

1. $(W \supset X) \supset Y$
2. $\sim X$

3. $\sim W$ 1, 2, MT (invalid—$W \supset X$ must first be obtained on a line by itself)

1. $L \supset M$
2. $L \supset N$

3. $M \cdot N$ 1, 2, Conj (invalid—M and N must first be obtained on lines by themselves)

1. $\sim(P \cdot Q)$
2. $\sim P$ 1, Simp (invalid—parentheses must be removed first)

1. $\sim(P \vee Q)$
2. $\sim P$

3. Q 1, 2, DS (invalid—parentheses must be removed first)

The use of addition in the $G \supset H$ example is called "improper" because the letter that is added is not added to the whole line. It turns out, however, that even though the addition rule is not correctly applied here, the inference is still valid. Hence, this inference is not called "invalid," as the others are. As for the last two examples, a rule will be presented in the next section (De Morgan's rule) that will allow us to remove parentheses preceded by negation signs. But even after the parentheses have been removed from these examples, the inferences remain invalid.

Like the previous section, this one ends with a few strategies for applying the last four rules of implication:

Strategy 6: If the conclusion contains a letter that appears in a conjunctive statement in the premises, consider obtaining that letter via simplification:

1. $A \supset B$
2. $C \cdot B$
3. $C \supset A$ / C
4. C 2, Simp

Strategy 7: If the conclusion is a conjunctive statement, consider obtaining it via conjunction by first obtaining the individual conjuncts:

1. $A \supset C$
2. B
3. $\sim C$ / $B \cdot \sim C$
4. $B \cdot \sim C$ 2, 3, Conj

Strategy 8: If the conclusion is a disjunctive statement, consider obtaining it via constructive dilemma or addition:

1. $(A \supset B) \cdot (C \supset D)$
2. $B \supset C$
3. $A \vee C$ / $B \vee D$
4. $B \vee D$ 1, 3, CD

1. $A \vee C$
2. B
3. $C \supset D$ / $B \vee D$
4. $B \vee D$ 2, Add

7

Strategy 9: If the conclusion contains a letter not found in the premises, addition *must* be used to introduce that letter. (See the second example under Strategy 8.)

Strategy 10: Conjunction can be used to set up constructive dilemma:

1. $A \supset B$
2. $C \supset D$
3. $A \lor C$ / $B \lor D$
4. $(A \supset B) \cdot (C \supset D)$ 1, 2, Conj
5. $B \lor D$ 3, 4, CD

EXERCISE 7.2

I. For each of the following lists of premises, derive the indicated conclusion and complete the justification. In problems 4 and 8 you can add any statement you choose.

★(1) 1. $S \lor H$
      2. $B \cdot E$
      3. $R \supset G$
      4. _____ _____, Simp

(2) 1. $(N \supset T) \cdot (F \supset Q)$
      2. $(N \supset R) \lor (F \supset M)$
      3. $N \lor F$
      4. _____ _____, CD

(3) 1. D
      2. W
      3. _____ _____, Conj

★(4) 1. H
      2. _____ _____, Add

(5) 1. $R \cdot (N \lor K)$
      2. $(G \cdot T) \lor S$
      3. $(Q \cdot C) \supset (J \cdot L)$
      4. _____ _____, Simp

(6) 1. $\sim R \lor P$
      2. $(P \supset \sim D) \cdot (\sim R \supset S)$
      3. $(\sim R \supset A) \cdot (P \supset \sim N)$
      4. _____ _____, CD

★(7) 1. $(Q \lor K) \cdot \sim B$
      2. $(M \cdot R) \supset D$
      3. $(W \cdot S) \lor (G \cdot F)$
      4. _____ _____, Simp

(8) 1. $E \cdot G$
      2. _____ _____, Add

(9) 1. $\sim B$
      2. $F \lor N$
      3. _____ _____, Conj

★(10) 1. $S \lor \sim C$
 2. $(S \supset \sim L) \cdot (\sim C \supset M)$
 3. $(\sim N \supset S) \cdot (F \supset \sim C)$
 4. _____ ____, CD

II. In the following symbolized arguments, derive the line needed to obtain the conclusion (last line), and supply the justification for both lines.

★(1) 1. $G \supset N$
 2. $G \cdot K$
 3. _____ ____
 4. $G \lor T$ ____

(2) 1. $\sim A$
 2. $A \lor E$
 3. _____ ____
 4. $\sim A \cdot E$ ____

(3) 1. $B \supset N$
 2. $B \lor K$
 3. $K \supset R$
 4. _____ ____
 5. $N \lor R$ ____

★(4) 1. T
 2. $T \supset G$
 3. $(T \lor U) \supset H$
 4. _____ ____
 5. H ____

(5) 1. $S \supset E$
 2. $E \lor (S \cdot P)$
 3. $\sim E$
 4. _____ ____
 5. S ____

(6) 1. N
 2. $N \supset F$
 3. $(N \supset A) \cdot (F \supset C)$
 4. _____ ____
 5. $A \lor C$ ____

★(7) 1. J
 2. $\sim L$
 3. $F \supset L$
 4. _____ ____
 5. $\sim F \cdot J$ ____

(8) 1. $(E \supset B) \cdot (Q \supset N)$
 2. $K \supset E$
 3. $B \supset K$
 4. _____ ____
 5. $E \supset K$ ____

(9) 1. $G \lor N$
 2. $\sim G$
 3. $\sim G \supset (H \cdot R)$
 4. _____ ____
 5. H ____

★(10) 1. M
 2. $(M \cdot E) \supset D$
 3. E
 4. _____ ____
 5. D ____

III. Use the first eight rules of inference to derive the conclusions of the following symbolized arguments:

★(1) 1. $\sim M \supset Q$
 2. $R \supset \sim T$
 3. $\sim M \lor R$ / $Q \lor \sim T$

(2) 1. $N \supset (D \cdot W)$
 2. $D \supset K$
 3. N / $N \cdot K$

(3) 1. $E \supset (A \cdot C)$
 2. $A \supset (F \cdot E)$
 3. E / F

★(4) 1. $(H \lor \sim B) \supset R$
 2. $(H \lor \sim M) \supset P$
 3. H / $R \cdot P$

(5) 1. $G \supset (S \cdot T)$
     2. $(S \lor T) \supset J$
     3. G / J

(6) 1. $(L \lor T) \supset (B \cdot G)$
     2. $L \cdot (K \equiv R)$ / $L \cdot B$

★(7) 1. $(\sim F \lor X) \supset (P \lor T)$
     2. $F \supset P$
     3. $\sim P$ / T

(8) 1. $(N \supset B) \cdot (O \supset C)$
     2. $Q \supset (N \lor O)$
     3. Q / $B \lor C$

(9) 1. $(U \lor W) \supset (T \supset R)$
     2. $U \cdot H$
     3. $\sim R \cdot \sim J$ / $U \cdot \sim T$

★(10) 1. $(D \lor E) \supset (G \cdot H)$
     2. $G \supset \sim D$
     3. $D \cdot F$ / M

(11) 1. $(B \lor F) \supset (A \supset G)$
     2. $(B \lor E) \supset (G \supset K)$
     3. $B \cdot \sim H$ / $A \supset K$

(12) 1. $(P \supset R) \supset (M \supset P)$
     2. $(P \lor M) \supset (P \supset R)$
     3. $P \lor M$ / $R \lor P$

★(13) 1. $(C \supset N) \cdot E$
     2. $D \lor (N \supset D)$
     3. $\sim D$ / $\sim C \lor P$

(14) 1. $F \supset (\sim T \cdot A)$
     2. $(\sim T \lor G) \supset (H \supset T)$
     3. $F \cdot O$ / $\sim H \cdot \sim T$

(15) 1. $(\sim S \lor B) \supset (S \lor K)$
     2. $(K \lor \sim D) \supset (H \supset S)$
     3. $\sim S \cdot W$ / $\sim H$

★(16) 1. $(C \lor \sim G) \supset (\sim P \cdot L)$
     2. $(\sim P \cdot C) \supset (C \supset D)$
     3. $C \cdot \sim R$ / $D \lor R$

(17) 1. $[A \lor (K \cdot J)] \supset (\sim E \cdot \sim F)$
     2. $M \supset [A \cdot (P \lor R)]$
     3. $M \cdot U$ / $\sim E \cdot A$

(18) 1. $\sim H \supset (\sim T \supset R)$
     2. $H \lor (E \supset F)$
     3. $\sim T \lor E$
     4. $\sim H \cdot D$ / $R \lor F$

★(19) 1. $(U \cdot \sim\sim P) \supset Q$
     2. $\sim O \supset U$
     3. $\sim P \supset O$
     4. $\sim O \cdot T$ / Q

(20) 1. $(M \lor N) \supset (F \supset G)$
     2. $D \supset \sim C$
     3. $\sim C \supset B$
     4. $M \cdot H$
     5. $D \lor F$ / $B \lor G$

(21) 1. $(F \cdot M) \supset (S \lor T)$
     2. $(\sim S \lor A) \supset F$
     3. $(\sim S \lor B) \supset M$
     4. $\sim S \cdot G$ / T

★(22) 1. $(\sim K \cdot \sim N) \supset$
          $[(\sim P \supset K) \cdot (\sim R \supset G)]$
     2. $K \supset N$
     3. $\sim N \cdot B$
     4. $\sim P \lor \sim R$ / G

(23) 1. $(\sim A \lor D) \supset (B \supset F)$
     2. $(B \lor C) \supset (A \supset E)$
     3. $A \lor B$
     4. $\sim A$ / $E \lor F$

(24) 1. $(J \supset K) \cdot (\sim O \supset \sim P)$
     2. $(L \supset J) \cdot (\sim M \supset \sim O)$
     3. $\sim K \supset (L \lor \sim M)$
     4. $\sim K \cdot G$ / $\sim P$

★(25) 1. $(\sim M \cdot \sim N) \supset [(\sim M \lor H) \supset (K \cdot L)]$
     2. $\sim M \cdot (C \supset D)$
     3. $\sim N \cdot (F \equiv G)$ / $K \cdot \sim N$

(26) 1. $(P \lor S) \supset (E \supset F)$
     2. $(P \lor T) \supset (G \supset H)$
     3. $(P \lor U) \supset (E \lor G)$
     4. P / $F \lor H$

(27) 1. $(S \supset Q) \cdot (Q \supset \sim S)$
     2. $S \lor Q$
     3. $\sim Q$ / $P \cdot R$

★(28) 1. $(D \supset B) \cdot (C \supset D)$
     2. $(B \supset D) \cdot (E \supset C)$
     3. $B \lor E$ / $D \lor B$

(29) 1. $(R \supset H) \cdot (S \supset I)$
     2. $(\sim H \cdot \sim L) \supset (R \lor S)$
     3. $\sim H \cdot (K \supset T)$
     4. $H \lor \sim L$ / $I \lor M$

(30) 1. $(W \cdot X) \supset (Q \lor R)$
    2. $(S \lor F) \supset (Q \lor W)$
    3. $(S \lor G) \supset (\sim Q \supset X)$
    4. $Q \lor S$
    5. $\sim Q \cdot H$ / R

IV. Translate the following arguments into symbolic form and use the first eight rules of inference to derive the conclusion of each. Use the letters in the order in which they are listed.

★1. If topaz is harder than quartz, then it will scratch quartz and also feldspar. Topaz is harder than quartz and it is also harder than calcite. Therefore, either topaz will scratch quartz or it will scratch corundum. (T, Q, F, C, O)

2. If clear-cutting continues in primary forests and the Endangered Species Act is not repealed, then either the Endangered Species Act will be repealed or thousands of animal species will become extinct. Clear-cutting continues in primary forests. The Endangered Species Act will not be repealed. Therefore, thousands of animal species will become extinct. (C, E, T)

3. If the rate at which rubidium becomes strontium or the rate at which potassium becomes argon are accurate indicators of age, then rocks from Greenland are 3.8 billion years old or rocks from the moon are 4.6 billion years old. The rate at which rubidium becomes strontium and the rate at which uranium becomes lead are accurate indicators of age. If rocks from Greenland are 3.8 billion years old, then the earth was formed more than 3.8 billion years ago; also, if rocks from the moon are 4.6 billion years old, then the earth was formed 4.6 billion years ago. If either the earth was formed more than 3.8 billion years ago or 4.6 billion years ago, then the creationists are wrong. Therefore, the creationists are wrong. (R, P, G, M, U, E, F, C)

★4. Either animals are mere mechanisms or they feel pain. If either animals feel pain or they have souls, then they have a right not to be subjected to needless pain and humans have a duty not to inflict needless pain on them. It is not the case that animals are mere mechanisms. Therefore, animals have a right not to be subjected to needless pain. (M, P, S, R, D)

5. If half the nation suffers from depression, then if either the insurance companies have their way or the psychiatrists have their way, then everyone will be taking antidepressant drugs. If either half the nation suffers from depression or sufferers want a real cure, then it is not the case that everyone will be taking antidepressant drugs. Half the nation suffers from depression. Therefore, it is not the case that either the insurance companies or the psychiatrists will have their way. (H, I, P, E, W)

6. If either parents get involved in their children's education or the school year is lengthened, then if the children learn phonics, their reading will improve and if they are introduced to abstract concepts earlier, their math will improve. If either parents get involved in their children's education or nebulous subjects are dropped from the curriculum, then either the children will learn phonics or they will be introduced to abstract concepts earlier. Parents will get involved

in their children's education, and writing lessons will be integrated with other subjects. Therefore, either the children's reading or their math will improve. (*P, S, L, R, I, M, N, W*)

★7. If either manufacturers will not concentrate on producing a superior product or they will not market their product abroad, then if they will not concentrate on producing a superior product, then the trade deficit will worsen. Either manufacturers will concentrate on producing a superior product or the trade deficit will not worsen. Manufacturers will not concentrate on producing a superior product. Therefore, today's business managers lack imagination. (*C, M, T, B*)

8. If either medical fees or malpractice awards escape restrictions, then health care costs will soar and millions of poor will go uninsured. If the lawyers get their way, then malpractice awards will escape restrictions. If the doctors get their way, then medical fees will escape restrictions. Either the doctors or the lawyers will get their way, and insurance companies will resist reform. Therefore, health care costs will soar. (*F, A, H, P, L, D, I*)

9. If we are less than certain the human fetus is a person, then we must give it the benefit of the doubt. If we are certain the human fetus is a person, then we must accord it the right to live. If either we must give the fetus the benefit of the doubt or accord it the right to live, then we are not less than certain the fetus is human and it is not merely a part of the mother's body. Either we are less than certain the human fetus is a person or we are certain about it. If we are certain the human fetus is a person, then abortion is immoral. Therefore, abortion is immoral. (*L, G, C, A, M, I*)

★10. If the assassination of terrorist leaders violates civilized values and also is not effective in the long run, then if it prevents terrorist atrocities, then it is effective in the long run. If the assassination of terrorist leaders violates civilized values, then it is not effective in the long run. The assassination of terrorist leaders violates civilized values and is also illegal. If the assassination of terrorist leaders is not effective in the long run, then either it prevents terrorist atrocities or it justifies acts of revenge by terrorists. Therefore, the assassination of terrorist leaders justifies acts of revenge by terrorists and also is not effective in the long run. (*V, E, P, I, J*)

7.3   Rules of Replacement I

Unlike the rules of implication, which are basic argument forms, the ten **rules of replacement** are expressed in terms of pairs of logically equivalent statement forms, either of which can replace the other in a proof sequence. To express these rules, a new symbol, called a **double colon** (::), is used to designate logical equivalence. This symbol is a *metalogical* symbol in that it makes an assertion not about things but about symbolized statements: It asserts that the expressions on either side of it have the same truth value regardless of the truth values of their components. Underlying the use of the rules of replacement is an **axiom of replacement,** which asserts that within the context of a proof, logically equivalent expressions may replace each other. The first five rules of replacement are as follows:

9. De Morgan's rule (DM):

$$\sim(p \cdot q) :: (\sim p \vee \sim q)$$
$$\sim(p \vee q) :: (\sim p \cdot \sim q)$$

10. Commutativity (Com):

$$(p \vee q) :: (q \vee p)$$
$$(p \cdot q) :: (q \cdot p)$$

11. Associativity (Assoc):

$$[p \vee (q \vee r)] :: [(p \vee q) \vee r]$$
$$[p \cdot (q \cdot r)] :: [(p \cdot q) \cdot r]$$

12. Distribution (Dist):

$$[p \cdot (q \vee r)] :: [(p \cdot q) \vee (p \cdot r)]$$
$$[p \vee (q \cdot r)] :: [(p \vee q) \cdot (p \vee r)]$$

13. Double negation (DN):

$$p :: \sim\sim p$$

De Morgan's rule (named after the nineteenth-century logician Augustus De Morgan) was discussed in Section 6.1 in connection with translation. There it was pointed out that "Not both *p* and *q*" is logically equivalent to "Not *p* or not *q*," and that "Not either *p* or *q*" is logically equivalent to "Not *p* and not *q*." When applying De Morgan's rule, one should keep in mind that it holds only for conjunctive and disjunctive statements (not for conditionals or biconditionals). The rule may be summarized as follows: When moving a tilde inside or outside a set of parentheses, a dot switches with a wedge and vice versa.

Commutativity asserts that the truth value of a conjunction or disjunction is unaffected by the order in which the components are listed. In other words, the component statements may be commuted, or switched for one another, without affecting the truth value. The validity of this rule should be immediately apparent. You may recall from arithmetic that the commutativity rule also applies to addition and multiplication and asserts, for example, that 3 + 5 equals 5 + 3, and that 2 × 3 equals 3 × 2. However, it does *not* apply to division; 2 ÷ 4 does not equal 4 ÷ 2. A similar lesson applies in logic: The commutativity rule applies only to conjunction and disjunction; it does *not* apply to implication.

Associativity states that the truth value of a conjunctive or disjunctive statement is unaffected by the placement of parentheses when the same operator is used throughout. In other words, the way in which the component propositions are grouped, or associated with one another, can be changed without affecting the truth value. The validity of this rule is quite easy to see, but if there is any doubt about it, it may be readily checked by means of a truth table. You may recall that the associativity rule also applies to addition and multiplication and asserts, for example, that 3 + (5 + 7) equals (3 + 5) + 7, and that 2 × (3 × 4) equals (2 × 3) × 4. But it does *not* apply to division: (8 ÷ 4) ÷ 2 does not equal 8 ÷ (4 ÷ 2). Analogously, in logic, the associativity rule applies only to conjunctive and disjunctive statements; it does *not* apply to conditional statements. Also note, when applying this rule, that the order of the letters remains unchanged; only the placement of the parentheses changes.

Distribution, like De Morgan's rule, applies only to conjunctive and disjunctive statements. When a proposition is conjoined to a disjunctive statement in parentheses or disjoined to a conjunctive statement in parentheses, the rule allows us to put that proposition together with each of the components inside the parentheses, and also to go in the reverse direction. In the first form of the rule, a statement is distributed through a disjunction, and in the second form, through a conjunction. While the rule may not be immediately obvious, it is easy to remember: The operator that is at first outside the parentheses goes inside, and the operator that is at first inside the parentheses goes outside. Note also how distribution differs from commutativity and associativity. The latter two rules apply only when the *same* operator (either a dot or a wedge) is used throughout a statement. Distribution applies when a dot and a wedge appear *together* in a statement.

Double negation is fairly obvious and needs little explanation. The rule states simply that pairs of tildes immediately adjacent to one another may be either deleted or introduced without affecting the truth value of the statement.

There is an important difference between the rules of implication, treated in the first two sections of this chapter, and the rules of replacement. The rules of implication derive their name from the fact that each is a simple argument form in which the premises imply the conclusion. To be applicable in natural deduction, certain lines in a proof must be interpreted as substitution instances of the argument form in question. Stated another way, the rules of implication are applicable only to *whole lines* in a proof. For example, step 3 in the following proof is not a legitimate application of *modus ponens*, because the first premise in the *modus ponens* rule is applied to only a *part* of line 1.

> 1. $A \supset (B \supset C)$
> 2. B
> 3. C 1, 2, MP (incorrect)

The rules of replacement, on the other hand, are not rules of implication but rules of logical equivalence. Since, by the axiom of replacement, logically equivalent statement forms can always replace one another in a proof sequence, the rules of replacement can be applied either to a whole line or to any part of a line. Step 2 in the following proof is a quite legitimate application of De Morgan's rule, even though the rule is applied only to the consequent of line 1:

> 1. $S \supset {\sim}(T \cdot U)$
> 2. $S \supset ({\sim}T \vee {\sim}U)$ 1, DM (valid)

Another way of viewing this distinction is that the rules of implication are "one-way" rules, whereas the rules of replacement are "two-way" rules. The rules of implication allow us to proceed only from the premise lines of a rule to the conclusion line, but the rules of replacement allow us to replace either side of an equivalence expression with the other side.

Application of the first five rules of replacement may now be illustrated. Consider the following argument:

> 1. $A \supset {\sim}(B \cdot C)$
> 2. $A \cdot C$ / ${\sim}B$

Examining the premises, we find *B* in the consequent of line 1. This leads us to suspect that the conclusion can be obtained via *modus ponens*. If this is correct, the tilde would then have to be taken inside the parentheses via De Morgan's rule and the resulting ~*C* eliminated by disjunctive syllogism. The following completed proof indicates that this strategy yields the anticipated result:

1. $A \supset \sim(B \cdot C)$
2. $A \cdot C$ / ~*B*
3. A 2, Simp
4. $\sim(B \cdot C)$ 1, 3, MP
5. $\sim B \vee \sim C$ 4, DM
6. $C \cdot A$ 2, Com
7. C 6, Simp
8. $\sim\sim C$ 7, DN
9. $\sim C \vee \sim B$ 5, Com
10. $\sim B$ 8, 9, DS

The rationale for line 6 is to get *C* on the left side so that it can be separated via simplification. Similarly, the rationale for line 9 is to get ~*C* on the left side so that it can be eliminated via disjunctive syllogism. Line 8 is required because, strictly speaking, the negation of ~*C* is ~~*C*—not simply *C*. Thus, *C* must be replaced with ~~*C* to set up the disjunctive syllogism. If your instructor permits it, you can combine commutativity and double negation with other inferences on a single line, as the following shortened proof illustrates. However, we will avoid this practice throughout the remainder of the book.

1. $A \supset \sim(B \cdot C)$
2. $A \cdot C$ / ~*B*
3. A 2, Simp
4. $\sim(B \cdot C)$ 1, 3, MP
5. $\sim B \vee \sim C$ 4, DM
6. C 2, Com, Simp
7. $\sim B$ 5, 6, Com, DN, DS

Another example:

1. $D \cdot (E \vee F)$
2. $\sim D \vee \sim F$ / $D \cdot E$

The conclusion requires that we get *D* and *E* together. Inspection of the first premise suggests distribution as the first step in achieving this. The completed proof is as follows:

1. $D \cdot (E \vee F)$
2. $\sim D \vee \sim F$ / $D \cdot E$
3. $(D \cdot E) \vee (D \cdot F)$ 1, Dist
4. $(D \cdot F) \vee (D \cdot E)$ 3, Com
5. $\sim(D \cdot F)$ 2, DM
6. $D \cdot E$ 4, 5, DS

Some proofs require that we use distribution in the reverse manner. Consider this argument:

1. $(G \cdot H) \vee (G \cdot J)$
2. $(G \vee K) \supset L$ / L

The conclusion can be obtained from line 2 via *modus ponens* if we first obtain $G \vee K$ on a line by itself. Since K does not occur in the first premise at all, it must be introduced by addition. Doing this requires in turn that we obtain G on a line by itself. Distribution applied to line 1 provides the solution:

1. $(G \cdot H) \vee (G \cdot J)$
2. $(G \vee K) \supset L$ / L
3. $G \cdot (H \vee J)$ 1, Dist
4. G 3, Simp
5. $G \vee K$ 4, Add
6. L 2, 5, MP

Application of the associativity rule is illustrated in the next proof:

1. $M \vee (N \vee O)$
2. $\sim O$ / M ∨ N
3. $(M \vee N) \vee O$ 1, Assoc
4. $O \vee (M \vee N)$ 3, Com
5. $M \vee N$ 2, 4, DS

Before O can be eliminated via disjunctive syllogism from line 1, it must be moved over to the left side. Associativity and commutativity together accomplish this objective.

In some arguments the attempt to "find" the conclusion in the premises is not immediately successful. When confronted with such an argument, one should often begin by "deconstructing" the conclusion using the rules of replacement. In other words, one should first apply the rules of replacement to the conclusion to see how it is put together. After this is done, how the premises entail the conclusion may be evident. This procedure is justified by the fact that the rules of replacement are two-way rules. As a result, after the conclusion is deconstructed, it can be derived by using the same rules in reverse order. Here is an example of such an argument:

1. $K \supset (F \vee B)$
2. $G \cdot K$ / (F · G) ∨ (B · G)

If immediate inspection does not reveal how the conclusion should be derived, we may begin by applying the rules of replacement to the conclusion. The form of the conclusion suggests the distribution rule, but first we must use commutativity to move the G's to the left-hand side. The deconstruction proceeds as follows:

$(F \cdot G) \vee (B \cdot G)$
$(G \cdot F) \vee (B \cdot G)$ Com
$(G \cdot F) \vee (G \cdot B)$ Com
$G \cdot (F \vee B)$ Dist

Now we see that if we can obtain *G* on a line by itself, and *F* ∨ *B* on a line by itself, we can combine them on a single line via the conjunction rule. We can then obtain the conclusion via distribution and commutativity. Inspection of the premises reveals that *G* can be obtained from line 2 of the premises by simplification, and *F* ∨ *B* can be obtained from line 1 by *modus ponens*. The completed proof is as follows:

1. $K \supset (F \lor B)$
2. $G \cdot K$ / $(F \cdot G) \lor (B \cdot G)$
3. G 2, Simp
4. $K \cdot G$ 2, Com
5. K 4, Simp
6. $F \lor B$ 1, 5, MP
7. $G \cdot (F \lor B)$ 3, 6, Conj
8. $(G \cdot F) \lor (G \cdot B)$ 7, Dist
9. $(F \cdot G) \lor (G \cdot B)$ 8, Com
10. $(F \cdot G) \lor (B \cdot G)$ 9, Com

Here are some strategies for applying the first five rules of replacement. Most of them show how these rules may be used together with other rules.

Strategy 11: Conjunction can be used to set up De Morgan's rule:

1. $\sim A$
2. $\sim B$
3. $\sim A \cdot \sim B$ 1, 2, Conj
4. $\sim (A \lor B)$ 3, DM

Strategy 12: Constructive dilemma can be used to set up De Morgan's rule:

1. $(A \supset \sim B) \cdot (C \supset \sim D)$
2. $A \lor C$
3. $\sim B \lor \sim D$ 1, 2, CD
4. $\sim (B \cdot D)$ 3, DM

Strategy 13: Addition can be used to set up De Morgan's rule:

1. $\sim A$
2. $\sim A \lor \sim B$ 1, Add
3. $\sim (A \cdot B)$ 2, DM

Strategy 14: Distribution can be used in two ways to set up disjunctive syllogism:

1. $(A \lor B) \cdot (A \lor C)$
2. $\sim A$
3. $A \lor (B \cdot C)$ 1, Dist
4. $B \cdot C$ 2, 3, DS

1. $A \cdot (B \lor C)$
2. $\sim (A \cdot B)$
3. $(A \cdot B) \lor (A \cdot C)$ 1, Dist
4. $A \cdot C$ 2, 3, DS

7

Strategy 15: Distribution can be used in two ways to set up simplification:

1. $A \lor (B \cdot C)$
2. $(A \lor B) \cdot (A \lor C)$ 1, Dist
3. $A \lor B$ 2, Simp

1. $(A \cdot B) \lor (A \cdot C)$
2. $A \cdot (B \lor C)$ 1, Dist
3. A 2, Simp

Strategy 16: If inspection of the premises does not reveal how the conclusion should be derived, consider using the rules of replacement to deconstruct the conclusion. (See the previous example.)

EXERCISE 7.3

I. For each of the following lists of premises, derive the indicated conclusion and complete the justification. For double negation, avoid the occurrence of triple tildes.

★(1) 1. $\sim(E \supset H)$
     2. $\sim(N \lor G)$
     3. $\sim A \lor D$
     4. _____ ____, DM

(2) 1. $G \supset (N \supset K)$
     2. $R \lor (D \supset F)$
     3. $S \cdot (T \lor U)$
     4. _____ ____, Dist

(3) 1. $M \lor (G \lor T)$
     2. $P \cdot (S \supset N)$
     3. $D \cdot (R \lor K)$
     4. _____ ____, Assoc

★(4) 1. $B \supset W$
     2. $G \equiv F$
     3. $S \cdot A$
     4. _____ ____, Com

(5) 1. $\sim\sim R \lor T$
     2. $\sim N \lor \sim B$
     3. $\sim A \supset \sim H$
     4. _____ ____, DN

(6) 1. $(F \lor N) \lor (K \cdot D)$
     2. $(H \cdot Z) \lor (H \cdot W)$
     3. $(P \supset H) \lor (P \supset N)$
     4. _____ ____, Dist

★(7) 1. $\sim(G \cdot \sim Q)$
     2. $\sim(K \equiv \sim B)$
     3. $\sim T \supset \sim F$
     4. _____ ____, DM

7

(8) 1. $G \supset (\sim L \supset T)$
   2. $L \equiv (\sim R \supset \sim C)$
   3. $J \supset (S \lor \sim N)$
   4. _____ ____, Com

(9) 1. $S \supset (M \supset D)$
   2. $(K \cdot G) \lor B$
   3. $(E \cdot H) \cdot Q$
   4. _____ ____, Assoc

★(10) 1. $\sim R \lor \sim P$
   2. $\sim F \supset \sim W$
   3. $G \cdot \sim A$
   4. _____ ____, DM

(11) 1. $\sim B \lor E$
   2. $\sim E \cdot \sim A$
   3. $\sim C \supset \sim R$
   4. _____ ____, DN

(12) 1. $\sim G \cdot (S \supset A)$
   2. $\sim S \supset (B \cdot K)$
   3. $\sim Q \lor (T \cdot R)$
   4. _____ ____, Dist

★(13) 1. $F \supset (\sim S \lor M)$
   2. $H \supset (\sim L \cdot \sim D)$
   3. $N \supset (\sim G \supset \sim C)$
   4. _____ ____, DM

(14) 1. $F \supset (P \supset \sim E)$
   2. $C \lor (S \cdot \sim B)$
   3. $M \cdot (R \cdot \sim T)$
   4. _____ ____, Assoc

(15) 1. $(D \lor \sim K) \cdot (D \lor \sim W)$
   2. $(S \lor \sim Z) \lor (P \lor \sim T)$
   3. $(Q \supset \sim N) \cdot (Q \supset \sim F)$
   4. _____ ____, Dist

II. In the following symbolized arguments, derive the line needed to obtain the conclusion (last line), and supply the justification for both lines.

★(1) 1. $K \lor C$
   2. $\sim C$
   3. _____ ____
   4. K ____

(2) 1. $G \supset (R \lor N)$
   2. $\sim R \cdot \sim N$
   3. _____ ____
   4. $\sim G$ ____

(3) 1. $H \cdot T$
   2. _____ ____
   3. T ____

★(4) 1. $(L \cdot S) \cdot F$
   2. _____ ____
   3. L ____

(5) 1. $\sim B \lor K$
   2. _____ ____
   3. $\sim (B \cdot \sim K)$ ____

(6) 1. $C \supset {\sim}A$
   2. A
   3. _____ ____
   4. ${\sim}C$ ____

★(7) 1. $(D \cdot M) \vee (D \cdot N)$
   2. _____ ____
   3. D ____

(8) 1. $(U \vee T) \supset R$
   2. $T \vee U$
   3. _____ ____
   4. R ____

(9) 1. ${\sim}L \vee M$
   2. L
   3. _____ ____
   4. M ____

★(10) 1. $D \vee (N \cdot H)$
   2. _____ ____
   3. $D \vee N$ ____

(11) 1. $(K \vee E) \cdot (K \vee G)$
   2. ${\sim}K$
   3. _____ ____
   4. $E \cdot G$ ____

(12) 1. $(N \supset T) \cdot (F \supset Q)$
   2. $F \vee N$
   3. _____ ____
   4. $T \vee Q$ ____

★(13) 1. $(M \vee G) \vee T$
   2. ${\sim}M$
   3. _____ ____
   4. $G \vee T$ ____

(14) 1. $({\sim}A \supset T) \cdot ({\sim}S \supset K)$
   2. ${\sim}(A \cdot S)$
   3. _____ ____
   4. $T \vee K$ ____

(15) 1. ${\sim}R$
   2. _____ ____
   3. ${\sim}(R \cdot T)$ ____

III. Use the first thirteen rules of inference to derive the conclusions of the following symbolized arguments.

★(1) 1. $({\sim}M \supset P) \cdot ({\sim}N \supset Q)$
   2. ${\sim}(M \cdot N)$ / $P \vee Q$

(2) 1. ${\sim}S$ / ${\sim}(F \cdot S)$

(3) 1. $J \vee (K \cdot L)$
   2. ${\sim}K$ / J

★(4) 1. ${\sim}(N \cdot T)$
   2. T / ${\sim}N$

(5) 1. $H \supset {\sim}A$
   2. A / ${\sim}(H \vee {\sim}A)$

(6) 1. $R \supset {\sim}B$
   2. $D \vee R$
   3. B / D

★(7) 1. $T \supset (B \vee E)$
   2. ${\sim}E \cdot T$ / B

(8) 1. $(O \vee M) \supset S$
   2. ${\sim}S$ / ${\sim}M$

(9) 1. $Q \vee (L \vee C)$
   2. ${\sim}C$ / $L \vee Q$

★(10) 1. $(K \cdot H) \vee (K \cdot L)$
   2. ${\sim}L$ / H

(11) 1. ${\sim}({\sim}E \cdot {\sim}N) \supset T$
   2. $G \supset (N \vee E)$ / $G \supset T$

(12) 1. $H \cdot (C \cdot T)$
   2. ${\sim}({\sim}F \cdot T)$ / F

★(13) 1. $(E \cdot I) \vee (M \cdot U)$
   2. ${\sim}E$ / ${\sim}(E \vee {\sim}M)$

(14) 1. ${\sim}(J \vee K)$
   2. $B \supset K$
   3. $S \supset B$ / ${\sim}S \cdot {\sim}J$

(15) 1. $(G \cdot H) \vee (M \cdot G)$
   2. $G \supset (T \cdot A)$ / A

★(16) 1. $(Q \cdot N) \vee (N \cdot T)$
   2. $(Q \vee C) \supset {\sim}N$ / T

(17) 1. ${\sim}(U \vee R)$
   2. $({\sim}R \vee N) \supset (P \cdot H)$
   3. $Q \supset {\sim}H$ / ${\sim}Q$

(18) 1. ${\sim}(F \cdot A)$
   2. ${\sim}(L \vee {\sim}A)$
   3. $D \supset (F \vee L)$ / ${\sim}D$

★(19) 1. $[(I \vee M) \vee G] \supset {\sim}G$
   2. $M \vee G$ / M

(20) 1. $E \supset {\sim}B$
   2. $U \supset {\sim}C$
   3. ${\sim}({\sim}E \cdot {\sim}U)$ / ${\sim}(B \cdot C)$

(21) 1. ~(K ∨ F)
     2. ~F ⊃ (K ∨ C)
     3. (G ∨ C) ⊃ ~H   / ~(K ∨ H)

★(22) 1. S ∨ (I • ~J)
     2. S ⊃ ~R
     3. ~J ⊃ ~Q   / ~(R • Q)

(23) 1. (J ∨ F) ∨ M
     2. (J ∨ M) ⊃ ~P
     3. ~F   / ~(F ∨ P)

(24) 1. (K • P) ∨ (K • Q)
     2. P ⊃ ~K   / Q ∨ T

★(25) 1. E ∨ ~(D ∨ C)
     2. (E ∨ ~D) ⊃ C   / E

(26) 1. A • (F • L)
     2. A ⊃ (U ∨ W)
     3. F ⊃ (U ∨ X)   / U ∨ (W • X)

(27) 1. (T • R) ⊃ P
     2. (~P • R) • G
     3. (~T ∨ N) ⊃ H   / H

★(28) 1. P ∨ (I • L)
     2. (P ∨ I) ⊃ ~(L ∨ C)
     3. (P • ~C) ⊃ (E • F)   / F ∨ D

(29) 1. B ∨ (S • N)
     2. B ⊃ ~S
     3. S ⊃ ~N   / B ∨ W

(30) 1. (~M ∨ E) ⊃ (S ⊃ U)
     2. (~Q ∨ E) ⊃ (U ⊃ H)
     3. ~(M ∨ Q)   / S ⊃ H

★(31) 1. (~R ∨ D) ⊃ ~(F • G)
     2. (F • R) ⊃ S
     3. F • ~S   / ~(S ∨ G)

(32) 1. ~Q ⊃ (C • B)
     2. ~T ⊃ (B • H)
     3. ~(Q • T)   / B

(33) 1. ~(A • G)
     2. ~(A • E)
     3. G ∨ E   / ~(A • F)

★(34) 1. (M • N) ∨ (O • P)
     2. (N ∨ O) ⊃ ~P   / N

(35) 1. (T • K) ∨ (C • E)
     2. K ⊃ ~E
     3. E ⊃ ~C   / T • K

IV. Translate the following arguments into symbolic form and use the first thirteen rules of inference to derive the conclusion of each. Use the translation letters in the order in which they are listed.

★1. Either health care costs are skyrocketing and they are attributable to greedy doctors, or health care costs are skyrocketing and they are attributable to greedy hospitals. If health care costs are skyrocketing, then both the government should intercede and health care may have to be rationed. Therefore, health care costs are skyrocketing and health care may have to be rationed. (S, D, H, I, R)

2. Either the ancient Etruscans were experienced city planners and they invented the art of writing or they were highly skilled engineers and they invented the art of writing. If the ancient Etruscans were bloodthirsty numskulls (as scholars once thought), they did not invent the art of writing. Therefore, the ancient Etruscans were not bloodthirsty numskulls (as scholars once thought). (C, I, H, B)

3. It is not the case that either the earth's molten core is stationary or that it contains no iron. If it is not the case that both the earth's molten core is stationary and has a regular topography, then either the earth's core contains no iron or the direction of the earth's magnetic field is subject to change. Therefore, the direction of the earth's magnetic field is subject to change. (S, C, R, D)

★4. Either mosquito genes can be cloned or mosquitoes will become resistant to all insecticides and the incidence of encephalitis will increase. If either mosquito genes can be cloned or the incidence of encephalitis increases, then mosquitoes will not become resistant to all insecticides. Therefore, either mosquito genes can be cloned or mosquitoes will multiply out of control. (G, R, E, M)

5. Protein engineering will prove to be as successful as genetic engineering, and new enzymes will be developed for producing food and breaking down industrial wastes. If protein engineering proves to be as successful as genetic engineering and new enzymes are developed for breaking down industrial wastes, then it is not the case that new enzymes will be developed for producing food but not medicines. Therefore, protein engineering will prove to be as successful as genetic engineering and new enzymes will be developed for producing medicines. (E, P, B, M)

6. If workers have a fundamental right to a job, then unemployment will be virtually nonexistent but job redundancy will become a problem. If workers have no fundamental right to a job, then production efficiency will be maximized but job security will be jeopardized. Workers either have or do not have a fundamental right to a job. Therefore, either unemployment will be virtually nonexistent or production efficiency will be maximized. (F, U, R, P, S)

★7. If Japan is to reduce its huge trade surplus, then it must either convince its citizens to spend more or it must move its manufacturing facilities to other countries. It is not the case that Japan will either increase its imports or convince its citizens to spend more. Furthermore, it is not the case that Japan will either allow foreign construction companies to compete on an equal footing or move its manufacturing facilities to other countries. Therefore, Japan will not reduce its huge trade surplus. (R, C, M, I, A)

8. If women are by nature either passive or uncompetitive, then it is not the case that there are lawyers who are women. If men are by nature either insensitive or without the ability to nurture, then it is not the case that there are kindergarten teachers who are men. There are lawyers who are women and kindergarten teachers who are men. Therefore, it is not the case that either women by nature are uncompetitive or men by nature are without the ability to nurture. (P, U, L, I, W, K)

9. It is not the case that either the sun's interior rotates faster than its surface or Einstein's general theory of relativity is wrong. If the sun's interior does not rotate faster than its surface and eccentricities in the orbit of Mercury can be explained by solar gravitation, then Einstein's general theory of relativity is wrong. Therefore, eccentricities in the orbit of Mercury cannot be explained by solar gravitation. (S, E, M)

★10. Either school dropout programs are not as effective as they could be, or they provide basic thinking skills and psychological counseling to their students. Either school dropout programs are not as effective as they could be, or they adequately prepare their students for getting a job and working effectively with others. Either school dropout programs do not provide psychological counseling to their students or they do not provide adequate preparation for working effectively with others. Therefore, school dropout programs are not as effective as they could be. (E, B, P, G, W)

The remaining five rules of replacement are as follows:

14. Transposition (Trans):
  $(p \supset q) :: (\sim q \supset \sim p)$

15. Material implication (Impl):
  $(p \supset q) :: (\sim p \lor q)$

16. Material equivalence (Equiv):
  $(p \equiv q) :: [(p \supset q) \cdot (q \supset p)]$
  $(p \equiv q) :: [(p \cdot q) \lor (\sim p \cdot \sim q)]$

17. Exportation (Exp):
  $[(p \cdot q) \supset r] :: [p \supset (q \supset r)]$

18. Tautology (Taut):
  $p :: (p \lor p)$
  $p :: (p \cdot p)$

Transposition asserts that the antecedent and consequent of a conditional statement may switch places if and only if tildes are inserted before both or tildes are removed from both. The rule is fairly easy to understand and is easily proved by a truth table.

Material implication is less obvious than transposition, but it can be illustrated by substituting actual statements in place of the letters. For example, the statement "If you bother me, then I'll punch you in the nose" ($B \supset P$) is logically equivalent to "Either you stop bothering me or I'll punch you in the nose" ($\sim B \lor P$). The rule states that a horseshoe may be replaced by a wedge sign if the left-hand component is negated, and the reverse replacement is allowed if a tilde is deleted from the left-hand component.

Material equivalence has two formulations. The first is the same as the definition of material equivalence given in Section 6.1. The second formulation is easy to remember through recalling the two ways in which $p \equiv q$ may be true. Either p and q are both true or p and q are both false. This, of course, is the meaning of $[(p \cdot q) \lor (\sim p \cdot \sim q)]$.

Exportation is also fairly easy to understand. It asserts that the statement "If we have p, then if we have q we have r" is logically equivalent to "If we have both p and q, we have r." As an illustration of this rule, the statement "If Bob told the truth, then if Sue told the truth, then Jim is guilty" is logically equivalent to "If Bob and Sue told the truth, then Jim is guilty."

Tautology, the last rule introduced in this section, is obvious. Its effect is to eliminate redundancy in disjunctions and conjunctions.

The following proofs illustrate the use of these five rules.

1. $\sim A$ / $A \supset B$

In this argument the conclusion contains a letter not found in the premise. Obviously, addition must be used to introduce the B. The material implication rule completes the proof:

1. $\sim A$ / $A \supset B$
2. $\sim A \lor B$ 1, Add
3. $A \supset B$ 2, Impl

Here is another example:

1. $F \supset G$
2. $F \lor G$ / G

To derive the conclusion of this argument, some method must be found to link the two premises together and eliminate the F. Hypothetical syllogism provides the solution, but first the second premise must be converted into a conditional. Here is the proof:

1. $F \supset G$
2. $F \lor G$ / G
3. $\sim\sim F \lor G$ 2, DN
4. $\sim F \supset G$ 3, Impl
5. $\sim F \supset \sim\sim G$ 4, DN
6. $\sim G \supset F$ 5, Trans
7. $\sim G \supset G$ 1, 6, HS
8. $\sim\sim G \lor G$ 7, Impl
9. $G \lor G$ 8, DN
10. G 9, Taut

Another example:

1. $J \supset (K \supset L)$ / $K \supset (J \supset L)$

The conclusion can be obtained by simply rearranging the components of the single premise. Exportation provides the simplest method:

1. $J \supset (K \supset L)$ / $K \supset (J \supset L)$
2. $(J \cdot K) \supset L$ 1, Exp
3. $(K \cdot J) \supset L$ 2, Com
4. $K \supset (J \supset L)$ 3, Exp

Another example:

1. $M \supset N$
2. $M \supset O$ / $M \supset (N \cdot O)$

As with the F and G example, some method must be found to link the two premises together. In this case, however, hypothetical syllogism will not work. The solution lies in setting up a distribution step:

1. $M \supset N$
2. $M \supset O$ / $M \supset (N \cdot O)$
3. $\sim M \lor N$ 1, Impl
4. $\sim M \lor O$ 2, Impl
5. $(\sim M \lor N) \cdot (\sim M \lor O)$ 3, 4, Conj
6. $\sim M \lor (N \cdot O)$ 5, Dist
7. $M \supset (N \cdot O)$ 6, Impl

Another example:

1. $P \supset Q$
2. $R \supset (S \cdot T)$
3. $\sim R \supset \sim Q$
4. $S \supset (T \supset P)$ / $P \equiv R$

The conclusion is a biconditional, and there are only two ways that a biconditional can be obtained from such premises—namely, via the two formulations of the material equivalence rule. The fact that the premises are all conditional statements suggests the first formulation of this rule. Accordingly, we must try to obtain $P \supset R$ and $R \supset P$. Again, the fact that the premises are themselves conditionals suggests hypothetical syllogism to accomplish this. Premises 1 and 3 can be used to set up one hypothetical syllogism; premises 2 and 4 provide the other. Here is the proof:

1.	$P \supset Q$	
2.	$R \supset (S \cdot T)$	
3.	$\sim R \supset \sim Q$	
4.	$S \supset (T \supset P)$	/ $P \equiv R$
5.	$Q \supset R$	3, Trans
6.	$P \supset R$	1, 5, HS
7.	$(S \cdot T) \supset P$	4, Exp
8.	$R \supset P$	2, 7, HS
9.	$(P \supset R) \cdot (R \supset P)$	6, 8, Conj
10.	$P \equiv R$	9, Equiv

As we saw in Section 7.3, if it is not readily apparent how the conclusion should be derived, we can use the rules of replacement to deconstruct the conclusion. This will usually provide insight on how best to proceed. Again, this technique is justified because the rules of replacement are two-way rules. As a result, they can be applied in reverse order in the completed proof. Here is an example:

1.	$\sim S \supset K$	
2.	$S \supset (R \vee M)$	/ $\sim R \supset (\sim M \supset K)$

In deconstructing the conclusion, the form of the conclusion suggests exportation, and the result of this step suggests De Morgan's rule. For further insight, we apply transposition to the latter step. Each step follows from the one preceding it:

$\sim R \supset (\sim M \supset K)$	
$(\sim R \cdot \sim M) \supset K$	Exp
$\sim (R \vee M) \supset K$	DM
$\sim K \supset \sim\sim (R \vee M)$	Trans
$\sim K \supset (R \vee M)$	DN

Now, examining the premises in light of the deconstruction suggests that we begin by setting up a hypothetical syllogism. This will give us the last step in the deconstruction. We can then obtain the conclusion by repeating the deconstruction steps in reverse order. The completed proof is as follows:

1.	$\sim S \supset K$	
2.	$S \supset (R \vee M)$	/ $\sim R \supset (\sim M \supset K)$
3.	$\sim K \supset \sim\sim S$	1, Trans
4.	$\sim K \supset S$	3, DN
5.	$\sim K \supset (R \vee M)$	2, 4, HS
6.	$\sim (R \vee M) \supset \sim\sim K$	5, Trans
7.	$\sim (R \vee M) \supset K$	6, DN
8.	$(\sim R \cdot \sim M) \supset K$	7, DM
9.	$\sim R \supset (\sim M \supset K)$	8, Exp

Here is another example:

1. $K \supset M$
2. $L \supset M$ / $(K \lor L) \supset M$

In deconstructing the conclusion, the form of the premises suggests that we use some procedure that will combine M separately with K and L. This, in turn, suggests distribution; but before we can use distribution, we must eliminate the horseshoe via implication. The deconstruction is as follows:

$(K \lor L) \supset M$	
$\sim(K \lor L) \lor M$	Impl
$(\sim K \cdot \sim L) \lor M$	DM
$M \lor (\sim K \cdot \sim L)$	Com
$(M \lor \sim K) \cdot (M \lor \sim L)$	Dist
$(\sim K \lor M) \cdot (M \lor \sim L)$	Com
$(\sim K \lor M) \cdot (\sim L \lor M)$	Com
$(K \supset M) \cdot (\sim L \lor M)$	Impl
$(K \supset M) \cdot (L \supset M)$	Impl

Now, examining the premises in light of the last line of the deconstruction suggests that we begin by joining the premises together via the conjunction rule. The conclusion can then be obtained by reversing the steps of the deconstruction:

1.	$K \supset M$	
2.	$L \supset M$	/ $(K \lor L) \supset M$
3.	$(K \supset M) \cdot (L \supset M)$	1, 2, Conj
4.	$(\sim K \lor M) \cdot (L \supset M)$	3, Impl
5.	$(\sim K \lor M) \cdot (\sim L \lor M)$	4, Impl
6.	$(M \lor \sim K) \cdot (\sim L \lor M)$	5, Com
7.	$(M \lor \sim K) \cdot (M \lor \sim L)$	6, Com
8.	$M \lor (\sim K \cdot \sim L)$	7, Dist
9.	$(\sim K \cdot \sim L) \lor M$	8, Com
10.	$\sim(K \lor L) \lor M$	9, DM
11.	$(K \lor L) \supset M$	10, Impl

Note that whenever we use this strategy of working backward from the conclusion, the rules of replacement are the *only* rules we may use. We may not use the rules of implication, because these rules are one-way rules.

This section ends with some strategies that show how the last five rules of replacement can be used together with various other rules.

Strategy 17: Material implication can be used to set up hypothetical syllogism:

1.	$\sim A \lor B$	
2.	$\sim B \lor C$	
3.	$A \supset B$	1, Impl
4.	$B \supset C$	2, Impl
5.	$A \supset C$	3, 4, HS

Strategy 18: Exportation can be used to set up *modus ponens:*

1. $(A \cdot B) \supset C$
2. A
3. $A \supset (B \supset C)$ 1, Exp
4. $B \supset C$ 2, 3, MP

Strategy 19: Exportation can be used to set up *modus tollens:*

1. $A \supset (B \supset C)$
2. $\sim C$
3. $(A \cdot B) \supset C$ 1, Exp
4. $\sim(A \cdot B)$ 2, 3, MT

Strategy 20: Addition can be used to set up material implication:

1. A
2. $A \vee \sim B$ 1, Add
3. $\sim B \vee A$ 2, Com
4. $B \supset A$ 3, Impl

Strategy 21: Transposition can be used to set up hypothetical syllogism:

1. $A \supset B$
2. $\sim C \supset \sim B$
3. $B \supset C$ 2, Trans
4. $A \supset C$ 1, 3, HS

Strategy 22: Transposition can be used to set up constructive dilemma:

1. $(A \supset B) \cdot (C \supset D)$
2. $\sim B \vee \sim D$
3. $(\sim B \supset \sim A) \cdot (C \supset D)$ 1, Trans
4. $(\sim B \supset \sim A) \cdot (\sim D \supset \sim C)$ 3, Trans
5. $\sim A \vee \sim C$ 2, 4, CD

Strategy 23: Constructive dilemma can be used to set up tautology:

1. $(A \supset C) \cdot (B \supset C)$
2. $A \vee B$
3. $C \vee C$ 1, 2, CD
4. C 3, Taut

Strategy 24: Material implication can be used to set up tautology:

1. $A \supset \sim A$
2. $\sim A \vee \sim A$ 1, Impl
3. $\sim A$ 2, Taut

Strategy 25: Material implication can be used to set up distribution:

1. $A \supset (B \cdot C)$
2. $\sim A \vee (B \cdot C)$ 1, Impl
3. $(\sim A \vee B) \cdot (\sim A \vee C)$ 2, Dist

I. For each of the following lists of premises, derive the indicated conclusion and complete the justification.

★(1) 1. $H \vee F$
2. $N \vee {\sim}S$
3. ${\sim}G \vee Q$
4. _____ ____, Impl

(2) 1. $R \supset (S \supset N)$
2. $T \supset (U \vee M)$
3. $K \cdot (L \supset W)$
4. _____ ____, Exp

(3) 1. $G \equiv R$
2. $H \supset P$
3. ${\sim}F \vee T$
4. _____ ____, Trans

★(4) 1. $(B \supset N) \cdot (N \supset B)$
2. $(R \vee F) \cdot (F \vee R)$
3. $(K \supset C) \vee (C \supset K)$
4. _____ ____, Equiv

(5) 1. $E \vee {\sim}E$
2. $A \vee A$
3. $G \cdot {\sim}G$
4. _____ ____, Taut

(6) 1. $S \vee {\sim}M$
2. ${\sim}N \cdot {\sim}T$
3. ${\sim}L \supset Q$
4. _____ ____, Trans

★(7) 1. ${\sim}C \supset {\sim}F$
2. $D \vee {\sim}P$
3. ${\sim}R \cdot Q$
4. _____ ____, Impl

(8) 1. $E \supset (R \cdot Q)$
2. $(G \cdot N) \supset Z$
3. $(S \supset M) \supset P$
4. _____ ____, Exp

(9) 1. $(D \cdot H) \vee ({\sim}D \cdot {\sim}H)$
2. $(F \supset J) \cdot ({\sim}F \supset {\sim}J)$
3. $(N \vee T) \cdot ({\sim}N \vee {\sim}T)$
4. _____ ____, Equiv

★(10) 1. $L \supset (A \supset A)$
2. $K \supset (R \vee {\sim}R)$
3. $S \supset (G \cdot G)$
4. _____ ____, Taut

(11) 1. $K \cdot (S \vee B)$
    2. $\sim F \supset \sim J$
    3. $\sim E \vee \sim M$
    4. _____ ____, Trans

(12) 1. $H \supset (K \cdot J)$
    2. $(N \vee E) \supset B$
    3. $C \supset (H \supset A)$
    4. _____ ____, Exp

★(13) 1. $(A \supset \sim C) \cdot (C \supset \sim A)$
    2. $(W \supset \sim T) \cdot (\sim T \supset W)$
    3. $(M \supset \sim E) \cdot (\sim M \supset E)$
    4. _____ ____, Equiv

(14) 1. $(\sim K \vee M) \equiv S$
    2. $T \vee (F \cdot G)$
    3. $R \equiv (N \cdot \sim H)$
    4. _____ ____, Impl

(15) 1. $(S \vee S) \supset D$
    2. $K \supset (T \cdot \sim T)$
    3. $(Q \supset Q) \supset M$
    4. _____ ____, Taut

II. In the following symbolized arguments, derive the line needed to obtain the conclusion (last line), and supply the justification for both lines.

★(1) 1. $\sim J \vee M$
    2. $M \supset B$
    3. _____ ____
    4. $J \supset B$ ____

(2) 1. $(J \cdot F) \supset N$
    2. J
    3. _____ ____
    4. $F \supset N$ ____

(3) 1. $C \supset A$
    2. $A \supset C$
    3. _____ ____
    4. $C \equiv A$ ____

★(4) 1. $(G \supset K) \cdot (T \supset K)$
    2. $G \vee T$
    3. _____ ____
    4. K ____

(5) 1. $(G \supset B) \cdot (\sim C \supset \sim H)$
    2. $G \vee H$
    3. _____ ____
    4. $B \vee C$ ____

(6) 1. $J \supset (M \supset Q)$
    2. $J \cdot M$
    3. _____ ____
    4. Q ____

★(7) 1. $H \supset (\sim C \vee R)$
    2. _____ ____
    3. $(H \cdot C) \supset R$ ____

(8) 1. $\sim G \supset \sim T$
    2. $G \supset N$
    3. _____ ____
    4. $T \supset N$ ____

(9) 1. $K \supset (A \supset F)$
    2. $\sim F$
    3. _____ ____
    4. $\sim (K \cdot A)$ ____

★(10) 1. $H \supset \sim H$
    2. _____ ____
    3. $\sim H$ ____

(11) 1. $\sim S$
    2. _____ ____
    3. $S \supset K$ ____

(12) 1. $M \supset (M \supset D)$
    2. _____ ____
    3. $M \supset D$ ____

★(13) 1. $(N \supset A) \cdot (\sim N \supset \sim A)$
    2. _____ ____
    3. $N \equiv A$ ____

(14) 1. $E \cdot R$
    2. _____ ____
    3. $E \equiv R$ ____

(15) 1. $Q \supset (\sim W \supset \sim G)$
    2. _____ ____
    3. $(Q \cdot G) \supset W$ ____

III. Use the eighteen rules of inference to derive the conclusions of the following symbolized arguments.

★(1) 1. $(S \cdot K) \supset R$
    2. K / $S \supset R$

(2) 1. $T \supset (F \lor F)$
    2. $\sim(F \cdot F)$ / $\sim T$

(3) 1. $G \supset E$
    2. $H \supset \sim E$ / $G \supset \sim H$

★(4) 1. $S \equiv Q$
    2. $\sim S$ / $\sim Q$

(5) 1. $\sim N \lor P$
    2. $(N \supset P) \supset T$ / T

(6) 1. $F \supset B$
    2. $B \supset (B \supset J)$ / $F \supset J$

★(7) 1. $(B \supset M) \cdot (D \supset M)$
    2. $B \lor D$ / M

(8) 1. $Q \supset (F \supset A)$
    2. $R \supset (A \supset F)$
    3. $Q \cdot R$ / $F \equiv A$

(9) 1. $T \supset (\sim T \lor G)$
    2. $\sim G$ / $\sim T$

★(10) 1. $(B \supset G) \cdot (F \supset N)$
    2. $\sim(G \cdot N)$ / $\sim(B \cdot F)$

(11) 1. $(J \cdot R) \supset H$
    2. $(R \supset H) \supset M$
    3. $\sim(P \lor \sim J)$ / $M \cdot \sim P$

(12) 1. T / $S \supset T$

★(13) 1. $K \supset (B \supset \sim M)$
    2. $D \supset (K \cdot M)$ / $D \supset \sim B$

(14) 1. $(O \supset C) \cdot (\sim S \supset \sim D)$
    2. $(E \supset D) \cdot (\sim E \supset \sim C)$ / $O \supset S$

(15) 1. $\sim(U \cdot W) \supset X$
    2. $U \supset \sim U$ / $\sim(U \lor \sim X)$

★(16) 1. $T \supset R$
    2. $T \supset \sim R$ / $\sim T$

(17) 1. $S \lor \sim N$
    2. $\sim S \lor Q$ / $N \supset Q$

(18) 1. $M \supset (U \supset H)$
    2. $(H \lor \sim U) \supset F$ / $M \supset F$

★(19) 1. $\sim R \lor P$
      2. $R \lor \sim P$ / $R \equiv P$

(20) 1. $\sim H \supset B$
    2. $\sim H \supset D$
    3. $\sim (B \cdot D)$ / H

(21) 1. $J \supset (G \supset L)$ / $G \supset (J \supset L)$

★(22) 1. $S \supset (L \cdot M)$
      2. $M \supset (L \supset R)$ / $S \supset R$

(23) 1. $F \supset (A \cdot K)$
    2. $G \supset (\sim A \cdot \sim K)$
    3. $F \lor G$ / $A \equiv K$

(24) 1. $(I \supset E) \supset C$
    2. $C \supset \sim C$ / I

★(25) 1. $T \supset G$
      2. $S \supset G$ / $(T \lor S) \supset G$

(26) 1. $H \supset U$ / $H \supset (U \lor T)$

(27) 1. $Q \supset (W \cdot D)$ / $Q \supset W$

★(28) 1. $P \supset (\sim E \supset B)$
      2. $\sim (B \lor E)$ / $\sim P$

(29) 1. $(G \supset J) \supset (H \supset Q)$
    2. $J \cdot \sim Q$ / $\sim H$

(30) 1. $I \lor (N \cdot F)$
    2. $I \supset F$ / F

★(31) 1. $K \equiv R$
      2. $K \supset (R \supset P)$
      3. $\sim P$ / $\sim R$

(32) 1. $C \supset (\sim L \supset Q)$
    2. $L \supset \sim C$
    3. $\sim Q$ / $\sim C$

(33) 1. $(E \supset A) \cdot (F \supset A)$
    2. $E \lor G$
    3. $F \lor \sim G$ / A

★(34) 1. $(F \cdot H) \supset N$
      2. $F \lor S$
      3. H / $N \lor S$

(35) 1. $T \supset (H \cdot J)$
    2. $(H \lor N) \supset T$ / $T \equiv H$

(36) 1. $T \supset \sim(A \supset N)$
2. $T \vee N$ / $T \equiv \sim N$

★(37) 1. $(D \supset E) \supset (E \supset D)$
2. $(D \equiv E) \supset \sim(G \cdot \sim H)$
3. $E \cdot G$ / $G \cdot H$

(38) 1. $(O \supset R) \supset S$
2. $(P \supset R) \supset \sim S$ / $\sim R$

(39) 1. $(L \vee P) \supset U$
2. $(M \supset U) \supset I$
3. P / I

★(40) 1. $A \equiv W$
2. $\sim A \vee \sim W$
3. $R \supset A$ / $\sim(W \vee R)$

(41) 1. $(S \vee T) \supset (S \supset \sim T)$
2. $(S \supset \sim T) \supset (T \supset K)$
3. $S \vee T$ / $S \vee K$

(42) 1. $G \equiv M$
2. $G \vee M$
3. $G \supset (M \supset T)$ / T

★(43) 1. $O \supset (Q \cdot N)$
2. $(N \vee E) \supset S$ / $O \supset S$

(44) 1. $H \equiv I$
2. $H \supset (I \supset F)$
3. $\sim(H \vee I) \supset F$ / F

★(45) 1. $P \supset A$
2. $Q \supset B$ / $(P \vee Q) \supset (A \vee B)$

IV. Translate the following arguments into symbolic form and use the eighteen rules of inference to derive the conclusion of each. Use the translation letters in the order in which they are listed.

★1. If sports shoe manufacturers decline to use kangaroo hides in their products, then Australian hunters will cease killing millions of kangaroos yearly. It is not the case that both Australian hunters will cease killing millions of kangaroos yearly and the kangaroo will not be saved from extinction. Therefore, if sports shoe manufacturers decline to use kangaroo hides in their products, then the kangaroo will be saved from extinction. (D, C, S)

2. If there is a direct correlation between what a nation spends for health care and the health of its citizens, then America has the lowest incidence of disease and the lowest mortality rates of any nation on earth. But America does not have the lowest mortality rates of any nation on earth. Therefore, there is not a direct correlation between what a nation spends for health care and the health of its citizens. (C, D, M)

3. It is not the case that strict controls exist on either the manufacture or the sale of handguns. Therefore, if strict controls exist on the sale of handguns, then the use of handguns in the commission of crimes has decreased. (*M, S, U*)

★4. If birth control devices are made available in high school clinics, then the incidence of teenage pregnancy will decrease. Therefore, if both birth control information and birth control devices are made available in high school clinics, then the incidence of teenage pregnancy will decrease. (*D, P, I*)

5. If Congress enacts a law that either establishes a religion or prohibits the free exercise of religion, then that law is unconstitutional. Therefore, if Congress enacts a law that establishes a religion, then that law is unconstitutional. (*E, P, U*)

6. If cigarette smokers are warned of the hazards of smoking and they continue to smoke, then they cannot sue tobacco companies for any resulting lung cancer or emphysema. Cigarette smokers are warned of the hazards of smoking. Therefore, if cigarette smokers continue to smoke, they cannot sue tobacco companies for any resulting lung cancer or emphysema. (*W, C, S*)

★7. If grade-school children are assigned daily homework, then their achievement level will increase dramatically. But if grade-school children are assigned daily homework, then their love for learning may be dampened. Therefore, if grade-school children are assigned daily homework, then their achievement level will increase dramatically but their love for learning may be dampened. (*G, A, L*)

8. If a superconducting particle collider is built, then the data yielded will benefit scientists of all nations and it deserves international funding. Either a superconducting particle collider will be built, or the ultimate nature of matter will remain hidden and the data yielded will benefit scientists of all nations. Therefore, the data yielded by a superconducting particle collider will benefit scientists of all nations. (*S, D, I, U*)

9. If parents are told that their unborn child has Tay-Sachs disease, then if they go ahead with the birth, then they are responsible for their child's pain and suffering. Therefore, if parents are not responsible for their child's pain and suffering, then if they go ahead with the birth, then they were not told that their unborn child had Tay-Sachs disease. (*T, G, R*)

★10. Vitamin E is an antioxidant and a useless food supplement if and only if it does not reduce heart disease. It is not the case either that vitamin E does not reduce heart disease or is not an antioxidant. Therefore, vitamin E is not a useless food supplement. (*A, U, R*)

7

7.5   Conditional Proof

Conditional proof is a method for obtaining a line in a proof sequence (either the conclusion or some intermediate line). This method frequently offers the advantage of being both shorter and simpler to use than the direct method. Moreover, some arguments have conclusions that cannot be derived by the direct method, so some form of conditional proof must be used on them. While in theory the method of conditional proof can be used to derive any line in a proof sequence, in practice it is usually reserved for obtaining lines that are expressed in the form of conditional statements. The method consists of assuming the antecedent of the required conditional statement on one line, deriving the consequent on a subsequent line, and then "discharging" this sequence of lines in a conditional statement that exactly replicates the one that was to be obtained.

Any argument whose conclusion is a conditional statement is an immediate candidate for conditional proof. Consider the following example:

1. $A \supset (B \cdot C)$
2. $(B \vee D) \supset E$ / $A \supset E$

Using the direct method to derive the conclusion of this argument would require a proof having at least twelve lines, and the precise strategy to be followed in constructing it might not be immediately obvious. Nevertheless, we need only give cursory inspection to the argument to see that the conclusion does indeed follow from the premises. The conclusion states that if we have A, we then have E. Let us suppose, for a moment, that we do have A. We could then obtain $B \cdot C$ from the first premise via *modus ponens*. Simplifying this expression we could obtain B, and from this we could get $B \vee D$ via addition. E would then follow from the second premise via *modus ponens*. In other words, if we assume that we have A, we can get E. But this is exactly what the conclusion says. Thus, we have just proved that the conclusion follows from the premises.

The method of conditional proof consists of incorporating this simple thought process into the body of a proof sequence. A conditional proof for this argument requires only eight lines and is substantially simpler than a direct proof:

1. $A \supset (B \cdot C)$
2. $(B \vee D) \supset E$ / $A \supset E$
    3. A ACP
    4. $B \cdot C$ 1, 3, MP
    5. B 4, Simp
    6. $B \vee D$ 5, Add
    7. E 2, 6, MP
8. $A \supset E$ 3–7, CP

Lines 3 through 7 are indented to indicate their hypothetical character: They all depend on the assumption introduced in line 3 via ACP (assumption for conditional proof). These lines, which constitute the conditional proof sequence, tell us that if we assume A (line 3), we can obtain E (line 7). In line 8 the conditional sequence is discharged in the conditional statement $A \supset E$, which simply reiterates the result of the conditional sequence. Since line 8 is not hypothetical, it is written adjacent to the original margin, under lines 1 and 2. A vertical line is added to the conditional sequence to emphasize the indentation.

The first step in constructing a conditional proof is to decide what should be assumed on the first line of the conditional sequence. While any statement whatsoever *can* be assumed on this line, only the right statement will lead to the desired result. The clue is always provided by the conditional statement to be obtained in the end. The antecedent of this statement is what must be assumed. For example, if the statement to be

Gottlob Frege 1848–1925

© akg-images

The German mathematician, logician, and philosopher Gottlob Frege (pronounced fray-ga) was born in Wismar, a small town in northern Germany on the Baltic Sea. His parents taught at a private girls' school, which his father had helped to found. Frege attended the local gymnasium, where he studied mathematics, and then the University of Jena, where he studied mathematics, philosophy, and chemistry. After two years he transferred to the University of Göttingen, earning a doctor's degree in mathematics at age twenty-four. He then returned to the University of Jena, where he taught until retiring in 1917. While there he married Margaret Liesburg, who bore him at least two children. The children died young, but years later the couple adopted a son, Alfred.

Frege spent his entire life analyzing the concept of number, developing theories of logic and language, and attempting to reduce arithmetic to logic. In 1879 he published the *Begriffschrift* ("Concept-script"), a work written in the tradition of Leibniz that develops a purely formal symbolic language to express any proposition in any area of human discourse. Five years later he published *Die Grundlagen der Arithmetik* ("The Foundations of Arithmetic"), a less technical work containing few symbols that outlined his goal of reducing arithmetic to logic. Then, nine years later he published Volume I of *Grundgesetze der Arithmetik* ("Basic Laws of Arithmetic"), which attempted to accomplish the first phase of this reduction.

None of these works were well received, for several reasons: They were ahead of their time, the symbolic notation of the technical works struck readers as bizarre, and they were written in German, while most of the new work in logic was being done by English speakers. In fact, the last of these works was so badly reviewed that Frege was forced to publish Volume II at his own expense. To make matters worse, in 1902, while Volume II was in proof, Frege received a letter from Bertrand Russell that left him "thunderstruck." He was later to remark that it had destroyed his entire life's work.

Basic Law V of the *Grundgesetze* provides for the creation of classes of things merely by describing the properties of their members. So Russell invited Frege to create the class of all classes that are not members of themselves, and he then asked whether this very class is a member of itself. If it is a member of itself, then it is one of those classes that are not members of themselves; but if is not a member of itself, then, again, it is one of those classes, and it is a member of itself. The derivation of this contradiction (which has come to be called Russell's paradox) meant that the axioms of the *Grundgesetze* were fatally inconsistent. Frege attempted a last-minute modification of his system, but the change proved unworkable.

Despite this setback, Frege is universally recognized today as one of the most important logicians and philosophers of all time. Single-handedly he developed quantification theory and predicate logic, and his analysis of the concept of number led to a general theory of meaning that introduced the important distinction between *Sinn* (sense) and *Beduetung* (reference). Also, his work on concept clarification initiated the current movement known as analytic philosophy.

7

obtained is $(K \cdot L) \supset M$, then $K \cdot L$ should be assumed on the first line. This line is always indented and tagged with the designation "ACP." Once the initial assumption has been made, the second step is to obtain the consequent of the desired conditional statement at the end of the conditional sequence. To do this, we simply apply the ordinary rules of inference to any previous line in the proof (including the assumed line), writing the result directly below the assumed line. The third and final step is to discharge the conditional sequence in a conditional statement. The antecedent of this conditional statement is whatever appears on the first line of the conditional sequence, and the consequent is whatever appears on the last line. For example, if $A \vee B$ is on the first line and $C \cdot D$ is on the last, the sequence is discharged by $(A \vee B) \supset (C \cdot D)$. This discharging line is always written adjacent to the original margin and is tagged with the designation "CP" (conditional proof) together with the numerals indicating the first through the last lines of the sequence.

Conditional proof can also be used to obtain a line other than the conclusion of an argument. The following proof, which illustrates this fact, incorporates two conditional sequences one after the other within the scope of a single direct proof:

1. $G \supset (H \cdot I)$	
2. $J \supset (K \cdot L)$	
3. $G \vee J$	/ $H \vee K$
4. G	ACP
5. $H \cdot I$	1, 4, MP
6. H	5, Simp
7. $G \supset H$	4–6, CP
8. J	ACP
9. $K \cdot L$	2, 8, MP
10. K	9, Simp
11. $J \supset K$	8–10, CP
12. $(G \supset H) \cdot (J \supset K)$	7, 11, Conj
13. $H \vee K$	3, 12, CD

The first conditional proof sequence gives us $G \supset H$, and the second $J \supset K$. These two lines are then conjoined and used together with line 3 to set up a constructive dilemma, from which the conclusion is obtained.

This proof sequence provides a convenient opportunity to introduce an important rule governing conditional proof. The rule states that after a conditional proof sequence has been discharged, no line in the sequence may be used as a justification for a subsequent line in the proof. If, for example, line 5 in the proof just given were used as a justification for line 9 or line 12, this rule would be violated, and the corresponding inference would be invalid. Once the conditional sequence is discharged, it is sealed off from the remaining part of the proof. The logic behind this rule is easy to understand. The lines in a conditional sequence are hypothetical in that they depend on the assumption stated in the first line. Because no mere assumption can provide any genuine support for anything, neither can any line that depends on such an assumption. When a conditional sequence is discharged, the assumption on which it rests is expressed as the antecedent of a conditional statement. This conditional statement *can* be used to support subsequent lines because it makes no claim that its antecedent is true. The conditional statement merely asserts that *if* its antecedent is true, then its consequent is true, and this, of course, is what has been established by the conditional sequence from which it is obtained.

Just as a conditional sequence can be used within the scope of a direct proof to obtain a desired statement, one conditional sequence can be used within the scope of another to obtain a desired statement. The following proof provides an example:

```
1. L ⊃ [M ⊃ (N v O)]
2. M ⊃ ~N                        / L ⊃ (~M v O)
    3. L                         ACP
    4. M ⊃ (N v O)              1, 3, MP
        5. M                     ACP
        6. N v O                 4, 5, MP
        7. ~N                    2, 5, MP
        8. O                     6, 7, DS
    9. M ⊃ O                     5–8, CP
   10. ~M v O                    9, Impl
11. L ⊃ (~M v O)                3–10, CP
```

The rule introduced in connection with the previous example applies unchanged to examples of this sort. No line in the sequence 5–8 could be used to support any line subsequent to line 9, and no line in the sequence 3–10 could be used to support any line subsequent to line 11. Lines 3 or 4 could, of course, be used to support any line in the sequence 5–8.

One final reminder regarding conditional proof is that every conditional proof must be discharged. It is absolutely improper to end a proof on an indented line. If this rule is ignored, any conclusion one chooses can be derived from any set of premises. The following invalid proof illustrates this mistake:

```
1. P                  / Q ⊃ R
    2. ~Q             ACP
    3. ~Q v R         2, Add
    4. Q ⊃ R          2, Impl
```

EXERCISE 7.5

I. Use conditional proof and the eighteen rules of inference to derive the conclusions of the following symbolized arguments. Having done so, attempt to derive the conclusions without using conditional proof.

★(1) 1. N ⊃ O
    2. N ⊃ P   / N ⊃ (O • P)

(2) 1. F ⊃ E
    2. (F • E) ⊃ R   / F ⊃ R

(3) 1. G ⊃ T
    2. (T v S) ⊃ K   / G ⊃ K

★(4) 1. (G v H) ⊃ (S • T)
    2. (T v U) ⊃ (C • D)   / G ⊃ C

(5) 1. A ⊃ ~(A v E)   / A ⊃ F

(6) 1. $J \supset (K \supset L)$
2. $J \supset (M \supset L)$
3. $\sim L$ / $J \supset \sim (K \lor M)$

★(7) 1. $M \lor (N \cdot O)$ / $\sim N \supset M$

(8) 1. $P \supset (Q \lor R)$
2. $(P \supset R) \supset (S \cdot T)$
3. $Q \supset R$ / T

(9) 1. $H \supset (I \supset N)$
2. $(H \supset \sim I) \supset (M \lor N)$
3. $\sim N$ / M

★(10) 1. $C \supset (A \cdot D)$
2. $B \supset (A \cdot E)$ / $(C \lor B) \supset A$

(11) 1. $M \supset (K \supset L)$
2. $(L \lor N) \supset J$ / $M \supset (K \supset J)$

(12) 1. $F \supset (G \cdot H)$ / $(A \supset F) \supset (A \supset H)$

★(13) 1. $R \supset B$
2. $R \supset (B \supset F)$
3. $B \supset (F \supset H)$ / $R \supset H$

(14) 1. $(F \cdot G) \equiv H$
2. $F \supset G$ / $F \equiv H$

(15) 1. $C \supset (D \lor \sim E)$
2. $E \supset (D \supset F)$ / $C \supset (E \supset F)$

★(16) 1. $Q \supset (R \supset S)$
2. $Q \supset (T \supset \sim U)$
3. $U \supset (R \lor T)$ / $Q \supset (U \supset S)$

(17) 1. $N \supset (O \cdot P)$
2. $Q \supset (R \cdot S)$ / $(P \supset Q) \supset (N \supset S)$

(18) 1. $E \supset (F \supset G)$
2. $H \supset (G \supset I)$
3. $(F \supset I) \supset (J \lor \sim H)$ / $(E \cdot H) \supset J$

★(19) 1. $P \supset [(L \lor M) \supset (N \cdot O)]$
2. $(O \lor T) \supset W$ / $P \supset (M \supset W)$

(20) 1. $A \supset [B \supset (C \cdot \sim D)]$
2. $(B \lor E) \supset (D \lor E)$ / $(A \cdot B) \supset (C \cdot E)$

II. Translate the following arguments into symbolic form, using the letters in the order in which they are listed. Then use conditional proof and the eighteen rules of inference to derive the conclusion of each. Having done so, attempt to derive the conclusion without using conditional proof.

★1. If high-tech products are exported to Russia, then domestic industries will benefit. If the Russians can effectively utilize high-tech products, then their standard of living will improve. Therefore, if high-tech products are exported to Russia and the Russians can effectively utilize them, then their standard of living will improve and domestic industries will benefit. (*H*, *D*, *U*, *S*)

2. If the police take you into custody, then if they inform you that you have the right to remain silent, then whatever you say will be used against you. If the police inform you that you have the right to remain silent, then if whatever you say will be used against you, then you should not say anything. Therefore, if the police take you into custody, then if they inform you that you have the right to remain silent, then you should not say anything. (*P, I, W, S*)

3. A doctor must disconnect a dying patient from a respirator if and only if the fact that patients are self-determining implies that the doctor must follow the patient's orders. If a dying patient refuses treatment, then the doctor must disconnect the patient from a respirator and the patient will die peacefully. Patients are self-determining. Therefore, if a dying patient refuses treatment, then the doctor must follow the patient's orders. (*D, S, F, R, P*)

★4. If jails are overcrowded, then dangerous suspects will be released on their own recognizance. If jails are overcrowded and dangerous suspects are released on their own recognizance, then crime will increase. If no new jails are built and crime increases, then innocent victims will pay the price of increased crime. Therefore, if jails are overcrowded, then if no new jails are built, then innocent victims will pay the price of increased crime. (*J, D, C, N, I*)

5. If astronauts attempt interplanetary space travel, then heavy shielding will be required to protect them from solar radiation. If massive amounts of either fuel or water are carried, then the spacecraft must be very large. Therefore, if heavy shielding is required to protect the astronauts from solar radiation only if massive amounts of fuel are carried, then if astronauts attempt interplanetary space travel, then the spacecraft must be very large. (*A, H, F, W, L*)

7.6   Indirect Proof

Indirect proof is a technique similar to conditional proof that can be used on any argument to derive either the conclusion or some intermediate line leading to the conclusion. It consists of assuming the negation of the statement to be obtained, using this assumption to derive a contradiction, and then concluding that the original assumption is false. This last step, of course, establishes the truth of the statement to be obtained. The following proof sequence uses indirect proof to derive the conclusion:

1. $(A \lor B) \supset (C \cdot D)$		
2. $C \supset {\sim}D$	/ ${\sim}A$	
3. A	AIP	
4. $A \lor B$	3, Add	
5. $C \cdot D$	1, 4, MP	
6. C	5, Simp	
7. ${\sim}D$	2, 6, MP	
8. $D \cdot C$	5, Com	
9. D	8, Simp	
10. $D \cdot {\sim}D$	7, 9, Conj	
11. ${\sim}A$	3–10, IP	

The indirect proof sequence (lines 3–10) begins by assuming the negation of the conclusion. Since the conclusion is a negated statement, it shortens the proof to assume *A* instead of ~~*A*. This assumption, which is tagged "AIP" (assumption for indirect proof), leads to a contradiction in line 10. Since any assumption that leads to a contradiction is false, the indirect sequence is discharged (line 11) by asserting the negation of the assumption made in line 3. This line is then tagged with the designation "IP" (indirect proof) together with the numerals indicating the scope of the indirect sequence from which it is obtained.

Indirect proof can also be used to derive an intermediate line leading to the conclusion. Example:

1.	$E \supset [(F \lor G) \supset (H \cdot J)]$	
2.	$E \cdot \sim(J \lor K)$	/ $\sim(F \lor K)$
3.	E	2, Simp
4.	$(F \lor G) \supset (H \cdot J)$	1, 3, MP
5.	$\sim(J \lor K) \cdot E$	2, Com
6.	$\sim(J \lor K)$	5, Simp
7.	$\sim J \cdot \sim K$	6, DM
8.	F	AIP
9.	$F \lor G$	8, Add
10.	$H \cdot J$	4, 9, MP
11.	$J \cdot H$	10, Com
12.	J	11, Simp
13.	$\sim J$	7, Simp
14.	$J \cdot \sim J$	12, 13, Conj
15.	$\sim F$	8–14, IP
16.	$\sim K \cdot \sim J$	7, Com
17.	$\sim K$	16, Simp
18.	$\sim F \cdot \sim K$	15, 17, Conj
19.	$\sim(F \lor K)$	18, DM

The indirect proof sequence begins with the assumption of *F* (line 8), leads to a contradiction (line 14), and is discharged (line 15) by asserting the negation of the assumption. One should consider indirect proof whenever a line in a proof appears difficult to obtain.

As with conditional proof, when an indirect proof sequence is discharged, no line in the sequence may be used as a justification for a subsequent line in the proof. In reference to the last proof, this means that none of the lines 8–14 could be used as a justification for any of the lines 16–19. Occasionally, this rule requires certain priorities in the derivation of lines. For example, for the purpose of deriving the contradiction, lines 6 and 7 could have been included as part of the indirect sequence. But this would not have been advisable, because line 7 is needed as a justification for line 16, which lies outside the indirect sequence. If lines 6 and 7 had been included within the indirect sequence, they would have had to be repeated after the sequence had been discharged to allow ~*K* to be obtained on a line outside the sequence.

Just as a conditional sequence may be constructed within the scope of another conditional sequence, so a conditional sequence may be constructed within the scope of an indirect sequence, and, conversely, an indirect sequence may be constructed within the scope of either a conditional sequence or another indirect sequence. The next example illustrates the use of an indirect sequence within the scope of a conditional sequence:

```
 1. L ⊃ [~M ⊃ (N • O)]
 2. ~N • P                    / L ⊃ (M • P)
    │ 3. L                    ACP
    │ 4. ~M ⊃ (N • O)         1, 3, MP
    │   │ 5. ~M               AIP
    │   │ 6. N • O            4, 5, MP
    │   │ 7. N                6, Simp
    │   │ 8. ~N               2, Simp
    │   │ 9. N • ~N           7, 8, Conj
    │ 10. ~~M                 5–9, IP
    │ 11. M                   10, DN
    │ 12. P • ~N              2, Com
    │ 13. P                   12, Simp
    │ 14. M • P               11, 13, Conj
15. L ⊃ (M • P)              3–14, CP
```

The indirect sequence (lines 5–9) is discharged (line 10) by asserting the negation of the assumption made in line 5. The conditional sequence (lines 3–14) is discharged (line 15) in the conditional statement that has the first line of the sequence as its antecedent and the last line as its consequent.

Indirect proof provides a convenient way for proving the validity of an argument having a tautology for its conclusion. In fact, the only way in which the conclusion of many such arguments can be derived is through either conditional or indirect proof.

For the following argument, indirect proof is the easier of the two:

```
 1. S                        / T v ~T
    │ 2. ~(T v ~T)           AIP
    │ 3. ~T • ~~T            2, DM
 4. ~~(T v ~T)               2–3, IP
 5. T v ~T                   4, DN
```

Here is another example of an argument having a tautology as its conclusion. In this case, since the conclusion is a conditional statement, conditional proof is the easier alternative:

```
 1. S                        / T ⊃ T
    │ 2. T                   ACP
    │ 3. T v T               2, Add
    │ 4. T                   3, Taut
 5. T ⊃ T                    2–4, CP
```

The similarity of indirect proof to conditional proof may be illustrated by returning to the first example presented in this section. In the proof that follows, conditional proof—not indirect proof—is used to obtain the conclusion:

```
1. (A ∨ B) ⊃ (C • D)
2. C ⊃ ~D                          / ~A
     3. A                          ACP
     4. A ∨ B                      3, Add
     5. C • D                      1, 4, MP
     6. C                          5, Simp
     7. ~D                         2, 6, MP
     8. D • C                      5, Com
     9. D                          8, Simp
    10. D ∨ ~A                     9, Add
    11. ~A                         7, 10, DS
12. A ⊃ ~A                         3–11, CP
13. ~A ∨ ~A                        12, Impl
14. ~A                             13, Taut
```

This example illustrates how a conditional proof can be used to derive the conclusion of *any* argument, whether or not the conclusion is a conditional statement. Simply begin by assuming the negation of the conclusion, derive contradictory statements on separate lines, and use these lines to set up a disjunctive syllogism yielding the negation of the assumption as the last line of the conditional sequence. Then, discharge the sequence and use tautology to obtain the negation of the assumption outside the sequence.

Indirect proof can be viewed as a variety of conditional proof in that it amounts to a modification of the way in which the indented sequence is discharged, resulting in an overall shortening of the proof for many arguments. The indirect proof for the argument just given is repeated as follows, with the requisite changes noted in the margin:

```
1. (A ∨ B) ⊃ (C • D)
2. C ⊃ ~D                          / ~A
     3.  A                         AIP
     4.  A ∨ B                     3, Add
     5.  C • D                     1, 4, MP
     6.  C                         5, Simp
     7.  ~D                        2, 6, MP
     8.  D • C                     5, Com
     9.  D                         8, Simp
    10.  D • ~D                    7, 9, Conj  ⎫
11. ~A                             3–10, IP    ⎬ ──────── changed
                                               ⎭
```

The reminder at the end of the previous section regarding conditional proof pertains to indirect proof as well: It is essential that every indirect proof be discharged. No proof can be ended on an indented line. If this rule is ignored, indirect proof, like conditional proof, can produce any conclusion whatsoever. The following invalid proof illustrates such a mistake:

```
1. P                               / Q
     2. Q                          AIP
     3. Q ∨ Q                      2, Add
     4. Q                          3, Taut
```

I. Use either indirect proof or conditional proof (or both) and the eighteen rules of inference to derive the conclusions of the following symbolized arguments. Having done so, attempt to derive the conclusions without using indirect proof or conditional proof.

★(1) 1. $(S \lor T) \supset \sim S$ / $\sim S$

(2) 1. $(K \supset K) \supset R$
    2. $(R \lor M) \supset N$ / N

(3) 1. $(C \cdot D) \supset E$
    2. $(D \cdot E) \supset F$ / $(C \cdot D) \supset F$

★(4) 1. $H \supset (L \supset K)$
    2. $L \supset (K \supset \sim L)$ / $\sim H \lor \sim L$

(5) 1. $S \supset (T \lor \sim U)$
    2. $U \supset (\sim T \lor R)$
    3. $(S \cdot U) \supset \sim R$ / $\sim S \lor \sim U$

(6) 1. $\sim A \supset (B \cdot C)$
    2. $D \supset \sim C$ / $D \supset A$

★(7) 1. $(E \lor F) \supset (C \cdot D)$
    2. $(D \lor G) \supset H$
    3. $E \lor G$ / H

(8) 1. $\sim M \supset (N \cdot O)$
    2. $N \supset P$
    3. $O \supset \sim P$ / M

(9) 1. $(R \lor S) \supset T$
    2. $(P \lor Q) \supset T$
    3. $R \lor P$ / T

★(10) 1. K / $S \supset (T \supset S)$

(11) 1. $(A \lor B) \supset C$
    2. $(\sim A \lor D) \supset E$ / $C \lor E$

(12) 1. $(K \lor L) \supset (M \cdot N)$
    2. $(N \lor O) \supset (P \cdot \sim K)$ / $\sim K$

★(13) 1. $[C \supset (D \supset C)] \supset E$ / E

(14) 1. F / $(G \supset H) \lor (\sim G \supset J)$

(15) 1. $B \supset (K \cdot M)$
    2. $(B \cdot M) \supset (P \equiv \sim P)$ / $\sim B$

★(16) 1. $(N \lor O) \supset (C \cdot D)$
    2. $(D \lor K) \supset (P \lor \sim C)$
    3. $(P \lor G) \supset \sim (N \cdot D)$ / $\sim N$

(17) 1. $(R \cdot S) \equiv (G \cdot H)$
    2. $R \supset S$
    3. $H \supset G$ / $R \equiv H$

(18) 1. $K \supset [(M \lor N) \supset (P \cdot Q)]$
    2. $L \supset [(Q \lor R) \supset (S \cdot \sim N)]$ / $(K \cdot L) \supset \sim N$

★(19) 1. $A \supset [(N \vee \sim N) \supset (S \vee T)]$
2. $T \supset \sim(F \vee \sim F)$ / $A \supset S$

(20) 1. $F \supset [(C \supset C) \supset G]$
2. $G \supset \{[H \supset (E \supset H)] \supset (K \cdot \sim K)\}$ / $\sim F$

II. Translate the following arguments into symbolic form, using the letters in the order in which they are listed. Then use indirect proof and the eighteen rules of inference to derive the conclusion of each. Having done so, attempt to derive the conclusion without using indirect proof.

★1. If government deficits continue at their present rate and a recession sets in, then interest on the national debt will become unbearable and the government will default on its loans. If a recession sets in, then the government will not default on its loans. Therefore, either government deficits will not continue at their present rate or a recession will not set in. (C, R, I, D)

2. If either the sea turtle population continues to decrease or rescue efforts are commenced to save the sea turtle from extinction, then nesting sanctuaries will be created and the indiscriminate slaughter of these animals will be halted. If either nesting sanctuaries are created or poachers are arrested, then if the indiscriminate slaughter of these animals is halted, then the sea turtle population will not continue to decrease. Therefore, the sea turtle population will not continue to decrease. (C, R, N, I, P)

3. If asbestos workers sue their employers, then if punitive damages are awarded, then their employers will declare bankruptcy. If asbestos workers sue their employers, then punitive damages will be awarded. If asbestos workers contract asbestosis, then either they will sue their employers or their employers will declare bankruptcy. Therefore, either asbestos workers will not contract asbestosis or their employers will declare bankruptcy. (S, P, B, C)

★4. If astronauts spend long periods in zero gravity only if calcium is resorbed in their bodies, then astronauts on a Mars voyage will arrive with brittle bones. If astronauts attempt a voyage to Mars only if they spend long periods in zero gravity, then astronauts on a Mars voyage will arrive with brittle bones. Therefore, astronauts on a Mars voyage will arrive with brittle bones. (Z, C, B, V)

5. Either deposits should be required on beer and soft drink containers, or these containers will be discarded along highways and the countryside will look like a dump. If these containers will be discarded either in parks or along highways, then deposits should be required on soft drink containers. Therefore, deposits should be required on soft drink containers. (B, S, H, C, P)

7.7   Proving Logical Truths

Both conditional and indirect proof can be used to establish the truth of a logical truth (tautology). Tautological statements can be treated as if they were the conclusions of arguments having no premises. Such a procedure is suggested by the fact that any argument having a tautology for its conclusion is valid regardless of what its premises are. As we saw in the previous section, the proof for such an argument does not use the premises at all but derives the conclusion as the exclusive consequence of either a conditional or an indirect sequence. Using this strategy for logical truths, we write the statement to be proved as if it were the conclusion of an argument, and we indent the first line in the proof and tag it as being the beginning of either a conditional or an indirect sequence. In the end, this sequence is appropriately discharged to yield the desired statement form.

Tautologies expressed in the form of conditional statements are most easily proved via a conditional sequence. The following example uses two such sequences, one within the scope of the other:

$$/ \; P \supset (Q \supset P)$$

```
│ 1.  P                   ACP
││ 2.  Q                  ACP
││ 3.  P ∨ P              1, Add
││ 4.  P                  3, Taut
│ 5.  Q ⊃ P               2–4, CP
6.  P ⊃ (Q ⊃ P)          1–5, CP
```

Notice that line 6 restores the proof to the original margin—the first line is indented because it introduces the conditional sequence.

Here is a proof of the same statement using an indirect proof. The indirect sequence begins, as usual, with the negation of the statement to be proved:

$$/ \; P \supset (Q \supset P)$$

```
│ 1.  ~[P ⊃ (Q ⊃ P)]           AIP
│ 2.  ~[~P ∨ (Q ⊃ P)]          1, Impl
│ 3.  ~[~P ∨ (~Q ∨ P)]         2, Impl
│ 4.  ~~P • ~(~Q ∨ P)          3, DM
│ 5.  P • ~(~Q ∨ P)            4, DN
│ 6.  P • (~~Q • ~P)           5, DM
│ 7.  P • (~P • ~~Q)           6, Com
│ 8.  (P • ~P) • ~~Q           7, Assoc
│ 9.  P • ~P                   8, Simp
10.  ~~[P ⊃ (Q ⊃ P)]          1–9, IP
11.  P ⊃ (Q ⊃ P)              10, DN
```

More-complex conditional statements are proved by merely extending the technique used in the first proof. In the following proof, notice how each conditional sequence begins by asserting the antecedent of the conditional statement to be obtained:

$$/ \; [P \supset (Q \supset R)] \supset [(P \supset Q) \supset (P \supset R)]$$

```
│ 1. P ⊃ (Q ⊃ R)                            ACP
││ 2.  P ⊃ Q                                 ACP
│││ 3.  P                                     ACP
│││ 4.  Q ⊃ R                                 1, 3, MP
│││ 5.  Q                                     2, 3, MP
│││ 6.  R                                     4, 5, MP
││ 7.  P ⊃ R                                  3–6, CP
│ 8. (P ⊃ Q) ⊃ (P ⊃ R)                       2–7, CP
9. [P ⊃ (Q ⊃ R)] ⊃ [(P ⊃ Q) ⊃ (P ⊃ R)]       1–8, CP
```

Tautologies expressed as equivalences are usually proved using two conditional sequences, one after the other. Example:

		/ $P \equiv [P \cdot (Q \supset P)]$
1.	P	ACP
2.	$P \lor \sim Q$	1, Add
3.	$\sim Q \lor P$	2, Com
4.	$Q \supset P$	3, Impl
5.	$P \cdot (Q \supset P)$	1, 4, Conj
6. $P \supset [P \cdot (Q \supset P)]$		1–5, CP
7.	$P \cdot (Q \supset P)$	ACP
8.	P	7, Simp
9. $[P \cdot (Q \supset P)] \supset P$		7–8, CP
10. {line 6} $\cdot$ {line 9}		6, 9, Conj
11. $P \equiv [P \cdot (Q \supset P)]$		10, Equiv

EXERCISE 7.7

Use conditional proof or indirect proof and the eighteen rules of inference to establish the truth of the following tautologies.

★1. $P \supset [(P \supset Q) \supset Q]$

2. $(\sim P \supset Q) \lor (P \supset R)$

3. $P \equiv [P \lor (Q \cdot P)]$

★4. $(P \supset Q) \supset [(P \cdot R) \supset (Q \cdot R)]$

5. $(P \lor \sim Q) \supset [(\sim P \lor R) \supset (Q \supset R)]$

6. $P \equiv [P \cdot (Q \lor \sim Q)]$

★7. $(P \supset Q) \lor (\sim Q \supset P)$

8. $(P \supset Q) \equiv [P \supset (P \cdot Q)]$

9. $[(P \supset Q) \cdot (P \supset R)] \supset [P \supset (Q \cdot R)]$

★10. $[\sim(P \cdot \sim Q) \cdot \sim Q] \supset \sim P$

11. $(P \supset Q) \lor (Q \supset P)$

12. $[P \supset (Q \supset R)] \equiv [Q \supset (P \supset R)]$

★13. $(P \supset Q) \supset [(P \supset \sim Q) \supset \sim P]$

14. $[(P \supset Q) \supset R] \supset [(R \supset \sim R) \supset P]$

15. $(\sim P \lor Q) \supset [(P \lor \sim Q) \supset (P \equiv Q)]$

★16. $\sim[(P \supset \sim P) \cdot (\sim P \supset P)]$

17. $P \supset [(Q \cdot \sim Q) \supset R]$

18. $[(P \cdot Q) \lor R] \supset [(\sim R \lor Q) \supset (P \supset Q)]$

★19. $P \equiv [P \lor (Q \cdot \sim Q)]$

20. $P \supset [Q \equiv (P \supset Q)]$

Summary

Natural deduction is a method for establishing the validity of arguments symbolized in terms of the five logical operators. The method consists in applying one or more rules of inference to the premises and deriving the conclusion as the last line in a sequence of lines. By studying such a derivation, one can see exactly how the premises imply the conclusion. Success in using the rules of inference depends on an intimate familiarity with the rules themselves and a working knowledge of how each rule can be used in conjunction with the other rules.

The eight rules of implication are "one-way" rules because the premises of each rule can be used to derive the conclusion, but the conclusion cannot be used to derive the premises. On the other hand, the ten rules of replacement are "two-way" rules. These rules are expressed as logical equivalences, and the axiom of replacement states that logically equivalent expressions may replace each other in a proof. Thus, if one of these rules is used to derive a conclusion, the process can be reversed, and the rule can be used to derive the premise. This fact allows us to use the rules of replacement to "deconstruct" the conclusion for insight into how best to derive it in a proof sequence.

Conditional proof is a simple procedure for deriving a line in a proof sequence— either the conclusion or some other line. The procedure consists in assuming a certain statement as the first line in a conditional sequence, using that line to derive one or more additional lines, and then discharging the conditional sequence in a conditional statement having the first line of that sequence as antecedent and the last line as consequent. The procedure expresses the basic idea that if the antecedent of a true conditional statement is true, then so is the consequent.

Indirect proof is another simple procedure for deriving a line in a proof sequence. It consists in assuming the negation of the line to be obtained as the first line in an indirect sequence, using that line to derive a contradiction, and then discharging the indirect sequence in a statement that is the negation of the first line in that sequence. The procedure expresses the idea that any assumption that necessarily leads to a contradiction is false.

Natural deduction can also be used to prove logical truths (tautologies). The technique employs conditional proof and indirect proof. Conditional proof is often used for logical truths expressed as conditionals. The antecedent of the logical truth is assumed as the first line of a conditional sequence, the consequent is derived, and the sequence is then discharged in a statement that expresses the logical truth to be proved. Indirect proof can be used for proving any logical truth. The negation of the logical truth is assumed as the first line of an indirect sequence, a contradiction is derived, and the sequence is then discharged in a statement consisting of the negation of the first line in that sequence.

7

Appendix:
Logic and Graduate-Level Admissions Tests

Fifty percent of the LSAT (Law School Admission Test) and a substantial part of the GMAT (Graduate Management Admission Test) relates to questions involving arguments. Of these questions, a significant majority ask the test taker to identify the conclusion implied by a set of premises, to identify a missing premise needed to draw a stated conclusion, or to identify a statement that either strengthens or weakens a given argument. Additionally, a few questions ask the test taker to identify a fallacy committed by an argument, to identify a reasoning process similar to that of a given argument, or to identify the form or method of reasoning of a given argument. Among these seven kinds of questions, a few can be done using natural deduction techniques. This appendix touches on all of these topics.

For all of the questions involving arguments, you need to be able to distinguish premises from conclusion. Section 1.1 of this textbook covers this topic. Also, for most of these questions, it is very helpful to be familiar with various inductive and deductive forms of argumentation. This topic is treated throughout the book, but some chapters and sections are particularly salient. These include Section 1.3 (deductive and inductive forms), Section 1.5 (deductive forms), Chapter 3 (fallacious forms), Sections 4.4 and 4.5 (immediate inference forms), Section 5.1 (syllogistic forms), Section 6.6 (propositional logic forms and fallacies), Chapter 9 (analogy), and Chapter 10 (Mill's methods).

Furthermore, it often helps to apply the methods of symbolic logic. This is treated in Section 6.1 (translation) and Chapter 7 (natural deduction).

The questions that follow have been taken from *Logic and Reading Review for the GRE, GMAT, LSAT, MCAT,* published by Thompson-Peterson's. The book contains four complete practice tests and an extensive set of instructions on how to approach the various kind of questions found in admissions tests for graduate school.

Missing-Conclusion Questions

Questions of this sort are similar to enthymemes, treated in Section 5.6 of this textbook, and also in Exercise 7.1 Part I and Exercise 7.2 Part I. The answer must be inferentially relevant to the premise or premises. Understanding the meaning of this requirement depends on a knowledge of the various forms of argumentation, but it is easy to give an example. If the premises have the form "All *A* are *B*," and "All *B* are *C*," then the implied conclusion has the form "All *A* are *C*." For another example, if the premises have the form "*A* has attribute *x*, and *A* is similar to *B*," then the conclusion has the form "*B* has attribute *x*." Here is an example of a missing-conclusion question:

> The earth-moon system, the satellites of Jupiter, and the moons of Saturn are all examples of planetary systems in which a satellite moves in the gravitational field of a much more massive body. In every

one of these systems the satellite moves in an elliptical orbit.

If the statements above are true, they provide the most support for which one of the following?

(A) The more massive a body the more gravitational pull it exerts on another body.
(B) Only elliptical orbits can account for the various phases of the moon as seen from earth.
(C) Non-elliptical orbits violate the laws of celestial mechanics.
(D) The moons of the planet Uranus move in elliptical orbits.
(E) All celestial bodies move in elliptical orbits.

An examination of the premises alone does not reveal the exact kind of conclusion implied. But a quick survey of the answers shows that this is an argument from analogy, with three primary analogues: the earth-moon system, the satellites of Jupiter, and the moons of Saturn. Thus, the correct answer is (D). None of the conclusions expressed in (A), (B), (C), or (E) follows by any standard form of reasoning.

See if you can get the correct answer to the numbered questions that follow. A list of answers together with an explanation of each appears at the end of this appendix.

1. Historians universally agree that all democracies in the past have eventually perished as a result of disputes between competing groups of special interests, coupled with gross inefficiency, waste and corruption in government, and a decline in the moral values of the society at large. Every day the news reports confirm that all of these maladies are currently present in the United States of America.

Given that the statements above are true, which of the following conclusions is most strongly supported?

(A) Communism is a better form of government than democracy.
(B) Nondemocratic societies do not suffer from the same problems as democratic societies.
(C) If the experience of past democracies is a reliable indicator, democracy in the United States is in decline.
(D) News reports generally focus only on negative news.
(E) In the future, the United States will be a dictatorship.

2. The average annual salary for executives at World-Wide Travel last year was $55,000, while the average salary for travel consultants was $47,000. The average annual salary for all employees was $38,000.

If the above information is correct, which one of the following conclusions can be properly inferred from it?

(A) There were fewer executives than travel consultants at World-Wide Travel last year.
(B) No travel consultants earned more than an executive last year.
(C) There was at least one employee who earned less than the average for a travel consultant.
(D) Some travel consultants earn more than the lowest paid executives.
(E) All executives earn more than travel consultants.

3. A recipe for cooking potatoes states that potatoes should be cooked in boiling water for 20 minutes to be properly prepared. This holds only for potatoes that have been diced into one-inch cubes—smaller cubes would require proportionately less cooking time and larger ones proportionately more. It is important that potatoes not be overcooked, since this greatly diminishes their food value. Undercooking also should be avoided because undercooked potatoes cannot be properly digested.

If the above statements are true, which of the following conclusions is most strongly supported?

(A) Whole potatoes, when properly cooked, cannot be properly digested.
(B) Potatoes that are diced into one-half-inch cubes and cooked in boiling water for 20 minutes will likely have little food value.
(C) Potatoes that are properly digestible must be cooked in boiling water for at least 20 minutes.
(D) Boiling in water is the only method of cooking potatoes that will ensure high food value and proper digestibility.
(E) To be prepared properly, potatoes must be boiled in water for at least 20 minutes.

Missing-Premise Questions

Questions of this sort are similar to enthymemes missing a premise. These are treated in Section 5.6 of this textbook, and also in Exercises 7.1 Part II and 7.2 Part II. For these arguments the missing premise, once supplied, will provide the link between a stated premise and the conclusion. For example, if a stated premise has the form "All *A* are *B*," and the conclusion has the form "All *A* are *C*," the missing premise has the form "All *B* are *C*." Here is an actual example of such an argument:

Analytic propositions provide no information about any matter of fact. This applies to all analytic propositions. In other words, they are entirely devoid of information about the world. It is for this reason that no empirical evidence can refute them.

Which of the following must be assumed for the above argument's conclusion to be properly drawn?

(A) The truth or falsity of analytic propositions cannot be determined by empirical evidence.
(B) Analytic propositions are neither true nor false.
(C) Analytic propositions are completely uninformative.
(D) Empirical evidence can only refute propositions that provide information about matters of fact.
(E) Propositions that are entirely devoid of information about the world are false.

This argument has the following structure:

Stated: Analytic propositions provide no information about matters of fact.
Missing: Any proposition that provides no information about matters of fact cannot be refuted by empirical evidence.
Stated: Therefore, analytic propositions cannot be refuted by empirical evidence.

Thus, the answer is (D). None of the statements expressed in (A), (B), (C), or (E) expresses a link between the stated premise and the stated conclusion.

4. Captive animals are more interesting research subjects than are wild animals. That's why researchers can learn more from studying captive animals than from studying wild animals.

Which of the following is an assumption upon which the above argument depends?

(A) Researchers study only subjects they are interested in.
(B) In general, the more that can be learned from a research subject, the more interesting it is to study.
(C) In general, the more interesting a research subject, the more that can be learned from studying it.
(D) Researchers learn less from studying subjects they are not interested in.
(E) In general, researchers prefer studying interesting subjects more than non-interesting subjects.

5. In order to ensure a successful vote on the issue of abortion rights, the governor is pressuring the leaders of the state political party to replace several delegates to the national convention. The governor is insisting that certain individuals with a history of voting in favor of abortion rights be replaced with new delegates who have voted against abortion rights in the past.

The governor's actions demonstrate that he is making which of the following assumptions?

(A) Voting on abortion issues is an important part of the national political agenda.
(B) The current delegates will probably not share the governor's views on such issues as the national budget or federal spending limits.
(C) The proposed new delegates will continue to vote on abortion issues in the same way that they have voted in the past.
(D) The national delegation will not have an opportunity to vote on any issues other than abortion rights.
(E) Governors of other states will be making similar changes to their states' delegations, so the issue of abortion rights will be guaranteed to be decided as this governor desires.

6. Unequal pay for men and women is a completely indefensible practice and one that must be stopped immediately. After all, can anyone seriously doubt that women have as much right to self-esteem as men? Surely this fact alone is reason enough to justify their right to earn as much money as men.

Which of the following is an assumption on which the above argument depends?

(A) A person who has less money than another has less self-esteem.
(B) People who do not have jobs lack self-esteem.
(C) Women and men who perform similar jobs should earn similar salaries.
(D) Equal pay for equal work is a constitutionally guaranteed right of all workers.
(E) High self-esteem is as important to women as it is to men.

Strengthen Questions

Questions of this sort always involve inductive arguments. With inductive arguments it often happens that additional information will either strengthen or weaken the argument. (See the example involving the barrel of apples in Section 1.4.) These questions differ from the missing premise questions in that the latter ask for a statement that is necessary to draw a conclusion, but here the needed statement merely renders the conclusion more probable. Here is an example of such a question:

An auto mechanic who is too thorough in checking a car is likely to subject the customer to unnecessary expense. On the other hand, one who is not thorough enough is likely to miss some problem that could cause a serious accident. Therefore, it's a good idea not to have your car checked until a recognizable problem develops.

Which one of the following, if true, provides the most support for the above argument?

(A) The more complete the mechanical checkup, the more likely a problem, if present, will be discovered.
(B) Some people have enough mechanical knowledge to recognize a problem with their car.
(C) Not all tests performed by mechanics are time consuming and expensive.
(D) Most mechanical problems that are potentially dangerous or expensive to repair cannot be detected by routine checkups no matter how thorough they are.
(E) Many auto mechanics lie to customers about the mechanical condition of their cars.

To select the right answer for this question it is essential to pay close attention to the conclusion: It's a good idea not to have your car checked until a recognizable problem develops. The chief reason to take the car in for a checkup is to catch a problem that could lead to an accident. But if such problems are unlikely to be found, then there is little reason to take the car in. Thus, the answer is (D). Answers (A) and (C) support the opposite conclusion, that it *is* a good idea to take the car in. Answer (B) is largely irrelevant because it may apply only to a handful of people, and (E) likely relates only to nonexistent problems for which the mechanic would like to bill the customer.

7. Parents cannot be with their teenage children every minute of the day and, even if they could, they would not always be able to stop them from doing things that might cause harm to other people or other people's property. That's why they should not be blamed or punished for crimes that their teenage children commit.

   Which of the following general principles, if established, would most help to justify the conclusion in the argument above?

   (A) All activities that teenage children engage in should be supervised by adults.
   (B) Teenage children should be treated as adults in the criminal justice system.
   (C) People should be held accountable for only those actions over which they have control.
   (D) Parents should supervise the activities of their teenage children as much as possible.
   (E) Parents have the responsibility to teach their teenage children the difference between right and wrong.

8. Scientists have found through experimentation that baby female gorillas who were "nurtured" by inanimate mother substitutes that performed some parenting functions were unable to function as mothers when they had offspring. This teaches us that in-

fants should not be placed in the care of babysitters and day-care centers but should only be raised by their natural mothers.

   The conclusion reached by the author would be strengthened by which of the following?

   (A) The scientists found that the baby gorillas in the experiments were very dependent on each other.
   (B) The gorilla babies in the experiments would only accept food from the scientists, not from the "surrogate" mothers.
   (C) Baby gorillas that had brief but regular exposure to their natural mothers were able to function as mothers later.
   (D) Baby gorillas raised by females other than their own mothers were unable to function as mothers when they had offspring.
   (E) Mature female gorillas that were "raised" by the mother substitutes could be taught many mothering functions when they had offspring.

Weaken Questions

Like those in the previous set, these questions always involve inductive arguments, but they ask the test taker to identify a statement that renders the conclusion *less* probable. Here is an example:

There is no such thing as one single scientific method. Instead, there is a jumble of methods ranging from careful observation and collection of data from which hypotheses are advanced to mere conjecture of the underlying causes. Moreover, no attempts to rationally justify the various methods of science as sources of truth have as yet proven fruitful. For these reasons it can be concluded that science is not preferable to religion or mythology when it comes to finding out the basic truths of the universe.

Which one of the following claims, if true, would most weaken the author's position in the passage?

(A) Science is based on reason, whereas religion and mythology are based on faith.
(B) Unlike religion and mythology, the various methods of science all yield accurate predictions, and yielding accurate predictions is an indicator of truth.
(C) Religion and mythology are based on superstition and ignorance.
(D) There is widespread agreement among scientists about the nature of the universe but little agreement among the practitioners of religion and mythology.
(E) More technological advances have been made in the past two centuries, during which science

has reigned, than in the preceding twenty centuries, in which mythology and religion reigned.

The conclusion of this argument is that science is no better than religion. Thus, to weaken this conclusion we look for a statement that supports the claim that science *is* better than religion. Answer (B) says that science always leads to truth (which is good), whereas religion does not. Thus, (B) is the correct answer. Answer (A) fails to state that reason is better than faith, (C) says nothing about science, (D) fails to state that widespread agreement is good, and (E) speaks only about time periods; it says nothing about science and religion as such.

9. Residential water use has been severely restricted in response to the current drought in our state. However, current reservoir levels are at the same height as during the drought that occurred here eight years ago. Because residential water use was not restricted then, it should not be restricted now.

 Which of the following, if true, would most seriously undermine the author's contention?

 (A) No new reservoirs have been constructed in the state since the last drought.
 (B) The population of the state has grown at a steady rate of more than two million people a year since the last drought.
 (C) Residential water use makes up more than 50 percent of the total water use.
 (D) The restrictions on residential water use are projected to last for only two months during the summer.
 (E) Since the last drought, water-conserving devices are required by law to be installed in all new residential construction.

10. Recent reports from waste management companies indicate that disposable plastic containers make up an increasingly large percentage of the waste they collect. As a result, landfills and incineration sites now deal almost exclusively with the disposal of plastics, whereas glass and metal containers previously made up the bulk of their refuse. It is evident from this radical change in disposal patterns that the use of plastic containers has virtually replaced the use of glass and metal containers.

 Which of the following, if true, would most seriously call into question the conclusion above?

 (A) Metal and glass containers are more expensive to manufacture than plastic containers.
 (B) An increasing proportion of metal and glass containers are now being recycled.
 (C) Plastic containers can be used over and over again before being discarded.
 (D) Plastic containers decompose faster than metal and glass containers.

 (E) Environmentalists have been unsuccessful in their attempts to decrease the production of plastic containers.

Fallacy Questions

A *fallacy* is a mistake in an argument that usually arises from an error in reasoning. Being familiar with the various kinds of formal and informal fallacies can help you recognize them. In this textbook formal fallacies are treated in Sections 4.3, 4.4, 4.5, 5.3, and 6.6. Informal fallacies are the subject of Chapter 3. Here is an example of an argument that contains a fallacy:

 The mean price of new cars in Heavenly Hills is $38,563; in Cargo the mean price is only $23,769. Therefore, if you are in the market for a new car, you are likely to get a better deal on it in Cargo.
  Which of the following best describes the flaw in the author's reasoning?

 (A) The author's conclusion is based on a comparison that does not necessarily involve comparable things.
 (B) The author assumes that the number of cars sold in Heavenly Hills is the same as the number sold in Cargo.
 (C) The author has confused the mean average price with the median average price.
 (D) The author assumes that new cars in Cargo are less expensive than new cars in Heavenly Hills.
 (E) The author assumes that new car dealers in Cargo are more willing than Heavenly Hills dealers to make good deals on new cars.

This argument commits the fallacy of weak analogy. The conclusion depends on the idea that the cars sold in Heavenly Hills are similar to (the same make and model as) those sold in Fargo, but there is no reason to believe that this is the case. Thus, the correct answer is (A). Answers (B) and (C) are irrelevant to the conclusion, (D) more or less restates the conclusion, and (E) rests on the prior assumption that the cars are similar.

11. It is the sacrosanct duty of the press to publish any news that is in the public interest to have published. There can be no doubt that the public has demonstrated considerable interest in the Adamson murder case, especially since the details of the private lives of the people involved have been displayed in the tabloid magazines and television talk shows every day. Thus, the press has an obligation to publish the details of the private lives of all of the people involved in this case.

A reasoning error in the argument is that:

(A) The reasons given in support of the conclusion presuppose the truth of that conclusion.

(B) The argument employs a key term or phrase in two different meanings.

(C) The argument assumes that just because the press has a duty to publish something, it should publish it.

(D) It bases the conclusion on the unwarranted assumption that whatever is in the public interest to have published ought to be published.

(E) It incorrectly assumes that just because the public is interested in some topic, they are also interested in the private lives of the people involved.

12. According to modern science, everything in the universe is composed of atoms that are exceedingly small; so small, in fact, that they cannot be seen even with the most powerful microscopes because they do not provide sufficient stimulus for the optic nerve, even when magnified. But if it is true that everything in the universe is composed of invisible atoms, surely it follows that everything in the universe is invisible. The patent absurdity of this, however, is clearly evidenced by the fact that tables, chairs, and everyday objects are visible. So it follows that modern science must be mistaken in claiming that everything is composed of atoms.

   Which of the following best describes a flaw in the author's reasoning?

(A) The author's reasoning depends upon the mistaken belief that just because something occurred prior to something else it must be the cause of it.

(B) The author's reasoning depends upon the mistaken belief that what is true of the parts is necessarily true of the whole.

(C) The author uses the word "invisible" in two different senses.

(D) The author's reasoning depends upon the mistaken belief that the origin of a view is relevant to its truth or falsity.

(E) The author's reasoning depends upon the mistaken belief that whatever cannot be proven to be true must be false.

Natural-Deduction Questions

In some questions the correct answer can be reached very quickly by first translating the various statements into the notation of symbolic logic and then using natural deduction to derive a conclusion. In this textbook, translation is cov-

ered in Section 6.1, and natural deduction is the subject of Chapter 7. Here is an example of a question that lends itself to this approach:

> Unless a settlement can be reached, the truce will be violated by one of the parties to the dispute. But a settlement can be reached only if the border issues can be resolved, and the border issues can be resolved only if both parties are willing to give up the territory they captured during the hostilities.
>
> If the statements above are true, but both parties are not willing to give up the territory they captured during the hostilities, then each of the following must also be true EXCEPT:

(A) A settlement can't be reached and the truce will be violated by one of the parties to the dispute.

(B) The border issues cannot be resolved.

(C) The truce will not be violated by either of the parties to the dispute.

(D) A settlement cannot be reached.

(E) The border issues cannot be resolved, nor can a settlement be reached.

After translating the four statements into symbols, we have

$S \lor T$
$S \supset B$
$B \supset W$
$\sim W$

After three quick steps consisting of *modus tollens*, *modus tollens*, and disjunctive syllogism, we derive the conclusion *T*. Therefore, since the question asks for a statement that is *false*, we look for $\sim T$ among the five answers. The correct answer is (C). It is easy to see by the same derivation that answers (A), (B), (D), and (E) contain statements that are *true*.

13. In a game of Monopoly, if a player owns a hotel on Boardwalk, he must own both Boardwalk and Park Place. If he owns a hotel in Marvin Gardens, he must own Marvin Gardens and either Boardwalk or Park Place. If he owns Park Place, he also owns Marvin Gardens.

   If the player described above does not own Park Place, which of the following conclusions may be drawn?

(A) The player owns a hotel on Boardwalk.

(B) The player owns a hotel in Marvin Gardens but does not own a hotel on Boardwalk.

(C) The player owns Marvin Gardens and Boardwalk but does not own a hotel on either property.

(D) The player does not own a hotel in Marvin Gardens.

(E) The player does not own a hotel on Boardwalk.

14. Price and wage controls are the only way to control inflation. But wage controls limit worker spending, which, in turn, results in reduced corporate profits if price controls are in place.

Assume the above statements are true. Which of the following statements also must be true if corporate profits are not decreasing?

(A) If there is inflation, wage controls are not in place.
(B) If there is inflation, it is not being controlled.
(C) Workers have less money to spend.
(D) Price controls are in effect.
(E) Wage controls are in effect.

Parallel-Reasoning Questions

Questions of this sort ask the test taker to identify an argument that involves a reasoning process similar to that of a given argument. With some questions (such as number 15 and number 16) this identification is facilitated by translating the given argument together with one or more of the answers into symbolic notation. With other questions such translation is not necessary. Here is an example of the latter kind of question:

Card games requiring more than one player, such as poker and bridge, employ strategies aimed at outwitting the opponent; however, card games that are played alone, such as games of solitaire, do not. Hence, strategies that aim at outwitting an opponent are not an essential feature of all card games.

Which of the following most closely parallels the reasoning in the above passage?

(A) Games of chance, such as roulette and craps, employ odds that are detrimental to the player, but favorable to the house. Since these are the only kinds of games that are found in gambling casinos, having odds that favor the house is an essential feature of all games played in gambling casinos.
(B) Most aircraft have wings, but others, such as helicopters, do not. Hence, having wings is not an essential property of all aircraft.
(C) Chez Bon's most celebrated features are its great food and extensive wine list. But, since these are features of many other fine restaurants as well, they are not the only features which define the essence of this outstanding restaurant.
(D) It has been reliably reported that deer occasionally eat meat, but if deer were not primarily vegetarians they would have much different

shaped teeth than they do. Hence, being a vegetarian is an essential feature of being a deer.
(E) All cats are meat eaters and being a meat eater is the defining characteristic of being a carnivore. Hence, being carnivorous is essential to being a cat.

The given argument has the following structure:

Some card games involve outwitting opponents, but others do not.

Therefore, outwitting an opponent is not essential to all card games.

It should be fairly clear that the reasoning process in (B) is closest to that of the given argument. Thus, the answer is (B).

15. Lying is morally justified only if it is done to save a person's life. Yet, most people lie not because a life is in danger, but only to avoid the unpleasant consequences of telling the truth. Thus, most lies that are told are morally unjustified.

In which of the following is the pattern of reasoning most parallel to that in the argument above?

(A) Capital punishment is justified if it deters people from taking another's life. But it has been demonstrated conclusively that capital punishment is not an effective deterrent. Thus, capital punishment is not justified.
(B) Capital punishment is justified only if we are certain that the convicted offender is actually guilty of the crime. But there are many cases in which persons who are not guilty are convicted of capital offenses. Therefore, in many cases capital punishment is unjustified.
(C) Capital punishment is morally wrong only if it does not promote the greatest good for the greatest number of people. But sacred religious texts do not condemn capital punishment as being morally wrong. Thus, capital punishment promotes the greatest good for the greatest number of people.
(D) If the defendant in a murder trial is determined to be guilty beyond a reasonable doubt, the maximum penalty allowed under the law can be imposed. But most defendants in murder trials are not determined to be guilty beyond a reasonable doubt. Therefore, the maximum penalty is seldom imposed.
(E) Corporal punishment for persons who commit violent crimes is justified if and only if the punishment will alter the persons' behavior in the future. But most persons who commit violent crimes are corporally punished not in order to alter their future behavior, but only to exact revenge. Therefore, most instances of corporal punishment are unjustified.

16. Whenever inflation increases, the stock market declines; and whenever interest rates decrease, the stock market advances. However, since interest rates have not decreased nor has inflation increased, the stock market will neither decline nor advance.

    Which one of the following arguments contains a flaw that is most similar to the one in the argument above?

    (A) Whenever it rains, the streets get wet. But casual observation confirms that the streets aren't wet, so it can be confidently concluded that it hasn't rained.

    (B) Whenever the president vetoes a bill, Congress attempts to override it; and whenever Congress attempt to override a veto, it runs into serious opposition from the president's supporters; so Congress rarely succeeds in overriding a presidential veto.

    (C) When students receive individual tutoring, they invariably get good grades, and, as a general rule, when students get good grades, their self-esteem is greatly enhanced. Thus, to enhance a student's self-esteem, it is necessary to provide individual tutoring.

    (D) When children study logic at an early age, they never have trouble learning mathematics, so if they have trouble learning mathematics, it's probably because they didn't study logic early on.

    (E) Lawyers lose their cases whenever they go to trial without proper preparation. Good lawyers never go to trial without proper preparation, which is why they never lose their cases.

Argument-Form/Method-of-Reasoning Questions

For these questions it helps if the test taker is familiar with as many argument forms as possible. This point was noted earlier in the introduction to this appendix. Here is an example of a question that asks about the method of reasoning:

A study of six patients who all suffer from a rare form of cancer revealed that though they all live in different locations in the county and have quite different medical histories, diet, and personal habits—two smoke cigarettes and three drink alcoholic beverages—they are all employed at a company that manufactures herbicides and pesticides. From this study it can be concluded that exposure to the chemicals produced by the company is the probable cause of the disease.

The argument proceeds by:

(A) reaching a general conclusion on the basis of insufficient evidence.

(B) isolating a common feature through a process of elimination and concluding that this feature is causally related to the event under investigation.

(C) reaching a general conclusion on the basis of the experiences of the six patients.

(D) providing information that allows the application of a general claim to a specific case.

(E) indirectly showing that exposure to the chemicals produced by the company is the likely cause by demonstrating that none of the other alternatives is the cause.

The method of reasoning used by this argument is John Stuart Mill's method of agreement (see Chapter 10). Thus, (B), which describes this method, is the correct answer.

17. In a recent medical experiment, 20 volunteers who were not immune to yellow fever lived for an extended period in a mosquito-proof environment with patients who had advanced cases of yellow fever. During this period, the volunteers were in constant contact with these patients, yet none of the volunteers developed the disease. When the experiment was repeated in a non-mosquito-proof environment, several of the volunteers were bitten by mosquitoes. In this instance, the ones bitten all developed yellow fever. That mosquito bites, and not contact with persons who have this disease, is the cause of yellow fever can be confidently concluded on the basis of these two experiments.

    The argument above employs which one of the following methods of argumentation?

    (A) Establishing a causal conclusion through a process of elimination of all but one of the candidate causes.

    (B) Establishing a causal conclusion on the basis of the identification of an event that precedes the effect.

    (C) Establishing a causal conclusion on the basis of an analogy between two different environments.

    (D) Establishing a causal conclusion.

    (E) Employing the expert testimony of the experimenters as grounds for the conclusion.

18. The medical licensing board of this state maintains that only medical schools that are accredited by the board should be permitted to train doctors. The primary reason given for this policy is that doctors who are trained at nonaccredited institutions may lack the training necessary to become competent practitioners. But since the licensing board is composed entirely of doctors and they obviously have a

financial interest in limiting the supply of new doctors, their reasoning cannot be taken seriously.

Which one of the following argumentative techniques is used in the passage?

(A) The licensing board's argument is undermined by pointing out that one of the statements used to support the conclusion is false.
(B) The licensing board's argument is discredited by questioning the motives of the board in advancing it.
(C) The licensing board's argument is discredited by showing that the board is not a reliable authority on the topic of the argument.
(D) The licensing board's argument is discredited by pointing out that other institutions besides those accredited by the board can train competent doctors.
(E) The licensing board's argument is challenged on the grounds that the major premise on which the board bases its conclusion is highly questionable.

Answers

1. The argument in this question has the form "All A are B; the USA is a member of A." Thus, the conclusion has the form "The USA is a member of B." Answer: (C).

2. This is a deductive argument based on mathematics (see Section 1.4), and the conclusion follows from the second and third premises alone. If the average salary for all employees is $38,000, and the average for the travel consultants is $47,000, then some employees must earn less than $38,000 to bring the average for all employees down to $38,000. Answer: (C).

3. From the premises it follows that potatoes diced smaller than one inch and cooked for 20 minutes are overcooked. Therefore, since all overcooked potatoes have greatly diminished food value, it follows that these one-half-inch potatoes will have greatly diminished food value. Answer: (B).

4. This argument has the following structure:

Stated:	Captive animals are more interesting.
Missing:	More interesting animals are better sources of knowledge.
Stated:	Therefore, captive animals are better sources of knowledge.

Answer: (C).

5. This argument has the following structure:

| Stated: | The new delegates have voted against abortion rights in the past. |

| Missing: | If they have voted against abortion rights in the past, they will continue to do so in the future. |
| Stated: | The new delegates will vote against abortion rights in the future. |

Answer: (C).

6. This argument has the following structure:

Stated:	Women have as much right to self-esteem as men.
Missing:	Money is an essential part of self-esteem.
Stated:	Women have as much right to money as men.

Answer: (A).

7. The conclusion of this argument is that parents should not be blamed for the actions of their children. The general principle that supports this conclusion is that people should be blamed only for actions they control. Answer: (C).

8. This is an argument from analogy: the analogy between humans and gorillas. The conclusion is that baby humans should be raised by their natural mothers. The evidence that most supports this conclusion is that baby gorillas should be raised by their natural mothers. Answer: (D).

9. The conclusion of this argument is that water use should not be restricted now. The argument assumes that water demand is the same today as it was earlier. The claim that the state's population has grown significantly undermines this assumption. Answer: (B).

10. The conclusion is that plastic containers have replaced glass and metal containers. The argument assumes that metal and glass containers are thrown into the garbage just as frequently as are plastic containers. The claim that metal and glass containers are now being recycled (and therefore not thrown into the garbage) undermines this assumption. Answer: (B).

11. This argument commits the fallacy of equivocation, which means that the conclusion depends on a word or phrase being used in two or more ways. In the first premise "public interest" means whatever is beneficial to the public, but in the second premise it means what has attracted the attention of the public. Answer: (B).

12. This argument commits the fallacy of composition, which means that the conclusion depends on the improper transference of an attribute from the parts of something onto the whole. In this case it is argued that because the atoms (parts) are invisible, the whole is invisible. Answer: (B).

13. After translating the four statements into symbols, we have

$$B \supset (B \cdot P)$$
$$M \supset [M \cdot (B \lor P)]$$
$$P \supset M$$
$$\sim P$$

From the first and fourth statement alone we can quickly derive the conclusion $\sim B$. Answer: (E).

14. After translating the four statements into symbols, we have

$$I \supset (P \cdot W)$$
$$W \supset L$$
$$L \supset (P \supset R)$$
$$\sim R$$

Next, if we assume I on the first line of a conditional sequence, by using only the first three symbolized statements, we can derive R on the last line. Discharging the sequence, we have $I \supset R$. Then, by *modus tollens*, we have $\sim I$. Answer: (B).

15. This argument is a case of *modus tollens*, and it has the following form:

$$J \supset L$$
$$\sim L$$
$$\overline{\sim J}$$

The only one of the answers that has this form is (B):

$$J \supset C$$
$$\sim C$$
$$\overline{\sim J}$$

Answer: (B).

16. This argument involves two cases of denying the antecedent. Let A = inflation increases, B = the stock market declines, C = interest-rates decrease, D = the stock market advances. Then, we have

$$A \supset B \qquad C \supset D$$
$$\underline{\sim A} \qquad\qquad \underline{\sim C}$$
$$\sim B \qquad\qquad \sim D$$

The only answer that involves denying the antecedent is (E):

$$T \supset L$$
$$\underline{\sim T}$$
$$\sim L$$

Answer: (E).

17. The method of reasoning employed by this argument is Mill's method of difference. The method proceeds by eliminating all of the factors that are common to two occurrences, leaving the one way in which they differ as the cause. Answer: (A).

18. This argument commits the fallacy of *ad hominem* circumstantial, which means that it attempts to discredit an argument by pointing out circumstances that predispose the arguer to argue in this way. Answer: (B).

Answers to Selected Exercises

Exercise 1.1

I.

1. P: Titanium combines readily with oxygen, nitrogen, and hydrogen, all of which have an adverse effect on its mechanical properties.

   C: Titanium must be processed in their absence.

4. P: When individuals voluntarily abandon property, they forfeit any expectation of privacy in it that they might have had.

   C: A warrantless search and seizure of abandoned property is not unreasonable under the Fourth Amendment.

7. P_1: After October 1963, when Hurricane Flora devastated the island and killed more than a thousand people, the Cuban government overhauled its civil defense system.

   P_2: It was so successful that when six powerful hurricanes thumped Cuba between 1996 and 2002 only 16 people died.

   P_3: And when Hurricane Ivan struck Cuba in 2004 there was not a single casualty, but the same storm killed at least 70 people in other Caribbean countries.

   C: Cuba's record on disaster prevention is impressive.

10. P_1: Punishment, when speedy and specific, may suppress undesirable behavior.

    P_2: Punishment cannot teach or encourage desirable alternatives.

    C: It is crucial to use positive techniques to model and reinforce appropriate behavior that the person can use in place of the unacceptable response that has to be suppressed.

13. P_1: Private property helps people define themselves.

    P_2: Private property frees people from mundane cares of daily subsistence.

    P_3: Private property is finite.

    C: No individual should accumulate so much property that others are prevented from accumulating the necessities of life.

16. P_1: The nations of planet earth have acquired nuclear weapons with an explosive power equal to more than a million Hiroshima bombs.

    P_2: Studies suggest that explosion of only half these weapons would produce enough soot, smoke, and dust to blanket the earth, block out the sun, and bring on a nuclear winter that would threaten the survival of the human race.

    C: Radioactive fallout isn't the only concern in the aftermath of nuclear explosions.

19. P_1: Antipoverty programs provide jobs for middle-class professionals in social work, penology, and public health.

    P_2: Such workers' future advancement is tied to the continued growth of bureaucracies dependent on the existence of poverty.

    C: Poverty offers numerous benefits to the nonpoor.

22. P: Take the nurse who alleges that physicians enrich themselves in her hospital through unnecessary surgery; the engineer who discloses safety defects in the braking systems of a
fleet of new rapid-transit vehicles; the Defense Department official who alerts Congress to
military graft and overspending: All know that they pose a threat to those whom they denounce and that their own careers may be at risk.

    C: The stakes in whistle-blowing are high.

25. P_1: It is generally accepted that by constantly swimming with its mouth open, the shark is
simply avoiding suffocation.

    P_2: This assures a continuous flow of oxygen-laden water into the shark's mouth, over its gills,
and out through the gill slits.

    C: Contrary to the tales of some scuba divers, the toothy, gaping grin on the mouth of an
approaching shark is not necessarily anticipatory.

28. P_1: Anyone familiar with our prison system knows that there are some inmates who behave
little better than brute beasts.

    P_2: If the death penalty had been truly effective as a deterrent, such prisoners would long ago
have vanished.

    C: The very fact that these prisoners exist is a telling argument against the efficacy of capital
punishment as a deterrent.

II.

1. College sports are as much driven by money as are professional sports.

4. Business majors are robbing themselves of the true purpose of collegiate academics, a sacrifice
that outweighs the future salary checks.

7. The religious intolerance of television preachers must not be tolerated.

10. Protecting the environment requires that we limit population growth.

Exercise 1.2

I.

1. Nonargument; explanation.

4. Nonargument; illustration.

7. Argument (conclusion: If stem-cell research is restricted, then people will die prematurely).

10. Nonargument; report.

13. Nonargument; opinion.

16. Nonargument; piece of advice.

19. Argument (conclusion: For organisms at the sea surface, sinking into deep water usually means death).

22. Argument (conclusion: Atoms can combine to form molecules whose properties generally are
very different from those of the constituent atoms).

25. Nonargument; explanation.

28. Argument (conclusion: A person never becomes truly self-reliant).

31. This passage could be both an argument and an explanation (conclusion: In areas where rats are
a problem, it is very difficult to exterminate them with bait poison).

34. Nonargument; loosely associated statements.

II.

1. Nonargument.

4. Nonargument.

7. Argument (conclusion: The poor quality of parenting and the lack in continuity of adult care
provided to many U.S. children contribute to a passivity and a sense of helplessness that hobbles
individuals for the remainder of their lives).

10. Nonargument.

VI.

1. Sufficient: If something is a tiger, then it is an animal.
4. Necessary: If a person has no racket, then he/she cannot play tennis. *Or,* If a person plays tennis, then he/she has a racket.
7. Sufficient: If leaves burn, then smoke is produced.
10. Necessary: If a person does not open the door, then he/she cannot cross the threshold. *Or,* If a person crosses the threshold, then he/she has opened the door.

Exercise 1.3

I.

1. Deductive (argument based on mathematics; also, conclusion follows necessarily from the premises).
4. Deductive (categorical syllogism; also, conclusion follows necessarily from the premises).
7. Inductive (causal inference; also, conclusion follows only probably from the premise).
10. Inductive (argument from analogy; also, conclusion follows only probably from the premise).
13. Inductive (argument from authority; also, conclusion follows only probably from the premise).
16. Deductive (conclusion follows necessarily from the premise).
19. Inductive (causal inference; also, conclusion follows only probably from the premises).
22. Deductive (conclusion follows necessarily from the premise; this example might also be interpreted as an argument from definition—the definition of "refraction").
25. Inductive (causal inference: The dog's familiarity with the visitor caused the dog to be silent).
28. Inductive (causal inference; also, the word "may" suggests a probabilistic inference).

Exercise 1.4

I.

1. Valid, unsound; false premises, false conclusion.
4. Valid, sound; true premises, true conclusion.
7. Invalid, unsound; true premise, true conclusion.
10. Valid, unsound; false premise, false conclusion.
13. Invalid, unsound; true premise, true conclusion.

II.

1. Strong, cogent; true premise, probably true conclusion.
4. Weak, uncogent; true premise, probably false conclusion.
7. Strong, uncogent; false premise, probably true conclusion.
10. Strong, cogent; true premise, probably true conclusion.
13. Weak, uncogent; true premises, probably false conclusion.

III.

1. Deductive, valid.
4. Deductive, valid.
7. Inductive, weak.
10. Deductive, invalid.
13. Inductive, weak.
16. Deductive, invalid.
19. Inductive, strong.

Exercise 1.5

I.

1. All *G* are *S*.
    All *Q* are *S*.
    All *G* are *Q*.

    All cats are animals. (T)
    All dogs are animals. (T)
    All cats are dogs. (F)

4. No *I* are *P*.
    Some *I* are not *F*.
    Some *F* are not *P*.

No fish are mammals. (T)
Some fish are not cats. (T)
Some cats are not mammals. (F)

7. No *P* are *H*.
    No *C* are *H*.
    No *P* are *C*.

No dogs are fish. (T)
No mammals are fish. (T)
No dogs are mammals. (F)

10. Some *S* are not *O*.
     Some *G* are not *O*.
     Some *S* are not *G*.

Some dogs are not fish. (T)
Some animals are not fish. (T)
Some dogs are not animals. (F)

II.

1. If *A* then *E*.
    Not *A*.
    Not *E*.

If George Washington was assassinated, then
George Washington is dead. (T)
George Washington was not assassinated. (T)
George Washington is not dead. (F)

4. If *E*, then either *D* or *C*.
    If *D*, then *I*.
    If *E*, then *I*.

If Tom Cruise is a man, then he is either
a mouse or a human. (T)
If Tom Cruise is a mouse, then he has a tail. (T)
If Tom Cruise is a man, then he has a tail. (F)

7. All *C* with *L* are either
    S or *I*.
    All *C* are *I*.

All cats with fur are either mammals or dogs. (T)
All cats are dogs. (F)

10. All *R* that are *F* are either
     L or *H*.
     All *R* are *H*.
     All *F* are *L*.

All cats that are mammals are either
dogs or animals. (T)
All cats are animals. (T)
All mammals are dogs. (F)

Exercise 1.6

I.

1.

4.

7.

10.

II.

1.

4.

7.

10.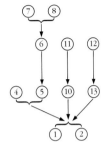

Note: Possible variations
exist for ⑤, ⑥, and ⑦.

13.

Exercise 2.1

II.

1. In dog sled races the dogs are tortured.
   Torturing animals is morally wrong.
   Therefore, dog sled races are morally wrong.

4. Free ownership of guns is as noble as belief in God and intestinal fortitude.
   Belief in God and intestinal fortitude made our country great and free.
   Continued belief in God and intestinal fortitude are necessary to keep our country the way it is.
   Free ownership of guns is no less important than God and intestinal fortitude.
   Therefore, gun control is wrong.

7. The celebration of cultural diversity causes social fragmentation.
   The celebration of cultural diversity is symptomatic of a split personality.
   The people who set this country up framed one nation, indivisible.
   The celebration of cultural diversity works against the intention of these people.
   The celebration of cultural diversity erodes national identity.
   Therefore, the celebration of cultural diversity is wrong.

10. Liberalism has excessively enlarged the welfare system.
    Liberalism has made welfare recipients indolent and irresponsible.
    The liberals refuse to acknowledge or correct the defects in this system.
    Liberalism has made the criminal justice system too sensitive to the criminal and too insensitive to the victim of crime.
    Liberalism has given more rights to the criminal than to the ordinary citizen.
    Liberalism has promoted sex and violence in the school system.
    Liberals have opposed prayer in the schools.
    Therefore, liberalism is bad.

III.

1. Probably verbal; ambiguity. Does "sound" designate a subjective perception or an objective disturbance of the air (or some other medium)?

4. Probably verbal; ambiguity. By "violence" do we mean intentional hostility exerted by one human against another, or the operation of blind physical forces? Possibly a combination of verbal and factual. Is human violence caused by the operation of physical forces just as other physical events are?

7. Factual. Did Paul go to Knoxville or Nashville?

10. Factual. When was the Battle of Trafalgar fought, and when did Nelson die?

13. Probably a combination of verbal (ambiguity) and factual. First, does "freedom" mean the absence of external constraint only, or the absence of both internal and external constraint? Second, given the former, is it appropriate to punish the perpetrator of evil acts even though those acts might be internally compelled?

16. Verbal; vagueness. What is the meaning of "overpaid"?

19. Verbal; vagueness. What is the meaning of "poverty"?

Exercise 2.2

I.

4a. Plant, tree, conifer, spruce, Sitka spruce.

Exercise 2.3

I.

1. Precising definition.
4. Lexical definition.
7. Persuasive definition.

10. Theoretical definition.
13. Stipulative definition.
16. Persuasive definition.

19. Lexical definition.
22. Precising definition.
25. Stipulative definition.

Exercise 2.4

I.

1. Definition by subclass.
4. Enumerative definition.
7. Demonstrative definition.
10. Operational definition.
13. Definition by genus and difference.

16. Etymological definition.
19. Enumerative definition.
22. Synonymous definition.
25. Definition by subclass.
28. Definition by genus and difference.

II.

1a. "Skyscraper" means the Empire State Building, Chrysler Building, Sears Tower, and so on. Nonsynonymous term: building.

3a. "Animal" means a horse, bear, lion, and so on. Nonsynonymous term: mammal.

5a. "Intersection" means crossing.

6a. A person is a "genius" if and only if that person can earn a score of 140 on an IQ test.

7a. "Drake" means a male duck.

8a. "Morphology" is derived from the Greek words *morphe*, meaning "form," and *logos*, meaning reason, speech, or account. The morphology of something (such as an animal or a plant) gives an account or explanation of the form or structure of that thing.

Exercise 2.5

1. Rule 3: too narrow; the definiens excludes images made of bronze, wood, plaster, and so on.
4. Rule 6: figurative language.
7. Rule 5: negative.

10. Rule 7: affective terminology.
13. Rule 1: improper grammar.
16. Rule 4: circular.
19. Rule 6: vague.
22. Rule 1: improper grammar; Rule 6: vague; Rule 3: too broad (the definiens also includes ketches, sloops, and yawls).
25. Rule 3: too broad (the definiens also describes violins, violas, and string basses).
28. Rule 2: fails to convey the essential meaning; the definition says nothing about the purpose of a clock, which is to tell the time; also too narrow: the definiens excludes twenty-four-hour clocks and clocks without twelve numerals on their face.
31. Rule 7: affective terminology.
34. Rule 3: both too narrow and too broad; the definiens excludes instruments used for writing on canvas, glass, metal, plastic, and so on, and it includes pencils, crayons, and so on.

Exercise 3.1

1. Formal fallacy.
4. Informal fallacy.
7. Informal fallacy.
10. Formal fallacy.

Exercise 3.2

I.
1. Appeal to pity.
4. Accident.
7. Appeal to force.
10. *Tu quoque* (you, too).
13. Red herring.

16. *Ad hominem* circumstantial.
19. Straw man.
22. Appeal to the people, indirect variety.
25. Missing the point.

Exercise 3.3

I.
1. Hasty generalization (converse accident).
4. Slippery slope.

7. Appeal to ignorance.
10. Appeal to unqualified authority.
13. Weak analogy.

III.
1. Hasty generalization.
4. *Ad hominem* circumstantial.
7. False cause (gambler's fallacy).
10. Straw man.
13. Red herring.

16. Missing the point.
19. Weak analogy.
22. No fallacy.
25. Appeal to ignorance.
28. False cause.

Exercise 3.4

I.
1. False dichotomy.
4. Amphiboly.
7. Begging the question.
10. Equivocation.
13. Composition.

16. Suppressed evidence.
19. Division.
22. Complex question.
25. Begging the question.

III.

1. *Ad hominem* circumstantial.
4. Equivocation.
7. Begging the question.
10. Division.
13. False cause (oversimplified cause).
16. Appeal to unqualified authority.
19. Composition.
22. Weak analogy.
25. Straw man.

28. Accident.
31. Red herring.
34. Amphiboly.
37. False cause (gambler's fallacy).
40. Begging the question.
43. Missing the point or suppressed evidence.
46. Hasty generalization.
49. Composition.

Exercise 3.5

I.

1. Missing the point or begging the question.
4. Composition.
7. No fallacy? Weak analogy?
10. Appeal to unqualified authority. The statement "Only a fool ..." involves an *ad hominem* abusive.
13. False cause, suppressed evidence, begging the question. There is little or no evidence of any causal connection between malpractice suits and the decision of some obstetricians to leave the field. An unmentioned factor is the inconvenience of being on call twenty-four hours per day waiting for patients to deliver. There is also little or no evidence of any genuine "lawsuit crisis."
16. Begging the question? (Strange argument!)
19. Slippery slope.
22. False cause? No fallacy?
25. False cause.
28. Suppressed evidence? Begging the question? No fallacy? The Commerce Clause of the U.S. Constitution and pertinent federal legislation prohibit unfair trade practices between states. No equivalent regulations exist for international trade.
31. Appeal to the people (direct variety). Also appeal to pity?
34. Appeal to the people (direct variety)?
37. False dichotomy? No fallacy?
40. Appeal to unqualified authority, slippery slope.
43. Several cases of weak analogy. Also, a possible case of *ad hominem* abusive.
46. Begging the question; straw man.
49. Appeal to unqualified authority. The last paragraph suggests a hasty generalization.
52. Hasty generalization. *Ad hominem* abusive? Also, begging the question or red herring?
55. Weak analogy.
58. Weak analogy? No fallacy?

Exercise 4.1

1. *Quantifier:* some; *subject term:* airport screeners; *copula:* are; *predicate term:* officials who harass frail grandmothers.
4. *Quantifier:* some; *subject term:* preachers who are intolerant of others' beliefs; *copula:* are not; *predicate term:* television evangelists.
7. *Quantifier:* no; *subject term:* sex education courses that are taught competently; *copula:* are; *predicate term:* programs that are currently eroding public morals.

Exercise 4.2

I.
1. E proposition, universal, negative, subject and predicate terms are distributed.
4. O proposition, particular, negative, subject term undistributed, predicate term distributed.
7. I proposition, particular, affirmative, subject and predicate terms undistributed.

II.
1. No drunk drivers are threats to others on the highway.
4. Some CIA operatives are champions of human rights.

III.
1. Some owners of pit bull terriers are people who can expect expensive lawsuits.
4. No residents of Manhattan are people who can afford to live there.

IV.
1. Some oil spills are not events catastrophic to the environment.
4. All corporate lawyers are people with a social conscience.

Exercise 4.3

I.
1.

4.

7.

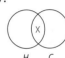

II.
1. Invalid.
4. Valid.
7. Invalid.
10. Valid.
13. Invalid.

III.
1. No S are B.

All S are B.
(invalid)

4. All M are C.

False: Some M are not C.
(valid)

7. No F are S.

False: All F are S.
(invalid, existential fallacy)

10. No V are A.

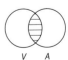

False: Some V are A.
(valid)

13. False: Some *S* are
not *O*.

Some *S* are *O*.
(invalid,
existential fallacy)

Exercise 4.4

I.

  1. No non-*B* are *A*. (true)

  4. All non-*B* are *A*. (false)

  7. Contraposition. (undetermined)

10. Obversion. (false)

II.

  1a. All storms intensified by global warming are hurricanes. (not logically equivalent)

  2a. No radically egalitarian societies are societies that preserve individual liberties. (logically equivalent)

  3a. All physicians eligible to practice are physicians with valid licenses. (logically equivalent)

III.

  1. Invalid (illicit conversion).   **13.** Invalid (illicit conversion).

  4. Invalid (illicit contraposition).   **16.** Invalid (illicit contraposition).

  7. Valid.   **19.** Valid.

10. Valid.

Exercise 4.5

I.

  1. (a) False, (b) True, (c) False.

  4. (a) Undetermined, (b) True, (c) Undetermined.

  7. (a) False, (b) Undetermined, (c) Undetermined.

II.

  1. Valid.   **10.** Invalid (illicit subcontrary).

  4. Invalid (existential fallacy).   **13.** Invalid (existential fallacy).

  7. Invalid (illicit contrary).

III.

  1. All non-*B* are *A*. (true)   **13.** Obversion. (false)

  4. Some non-*A* are *B*. (undetermined)   **16.** Contradiction. (true)

  7. No non-*A* are *B*. (false)   **19.** Contrary. (undetermined)

10. Some non-*A* are not non-*B*. (true)

IV.

  1. Valid.   **10.** Invalid (illicit contrary).

  4. Invalid (illicit contraposition).   **13.** Invalid (illicit subcontrary).

  7. Valid.

V.

1. All *I* are *C*.
   Some *I* are *C*. (subalternation)
   Some *C* are *I*. (conversion)
4. All *E* are *A*.
   False: No *E* are *A*. (contrary)
   False: No *A* are *E*. (conversion)
   False: All *A* are non-*E*. (obversion)

7. Some *P* are not non-*S*.
   Some *P* are *S*. (obversion)
   Some *S* are *P*. (conversion)
   False: No *S* are *P*. (contradiction)
10. False: Some *F* are not *A*.
    False: No *F* are *A*. (subalternation)
    False: No *A* are *F*. (conversion)
    False: All *A* are non-*F*. (obversion)

Exercise 4.6

I.

1. Some *A* are not *B*.

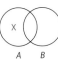

   No *A* are *B*.
   (invalid)

4. All *A* are *B*.

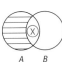

   False: No *A* are *B*.
   (invalid, Boolean;
   conditionally valid,
   Aristotelian)

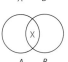

7. False: Some *A* are *B*.

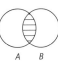

   No *A* are *B*.
   (valid, Boolean)

10. No *A* are *B*.

   Some *A* are not *B*.
   (invalid, Boolean;
   conditionally valid,
   Aristotelian)

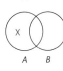

II.

1. No *S* are *B*.

   False: Some *S* are *B*.
   (valid, Boolean)

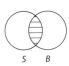

4. False: Some *D* are *A*.

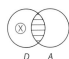

   Some *D* are not *A*.
   (invalid, Boolean; valid,
   Aristotelian; existential
   fallacy, Boolean)

7. All *P* are *F*.

   False: No *P* are *F*.
   (invalid; existential
   fallacy, Boolean and
   Aristotelian)

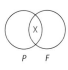

10. False: Some *T* are *Q*.

   All *T* are *Q*.
   (invalid)

13. False: Some *P* are *T*.

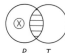

P   T

False: All *P* are *T*.
(invalid, Boolean;
valid; Aristotelian;
existential fallacy,
Boolean)

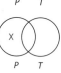

P   T

Exercise 4.7

I.

1. All banks that make too many risky loans are banks that will fail.
4. All substances identical to bromine are substances extractable from seawater.
7. No halogens are chemically inert elements.
10. All ships that fly the Jolly Roger are pirate ships.
13. All bachelors are unmarried men.
16. Some organic silicones are things used as lubricants.
19. Some giant stars are things in the Tarantula Nebula. *Or* All things identical to the Tarantula Nebula are things that contain a giant star.
22. All people who require insulin treatments are diabetics.
25. All cities identical to Berlin are cities that were the setting for the 1936 Olympic Games.
    Or All events identical to the 1936 Olympic Games are events that took place in Berlin.
28. All places there is smoke are places there is fire.
31. All ores identical to pitchblende are radioactive ores.
34. All novels written by John Grisham are are novels about lawyers.
37. All times a rainbow occurs are times the sun is shining.
40. Some corporate raiders are people known for their integrity, and some corporate raiders are not people known for their integrity.
43. All people identical to me are people who like strawberries. *Or* All things identical to strawberries are things I like.
46. All places Cynthia wants to travel are places Cynthia travels.
49. No physicists are people who understand the operation of superconductors.
52. All measures that increase efficiency are measures that improve profitability.
55. Some picnics are events entirely free of ants, and some picnics are not events entirely free of ants.
58. Some contestants are people who won prizes.

II.

1. Some third-generation computers are machines that take dictation.
4. No downhill skiers who suffer from altitude sickness are effective competitors.
7. No matadors are performers who succumb easily to fear.
10. All hungry crocodiles are dangerous animals.

Exercise 5.1

I.

1. *Major term:* things that produce intense gravity.
   Minor term: extremely dense objects.
   Middle term: neutron stars.
   Mood, figure: **AAA**-3; invalid.
4. *Major term:* good witnesses.
   Minor term: hypnotized people.
   Middle term: people who mix fact with fantasy.
   Mood, figure: **EIO**-1; valid, Boolean.

II.

1. All *B* are *D.*
   No *R* are *D.*
   No *R* are *B.*
   AEE-2
   valid, Boolean
4. No *M* are *F.*
   All *M* are *I.*
   Some *I* are not *F.*
   EAO-3
   invalid, Boolean;
   valid, Aristotelian

7. All *P* are *E.*
   All *L* are *P.*
   Some *L* are *E.*
   AAI-1
   invalid
10. Some *O* are not *C.*
    All *S* are *O.*
    Some *S* are *C.*
    OAI-1
    invalid

III.

1. Some *M* are not *P.*
   All *M* are *S.*
   No *S* are *P.*
4. Some *M* are *P.*
   All *S* are *M.*
   No *S* are *P.*

7. All *M* are *P.*
   All *S* are *M.*
   All *S* are *P.*
10. Some *P* are not *M.*
    No *M* are *S.*
    All *S* are *P.*

IV.

1. No dogmatists are scholars who encourage free thinking.
   Some theologians are scholars who encourage free thinking.
   Some theologians are not dogmatists.
4. Some viruses are not things capable of replicating by themselves.
   All viruses are structures that invade cells.
   Some structures that invade cells are not things capable of replicating by themselves.

Exercise 5.2

I.

1. All *C* are *U.*
   Some *U* are *I.*
   Some *I* are *C.*
   AII-4
   invalid

4. All *H* are *D.*
   Some *D* are not *P.*
   Some *P* are not *H.*
   AOO-4
   invalid

7. No *P* are *I*.
  All *F* are *I*.
  No *F* are *P*.
   EAE-2
   valid, Boolean

16. All *C* are *G*.
  All *G* are *E*.
  Some *E* are *C*.
   AAI-4
   invalid

10. No *C* are *O*.
  Some *D* are not *O*.
  Some *D* are not *C*.
   EOO-2
   invalid

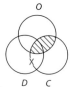

19. No *S* are *I*.
  All *S* are *N*.
  Some *N* are not *I*.
   EAO-3
   invalid, Boolean;
   valid, Aristotelian

13. No *P* are *W*.
  All *D* are *P*.
  No *D* are *W*.
   EAE-1
   valid, Boolean

II.

1.

Conclusion: No *S* are *P*.

7.

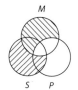

Conclusion: All *S* are *P*.

4.

Conclusion: Some *S* are not *P*.

10.

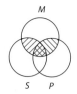

Conclusion: None.

Exercise 5.3

I.

1. All *M* are *P*.
  All *M* are *S*.
  All *S* are *P*.
   invalid;
   illicit minor

4. All *P* are *M*.
  All *S* are *M*.
  Some *S* are *P*.
   invalid;
   undistributed middle

7. No *M* are *P*.

　　All *S* are *M*.

　　All *S* are *P*.

　　invalid;

　　drawing affirmative

　　conclusion from

　　negative premise

16. No *M* are *P*.

　　No *S* are *M*.

　　No *S* are *P*.

　　invalid;

　　exclusive premises

10. Some *M* are *P*.

　　All *M* are *S*.

　　Some *S* are not *P*.

　　invalid;

　　illicit major;

　　drawing negative

　　conclusion from

　　affirmative premises

19. All *P* are *M*.

　　Some *S* are not *M*.

　　Some *S* are not *P*.

　　valid, Boolean;

　　no rules broken

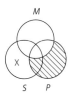

13. All *P* are *M*.

　　No *M* are *S*.

　　No *S* are *P*.

　　valid, Boolean;

　　no rules broken

II.

1. Some *N* are *C*.

　　Some *C* are *O*.

　　Some *O* are *N*.

　　invalid;

　　undistributed middle

7. No *S* are *V*.

　　Some *W* are *V*.

　　Some *W* are not *S*

　　valid, Boolean

　　no rules broken

4. Some *C* are not *M*.

　　No *C* are *I*.

　　Some *I* are not *M*.

　　invalid;

　　exclusive premises

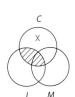

10. All *S* are *M*.

　　All *M* are *P*.

　　Some *P* are *S*.

　　invalid, Boolean;

　　valid, Aristotelian;

　　existential fallacy,

　　Boolean

Exercise 5.4

1. Some non-*T* are *M*. (convert, obvert)

　　All non-*I* are non-*M*. (contrapose)

　　Some *I* are *T*.

Some *M* are not *T*.

All *M* are *I*.

Some *I* are *T*.

　　invalid; drawing affirmative conclusion

　　from negative premise

4. Some *I* are *C*.
All *C* are non-*P*.
_____
Some non-*I* are not *P*. (contrapose)

Some *I* are *C*.
All *C* are non-*P*.
_____
Some non-*P* are not *I*.
   invalid; illicit major

7. All non-*M* are non-*E*. (contrapose)
Some *P* are not *M*.
_____
Some *P* are non-*E*. (obvert)

All *E* are *M*.
Some *P* are not *M*.
_____
Some *P* are not *E*.
   valid

10. Some *F* are non-*D*. (obvert)
No *D* are *V*.
_____
Some non-*V* are *F*. (convert, obvert)

Some *F* are not *D*.
No *D* are *V*.
_____
Some *F* are not *V*.
   invalid; exclusive premises

Exercise 5.5

1. All scientists who theorize about the nature of time are physicists.
All people identical to Stephen Hawking are scientists who theorize about the nature of time.
_____
All people identical to Stephen Hawking are physicists.
   valid

4. All people who wrote the Declaration of Independence are people who had a big impact on civilization.
All people identical to Thomas Jefferson are people who had a big impact on civilization.
_____
All people identical to Thomas Jefferson are people who wrote the Declaration of Independence.
   invalid, undistributed middle

7. Some songs Shania Twain sings are country songs.
All songs Shania Twain wants to sing are songs Shania Twain sings.
_____
Some songs Shania Twain wants to sing are country songs.
   invalid, undistributed middle

10. All TV viewers who receive scrambled signals are viewers with a decoder.
All people who receive digital satellite signals are TV viewers who receive scrambled signals.
_____
All people who receive digital satellite signals are viewers with a decoder.
   valid

13. All diseases carried by recessive genes are diseases that can be inherited by offspring of two carriers.
All diseases identical to cystic fibrosis are diseases carried by recessive genes.
_____
All diseases identical to cystic fibrosis are diseases that can be inherited by offspring of two carriers.
   valid

Exercise 5.6

I.

1. Premise missing: Some police chiefs fix parking tickets.

4. Conclusion missing: A few fraternities have no legitimate role in campus life.

7. Conclusion missing: Some phone calls are not from friends.

10. Premise missing: Whenever the humpback whale is overhunted, the humpback whale population decreases.

13. Premise missing: No one who thinks that everything is governed by deterministic laws believes in free will.

II.

1. All people who fix parking tickets are people who undermine the evenhanded enforcement of the law.

   Some police chiefs are people who fix parking tickets.

   Some police chiefs are people who undermine the evenhanded enforcement of the law.

   valid

4. No groups that have dangerous initiation rites are groups that have a legitimate role in campus life.

   Some fraternities are groups that have dangerous initiation rites.

   Some fraternities are not groups that have a legitimate role in campus life.

   valid

7. All calls from friends are welcome calls.

   Some phone calls are not welcome calls.

   Some phone calls are not calls from friends.

   valid

10. All times the humpback whale is overhunted are times the humpback whale population decreases.

    All recent years are times the humpback whale is overhunted.

    All recent years are times the humpback whale population decreases.

    valid

13. No people who think that everything is governed by deterministic laws are people who believe in free will.

    All mechanistic materialists are people who think everything is governed by deterministic laws.

    No mechanistic materialists are people who believe in free will.

    valid

III.

1. No organizations that make alcohol readily available and acceptable are organizations that are serious about fighting alcohol abuse.

   All organizations identical to the Defense Department are organizations that make alcohol readily available and acceptable.

   No organizations identical to the Defense Department are organizations that are serious about fighting alcohol abuse.

4. All efforts to ban books are efforts that ensure those books will be read.

   All efforts by the fundamentalist families in Church Hill, Tennessee, to remove *Macbeth*, etc. from the libraries are efforts to ban books.

   All efforts by the fundamentalist families in Church Hill, Tennessee, to remove *Macbeth*, etc. from the libraries are efforts that ensure those books will be read.

7. All policies that promote more college graduates tomorrow are policies that result in higher tax revenues tomorrow.

   All policies that offer financial aid to college students today are policies that promote more college graduates tomorrow.

   All policies that offer financial aid to college students today are policies that result in higher tax revenues tomorrow.

   and

   All policies that result in higher tax revenues tomorrow are good investments in the future.

   All policies that offer financial aid to college students today are policies that result in higher tax revenues tomorrow.

   All policies that offer financial aid to college students today are good investments in the future.

10. All people who act in ways that decrease their chances of survival are people who will die out through natural selection.

All smokers who continue smoking are people who act in ways that decrease their chances of survival.

All smokers who continue smoking are people who will die out through natural selection.

and

All people who act in ways that increase their chances of survival are people who will survive through natural selection.

All smokers who quit are people who act in ways that increase their chances of survival.

All smokers who quit are people who will survive through natural selection.

Exercise 5.7

I.

1. All *A* are *B*. ⎫
   No *B* are *C*. ⎬ No *C* are *A*. ⎫
   Some *D* are *C*. ─────→ ⎬
   ─────────── ⎭
   Some *D* are not *A*.
   valid

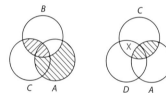

4. No *K* are *N*. ⎫
   Some *T* are *K*. ⎬ Some *T* are not *N*. ⎫
   All *T* are *C*. ──────────────→ ⎬ Some *C* are not *N*. ⎫
   Some *C* are *Q*. ──────────────────────→ ⎬
   ────────────── ⎭
   Some *Q* are not *N*.
   invalid

  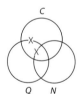

7. After contraposing the first premise, obverting the second premise and the conclusion, and rearranging the premises, we have

No *X* are *W.* ⎫
All *U* are *W.* ⎭   No *U* are *X.* ⎫
All *V* are *U.* ⟶   ⎭   No *V* are *X.* ⎫
All *V* are *Y* ⟶⟶⟶⟶⟶⟶⟶⟶ ⎭
―――――――――
No *Y* are *X.*
  invalid

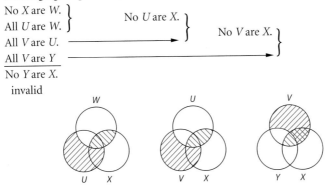

10. After converting and obverting the second and fourth premises, obverting the third and fifth premises and the conclusion, and rearranging the premises, we have

All *P* are *Q.* ⎫
All *Q* are *R.* ⎭   All *P* are *R.* ⎫
All *R* are *S.* ⟶   ⎭   All *P* are *S.* ⎫
No *T* are *S.* ⟶⟶⟶⟶⟶⟶ ⎭   No *P* are *T.* ⎫
All *T* are *V.* ⟶⟶⟶⟶⟶⟶⟶⟶⟶⟶⟶ ⎭
―――――――――
No *V* are *P.*
  invalid

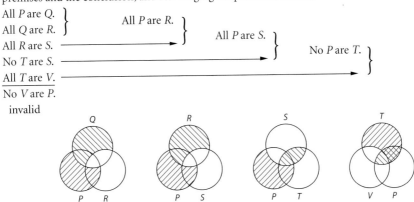

II.

  1. Valid—no rules broken.
  4. Invalid—breaks Rule 1: *C* is undistributed in both premises.
  7. Invalid—breaks Rule 2: *Y* is distributed in the conclusion but not in the premise.
  10. Invalid—breaks Rule 2: *V* is distributed in the conclusion but not in the premise.

III.

  1. All things that produce oxygen are things that support human life.   All *O* are *S.*
     All rain forests are things that produce oxygen.   All *R* are *O.*
     No things that support human life are things that should be destroyed.   No *S* are *D.*
     ―――――――――――――――――――――――   No *R* are *D.*
     No rain forests are things that should be destroyed.

   After rearranging the premises, we have

   No *S* are *D.* ⎫
   All *O* are *S.* ⎭   No *O* are *D.* ⎫
   All *R* are *O.* ⟶   ⎭
   ―――――――――
   No *R* are *D.*
     no rules broken

4. No brittle things are ductile things.
All superconductors are ceramics.
All things that can be pulled into wires are ductile things.
All ceramics are brittle things.
No superconductors are things that can be pulled into wires.

No B are D.
All S are C.
All P are D.
All C are B.
No S are P.

After rearranging the premises, we have

All P are D.
No B are D. } No B are P.
All C are B. ⟶ } No C are P.
All S are C. ⟶
No S are P.

no rules broken

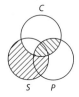

7. All people who give birth to crack babies are people who increase future crime rates.
Some pregnant women are pregnant crack users.
All people who increase future crime rates are criminals.
No pregnant crack users are people who fail to give birth to crack babies.
Some pregnant women are criminals.

All B are I.
Some P are U.
All I are C.

No U are non-B.
Some P are C.

After obverting the fourth premise and rearranging the premises, we have

All I are C. }
All B are I. } All B are C. }
All U are B. ⟶ } All U are C. }
Some P are U. ⟶
Some P are C.

no rules broken

10. All things that promote skin cancer are things that cause death.
All things that preserve the ozone layer are things that prevent the release of CFCs.
No things that resist skin cancer are things that increase UV radiation.
All things that do not preserve the ozone layer are things that increase UV radiation.
Some packaging materials are things that release CFCs.
No things that cause death are things that should be legal.
Some packaging materials are things that should not be legal.

All S are C.

All O are non-R.
No non-S are U.

All non-O are U.
Some M are R.
No C are L.
Some M are non-L.

After contraposing the second premise, converting and obverting the third premise, and obverting the conclusion, we have

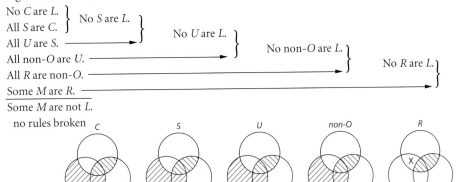

No C are L. }
All S are C. } No S are L.
All U are S. ──────→ } No U are L.
All non-O are U. ──────→ } No non-O are L.
All R are non-O. ──────→ } No R are L.
Some M are R. ──────→
Some M are not L.
no rules broken

IV.

1. No ducks are waltzers.
   No officers are non-waltzers.
   All poultry of mine are ducks.
   No poultry of mine are officers.

   No D are W.
   No O are non-W.
   All P are D.
   No P are O.

   After obverting the second premise and rearranging the premises, we have

   All O are W. }
   No D are W. } No D are O.
   All P are D. ──────→ }
   No P are O.
   no rules broken

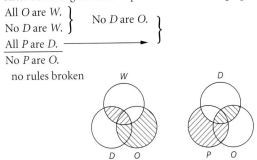

4. All hummingbirds are richly colored birds.
   No large birds are birds that live on honey.
   All birds that do not live on honey are birds that are dull in color.
   All hummingbirds are small birds.

   All H are R.
   No L are O.
   All non-O are non-R.
   All H are non-L.

   After contraposing the third premise, obverting the conclusion, and rearranging the premises, we have

   No L are O. }
   All R are O. } No L are R.
   All H are R. ──────→ }
   No H are L.
   no rules broken

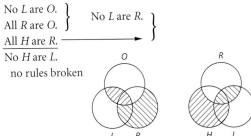

7. All books in this library that I do not recommend are books that are unhealthy in tone.
   All the bound books are well-written books.
   All the romances are books that are healthy in tone.
   All the unbound books are books in this library that I do not recommend.

   ————————————————————————

   All the romances are well-written books.

   All non-R are non-H.
   All B are W.
   All O are H.

   ——————————

   All non-B are non-R.
   All O are W.

   After contraposing the first and fourth premises, we have

   All B are W. ⎫
   All R are B. ⎬ All R are W. ⎫
   All H are R. ——————————→ ⎬ All H are W. ⎫
   All O are H. ——————————————————————→ ⎬
   ————————
   All O are W.
   no rules broken

10. All animals that belong to me are animals I trust.
    All dogs are animals that gnaw bones.
    All animals I admit to my study are animals that beg when told to do so.
    All the animals in the yard are animals that belong to me.
    All animals I trust are animals I admit into my study.
    All animals that are willing to beg when told to do so are dogs.

    ——

    All the animals in the yard are animals that gnaw bones.

    All A are T.
    All D are G.
    All S are B.
    All Y are A.
    All T are S.
    All B are D.

    ——————————

    All Y are G.

    After rearranging the premises, we have

    All D are G. ⎫
    All B are D. ⎬ All B are G. ⎫
    All S are B. ——————————→ ⎬ All S are G. ⎫
    All T are S. ——————————————————→ ⎬ All T are G. ⎫
    All A are T. ——————————————————————————→ ⎬ All A are G. ⎫
    All Y are A. ——————————————————————————————————→ ⎬
    ————————
    All Y are G.
    no rules broken

Exercise 6.1

I.
  1. ~C
  4. H · B
  7. L ≡ B
  10. C ⊃ P
  13. M · (E ∨ D)
  16. ~J · ~P
  19. ~(F ∨ M) or ~F · ~M
  22. (B ⊃ K) ⊃ P
  25. ~R ∨ (M ⊃ P)
  28. (~P · ~C) ⊃ M
  31. (T · B) ∨ (~Z · ~K)
  34. ~H · [I ⊃ (B ∨ C)]
  37. S ⊃ [D ⊃ (P · M)]
  40. ~[(K ∨ S) · (L ∨ B)]
  43. I ≡ P
  46. ~[(A ⊃ N) · (S ⊃ C)]
  49. [(C · J) ≡ K] ⊃ ~(B ∨ S)

II.
  1. R ∨ F
  4. ~(H ∨ S)
  7. S ⊃ G
  10. A ⊃ (~N ⊃ M)
  13. (C · K) ≡ P
  16. [(T · L) ⊃ H] · (H ⊃ I)
  19. (B ⊃ M) · [(M · I) ⊃ (C · P)]

Exercise 6.2

I.
  1. Dot. 4. Triple bar. 7. Horseshoe. 10. Wedge.

II.
  1. ~ H
     Ⓕ T
  4. H · ~ N
     T Ⓕ F T
  7. W ⊃ E
     F Ⓣ F
  10. H ⊃ (C ∨ E)
     T Ⓣ T T F
  13. ~ (E ∨ F) ⊃ (H · L)
     T F F F Ⓣ T T T

III.

1. $A \cdot X$
   T Ⓕ F

4. $\sim C \vee Z$
   F T Ⓔ F

7. $\sim X \supset Z$
   T F Ⓕ F

10. $\sim (A \cdot \sim Z)$
    Ⓕ T T T F

13. $(A \cdot Y) \vee (\sim Z \cdot C)$
    T F F Ⓣ T F T T

16. $(C \equiv \sim A) \vee (Y \equiv Z)$
    T F F T Ⓣ F T F

19. $\sim [\sim (X \supset C) \equiv \sim (B \supset Z)]$
    Ⓣ F F T T T F T F F

22. $\sim [(A \equiv X) \vee (Z \equiv Y)] \vee [(\sim Y \supset B) \cdot (Z \supset C)]$
    F T F F T F T F Ⓣ T F T T T F T T

25. $(Z \supset C) \supset \{[(\sim X \supset B) \supset (C \supset Y)] \equiv [(Z \supset X) \supset (\sim Y \supset Z)]\}$
    F T T Ⓣ T F T T F T F F T F T F F T F F F

IV.

1. $A \vee P$
   T Ⓣ ?

4. $Q \cdot A$
   ? Ⓕ T

7. $A \supset P$
   T Ⓕ ?

10. $(P \supset A) \equiv (Q \supset B)$
    ? T T Ⓣ ? T T

13. $\sim (Q \cdot Y) \equiv \sim (Q \vee A)$
    T ? F F Ⓕ F ? T T

Exercise 6.3

I.

1. $N \supset (N \supset N)$

T	T	T T T

   T $\boxed{T}$ T T T
   F $\boxed{T}$ F T F
   tautologous

4. $[(E \supset F) \supset F] \supset E$

   T T T T T $\boxed{T}$ T
   T F F T F $\boxed{T}$ T
   F T T T F $\boxed{F}$ F
   F T F F F $\boxed{T}$ F
   contingent

7. $[(Z \supset X) \cdot (X \vee Z)] \supset X$

   T T T T T T T $\boxed{T}$ T
   T F F F F T T $\boxed{T}$ F
   F T T T T T F $\boxed{T}$ T
   F T F F F F F $\boxed{T}$ F
   tautologous

10. $[G \supset (N \supset \sim G)] \cdot [(N \equiv G) \cdot (N \vee G)]$

T F	T F F T	**F**	T T T	T T T
T T	F T F T	**F**	F F T	F F T T
F T	T T T F	**F**	T F F	F T T F
F T	F T T F	**F**	F T F	F F F F

self-contradictory

13. $[U \cdot (T \vee S)] \equiv [(\sim T \vee \sim U) \cdot (\sim S \vee \sim U)]$

T T T T T	**F**	F T F F T F	F T F F T
T T T T F	**F**	F T F F T F	T F T F T
T T F T T	**F**	T F T F T F	F T F F T
T F F F F	**F**	T F T F T T	T F T F T
F F T T T	**F**	F T T T F T	F T T T F
F F T T F	**F**	F T T T F T	T F T T F
F F F T T	**F**	T F T T F T	F T T T F
F F F F F	**F**	T F T T F T	T F T T F

self-contradictory

II.

1. $\sim D \vee B$ $\sim (D \cdot \sim B)$

F T **T** T	**T** T F F T
F T **F** F	**F** T T T F
T F **T** T	**T** F F F T
T F **T** F	**T** F F T F

logically equivalent

4. $R \vee \sim S$ $S \cdot \sim R$

T **T** F T	T **F** F T
T **T** T F	F **F** F T
F **F** F T	T **T** T F
F **T** T F	F **F** T F

contradictory

7. $(E \supset C) \supset L$ $E \supset (C \supset L)$

T T T **T** T	T **T** T T T
T T T **F** F	T **F** T F F
T F F **T** T	T **T** F T T
T F F **T** F	T **T** F T F
F T T **T** T	F **T** T T T
F T T **F** F	F **T** T F F
F T F **T** T	F **T** F T T
F T F **F** F	F **T** F T F

consistent

10. $W \equiv (B \cdot T)$ $W \cdot (T \supset \sim B)$

T **T** T T T	T **F** T F F T
T **F** T F F	T **T** F T F T
T **F** F F T	T **T** T T T F
T **F** F F F	T **T** F T T F
F **F** T T T	F **F** T F F T
F **T** T F F	F **F** F T F T
F **T** F F T	F **F** T T T F
F **T** F F F	F **F** F T T F

inconsistent

13. $H \cdot (K \lor J)$ $(J \cdot H) \lor (H \cdot K)$

```
T T  T T T        T T T  T  T T T
T T  T T F        F F T  T  T T T
T T  F T T        T T T  T  T F F
T F  F F F        F F T  F  T F F
F F  T T T        T F F  F  F F T
F F  T T F        F F F  F  F F T
F F  F T T        T F F  F  F F F
F F  F F F        F F F  F  F F F
```

logically equivalent

III.

1. Carlson's prediction is false (self-contradictory).

4. It is possible that both astronomers are correct. If they are, a supernova will not occur within 10 light years of the earth.

7. It is possible that both stockbrokers are correct. If they are, then Datapro will cut back its work force. We can conclude nothing about Netmark and Compucel.

10. It is possible that Nicole's philosophy makes sense. If it does, then the mind is not identical to the brain, personal freedom exists, and humans are responsible for their actions.

Exercise 6.4

I.

1. $N \supset S \ / \ / \ \sim N \supset \sim S$

```
T T  T      F T T  F T
T F  F      F T T  T F
F T  T      T F F  F T
F T  F      T F T  T F
```
invalid

4. $D \supset W \ / \ D \ / \ W$

```
T T  T     T     T
T F  F     T     F
F T  T     F     T
F T  F     F     F
```
valid

7. Invalid (fails on first line).

10. Valid.

II.

1. Valid.

4. Valid.

7. Invalid (fails on fourth line).

10. Invalid (fails on fourth and sixth lines).

13. Valid.

16. Invalid (fails on third line).

19. Valid.

Exercise 6.5

Note: Truth values may vary depending on how the problem is done.

1. $B \supset C \ / \ \sim C \ / \ / \ \sim B$

```
T T F     T F     F T
```
valid

4. $\sim (I \equiv J) \ / \ / \ \sim (I \supset J)$

```
T  T F F      F T F  F
T  F F T      F F T T
```
invalid

7. $G \supset H \ / \ H \supset I \ / \ \sim J \supset G \ / \ \sim I \ / \ / \ J$

```
T T T     T T T    T F T T    T T      F
```
valid

10. $(M \lor N) \supset O$ / $O \supset (N \lor P)$ / $M \supset (\sim Q \supset N)$ / $(Q \supset M) \supset \sim P$ / / $N \equiv O$

T T T F   T   T   T   T F F

      T T   T T   F T T   F T   T F F T F T   F F T

invalid

13. $(A \lor B) \supset (C \cdot D)$ / $(X \lor \sim Y) \supset (\sim C \cdot \sim W)$ / $(X \lor Z) \supset (A \cdot E)$ / / $\sim X$

T (T   T   F F)   T T   T   T F T T F   T T   T   T T T   F T

valid

II.

1. $K \equiv (R \lor M)$ / $K \cdot \sim R$ / $M \supset \sim K$

T T F T T   T T T F   (T T F) T

inconsistent

4. $(N \lor C) \equiv E$ / $N \supset \sim (C \lor H)$ / $H \supset E$ / $C \supset H$

F T T   T T   F T F   T T T   T T T   T T T

                                              F T T

                                              F T F

consistent

7. $S \supset (R \equiv A)$ / $A \supset (W \cdot \sim R)$ / $R \equiv (W \lor T)$ / $S \cdot U$ / $U \supset T$

T T (T T F)   F T   F F T   T T   T T   T T T   T T T

inconsistent

10. $A \lor Z$ / $A \supset (T \cdot F)$ / $Z \supset (M \cdot Q)$ / $Q \supset \sim F$ / $T \supset \sim M$ / $M \supset A$

T T T   (T T F F) F   T T   T T T   T T T F   F T F T   T T T

T T F   T T   T T T   F T   F F F   F T F T   T T T F   F T T

                                                        F T F

consistent

Exercise 6.6

I.

1. MT—valid.   **7.** DD—valid.   **13.** DS—valid.   **19.** Invalid.

4. CD—valid.   **10.** DA—invalid.   **16.** AC—invalid.

Numbers 7 and 13 must be rewritten as follows:

7. $(E \supset N) \cdot (\sim L \supset \sim K)$

$\underline{\sim N \lor \sim \sim K \qquad\qquad}$

$\sim E \lor \sim \sim L$

13. $\sim S \lor P$

$\underline{\sim \sim S}$

P

II.

1. $F \supset T$

$\underline{\sim T}$

$\sim F$ MT—valid

4. $W \lor \sim M$

$\underline{\sim W}$

$\sim M$ DS—valid

7. T

$\underline{T \supset \sim H}$

$\sim H$ MP—valid

10. $(L \supset \sim A) \cdot (C \supset F)$

$\underline{\sim L \cdot \sim C \qquad\qquad}$

$A \cdot \sim F$ invalid

13. $(A \supset E) \cdot (P \supset \sim E)$

$\underline{E \lor \sim E \qquad\qquad}$

$\sim A \lor \sim P$

rewritten:

$(A \supset E) \cdot (P \supset \sim E)$

$\underline{\sim E \lor \sim \sim E \qquad}$

$\sim A \lor \sim P$ DD—valid

16. $\sim M \supset U$

$\underline{U}$

$\sim M$ AC—invalid

19. $S \supset C$

$\underline{I \supset S}$

$I \supset C$ HS—valid

III.

1. $(S \supset M) \cdot (\sim S \supset F)$

$\dfrac{S \vee \sim S}{M \vee F}$ CD

Since the second premise is a tautology, it is impossible to escape between the horns. The two available strategies are therefore grasping by the horns and constructing a counterdilemma. If Melinda adequately prepares for the test before the party, then she does not spend the party night studying and she does not fail the test. This would falsify the right-hand conjunct of the first premise, thus falsifying the entire premise. Here is a counterdilemma:

> If Melinda spends the night studying, she will pass the test tomorrow; and if she doesn't spend the night studying, she will go to the party. She will either spend the night studying or not studying. Therefore, she will either pass the test or go to the party.

4. $(C \supset \sim S) \cdot (E \supset S)$ rewritten: $(C \supset \sim S) \cdot (E \supset S)$

$\dfrac{S \vee \sim S}{\sim C \vee \sim E}$ $\dfrac{\sim\sim S \vee \sim S}{\sim C \vee \sim E}$ DD

The second premise is a tautology, so it is impossible to escape between the horns. One could grasp the dilemma by the horns by arguing that corporations could share the cost of neutralizing toxic waste, thus preserving the competitive edge. Here is a constructive counterdilemma:

> If corporations spend money to neutralize their toxic waste, then the environment will be preserved; but if corporations do not spend money to neutralize their toxic waste, then they will remain competitive. Corporations will do one or the other. Therefore, either the environment will be preserved or corporations will remain competitive.

7. $(C \supset L) \cdot (J \supset B)$

$\dfrac{\sim L \vee \sim B}{\sim C \vee \sim J}$ DD

Here the second premise is not a tautology, so it is possible to escape between the horns. Perhaps students could take a double major in liberal arts and business. One could also grasp the dilemma by the horns by arguing that students could major in a liberal arts field where a job *would* be available upon graduation. Here is a constructive counterdilemma:

> If students major in liberal arts, then they will take courses that are interesting and rewarding; but if they major in business, then they will have a job when they graduate. Students will either major in liberal arts or business. Therefore, either they will take courses that are interesting and rewarding or they will have a job when they graduate.

10. $(P \supset R) \cdot (T \supset E)$

$\dfrac{P \vee T}{R \vee E}$ CD

The second premise is not a tautology, so it is at least possible to escape between the horns. If we instructed counterterrorist squads to execute terrorists on the spot, we would neither prosecute them nor release them. Can you think of a way to grasp the dilemma by the horns? Here is a counterdilemma:

> If we prosecute suspected terrorists, then we discourage terrorism; but if we release them, then we avoid the risk of retaliation by other terrorists. We must either prosecute or release suspected terrorists. Therefore, either we will discourage terrorism or we will avoid the risk of retaliation by other terrorists.

IV.

1. If Oral Roberts actually receives messages from God, then he would not have sent the letter. Oral Roberts did send the letter. Therefore, he does not actually receive messages from God. (MT)

4. If group problem solving is important, then we should not emphasize individual testing. Group problem solving is important. Therefore, we should not emphasize individual testing. (MP)

   If we should not emphasize individual testing, then the national math test is a mistake. We should not emphasize individual testing. Therefore, the national math test is a mistake. (MP)

7. If we close the library at Central Juvenile Hall, then delinquents will be deprived of an opportunity to read. If delinquents are deprived of an opportunity to read, then they will not have access to ideas, dreams, and alternative ways of living. Therefore, if we close the library at Central Juvenile Hall, then delinquents will not have access to ideas, dreams, and alternative ways of living. (HS)

   If we close the library at Central Juvenile Hall, then delinquents will not have access to ideas, dreams, and alternative ways of living. Delinquents must have access to ideas, dreams, and alternative ways of living. Therefore, we must not close the library at Central Juvenile Hall. (MT)

10. If viewing adult videocassettes led to violent sex crimes, then there would be over a million violent sex crimes per week. It is not the case that there are over a million violent sex crimes per week. Therefore, viewing adult videocassettes does not lead to violent sex crimes. (MT)

Exercise 7.1

I.

1.	$\sim G$	1, 2, MT
4.	C	1, 2, DS
7.	$F \supset D$	1, 3, HS
10.	$G \supset A$	1, 4, HS

13.	$\sim\sim C$	1, 3, MT
16.	$\sim P$	1, 2, MP
19.	$\sim(S \vee C)$	1, 3, MT

II.

1.	$\sim B$	
		1, 2, DS
4.	$R \supset C$	
		1, 2, HS
7.	Q	
		2, 3, MP
10.	$\sim A$	
		1, 4, MT

13.	$\sim\sim S$	
		3, 4, MT
16.	$\sim Z$	
		3, 4, MP
19.	$H \vee G$	
		2, 4, MP

III.

(1) 1. $\sim C \supset (A \supset C)$
    2. $\sim C$ / $\sim A$
    3. $A \supset C$ 1, 2, MP
    4. $\sim A$ 2, 3, MT

(4) 1. $P \supset (G \supset T)$
    2. $Q \supset (T \supset E)$
    3. P
    4. Q / $G \supset E$
    5. $G \supset T$ 1, 3, MP
    6. $T \supset E$ 2, 4, MP
    7. $G \supset E$ 5, 6, HS

(7) 1. $\sim S \supset D$
    2. $\sim S \vee (\sim D \supset K)$
    3. $\sim D$ / K
    4. $\sim\sim S$ 1, 3, MT
    5. $\sim D \supset K$ 2, 4, DS
    6. K 3, 5, MP

(10) 1. $N \supset (J \supset P)$
2. $(J \supset P) \supset (N \supset J)$
3. N / P
4. $J \supset P$ 1, 3, MP
5. $N \supset J$ 2, 4, MP
6. $N \supset P$ 4, 5, HS
7. P 3, 6, MP

(13) 1. $R \supset (G \lor {\sim}A)$
2. $(G \lor {\sim}A) \supset {\sim}S$
3. $G \supset S$
4. R / ${\sim}A$
5. $G \lor {\sim}A$ 1, 4, MP
6. ${\sim}S$ 2, 5, MP
7. ${\sim}G$ 3, 6, MT
8. ${\sim}A$ 5, 7, DS

(16) 1. $(B \supset {\sim}M) \supset (T \supset {\sim}S)$
2. $B \supset K$
3. $K \supset {\sim}M$
4. ${\sim}S \supset N$ / $T \supset N$
5. $B \supset {\sim}M$ 2, 3, HS
6. $T \supset {\sim}S$ 1, 5, MP
7. $T \supset N$ 4, 6, HS

(19) 1. ${\sim}G \supset [G \lor (S \supset G)]$
2. $(S \lor L) \supset {\sim}G$
3. $S \lor L$ / L
4. ${\sim}G$ 2, 3, MP
5. $G \lor (S \supset G)$ 1, 4, MP
6. $S \supset G$ 4, 5, DS
7. ${\sim}S$ 4, 6, MT
8. L 3, 7, DS

(22) 1. $(C \supset M) \supset (N \supset P)$
2. $(C \supset N) \supset (N \supset M)$
3. $(C \supset P) \supset {\sim}M$
4. $C \supset N$ / ${\sim}C$
5. $N \supset M$ 2, 4, MP
6. $C \supset M$ 4, 5, HS
7. $N \supset P$ 1, 6, MP
8. $C \supset P$ 4, 7, HS
9. ${\sim}M$ 3, 8, MP
10. ${\sim}C$ 6, 9, MT

(25) 1. ${\sim}N \supset [(B \supset D) \supset (N \lor {\sim}E)]$
2. $(B \supset E) \supset {\sim}N$
3. $B \supset D$
4. $D \supset E$ / ${\sim}D$
5. $B \supset E$ 3, 4, HS
6. ${\sim}N$ 2, 5, MP
7. $(B \supset D) \supset (N \lor {\sim}E)$ 1, 6, MP
8. $N \lor {\sim}E$ 3, 7, MP
9. ${\sim}E$ 6, 8, DS
10. ${\sim}D$ 4, 9, MT

IV.

(1) 1. $W \supset (P \lor C)$
2. ${\sim}P$
3. W / C
4. $P \lor C$ 1, 3, MP
5. C 2, 4, DS

(7) 1. $H \supset (D \equiv A)$
2. $V \lor (R \supset V)$
3. $R \lor H$
4. ${\sim}V$ / $D \equiv A$
5. $R \supset V$ 2, 4, DS
6. ${\sim}R$ 4, 5, MT
7. H 3, 6, DS
8. $D \equiv A$ 1, 7, MP

(4) 1. $(R \supset L) \supset (L \supset {\sim}F)$
2. ${\sim}F \lor (R \supset L)$
3. ${\sim}{\sim}F$ / ${\sim}R$
4. $R \supset L$ 2, 3, DS
5. $L \supset {\sim}F$ 1, 4, MP
6. ${\sim}L$ 3, 5, MT
7. ${\sim}R$ 4, 6, MT

(10) 1. ${\sim}C \supset [C \lor (J \supset D)]$
2. $C \supset (C \cdot U)$
3. ${\sim}(C \cdot U)$
4. ${\sim}D$ / ${\sim}J$
5. ${\sim}C$ 2, 3, MT
6. $C \lor (J \supset D)$ 1, 5, MP
7. $J \supset D$ 5, 6, DS
8. ${\sim}J$ 4, 7, MT

Exercise 7.2

I.

1. B	2	
4. $H \lor F$	1	

7. $Q \lor K$	1	
10. $\sim\!L \lor M$	1, 2	

II.

1. G	2, Simp
	3, Add
4. $T \lor U$	1, Add
	3, 4, MP

7. $\sim\!F$	2, 3, MT
	1, 4, Conj
10. $M \cdot E$	1, 3, Conj
	2, 4, MP

III.

(1)
1. $\sim\!M \supset Q$		
2. $R \supset \sim\!T$		
3. $\sim\!M \lor R$	$/\ Q \lor \sim\!T$	
4. $(\sim\!M \supset Q) \cdot (R \supset \sim\!T)$	1, 2, Conj	
5. $Q \lor \sim\!T$	3, 4, CD	

(4)
1. $(H \lor \sim\!B) \supset R$	
2. $(H \lor \sim\!M) \supset P$	
3. H	$/\ R \cdot P$
4. $H \lor \sim\!B$	3, Add
5. R	1, 4, MP
6. $H \lor \sim\!M$	3, Add
7. P	2, 6, MP
8. $R \cdot P$	5, 7, Conj

(7)
1. $(\sim\!F \lor X) \supset (P \lor T)$	
2. $F \supset P$	
3. $\sim\!P$	$/\ T$
4. $\sim\!F$	2, 3, MT
5. $\sim\!F \lor X$	4, Add
6. $P \lor T$	1, 5, MP
7. T	3, 6, DS

(10)
1. $(D \lor E) \supset (G \cdot H)$	
2. $G \supset \sim\!D$	
3. $D \cdot F$	$/\ M$
4. D	3, Simp
5. $D \lor E$	4, Add
6. $G \cdot H$	1, 5, MP
7. G	6, Simp
8. $\sim\!D$	2, 7, MP
9. $D \lor M$	4, Add
10. M	8, 9, DS

(13)
1. $(C \supset N) \cdot E$	
2. $D \lor (N \supset D)$	
3. $\sim\!D$	$/\ \sim\!C \lor P$
4. $N \supset D$	2, 3, DS
5. $\sim\!N$	3, 4, MT
6. $C \supset N$	1, Simp

7. $\sim\!C$	5, 6, MT
8. $\sim\!C \lor P$	7, Add

(16)
1. $(C \lor \sim\!G) \supset (\sim\!P \cdot L)$	
2. $(\sim\!P \cdot C) \supset (C \supset D)$	
3. $C \cdot \sim\!R$	$/\ D \lor R$
4. C	3, Simp
5. $C \lor \sim\!G$	4, Add
6. $\sim\!P \cdot L$	1, 5, MP
7. $\sim\!P$	6, Simp
8. $\sim\!P \cdot C$	4, 7, Conj
9. $C \supset D$	2, 8 MP
10. D	4, 9, MP
11. $D \lor R$	10, Add

(19)
1. $(U \cdot \sim\!\sim\!P) \supset Q$	
2. $\sim\!O \supset U$	
3. $\sim\!P \supset O$	
4. $\sim\!O \cdot T$	$/\ Q$
5. $\sim\!O$	4, Simp
6. U	2, 5, MP
7. $\sim\!\sim\!P$	3, 5, MT
8. $U \cdot \sim\!\sim\!P$	6, 7, Conj
9. Q	1, 8, MP

(22)
1. $(\sim\!K \cdot \sim\!N) \supset [(\sim\!P \supset K) \cdot (\sim\!R \supset G)]$	
2. $K \supset N$	
3. $\sim\!N \cdot B$	
4. $\sim\!P \lor \sim\!R$	$/\ G$
5. $\sim\!N$	3, Simp
6. $\sim\!K$	2, 5, MT
7. $\sim\!K \cdot \sim\!N$	5, 6, Conj
8. $(\sim\!P \supset K) \cdot (\sim\!R \supset G)$	1, 7, MP
9. $K \lor G$	4, 8, CD
10. G	6, 9, DS

(25)
1. $(\sim\!M \cdot N) \supset [(\sim\!M \lor H) \supset (K \cdot L)]$	
2. $\sim\!M \cdot (C \supset D)$	
3. $\sim\!N \cdot (F \equiv G)$	$/\ K \cdot \sim\!N$
4. $\sim\!M$	2, Simp

5. ~N	3, Simp	
6. ~M • ~N	4, 5, Conj	
7. (~M v H) ⊃ (K • L)	1, 6, MP	
8. ~M v H	4, Add	
9. K • L	7, 8, MP	
10. K	9, Simp	
11. K • ~N	5, 10, Conj	

(28)
1. (D ⊃ B) • (C ⊃ D)
2. (B ⊃ D) • (E ⊃ C)
3. B v E   / D v B
4. D v C   2, 3, CD
5. B v D   1, 4, CD
6. B ⊃ D   2, Simp
7. D ⊃ B   1, Simp
8. (B ⊃ D) • (D ⊃ B)   6, 7, Conj
9. D v B   5, 8, CD

IV.

(1)
1. T ⊃ (Q • F)
2. T • C   / Q v O
3. T   2, Simp
4. Q • F   1, 3, MP
5. Q   4, Simp
6. Q v O   5, Add

(7)
1. (~C v ~M) ⊃ (~C ⊃ T)
2. C v ~T
3. ~C   / B
4. ~C v ~M   3, Add
5. ~C ⊃ T   1, 4, MP
6. T   3, 5, MP
7. T v B   6, Add
8. ~T   2, 3, DS
9. B   7, 8, DS

(4)
1. M v P
2. (P v S) ⊃ (R • D)
3. ~M   / R
4. P   1, 3, DS
5. P v S   4, Add
6. R • D   2, 5, MP
7. R   6, Simp

(10)
1. (V • ~E) ⊃ (P ⊃ E)
2. V ⊃ ~E
3. V • I
4. ~E ⊃ (P v J)   / J • ~E
5. V   3, Simp
6. ~E   2, 5, MP
7. V • ~E   5, 6, Conj
8. P ⊃ E   1, 7, MP
9. ~P   6, 8, MT
10. P v J   4, 6, MP
11. J   9, 10, DS
12. J • ~E   6, 11, Conj

Exercise 7.3

I.

1. ~N • ~G	2
4. A • S	3
7. ~G v ~~Q	1
10. ~(R • P)	1
13. H ⊃ ~(L v D)	2

II.

1. C v K	1, Com
	2, 3, DS
4. L • (S • F)	1, Assoc
	2, Simp
7. D • (M v N)	1, Dist
	2, Simp
10. (D v N) • (D v H)	1, Dist
	2, Simp
13. M v (G v T)	1, Assoc
	2, 3, DS

III.

(1)
1. $(\sim M \supset P) \cdot (\sim N \supset Q)$
2. $\sim(M \cdot N)$ / $P \vee Q$
3. $\sim M \vee \sim N$ 2, DM
4. $P \vee Q$ 1, 3, CD

(4)
1. $\sim(N \cdot T)$
2. T / $\sim N$
3. $\sim N \vee \sim T$ 1, DM
4. $\sim T \vee \sim N$ 3, Com
5. $\sim\sim T$ 2, DN
6. $\sim N$ 4, 5, DS

(7)
1. $T \supset (B \vee E)$
2. $\sim E \cdot T$ / B
3. $T \cdot \sim E$ 2, Com
4. T 3, Simp
5. $B \vee E$ 1, 4 MP
6. $E \vee B$ 5, Com
7. $\sim E$ 2, Simp
8. B 6, 7, DS

(10)
1. $(K \cdot H) \vee (K \cdot L)$
2. $\sim L$ / H
3. $K \cdot (H \vee L)$ 1, Dist
4. $(H \vee L) \cdot K$ 3, Com
5. $H \vee L$ 4, Simp
6. $L \vee H$ 5, Com
7. H 2, 6, DS

(13)
1. $(E \cdot I) \vee (M \cdot U)$
2. $\sim E$ / $\sim(E \vee \sim M)$
3. $\sim E \vee \sim I$ 2, Add
4. $\sim(E \cdot I)$ 3, DM
5. $M \cdot U$ 1, 4, DS
6. M 5, Simp
7. $\sim\sim M$ 6, DN
8. $\sim E \cdot \sim\sim M$ 2, 7, Conj
9. $\sim(E \vee \sim M)$ 8, DM

(16)
1. $(Q \cdot N) \vee (N \cdot T)$
2. $(Q \vee C) \supset \sim N$ / T
3. $(N \cdot Q) \vee (N \cdot T)$ 1, Com
4. $N \cdot (Q \vee T)$ 3, Dist
5. N 4, Simp
6. $\sim\sim N$ 5, DN
7. $\sim(Q \vee C)$ 2, 6, MT
8. $\sim Q \cdot \sim C$ 7, DM
9. $\sim Q$ 8, Simp
10. $(Q \vee T) \cdot N$ 4, Com
11. $Q \vee T$ 10, Simp
12. T 9, 11, DS

(19)
1. $[(I \vee M) \vee G] \supset \sim G$
2. $M \vee G$ / M
3. $(M \vee G) \vee I$ 2, Add
4. $I \vee (M \vee G)$ 3, Com
5. $(I \vee M) \vee G$ 4, Assoc
6. $\sim G$ 1, 5, MP
7. $G \vee M$ 2, Com
8. M 6, 7, DS

(22)
1. $S \vee (I \cdot \sim J)$
2. $S \supset \sim R$
3. $\sim J \supset Q$ / $\sim(R \cdot Q)$
4. $(S \vee I) \cdot (S \vee \sim J)$ 1, Dist
5. $(S \vee \sim J) \cdot (S \vee I)$ 4, Com
6. $S \vee \sim J$ 5, Simp
7. $(S \supset \sim R) \cdot (\sim J \supset Q)$ 2, 3, Conj
8. $\sim R \vee \sim Q$ 6, 7, CD
9. $\sim(R \cdot Q)$ 8, DM

(25)
1. $E \vee \sim(D \vee C)$
2. $(E \vee \sim D) \supset C$ / E
3. $E \vee (\sim D \cdot \sim C)$ 1, DM
4. $(E \vee \sim D) \cdot (E \vee \sim C)$ 3, Dist
5. $E \vee \sim D$ 4, Simp
6. C 2, 5, MP
7. $(E \vee \sim C) \cdot (E \vee \sim D)$ 4, Com
8. $E \vee \sim C$ 7, Simp
9. $\sim C \vee E$ 8, Com
10. $\sim\sim C$ 6, DN
11. E 9, 10, DS

(28)
1. $P \vee (I \cdot L)$
2. $(P \vee I) \supset \sim(L \vee C)$
3. $(P \cdot \sim C) \supset (E \cdot F)$ / $F \vee D$
4. $(P \vee I) \cdot (P \vee L)$ 1, Dist
5. $P \vee I$ 4, Simp
6. $\sim(L \vee C)$ 2, 5, MP
7. $\sim L \cdot \sim C$ 6, DM
8. $\sim L$ 7, Simp
9. $(P \vee L) \cdot (P \vee I)$ 4, Com
10. $P \vee L$ 9, Simp
11. $L \vee P$ 10, Com
12. P 8, 11, DS
13. $\sim C \cdot \sim L$ 7, Com
14. $\sim C$ 13, Simp
15. $P \cdot \sim C$ 12, 14, Conj
16. $E \cdot F$ 3, 15, MP
17. $F \cdot E$ 16, Com
18. F 17, Simp
19. $F \vee D$ 18, Add

(31) 1. $(\sim R \lor D) \supset \sim(F \cdot G)$
   2. $(F \cdot R) \supset S$
   3. $F \cdot \sim S$ $/ \sim(S \lor G)$
   4. $\sim S \cdot F$ 3, Com
   5. $\sim S$ 4, Simp
   6. $\sim(F \cdot R)$ 2, 5, MT
   7. $\sim F \lor \sim R$ 6, DM
   8. F 3, Simp
   9. $\sim\sim F$ 8, DN
  10. $\sim R$ 7, 9, DS
  11. $\sim R \lor D$ 10, Add
  12. $\sim(F \cdot G)$ 1, 11, MP
  13. $\sim F \lor \sim G$ 12, DM
  14. $\sim G$ 9, 13, DS
  15. $\sim S \cdot \sim G$ 5, 14, Conj
  16. $\sim(S \lor G)$ 15, DM

(34) 1. $(M \cdot N) \lor (O \cdot P)$
   2. $(N \lor O) \supset \sim P$ $/ N$
   3. $[(M \cdot N) \lor O] \cdot [(M \cdot N) \lor P]$ 1, Dist
   4. $(M \cdot N) \lor O$ 3, Simp
   5. $O \lor (M \cdot N)$ 4, Com
   6. $(O \lor M) \cdot (O \lor N)$ 5, Dist
   7. $(O \lor N) \cdot (O \lor M)$ 6, Com
   8. $O \lor N$ 7, Simp
   9. $N \lor O$ 8, Com
  10. $\sim P$ 2, 9, MP
  11. $[(M \cdot N) \lor P] \cdot [(M \cdot N) \lor O]$ 3, Com
  12. $(M \cdot N) \lor P$ 11, Simp
  13. $P \lor (M \cdot N)$ 12, Com
  14. $M \cdot N$ 10, 13, DS
  15. $N \cdot M$ 14, Com
  16. N 15, Simp

IV.

(1) 1. $(S \cdot D) \lor (S \cdot H)$
   2. $S \supset (I \cdot R)$ $/ S \cdot R$
   3. $S \cdot (D \lor H)$ 1, Dist
   4. S 3, Simp
   5. $I \cdot R$ 2, 4, MP
   6. $R \cdot I$ 5, Com
   7. R 6, Simp
   8. $S \cdot R$ 4, 7, Conj

(4) 1. $G \lor (R \cdot E)$
   2. $(G \lor E) \supset \sim R$ $/ G \lor M$
   3. $(G \lor R) \cdot (G \lor E)$ 1, Dist
   4. $(G \lor E) \cdot (G \lor R)$ 3, Com
   5. $G \lor E$ 4, Simp
   6. $\sim R$ 2, 5, MP
   7. $G \lor R$ 3, Simp
   8. $R \lor G$ 7, Com
   9. G 6, 8, DS
  10. $G \lor M$ 9, Add

(7) 1. $R \supset (C \lor M)$
   2. $\sim(I \lor C)$
   3. $\sim(A \lor M)$ $/ \sim R$
   4. $\sim I \cdot \sim C$ 2, DM
   5. $\sim A \cdot \sim M$ 3, DM
   6. $\sim C \cdot \sim I$ 4, Com
   7. $\sim C$ 6, Simp
   8. $\sim M \cdot \sim A$ 5, Com
   9. $\sim M$ 8, Simp
  10. $\sim C \cdot \sim M$ 7, 9, Conj
  11. $\sim(C \lor M)$ 10, DM
  12. $\sim R$ 1, 11, MT

(10) 1. $\sim E \lor (B \cdot P)$
   2. $\sim E \lor (G \cdot W)$
   3. $\sim P \lor \sim W$ $/ \sim E$
   4. $(\sim E \lor B) \cdot (\sim E \lor P)$ 1, Dist
   5. $(\sim E \lor P) \cdot (\sim E \lor B)$ 4, Com
   6. $\sim E \lor P$ 5, Simp
   7. $(\sim E \lor G) \cdot (\sim E \lor W)$ 2, Dist
   8. $(\sim E \lor W) \cdot (\sim E \lor G)$ 7, Com
   9. $\sim E \lor W$ 8, Simp
  10. $(\sim E \lor P) \cdot (\sim E \lor W)$ 6, 9, Conj
  11. $\sim E \lor (P \cdot W)$ 10, Dist
  12. $(P \cdot W) \lor \sim E$ 11, Com
  13. $\sim(P \cdot W)$ 3, DM
  14. $\sim E$ 12, 13, DS

7

I.
1. $G \supset Q$ 3
4. $B \equiv N$ 1
7. $\sim\sim C \vee \sim F$ 1

10. $S \supset G$ 3
13. $W \equiv \sim T$ 2

II.
1. $J \supset M$ 1, Impl
     2, 3, HS
4. $K \vee K$ 1, 2, CD
     3, Taut
7. $H \supset (C \supset R)$ 1, Impl
     2, Exp

10. $\sim H \vee \sim H$ 1, Impl
     2, Taut
13. $(N \supset A) \cdot (A \supset N)$ 1, Trans
     2, Equiv

III.
(1) 1. $(S \cdot K) \supset R$
  2. K $/ S \supset R$
  3. $(K \cdot S) \supset R$ 1, Com
  4. $K \supset (S \supset R)$ 3, Exp
  5. $S \supset R$ 2, 4, MP

(4) 1. $S \equiv Q$
  2. $\sim S$ $/ \sim Q$
  3. $(S \supset Q) \cdot (Q \supset S)$ 1, Equiv
  4. $(Q \supset S) \cdot (S \supset Q)$ 3, Com
  5. $Q \supset S$ 4, Simp
  6. $\sim Q$ 2, 5, MT

(7) 1. $(B \supset M) \cdot (D \supset M)$
  2. $B \vee D$ $/ M$
  3. $M \vee M$ 1, 2, CD
  4. M 3, Taut

(10) 1. $(B \supset G) \cdot (F \supset N)$
  2. $\sim(G \cdot N)$ $/ \sim(B \cdot F)$
  3. $\sim G \vee \sim N$ 2, DM
  4. $(\sim G \supset \sim B) \cdot (F \supset N)$ 1, Trans
  5. $(\sim G \supset \sim B) \cdot (\sim N \supset \sim F)$ 4, Trans
  6. $\sim B \vee \sim F$ 3, 5, CD
  7. $\sim(B \cdot F)$ 6, DM

(13) 1. $K \supset (B \supset \sim M)$
  2. $D \supset (K \cdot M)$ $/ D \supset \sim B$
  3. $K \supset (\sim\sim M \supset \sim B)$ 1, Trans
  4. $K \supset (M \supset \sim B)$ 3, DN
  5. $(K \cdot M) \supset \sim B$ 4, Exp
  6. $D \supset \sim B$ 2, 5, HS

(16) 1. $T \supset R$
  2. $T \supset \sim R$ $/ \sim T$
  3. $\sim\sim R \supset \sim T$ 2, Trans
  4. $R \supset \sim T$ 3, DN
  5. $T \supset \sim T$ 1, 4, HS
  6. $\sim T \vee \sim T$ 5, Impl
  7. $\sim T$ 6, Taut

(19) 1. $\sim R \vee P$
  2. $R \vee \sim P$ $/ R \equiv P$
  3. $R \supset P$ 1, Impl
  4. $\sim P \vee R$ 2, Com
  5. $P \supset R$ 4, Impl
  6. $(R \supset P) \cdot (P \supset R)$ 3, 5, Conj
  7. $R \equiv P$ 6, Equiv

(22) 1. $S \supset (L \cdot M)$
  2. $M \supset (L \supset R)$ $/ S \supset R$
  3. $(M \cdot L) \supset R$ 2, Exp
  4. $(L \cdot M) \supset R$ 3, Com
  5. $S \supset R$ 1, 4, HS

(25) 1. $T \supset G$
  2. $S \supset G$ $/ (T \vee S) \supset G$
  3. $\sim T \vee G$ 1, Impl
  4. $\sim S \vee G$ 2, Impl
  5. $G \vee \sim T$ 3, Com
  6. $G \vee \sim S$ 4, Com
  7. $(G \vee \sim T) \cdot (G \vee \sim S)$ 5, 6, Conj
  8. $G \vee (\sim T \cdot \sim S)$ 7, Dist
  9. $(\sim T \cdot \sim S) \vee G$ 8, Com
  10. $\sim(T \vee S) \vee G$ 9, DM
  11. $(T \vee S) \supset G$ 10, Impl

(28) 1. $P \supset (\sim E \supset B)$
  2. $\sim(B \vee E)$ $/ \sim P$
  3. $\sim(E \vee B)$ 2, Com
  4. $\sim(\sim\sim E \vee B)$ 3, DN
  5. $\sim(\sim E \supset B)$ 4, Impl
  6. $\sim P$ 1, 5, MT

(31) 1. $K \equiv R$
  2. $K \supset (R \supset P)$
  3. $\sim P$ $/ \sim R$
  4. $(K \cdot R) \vee (\sim K \cdot \sim R)$ 1, Equiv
  5. $(K \cdot R) \supset P$ 2, Exp
  6. $\sim(K \cdot R)$ 3, 5, MT

7. ~K • ~R   4, 6, DS
8. ~R • ~K   7, Com
9. ~R   8, Simp
(34) 1. (F • H) ⊃ N
2. F ∨ S
3. H   / N ∨ S
4. (H • F) ⊃ N   1, Com
5. H ⊃ (F ⊃ N)   4, Exp
6. F ⊃ N   3, 5, MP
7. ~N ⊃ ~F   6, Trans
8. ~~F ∨ S   2, DN
9. ~F ⊃ S   8, Impl
10. ~N ⊃ S   7, 9, HS
11. ~~N ∨ S   10, Impl
12. N ∨ S   11, DN
(37) 1. (D ⊃ E) ⊃ (E ⊃ D)
2. (D ≡ E) ⊃ ~(G • ~H)
3. E • G   / G • H
4. E   3, Simp
5. E ∨ ~D   4, Add
6. ~D ∨ E   5, Com
7. D ⊃ E   6, Impl
8. E ⊃ D   1, 7, MP
9. (D ⊃ E) • (E ⊃ D) 7, 8, Conj
10. D ≡ E   9, Equiv
11. ~(G • ~H)   2, 10, MP
12. ~G ∨ ~~H   11, DM
13. ~G ∨ H   12, DN
14. G • E   3, Com
15. G   14, Simp
16. ~~G   15, DN
17. H   13, 16, DS
18. G • H   15, 17, Conj
(40) 1. A ≡ W
2. ~A ∨ ~W
3. R ⊃ A   / ~(W ∨ R)
4. (A • W) ∨ (~A • ~W) 1, Equiv
5. ~(A • W)   2, DM
6. ~A • ~W   4, 5, DS

IV.
(1) 1. D ⊃ C
2. ~(C • ~S)   / D ⊃ S
3. ~C ∨ ~~S   2, DM
4. C ⊃ ~~S   3, Impl
5. C ⊃ S   4, DN
6. D ⊃ S   1, 5, HS

7. ~A   6, Simp
8. ~R   3, 7, MT
9. ~W • ~A   6, Com
10. ~W   9, Simp
11. ~W • ~R   8, 10, Conj
12. ~(W ∨ R)   11, DM
(43) 1. O ⊃ (Q • N)
2. (N ∨ E) ⊃ S   / O ⊃ S
3. ~O ∨ (Q • N)   1, Impl
4. (~O ∨ Q) • (~O ∨ N) 3, Dist
5. (~O ∨ N) • (~O ∨ Q) 4, Com
6. ~O ∨ N   5, Simp
7. O ⊃ N   6, Impl
8. ~(N ∨ E) ∨ S   2, Impl
9. (~N • ~E) ∨ S   8, DM
10. S ∨ (~N • ~E)   9, Com
11. (S ∨ ~N) • (S ∨ ~E) 10, Dist
12. S ∨ ~N   11, Simp
13. ~N ∨ S   12, Com
14. N ⊃ S   13, Impl
15. O ⊃ S   7, 14, HS
(45) 1. P ⊃ A
2. Q ⊃ B   / (P ∨ Q) ⊃ (A ∨ B)
3. ~P ∨ A   1, Impl
4. ~Q ∨ B   2, Impl
5. (~P ∨ A) ∨ B   3, Add
6. (~Q ∨ B) ∨ A   4, Add
7. ~P ∨ (A ∨ B)   5, Assoc
8. (A ∨ B) ∨ ~P   7, Com
9. ~Q ∨ (B ∨ A)   6, Assoc
10. ~Q ∨ (A ∨ B)   9, Com
11. (A ∨ B) ∨ ~Q   10, Com
12. [(A ∨ B) ∨ ~P] • [(A ∨ B) ∨ ~Q]
                    8, 11, Conj
13. (A ∨ B) ∨ (~P • ~Q) 12, Dist
14. (~P • ~Q) ∨ (A ∨ B) 13, Com
15. ~(P ∨ Q) ∨ (A ∨ B) 14, DM
16. (P ∨ Q) ⊃ (A ∨ B) 15, Impl

(4) 1. D ⊃ P   / (I • D) ⊃ P
2. ~D ∨ P   1, Impl
3. (~D ∨ P) ∨ ~I   2, Add
4. ~I ∨ (~D ∨ P)   3, Com
5. (~I ∨ ~D) ∨ P   4, Assoc
6. ~(I • D) ∨ P   5, DM
7. (I • D) ⊃ P   6, Impl

(7) 1. $G \supset A$
     2. $G \supset L$ / $G \supset (A \cdot L)$
     3. $\sim G \vee A$ 1, Impl
     4. $\sim G \vee L$ 2, Impl
     5. $(\sim G \vee A) \cdot (\sim G \vee L)$ 3, 4, Conj
     6. $\sim G \vee (A \cdot L)$ 5, Dist
     7. $G \supset (A \cdot L)$ 6, Impl
(10) 1. $(A \cdot U) \equiv \sim R$
     2. $\sim(\sim R \vee \sim A)$ / $\sim U$
     3. $[(A \cdot U) \supset \sim R] \cdot [\sim R \supset (A \cdot U)]$ 1, Equiv
     4. $(A \cdot U) \supset \sim R$ 3, Simp
     5. $\sim\sim R \cdot \sim\sim A$ 2, DM
     6. $\sim\sim R$ 5, Simp
     7. $\sim(A \cdot U)$ 4, 6, MT
     8. $\sim A \vee \sim U$ 7, DM
     9. $\sim\sim A \cdot \sim\sim R$ 5, Com
    10. $\sim\sim A$ 9, Simp
    11. $\sim U$ 8, 10, DS

Exercise 7.5

I.

(1) 1. $N \supset O$
    2. $N \supset P$ / $N \supset (O \cdot P)$
       | 3. N ACP
       | 4. O 1, 3, MP
       | 5. P 2, 3, MP
       | 6. $O \cdot P$ 4, 5, Conj
    7. $N \supset (O \cdot P)$ 3–6, CP
(4) 1. $(G \vee H) \supset (S \cdot T)$
    2. $(T \vee U) \supset (C \cdot D)$ / $G \supset C$
       | 3. G ACP
       | 4. $G \vee H$ 3, Add
       | 5. $S \cdot T$ 1, 4, MP
       | 6. $T \cdot S$ 5, Com
       | 7. T 6, Simp
       | 8. $T \vee U$ 7, Add
       | 9. $C \cdot D$ 2, 8, MP
       | 10. C 9, Simp
    11. $G \supset C$ 3–10, CP
(7) 1. $M \vee (N \cdot O)$ / $\sim N \supset M$
       | 2. $\sim M$ ACP
       | 3. $N \cdot O$ 1, 2, DS
       | 4. N 3, Simp
    5. $\sim M \supset N$ 2–4, CP
    6. $\sim N \supset \sim\sim M$ 5, Trans
    7. $\sim N \supset M$ 6, DN

(10) 1. $C \supset (A \cdot D)$
    2. $B \supset (A \cdot E)$ $/ (C \lor B) \supset A$
        3. $C \lor B$ ACP
        4. $[C \supset (A \cdot D)] \cdot [B \supset (A \cdot E)]$ 1, 2, Conj
        5. $(A \cdot D) \lor (A \cdot E)$ 3, 4, CD
        6. $A \cdot (D \lor E)$ 5, Dist
        7. A 6, Simp
    8. $(C \lor B) \supset A$ 3–7, CP

(13) 1. $R \supset B$
    2. $R \supset (B \supset F)$
    3. $B \supset (F \supset H)$ $/ R \supset H$
        4. R ACP
        5. B 1, 4, MP
        6. $B \supset F$ 2, 4, MP
        7. F 5, 6, MP
        8. $F \supset H$ 3, 5, MP
        9. H 7, 8, MP
   10. $R \supset H$ 4–9, CP

(16) 1. $Q \supset (R \supset S)$
    2. $Q \supset (T \supset {\sim}U)$
    3. $U \supset (R \lor T)$ $/ Q \supset (U \supset S)$
        4. Q ACP
           5. U ACP
           6. $R \supset S$ 1, 4, MP
           7. $T \supset {\sim}U$ 2, 4, MP
           8. ${\sim}{\sim}U$ 5, DN
           9. ${\sim}T$ 7, 8, MT
          10. $R \lor T$ 3, 5, MP
          11. $T \lor R$ 10, Com
          12. R 9, 11, DS
          13. S 6, 12, MP
        14. $U \supset S$ 5–13, CP
   15. $Q \supset (U \supset S)$ 4–14, CP

(19) 1. $P \supset [(L \lor M) \supset (N \cdot O)]$
    2. $(O \lor T) \supset W$ $/ P \supset (M \supset W)$
        3. P ACP
          4. M ACP
          5. $(L \lor M) \supset (N \cdot O)$ 1, 3, MP
          6. $M \lor L$ 4, Add
          7. $L \lor M$ 6, Com
          8. $N \cdot O$ 5, 7, MP
          9. $O \cdot N$ 8, Com
         10. O 9, Simp
         11. $O \lor T$ 10, Add
         12. W 2, 11, MP
       13. $M \supset W$ 4–12, CP
   14. $P \supset (M \supset W)$ 3–13, CP

II.
(1) 1. $H \supset D$
    2. $U \supset S$ $/ (H \cdot U) \supset (S \cdot D)$
         3. $H \cdot U$ ACP
         4. H 3, Simp
         5. D 1, 4, MP
         6. $U \cdot H$ 3, Com
         7. U 6, Simp
         8. S 2, 7, MP
         9. $S \cdot D$ 5, 8, Conj
    10. $(H \cdot U) \supset (S \cdot D)$ 3–9, CP

(4) 1. $J \supset D$
    2. $(J \cdot D) \supset C$
    3. $(N \cdot C) \supset I$ $/ J \supset (N \supset I)$
         4. J ACP
            5. N ACP
            6. D 1, 4, MP
            7. $J \cdot D$ 4, 6, Conj
            8. C 2, 7, MP
            9. $N \cdot C$ 5, 8, Conj
          10. I 3, 9, MP
        11. $N \supset I$ 5–10, CP
    12. $J \supset (N \supset I)$ 4–11, CP

Exercise 7.6

I.

(1) 1. $(S \lor T) \supset {\sim}S$ $/ {\sim}S$
         2. S AIP
         3. $S \lor T$ 2, Add
         4. ${\sim}S$ 1, 3, MP
         5. $S \cdot {\sim}S$ 2, 4, Conj
       6. ${\sim}S$ 2–5, IP

(4) 1. $H \supset (L \supset K)$
    2. $L \supset (K \supset {\sim}L)$ $/ {\sim}H \lor {\sim}L$
         3. $H \cdot L$ AIP
         4. H 3, Simp
         5. $L \supset K$ 1, 4, MP
         6. $L \cdot H$ 3, Com
         7. L 6, Simp
         8. $K \supset {\sim}L$ 2, 7, MP
         9. K 5, 7, MP
       10. ${\sim}L$ 8, 9, MP
       11. $L \cdot {\sim}L$ 7, 10, Conj
    12. ${\sim}(H \cdot L)$ 3–11, IP
    13. ${\sim}H \lor {\sim}L$ 12, DM

(7) 1. $(E \lor F) \supset (C \cdot D)$
    2. $(D \lor G) \supset H$
    3. $E \lor G$ $/ H$
         4. ${\sim}H$ AIP
         5. ${\sim}(D \lor G)$ 2, 4, MT
         6. ${\sim}D \cdot {\sim}G$ 5, DM
         7. ${\sim}D$ 6, Simp
         8. ${\sim}D \lor {\sim}C$ 7, Add
         9. ${\sim}C \lor {\sim}D$ 8, Com
       10. ${\sim}(C \cdot D)$ 9, DM
       11. ${\sim}(E \lor F)$ 1, 10, MT
       12. ${\sim}E \cdot {\sim}F$ 11, DM
       13. ${\sim}E$ 12, Simp
       14. G 3, 13, DS
       15. ${\sim}G \cdot {\sim}D$ 6, Com
       16. ${\sim}G$ 15, Simp
       17. $G \cdot {\sim}G$ 14, 16, Conj
    18. ${\sim}{\sim}H$ 4–17, IP
    19. H 18, DN

(10) 1. K $/ S \supset (T \supset S)$

   2. S ACP
   3. $S \lor {\sim}T$ 2, Add
   4. ${\sim}T \lor S$ 3, Com
   5. $T \supset S$ 4, Impl
  6. $S \supset (T \supset S)$ 2–5, CP

(13) 1. $[C \supset (D \supset C)] \supset E$ $/ E$

   2. C ACP
   3. $C \lor {\sim}D$ 2, Add
   4. ${\sim}D \lor C$ 3, Com
   5. $D \supset C$ 4, Impl
  6. $C \supset (D \supset C)$ 2–5, CP
  7. E 1, 6, MP

(16) 1. $(N \lor O) \supset (C \cdot D)$
  2. $(D \lor K) \supset (P \lor {\sim}C)$
  3. $(P \lor G) \supset {\sim}(N \cdot D)$ $/ {\sim}N$

   4. N AIP
   5. $N \lor O$ 4, Add
   6. $C \cdot D$ 1, 5, MP
   7. $D \cdot C$ 6, Com
   8. D 7, Simp
   9. $D \lor K$ 8, Add
   10. $P \lor {\sim}C$ 2, 9, MP
   11. C 6, Simp
   12. ${\sim}C \lor P$ 10, Com
   13. ${\sim}{\sim}C$ 11, DN
   14. P 12, 13, DS
   15. $P \lor G$ 14, Add
   16. ${\sim}(N \cdot D)$ 3, 15, MP
   17. ${\sim}N \lor {\sim}D$ 16, DM
   18. ${\sim}{\sim}N$ 4, DN
   19. ${\sim}D$ 17, 18, DS
   20. $D \cdot {\sim}D$ 8, 19, Conj
  21. ${\sim}N$ 4–20, IP

(19) 1. $A \supset [(N \lor {\sim}N) \supset (S \lor T)]$
  2. $T \supset {\sim}(F \lor {\sim}F)$ $/ A \supset S$

   3. $A \cdot {\sim}S$ AIP
   4. A 3, Simp
   5. $(N \lor {\sim}N) \supset (S \lor T)$ 1, 4, MP
     6. N ACP
     7. $N \lor N$ 6, Add
     8. N 7, Taut
   9. $N \supset N$ 6–8, CP
   10. ${\sim}N \lor N$ 9, Impl
   11. $N \lor {\sim}N$ 10, Com
   12. $S \lor T$ 5, 11, MP
   13. ${\sim}S \cdot A$ 3, Com
   14. ${\sim}S$ 13, Simp
   15. T 12, 14, DS
   16. ${\sim}(F \lor {\sim}F)$ 2, 15, MP
   17. ${\sim}F \cdot {\sim}{\sim}F$ 16, DM
  18. ${\sim}(A \cdot {\sim}S)$ 3–17, IP
  19. ${\sim}A \lor {\sim}{\sim}S$ 18, DM
  20. ${\sim}A \lor S$ 19, DN
  21. $A \supset S$ 20, Impl

II.

(1) 1. $(C \cdot R) \supset (I \cdot D)$
  2. $R \supset {\sim}D$ $/ {\sim}C \lor {\sim}R$

   3. $C \cdot R$ AIP
   4. $I \cdot D$ 1, 3, MP
   5. $D \cdot I$ 4, Com
   6. D 5, Simp
   7. $R \cdot C$ 3, Com
   8. R 7, Simp
   9. ${\sim}D$ 2, 8, MP
   10. $D \cdot {\sim}D$ 6, 9, Conj
  11. ${\sim}(C \cdot R)$ 3–10, IP
  12. ${\sim}C \lor {\sim}R$ 11, DM

(4) 1. $(Z \supset C) \supset B$
  2. $(V \supset Z) \supset B$ $/ B$

   3. ${\sim}B$ AIP
   4. ${\sim}(Z \supset C)$ 1, 3, MT
   5. ${\sim}({\sim}Z \lor C)$ 4, Impl
   6. ${\sim}{\sim}Z \cdot {\sim}C$ 5, DM
   7. ${\sim}{\sim}Z$ 6, Simp
   8. ${\sim}(V \supset Z)$ 2, 3, MT
   9. ${\sim}({\sim}V \lor Z)$ 8, Impl
   10. ${\sim}{\sim}V \cdot {\sim}Z$ 9, DM
   11. ${\sim}Z \cdot {\sim}{\sim}V$ 10, Com
   12. ${\sim}Z$ 11, Simp
   13. ${\sim}Z \cdot {\sim}{\sim}Z$ 7, 12, Conj
  14. ${\sim}{\sim}B$ 3–13, IP
  15. B 14, DN

Exercise 7.7

(1)   / $P \supset [(P \supset Q) \supset Q]$

    1. P ACP
      2. $P \supset Q$ ACP
      3. Q 1, 2, MP
    4. $(P \supset Q) \supset Q$ 2–3, CP
  5. $P \supset [(P \supset Q) \supset Q]$ 1–4, CP

(4)   / $(P \supset Q) \supset [(P \cdot R) \supset (Q \cdot R)]$

    1. $P \supset Q$ ACP
      2. $P \cdot R$ ACP
      3. P 2, Simp
      4. Q 1, 3, MP
      5. $R \cdot P$ 2, Com
      6. R 5, Simp
      7. $Q \cdot R$ 4, 6, Conj
    8. $(P \cdot R) \supset (Q \cdot R)$ 2–7, CP
  9. $(P \supset Q) \supset [(P \cdot R) \supset (Q \cdot R)]$ 1–8, CP

(7)   / $(P \supset Q) \lor (\sim Q \supset P)$

    1. $\sim[(P \supset Q) \lor (\sim Q \supset P)]$ AIP
    2. $\sim(P \supset Q) \cdot \sim(\sim Q \supset P)$ 1, DM
    3. $\sim(P \supset Q)$ 2, Simp
    4. $\sim(\sim P \lor Q)$ 3, Impl
    5. $\sim\sim P \cdot \sim Q$ 4, DM
    6. $P \cdot \sim Q$ 5, DN
    7. P 6, Simp
    8. $\sim(\sim Q \supset P) \cdot \sim(P \supset Q)$ 2, Com
    9. $\sim(\sim Q \supset P)$ 8, Simp
    10. $\sim(\sim\sim Q \lor P)$ 9, Impl
    11. $\sim(Q \lor P)$ 10, DN
    12. $\sim Q \cdot \sim P$ 11, DM
    13. $\sim P \cdot \sim Q$ 12, Com
    14. $\sim P$ 13, Simp
    15. $P \cdot \sim P$ 7, 14, Conj
  16. $\sim\sim[(P \supset Q) \lor (\sim Q \supset P)]$ 1–15, IP
  17. $(P \supset Q) \lor (\sim Q \supset P)$ 16, DN

(10)   / $[\sim(P \cdot \sim Q) \cdot \sim Q] \supset \sim P$

    1. $\sim(P \cdot \sim Q) \cdot \sim Q$ ACP
    2. $\sim(P \cdot \sim Q)$ 1, Simp
    3. $\sim P \lor \sim\sim Q$ 2, DM
    4. $\sim P \lor Q$ 3, DN
    5. $\sim Q \cdot \sim(P \cdot \sim Q)$ 1, Com
    6. $\sim Q$ 5, Simp
    7. $Q \lor \sim P$ 4, Com
    8. $\sim P$ 6, 7, DS
  9. $[\sim(P \cdot \sim Q) \cdot \sim Q] \supset \sim P$ 1–8, CP

(13)   / $(P \supset Q) \supset [(P \supset \sim Q) \supset \sim P]$

    1. $P \supset Q$ ACP
      2. $P \supset \sim Q$ ACP
      3. $\sim\sim Q \supset \sim P$ 2, Trans
      4. $Q \supset \sim P$ 3, DN
      5. $P \supset \sim P$ 1, 4, HS
      6. $\sim P \vee \sim P$ 5, Impl
      7. $\sim P$ 6, Taut
    8. $(P \supset \sim Q) \supset \sim P$ 2–7, CP
  9. $(P \supset Q) \supset [(P \supset \sim Q) \supset \sim P]$ 1–8, CP

(16)   / $\sim[(P \supset \sim P) \cdot (\sim P \supset P)]$

    1. $(P \supset \sim P) \cdot (\sim P \supset P)$ AIP
    2. $(\sim P \vee \sim P) \cdot (\sim P \supset P)$ 1, Impl
    3. $\sim P \cdot (\sim P \supset P)$ 2, Taut
    4. $\sim P \cdot (\sim\sim P \vee P)$ 3, Impl
    5. $\sim P \cdot (P \vee P)$ 4, DN
    6. $\sim P \cdot P$ 5, Taut
    7. $P \cdot \sim P$ 6, Com
  8. $\sim[(P \supset \sim P) \cdot (\sim P \supset P)]$ 1–7, IP

(19)   / $P \equiv [P \vee (Q \cdot \sim Q)]$

    1. P ACP
    2. $P \vee (Q \cdot \sim Q)$ 1, Add
  3. $P \supset [P \vee (Q \cdot \sim Q)]$ 1–2, CP
    4. $P \vee (Q \cdot \sim Q)$ ACP
      5. $\sim P$ AIP
      6. $Q \cdot \sim Q$ 4, 5, DS
    7. $\sim\sim P$ 5–6, IP
    8. P 7, DN
  9. $[P \vee (Q \cdot \sim Q)] \supset P$ 4–8, CP
  10. {line 3} $\cdot$ {line 9}   3, 9, Conj
  11. $P \equiv [P \vee (Q \cdot \sim Q)]$ 10, Equiv

Exercise 8.1

1. Ce
4. $Jr \vee Nr$
7. $(x)(Mx \supset Tx)$
10. $(\exists x)(Hx \cdot \sim Rx)$
13. $(\exists x)Tx$
16. $(\exists x)(Sx \cdot \sim Gx)$
19. $(x)(Sx \supset Vx)$
22. $(x)(Cx \supset \sim Hx)$
25. $(x)(Tx \supset Hx)$
28. $(x)(Hx \supset \sim Ex)$

31. $(\exists x)[Cx \cdot \sim(Sx \vee Bx)]$
34. $(\exists x)[Dx \cdot (Bx \equiv Tx)]$
37. $(\exists x)[Cx \cdot (Ax \supset Tx)]$
40. $(x)[(Wx \cdot Cx) \supset Rx]$
43. $(x)[(Vx \vee Cx) \supset (Sx \cdot Ix)]$
46. $(\exists x)[(Fx \cdot Rx) \cdot Ex]$
49. $Gt \equiv (x)(Wx \supset Cx)$
52. $(\exists x)(Ix \cdot Mx) \supset Ir$
55. $(x)[(Bx \cdot Mx) \supset Sx] \supset Sc$
58. $(\exists x)(Ex \cdot Rx) \equiv (\exists x)(Mx \cdot Ox)$

8

Glossary / Index

the thing or situation that the sign symbolizes, 35

Argument form: (1) An arrangement of words and letters such that the uniform substitution of terms or statements in place of the letters results in an argument, 54–60; (2) an arrangement of statement variables and operators such that the uniform substitution of statements in place of the variables results in an argument, 333–336, 339–343; invalid, 55–60, 335, 338–339; valid, 54–55, 333–336, 339–340

Argument from analogy: An inductive argument that depends on the existence of a similarity between two things or states of affairs, 35–36, 468–471

Argument from authority: An inductive argument in which the conclusion rests on a statement made by some presumed authority or witness, 35

Argument from compassion, 117–118

Argument from definition: A deductive argument in which the conclusion is claimed to depend merely on the definition of some word or phrase used in the premise or conclusion, 34

Argument from example: An argument that purports to prove something by giving one or more examples of it, 19–20

Argumentum ad bacculum. See Appeal to force

Argumentum ad hominem. See Argument against the person

Argumentum ad ignorantiam. See Appeal to ignorance

Argumentum ad misericordiam. See Appeal to pity

Argumentum ad populum. See Appeal to the people

Argumentum ad verecundiam. See Appeal to unqualified authority

Aristotelian sorites, 282n

Aristotelian standpoint/interpretation (traditional standpoint), 196, 198, 215–216, 218–220, 225–231, 247, 259–261, 267–268, 270; in predicate logic, 410; Venn diagrams for, 225–226

Aristotle, 5–6, 36, 50, 115, 196, 264, 547, 551–552

Associativity: A valid rule of inference that allows for the relocation of parentheses in conjunctions and disjunctions, 371, 374

Atmospheric pressure, discovery of, 551–552

Autokinetic effect, 577

Average, meaning of, 530–532

Avoiding fallacies, 173–178

Axiom of replacement: An axiom that states that logically equivalent expressions may replace one another in a proof sequence, 370

Baliani, Giovanni, 551

Bandwagon argument: A variety of the appeal-to-the-people fallacy that occurs when the arguer plays on the reader's or listener's need to feel part of a group, 118-119

"Barbara" syllogism, 7, 248, 275

Barometer, invention of, 551–552

Bayes, Thomas, 519

Bayes's theorem: In probability theory, a rule for evaluating the conditional probability of two or more mutually exclusive and jointly exhaustive events, 519–521

"Because," 3, 20

Becquerel, Henri, 549

Begging the question: An informal fallacy that occurs when the arguer creates the illusion that inadequate premises provide adequate support for the conclusion—by leaving out a key premise, by restating the conclusion as a premise, or by reasoning in a circle, 149–152, 173, 175–176

Benassi, Victor A., 574

Bentham, Jeremy, 491

Berti, Gasparo, 551

Biased sample: A sample that is not representative of the population from which it was selected, 527

Biconditional statement (biconditional): A statement having a triple bar as its main operator, 292, 295; comparison of with ordinary language, 310–311; relating logically equivalent statements, 318, subjunctive, 311; truth-functional definition of, 305–306

Boethius, 5

Bolzano, Bernard, 7

Boole, George, 7, 196-197, 252

Boolean standpoint/interpretation (modern standpoint), 196, 198, 212, 215, 219–220, 225, 246, 254–259, 264-270; in predicate logic, 408–410

"Both . . . not," 296–297

Bound variable: A variable that is bound by a quantifier, 409

Bouvard, Alexis, 550

Boyle, Robert, 503

Braces, 295

Brackets, 295-296

Broad definitions, 107

Broad hypotheses, 571

Bruner, Jerome S., 576

Campbell, Stephen K., 540n

Cantril, Albert H., 528n

Carroll, Lewis, 287

Categorical proposition: A proposition that relates two classes (or categories), 189–243; letter names of, 192, 195; standard form of, 189–190

Categorical syllogism: A syllogism in which all three statements are categorical propositions, 34, 244–289; exceptive propositions in, 276; figure of, 246–247; form of, 246–247; in ordinary language, 274–276; mood of, 245–246; proving the rules for, 268–270; reconstruction of, from mood and figure, 248; reducing the number of terms in, 272–273; rules for, 264–270; standard form of, 244–245; Venn diagrams for, 251–261

Causal inference: An inductive inference that proceeds from knowledge of a cause to a claim about an effect, or from knowledge of an effect to a claim about a cause, 35-36

Causality, 487–488

Change of quantifier rule: A rule of inference that allows one kind of quantifier to be replaced by another, provided that certain negation signs are deleted or introduced, 425–428; with overlapping quantifiers, 446, 448

Charles, Jacques Alexandre, 503

Cicero, 50

Chrysippus, 5, 7, 50

Circular definitions, 107–108

Circular reasoning. *See* Begging the question

Class complement, 208

Class statement, 160-161

Classical theory of probability: The theory according to which probabilities are computed a priori by dividing the number of favorable outcomes by the number of possible outcomes, 510–513, 521

Cleanthes, 50

Cogent argument: An inductive argument that is strong and has all true premises, 48–49

Cognitive meaning: The meaning by which terminology conveys information, 74–76

Coherence. *See* Internal coherence

Cold reading, 579–580

Collective hallucination, 577

Collective predication: An attribute is predicated collectively when it is assigned to a class as a whole, 160-161

Common names, 84

Commutativity: A valid rule of inference that provides for the rearrangement of conjunctions and disjunctions, 341, 371–375

Complex question: An informal fallacy that occurs when a single question that is really *two* or more questions is asked, and a single answer is applied to both questions, 149, 152–153, 173

Composition: An informal fallacy that occurs when the conclusion of an argument depends on the erroneous transference of an attribute from the parts of something onto the whole, 149, 159–161

Compound statement: A statement that contains at least one simple statement as a component, 290–291; truth values of, 302–308

Conclusion: The statement in an argument that the premises are claimed to support or imply, 2–5; tautologous, 323

Conclusion indicator: A word that provides a clue to identifying a conclusion, 2–3

Conditional proof: A method of proof that consists of assuming the antecedent of a required conditional statement on the first line of an indented sequence, deriving the consequent on a subsequent line, and then discharging the indented sequence in a conditional statement that exactly replicates the one to be obtained, 391–395; in predicate logic, 430–434, 447, 459; incorrect use of, 395; indirect proof and, 398–400; to prove logical truths, 403–404

Conditional statement (conditional): (1) An "if . . . then" statement, 21–23; (2) a statement having a horseshoe as its main operator, 292, 294–295; comparison of with ordinary language, 309–310; in propositional logic, 292, 294-295, 304–305, subjunctive, 310; translating into categorical propositions, 237; truth-functional definition of, 304–305. *See also* Corresponding conditional

Conditionally valid: Valid from the Aristotelian standpoint on condition that the subject term of the premise (or premises) denotes actually existing things; conditionally valid inferences, 229–230; conditionally valid syllogisms, 247, 259–261

Confabulation, 577-578

Conjoint premises, 63

Conjunct: The component in a conjunctive statement on either side of the main operator, 292

Conjunction: (1) A statement having a dot as its main operator, 292-293; (2) a valid rule of inference: "*p* / *q* // *p* and *q*" 361–362, 364–366; truth-functional definition of, 303

Conjunctive statement (conjunction): A statement having a dot as its main operator, 292

Connectives: Symbols used to connect or negate propositions in propositional logic, 290

Connotation: Intensional meaning or intension, 85–86; conventional, 85–86

Connotative definition. *See* Intensional definition

Consequent: (1) The component of a conditional statement immediately following the word "then"; the component of a conditional statement that is not the antecedent, 21–22; (2) the component of a conditional statement to the right of the horseshoe, 292

Consistent statements: Statements for which there is at least one line on their truth tables in which all of them are true, 317–319, 329–331

Consistency, indirect truth tables for, 329–331; truth tables for, 317–318. *See also* External consistency

Constant. *See* Individual constant

Constructive dilemma: A valid argument form/rule of inference: "If *p* then *q*, and if *r* then *s* / *p* or *r* // *q* or *s*" 336, 340-342, 361, 363, 365-366; refuting, 336–338

Context, definitions and, 109-110

Contingent statement: A statement that is neither necessarily true nor necessarily false, 316–317

Contradictory relation: The relation that exists between statements that necessarily have opposite truth values, 201, 216, 219, 226–227

Contradictory statements: Statements that necessarily have opposite truth values, 201, 216, 317–318

Contraposition: An operation that consists in switching the subject and predicate terms in a standard-form categorical proposition and replacing each with its term complement, 210–213; to reduce number of terms in a syllogism, 272–273

Contrapositive, 210–211

Contrary relation: The relation that exists between two statements that are necessarily not both true, 216–220, 227

Controlled experiments, 498–501, 503

Conventional connotation: The intensional meaning conventionally agreed on by the members of the community who speak the language in question, 85–86

Converse, 206–207

Converse accident. *See* Hasty generalization

Conversion: An operation that consists in switching the subject and predicate terms in a standard-form categorical proposition, 206–207, 212-213; to reduce number of terms in a syllogism, 272–273

Copernicus, Nicholaus, 547, 556, 558, 569, 581

Copula: In standard-form categorical propositions, the words "are" and "are not," 190

Correlation coefficient, 502

Correlational method, 501–504

Corresponding conditional: The conditional statement having the conjunction of an argument's premises as its antecedent and the conclusion as its consequent, 323-324

Counteranalogy, 470

Counterdilemma, 337–338

Counterexample method: A method for proving invalidity; consists in constructing a substitution instance having true premises and false conclusion, 57–60; in predicate logic, 436–437

Curie, Marie, 548–550, 558

Curie, Pierre, 548–550

Dalton, John, 547

Däniken, Erich von, 573

Darwin, Charles, 547

Decreasing extension: The order of decreasing class size, 87

Decreasing intension: The order of decreasing specificity or increasing generality, 87

Deduction. *See* Deductive argument; Natural deduction

Deductive argument: An argument incorporating the claim that it is impossible for the conclusion to be false given that the premises are true, 32–34, 36–38; invalid, 42–45, 49; sound, 44–45, 49; valid, 42–45, 49

Definiendum: In a definition, the word or group of words that are proposed to be defined, 89

Definiens: In a definition, the word or group of words that do the defining, 87

Definite description, 458–459

Definition: A group of words that assigns a meaning to a word or group of words, 89; argument and, 77–78; by genus and difference, 101–103, 107–108; by subclass, 98–99, 103; circular, 107–108; criteria for, 106–110; demonstrative (ostensive), 97–99, 103; enumerative, 98–99, 103; etymological, 100, 103; extensional (denotative), 97–99, 107; intensional, 99–103; lexical, 91, 98, 102–103; negative, 108; operational, 100–103, 107–108; persuasive, 94, 99, 102–103; precising, 91, 93, 99, 102–103; purposes of, 88–91, 93–94; stipulative, 89–91, 94, 98–99, 102–103; synonymous, 99–100, 102–103, 107–108; theoretical, 93–94, 99, 102–103

Definition by genus and difference: A definition that assigns a meaning to a term by identifying a genus term and one or more difference words that, when combined, convey the same meaning as the term being defined, 101–103, 107–108

Definition by subclass: A definition that assigns a meaning to a term by naming subclasses of the class that the term denotes, 98-99, 103

Definitional techniques, 97–103

Definitions of the logical operators, 302–306

Demonstrative (ostensive) definition: A definition that assigns a meaning to a word by pointing to members of the class that the word denotes, 97–99, 103

De Morgan, Augustus, 7, 50, 252, 330, 555

De Morgan's rule: A valid rule of inference that allows tildes to be moved inside and outside of parentheses, 141, 296-297, 371–375

Denotation: Extensional meaning or extension, 85

Denotative definition. *See* Extensional (denotative) definition

Denying the antecedent: An invalid argument form: "If p then q / not p // not q" 335, 340, 342

Dependent events, 515

Descartes, René, 552, 558

Descriptive phrases, 84

Destructive dilemma: A valid argument form/rule of inference: "If p then q, and if r then s / not q or not s // not p or not r" 336, 340; refuting, 336–338

Detecting fallacies, 172–173

Difference, 101–102

Dilemma. *See* Constructive dilemma; Destructive dilemma

Disanalogy, 469

Disconfirmability, 571

Disjunct: The component in a disjunctive statement on either side of the main operator, 292

Disjunctive statement (disjunction): A statement having a wedge as its main operator, 292, 293; comparison of disjunction with ordinary language, 308-309; exclusive, 304, 308; inclusive, 293, 304, 308, 334; truth-functional definition of, 303–304

Disjunctive syllogism: (1) A syllogism having a disjunctive statement for one or both of its premises, 34; (2) a valid argument form/rule of inference: "p or q / not p // q" 333, 339–343, 350, 352–356

Dispersion: In statistics, an indicator of how spread out the data are in regard to numerical value, 532–537

Disputes, 78

Distribution: (1) An attribute possessed by a term in a categorical proposition if and only if the proposition makes a claim about all the members of the class denoted by the term, 192–195, 264; (2) a valid rule of inference that allows a conjunct/disjunct to be distributed through a disjunction/conjunction, 371–376, 385

Distributive predication: An attribute is predicated distributively when it is assigned to each and every member of a class, 160-161

Division: An informal fallacy that occurs when the conclusion of an argument depends on the erroneous transference of an attribute from a whole (or class) onto its parts (or members), 149, 161–163

Dot, 291–293; truth-functional definition of, 303; comparison of with ordinary language, 308; use in predicate logic, 410

Double blind studies, 500, 529-530

Double colon: The metalogical symbol that designates logical equivalence, 370

Double colon with superscribed "c," 437

Double negation: A valid rule of inference that allows the introduction or deletion of pairs of negation signs, 341, 371–373

Drawing an affirmative/negative conclusion from negative/affirmative premises: A formal fallacy that occurs in a categorical syllogism when an affirmative conclusion is drawn from a negative premise or a negative conclusion is drawn from affirmative premises, 266–267

Duns Scotus, 141

E proposition: A categorical proposition having the form "No S are P" 192

Edmonstone, Susanna Carnegie, 252

Einstein, Albert, 454, 547, 557-559, 573

Emotional disposition and avoiding fallacies, 174, 177–178

Emotive meaning: The meaning by which terminology expresses or evokes feelings, 74–76

Empirical hypotheses: Hypotheses that concern the production of some thing or the occurrence of some event that can be observed, 554, 556–557

Empty extension: The extension of a term that denotes something that does not exist; the null class, 86

Empty intension, 86

Enthymeme: A categorical syllogism that is missing a premise or conclusion, 277–279; an argument that is missing a premise or conclusion, 22n, 277–279

Enumerative definition: A definition that assigns a meaning to a word by naming the members of the class that the word denotes, 98–99, 103

Equivalence. *See* Biconditional statement; Logically equivalent statements; Material equivalence

Equivocation: An informal fallacy that occurs because some word or group of words is used either implicitly or explicitly in two different senses, 149, 156–157, 177, 540; division and, 162

Escaping between the horns of a dilemma, 337

Essential meaning, definitions and, 107

Etymological definition: A definition that assigns a meaning to a word by disclosing the word's ancestry in both its own language and other languages, 100, 103

Everest, Mary, 197

Evidentiary support, 568–573

Goclenian sorites, 282n

Gödel, Kurt, 8, 454

Grammar, definitions and, 106–107

Grammatical analogy, fallacies of. *See* Fallacies of grammatical analogy

Graphs, 537–538

Grasping a dilemma by the horns, 336–337

Hallucination, 577

Hasty generalization: An informal fallacy that occurs when a general conclusion is drawn from atypical specific cases, 134–136, 160–161, 175, 575

Helmont, Jan Baptista Van, 552

Heloise, 92

Herschel, William, 550

History of logic, 5–8

Horizontal pattern, 63

Horns of a dilemma, 336

Horseshoe, 291, 294–295; comparison of with ordinary language, 309–310; truth-functional definition of, 304–305; use in predicate logic, 408

Huff, Darrell, 533n

Hyman, Ray, 580

Hypnagogic hallucination, 577

Hypnopompic hallucination, 577

Hypotheses: Conjectures offered as possible explanations for a phenomenon, 546–548; broad, 571; empirical, 554–557; proof of, 554–557; tentative acceptance of, 557–559; theoretical, 554–557; vague, 570-571

Hypothetical reasoning: The reasoning process used to produce hypotheses, 546–567

Hypothetical syllogism: A syllogism having a conditional statement for one or both of its premises, 34. *See also* Pure hypothetical syllogism

I proposition: A categorical proposition having the form "Some *S* are *P*" 192

Identity, 453–462; rules of, 459–462

Ignoratio elenchi. See Missing the point

Illicit contradictory, 218

Illicit contraposition: A formal fallacy that occurs when the conclusion of an argument depends on the contraposition of an **E** or **I** statement, 212

Illicit contrary: A formal fallacy that occurs when the conclusion of an argument depends on an incorrect application of the contrary relation, 218

Illicit conversion: A formal fallacy that occurs when the conclusion of an argument depends on the conversion of an **A** or **O** statement, 207, 212

Illicit major: A formal fallacy that occurs when the major term in a categorical syllogism is distributed in the conclusion but not in the premise, 265–266

Illicit minor: A formal fallacy that occurs when the minor term in a categorical syllogism is distributed in the conclusion but not in the premise, 265–266

Illicit subalternation: A formal fallacy that occurs when the conclusion of an argument depends on an incorrect application of the subalternation relation, 218

Illicit subcontrary: A formal fallacy that occurs when the conclusion of an argument depends on an incorrect application of the subcontrary relation, 218

Illustration: An expression involving one or more examples that is intended to show what something means or how it is done, 19–20

Immediate inference: An argument having a single premise, 202–204, 228–231

Implication, rules of, 351–356, 361–366. *See also* Material implication

Inclusive disjunction, 293, 304, 308, 334

Inconsistent premises, 323, 364

Inconsistent statements: Statements such that there is no line on their truth tables in which all of them are true, 317–319, 329-331

Increasing extension: The order of increasing class size, 87

Increasing intension: The order of increasing specificity, 86–87

Independent events, 514

Indirect proof: A method of proof that consists of assuming the negation of a required statement on the first line of an indented sequence, deriving a contradiction on a subsequent line, and then discharging the indented sequence by asserting the negation of the assumed statement, 397–400; in predicate logic, 430–434, 447–448, 459–461; incorrect use of, 400; to prove logical truths, 403

Indirect truth tables, for arguments, 325–329; for series of statements, 329–331; in predicate logic, 438–440

Individual constant: A lowercase letter (*a, b, c . . . u, v, w*) used to name individuals, 407

Individual variable: A lowercase letter (*x, y, z*) used to represent anything at random in the universe, 408

Inductive argument: An argument incorporating the claim that it is improbable that the conclusion is false given that the premises are true, 32–38; cogency of, 48–49; strong, 45–49

Inference: The reasoning process expressed by an argument, 5; conditional statements and, 22–23; rules of, 351–356, 361–366, 370–376, 381–385

Inferential claim: A claim that alleged evidence or reasons support or imply something, 15–18

Informal fallacy: A fallacy that can be detected only through analysis of the content of an argument, 114–115; avoiding, 173–178; detecting in ordinary language, 172–173; generally, 113–188; summary of, 163–164. *See also* Fallacies (of various kinds)

Instantial letter: The letter (a variable or constant) introduced by universal instantiation or existential instantiation, 416

Instantiation, 416. *See also* Existential instantiation; Universal instantiation

Integrity, 569–578-583

Intensional definition: A definition that assigns a meaning to a word by indicating the qualities or attributes that the word connotes, 99–103

Intensional meaning (intension): The qualities or attributes that a term connotes, 85–87, 99

Intent, role of, in fallacies, 173–174, 177

Internal coherence: The extent to which the ideas or terms in a hypothesis are rationally interconnected, 557–558, 568–569

Invalid argument forms, 55–60, 335, 338–339

Invalid deductive argument: A deductive argument in which it is possible for the conclusion to be false given that the premises are true, 42–45, 49

Invalidity, proving, 54–60; proving in predicate logic, 435–440

Jevons, William Stanley, 7

Joint method of agreement and difference: A method for identifying a causal connection between an effect and a single factor that is present in two or more occurrences in which the effect is present and absent from two or more occurrences in which the effect is absent, but never present when the effect is absent nor absent when the effect is present, 493–495, 499, 501

Kant, Immanuel, 6, 547
Kepler, Johannes, 557
Kuhn, Thomas, 580–581

Lakatos, Imre, 573
Lalande, J. J., 556
Laplace, Pierre, 550
Leading question, 153
Leavitt, Henrietta Swan, 503-504
Legal reasoning, 471–475
Leibniz, Gottfried Wilhelm, 7, 298, 393, 547
Leikind, Bernard J., 579
Letter names of categorical propositions, 192, 195
Leverrier, U. J. J., 548–550, 556-558
Lexical definition: A definition intended to report the way a word is actually used in a language, 91, 98, 102–103; criteria for, 106–110
Liesburg, Margaret, 393
Literary Digest poll, 529
Logic: The science that evaluates arguments, 1; history of, 5–8
Logical operators, definitions of, 302–306
Logically equivalent statements: (1) Statements that necessarily have the same truth value, 206–207, 209, 212; (2) statements having the same truth value on each line under their main operators, 317–318; consistency and, 318
Logically false statement: A statement that is necessarily false, a self-contradictory statement, 316-317
Logically true statement: A statement that is necessarily true; a tautology, 316–317; proving, 402–404
Logically undetermined truth value: A condition that exists when a certain statement is not necessarily either true or false, given the truth value of some related statement, 201, 207, 211, 213, 216–218, 227–228
Loosely associated statements: Statements that are about the same general subject and that lack an inferential relationship, 17
Ludwig of Bavaria, 141
Lyons, Eugene, 540n

Maharishi Mahesh Yogi, 582
Main operator: The operator (connective) in a compound statement that governs the largest component(s) in the statement, 292, 306–307
Major premise: In a categorical syllogism, the premise that contains the major term, 244–245
Major term: In a standard-form categorical syllogism, the predicate of the conclusion, 244–245
Material equivalence: (1) The relation expressed by a truth-functional biconditional, 292, 295; comparison with ordinary language, 310–311; truth-functional definition of, 305-306; (2) a valid rule of inference that allows an equivalence statement to be replaced by a conjunctive statement or a disjunctive statement, 381, 383
Material implication: (1) The relation expressed by a truth-functional conditional, 292, 294-295; comparison with ordinary language, 309-310; truth-functional definition of, 304–305; (2) a valid rule of inference that allows an implication sign to be replaced by a disjunction sign if and only if the antecedent is negated, 381-382, 384-385
Maxwell, James Clerk, 558–559
Mean: The arithmetical average, 530–537
Meaning, 74–78, 85; cognitive, 74–76; emotive, 74–76; extensional, 85–87, 99; intensional, 85–87, 99; varieties of, 74–78
Median: The middle point when data are arranged in ascending order, 530–533, 536
Mendeleev, Dmitri, 558
Mental carelessness, 174
Mention of a word, 84–85
Method of agreement: A method for identifying a causal connection between an effect and a single factor that is present in several occurrences in which the effect is present, 489–490
Method of concomitant variation: A method for identifying a causal connection between two conditions by matching variations in one condition with variations in another, 496–498, 501, 503
Method of difference: A method for identifying a causal connection between an effect and a single factor that is present in an occurrence in which the effect is present and absent from an occurrence in which the effect is absent, 490–493, 499–501

Method of residues: A method of identifying a causal connection by subtracting already-known strands of causal connection from a compound causal connection, 495–496
Michael of Cesena, 141
Middle term: In a standard-form categorical syllogism, the term that occurs only in the premises, 244
Mill, James, 491
Mill, John Stuart, 7, 252, 488, 491
Mill's methods and science, 498–504
Mill's methods of induction, 488–504
Minor premise: In a categorical syllogism, the premise that contains the minor term, 244–245
Minor term: In a standard-form categorical syllogism, the subject of the conclusion, 244–245
Missing the point: An informal fallacy that occurs when the premise of an argument entails one particular conclusion but a completely different conclusion is actually drawn, 124–125, 173, 175, 177-178, 541
Mnemonic device, for distribution, 194–195; for sufficient conditions, necessary conditions, 295
Mob mentality, 118
Modal logic: A kind of logic that deals with concepts such as possibility, necessity, belief, and doubt, 5–6, 8
Mode: The value that occurs with the greatest frequency in a set of data, 530–531, 536
Modern square of opposition: A diagram that illustrates the necessary relations that prevail between the four kinds of standard-form categorical propositions as interpreted from the Boolean standpoint, 201
Modus ponens: A valid argument form/rule of inference: "If p then q / p // q" 334, 338–340, 342-343, 350–355; in predicate logic, 416
Modus tollens: A valid argument form/rule of inference: "If p then q / not q // not p" 334–335, 339, 342, 350–352, 354–355
Monadic predicate: A predicate used to assign an attribute to individual things, 442
Mood: An attribute of a categorical syllogism that specifies the kind of statements (A, E, I, O) that make it up, 245–246
Moral reasoning, 475–479
Multiple conclusion, 63
Mutually exclusive events, 515

Names, 84, 86; existential, 419–421

Narrow definitions, 107

Natural deduction: A proof procedure by which the conclusion of an argument is derived from the premises through use of rules of inference, 350; in predicate logic, 415–467; in propositional logic, 350–405

Necessary and sufficient condition, 295; causality and, 487–488, 494–495

Necessary condition: The condition represented by the consequent in a conditional statement, 23, 294–295; causality and, 487–490

Needham, John, 553–554

Negation: A statement having a tilde as its main operator, 292; truth-functional definition of, 303

Negation rule: A rule for computing the probability of an event from the probability of the event *not* happening, 518, 521

Negative definitions, 108

Negative statement: A statement that denies class membership, 191–192, 195

"Neither . . . nor," 296–297

Neptune, discovery of, 550, 557

Neurolinguistic programming, 579

Newton, Isaac, 552–553, 557–559, 571

"No . . . except," 237, 455

Non causa pro causa, 136–137

Non sequitur, 113

Nonarguments, typical kinds of, 16–24

"None but," 237–238; in predicate logic, 411

"None except," 237–238

Nonstandard quantifiers, 236

Nonstandard verbs, translation of, 233

Normal probability distribution: A distribution of random phenomena that has the shape of a bell, 500, 535–536

"Not both," 296–297

"Not either," 296–297

Numerical statement, 456–458

O proposition: A categorical proposition having the form "Some *S* are not *P*" 192

Objectivity, 568, 573–578

Obscure definitions, 108–109

Obverse, 208–209

Obversion: An operation that consists of changing the quality of a standard-form categorical proposition and replacing the predicate term with its term complement, 208–210, 213; to

reduce the number of terms in a syllogism, 272–273

Ockham, William of, 7, 141, 572

Ockham's razor, 141, 572-573

Odds of an event happening, 511

Oerstead, Hans Christian, 503

"Only," 237–238; in predicate logic, 411–412, 455

"Only if," 237, 291, 294

Operational definition: A definition that assigns a meaning to a word by specifying experimental procedures that determine whether or not the word applies to a certain thing, 100–103, 107–108

Operators: Symbols used to connect simple propositions in propositional logic, 290–291; truth-functional definitions of, 302–306

Opinion, 16–17

Ostensive definition. *See* Demonstrative (ostensive) definition

Overlapping quantifiers: Quantifiers that lie within the scope of one another, 443–450

Oversimplified cause, 137-138

Parameter: A phrase that, when introduced into a statement, affects the form but not the meaning, 234–235

Pareidolia, 576

Parentheses, 295–297

Particular statement: A statement that makes a claim about one or more (but not all) members of a class, 37, 192, 195; in a restricted universe, 437-438; in predicate logic, 409–411

Pascal, Blaise, 510, 552

Pasteur, Louis, 548-549, 553–554, 556-558

Peirce, Charles Sanders, 7, 197, 555

Percentages, 539–541

Perceptual set, 576–577

Perier, F., 552

Persuasive definition: A definition intended to engender a favorable or unfavorable attitude toward what is denoted by the definiendum, 94, 99, 102–103

Peter of Spain, 7

Petitio principii. See Begging the question

Pictogram: A diagram that compares two situations through drawings that differ in either size or number, 539

Piece of advice: A form of expression that makes a recommendation about some future decision or course of conduct, 16

Placebo effect, 576

Plato, 6, 88, 547, 568, 582

Pope John XXII, 141

Post, Emile, 7

Post hoc ergo propter hoc, 136, 569

Postman, Leo J., 576

Popper, Karl, 571

Precising definition: A definition intended to reduce the vagueness of a word, 91, 93, 99, 102–103

Predicate: An expression of the form "is a bird," "is a house," and "are fish," 407; monadic, 442, relational, 442–450

Predicate logic: A kind of logic that combines the symbolism of propositional logic with symbols used to translate predicates, 406–467

Predicate symbol: An uppercase letter used to translate a predicate, 407; relational, 442

Predicate term: In a standard-form categorical proposition, the term that comes immediately after the copula, 189–190

Predication. *See* Collective predication; Distributive predication

Prediction: An inductive argument that proceeds from knowledge of some event in the relative past to a claim about some other event in the relative future, 35-36

Premise: A statement in an argument that sets forth evidence, 2–5; exclusive, 266; inconsistent, 323, 364

Premise indicator: A word that provides a clue to identifying a premise, 3

Presumption, fallacies of. *See* Fallacies of presumption

Presuppositions, 175–177

Primary analogue, 469–470

Principle of indifference: In the classical theory of probability, the principle that the various possible outcomes are equally probable, 511

Probability, 510–522; classical theory of, 510–513, 521; relative frequency theory of, 510, 512-513, 521; subjectivist theory of, 510, 513, 521

Probability calculus: A set of rules for computing the probability of compound events from the probabilities of simple events, 513–514

Probability of a necessary event, 514

Probability of an impossible event, 514

Progress in science, 573

Pronouns, translation of, 235

Proper names, 84; intension of, 86

Proposition: The information content of a statement, 5; exceptive, 239, 276, 455; exclusive, 237–238, 411–412, 455. *See also* Categorical proposition

Propositional logic: A kind of logic in which the fundamental components are whole statements or propositions, 290

Prospective study, 501

Proving invalidity, 54–60; in predicate logic, 435–440

Proving logical truths, 402–404

Proving the rules for categorical syllogisms, 268–270

Psychological factors affecting a sample, 529

Ptolemy, 547, 556, 558, 569

Pure hypothetical syllogism: A valid argument form/rule of inference: "If *p* then *q* / If *q* then *r* // If *p* then *r*" 334, 339, 342, 350, 352–356

Quality: The attribute of a categorical proposition by which it is either affirmative or negative, 191–192

Quantifier: In standard-form categorical propositions, the words "all," "no," and "some," 190; existential, 409–410; nonstandard 236; overlapping, 443–450; rule for change of, 425–428; unexpressed, 235–236; universal, 408

Quantity: The attribute of a categorical proposition by which it is either universal or particular, 191–192

Quine, Willard Van Orman, 426

Radium, discovery of, 549–550, 557

Randi, James, 578

Random sample: A sample in which every member of the population has an equal chance of being selected, 527–528

Range: In statistics, the difference between the largest and smallest values in a set of data, 532–533

Red herring: A fallacy that occurs when the arguer diverts the attention of the reader or listener by addressing extraneous issues and finishes by presuming that some conclusion has been established, 125–126, 173

Redi, Francesco, 553

Reducing the number of terms in a categorical syllogism, 272–273

Reference, 85

Regression line, 502

Relation, 442–443

Relational predicate: A predicate that expresses a connection between or among two or more individuals, 441–450

Relative frequency theory of probability: The theory according to which probabilities are computed by dividing the number of observed favorable events by the number of observed events, 510, 512–513, 521

Relevance, fallacies of. *See* Fallacies of relevance

Replacement, axiom of, 370; rules of, 370–376, 381–385

Replicability, 570

Report: A kind of nonargument consisting of one or more statements that convey information about some topic or event, 17–18

Restricted conjunction rule: In probability theory, a rule for computing the probability of two independent events occurring together, 514–515, 521

Restricted disjunction rule: In probability theory, a rule for computing the probability of either of two mutually exclusive events, 515–516

Retrospective study, 501

Robbins, Tony, 579

Roll, Charles W., 528n

Rule of implication: A rule consisting of a basic argument form by means of which the conclusion of an argument is derived from the premises, 351–356, 361–366

Rule of inference: A rule by means of which the conclusion of an argument is derived from the premises, 351–356, 361–366, 370–376, 381–385; for identity, 459–461; for relational predicates and overlapping quantifiers, 446–450; in predicate logic, 415–424; misapplications of, 364–365

Rule of replacement: A rule consisting of two logically equivalent statement forms by means of which the conclusion of an argument is derived from the premises, 370–376, 381–385

Rules for categorical syllogisms, 268–270

Rules for sorites, 283–284

Russell, Bertrand, 6-7, 330, 393, 426, 555

Russell's paradox, 393

Samples, 526–530

Sampling error: The difference between the relative frequency with which some characteristic occurs in a sample and the relative frequency with which

the same characteristic occurs in the population, 528–529

Scatter diagram, 502

Science and superstition, 568–594

Scientific arguments, 36

Scientific progress, 573

Scientific reasoning, 546–567

Secondary analogue, 469

Self-contradictory statement: A statement that is necessarily false, a logically false statement, 316-317; and inconsistency, 318-319

Sense, 85

Shannon, Claude, 197

Sherwood, William of, 7

Shirt-collar model, 246

Sidgwick, Henry, 252

Simple identity statements, 453-455

Simple noninferential passages, 16–18

Simple statement: A statement that does not contain any other statement as a component, 290

Simplification: A valid rule of inference, "*p* and *q* // *p*" 361–365, 376

"Since," 3, 15

Singer, Barry F., 574

Singleton, Donald, 579

Singular proposition (statement): A proposition (statement) that makes an assertion about a specifically named person, place, thing, or time, 234–235; in predicate logic, 407

Size of sample, 528

Slippery slope: An informal fallacy that occurs when the conclusion of an argument rests on an alleged chain reaction, and there is not sufficient reason to think that the chain reaction will actually take place, 139–140, 175

"Some," 58, 190, 198n

Sorites: A chain of categorical syllogisms in which the intermediate conclusions have been left out, 282–284; Aristotelian, 282n; Goclenian, 282n; rules for, 283-284; standard form of, 282

Sound argument: A deductive argument that is valid and has all true premises, 45, 49

Spallanzani, Lazzaro, 553

Species, 101–102

Specific difference, 101–102

Spinoza, Benedict, 558

Spontaneous generation, 552–554

Square of opposition. *See* Modern square of opposition; Traditional square of opposition

Stalin, Joseph, 540

Standard deviation: In statistics, a measure of how far the data vary or deviate from the mean value; the square root of the variance, 532–537

Standard-form categorical proposition: A proposition that has one of the following forms: "All *S* are *P*" "No *S* are *P*" "Some *S* are *P*" "Some *S* are not *P*" 189–190

Standard-form categorical syllogism: A categorical syllogism in which all three statements are standard-form categorical propositions, the two occurrences of each term are identical, each term is used in the same sense throughout the argument, and the major premise is listed first, the minor premise second, and the conclusion last, 244–245

Standard-form sorites: A sorites in which each of the component propositions is in standard form, each term occurs twice, the predicate of the conclusion is in the first premise, and each successive premise has a term in common with the preceding one, 282

Statement: (1) A sentence that is either true or false, 1–2, 49; (2) in predicate logic, an expression involving bound variables or constants throughout, 407–413, 421. *See also* Compound statement; General statement; Numerical statement; Particular statement; Simple statement; Singular proposition; Superlative statement; Universal statement

Statement form: An arrangement of statement variables and operators such that the uniform substitution of statements in place of the variables results in a statement, 303

Statement function: In predicate logic, the expression that remains when a quantifier is removed from a statement, 409, 420–421

Statement of belief, statement of opinion: A kind of nonargument composed of statements that express the personal conviction of a speaker or writer without giving any evidence in support of that conviction, 16–17

Statement variable: A lowercase letter, such as *p* or *q*, that can represent any statement, 302-303

Statistical reasoning, 526–545

Stellar parallax, 581

Stipulative definition: A definition that assigns a meaning to a word for the first time, 89–91, 94, 98–99, 102–103

Stipulative use of a word, 90–91

Stoicism, 50

Straw man: A fallacy that occurs when the arguer misinterprets an opponent's position for the purpose of more easily attacking it, demolishes the misinterpreted argument, and then proceeds to conclude that the original argument has been demolished, 123–124, 126, 173, 175

Striking predictions, 573

Strong inductive argument: An inductive argument in which it is improbable that the conclusion be false given that the premises are true 45–49

Study, 501

Subalternation relation: The relation by which a true **A** or **E** statement necessarily implies a true **I** or **O** statement, respectively, and by which a false **I** or **O** statement necessarily implies a false **A** or **E** statement, respectively, 217–220, 228

Subcontrary relation: The relation that exists between two statements that are necessarily not both false, 216–220, 228

Subject, 190

Subject term: In a standard-form categorical proposition, the term that comes immediately after the quantifier, 189–190

Subjectivist theory of probability: The theory according to which probabilities are computed from the odds that people would accept on a bet, 510, 513, 521

Subjunctive biconditionals, 311

Subjunctive conditionals, 310

Substitution instance: An argument or statement that has the same form as a given argument form or statement form; of an argument form, 55–59, 333–336, of a statement form, 303

Sufficient and necessary condition, 295; causality and, 487-488, 494–495

Sufficient condition: The condition represented by the antecedent in a conditional statement, 23, 294–295; causality and, 487–488, 492–493

Superfluous distribution rule, 268

Superlative statement, 456

Superstition, 568–583

Suppressed evidence: A fallacy that occurs when the arguer ignores relevant evidence that outweighs the presented evidence and entails a very different conclusion, 149, 155–156, 173, 175, 541

Syllogism: A deductive argument consisting of two premises and one conclusion, 244. *See also* Categorical syllogism; Disjunctive syllogism; Hypothetical syllogism; Pure hypothetical syllogism

Syllogistic logic: The logic that deals with categorical propositions and categorical syllogisms, 5; predicate logic and, 406

Synonymous definition: A definition in which the definiens is a single word that connotes the same attributes as the definiendum, 99–100, 102–103, 107–108

Tautologous conclusion, 323

Tautologous statement: A statement that is necessarily true; a logically true statement, 316-317

Tautology: (1) A tautologous statement, 316; (2) A rule of inference that eliminates redundancy in conjunctions and disjunctions, 381–382, 385; with relational predicates, 447–448

Taylor, Harriet, 491

Term: A word or group of words that can serve as the subject of a statement, 84. *See also* Predicate term; Subject term

Term complement: The word or group of words that denotes the class complement, 208

Terms without nouns, translation of, 233

"The only," 238, 455

Theophrastus, 50

Theoretical definition: A definition that assigns a meaning to a word by suggesting a theory that gives a certain characterization to the entities that the term denotes, 93–94, 99, 102–103

Theoretical hypotheses: Hypotheses that concern how something should be conceptualized, 554–557

"Thus," 2, 15, 19

Tilde, 291–292, 296; truth-functional definition of, 303

Torricelli, Evangelista, 548, 551–552, 556–559

Total evidence requirement, 48–49

Traditional square of opposition: A diagram that illustrates the necessary relations that prevail between the four kinds of standard-form categorical propositions as interpreted from the Aristotelian standpoint, 215–220; proof of, 226–228

Traditional standpoint. *See* Aristotelian standpoint

Traditional Square of Opposition

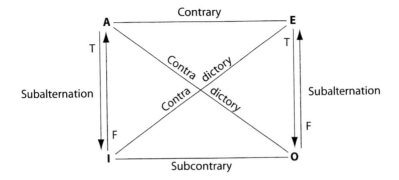

Logically Equivalent Statement Forms

Conversion	*Given statement*	*Converse*
	E: No *S* are *P*.	No *P* are *S*.
	I: Some *S* are *P*.	Some *P* are *S*.

Obversion	*Given statement*	*Obverse*
	A: All *S* are *P*.	No *S* are non-*P*.
	E: No *S* are *P*.	All *S* are non-*P*.
	I: Some *S* are *P*.	Some *S* are not non-*P*.
	O: Some *S* are not *P*.	Some *S* are non-*P*.

Contraposition	*Given statement*	*Contrapositive*
	A: All *S* are *P*.	All non-*P* are non-*S*.
	O: Some *S* are not *P*.	Some non-*P* are not non-*S*.

Valid Syllogistic Forms

Unconditionally Valid Forms

Figure 1	Figure 2	Figure 3	Figure 4
AAA	EAE	IAI	AEE
EAE	AEE	AII	IAI
AII	EIO	OAO	EIO
EIO	AOO	EIO	

Conditionally Valid Forms

	Figure 1	Figure 2	Figure 3	Figure 4	Required condition
	AAI	AEO		AEO	*S* exist
	EAO	EAO			
			AAI	EAO	*M* exist
			EAO		
				AAI	*P* exist

Rules for Categorical Syllogisms

Rule 1:   *The middle term must be distributed at least once.*
Fallacy: Undistributed middle

Rule 2:   *If a term is distributed in the conclusion, then it must be distributed in the premise.*
Fallacy: Illicit major; illicit minor

Rule 3:   *Two negative premises are not allowed.*
Fallacy: Exclusive premises

Rule 4:   *A negative premise requires a negative conclusion, and a negative conclusion requires a negative premise.*
Fallacy: Drawing an affirmative conclusion from a negative premise; drawing a negative conclusion from affirmative premises

Rule 5:   *If both premises are universal, the conclusion cannot be particular.*
Fallacy: Existential fallacy

NOTE: If only Rule 5 is broken, the syllogism is valid from the Aristotelian standpoint if the critical term denotes actually existing things.

Truth Tables for the Propositional Operators

p	q	$\sim p$	$p \cdot q$	$p \vee q$	$p \supset q$	$p \equiv q$
T	T	F	T	T	T	T
T	F	F	F	T	F	F
F	T	T	F	T	T	F
F	F	T	F	F	T	T

Rules for the Probability Calculus

1. $P(A \text{ or not } A) = 1$
2. $P(A \text{ and not } A) = 0$
3. $P(A \text{ and } B) = P(A) \times P(B)$ (when A and B are independent)
4. $P(A \text{ and } B) = P(A) \times P(B \text{ given } A)$
5. $P(A \text{ or } B) = P(A) + P(B)$ (when A and B are mutually exclusive)
6. $P(A \text{ or } B) = P(A) + P(B) - P(A \text{ and } B)$
7. $P(A) = 1 - P(\text{not } A)$

Conditional Proof

$$
\begin{array}{l}
\underline{} \\
\underline{} \\
\underline{} \quad\quad /\underline{} \\
\quad p \quad\quad \text{ACP} \\
\quad \underline{} \\
\quad \underline{} \\
\quad \underline{} \\
\quad q \\
\underline{p \supset q} \quad\quad \text{CP}
\end{array}
$$

Indirect Proof

$$
\begin{array}{l}
\underline{} \\
\underline{} \\
\underline{} \quad\quad /\underline{} \\
\quad p \quad\quad \text{AIP} \\
\quad \underline{} \\
\quad \underline{} \\
\quad q \cdot {\sim}q \\
\underline{{\sim}p} \quad\quad \text{IP}
\end{array}
$$

Rules for Removing and Introducing Quantifiers

($a, b, c, \ldots u, v, w$ are individual constants; x, y, z are individual variables)

1. Universal instantiation (UI)

$$\frac{(x)\mathscr{F}x}{\mathscr{F}y} \qquad\qquad \frac{(x)\mathscr{F}x}{\mathscr{F}a}$$

2. Universal generalization (UG)

$$\frac{\mathscr{F}y}{(x)\mathscr{F}x} \quad \begin{array}{c}\textit{not}\\ \textit{allowed:}\end{array} \quad \frac{\mathscr{F}a}{(x)\mathscr{F}x}$$

Restrictions:
(conditional and indirect proof)

(1) UG must not be used within the scope of an indented sequence if the instantial variable y is free in the first line of that sequence.

(overlapping quantifiers)

(2) UG must not be used if the instantial variable y is free in any preceding line obtained by EI.

3. Existential instantiation (EI)

$$\frac{(\exists x)\mathscr{F}x}{\mathscr{F}a} \quad \begin{array}{c}\textit{not}\\ \textit{allowed:}\end{array} \quad \frac{(\exists x)\mathscr{F}x}{\mathscr{F}y}$$

Restriction: The existential name a must be a new name that has not occurred in any previous line (including the conclusion line).

4. Existential generalization (EG)

$$\frac{\mathscr{F}a}{(\exists x)\mathscr{F}x} \qquad\qquad \frac{\mathscr{F}y}{(\exists x)\mathscr{F}x}$$

Change of Quantifier Rules

$$(x)\mathscr{F}x \ ::\ {\sim}(\exists x){\sim}\mathscr{F}x \qquad\qquad (\exists x)\mathscr{F}x \ ::\ {\sim}(x){\sim}\mathscr{F}x$$
$$ {\sim}(x)\mathscr{F}x \ ::\ (\exists x){\sim}\mathscr{F}x \qquad\qquad {\sim}(\exists x)\mathscr{F}x \ ::\ (x){\sim}\mathscr{F}x$$

Identity Rules

1. $\dfrac{\text{Prem.}}{a = a}$
2. $a = b \ ::\ b = a$
3. $\dfrac{\mathscr{F}a}{\begin{array}{c}a = b\\ \hline \mathscr{F}b\end{array}}$

Rules of Implication

1. *Modus ponens* (MP)

$p \supset q$

$\dfrac{p}{q}$

2. *Modus tollens* (MT)

$p \supset q$

$\dfrac{\sim q}{\sim p}$

3. Hypothetical syllogism (HS)

$p \supset q$

$\dfrac{q \supset r}{p \supset r}$

4. Disjunctive syllogism (DS)

$p \lor q$

$\dfrac{\sim p}{q}$

5. Constructive dilemma (CD)

$(p \supset q) \cdot (r \supset s)$

$\dfrac{p \lor r}{q \lor s}$

6. Simplification (Simp)

$\dfrac{p \cdot q}{p}$

7. Conjunction (Conj)

p

$\dfrac{q}{p \cdot q}$

8. Addition (Add)

$\dfrac{p}{p \lor q}$

Rules of Replacement

9. De Morgan's rule (DM)

$\sim(p \cdot q) :: (\sim p \lor \sim q)$
$\sim(p \lor q) :: (\sim p \cdot \sim q)$

10. Commutativity (Com)

$(p \lor q) :: (q \lor p)$
$(p \cdot q) :: (q \cdot p)$

11. Associativity (Assoc)

$[p \lor (q \lor r)] :: [(p \lor q) \lor r]$
$[p \cdot (q \cdot r)] :: [(p \cdot q) \cdot r]$

12. Distribution (Dist)

$[p \cdot (q \lor r)] :: [(p \cdot q) \lor (p \cdot r)]$
$[p \lor (q \cdot r)] :: [(p \lor q) \cdot (p \lor r)]$

13. Double negation (DN)

$p :: \sim\sim p$

14. Transposition (Trans)

$(p \supset q) :: (\sim q \supset \sim p)$

15. Material implication (Impl)

$(p \supset q) :: (\sim p \lor q)$

16. Material equivalence (Equiv)

$(p \equiv q) :: [(p \supset q) \cdot (q \supset p)]$
$(p \equiv q) :: [(p \cdot q) \lor (\sim p \cdot \sim q)]$

17. Exportation (Exp)

$[(p \cdot q) \supset r] :: [p \supset (q \supset r)]$

18. Tautology (Taut)

$p :: (p \lor p)$
$p :: (p \cdot p)$